AF569565

Greenville County Museum of Art

THE SOUTHERN COLLECTION 

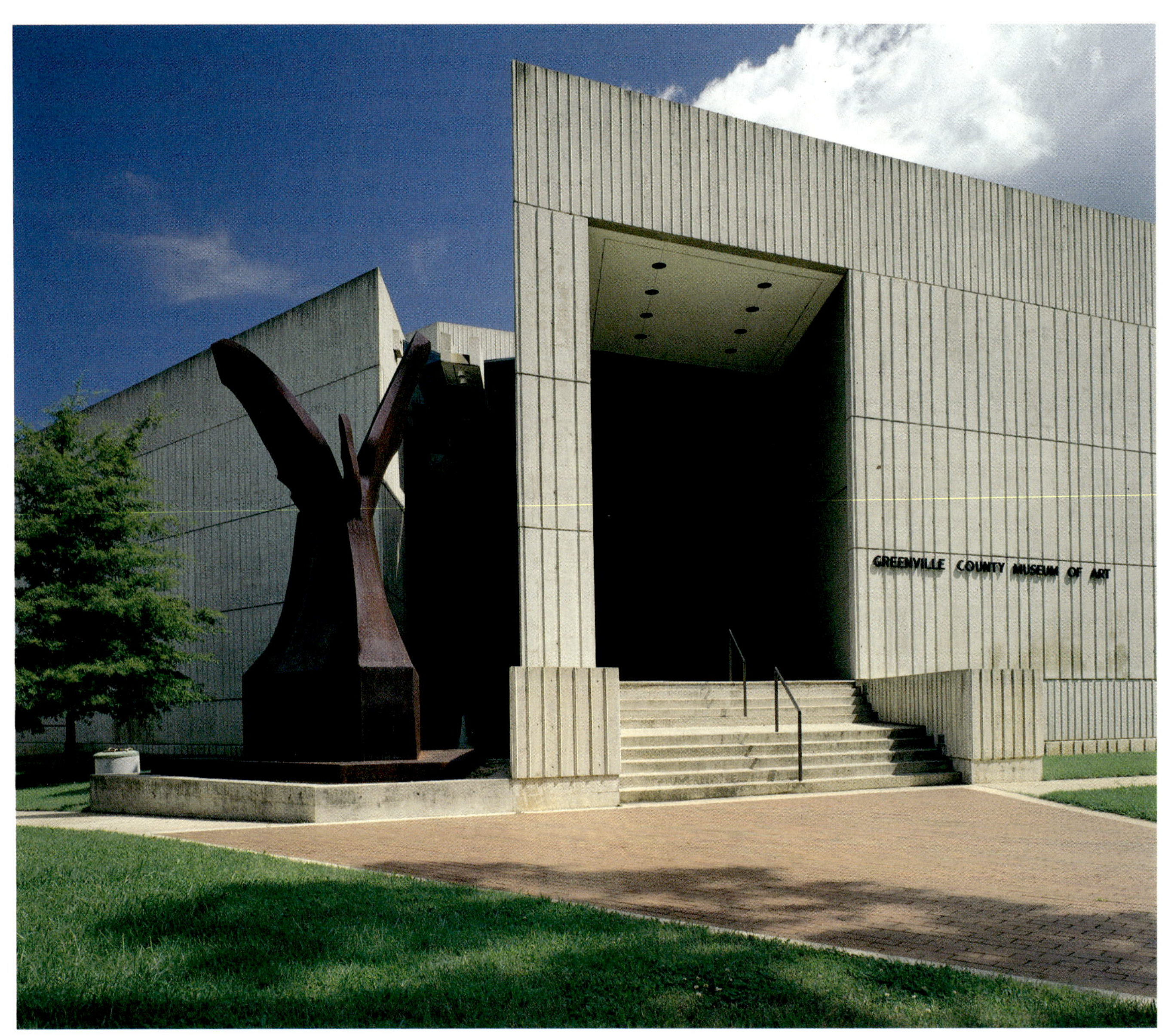
GREENVILLE COUNTY MUSEUM OF ART

Greenville County Museum of Art

THE SOUTHERN COLLECTION

by Martha R. Severens

Introduction by William H. Gerdts

Hudson Hills Press, New York

in association with the Greenville County Museum of Art

Carolina First has supported the publication of *Greenville County Museum of Art: The Southern Collection* through a generous grant to the Greenville County Museum of Art.

First Edition

Published in the United States by Hudson Hills Press, Inc., Suite 1308,
230 Fifth Avenue, New York, NY 10001-7704.

Distributed in the United States, its territories and possessions, Canada, Mexico,
and Central and South America by National Book Network.
Distributed in the United Kingdom and Eire by Art Books International Ltd.
Exclusive representation in Asia, Australia, and New Zealand by EM International.

Editor and Publisher: Paul Anbinder

Copy Editor: Fronia W. Simpson

Proofreader: Lydia Edwards

Photographer: Blake Praytor

Designer: Sisco & Evans, Ltd., New York

Composition: Angela Taormina

Manufactured in Japan by Toppan Printing Company.

Library of Congress Cataloguing-in-Publication Data

Severens, Martha R., 1945–

Greenville County Museum of Art : the Southern Collection /
by Martha R. Severens ; introduction by Williams H. Gerdts.—1st ed.
p. cm.
Includes bibliographical references and index.
ISBN 1-55595-102-3
1. Art, American—Southern States—Catalogues. 2. Regionalism in art—Southern States—Catalogues. 3. Art—South Carolina—Greenville—Catalogues. 4. Greenville County Museum of Art—Catalogues.
I. Greenville County Museum of Art. II. Title.
N6520.S48 1995
709'.75'07475727—dc20 94-48053
CIP

This project has been made possible, in part, by the National Endowment for the Arts, a federal agency, and the South Carolina Arts Commission.

Contents

Color Plates

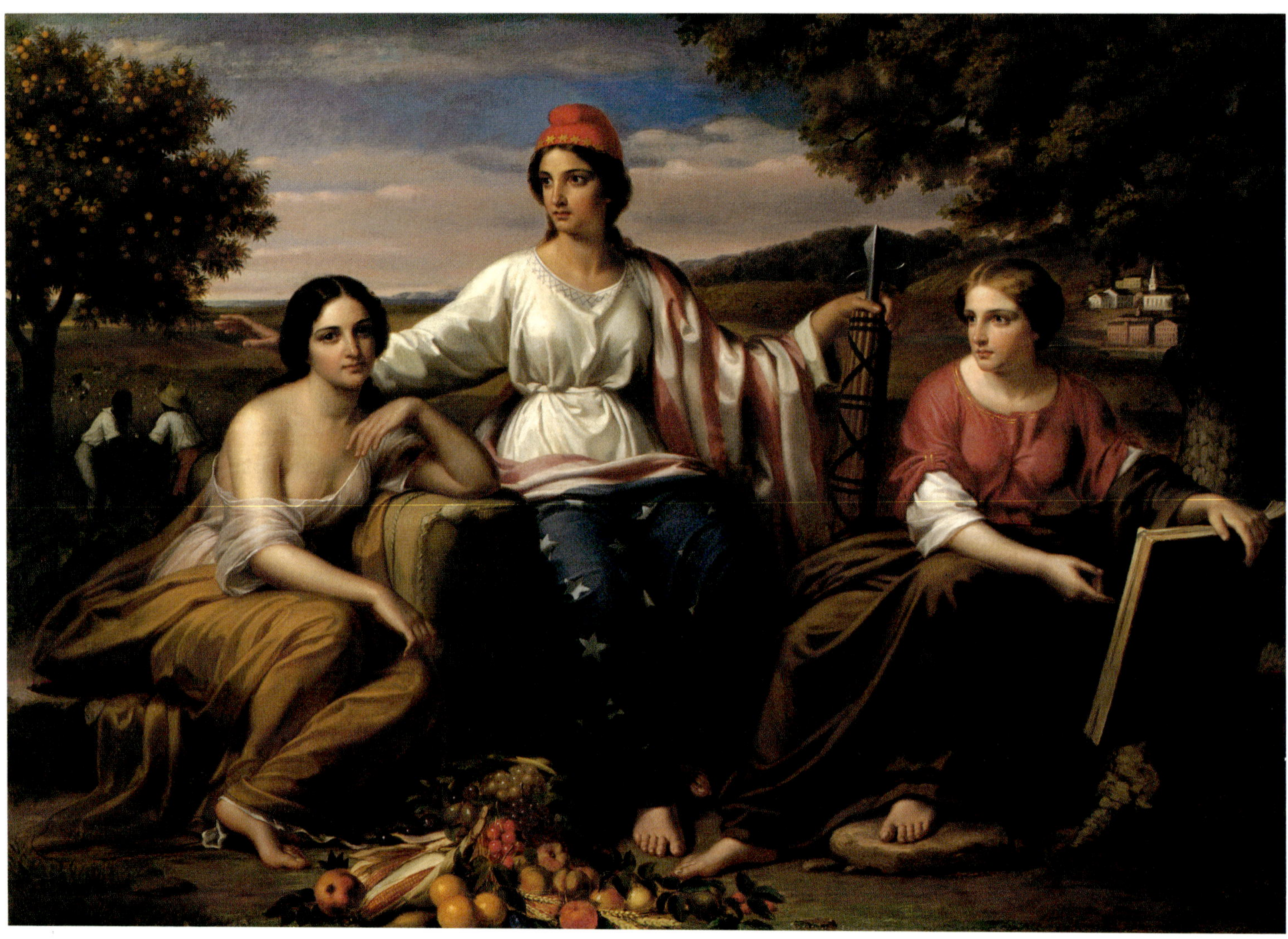

Luther Terry 1813–1900

***An Allegory of the North and the South*, 1858**
oil on canvas, 50 × 70 inches
signed, left of center: *LT/58*
Gift of Mr. and Mrs. Charles C. Mickel

Serving as a capstone to the Museum's collection, Luther Terry's large canvas, *An Allegory of the North and South*, is the latest addition to the Southern Collection. Terry, a native of Connecticut, was based in Rome, where he joined a distinguished group of painters, sculptors, and writers who discovered the allure and advantages of working in Italy. Toward the middle of his career, Terry devised the Museum's painting, unusual in the history of American art and atypical of his own work. The composition, possibly inspired by Raphael, features three women: personifications of the two regions flank a flag-draped figure identifiable as either Liberty or America. A slightly seductive South reclines on a bale of cotton while slaves labor in the background. The prim figure of the north holds a large volume entitled *Useful Arts and Sciences* and sits in front of a scenic New England village dominated by a textile mill and a white church. Dated 1858, the painting can be viewed as Terry's allegorical plea for preserving the Union.

Foreword

About fifteen years ago, while I was ensconced in my curatorial office at the Chrysler Museum in Norfolk, Virginia, Walter P. Chrysler, Jr., rushed in with a transparency of the painting *Bombardment of Fort Sumter,* considered at the time to be a major early Luminist work by Albert Bierstadt. Walter was anxious to make a deal for it, and he wanted me to dream up a way to cinch the acquisition. I suggested that we already owned a perfectly good Bierstadt, that this painting didn't look much like Bierstadt to me, and bravely wondered aloud why we should go out on a limb for such an odd subject anyway. Walter indignantly insisted, "We're an important Southern museum, and important Southern museums ought to have important Southern paintings!" Because the mainstream of American art history was so well represented in the Chrysler collection, I simply was not interested in what I considered to be marginal issues. I therefore worked diligently and surreptitiously (and successfully, I am happy to say) to undermine the transaction. I just didn't get it; fortunately, later, I did. I have begun to take some comfort in knowing how wrong I can be.

In 1983, I enthusiastically accepted the directorship of the Greenville County Museum of Art. Assuming that the mandate of the Museum's programming was the exhibition of contemporary American art, I quickly organized a show that reflected the urban street sensibilities of the current New York graffiti and Neo-expressionist painters. There were very nearly riots in Greenville's streets. In the wake of my misunderstanding I decided that the Greenville audience needed historical grounding in the evolution of American art so that contemporary art might be seen more clearly as a dialectical emanation from traditional sources rather than as a crude insult coming out of nowhere. A comprehensive permanent collection of American art was the obvious answer; the lack of money to support such a dream was the obvious roadblock. Nonetheless, we began to dream.

The formulation of a regional theme for Greenville's collection derived from my admiration for both The Oakland Museum's effective focus on California art and the contemporaneous curatorial efforts of the Virginia Museum of Fine Arts in Richmond in organizing the exhibition *Painting in the South, 1564–1980.* My introductions to Robert M. Hicklin, Jr., and to the late Dr. Robert P. Coggins, a regional dealer and collector, respectively, of Southern art, further solidified my resolve to pursue this direction. And, as a practical matter, purchasing major works by lesser-known artists was then possible on a shoestring budget. Leaping penniless into the mainstream market was not only absurd, but also wholly lacking in intellectual challenge. The prospect of unearthing aesthetic gems of Southern-related art was stimulating for everyone involved in the effort, and it has proven to be a most satisfying accomplishment.

The Greenville County Museum Commission and The Museum Association embraced the Southern Collection concept eagerly, endorsed it unhesitatingly, and have supported it financially over the past decade. It is a miracle to me that the collection has been built, almost from scratch, in so short a time. But Greenville is a place where miracles seem to happen with some regularity due to the vision, courage, and generosity of its civic leaders.

More than ninety percent of the works featured herein have been acquired since 1983. Since then, millions of dollars have been provided as direct contributions from individuals to purchase art, and although no tax money has been used for art acquisitions, the citizens of Greenville County through their tax millage have generously supported Museum operations. On behalf of the Museum Commission, staff, and membership I am pleased to express our gratitude for the community's investment. It is apparent in the credit lines throughout the book that on occasion many contributors have worked together to make an acquisition possible, and several donors have given repeatedly. Theirs is a legacy to be proud of. I especially want to single out Holly and Arthur Magill, who, through thick and thin, have made such a profound difference in the life of the Museum as well as in the lives of present and future generations of Greenvillians.

The goal of building a permanent collection that surveys the major issues in American art history through Southern-related examples is fulfilled in this book. For our purposes, the South includes the states of Virginia, West Virginia, Kentucky, Tennessee, North Carolina, South Carolina, Georgia, Florida, Alabama, Mississippi, Arkansas, Louisiana, and the District of Columbia. We have defined the Southern connections in generous terms: an artist may have been born in the South, worked or taught here, or portrayed a subject of significance to Southern culture or history. Through this collection of carefully selected acquisitions, the South is seen to be simultaneously unique as a region yet indivisible from the whole of the nation. We are recognized by who we are as Southerners, and we are strengthened by what we share as Americans. This collection is no mere accumulation of sentimental illustrations of swamps, plantations, and moss-laden live oaks, but is, rather, a meaningful testament to the ongoing cross-pollination of ideas that inspires the greatest achievements in American creativity. The task of telling this story has been admirably met by Martha Severens. Paula Hysinger likewise has edited it with skill. Together, Martha and Paula have created an accessible history of American art that also stands as a new scholarly contribution to the field. I commend them for this milestone publication. Indeed, the entire Museum staff has contributed in innumerable ways to this project, and in particular, Mary Lawson, through her singular energy and drive as a successful fund-raiser, deserves special thanks.

In 1989 the Greenville County Museum purchased the same *Bombardment of Fort Sumter* that Walter Chrysler had so desperately wanted. It is now known to be the masterpiece of John Ross Key's career rather than that of Albert Bierstadt's. By any author it is a superior work. Many such masterpieces have come to reside in Greenville, South Carolina; and it now can be stated with confidence and authority that we are an important museum because we have important paintings.

Thomas W. Styron
Executive Director

Preface

"The Book," as this publication has come to be called, is the fulfillment of the ingenious plan of Thomas W. Styron, the Museum's director, whose vision and commitment have shaped the Southern Collection. Assembled within a decade, the collection focuses on the art of the South, a region that many believe has been overlooked for generations. One goal of this volume is to set the record straight, in essence, to re-tell the history of American art. To achieve this ambitious goal, "the South" has been broadly defined. In addition to the obvious category of artists born in the South, we have included individuals who worked in the region in a variety of capacities: as immigrants and itinerants, tourists and retirees, on commission, and, most important, as teachers. The last group is particularly significant because their legacy lives on among their many students. In addition, a few paintings are included because their subject matter is specifically Southern.

To convey clearly the idea that the collection surveys the history of American art, the entries are arranged chronologically. On occasion, strict chronology has been circumvented to permit the orderly flow of the narrative; for example, painters who worked as Abstract Expressionists are introduced after artists who maintained pre-World War II sentiments. All works are dated as specifically as possible; *circa* is used to indicate a period of five years preceding or following the date given.

This project would not have been possible without the assistance of many, from the taxpayers of Greenville County and their elected and appointed officials, including members of the County Council and the Museum Commission, to the many scholars whose research serves as the foundation for the ensuing entries. To express appreciation for their scholarship and to offer suggestions for further reading, an extensive bibliography is located at the end of the book. The Southern Collection could have never been built without the considerable support of numerous individuals and corporations who made possible the acquisition of the works of art. Their generosity is reflected in the extensive credit lines accompanying each work of art. And even as the book was in production the collection continued to grow; the generous gift of Luther Terry's *Allegory of the North and the South* serves as a fitting late addition to the Southern Collection.

The hardworking staff of the Greenville County Museum of Art has diligently provided support in many ways, from technical assistance with photographs and credit lines to intellectual and emotional support. Although all have been generous with their time, two individuals have excelled in their commitment to the project: Tom Styron, who provided substance and humor, and Paula Hysinger, whose patient and persistent editing is a model of its kind. Both have been a joy to work with.

The staff of the Greenville County Library, especially those members at the reference desk and in the interlibrary-loan office, have been most accommodating and inventive in their responses to myriad questions. Beyond the confines of Greenville, many other individuals have participated in this catalogue. Noted scholar and authority on regional art, Dr. William H. Gerdts, Professor of Art History at the Graduate School and University Center, The City University of New York, has put the collection into perspective with an insightful and personal introductory essay. Paul Anbinder of Hudson Hills Press has contributed his extensive knowledge of collections catalogues to the project, and deserves special recognition. I would also like to thank Kenneth Severens for his knowledgeable support. Many friends and colleagues at other museums and libraries, as well as artists and dealers, have offered their time and resources to the successful completion of this catalogue. Staff members of the Archives of American Art, the Frick Art Reference Library, and the Gibbes Museum of Art have provided additional assistance.

Among those colleagues who have exceeded the normal duties of their profession are the following: George Adams and Allan Frumkin, Frumkin/Adams Gallery; Jeremy Adamson, Renwick Gallery of the National Museum of American Art; Fred Adelson, Rowan College of New Jersey; John Ahearn; Bo Bartlett; Jack Beal; Doreen Bolger, Museum of Art, Rhode Island School of Design; Judith H. Bonner, Historic New Orleans Collection; Roger Brown; Lana Burgess; Kathleen Burnside, Stuart Feld, and M. P. Naud, Hirschl & Adler Galleries; Carol Burtner, Virginia Museum of Fine Arts; Jay Cantor, Christie's; Bruce Chambers; Margaret Christman and Ellen G. Miles, National Portrait Gallery; Jeanne-Claude Christo; John Coffey, North Carolina Museum of Art; Janet Comey, Museum of Fine Arts, Boston; Regina Coppola, University Gallery, University of Massachusetts at Amherst; Anne Crookshank, Trinity College, Dublin; Edna W. Dennis; Lisa Dent, The Whitney Museum of American Art at Philip Morris; John Driscoll, Babcock Galleries; Evan Firestone, University of Georgia; Ross Fox, Mead Art Museum, Amherst College; Wendell Garrett, Sotheby's; Howard Godel, Godel & Company; Jonathan Greenberg, Jonathan Greenberg, Inc.; Robert M. Hicklin, Jr., Robert M. Hicklin, Jr., Inc.; J. Richard Gruber and E. C. Pennington, Morris Museum of Art; Sam Gilliam; William Henning, University of Kentucky Art Museum; Melinda Herzog, New Jersey Museum of Agriculture; Valerie Jaudon; Elizabeth Johns, University of Pennsylvania; Walter J. Karcheski, Jr., Higgins Armory Museum; David Karel, Cité Universitaire, Québec; Berta Borgenicht Kerr, Grace Borgenicht Gallery; April Kingsley, American Craft Museum; Robert K. Krick, Fredericksburg and Spotsylvania National Military Park; Melvin P. Lader, George Washington University; Cheryl Leibold, Pennsylvania Academy of the Fine Arts; Edmund Lewandowski; Gladys Lippincott, Peachtree Gallery, Ltd.; Katherine Manthorne, University of Illinois at Urbana-Champaign; Jerald Melberg, Jerald Melberg Gallery, Inc.; Rosalyn Moss, The Valentine Museum; Judith Hansen O'Toole, Westmoreland Museum of Art; David Parrish; Alice Patrick; Stephen Patrick, Hammond-Harwood House; William D. Pattison, University of Chicago; Glenn C. Peck and Franklin Riehlman, H. V. Allison Gallery; Candace Perry, The Filson Club; Gerald Peters, Gerald Peters Gallery; Charles K. Piehl, Mankato State University; Richard J. Powell, Duke University; Lewis Hoyer Rabbage; Margaret Reneke, Inventories of American Painting and Sculpture; Scott Richter; Tom Robinson; Joel Rosenkrantz, Conner & Rosenkrantz; Robin R. Salmon, Brookgreen Gardens; Linda Crocker Simmons, The Corcoran Gallery of Art; John Smith, The Art Institute of Chicago; Elisa Kay Sparks, Clemson University; Jacob Simon and Jill Springall, National Portrait Gallery, London; Bob Stanley; Deedee Wigmore, D. Wigmore Fine Art, Inc.; Joan E. Wight; Manning Williams; Evan Wilson; John Wilson, Cincinnati Art Museum; Philip Wofford; Richard York, Richard York Gallery; Scott Young; Daisy Youngblood.

The Greenville County Museum of Art also wishes to acknowledge grant assistance from the National Endowment for the Arts, a federal agency, and the South Carolina Arts Commission.

Martha R. Severens
Curator

History of the Greenville County Museum of Art

Pinpointing the beginning of the Greenville County Museum of Art is a difficult task. Greenville has long had a thriving, if at times small, visual arts community. As early as 1855 the town hosted a small exhibition of paintings by the internationally acclaimed artist Thomas Rossiter. Interest in the visual arts is, indeed, a local tradition, but to imply that the Museum's origins can be traced to such an early date would be misleading.

Organized art activity in Greenville did not begin in earnest until 1935, when three local artists and collectors, Marshall Prevost, Abe Wolfe Davidson, and Margaret Moore Walker, established the Greenville Fine Arts League. Boasting twenty-two members, all of whom were active artists, the league presented its first exhibition at the public library, then located on North Main Street. Only a year later, the Federal Art Project of the Works Progress Administration, part of Franklin Delano Roosevelt's New Deal, opened an art gallery on Furman University's Men's Campus. Despite the fact that the federally funded gallery moved frequently over the next several years, Fine Arts League members became quite involved in the Civic Art Gallery, which provided them with a meeting site as well as exhibition space. It was the loyalty of league members that enabled the gallery to remain open after federal moneys were withdrawn in 1939. Creating a historic model for the public-private partnership that ultimately brought the Museum into being, league members not only persuaded city and county officials to fund a director's salary, but they also raised, from private sources, the money needed to cover daily operating expenses. Sue Ferguson Mason, the league's first nonartist member, assumed the role of gallery director, a post she filled for more than twenty years.

Although World War II was to occupy the minds of Greenvillians for much of the next decade, the 1940s proved to be active years for the local arts community. The Junior League of Greenville initiated a regular program of children's art classes that evolved into the Museum School of Art. Soon after its success at saving the Civic Art Gallery, the Fine Arts League obtained a charter from the State of South Carolina as the Fine Arts League of the Carolinas, and in 1945 the group voted to accept nonartist members. That same year, the Greenville Art Association was formed, and four years later the organization was chartered and incorporated. The forerunner of The Museum Association, Inc., the Art Association immediately began to make preparations to ask the City of Greenville to help finance the purchase of a building for an art museum.

Increasingly aware that they were working toward the same goals and unnecessarily duplicating efforts, in 1953 the Fine Arts League voted to become the Creative Artists Committee of the Greenville Art Association. In 1954 the committee's chairman, Charles Blackwood, organized a spring sidewalk art show that has become Greenville's annual River Place Festival. In the meantime, the Civic Art Gallery was moved yet again, this time to the County Office Building on South Main Street, where it remained until 1958.

Spearheaded by Byrd B. Holmes, the Greenville Art Association resumed its quest to secure a suitable building to house a museum, and in 1958 the group purchased the forty-room Gassaway Mansion and the surrounding six acres on DuPont Drive for $68,000. Paying less than one-tenth of what the home cost to build in the early 1920s, the Art Association retired its debt in less than a year. Nevertheless, upkeep and renovation costs were high, and in 1962 the Association petitioned the state legislative delegation to create public management for the Museum, so that it could benefit from public funds. In 1963 the Greenville County Museum Commission was established by an act of the South Carolina General Assembly, and the Gassaway Mansion and its grounds were then donated to the Museum by the Art Association. Two years later, Jack Morris was hired as Museum director, and he began to tackle the challenges of expanding the base of Museum support in the community. One important component of the Museum's outreach program, the Museum School of Art, began to come into its own at this time. In 1970 the renowned artist and critic Elaine de Kooning taught a workshop at the Museum School, and the University of South Carolina approved academic credit for courses taught at the Museum. The South Carolina Veteran's Administration followed with its endorsement.

After ten years in the Gassaway Mansion, Museum staff and volunteers realized that to attract important traveling exhibitions and to assure donors and lenders that their works of art would be properly housed and safeguarded, the Museum must move again. To get the ball rolling, the Art Association transferred its assets to the Museum Commission for the purpose of acquiring a new building. Again echoing the theme of public-private partnership, the County of Greenville matched Holly and Arthur Magill's donation of $750,000 to build a new museum on Heritage Green. Ground was broken in 1972, and on 9 March 1974 the Greenville County Museum of Art opened the doors of its new College Street building. Designed by the local architectural firm of Craig, Gaulden, & Davis, the facility provided 80,000 square feet of exhibition, educational, office, and storage space.

As expected, the Museum's new building heightened Greenville's interest in and enthusiasm for the visual arts, but it was not until 1979 that the Museum truly became a focus of pride for upstate citizens. That year, Holly and Arthur Magill announced their purchase of twenty-six paintings by America's best-loved living artist, Andrew Wyeth. The Magills loaned the paintings to the Museum along with their second acquisition of 230 Wyeth drawings, sketches, and studies, and the Magill Collection quickly became known as the largest concentration of Wyeth works outside Pennsylvania's Brandywine Valley. The collection, which remained at the Museum until its sale by the Magills in 1989, not only put Greenville on the national map but also enabled the Museum to build its credibility as an institution with professional standards regarding the protection and care of fine artworks. This reputation became increasingly important in the 1980s and 1990s as the Museum successfully competed for traveling exhibitions from such museums as the Metropolitan Museum of Art, the Pennsylvania Academy of the Fine Arts, and the National Museum of American Art, Smithsonian Institution.

In 1983 Thomas W. Styron was named director of the Museum, and it was Styron who, in addition to establishing Greenville as a venue for touring exhibitions from the country's finest museums and collections, set the Museum on its course of building a Southern Collection. Shortly after his arrival, the collections philosophy was updated and refined to include the pursuit of a historical survey collection of Southern-related art. Appropriately, in addition to approving the new acquisitions policy in 1985, the Museum Commission officially recognized the

Greenville Art Association as the Museum's membership organization, and its name was changed to The Museum Association, Inc. The Museum Association has played the central role in the success of the Southern Collection. In less than ten years, the Museum has acquired almost two hundred works of art. Many of these acquisitions were made possible through the Association and its generous corporate and individual members. Of special note are works purchased with funds donated by the Arthur and Holly Magill Foundation. The Magills' 1990 contribution to the Museum of six million dollars was, at the time, the largest single-donor gift to an arts agency in South Carolina's history. Further reflecting the support of the community are the works whose purchase was made possible with funds from the Museum Antiques Show. Begun in 1986 with the express purpose of raising funds for acquisitions for the Southern Collection, the annual Antiques Show is a three-day event whose success—to date raising more than half a million dollars—has been ensured not only by the financial contributions of Greenville businesses and individuals but also by the donations of time and expertise by hundreds of volunteers.

Although a remarkable accomplishment, the achievement of a nationally recognized regional collection is neither the end of the Museum's aspirations nor the completion of its mission. The continued enhancement of its permanent collection, the educational needs of its constituents, and the cultural enrichment of the entire community will remain priorities as the Museum presses toward the twenty-first century.

Paula Casteel Hysinger
Editor

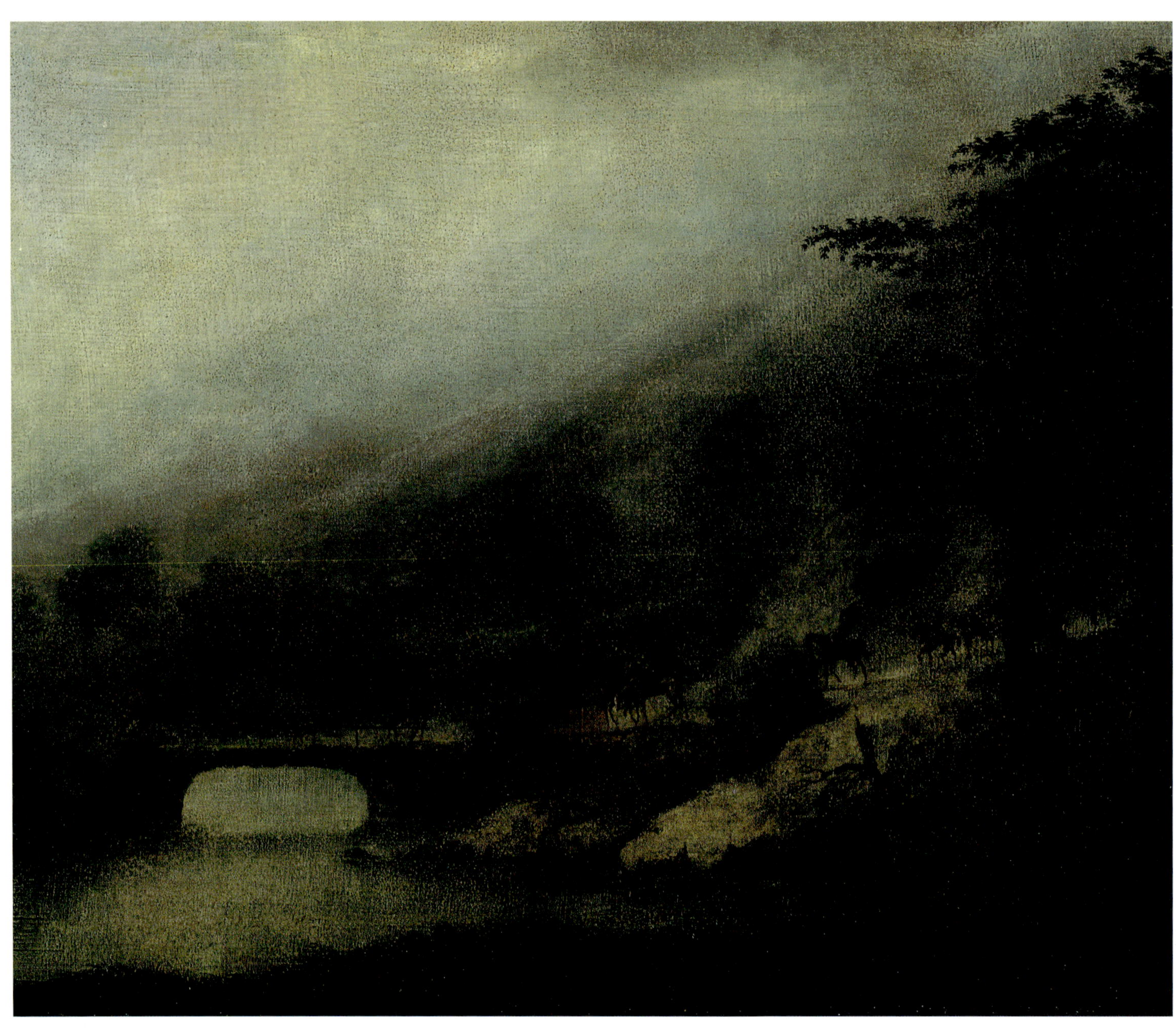

Washington Allston
Landscape with Banditti, 1798
(see page 36)

Introduction

I am honored to have been invited to write the introduction for the present volume, which presents a truly distinguished collection of regional painting. My own interest in the subject of regional art goes back a long way, to my twelve years as curator at the Newark Museum in Newark, New Jersey, beginning in 1954. Although Newark's is an all-encompassing American collection, as the leading public art museum in the state, the institution necessarily adopted a regional focus to some degree, and in 1957 I eagerly took on the project of the exhibition *Early New Jersey Artists,* and a book for the state's tricentennial in 1964, *Painting and Sculpture in New Jersey.*

Now, New Jersey is a very small state, and yet we uncovered more than a thousand artists who worked in the period before 1900. Research methodology was far less sophisticated then, and the current Ohio Artists' Project, headed by Mary Haverstock and working out of the Oberlin College Library, has uncovered more than sixteen thousand Ohio artists before 1900, although that does, admittedly, include architects, photographers, and some other categories that our endeavor in New Jersey omitted. Still, the difference testifies not only to the greater availability of resources but also to the vast increase in interest in regional art in the United States, allowing for a good deal of interchange among professionals, who are willing and even eager to abet such projects, and an art-conscious public concerned with the cultural history of their community, their state, and their region.

Such a public can and does express that concern in a variety of ways. Some become collectors and specialize regionally, in art chosen from among one or more categories such as painting, graphics, photography, and the decorative arts (I have not come across collectors or collections of regional sculpture, but that is not inconceivable, either). Others offer their support to public institutions that have either chosen to specialize in regional art or, as at the Newark Museum, added that mandate to a broader one. My general experience has been—and this *is* a generalization—that the more ambitious an institution is in regard to its collections and its exhibition policy—that is, if it sees its focus in a national or even an international perspective—the less energy is expended there toward regional art developments, even if the museum or gallery is the leading, or even the only, art institution in its area and often, by gift and bequest, has become the recipient of significant regional holdings.

Other factors enter into the decision of an institution to specialize in regional art—factors not dissimilar to those facing private collectors. Economics is one; regional art generally is not as expensive as art created by figures of national or international reputation. A superb Impressionist landscape by the renowned (although primarily locally celebrated) Hoosier painter, Theodore Steele, may cost less than one-tenth of what a similar picture by Childe Hassam would bring—and qualitatively, a first-rate Steele can be a finer work than an acceptable but perhaps undistinguished Hassam. But these economic considerations are changing, at least selectively.

But far more significant is the sentiment generated by regional art. "Patriotism" is not limited to national pride, and all of us, privately and corporately, must feel some affection and allegiance to our heritage or our adopted homeland. To support an understanding of the cultural achievements of a community or region is doubly compelling if those manifestations have been slighted or ignored. And corollary to that is the fascination of discovery: bringing to light the work of little-known, or unknown, artists and discovering information about both individual creators and cultural communities that previously have been passed over in favor of spotlighting painters and sculptors of international reputation are stimulating to both collectors and curators.

Until the past decade or two, regional investigation and regional collecting were sporadic, but the situation is rapidly changing. My discussion of artists from California, Indiana, and the South is not accidental. California, after all, is home to perhaps the best-known art museum with a steadfast regional direction: The Oakland Museum. It was founded in 1916, in the wake of the Panama-Pacific International Exposition, held in San Francisco the previous year, but although California art figured strongly in Oakland's exhibition and collection policy—after all, the significant Bay-Area artist, William H. Clapp, a member of the avant-garde Society of Six, was the director there from 1918 to 1949—it was not until Paul Mills assumed the directorial post in 1953 that the art of California became its official mandate. Oakland has since pursued that goal with a commitment matched only by the Greenville County Museum of Art.

The support for Indiana art in the Hoosier state is different and has developed through the efforts of private collectors and responsible and responsive dealers, especially Jane and Henry Eckert. From their efforts evolved the Hoosier Group, Inc., an organization that has successfully pursued its goal of sponsoring regional scholarship through publications, lectures, and exhibitions, and the encouragement of public institutions in the state to adopt a more regional focus, while enriching their own private collections. In both cases, The Oakland Museum and the Hoosier Group, Inc., have been successful. Present-day awareness of the accomplishments of California and Indiana art is remarkable; The Fine Arts Museums of San Francisco and the Indianapolis Museum of Art are both much more active in exhibiting and promoting the art of their respective states than they were two or three decades ago.

What I have found fascinating, if perplexing, since I became critically involved with regional art history, is the sporadic nature of the interest that has been generated. The Portland Art Museum is in the largest city in Oregon, but to date it has evinced almost none of the awareness or concern for the state's artistic history that has developed in California, leaving that responsibility up to the local historical society. One might attribute this disregard to the paucity of professional artists that marks the relatively short cultural history of Oregon, as well as to its rural nature and relative isolation—although, in fact, Oregon art has enjoyed both able practitioners and pictorial distinction. But such arguments hardly hold true in comparing the richness of Indiana's support for its art with the dearth of interest in neighboring Illinois; Chicago has numbered many, many more professional artists, art organizations, art periodicals, as well as patrons and critics, than has Indianapolis, but no Illinois institution has made regional art a focus, nor to my knowledge has any dealer in that state. I have only recently identified a single private collector of Illinois Impressionist painting.

The most comprehensive scholarly survey in recent years is probably the aforementioned Ohio Artists' Project, which in turn appears to be stimulating similar projects in other states; both Colorado and Connecticut have expressed interest in adopting the methodology of the OAP. Presumably, however, each state that undertakes such an examination of its artistic past will have individual guidelines; Colorado, for instance, with a limited pre-1900 history, may well extend their cut-off date to more recent times. And the Vose Archives Project in Massachusetts, after failing to find sufficient funding for updating and enlarging George Groce and David Wallace's 1956 *Dictionary of Artists in America, 1564–1860,* has modified its goals toward a more limited Massachusetts Artists' Project, still extremely ambitious and perhaps ultimately even more beneficial.

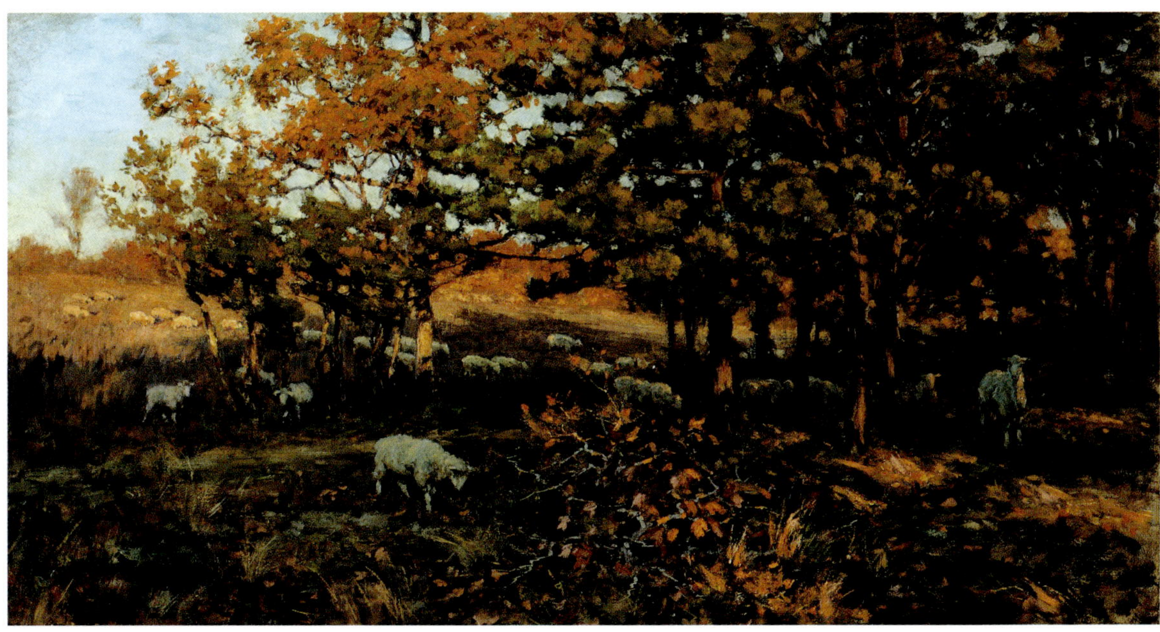

Gaines Ruger Donoho
Sheep, Late Afternoon, 1891
(see page 102)

To date, the great majority of scholarly regional projects have been based on statewide investigations, the direction also assumed by private and institutional collecting and exhibiting. The principal exception to this pattern has occurred in the South. It is true that the most serious contributions to the knowledge of Southern art in decades past were made in the surveys supported by the Colonial Dames of America in locating portraits owned in individual states. Contrary to common belief, this was a nationwide project, but the results outside of the South were sporadic and often fragmentary, while in some, although not all, of the Southern states, the volumes of documentation produced have been extremely impressive. It must be acknowledged, however, that the located works of art, restricted to portraiture, were not necessarily Southern—the pictures need only to have been located in the South.

And yet it has become customary to think of Southern art in a way quite distinctive to that region. If we exchange our consideration of artistic developments on a state-by-state basis for broader, regional accounts, the South really stands unique. Although recent regional scholarship might actually be said to have begun with the superb show *Currents of Expansion: Painting in the Midwest, 1820–1940,* which was held at the Saint Louis Art Museum in 1977, the exhibition did not really define any regional Midwestern artistic identity; it did, however, bring to light a number of superb, hitherto forgotten, artists. Likewise, there is no concept of New England art after the colonial era, or Middle Atlantic painting either. Artists of the Pacific Northwest occasionally have been grouped together, but more by the paucity of painters and information about them than by any conviction of regional cohesiveness. It is true that much literature on Western art exists, but it is chiefly concerned with such subject matter as Rocky Mountain landscapes and Native Americans and buffaloes, rather than with communities of resident artists. Perhaps the closest parallel to the concept of a uniquely Southern art is the painting of the Southwest, but in historical terms, this "school" is limited, actually, to one state and two centers—Taos and Santa Fe—and to a restricted time period of about thirty years. These last three groupings—Pacific Northwest, Western, and Southwestern art—have engendered both specialized collections and a good many regional exhibitions.

The fact remains, however, that my library houses, by *region,* more substantial studies of Southern art (to which this volume will be added) than of any other region, though individual Southern *states* are, for the most part, meagerly represented, especially if we subtract Alexander Wilbourne Weddell's 1930 volume, *Virginia Historical Portraiture, 1585–1830,* the largest (and heaviest!) of all publications in my regional library—prior to my own three-volume *Art Across America* of 1990. (But then, anomalies do occur; after all, the next largest volume, for almost unfathomable reasons, is Joseph Stuart's 1974 *Index of South Dakota Artists.*) The point here is that the perception of a distinctly Southern art as a valid cultural concept appears not only to be unique but also to enjoy considerable legitimacy. It goes back at least to 1921, with the founding of the Southern States Art League, which had as its purpose the encouragement of art by Southern artists, especially in their depiction of Southern subject matter, to be exhibited before a Southern audience, who it was hoped would be encouraged to become patrons of Southern art.[1] That concept has been underscored in recent years by the professional vitality of public collections devoted solely to the art of the South, the Greenville County Museum of Art especially, and also the Morris Museum of Art in Augusta, Georgia; by private collectors such as Roger Houston Ogden in New Orleans and the late Robert P. Coggins in Marietta, Georgia; and such dealers as Robert M. Hicklin, Jr., in Spartanburg, South Carolina.

One could probably debate forever the parameters of Southern art, both geographically and conceptually. Does it include Texas? Does it encompass such border states as Missouri, Kentucky, West Virginia, and Maryland, as well as the District of Columbia? If an artist was born in the South, but left at an early age, never to return, is that artist a Southern artist? If artists from the North, or elsewhere, visited the South as active professionals, are they Southern artists? How extended a visit is necessary to confirm their Southern identity? And similar questions address the works of art themselves. Is a work painted elsewhere by a Southern artist—a Northern portrait, a Western landscape, a European peasant scene—a Southern work of art? Can a Northern subject by a Northern painter who occasionally visited the South be acceptable as a Southern picture?

These questions may seem to generate pretty straightforward responses, but in actuality they can be extremely tricky, given the exigencies and practical economics of the marketplace that regional collectors, public or private, must face. Winslow Homer's Virginia paintings are among his most powerful images as well as some of the most Southern of great paintings, but they are also exceedingly few in number, and his time spent in Virginia was very limited; would a Southern collection then be justified in acquiring and exhibiting one of his Gloucester, Massachusetts, or Prout's Neck, Maine, pictures? Actually, Homer is not so difficult a problem, since he also spent time fishing—and painting—in Florida, and perhaps even one of his Bermuda or Bahamian watercolors might satisfy.

I suspect the solution for a truly Southern Collection is perceptive inclusivity. That is, when in doubt, include, rather than exclude, but at the same time direct greater focus toward artists whose Southern connections were stronger and more enduring than visitors and "pass-throughs." Likewise, preference should be given to subject matter that is indigenous—portraits should preferably be *of* Southerners as well as *by* Southern artists; landscapes should rather be Southern scenes, and ideally distinctly so—bayous, the Smokies, the South Atlantic and Gulf coasts, and so on. Regional genre subjects—cotton fields, plantation life, but also the steel mills of Birmingham—are more meaningful to a Southern audience and therefore are more fitting for a Southern Collection than Long Island farmers and Hopi Snake Dances. Likewise, still lifes of camellias, orchids, and cherokee roses have greater Southern resonances than chrysanthemums and lupines. And while national history is also Southern history, Southern historical themes are special to the region.

That the art of the South evolved separately from that of the North or from other regions of the nation is unquestionable, given its agricultural base and its diverse heritage early on—not only English, but French, French Huguenot, and Spanish—before the Civil War, along with the tragic aftermath of that struggle. Ellsworth Woodward, not only a significant painter in the New Orleans art world of the early twentieth century but also a major spokesman and writer on Southern art, addressed this situation a number of times, noting "the tragic dissipation by the Civil War of all material resources, the collapse of social momentum, the isolation of the South for two generations from the stimulating contact of world events."[2] And he acknowledged that, although the spirit of the South was not eclipsed but rather intensified in its peculiar individuality, the arts remained relatively inactive. Woodward believed the solution lay in the development of art schools, but at the same time he decried the abandonment by Southern artists of their heritage or at least of their environment. In speaking to the members of the Southern States Art League in 1935, he admonished: "Those beautiful pictures produced in New England or in France are not yours, for after all they speak of another land. What of the Southern land you know? What Southern artist has made a symbol of it? Dixie, the greatest symbol of the South, was not written in the South nor by a Southerner. . . . When you Southerners go to Cape Cod, Providence, and Gloucester, you can paint your heads off, but New England artists can paint those scenes better than you ever will. . . . Now, I tell you candidly no Yankee artist, however skillful, can paint the South."[3]

None of this, of course, addresses the underlying question of a distinctly *Southern* art—if this exists beyond an aggregate of all the works painted by resident and visiting artists within whatever regional boundaries are accepted, combined with subject matter distinctive to that region. This itself has generated a dialogue, with Estill Curtis Pennington speaking out for a truly Southern sensibility. This was the subtext for his 1989 study, *Look Away: Reality and Sentiment in Southern Art,* the subtitle of which expressed his definition of the Southern sensibility as "the sharp division between things as they really were and things as we now imagine them to have been."[4] But certainly this disparity is characteristic of the art of all American regions: the contrast in the North of the vigorous naturalism of Winslow Homer with the re-creations of colonial and early-nineteenth-century life painted by Edward Lamson Henry, both in the late nineteenth century, or Charles Nahl's impossibly cheery California vaqueros and the gritty reality of William Hahn's contemporaneous urban scenes in San Francisco and Sacramento.[5]

I rather favor, instead, the position taken by Bruce Chambers, writing about the Coggins collection in 1984:

> It would be utterly fascinating if there were neat correlations between the art of the South and the dominant myths of Southern culture. . . . Just as the profound simplifications of Southern mythology continue to distort the perceptions of Northerners and Southerners alike, so do they also deflect any objective assessment of Southern art. In a phrase, if we continue looking for images that illustrate our time-honored fantasies of the region, we are bound to be locked into those few examples of Southern art in which our expectations are realized and to ignore the vast majority of instances where the art of the South does not correspond to our mythologies.[6]

One of the problems with the demand for a single, overall Southern artistic sensibility is lodged in its exclusivity. Obviously, outsiders visiting for only some months—for instance, Samuel F. B. Morse in Charleston; John Wesley Jarvis in New Orleans; Winslow Homer in Petersburg; Birge Harrison also in Charleston—could not truly become seasonal Southerners, though the first two painted portraits of eminent Southern ladies and gentlemen, while Homer recorded Southern African-American life and Harrison recorded Charleston's harbors and churches. Yet, their impact in the South—Morse and Harrison particularly—is undeniable; Charleston's portrait tradition was incredibly enriched by Morse, and Alice Ravenel Huger Smith, who spearheaded the painting renaissance in Charleston during the 1910s and 1920s, was much indebted to Harrison. Whatever sensibility Morse brought to Charleston is equally apparent in his New York portraits, and the same is true with Harrison's Tonalist landscapes, whether painted in Charleston or in Woodstock, New York. George Inness's great Tarpon Springs, Florida, landscapes are Southern in their foliage and architectural details, but in essence they are no different from his Montclair, New Jersey, scenes, the aesthetic and religious philosophies of which were irrelevant to regional considerations. Martin Johnson Heade's Florida landscapes are distinct from their Newburyport, Massachusetts, marsh scene counterparts because of their palm trees and swampy settings, but Heade's Luminist aesthetic strategies remain intact.

Our admiration for individual Southern artists transcends their regional identification. Charles Fraser was a great American miniature painter, *not* a great Southern miniaturist; John Ross Key's *Bombardment of Fort Sumter* is as great a landscape and history painting now as when it was misattributed to the *Northern* master Albert Bierstadt. Catherine Wiley of Knoxville was a marvelous American Impressionist; her identification should not be restricted to a "Southern Impressionist," any more than it should be to a "woman Impressionist."

I am convinced of the importance of qualitative regional collections like the one featured in this publication. Regional art, championed by such institutions as The Oakland Museum and the Greenville County Museum of Art, is only beginning to receive the attention it deserves. What is needed now is a greater national focus on those achievements. One solution may be the creation of a center for the collection and exhibition of the art of *all* regions, together with the organization of traveling exhibitions of regional art. For the most part, Southern art has been seen only in the South, just as displays of California painting travel among museums in that state, and Indiana art is seen exclusively in Indiana. Rather, exhibits of the *best* art—best as defined in Greenville's Southern Collection—should tour to Indianapolis, and San Francisco, and, yes, New York and Boston.

Until now Southern accomplishments have been too little recognized. Yet here in the Greenville County Museum's collection, where each work of art is of consistently high quality, a most compelling argument is advanced for redressing this oversight. In this union of the South's finest artistic efforts, the stereotypical limitations of both regional and mainstream culture are dispelled in the revelation that the true spirit of America resides in the rich diversity of its land and its people.

William H. Gerdts
Professor of Art History
The Graduate School and University Center
The City University of New York

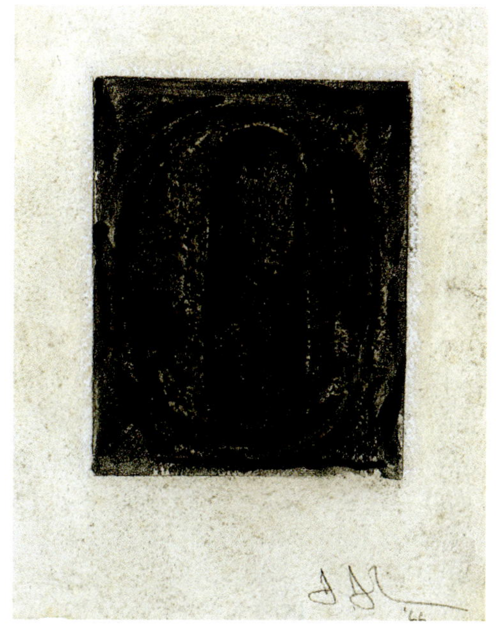

Jasper Johns
0, 1966
(see page 238)

---

1. A few considerations of Southern art were published even in the nineteenth century. See Samuel D. Davis, "The Fine Arts in the South," *Southern Literary Messenger* 34 (November–December 1862): 657–661; Margaret J. Preston, "Art in the South," *Southern Review* 26 (July 1879): 394–408; William Sartain, "Art in the South," *Southern Magazine* 5 (September 1894): 115–133.

2. Ellsworth Woodward, "Present Day Art in the South: Cause and Effect," *Art Bulletin* 6 (September 1923): 8.

3. Woodward, as quoted in "Advice to the South," *Art Digest* 10 (1 December 1935): 9.

4. Estill Curtis Pennington, *Look Away: Reality and Sentiment in Southern Art* (Spartanburg, S.C.: Peachtree Publishers, 1989), 3. One notes, parenthetically, that Pennington earlier rhetorically answered the question, "Is there a Southern art?" by stating that "the question is somewhat unimportant" and hoping rather that "the enduring formal qualities in Southern art can take their place within the larger canon." See Pennington, *The South on Paper: Line, Color and Light* (Spartanburg, S.C.: Robert M. Hicklin, Jr., Inc., 1985), 1 and 4.

5. See also the objections to Pennington's anomalies and generalizations in a review of Pennington's book by the dean of the South's art historians, Jessie Poesch, "Art: A Subjective Southern Look," *Mississippi Quarterly* 43 (Fall 1990): 529–537.

6. Bruce W. Chambers, *Art of the South: The Robert P. Coggins Collection* (Columbia: University of South Carolina Press, 1984), 2.

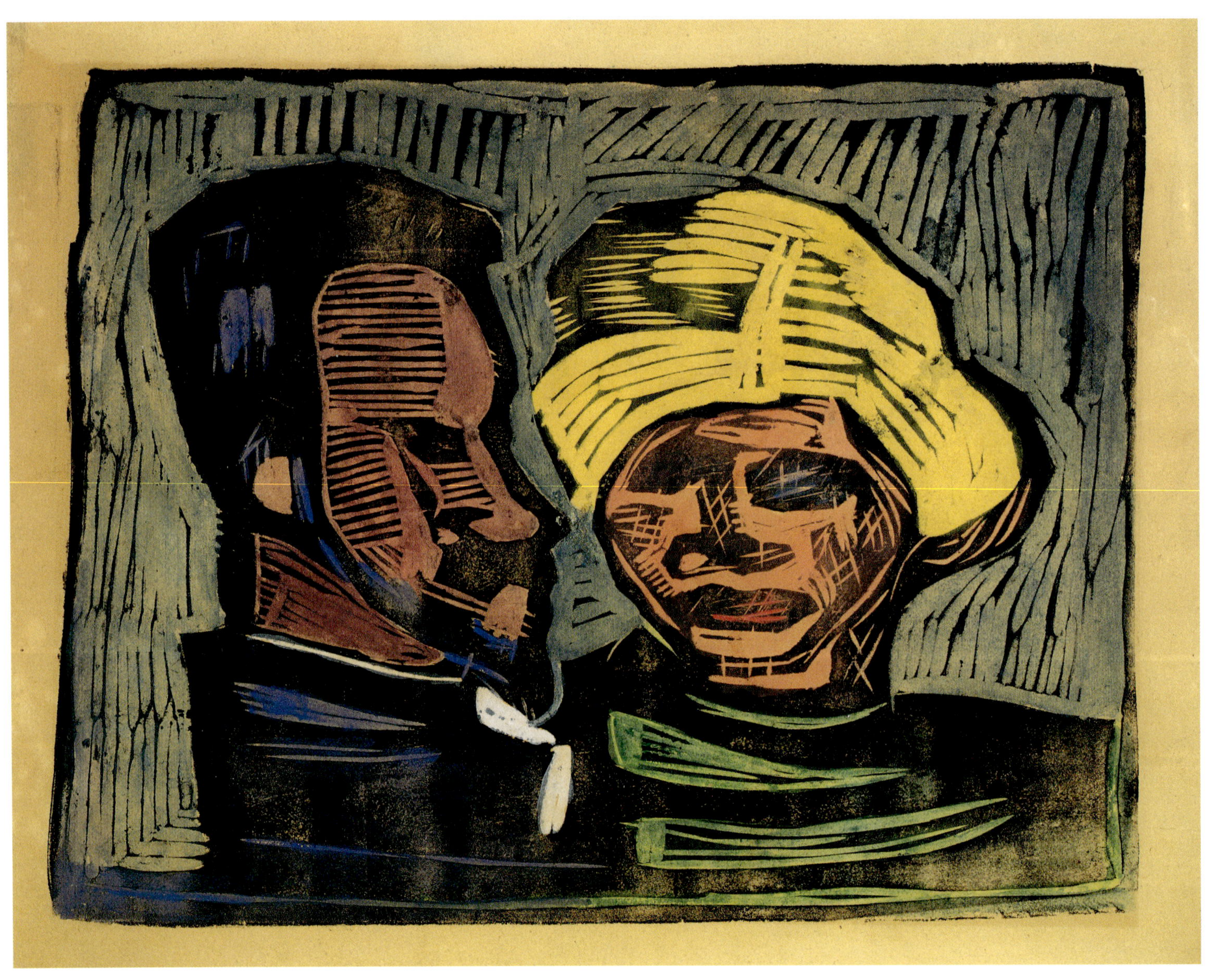

William Henry Johnson
Little Talk, circa 1935
(see page 160)

Greenville County Museum of Art

THE SOUTHERN COLLECTION 

Henrietta de Beaulieu Dering Johnston

circa 1674–1729

Man in Armor, 1726

pastel on paper, 11 7/8 × 8 15/16 inches
signed, on reverse: *Henrietta Johnston fecit / South Carolina Ano 17. . ;*
copied in later hand: *Henrietta Johnston fecit / South Carolina Ano 1726*
Museum purchase with funds from the 1988 Museum Antiques Show, Elliott, Davis & Company, CPAs, sponsor, and donated by The Museum Association, Inc.

Most of the artists working in the American colonies were born and trained abroad, so it is not surprising that many of the conventions used by colonial painters derived from European examples. As an extension of England, the colonies not only adapted the governance, currency, and legal system from the mother country but also subscribed to prevailing attitudes and ideas about art. Artists in America faced a number of challenges, including the practical concerns of obtaining supplies and developing a clientele for their paintings. The latter often proved particularly difficult since many early settlers were preoccupied with basic survival in bleak and often hostile surroundings. For these reasons, Henrietta Dering Johnston is a remarkable figure in American art history—not only because she was the country's first professional woman artist, but also because she worked in pastel, a medium not yet popular in Europe.

Exactly when and where Johnston began to paint and with whom she studied have not been discovered. Her maiden name, de Beaulieu, suggests that she was from a French Huguenot family. Neither the date nor location of her birth has been determined, but immigration records for London dated December 1687 granted certain rights of citizenship to Francis and Suzanna de Beaulieu and their children, Henry and Henrietta. Robert Dering, a member of a distinguished English family, married the artist in 1694. Ten years later she was a widow living in Dublin, where she painted portraits, perhaps to support herself. Conspicuous for their sophistication and stylishness, her Irish pastels have remained in exceptionally good condition.[1]

In 1705 the artist married the Reverend Gideon Johnston. Three years later the couple arrived in Charleston, where he became rector of St. Philip's Episcopal Church. The minister's letters suggest that his journey to the New World was motivated by his eagerness for a steady income rather than his missionary zeal. Nonetheless, his pay apparently was insufficient, and his wife supplemented the family income with her portrait commissions.

Johnston's American portraits are less complicated versions of her Irish examples. They are also smaller, which may have been the result of Johnston's wish to use her materials, imported from England, sparingly. Her style is a clearly recognizable one, derived from a type made popular among the English gentry by Sir Godfrey Kneller. Johnston's female subjects usually wore delicate chemises, while the male sitters were dressed in street clothes or, occasionally, armor. Each sitter's posture is erect, with the head often turned slightly toward the viewer. Typically, large oval eyes dominate the subject's face.

The sitter in the Museum's portrait has not been identified. Johnston's other sitters were members of her family's circle, namely members of the Dering family living in Dublin; parishioners at St. Philip's; French Huguenots, with whom the artist would have had a shared background; and the daughters of the Johnston family physician. It is likely that the subject of *Man in Armor* was also an acquaintance, possibly a military officer, although his outfit should not be interpreted too literally. His armor represents a pastiche, or collection of varied elements, from sixteenth- and seventeenth-century Italian and English motifs.[2]

---

1. Professor Anne Crookshank, Trinity College, Dublin, to author. See Forsyth Alexander, ed., *Henrietta Johnston* (Winston-Salem, N.C.: Museum of Early Southern Decorative Arts, 1991).

2. Walter J. Karcheski, Jr., curator, Higgins Armory Museum, Worcester, Mass., to author, 2 April 1993.

Born, probably France, circa 1674; emigrated to England, 1687; in Dublin, Ireland, circa 1700–1707; to Charleston, South Carolina, 1708–1729; died, Charleston, 1729.

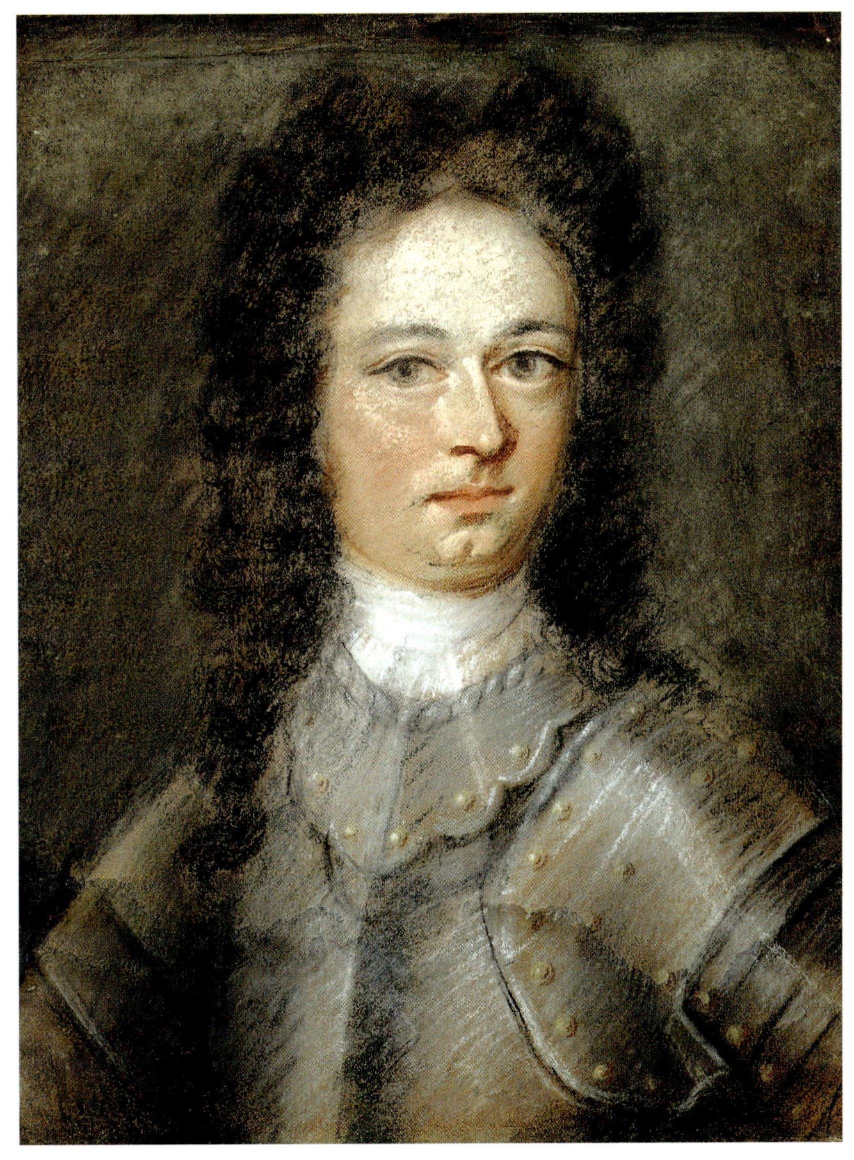

Mark Catesby

1679–1749

The Largest White Billed Woodpecker (Picus Maximus Rostro Albo) with Willow Oak, circa 1735

hand-colored engraving: image, 15 × 10⅛ inches; paper, 16⅞ × 12 inches
Museum purchase with funds donated by the Arthur and Holly Magill Foundation

The first European artists to come to the American continent were members of exploration and cartography teams. Their function was to record the flora and fauna as well as the inhabitants of the New World. In the mid-sixteenth century, as an emissary of Sir Walter Raleigh, John White voyaged to the Roanoke Colony; his firsthand watercolors later became the basis for a series of engravings by Theodore de Bry, which were widely circulated. Although designed to promote settlement, these images sensationalized the life-style of the natives. A century later the Enlightenment fostered a scientific interest in the documentation and publication of the plant and animal life of the colonies.

Often described as the forerunner of John James Audubon, Mark Catesby made two trips to the Southern colonies with the express purposes of recording the area's natural history and procuring specimens and seeds to send back to England. As a field botanist, his approach was studious; he visited different locales at different seasons both to see plants in various stages of growth and to facilitate the collection of seeds for his sponsors. He experimented with transplanting American plants in England and was successful with eighty-five varieties.

Catesby's first trip was to Virginia in 1712. At Westover, he assisted William Byrd II with his gardens in return for information about American species. Byrd, a naturalist who had been educated in England, remained an important supporter and resource for Catesby. During the ensuing seven years Catesby traveled inland to the Appalachians as well as south to Jamaica and Bermuda. After a short interval in England devoted primarily to soliciting sponsors, Catesby returned for three years of intense study and travel through the Carolinas, which at the time included Georgia and Florida. His goal was to publish his findings, and, when financial backing was not forthcoming, Catesby learned to engrave his watercolors. The result is a singular volume of 220 plates for which one individual procured and sketched the specimens, completed the engravings, and wrote the text. A true labor of love, Catesby's *Natural History of Carolina, Florida, and the Bahama Islands* was published in installments between 1731 and 1743.

Primarily a self-taught artist, Catesby created images that are remarkable for their detail and freshness. At times his arrangements verge on the naïve, but, like Audubon, who worked a century later, his purpose was not aesthetic but illustrative. Recognizing his artistic shortcomings, Catesby apologized in his text: "As I was not bred a Painter I hope some faults in perspective, and other niceties, may be more readily excused: for I humbly conceive that Plants and other Things done in a Flat, tho' exact manner, may serve the Purpose of Natural History, better in some Measure, than in a more bold and Painter-like Way."[1] Catesby's major invention that others, including Audubon, would follow was the placement of birds and animals among appropriate vegetation. His diligence toward the study of birds was rewarded with the appellation "founder of American ornithology."

In most of his renderings, Catesby elected to show the birds in profile. Although in his introduction he claims, "the Animal, particularly the Bird, I painted while alive (except a very few) and gave them their Gestures peculiar to every kind of Bird,"[2] his birds often appear as specimens, laid out for the viewer's examination. In *The Largest White Billed Woodpecker,* however, he succeeded in capturing the bird's characteristic stiff-necked posture, while implying its persistent pecking motion. The small oak leaves, which add both color and pattern to Catesby's design, also serve to make the bird appear more imposing.

Although little is known about Catesby's biography, he provided insight into why he devoted so much attention to birds: "As there is a greater variety of the feather'd Kind than of any other Animals . . . and as they excel in the Beauty of their Colours, and have a nearer relation to the Plants of which they feed on and frequent; I was induced chiefly (so far as I was able) to compleat an Account of them."[3] The importance of color to Catesby is witnessed by the fact that he personally hand-colored at least one set of the engravings and supervised the coloring of the others. In *Woodpecker* the brilliance of the red crest enlivens the entire composition, while the bird's angular shape is artfully mirrored by the tail and the spiky contours of the oak leaves.

---

1. Mark Catesby, *Natural History of Carolina, Florida, and the Bahama Islands . . . by the late Mark Catesby, F.R.S.,* with an introduction by George Frick and note by Joseph Ewan (1771; reprint, Savannah, Ga.: Beehive Press, 1974), vi.

2. Catesby, *Natural History,* vi.

3. Catesby, *Natural History,* iv.

Born, London, 1679; traveled to Virginia, Appalachia, Jamaica, and possibly Bermuda, 1712–1719; in England, 1719–1722, returned to Carolina, Florida, and the Bahamas, 1722–1725; in England, 1725–1749; named a fellow of the Royal Society, 1733; died, London, 1749.

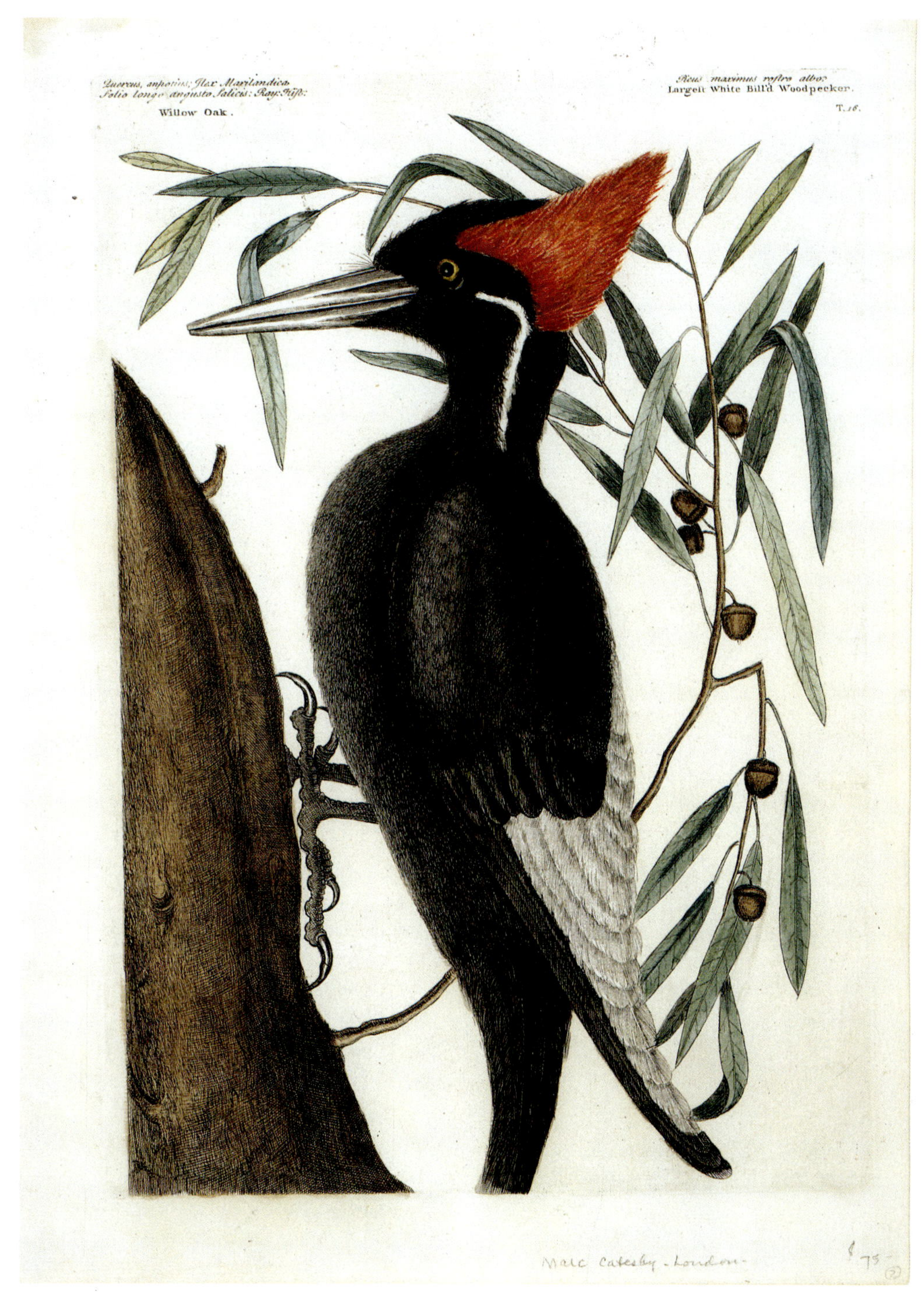
Quercus, an potius; Ilex Marilandica
Folio longo angusto Salicis: Ray Hist:
Willow Oak.
Picus maximus rostro albo
Largest White Bill'd Woodpecker.
T. 16.

Jeremiah Theus

1716–1774

Mrs. Henry Izard (Charlotte Broughton)
(circa 1729–1801), 1757

oil on canvas, 29½ × 24⅝ inches
signed, lower left: *J. Theus, 1757*
Museum purchase with funds donated by the Arthur and Holly Magill Foundation

Colonial artists were primarily portraitists who responded to the desires of well-to-do citizens. Portraits served several purposes: hanging in parlors, they were overt signs of affluence; and in a time of high mortality, they perpetuated the memory of individual family members. Portraits also provided a tie with the old country, and their popularity mirrored European taste. Many colonial painters were born abroad, some even had rudimentary training overseas, and most modeled their work on European examples. The preeminent American-born colonial painters were Benjamin West and John Singleton Copley, both of whom became frustrated by the restraints imposed by portraiture and moved to England, where they created monumental history paintings and found great success. Nonetheless, the demand for portraiture among American patrons grew, and throughout the colonies painters sought to accommodate this rising interest.

In New England several painters, including Robert Feke, Joseph Blackburn, and John Smibert, produced fashionable likenesses, many of which were based on English prototypes. John Wollaston, a London-trained drapery painter, built his reputation by traveling the East Coast in pursuit of portrait commissions, depicting countless sitters with his hallmark almond-shaped eyes. In South Carolina, Jeremiah Theus emerged as the exalted painter of successful merchants and plantation owners and their families. Like their Northern counterparts, Theus and his patrons aspired to create images in the latest fashion, a task accomplished by the shrewd adaptation of motifs found in contemporaneous English portraits. Although geographically isolated from his peers, Theus had access both to portraits of Charlestonians painted in London and to mezzotints, a highly refined form of engraving, of English notables. Just as colonial architecture and furniture reflect the use of published handbooks as source material, portraits painted before the Revolution reveal a reliance upon prints for details of costume and pose.

Born in Switzerland, Theus came to the Carolina colony in his late teens. There is no record of his formal training, but Theus knew how to procure materials and prepare pigments and canvas. The earliest known reference to the artist is a newspaper advertisement in which he offers his services as a portraitist as well as a painter of signs, crests, and coats of arms. Theus was eager to please, advertising, "likewise for the conveniency of those who live in the country, he is willing to wait on them at their respective plantations."[1] Theus succeeded in his endeavor to become the equivalent of Charleston's court painter, a position he achieved by depicting his sitters adorned in elegant jewels and fine fabrics, occasionally even in ermine-lined dresses.

Over a career that spanned three decades, Theus created a veritable social register of Charleston, a cosmopolitan city described by a contemporary as "a polite agreeable place, the people live very much in the English taste."[2] Theus's portraits, in their use of such conventions as the illusion of an oval frame and erect posture for the sitter, reflect this predilection. In about thirty extant portraits he employed motifs derived directly from mezzotints after contemporary English portraits. Specific details of clothing, jewelry, and bouquets document Theus's visual plagiarism, a methodology that did not perturb his sitters. Theus's patrons, in their desire to be fashionable, may even have encouraged him in this deceit. His paraphrasing from English examples eased his transition from sign painter to well-respected portraitist.[3]

Not all of Theus's portraits reflect his penchant for copying. *Mrs. Henry Izard,* painted in midcareer, is an unpretentious example in which the sitter's physiognomy is portrayed with remarkable honesty. Although the painter may have been loath to idealize her facial features, his skillful rendering of her dress and bonnet betray his desire to flatter. However, Theus portrays her as far more than a clotheshorse, capturing a wistful expression, perhaps reflecting the sad facts of her life. She was married at age eighteen, had two children who died in infancy, and was left a widow by her early twenties. She never remarried and lived until 1801, dying in her seventies. Several other members of her own family, the Broughtons, were painted by Theus, as was her stepson Ralph Izard, at age twelve. Sent to England for his education, Izard later became an important art patron and, in 1775, along with his young wife, was depicted by Copley in Rome. This painting, a conversation piece in which the couple gaze at each other, both reflects the Englishness of American taste and depicts the Izards as classical connoisseurs making the grand tour, a key ingredient in the education of a gentleman.

---

1. *South Carolina Gazette,* 20 August 1740.

2. Eliza Lucas to Mrs. Boddicott, 2 May [probably] 1740, as quoted in Harriott Horry Ravenel, *Eliza Pinckney* (New York: Scribner's, 1896), 5.

3. See Martha R. Severens, "Jeremiah Theus of Charleston: Plagiarist or Pundit?" *The Southern Quarterly: A Journal of the Arts of the South* 24, nos. 1–2 (Fall–Winter 1985): 56–70.

Born, Chur, Switzerland, 1716; immigrated to Orangeburg Township, Carolina, 1735; moved to Charleston, 1740; died, Charleston, 1774.

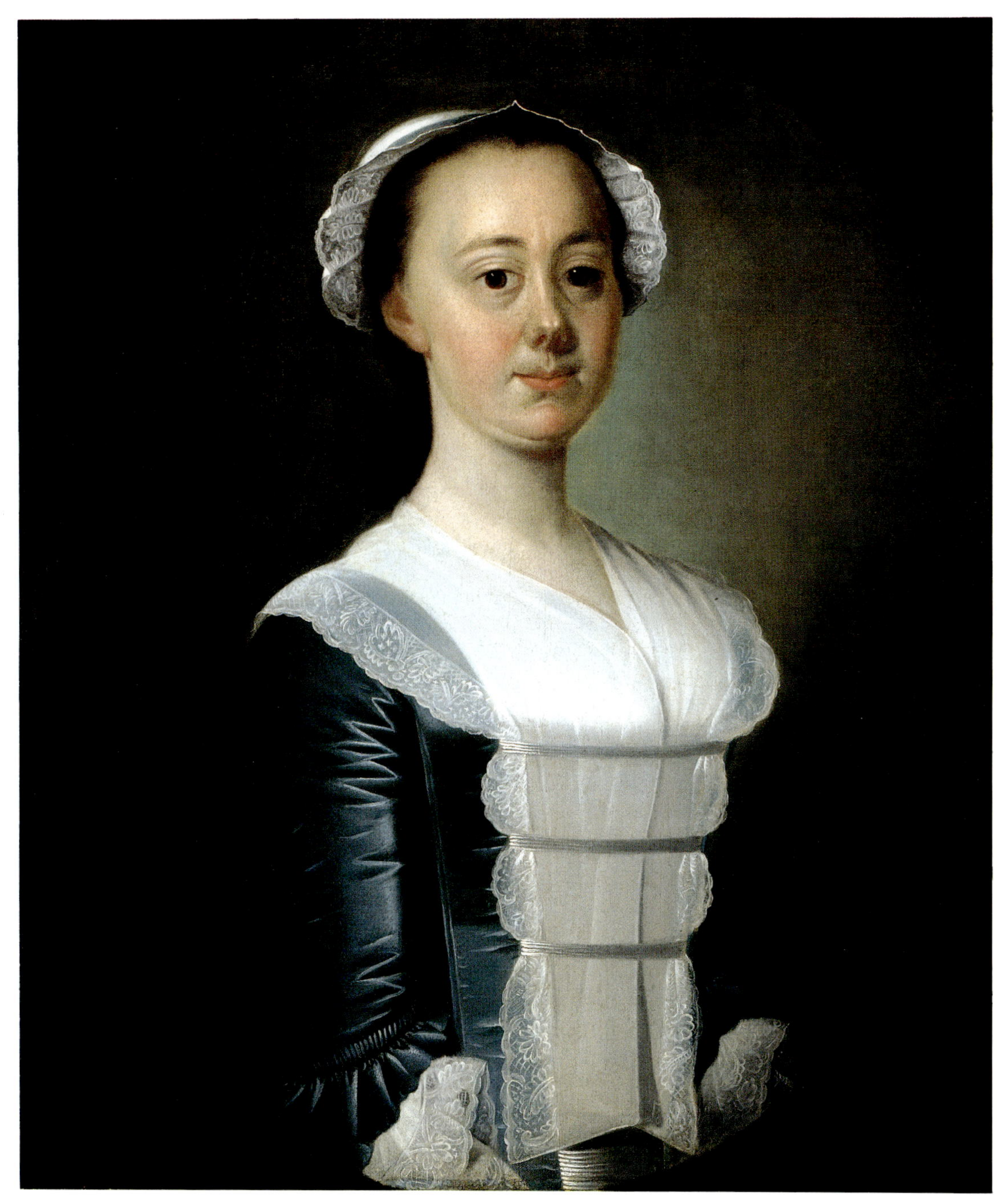

Charles Peale Polk

1767–1822

General Nathanael Greene (1742–1786), circa 1794

oil on canvas, 21 × 18 inches
Museum purchase with funds donated by the Daniel Foundation

In contrast to colonial portraits, which were dependent on English prototypes, the images created after the Revolution were intended as direct statements and realistic portrayals of American citizens. In fact, portraits of military officers and statesmen were so much in demand that, after an absence of eighteen years, Gilbert Stuart returned to the United States, where he established himself as one of the foremost portraitists of American notables. Similarly, Charles Willson Peale and his son Rembrandt painted numerous likenesses of President George Washington as well as of other important figures of the day.

Charles Peale Polk's portrait of General Nathanael Greene reflects this demand for patriotic portraits. The painting also demonstrates the training available to a young American artist in the 1780s. Polk was a nephew of Charles Willson Peale, the paterfamilias of a clan of painters, naturalists, and museum founders. From early childhood Polk lived in his uncle's household, where he may have received instruction in the rudiments of painting. This training almost certainly would have included copying his uncle's work, and Polk's earliest known works are 1783 copies of Peale's portraits.[1] Ten years later, advertising in Baltimore, Polk invited prospective patrons to visit his exhibition room to view likenesses of Washington and Thomas Jefferson. Polk's portrait of Greene may also have been copied for this occasion from his uncle's 1783 life study.

Polk's painting is a simplification of Peale's original, a painting that was part of Peale's Gallery of Great Men, and that is now in the collection of Independence Hall, Philadelphia. Polk has reduced the size of the canvas slightly, sharpened the contours, and flattened the image. He appears to have had some difficulty with foreshortening as well as with the modeling of the face. These sorts of challenges often troubled unsophisticated portrait painters, today referred to as limners.

A portrait of Nathanael Greene is important to the South, and particularly to Greenville. Having fought at Boston, Trenton, and Monmouth, Greene was given command of the American forces in the South in October 1780, following the defeat of Horatio Gates by Cornwallis at Camden, South Carolina. Skilled at supply management, Greene recognized the need not only for an expert cavalry but also for an efficient communication system. Two years after Greene's appointment, Charleston, the last British post in the South, fell. In gratitude for his exemplary service, both South Carolina and Georgia voted him extensive tracts of land. As further tribute, towns through the Southeast, including Greenville, South Carolina, were named or renamed in his honor.[2]

1. Linda Crocker Simmons, *Charles Peale Polk, 1767–1822* (Washington, D.C.: The Corcoran Gallery of Art, 1981), 3.

2. A. V. Huff, "A History of Greenville County," unpublished manuscript, 79.

Born, Annapolis, Maryland, 1767; by 1776 living in Charles Willson Peale's household, Philadelphia; began professional career in Philadelphia, 1785–1790, followed by five years in Baltimore, 1791–1796; itinerant painter in western Maryland until 1802; government clerk, Washington, D.C., 1802–1819; died, Richmond County, Virginia, 1822.

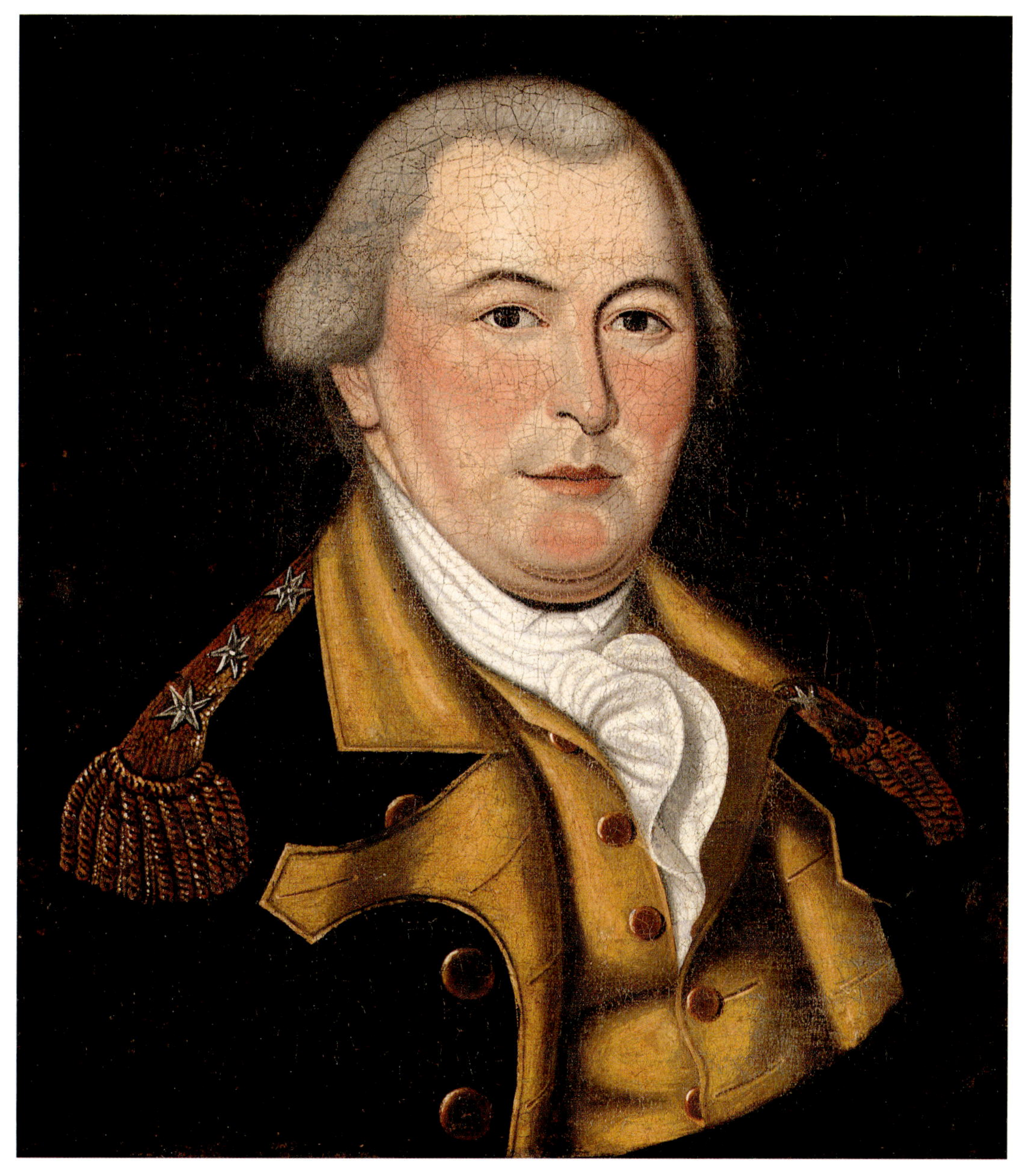

Unidentified artist

active circa 1805

Benjamin Hawkins and the Creek Indians, circa 1805

oil on canvas, 35⅞ × 49⅞ inches
Gift of The Museum Association, Inc., with funds donated by Corporate Partners: Ernst and Young; Fluor Daniel; Director's Circle Members: Mr. and Mrs. Alester G. Furman III; Mr. and Mrs. M. Dexter Hagy; Thomas P. Hartness; Mr. and Mrs. E. Erwin Maddrey II; Mary M. Pearce; Mr. and Mrs. John D. Pellett, Jr.; Mr. W. Thomas Smith; Mr. and Mrs. Edward H. Stall; Eleanor and Irvine Welling; Museum Antiques Show, 1989, 1990, 1991, Elliott, Davis & Company, CPAs, sponsor; Collector's Group 1990, 1991

Until the antebellum period, paintings that recorded specific events in American history were rare, as they required both patrons and a suitable place for display. Even such important works as Benjamin West's *William Penn's Treaty with the Indians* was created without American patronage. A veritable icon of American history, it was painted in England, for an Englishman, and remained there until 1850. Its peacemaking image, however, became well known through widely circulated engravings as well as through several copies.

In this light, the canvas portraying Benjamin Hawkins and members of the Creek tribe is even more remarkable. Rather than embracing a topic about which Americans concurred, the painting deals with a sensitive and controversial issue: white settlers' treatment of Native Americans. Regrettably, the circumstances of the painting's commission and its authorship are today unknown. Even its subject matter was misunderstood for much of its recent history.[1]

Benjamin Hawkins (1754–1818), a well-educated and well-to-do North Carolinian, served as George Washington's French interpreter. In his native state he performed several public duties, first as a delegate to the Congress of Confederation and then as North Carolina's first full-term senator. Perhaps because of his linguistic skills and his humanitarian outlook, Hawkins was appointed by Washington as superintendent for Indian affairs in the South, a vast area extending as far west and north as the Ohio River. Ideologically, Hawkins was closely aligned with Thomas Jefferson, and together they believed the solution to the "Indian problem" was education and the cultivation of land rather than forced removal. In one of several lengthy letters to Hawkins, Jefferson articulated his philosophy about native peoples: "The promotion of agriculture, therefore, and household manufacture, are essential to their preservation, and I am disposed to aid and encourage it liberally."[2]

Hawkins labored after these ideals for more than two decades and, to a large degree, was successful in introducing staple agriculture and animal husbandry to the Creeks. Like Jefferson at Monticello, Hawkins, with his own resources, established a model farm that he actively cultivated: "I have commenced a garden on a large scale in which I am planting everything I can gather. I have now of my own raising pumpkins, turnips, beets, radishes, cabbages, coleworts, carrots, shallots, lettuce and parsley."[3]

The Museum's painting can be viewed as both an idealistic tribute to Hawkins's endeavor and as propaganda for Jefferson's policy. As such, it must date to before 1811, when the plan was undermined by tensions preceding the War of 1812; the rebellious Tecumseh attempted to incite the Creeks as they were wooed by the British. The scene depicted is Hawkins's model plantation along the Flint River in central Georgia and its abundant results. In the foreground Hawkins instructs a pair of Creeks in the use of the plow; another plow behind this group serves as the intentionally emblematic focal point. Although Hawkins dominates the composition as the tallest figure dressed in a slightly old-fashioned formal waistcoat, he is significantly outnumbered by Creeks, who wear a combination of tribal and colonial clothing. The background consists of a richly cultivated and orderly landscape that has been improved through Hawkins's efforts; the overriding theme of the painting is civilization, and the mood is one of harmony.

Benjamin Hawkins and the Creek Indians is a combination of several different types of painting: portraiture, landscape, still life, and even genre, in its depiction of everyday people in typical postures. Thus, the painting is something of a pastiche, which suggests that it may have been painted by more than one artist. Such passages as the rendering of Hawkins, the conversing Creeks, and the nursing mother may derive from paintings or engravings; they parallel similar elements in West's *Penn's Treaty*. The friezelike arrangement of figures, standing as if on the edge of a stage, along with their insufficient integration with the landscape, indicate the lack of a single artistic vision. And whereas many of the details, like the turnips and the Creeks' clothing, are studiously and realistically painted, certain aspects of the landscape suggest that the painter never visited the site but worked instead from a verbal description or visual representations.

Numerous artists have been suggested as the author of the Museum's painting, including William Bowles, an adversary of Hawkins and an amateur painter who lived among the Seminoles and was reportedly more interested in exploiting them than in lending assistance. The landscape with its modest, steep-roofed dwellings resembles the views of Mulberry Plantation by the Charleston painter Thomas Coram, although most of his work was on a small scale. Both the figure of Hawkins and landscape details are reminiscent of the work of Ralph Earl, a Connecticut portraitist known for his inclusion of scenery. Earl, however, died in 1801, just as Hawkins established himself on the Flint River. Among other artists whose names have been put forward are Robert Edge Pine, whose 1784 portrait of Hawkins is now lost, and Edward Savage, more for circumstantial than stylistic reasons. Pine painted a large multifigured history painting, *Congress Voting for Independence*, which Savage finished after Pine's death in 1788. This work was a centerpiece of Savage's enterprise, the Columbian Gallery, a venue suitable for the Museum's painting, although the work is not listed in the gallery's catalogues or announcements.

The painting's lack of a signature, a circumstance not unusual for a painting from this period, adds to the puzzle. Without such firm documentary evidence as contracts, bills and receipts, or letters, and in the absence of a verbal tradition, the attribution of a painting as unusual as *Benjamin Hawkins and the Creek Indians* becomes a connoisseur's dilemma. However, the painting serves as a reminder that there were a few enlightened individuals, including Hawkins and Jefferson, whose humanitarian approach to the "Indian problem" was erased in the name of progress.

---

1. See Linda Crocker Simmons, "The Emerging Nation, 1790–1830," in *Painting in the South, 1564–1980* (Richmond: Virginia Museum of Fine Arts, 1983), 42 and 202.

2. Jefferson to Hawkins, 18 February 1803, in Andrew A. Lipscomb, ed., *The Writings of Thomas Jefferson* (Washington, D.C.: The Thomas Jefferson Memorial Association, 1903), 20:362–363.

3. Hawkins to Silas Dinsmoor, 6 January 1799, in C. L. Grant, ed., *Letters, Journals and Writings of Benjamin Hawkins, 1796–1801* (Savannah, Ga.: The Beehive Press, 1980), 1:236.

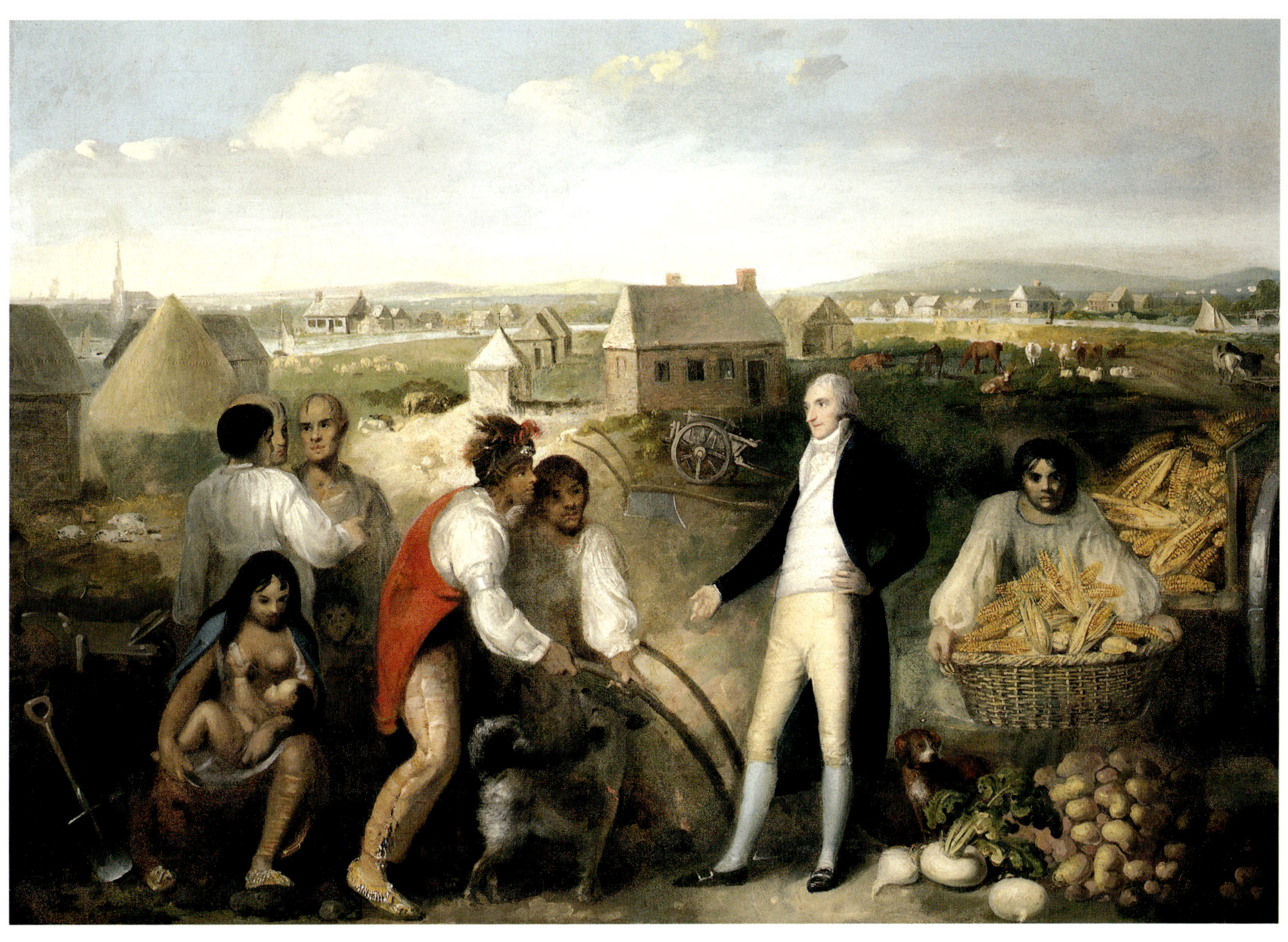

Washington Allston

1779–1843

Landscape with Banditti, 1798

oil on canvas, 11 5/8 × 13 3/8 inches
signed, on reverse before relining: *W. Allston designed and painted / Nov. 1798, Harvard College / Cambridge*
Gift of Mr. and Mrs. Alester G. Furman III
(illustrated on page 16)

Isaac of York, 1817

oil on canvas, 30 × 25 inches
Gift of Mrs. Charles E. Daniel

Portraiture dominated American art from the colonial period well into the nineteenth century. The preference for portraiture may be explained by its practical nature, that of recording for posterity the likeness of an important figure or of a loved one. An American taste for landscape and other subjects developed slowly, and many artists, especially those who spent extended periods in England and France, including Samuel F. B. Morse, John Vanderlyn, and Washington Allston, were frustrated by the reluctance on this side of the Atlantic to abandon portraits in favor of other, more uplifting, imagery. Of these, it was Allston who relied least on portrait painting, preferring instead grandly conceived narrative paintings based on religious or literary themes.

A native of South Carolina, Allston was born on his family's plantation, Brookgreen, along the Waccamaw River. He left the state as a boy to pursue his education in New England, and it was while he was a student at Harvard College that he painted the small canvas *Landscape with Banditti,* demonstrating not only his romantic inclination but also his allegiance to the old masters, in this case Salvator Rosa. The misty atmosphere, gesturing figures, and dead trees clearly relate to the works of Rosa, whom Allston is known to have admired. Inscribed on the reverse, "W. Allston designed and painted / Nov. 1798, Harvard College / Cambridge," the painting is virtually contemporary with a paper written by the artist the following year. Titled "Procrastination Is the Thief of Time," the essay tells the story of an artist who makes his way to Rome and falls under the spell of Raphael, Michelangelo, Correggio, Claude Lorrain, and, in particular, Rosa. The protagonist felt that "the Soul of this master was in unison with his own; he felt a strange pleasure in brooding over his dark rocks and gloomy wildness and shuddered at, yet could not but admire the noble ferocity of his banditti."[1] A dark and moody composition, Allston's painting is more an evocation than the depiction of an actual story. It is unclear whether the figures in the painting are soldiers or thieves.

The influence of seventeenth-century art on Allston's work is clear throughout his career and is also evident in the works of other members of his circle. In England from 1811 to 1818, Allston was there during what must have been a rich and stimulating time that included the early formation of the London National Gallery. In Paris, he saw the vast art treasures assembled by Napoleon. Allston's taste was eclectic; he was inspired not only by the stylistic and technical qualities of old-master paintings but also by their subject matter. He had a tremendous capability for synthesizing various styles, absorbing them, and making them his own. *Isaac of York* resembles the work of Rembrandt, without relying on a specific painting. Allston, like Rembrandt, was intrigued by the ethnicity of Polish Jews, whom he encountered in London. The Museum's painting is one of four contemporaneous canvases devoted to this theme, and all relate to *Belshazzar's Feast,* Allston's magnum opus.[2] About to embark on a major theme from the Old Testament, Allston's emulation of Rembrandt was logical and his admiration for the Dutch master was profound: "Rembrandt, as you know, had no excellence in form, though no one ever surpassed him in expression, even in the widest sense; for he was a poet in all else."[3]

Reminiscent of Rembrandt's high priests, the figure projects an otherworldly, inspired gaze that radiates spirituality. Allston's manner of painting, with its many glazes, is akin to the technique of the Venetian painters whose work he studied. Entitled *Isaac of York,* a designation given by the artist at the time of its exhibition at the Boston Athenaeum in 1833, the painting evokes a literary association with Sir Walter Scott's *Ivanhoe,* which was issued in 1819, two years after the painting was completed. Although the four paintings are typologically related to *Belshazzar's Feast,* they were never incorporated into the huge painting, which was begun in England in 1817 and remained unfinished at Allston's death.

---

1. William H. Gerdts and Theodore H. Stebbins, Jr., *"A Man of Genius": The Art of Washington Allston (1779–1843)* (Boston: Museum of Fine Arts, 1979), 19.

2. The other three paintings belong to the Corcoran Gallery of Art, Washington, D.C., the Museum of Fine Arts, Boston, and a private collector; *Belshazzar's Feast* is in the collection of the Detroit Institute of Arts. The Greenville Museum's painting was acquired by the Boston Athenaeum in 1833 and remained on deposit at the Museum of Fine Arts, Boston, from 1876 to 1986. See David Bjelajac, *Millennial Desire and the Apocalyptic Vision of Washington Allston* (Washington, D.C.: Smithsonian Institution Press, 1987).

3. Allston to John S. Cogdell, in Jared B. Flagg, ed., *The Life and Letters of Washington Allston* (1892; reprint, New York: Benjamin Blom, 1969), 297.

Born, Brookgreen Plantation, near Georgetown, South Carolina, 1779; graduated from Harvard College in 1800; to England with Edward Greene Malbone, 1801; studied with Benjamin West at the Royal Academy, London; Europe, 1804–1808; after three years in Boston, returned to England, 1811–1818; resided in the Boston area, 1818–1843; died, Cambridgeport, Massachusetts, 1843.

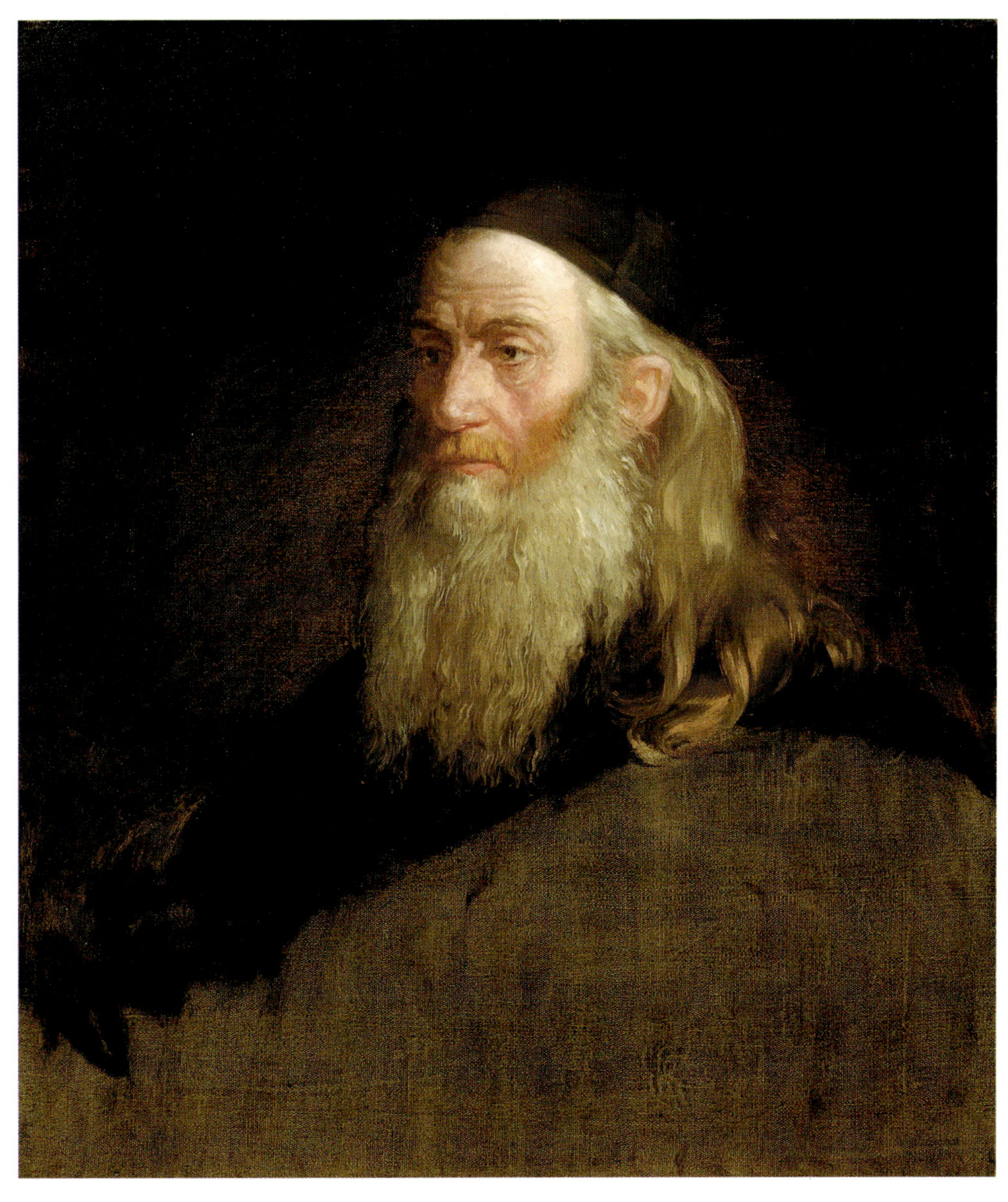

Thomas Sully

1783–1872

Ganymede, 1822

oil on canvas, 18 × 14½ inches
signed, on headband: *T. S. Guido*
Gift of the Director's Associates: Mr. and Mrs. R. Glenn Hilliard; Dr. and Mrs. Jeffrey G. Lawson; Alice and Hal Lonnecker; Mr. and Mrs. Thomas A. Roe; Mr. and Mrs. Robert Scott Small; Mr. and Mrs. Wilson C. Wearn

The American appetite for portraits spawned a veritable industry of portraitists in the late eighteenth century that persisted until the 1840s, when photography became an affordable alternative. Although many artists, including Washington Allston and Samuel F. B. Morse, shunned portraiture, others reveled in it, frequently traveling great distances in pursuit of commissions. As the economy expanded, more and more people wanted their portraits painted; portraits proliferated to such an extent that one critic decried the fact that parlors were soon overwhelmed by them: "You can hardly open the door of a best-room any where, without surprizing or being surprized by, the picture of some body, plastered to the wall and staring at you with both eyes and a bunch of flowers."[1]

Thomas Sully dominated portraiture not only as a popular and prolific artist, painting more than two thousand likenesses, but also as a teacher, whose many students disseminated his flattering and fluid painting style beyond the eastern seaboard. He was acclaimed by William Dunlap, the first historian of American art, as "the prince of American portrait painting." Born in England, Sully spent his childhood in Charleston, South Carolina, where he enjoyed the friendship of Charles Fraser, whom Sully called "the first person that ever took pains to instruct me in the rudiments of the art, and although himself a mere tyro, his kindness, and the progress made in the consequence of it, determined the course of my future life."[2]

Like many of his peers, Sully went to England to further his education, working in the studio of Benjamin West for about nine months. Despite the fact that he was in London when history painting was all the rage, Sully persisted with portrait painting, admiring the fashionable Sir Thomas Lawrence. His trip had been underwritten by six sponsors who were each to receive a copy by Sully of an old master. The artist easily gained invitations to view several London collections, but permission to copy was more difficult to obtain. West came to his rescue, permitting Sully to make copies from the collection he had assembled. From this experience Sully developed a taste for old-master paintings, and he learned from West the value of an exhibition space adjoining his studio—for his own enjoyment, for his students, and for prospective clients.

Understandably, Sully's copies gained him less recognition than his highly successful work in portraiture, but his register indicates that one-fifth of his work was devoted to "fancy pieces," landscapes, and history painting. Many of the paintings were done specifically for his own use, including the Museum's *Ganymede.* Register entry number 2252 reads: "Ganymede. Copied from painting by Guido for the artist's collection. Begun Oct. 29th, 1822, finished Nov. 11th, 1822. Head. Price, $80.00."[3] Others in this category were painted as demonstration pieces for his students, and some were offered for sale in the exhibitions of the Pennsylvania Academy of the Fine Arts.

Upon his return to America, Sully resided in Philadelphia, where he participated regularly in the Academy's exhibitions and was an active supporter, serving as a member of the board of directors and as an instructor for more than thirty years. As the source for his copy Sully used the *Ganymede* by Guido Reni presented to the Academy in 1812 by Joseph Allen Smith, one of the preeminent collectors of the period and a native of Charleston who had amassed his collection of Italian paintings, engravings, and gems during a fourteen-year stay in Europe.[4]

The selection of Reni's *Ganymede* is of interest because the Italian Baroque painter's reputation was variously regarded. Sir Joshua Reynolds, who established taste among artists and collectors in the late eighteenth century, disdained him, but the English Romantic painter, Henry Fuseli, commended his refinement, saying, "Grace attracted Guido, but it was not the studied grace of the theatres; his female forms are abstractions of antique beauty attended by languishing attitudes, arrayed by voluptuous fashions."[5] Perhaps it was these very qualities that appealed to Sully, who was later celebrated for his languid, flattering depictions, especially those of women.

Sully's copy of Reni's *Ganymede* is faithful and was evidently something of a favorite, as he repeated it at least five times. The subject of the painting derives from Homer, who recounted Zeus's many liaisons and affairs. A peasant boy, Ganymede, "handsomest of mortals," was loved by Zeus for his beauty. He was captured by the god disguised as an eagle and given the role of cup bearer to the gods. Both Reni and Sully present the sexually ambiguous nature of the figure, which is augmented by the latter's soft handling and delicate use of color.

---

1. John Neal, "Observations on Writings of John Neal, 1793–1876," *Pennsylvania State College Bulletin* 37 (5 February 1943): 42.

2. William Dunlap, *A History of the Rise and Progress of the Arts of Design in the United States* (1834; reprint, New York: Benjamin Blom, 1965), 2:237.

3. Edward Biddle and Mantle Fielding, *The Life and Works of Thomas Sully, 1783–1872* (Lancaster, Pa.: Wickersham Press, 1921), 353.

4. George C. Rogers, Jr., "Joseph Allen Smith," *Art in the Lives of South Carolinians* (Charleston, S.C.: Carolina Art Association, 1979).

5. Henry Fuseli, *Lectures on Painting,* London 1801, in *Guido Reni, 1572–1642* (Los Angeles: Los Angeles County Museum of Art, 1988), 335.

Born, Horncastle, Lincolnshire, England, 1783; childhood in Charleston, South Carolina, 1794–1799; studied in Virginia with his brother Lawrence, 1799–1804, and in London with Benjamin West, 1809–1810; based in Philadelphia, 1810–1872, traveled in pursuit of commissions to Baltimore, Richmond, Charleston, and London; died, Philadelphia, 1872.

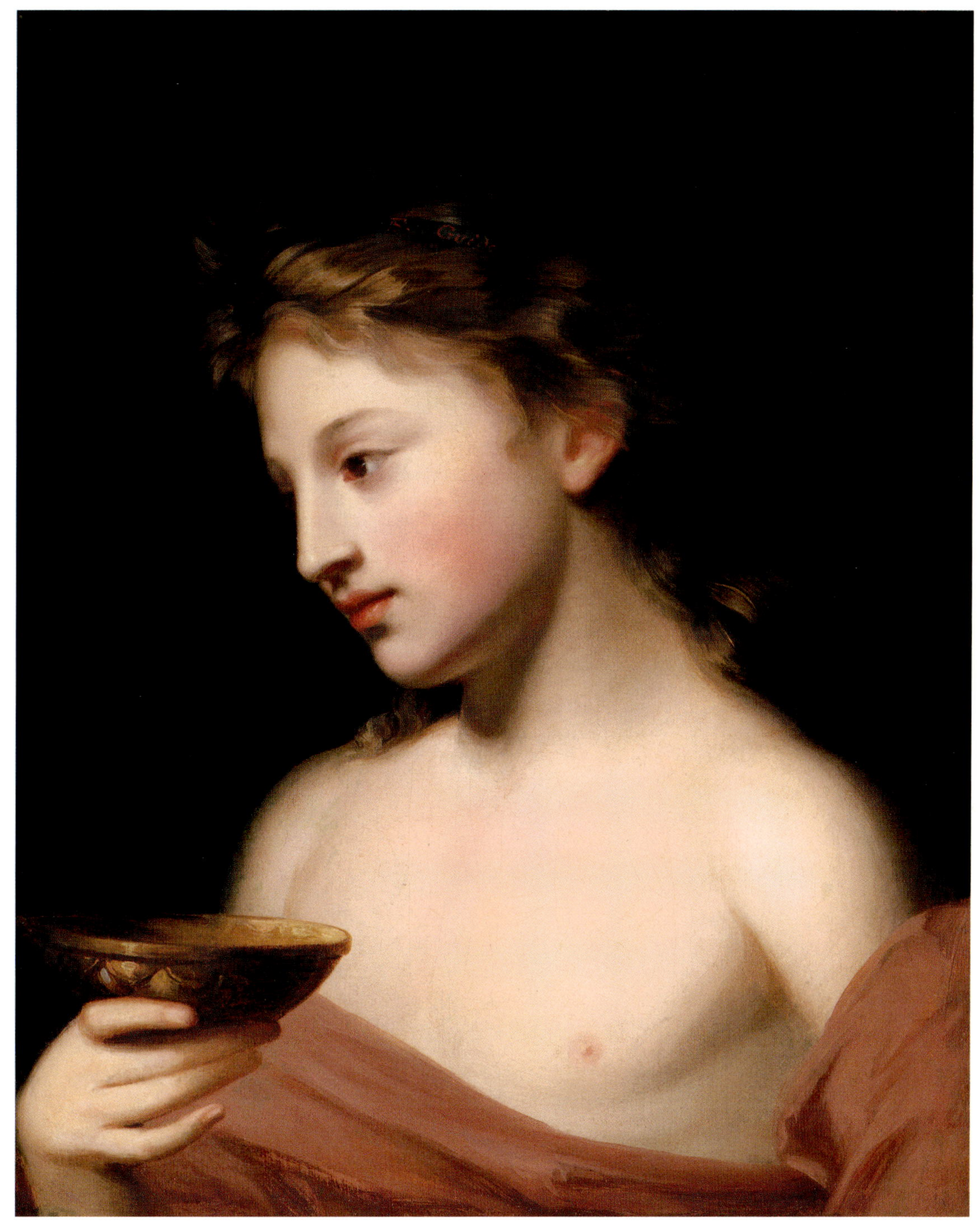

Charles Fraser

1782–1860

Niagara Falls from Goat Island Looking toward Canadian Side, 1820 [A]

watercolor on paper, 10 15/16 × 17 7/8 inches

Niagara Falls from Goat Island Looking toward Prospect Point, 1820 [B]

watercolor on paper, 10 15/16 × 17 15/16 inches

Niagara Falls from Prospect Point, 1820 [C]

watercolor on paper, 11 15/16 × 17 15/16 inches
signed, lower left: *C. Fraser, 1820*

Niagara Falls below the Falls, 1820 [D]

watercolor on paper, 10 5/16 × 16 3/8 inches

Museum purchase with funds donated by the Arthur and Holly Magill Foundation

The earliest American landscapes were topographical views meant to record specific places. Often intended to promote the commerce of an area or to document a noteworthy site, they frequently appeared as illustrations in books or periodicals. The single most popular and the oldest landscape image was that of Niagara Falls. As early as 1697 an unidentified Dutch artist produced an image of Niagara from an explorer's verbal description.[1] The depiction of Niagara Falls presented particular challenges: its vastness defies reduction, and its most memorable aspect, the great roar of water, cannot be re-created.

Among the many artists attracted to Niagara were John Trumbull, John Vanderlyn, and Charles Fraser, all primarily portraitists. Fraser, of Charleston, South Carolina, specialized in miniatures and was largely self-taught, although as a schoolboy he took art lessons from Thomas Coram. Perhaps at Coram's instigation, while still a teenager, Fraser began a series of sketchbooks. Many of the pen-and-ink sketches are direct copies from travel books of foreign places like Portugal and Wales that Fraser would never see. These copies served as exercises in perspective and in the conventions of landscape. More significant, however, are the many watercolor views of Charleston and its environs that record plantations belonging to family and friends. Dating to about 1800, these remarkable sketches are precocious examples of an emerging landscape tradition. Their purpose, however, was much like that of the artist's miniatures, to provide small-scale likenesses.[2] Fraser produced a series of topographical views of Boston, Richmond, Passaic Falls, and the Hudson River, which was engraved and published in *Analectic Magazine* between 1815 and 1818.

Although he left no record of having traveled to Niagara, Fraser was fascinated by it. The key to understanding this preoccupation may lie in a fellow artist, Alvan Fisher from Boston, and a British patron, Sir James Wright. Fisher visited Charleston in early 1819 and exhibited a variety of landscape and genre paintings. The following year Fraser painted a miniature portrait of Fisher, gratis, and both painted views of Niagara. It is conceivable that they traveled to the falls together, and that the miniature portrait is a testament of their friendship. Three years later, in 1823, Fraser noted in his account book the sale of a "View of the Falls . . . [and] a Portfolio of the views of Niagara to Sir James Wright for—$100."[3] The connection between Wright and Fraser is unclear; it is possible that Wright, like many Europeans, was captivated by the grandeur of the American landscape as exemplified by Niagara.

The Museum's four watercolors of Niagara present the site from a variety of viewpoints. Fraser, like many other artists who worked in sets of four, endeavored to portray the scene completely.[4] Standing on Goat Island, which divides the Niagara River, Fraser looked toward both the American and Canadian sides of the falls for two of his views. From the American side he portrayed the drama of the horseshoe falls with spray rising. The fourth scene, a quiet departure from the drama of the falls themselves, depicts pleasure boats on the river and the village of Queenston, Canada, nestled on the shore. Together the four views may have composed the portfolio acquired by Wright; Fraser may have planned to develop them for publication.

Fraser liberally employed a variety of landscape conventions. Most notable are the gesturing man overlooking the falls in the foreground, the dead stump that directs the viewer's gaze into the composition, and the use of *repoussoir* in three of the four works. Translated literally, *repoussoir* means "to push back." As an art term it describes the placement of such landscape elements as trees and rocks in the corners of the foreground, a device that aids in creating the illusion of space. Clearly Fraser used the technique to convey a sense of the vastness and expansiveness of Niagara.

---

1. See Jeremy Elwell Adamson, *Niagara* (Washington, D.C.: The Corcoran Gallery of Art, 1985).

2. See Alice R. Huger Smith, *A Charleston Sketchbook, 1796–1806* (Charleston, S.C.: Carolina Art Association, 1940), and Martha R. Severens, "Sketches and Oil Paintings," in Martha R. Severens and Charles L.Wyrick, eds., *Charles Fraser of Charleston* (Charleston, S.C.: Carolina Art Association/Gibbes Art Gallery, 1983), 75–104.

3. For Fraser's account book see Severens and Wyrick, *Fraser,* 115–146.

4. Adamson, *Niagara,* 38–41.

Born, Charleston, South Carolina, 1782; took drawing lessons from Thomas Coram, 1795; studied and practiced law, 1801–1818; traveled to New York and Connecticut, 1816; to Boston, 1824; to Hartford, Connecticut, 1831; and New England, 1833; died, Charleston, 1860.

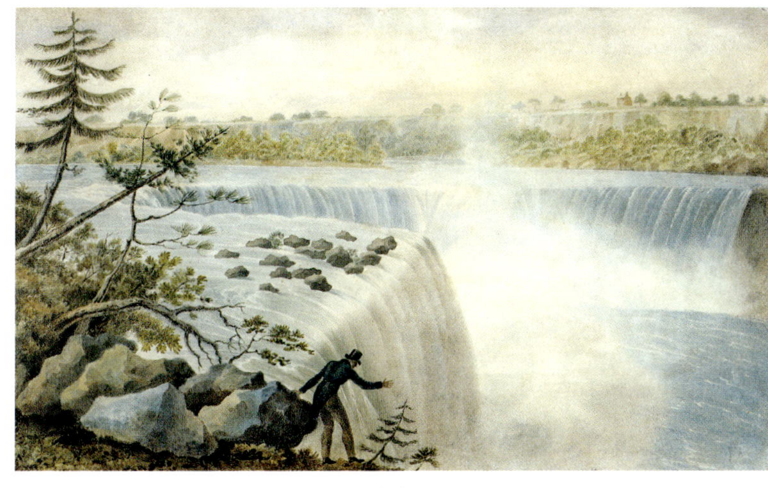

[A]

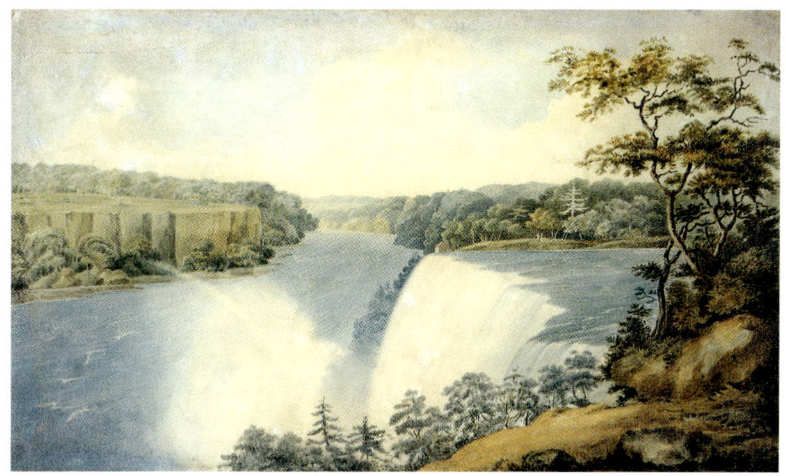

[B]

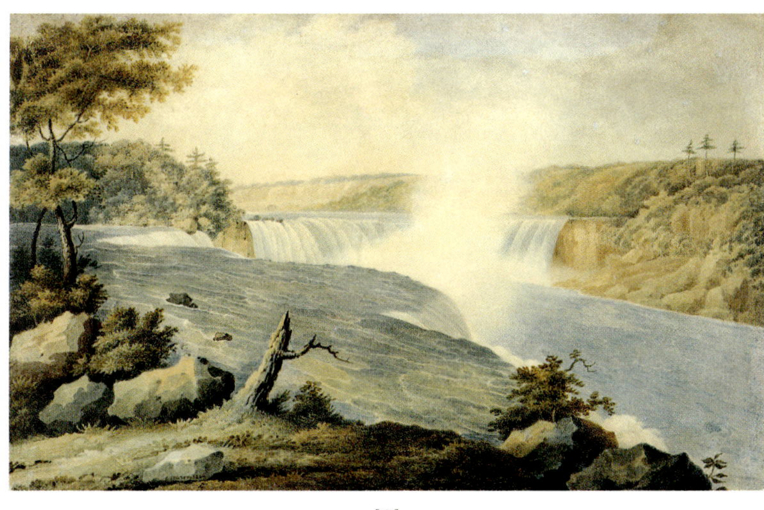

[C]

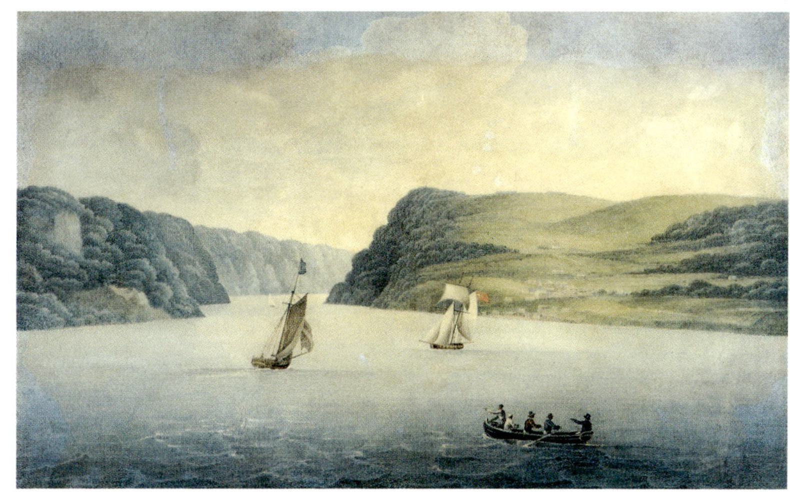

[D]

Alvan Fisher

1792–1863

Under the Bridge, 1828

oil on canvas, 30 × 25 inches
signed, lower center: *A. Fisher, 1828*
Museum purchase with funds donated by the Arthur and Holly Magill Foundation

The transition from topographical renderings of particular sites to full-fledged landscapes was slow, and it was not until the 1830s, under the leadership of Thomas Cole, that landscape painting was widely accepted. Initially, American landscapes mirrored European prototypes, and stylistic conventions abounded in these earliest depictions, indicating that artists used other paintings rather than nature as their model.

The frustrations encountered by aspiring landscape painters are cogently recounted by Alvan Fisher. After some initial success, he returned to portrait painting to earn a steady income:

> I then [in 1815] began painting a species of pictures which had not been practised much, if any, in this country, viz: barnyard scenes belonging to rural life, winter pieces, portraits of animals, etc. This species of painting being novel in this part of the country, I found it a more lucrative, pleasant and distinguishing branch of the art than portrait painting, which I then pursued. I continued this course until 1819–1820, when I gradually resumed portrait painting, which I have practised more or less to this time, so that at present my principal business is portraiture. It is seldom that I am without orders for painting other than portraits.[1]

The turning point that Fisher cites, 1819–1820, came as he was exploring other markets. Like many itinerant artists who traveled in pursuit of commissions, Fisher went to Charleston, South Carolina, a conservative but cosmopolitan city, and there he placed notices in the local paper, where he advertised his services as both a portraitist and a landscape painter. Fisher continued to exhibit in Charleston, showing a series devoted to Niagara Falls along with more rustic images of farms. Fisher's work was praised by a local critic, who both bemoaned and explained the lack of patronage for landscape imagery:

> You will recognize them by their beautiful resemblance of life and nature, the chaste foliage of the trees, and the delicate softness of the distant horizon. It is a pity that Mr. Fisher should be deterred from landscape painting, by the small comparative demand for such productions, and the great popularity of portrait painting, yet one cannot complain—a cow, however innocent,—can never be as attractive as a beautiful girl—trees are too much like each other to possess individual interest—and water, except in the midst of the ocean, is green everywhere.[2]

Despite this somewhat discouraging attitude, Fisher persisted in the painting of landscapes. Of the more than eight hundred paintings listed in his notebooks, more than half were landscapes.[3] Few, however, exemplify pure landscape, that is, with no trace of human involvement. Many have small figures, often couples picnicking or youths skating, but the motif that Fisher favored most was fishing. This preoccupation may be a pun on the part of the artist, in which he refers to his own name.[4] In *Under the Bridge* the theme of fishing dominates, providing an anecdotal interest that supplements the landscape. In addition to the figures of the boys and their playful dog in the foreground, men engaged in fishing on a larger scale, with nets and boats, are evident in the middle distance. Fisher may have intentionally juxtaposed the pastime activities of the boys with the more serious commercial endeavor of the men. The boys are placed in a partially sunny spot, while their older counterparts work in the shadows. The most revealing emblem, however, is the shipwrecked hull. Indicative of the life-threatening nature of commercial fishing, this haunting reminder of the dangers of the sea is placed at the midpoint of Fisher's canvas.

In addition to the anecdotal and symbolic elements of *Under the Bridge,* the painting is interesting because of its vertical format. Typically, portraits are painted vertically and landscapes horizontally, although there are exceptions. In the Museum's painting Fisher has employed a strong arch motif, possibly inspired by images of classical architecture, especially those popularized by the prints of Giovanni Battista Piranesi. This imposing foreground element serves to frame the scene and to enhance the illusion of spatial recession. By moving from a light foreground to a darker background, Fisher uses another age-old convention to convey depth. Both the cliffs, as they come down to the sea, and the sail on the boat reflect the shape of the arch and the large tree looming in the foreground.

Fisher's reliance on these conventions reveals not only the newness of American landscape painting but also his own training. A native of the Boston area, Fisher apprenticed for two years with John R. Penniman, an ornamental painter. Among the tasks that Penniman performed was the painting of clock faces, a formulaic form of decoration. In his letter to William Dunlap, Fisher admits, "from him [Penniman] I acquired a style which required years to shake off—I mean a mechanical ornamental touch, and manner of coloring."[5]

---

1. Fisher to William Dunlap, as quoted in *A History of the Rise and Progress of the Arts of Design in the United States* (1834; reprint, New York: Benjamin Blom, 1965), 3:32–33.
2. *Charleston Courier,* 20 March 1822.
3. Mabel Munson Swan, "The Unpublished Notebooks of Alvan Fisher," *The Magazine Antiques,* August 1955, 126.
4. Dr. Fred Adelson, telephone conversation with author, August 1993.
5. Dunlap, *History,* 32.

Born, Needham, Massachusetts, 1792; apprenticed to John R. Penniman, Boston, 1812–1814; traveled to Charleston, South Carolina, 1819 and 1820; to Niagara Falls, 1820; and abroad, 1825; settled in Boston; died, Dedham, Massachusetts, 1863.

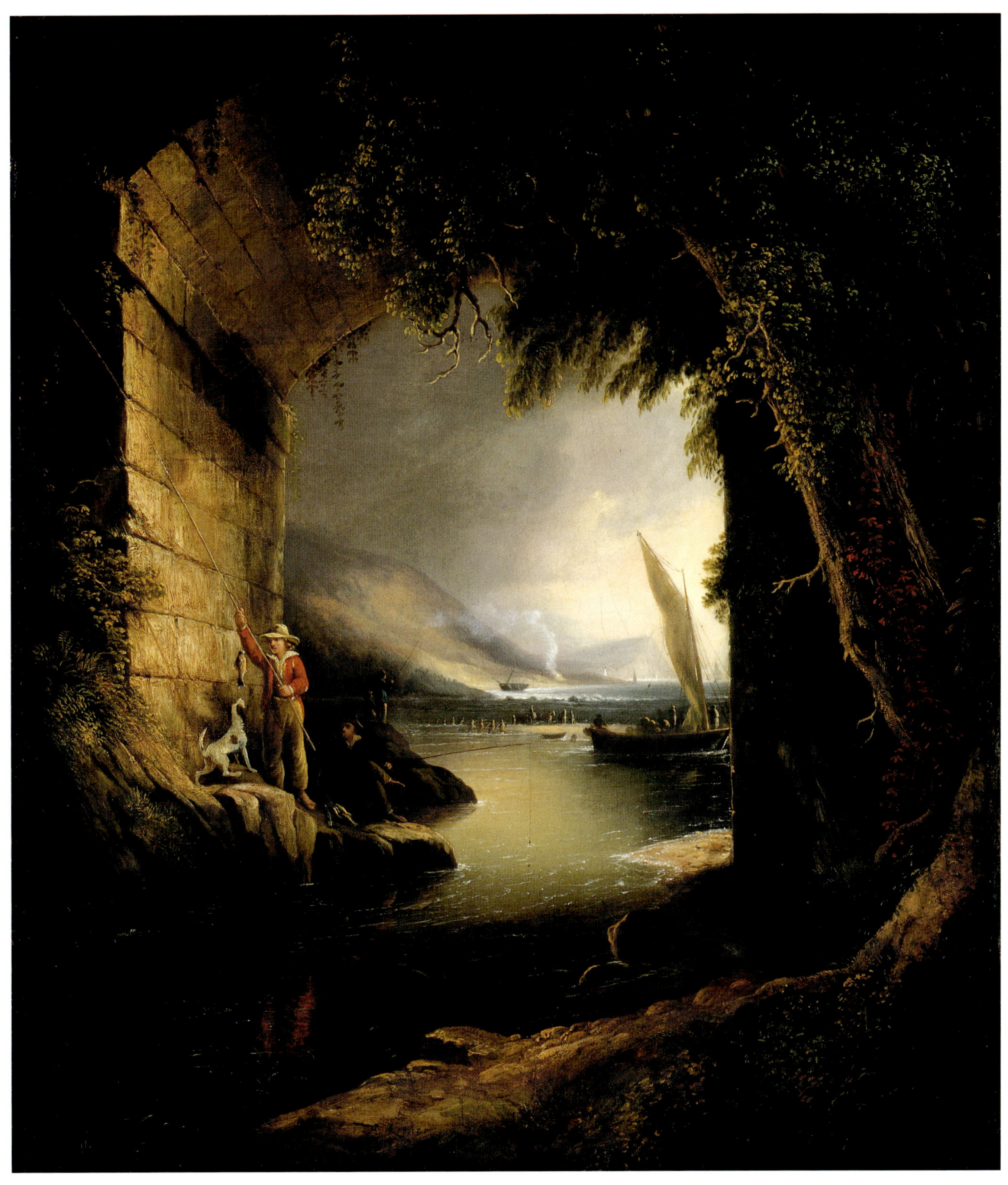

John Gadsby Chapman

1808–1889

The Coronation of Powhatan, circa 1835

oil on canvas, 22¼ × 29⅛ inches
Museum purchase with funds donated by the Arthur and Holly Magill Foundation

Although history painting was revered as the most venerable art form in Europe, Americans were slow to acquire a taste for esoteric themes. Embraced by Washington Allston, Samuel F. B. Morse, and other artists who worked abroad, paintings with lofty historical imagery were exceptional in America before the 1830s. Paintings depicting American history gained visibility in 1836 when Congress commissioned murals for the rotunda of the United States Capitol. This action coincided with a period of intense nationalistic pride that was ignited by the Monroe Doctrine, which was aimed at ending European control of American soil, and further fueled by the reelection of a populist president, Andrew Jackson. In response to these events as well as to the pervasive spirit of Manifest Destiny, many history paintings reflected the nationalist sentiment of the period. Yet, in hindsight, some of these works may be interpreted as propagandistic.[1]

Chosen on the basis of his successful illustrations for George Bancroft's ten-volume *History of the United States,* John Gadsby Chapman was one of four artists selected to decorate the Capitol rotunda. Collectively these murals review American history: from exploration (*The Landing of Columbus* by John Vanderlyn); to discovery (*Discovery of the Mississippi by de Soto* by William H. Powell); and finally to settlement (*Embarkation of the Pilgrims* by Robert Weir and *Baptism of Pocahontas* by Chapman).

A student of Charles Bird King, who in 1821 had begun an extensive series of portraits of Native Americans, Chapman would have been familiar with his teacher's interpretations of the "noble savage." *The Coronation of Powhatan,* which was completed slightly earlier than the rotunda mural, represents an episode in the life of Pocahontas's father, the chief of the Powhatan Indians. A strong ruler responsible for uniting several tribes, Chief Powhatan was described by Captain John Smith as "a tall, well proportioned man, with a sower looke; his head somewhat gray, his beard so thinne that it seemth none at al. His age neare 60, of a very able and hardy body."[2] At the instruction of the English king, Smith and the other colonists were to present gifts to Powhatan, in hopes that he would lead them to a neighboring tribe renowned for its wealth. In addition, Smith was to bestow a crown upon Powhatan, who only reluctantly agreed to this white man's honor.

When Chapman painted the Powhatans, Native Americans were still viewed paternalistically as children of nature. However, as settlements expanded westward, this attitude changed dramatically, and by midcentury Native Americans were shown as hostile obstructions to civilization. Drawing upon his knowledge of Charles Bird King's paintings as well as European models, Chapman portrays the narrative in explicit terms, from left to right, emphatically juxtaposing Europe and America. The English ambassadors, whose depictions recall royal portraits by Anthony van Dyck, are silhouetted against an open sky. They are balanced by the Powhatans who, more simply dressed, occupy a natural setting. The poses of the latter are reminiscent of Benjamin West's *William Penn's Treaty with the Indians,* an image well known through copies and engravings.

The Coronation of Powhatan was also widely circulated as an engraving. Chapman himself was a skilled printmaker and during his lifetime designed more than 1,400 illustrations. Actively concerned for art education in America, Chapman authored three manuals on making art, including *The American Drawing Book: A Manual for the Amateur and Basis of Study for the Professional Artist.* Convinced that this country needed organizations for the support of artists, Chapman was a founder of both the American Art Union and the Century Club. Despite these commitments, Chapman left the United States in 1848, eventually settling in Italy, where he depicted the Roman countryside, primarily for American tourists.

---

1. See Susan Danly, *Telling Tales: Nineteenth-Century Narrative Painting from the Collection of the Pennsylvania Academy of the Fine Arts* (Philadelphia: Pennsylvania Academy of the Fine Arts, 1991), and William H. Truettner, ed., *The West as America: Reinterpreting Images of the Frontier, 1820–1920* (Washington, D.C.: Smithsonian Institution Press, 1991).

2. Captain John Smith, *The Generall Historie of Virginia, New England, and the Summer Isles* (Glasgow: James MacLehose & Sons, 1907), 1:77.

Born, Alexandria, Virginia, 1808; studied with Charles Bird King at the Pennsylvania Academy of the Fine Arts, Philadelphia, then in Florence and Rome, 1828–1831; divided time between New York and Washington, D.C., until 1848; lived abroad, primarily in Rome, 1848–1884; returned to the United States, 1884; died, Brooklyn, 1889.

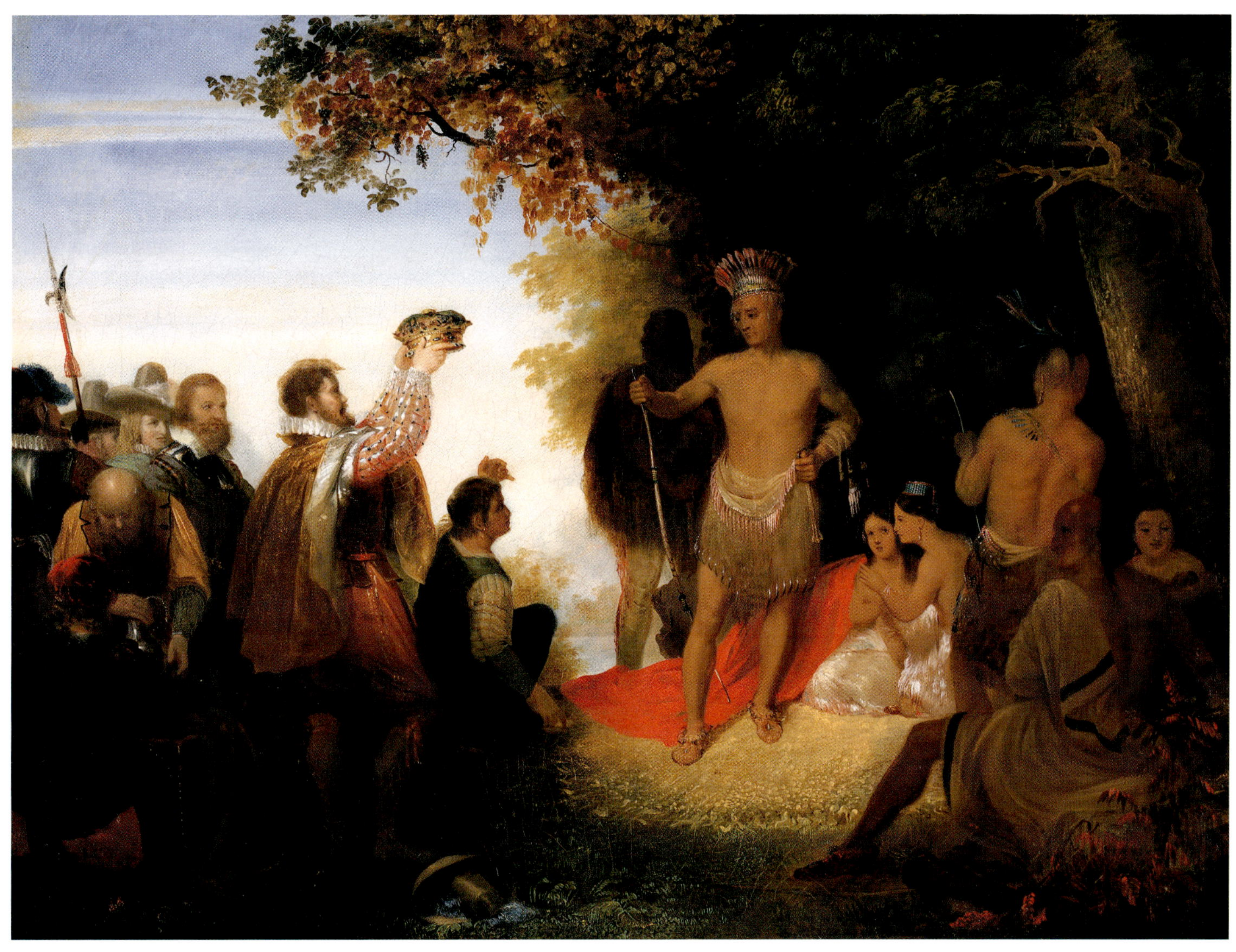

William Edward West

1788–1857

Portrait of Two Ladies, circa 1840

oil on canvas, 36¼ × 28 inches
Gift of The Museum Association, Inc., with funds from the 1990 Museum Antiques Show, Elliott, Davis & Company, CPAs, sponsor; Corporate Benefactors: Barker Air and Hydraulics; Greenville News–Piedmont Company; Hartness International; KPMG Peat Marwick; Liberty Corporation, Liberty Life Insurance Company, Cosmos Broadcasting Company, Liberty Properties Group and Liberty Capital Advisors; Pepsi-Cola; Republic Locomotive

As prosperity extended into the deep South during the antebellum period, itinerant portrait painters followed. Patrons with newly acquired means were eager to have their likenesses painted, preferably by the most fashionable artists of the day. With its emphasis on ancestry and its appetite for status symbols, the South was especially fertile ground for these portraitists who traveled by boat from seaport to seaport and along rivers, by horseback, and later by railroad. It was not until the 1840s that the availability of modestly priced photographs jeopardized the painted portrait.

Itinerants like William Edward West were responsible for importing the latest painting styles from the eastern seaboard to the western boundaries of the South. A native of Lexington, Kentucky, West found encouragement for his fledgling career from Thomas Sully in Philadelphia. Although West never became a formal student of the artist, he painted in Sully's studio, and his debt to the master is apparent throughout his career. West maintained a residence in Philadelphia, but he returned to the South and traveled the Mississippi River from New Orleans to Natchez in pursuit of portrait commissions.

In 1819 West left for Europe to study, where he remained until 1837. Unlike the many other American artists who chose to train in England, West studied at the Academy in Florence, a city renowned for its Renaissance masterpieces. In explanation of his decision to study in Italy, West wrote, "[H]ere are the old masters and here is nature in perfection. As for the Academy it might be better. There are no lectures on anatomy, yet for a man with a light pocket Florence has much to recommend it. One can live here for very little and [have] the finest models always before him at the same price."[1] Of the old masters, Parmigianino, a sixteenth-century Mannerist, exerted the greatest influence on West. He may also have been inspired by the paintings of the French Neoclassicist Jean-Auguste-Dominique Ingres, who was in Florence from 1820 to 1824.

While in Italy West painted the last portrait of the famous expatriate English poet Lord Byron. This painting endeared West to English patrons and served to enhance his reputation. He opened a studio in Paris in 1824 but left shortly afterward for London, where he came under the influences of Sir Thomas Lawrence, the most fashionable portraitist of the day and president of the Royal Academy. After encountering economic difficulties, West returned to the United States. He spent four years in Baltimore, working to recover his finances, before he settled in New York, where he cultivated friendships with some of the city's well-known families, including the Astors, the Schuylers, and the Van Rensselaers.

The sitters in the Museum's portrait have yet to be identified, but it is possible that they are sisters from one of these families. Sharing similar features, coloring, and hairstyles, they are clearly fashionable members of high society, whose languid and attenuated proportions reflect the influences of Parmigianino and Ingres. West handled the challenge of placing two sitters within one composition adroitly. While the ascendant sister sits with her body at a right angle, her face turned slightly toward the viewer, the other sister is shown full-face. The entire canvas is enlivened by broken brushstrokes, reminiscent of both Sully and Lawrence.

---

1. West to Edward West, 4 February 1820. Archives of American Art, as quoted in Estill Curtis Pennington, *William Edward West, 1788–1857* (Washington, D.C.: National Portrait Gallery, 1985), 15.

Born, Lexington, Kentucky, 1788; based in Philadelphia, pursued commissions along the Mississippi River, circa 1808–1817; painted with Thomas Sully, 1815–1816; studied in Florence at the Academy beginning in 1819; to Paris in 1824, then to London, 1825–1837; returned to Baltimore, 1837–1841; New York, 1841–1845; died, Nashville, Tennessee, 1857.

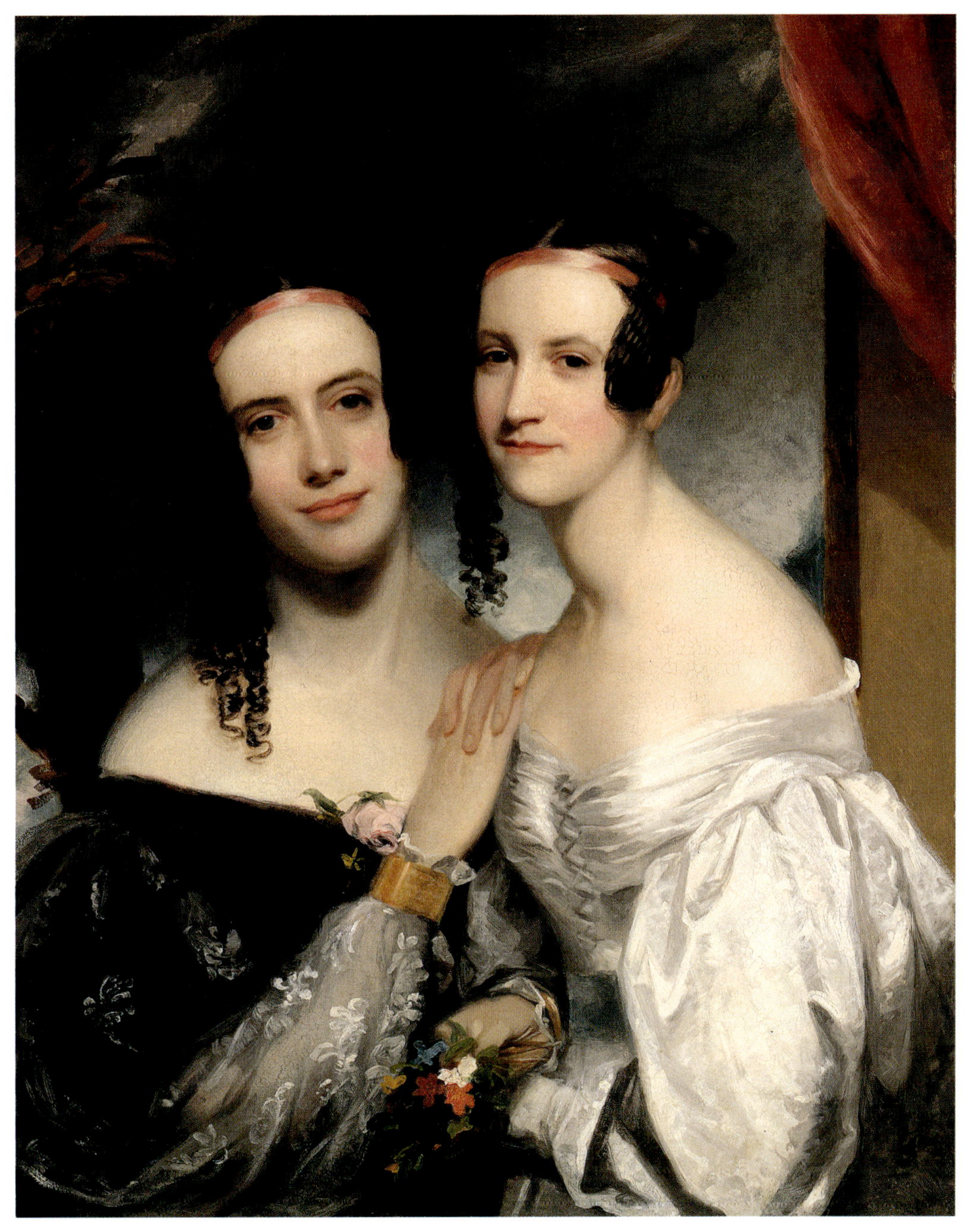

William Harrison Scarborough

1812–1871

Governor William Henry Gist (1807–1874), circa 1845

oil on canvas, 30 × 25 inches
Museum purchase with funds raised by the 1988 Museum Antiques Show, Elliott, Davis & Company, CPAs, sponsor, and donated by The Museum Association, Inc.

Mary Rice Gist (Mrs. William Henry Gist) (1813–1889), circa 1845

oil on canvas, 30 × 25 inches
Museum purchase with funds raised by the 1988 Museum Antiques Show, Elliott, Davis & Company, CPAs, sponsor, and donated by The Museum Association, Inc.

Although many artists, including Washington Allston, Thomas Sully, William Edward West, and later George Healy, sought training, exposure, and commissions in the fashionable capitals of Europe, others contentedly established their practices in the smaller urban centers of America. Despite modest training these painters often achieved considerable success. The viability of the art market during the mid-1830s is underscored by the impressive number of artists, more than 450, that William Dunlap included in his 1834 history of American art.

William Harrison Scarborough in Columbia and Charles Fraser in Charleston attained success by painting likenesses of South Carolinians. They earned both the respect of their fellow citizens and substantial incomes. By midcareer, Scarborough's prosperity enabled him to travel to Europe. He went primarily as a tourist to see the masterpieces of Renaissance and Baroque art that he admired. His overall impression of Europe, however, was somewhat parochial: "For a time, and as a visitor I like Paris—But to be a citizen? No! Give me quiet Columbia, where there less of the bad of human nature is conspicuous; where there is less gloss, less misery, less vice."[1] Upon his return to the state capital, he sought to establish an art gallery, a project that was doomed by the onset of the Civil War.

The war also jeopardized Scarborough's career, and his investments in the Confederate cause put him at severe financial risk. In his account book, he made the following entry for 5 February 1865: "There is no use in keeping accounts. Our currency is almost worthless, everything unpromising for the success of our cause. The enemy approaches and our small forces seem impotent to effect anything good. And are we after all to be a subjugated people? . . . If our armies are defeated, I, with thousands of others, are ruined."[2]

Scarborough concentrated on painting portraits of prominent citizens living in the central and piedmont areas of the state. Although his career was centered in Columbia, he pursued commissions in other locations, often advertising in the local press and staying as a guest of the family he was painting. In addition to his regional travels, he made annual pilgrimages to New York for supplies and frames.

In his paintings of Governor and Mrs. William Henry Gist, Scarborough confronted the perennial challenge for portraitists, that is, how to create a pair in which the husband and wife complement each other. By using the same somber background and by placing the sitters facing each other with their heads on the same line, Scarborough has balanced these two portraits. Furthermore, by presenting equivalent characterizations of the Gists, Scarborough avoided a fault common to many portrait painters, who tended to endow their male sitters with personalities while portraying the female sitters as decorative objects. Both sitters are fashionably dressed, although Mary Rice Gist's costume is the more elegant of the two. Scarborough's rather severe and sober style is appropriate for individuals who were upstanding members of their community. Active in the temperance movement, Gist was a strong advocate for states' rights and, ultimately, an ardent secessionist. A lawyer by training, Gist served in the state legislature for sixteen years before becoming the last antebellum governor of South Carolina. It was at the conclusion of his gubernatorial service, on 20 December 1860, that he signed the Ordinance of Secession, realizing an earlier expressed hope that "by the twenty-fifth of December no flag but the Palmetto will float over any part of South Carolina."[3]

1. Scarborough, "Memorandum of Travel," as quoted in Helen Kohn Hennig, *William Harrison Scarborough* (Columbia, S.C.: R. L. Bryan, 1937), 50.

2. Hennig, *Scarborough,* 18–19.

3. *Journal of the Senate of South Carolina* (Columbia, S.C.: R. W. Gibbes, 1860), 68.

Born, Dover, Tennessee, 1812; studied with John Grimes in Nashville and Horace Harding in Cincinnati; moved to South Carolina, first to Charleston, then Darlington; settled in Columbia, 1846–1871; traveled abroad, 1857; died, Columbia, 1871.

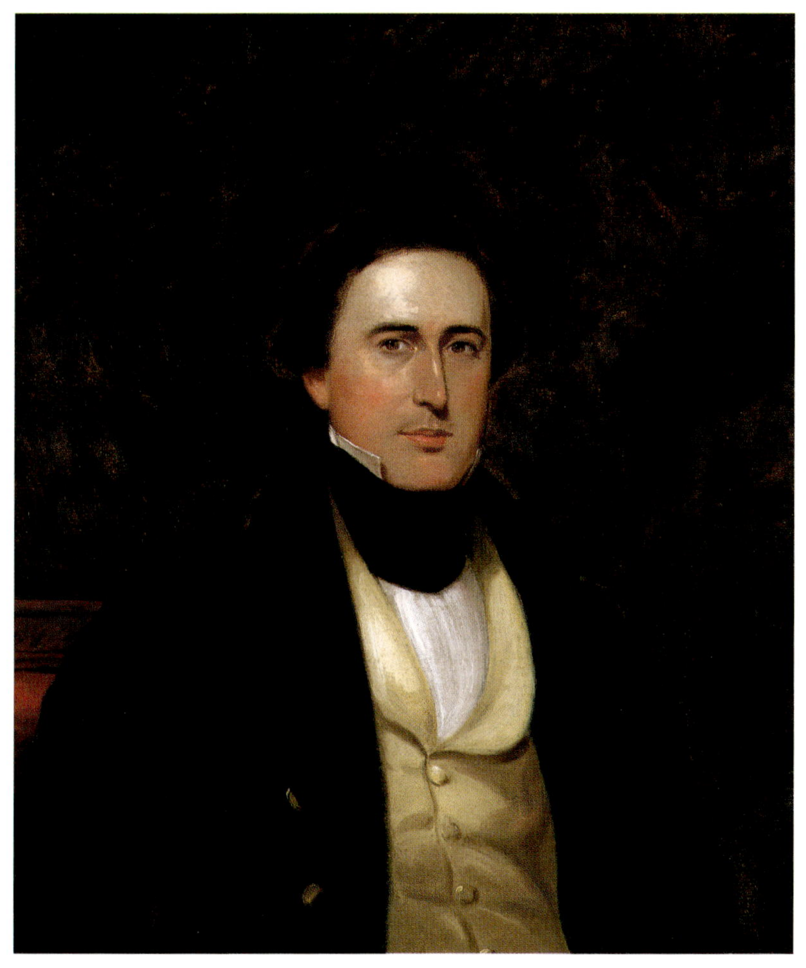

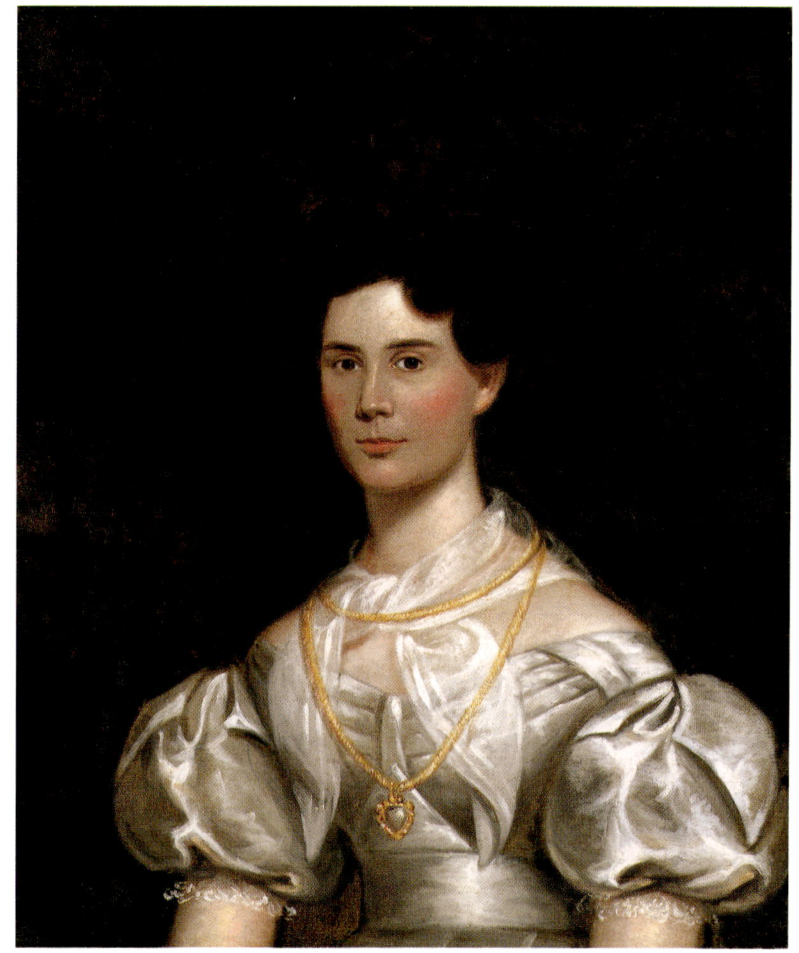

Charles Fraser

1782–1860

Still Life–Duck and Partridges, circa 1840

oil on canvas, 24 × 20⅛ inches
Gift of Christie and Jean Prevost in memory of Mr. and Mrs. Marshall Blair Prevost

The phrase "the burden of portraiture" has been used to describe the dominance of portrait painting throughout the first four decades of the nineteenth century.[1] In addition to oil paintings on canvas, miniature watercolor portraits on ivory were also popular, especially in the South. Often encased in gold lockets or small leather cases, these delicate images were intimate expressions of affection shared by couples during courtship or by parents and their children.

Charles Fraser of Charleston, South Carolina, was an accomplished miniature painter who found among his friends and fellow residents a devoted clientele. Although Fraser took art lessons as a schoolboy from Thomas Coram, he was largely self-taught. His friend, the exalted miniature painter Edward Greene Malbone, provided inspiration as well as examples from which Fraser could learn. Fraser's skill at miniatures was acclaimed by his fellow painters, including both Gilbert Stuart and Washington Allston, who commented, "I had the pleasure to meet . . . Fraser, who by the by paints an admirable miniature."[2]

Despite his obvious talent, Fraser, like many artists of the day, was not encouraged by his family to pursue a career in art. Instead, he was trained in law and practiced for eleven years before abandoning the profession to become Charleston's preeminent antebellum artist. Charlestonians recognized his ability and commissioned miniature portraits that provide a veritable social register for the period. In 1857 the community paid tribute to him with a major retrospective exhibition of his work, an honor granted only a handful of artists before the Civil War.

By about 1830 Fraser began to shift his focus. He did fewer portraits and more landscapes and "fancy pieces," namely still lifes and paintings with literary themes, possibly reflecting a general change in taste. Fraser's failing eyesight, partially a result of working on such a small scale, and the 1839 invention of the daguerreotype may have been further inducements to diversify his subject matter. The change, however, did not produce tremendous financial rewards. In 1820 Fraser charged fifty dollars for a miniature portrait; by 1844 a still life of game brought only forty dollars, more than half of which went toward the frame.

Fraser's still-life compositions are limited to images of game, a subject that would have had a particular appeal among his planter patrons. Depictions of dead game were also made popular by the great naturalist John James Audubon, who frequented Charleston in the 1830s. For his model, Fraser may have used a seventeenth-century Dutch painting or engraving. Fraser's early sketchbooks document his dependence on European examples, a logical source for the game paintings. The stiff paint handling and elemental compositions reiterate the fact that Fraser was self-taught.

At times the artist introduced a threatening cat or favorite hunting dog into his compositions, but usually the arrangements are simple attempts at trompe l'oeil, or "fool the eye." In the Museum's painting Fraser created an illusion of wood paneling, a common motif in his depictions of dead fowl. In these works Fraser was ahead of his time; only toward the end of the century did trompe l'oeil still lifes become popular, most notably in the hands of William M. Harnett.

---

1. See Neil Harris, *The Artist in American Society* (Chicago: University of Chicago Press, 1982), 56–88.

2. William Dunlap, *A History of the Rise and Progress of the Arts of Design in the United States* (1834; reprint, New York: Benjamin Blom, 1965), 2:301.

Born, Charleston, South Carolina, 1782; took drawing lessons from Thomas Coram, 1795; studied and practiced law 1801–1818; traveled to New York and Connecticut, 1816; to Boston, 1824; to Hartford, Connecticut, 1831; and New England, 1833; died, Charleston, 1860.

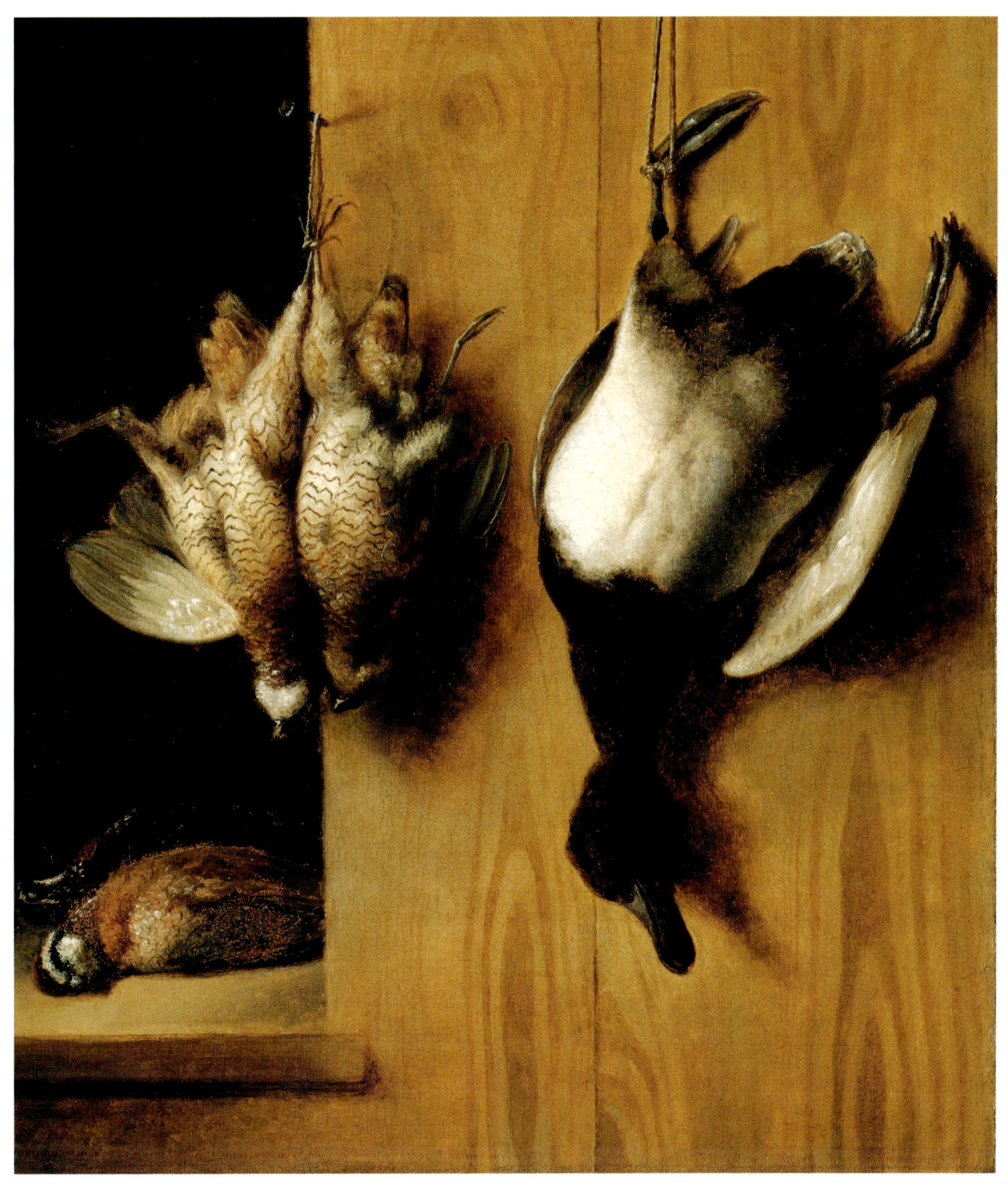

Thomas Wightman

1811–1888

Still Life, circa 1845

oil on canvas, 29 × 36 inches
Gift of E. D. Sloan, Jr.

By the 1830s American artists had begun to vary the subjects of their paintings to include landscape and still-life themes that not only reflected pride in the beauty and abundance of the land but also mirrored a positive nationalistic attitude that lasted until the onset of the Civil War. In its earliest phases American still-life painting focused on fruits rather than on flowers or household objects. The Charles Willson Peale family, as in other arenas, was in the forefront of developing an interest in still-life paintings. James Peale and his nephew Raphaelle painted unpretentious but luscious arrangements of common fruits. A generation later, Severin Roesen painted ambitious and imposing fruit and floral compositions that demonstrate his remarkable virtuosity.

Using fruit as his imagery Thomas Wightman indulged in the same theme of abundance as Roesen, who did not arrive in America until 1848. Little is known about Wightman except that he was born in Charleston, South Carolina, and that he studied in New York with the noted painter Henry Inman. Inman, a painter of portraits and "fancy pieces," was a founding member of the National Academy of Design, where Wightman exhibited regularly from 1836 to 1854. When he exhibited his first fruit painting there in 1844 he was one of very few artists painting still lifes.[1]

In composing his still lifes Wightman regularly employed several long-standing conventions; both the projecting tabletop and the half-peeled lemon relate to seventeenth-century Dutch paintings. The calligraphic tendrils, a device closely associated with Roesen, help to extend the composition beyond the central cascade of fruit. Wightman's still lifes typically feature a watermelon, a fruit often associated with the South. Frequently a half-watermelon pierced with a knife is the dramatic focus of the canvas. More subtle than other examples, the Museum's painting, with its lavish display, emphasizes the bounty of the land. Although the arrangement is precarious and the impossibility of the simultaneous availability of all the fruits makes the painting unrealistic, each of the seventeen species is painted with compelling veracity.

---

1. See Bartlett Cowdrey, *National Academy of Design Exhibition Record 1826–1860* (New York: The New-York Historical Society, 1943).

Born, Charleston, South Carolina, 1811; student of Henry Inman in New York; exhibited at the National Academy of Design, 1836–1854; returned to the South upon the outbreak of the Civil War; died, Augusta, Georgia, 1888.

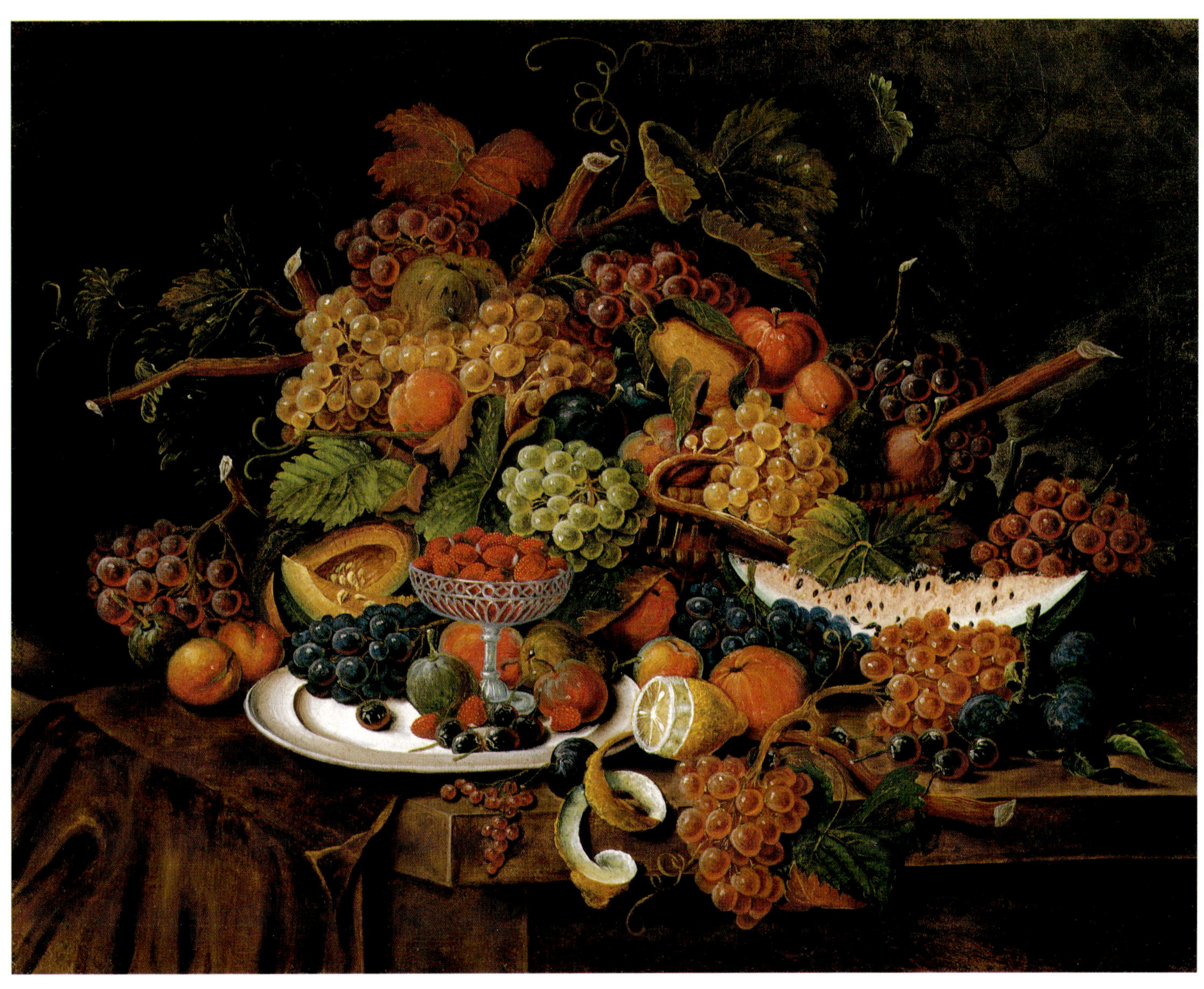

Christian Mayr

circa 1805–1851

The First Step in Life, circa 1847

oil on canvas, 26¾ × 31⅞ inches
Museum purchase with funds from the 1993 Museum Antiques Show, Elliott, Davis & Company, CPAs, sponsor; Corporate Benefactors: Alice Manufacturing Company, Inc.; Barker Air and Hydraulics, Inc.; BB&T; Carolina First Bank; The First Union Foundation; Greenville News–Piedmont Company; Hartness International; Insignia Financial Group, Inc.; KEMET Corporation; Liberty Life Insurance; Michelin North America; Odell Associates, Inc.; Pepsi-Cola Bottling Company of Greenville; Portman Marina, Inc.; Provence Printing, Inc.; Suitt Construction Company; Thoracic and Cardiovascular Associates

Genre painting, or the depiction of everyday life, began to appear in American art around 1830, and its popularity continued throughout the nineteenth century. Its enthusiastic acceptance by the public reflected both the rise of nationalism and the emphasis on homespun values embodied by President Andrew Jackson. Realistic in style, genre paintings usually illustrated familiar American subjects, and they often satirically exploited certain stereotypes. Frequently these works included a narrative, or storytelling, component that contained veiled references to contemporary mores or politics. More than any other artist, William Sidney Mount popularized vernacular subjects while simultaneously grappling with such challenging issues as race relations and the dichotomy of urban and rural life.[1]

Like many artists who undertook genre paintings, Christian Mayr painted portraits and also produced daguerreotypes. Born in Bavaria, Germany, Mayr studied in Munich, where he received his initial training in architectural draftsmanship and painting. Traditional German painting emphasized clear, crisp rendering of details and bright colors, qualities evident in Mayr's work. Within six months of his arrival in this country, Mayr exhibited six paintings at the National Academy of Design. His productivity was noted by William Dunlap, who commented that Mayr painted "with great rapidity."[2]

Mayr spent the early 1840s in Charleston, South Carolina, where he painted his masterpiece, *Officers of the Volunteer Fire Department,* which depicts the organization's thirty-three members standing before three preeminent examples of the city's architecture. Taking advantage of his skills and talents, Mayr probably used daguerreotypes to create the portraits of the firefighters, while the streetscape behind the figures demonstrates his facility with architectural rendering. It is colorfully painted, with faithful attention to detail. Unlike portraitists who were assured a commission, Mayr worked on speculation and displayed a flair for showmanship. He once conducted a raffle for thirty of his paintings, and he even charged the public an admission fee to view his painting of the fire department, which he later awarded as a prize.[3]

For subject matter Mayr relied on a variety of sources, including religion, literature, and rural life. Collectively his works demonstrate his desire to entertain, as in *It's Too Tight,* and to inspire, as in *Reading the Bible.* The Museum's painting, *The First Step in Life,* depicts a bucolic home in which a familiar scene takes place. The young parents appear eager, apprehensive, and proud; the child is both tentative and excited. The older man, whose identity is unclear, seems amused but remains aloof from the action as he stuffs his pipe. Once again, Mayr's training and background are evident in the carefully apportioned interior, with its profusion of household objects and painstaking regard for minutiae. The domestic setting, warmed by its cozy fire, is reminiscent of Dutch interiors of the seventeenth century.

Like Mount, Mayr may have been commenting on contemporary issues; clearly, *The First Step in Life* is a reassuring depiction of domestic harmony and familial continuity. It affirms the woman's central role in the family and, simultaneously, implies her confinement to the home by housekeeping chores. Included in the annual exhibition of the National Academy of Design in 1847, *The First Step in Life* may, with its abundance of functional and decorative items, also allude to the burgeoning consumerism of the nineteenth century.[4]

---

1. See Elizabeth Johns, *American Genre Painting: The Politics of Everyday Life* (New Haven: Yale University Press, 1991).
2. William Dunlap, *A History of the Rise and Progress of the Arts of Design in the United States* (1834; reprint, New York: Benjamin Blom, 1965), 3:269.
3. Anna Wells Rutledge, *Artists in the Life of Charleston* (1949; reprint, Columbia: University of South Carolina Press, 1980), 105; newspaper references assembled by Rutledge in the files at Gibbes Museum of Art, Charleston, include lists of Mayr's paintings.
4. See Johns, *American Genre,* chapter 5.

Born, Bavaria, Germany, circa 1805; studied in Nuremberg and Munich; immigrated to the United States, 1833; New York, 1834–1840; three years in Charleston, South Carolina, then New Orleans, 1840–1845; in New York, 1845–1851; died, New York, 1851.

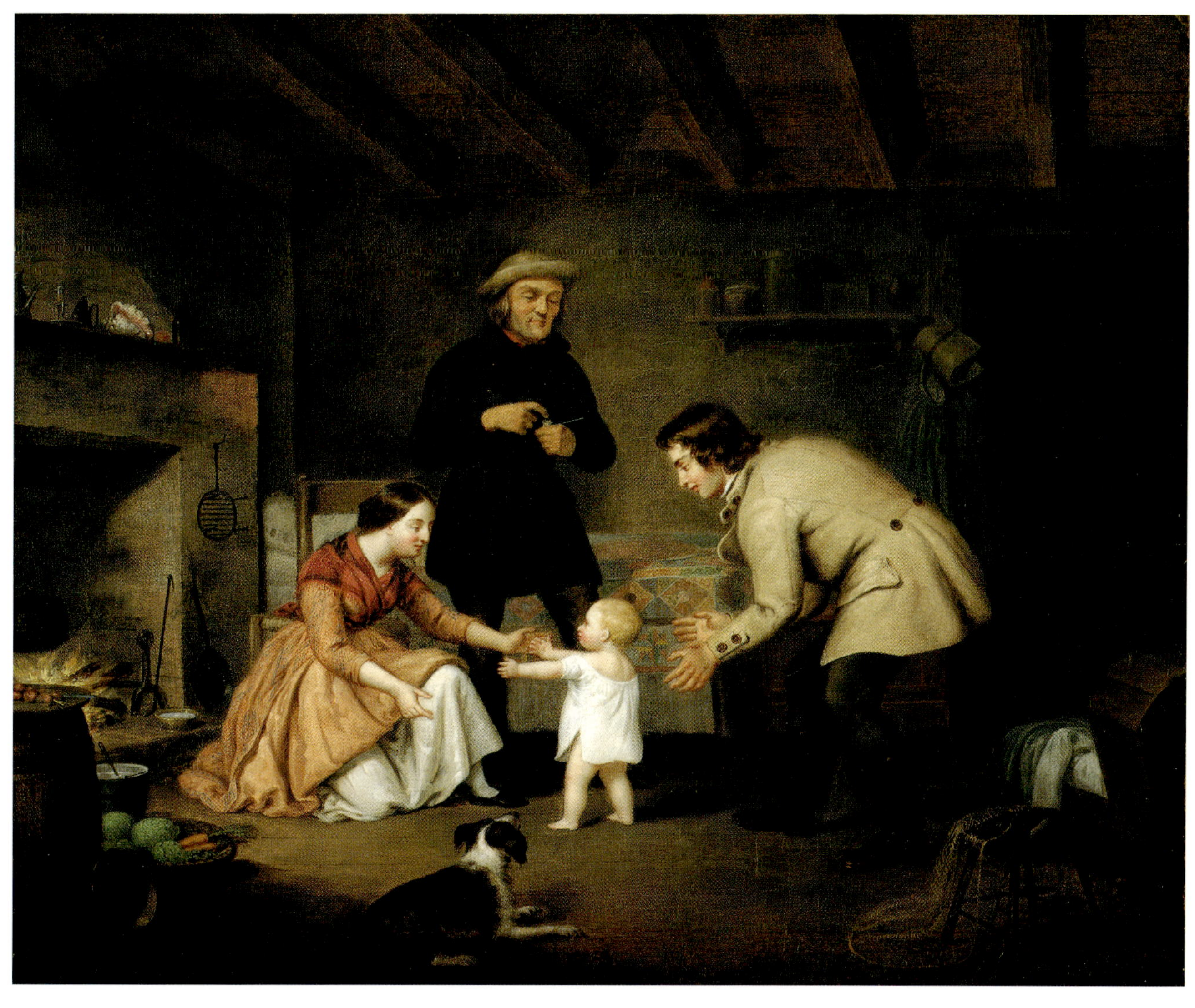

William Tylee Ranney

1813–1857

Marion Crossing the Pedee, 1849

oil on canvas, 16 × 21 inches
signed, on boat: *W. Ranney*
Gift of Dr. and Mrs. DeWitt Harper

As nationalistic sentiment grew across the country, interest in American art with American subject matter flourished. Aristocratic portraiture became less popular, and paintings of landscape and genre subjects acquired new audiences. Often the works were filled with overt references to the grandeur of the new republic or to the resourcefulness of her citizens. This popularization of art was accompanied not only by traveling displays of panoramic vistas like John Vanderlyn's *View of Versailles* but also by a burgeoning number of illustrated magazines and books. These publications, along with the introduction of photography and the dissemination of prints, made art more accessible. The two most important organizations for the promotion of American art were the National Academy of Design and the American Art Union. Indicative of the democratization of art, by 1849 the latter boasted almost 19,000 members, who received prints based on paintings. In addition, the Art Union's five-dollar membership fee afforded individuals the opportunity to win an original painting, most often a genre scene, in an annual lottery.

Paintings about the West, portraying pioneer families, valiant frontiersmen, and Native Americans, were extremely popular. William Ranney made the West his primary subject, but unlike George Catlin and Alfred Jacob Miller, who depicted Native Americans, Ranney focused on settlers and trappers. His interest in frontiersmen paralleled the popular narratives of Daniel Boone and Davy Crockett. Ranney, while still an art student in New York, went to Texas in 1836 shortly after the fall of the Alamo. Responding to a call for volunteers, he served in the Texas Army for nine months. By the mid-1840s, when Ranney painted most of his Western works, Texas and westward expansion were still in the forefront of the national consciousness.

Ranney and his colleagues also found new American heroes in their romantic revisitation of the revolutionary era. Thus, in 1840 the American Art Union selected John Blake White's *General Francis Marion Inviting a British Officer to Dinner* as its first engraving; twelve years later Emanuel Leutze would exhibit in the United States Capitol, with resounding success, his monumental canvas of *Washington Crossing the Delaware.* The 1848 political uprisings in France made revolutionary subjects even more timely. The heroic efforts of Francis Marion gained him a mythic reputation throughout the Carolinas, Ranney's boyhood home. Marion, who earned the nickname the "Swamp Fox," led a ragtag band of patriots who conducted guerrilla attacks on the British in South Carolina. Not unlike the heroes of the West who emerged in Ranney's day, Marion's success was a result of his daring leadership and his reliance on his wits.

The Museum's painting is a preliminary oil study for a larger canvas in the collection of the Amon Carter Museum in Fort Worth. The fact that the study bears Ranney's signature, at the midpoint of the boat, indicates that he valued this work as a completed composition. The final version, which includes a second boat and more figures, is a more grandiose depiction. As might be expected, in the larger painting the overall color is more intense, details are more defined, and reflections are clearer. In its simplicity and directness, however, Ranney's initial conception more accurately reflects the actual circumstances of Marion's military tactics. Inadequately equipped, Marion and his men often hid in the swamps and traveled the rivers in the mist, succeeding against the British through stealth and surprise.

Steel engravings based on *Marion Crossing the Pedee* were distributed by the American Art Union, the organization that advanced Ranney's career by purchasing twenty-six of his paintings. In 1858, a year after his death, a sale of more than two hundred paintings, half by Ranney and half by such friends and colleagues as Asher B. Durand, Frederic Edwin Church, and George Inness, was held for the support of his family. In his obituary he was saluted as "in every sense of the word, an American artist."[1]

1. *The New York Times*, 5 December 1857 as quoted in Linda Ayres, "William Ranney," in *American Frontier Life: Early Western Painting and Prints* (Fort Worth: Amon Carter Museum; Cody, Wyo.: Buffalo Bill Historical Center, 1987), 102.

Born, Middletown, Connecticut, 1813; adolescence in Fayetteville, North Carolina, apprenticed to a tinsmith; studied art in Brooklyn, and in 1836 served in the Texas Army; returned North, settled in New Jersey, 1836–1857; died, West Hoboken, 1857.

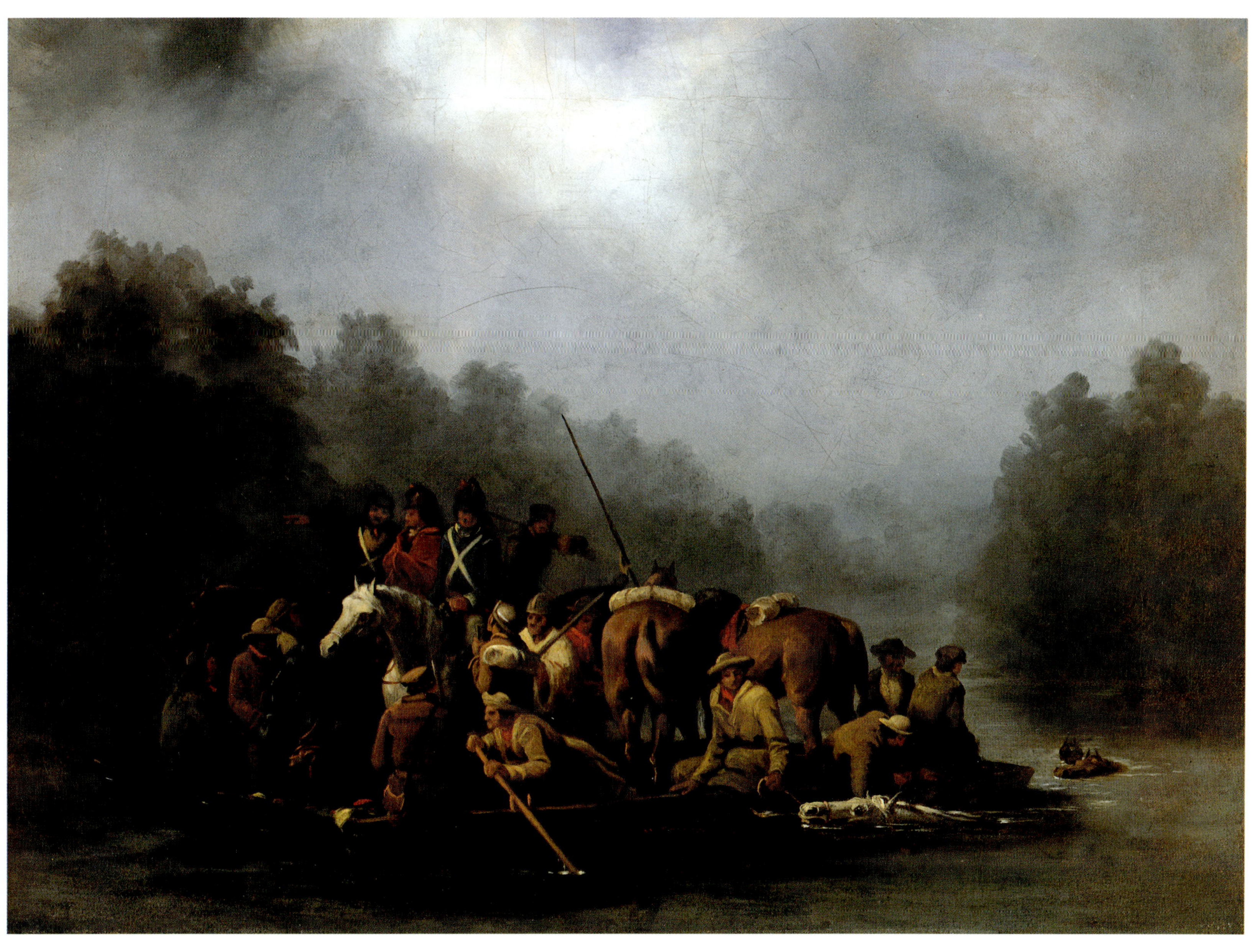

George Peter Alexander Healy

1813–1894

Portrait of John C. Calhoun (1782–1850), 1845

oil on canvas, 30 × 25 inches
signed, upper left: *G. P. A. Healy, / 1845*
Gift of W. Thomas Smith

Throughout the nineteenth century painters made copies of works by other artists as well as replicas of their own paintings. In this country the absence of formal art education, such as that offered by the academies in Europe, made copying a crucial component in the acquisition of basic skills. By copying, an artist trained himself to follow prescribed conventions and techniques. In this way Charles Willson Peale's brothers, sons, and nephew learned to paint. Copying was also a means for artists and patrons to have reproductions of important works of art, whether old-master paintings or images of well-known Americans. Somewhat different, the term *replica* usually applies to an artist's second or subsequent version of his own work. Thus, Gilbert Stuart's many portraits of George Washington are considered replicas of his original portrait, which was taken from life.

Another prolific portraitist, George Healy, made copies of important paintings by others as well as replicas of his own work, which explains the multitude of canvases he painted over his long and productive career. Among Healy's patrons the most notable was Louis-Philippe, king of France, whose ambition was to build a collection that featured the likenesses of distinguished Americans. For almost a decade Healy served the French monarch, traversing the Atlantic to execute portraits of American statesmen.

With Louis-Philippe as his sponsor, Healy traveled throughout the South, painting former President Andrew Jackson at his Tennessee home, the Hermitage, and Henry Clay at his Kentucky plantation, Ashland. Healy also devised two major narrative paintings for the king's gallery: one depicted Benjamin Franklin at the court of Louis XVI, the other represented the notorious Robert Hayne–Daniel Webster debates of 1830.

As a student of the French Romantic painter Baron Antoine Gros, Healy learned the importance of creating dynamic images. His most compelling portraits are those in which the sitter is involved in a characteristic activity. For his portrait of John C. Calhoun, Healy selected a pose that suggests the great orator is about to speak. Healy has enhanced the sense of drama by the emphatic highlighting of Calhoun's chiseled features; the unkempt hair and the unsettled sky in the background add to the intensity of the painting.

The Museum's portrait of Calhoun was done directly from life, probably in Washington, in 1845. Calhoun had already served as vice-president, from 1825 to 1832, under presidents John Quincy Adams and Andrew Jackson, both of whom were painted by Healy. Having resigned over the nullification controversy, the fiery politician served during the 1840s in the United States Senate where he felt he could better represent South Carolina. Healy later made three bust-length replicas, one of which remains in France at the museum at Versailles. Of the four canvases, the Greenville painting is the only one that bears a signature and a date; it also has several details that do not appear in the others. The intricate turning of the edges of Calhoun's collar are unique to the Museum's painting, suggesting that in making the replicas Healy abbreviated some of the particulars.

From this image Healy also developed a full-length posthumous portrait, commissioned by the City of Charleston in 1850. The artist wrote to the mayor of Charleston: "It is with the greatest pleasure I accept this commission to paint a man for whom I entertained so deep an admiration, and in whose society I derived so much benefit."[1] Eleven years later, in April 1861, Healy was in Charleston to complete his portrait of Confederate General P. G. T. Beauregard, just as Fort Sumter was under attack. A Northerner, Healy was advised to leave the city as soon as possible.

---

1. Healy to T. Leger Hutchinson, 1 August 1850, as quoted in Anna Wells Rutledge, *Catalogue of Paintings and Sculpture in the Council Chamber, City Hall, Charleston, South Carolina* (Charleston, S.C.: The City Council, 1943), 12. The other three bust-length portraits are in the collections of the Virginia Museum of Fine Arts, Richmond; the National Portrait Gallery, Washington, D.C.; and the Musée National, Versailles.

Born, Boston, 1813; kept a studio in Boston, 1830–1834; to Paris to study under Baron Gros; studied and traveled, to Italy, England, Switzerland, 1835–1839; served King Louis-Philippe of France, 1840–1848; traveled between Paris, London, and the United States regularly, until 1856; settled in Chicago, 1856–1865; to Paris, 1867; Rome, 1868–1869; traveled to Spain, Germany, and Rumania in the 1870s; also to the United States and London; died, Chicago, 1894.

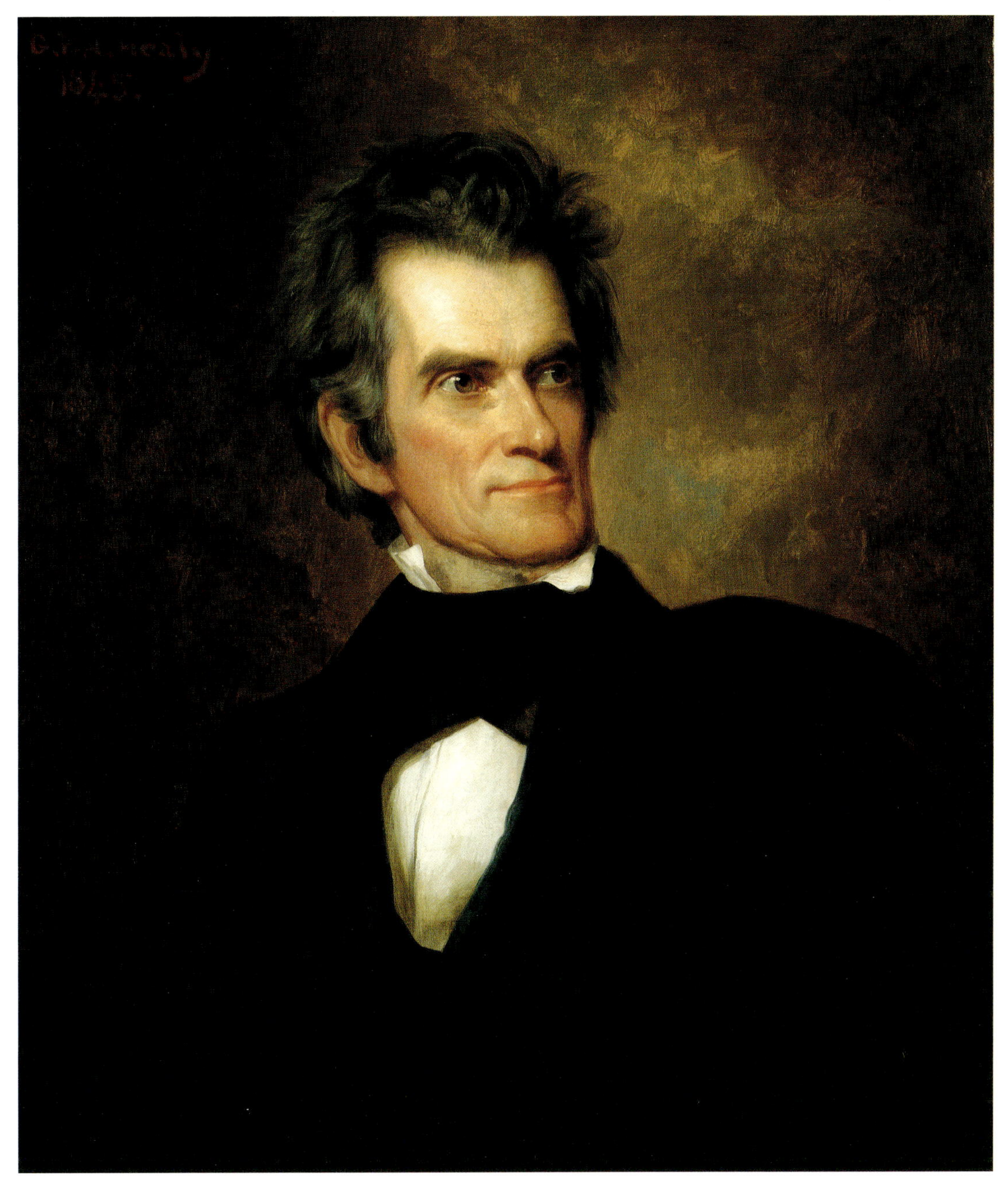

Clark Mills

1815–1883

Andrew Jackson (1767–1845), 1855

bronze, 24½ × 19½ × 8 inches
stamped, on base: *Patented May 15, 1855* and *Cornelius and Baker, Philadelphia*
Museum purchase with funds donated by the John I. Smith Charities

Primarily associated with architecture and tombstones, or reserved for public commissions, sculpture was much less common than painting in the United States. Although in the eighteenth century wood-carvers produced allegorical figures on a modest scale and by the beginning of the next century William Rush was carving life-size works in Philadelphia, most of the earliest marble sculpture was made by European artists. John Wilton's statues of William Pitt and Antonio Canova's and Jean-Antoine Houdon's portrayals of George Washington are three examples. By the 1830s the leading American sculptors, Horatio Greenough and Hiram Powers, were working in Italy. Not only were they strongly influenced by ancient models, but they were also dependent on local craftsmen to do the actual carving from the world's best marble.

The emergence of Clark Mills, virtually a self-taught sculptor, is remarkable, and his most important commission became this country's first monumental equestrian statue to be cast in bronze. As a self-made man, Mills exemplified those qualities so admired in America, qualities he shared with his subject, Andrew Jackson. Like Mills, Jackson had endured a troubled childhood and, although inexperienced, achieved success. Jackson was the victorious general at the Battle of New Orleans, a military hero of the War of 1812, and first populist president.

According to tradition, Mills had never seen an equestrian statue. Although he did not travel abroad, where examples could be seen from ancient Rome, Renaissance Venice, or Napoleonic Paris, he may have seen engravings. Nonetheless, in 1847 Mills was selected by the Jackson Monument Committee to create a life-size statue to be placed in Lafayette Park, across from the White House. The format of horse and rider presented both aesthetic and engineering challenges. Mills studied the pose carefully, even training a horse to rear so that he could achieve verisimilitude. He solved structural problems by placing most of the weight of the statue on the horse's rear legs. A further challenge was the task of adapting Jackson's likeness from a painting, possibly from the full-length portrait by John Vanderlyn in the City Hall, Charleston, South Carolina, where Mills had worked from 1837 until 1847 as an ornamental plasterer. It was during this time that he invented a process for casting life masks, further demonstrating his ingenuity.

Although commissioned for a prime location in the nation's capital, Mills's statue does not portray Jackson in his role as president but rather as a young, virile general addressing his troops. Mills explained the actual moment as he envisioned it:

> General Jackson is there represented as he appeared on the morning of the 8th of January, forty-one years ago. He had advanced to the centre of the line in the act of review; the lines have come to present arms as a salute to their commander, who is acknowledging it by raising his chapeau, according to the military etiquette of that day. His restive horse, anticipating the next move, attempts to dash down the line; the bridle hand of the dauntless hero being turned under, shows that he is restraining the horse, whose mouth and curved neck indicate that the animal is feeling the bit.[1]

The resulting image, both energetic and heroic, became the basis for countless equestrian figures erected in Washington and in other cities throughout the country.

Although bronze foundries existed in the United States, most was used for the production of arms; none was suitable for the manufacture of monumental sculpture. Mills set up his own facility, obtained some of the raw material from British cannons confiscated in the War of 1812, and after six casts of the horse, succeeded in producing his monument. He fabricated additional versions for New Orleans and Nashville and later cast a similar figure of George Washington for the nation's capital. Perhaps to recoup his considerable investment, Mills produced a series of about ten small-scale replicas of the Jackson monument. Although stamped "Patented May 15 1855," the actual patent requested was for the larger monument.[2] Manufactured by Cornelius and Baker, a Philadelphia firm that specialized in gas lamps, the replicas represent the beginning of cast-bronze statuary and foreshadow Frederic Remington's later success with his bronze Western subjects.[3] With the exception of the addition of a rocky base, the replica of Mills's Andrew Jackson is an intimate and accessible, yet dynamic, version of the original public monument.

---

1. As quoted in W. O. Hart, "Clark Mills," *Louisiana Historical Quarterly* 3 (1920): 615.

2. Ellen Miles, National Portrait Gallery, to author, 18 March 1993.

3. Michael Edward Shapiro, *Bronze Casting and American Sculpture, 1850–1900* (Newark: University of Delaware Press, 1985), 41–42.

Born, near Syracuse, New York, 1815; worked as a plasterer in Charleston, South Carolina, 1837–1847; to Washington, D.C., 1847; died, Washington, 1883.

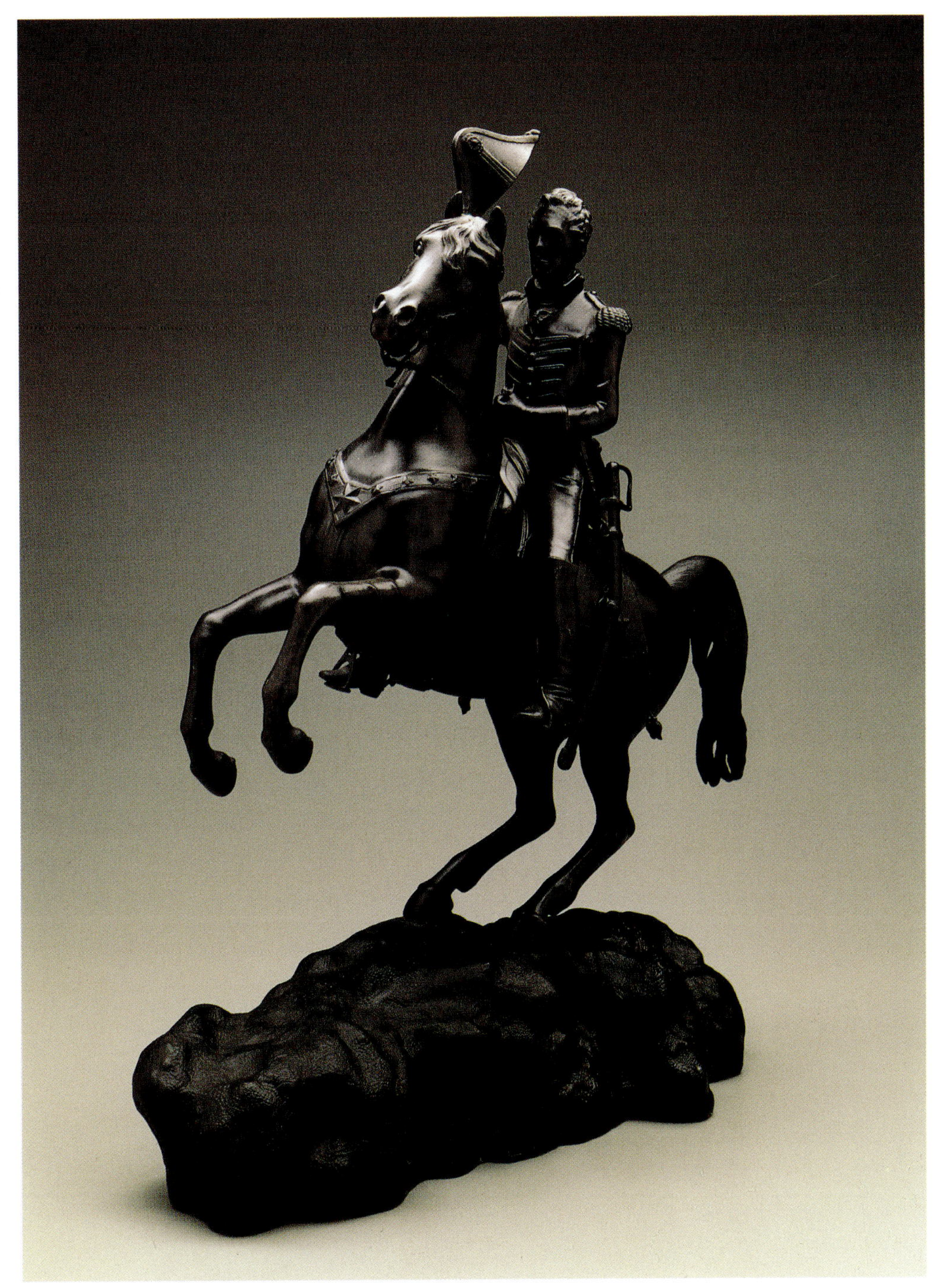

Thomas Addison Richards

1820–1900

The Edisto River, South Carolina, 1858

oil on canvas, 20¾ × 16⅞ inches
signed, lower right: *1858 T. Addison Richards*
Museum purchase with funds donated by the Arthur and Holly Magill Foundation

Despite landscape painting's noble tradition in Europe, Americans were reluctant to regard it as a significant art form. The depiction of natural scenery held little interest until Thomas Cole and other members of the Hudson River School rendered evocative landscapes that, at times, were infused with religious and philosophical overtones. Recognized as the leader of the Hudson River School, Cole created paintings that were consistent with the writings of the Transcendentalists. Originally intended as a derogatory description, the term *Hudson River School,* which was first used in the 1870s, refers not to a school but rather to a group of painters who shared ideals about depicting the outdoors.[1]

The painters of the so-called Hudson River School made frequent trips together, keeping sketchbooks of scenery that they would later develop into larger oil paintings. Thomas Addison Richards joined Sanford Robinson Gifford, a noted landscape painter, in several sketching trips to the Catskills and the Green Mountains. The material gathered from such expeditions was used by Richards in the travel books he wrote and illustrated, including *Appleton's Illustrated Hand-book of American Travel,* published in 1857. He also produced a series of illustrated articles about famous authors, including Washington Irving and William Gilmore Simms, and their homes. Simms described Richards as "an amiable young man who paints a good landscape, and who is modest and intelligent."[2]

Early in his career Richards was a champion of Southern scenery. Born in England, he went as a youth to South Carolina and Georgia. With his brother, William C. Richards, he published *Georgia Illustrated,* which praised the beauty of their adopted state: "The upper part of the State abounds with romantic and picturesque views. Mountains and vallies, glens and waterfalls, caverns and cliffs, with pastoral landscapes, are met with through all that region. Nor is it alone in the upper part of the State that Nature has lavished her beauties. There are scenes of loveliness peculiar to the 'sunny South,' among green savannas and dense forests of the 'low country.'"[3]

In addition to his numerous illustrations, which gained wide circulation, many of Richards's paintings, including *The Edisto River,* were exhibited at the National Academy of Design, further stimulating an interest in Southern landscape. A newspaper notice suggests that Richards developed his oils, often of a modest size, from sketches: "He has numerous original drawings of Landscape scenes in the Carolinas and Georgia, from which he will be pleased to execute [in]to connoisseur cabinet pictures in water or oil colors. These views are from scenes of rare beauty."[4] His compositions are generally uncomplicated, appropriate for the decoration of parlors. Although such details as the indigenous Spanish moss and palmettos are carefully rendered, Richards's real achievement is his ability to evoke accurately the atmosphere of the coastal low country.

To become successful, landscape painters needed patrons and opportunities to exhibit their work, both of which were provided by the National Academy of Design. Founded in 1825, the Academy was an integral part of Richards's career for more than half a century. He took classes in the mid-1840s, exhibited there regularly, and for forty years served as its corresponding secretary. The rise of the Hudson River School coincided with the success of the Academy, and as collectors embraced this new art form because of its nationalistic associations, the decade of the 1850s became the heyday of American landscape painting.

---

1. See Kevin Avery, "A Historiography of the Hudson River School," in *American Paradise: The World of the Hudson River School* (New York: The Metropolitan Museum of Art, 1987), 3–20.

2. Simms to James Lawson, 2 March 1847, as quoted in Mary Simms Oliphant, Alfred Taylor Odell, and T. C. Duncan Eaves, eds., *The Letters of William Gilmore Simms* (Columbia: University of South Carolina Press, 1952), 2:275.

3. William C. Richards, ed., *Georgia Illustrated* (Penfield, Ga., 1842), 1.

4. *Charleston Mercury,* 12 December 1843.

Born, London, 1820; immigrated to New York, 1831; settled in Penfield, Georgia, 1835; studied for two years at the National Academy of Design, elected full Academician, 1851; corresponding secretary, 1852–1892; taught at the University of the City of New York, 1867–1887; died, Annapolis, Maryland, 1900.

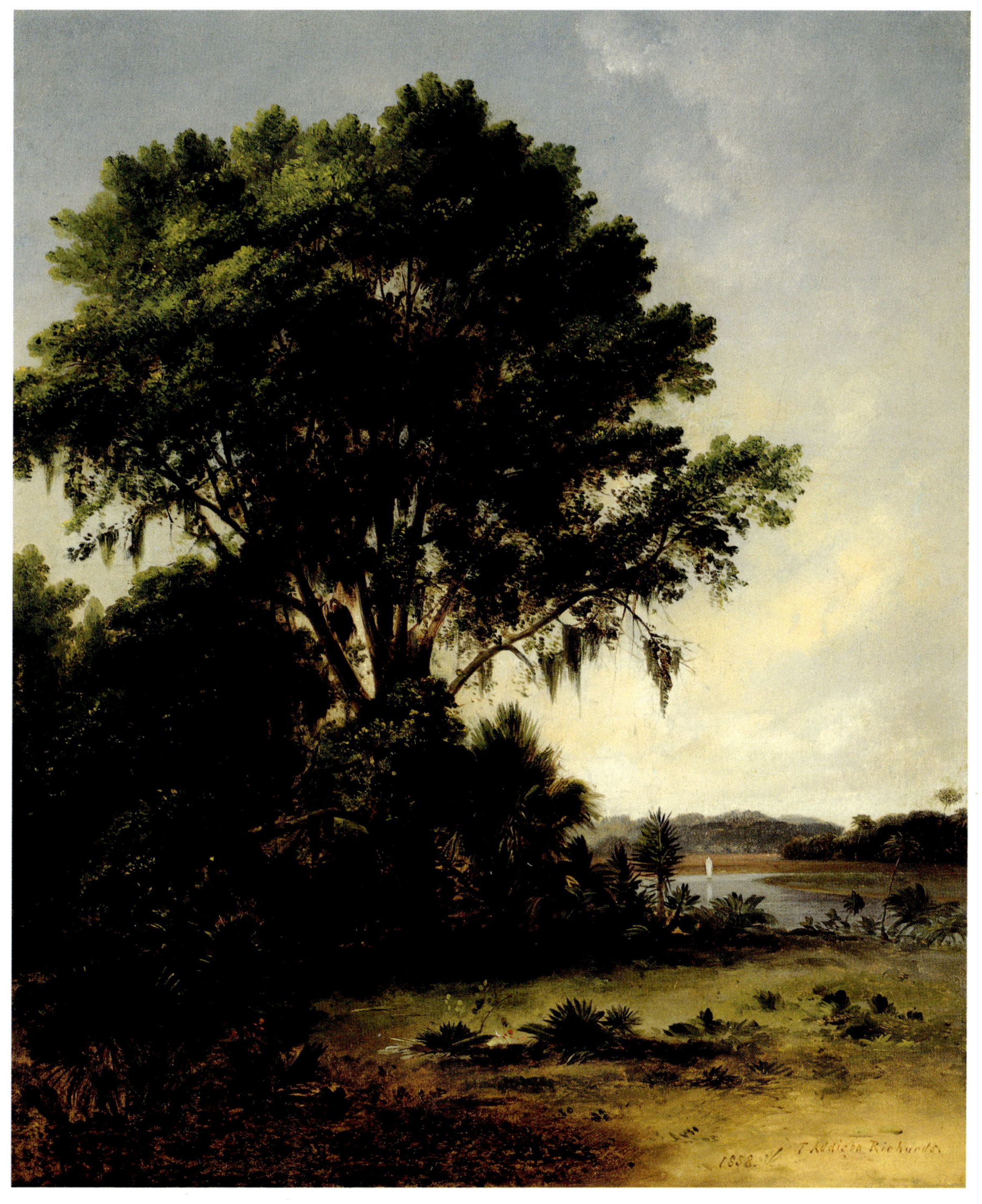
1858.
T. Addison Richards.

William Charles Anthony Frerichs

1829–1905

Mountain Falls, circa 1860

oil on canvas, 54 × 69¾ inches
signed, lower right: *W. C. A. Frerichs*
Museum purchase with funds donated by Southern Bank and the estate of Byrd B. Holmes

By the time of the Civil War, landscape painting had gained wide acceptance among patrons, critics, and the public. An inherently democratic art form that required the viewer to have little background in history or literature, landscape was soon established as a part of America's national identity. Although the artists affiliated with the National Academy of Design and the Hudson River School logically focused on New York and its surroundings, such artists as Thomas Addison Richards explored other regions, including the South. The Blue Ridge and Smoky Mountains were still sparsely settled, and the scenery offered compelling images of untamed nature, as rugged and inaccessible as the territory embraced by Henry David Thoreau. Another inveterate traveler, Frederic Edwin Church enjoyed excursions from the Natural Bridge in Virginia to Mount Katahdin in Maine.

One of the few to paint the Southern mountain wilderness was William C. A. Frerichs, who arrived in Greensboro, North Carolina, in 1855 to teach at Greensboro Female College. A native of the Netherlands, he attended the Academy at The Hague, one of Holland's major art centers, where he would have had the opportunity to study the work of the Dutch seventeenth-century master of landscape, Jacob van Ruisdael.

Whereas the painters of the Hudson River School often depicted pastoral scenes from an elevated perspective, Frerichs's viewpoint was usually lower, and the mood he created was more foreboding. He seems to have delighted in the wilderness. One of his favorite motifs, and a device common in Ruisdael's works, was a swift stream rushing from the center of the canvas toward the viewer. The large scale and lack of human presence in the Museum's *Mountain Falls* is in keeping with the work of the younger generation of the Hudson River School painters, whose work sought to glorify the majestic splendors of the American wilderness. The painting's impact is heightened by bold and expressive brushwork.

Later in life, Frerichs settled on Staten Island, New York, where a small community of Hudson River School painters lived. He traveled north to the Connecticut Valley and the White Mountains, and even painted the Oxbow near Northampton, Massachusetts, a scene immortalized by Thomas Cole.

Born, Ghent, the Netherlands, 1829; studied at the Academy, The Hague; immigrated to New York, 1850; taught at the Greensboro Female College, 1855–1863; New York, 1865–1869; Staten Island, New York, 1869–1880; moved to Newark, New Jersey, 1880; died, Tottenville, New York, 1905.

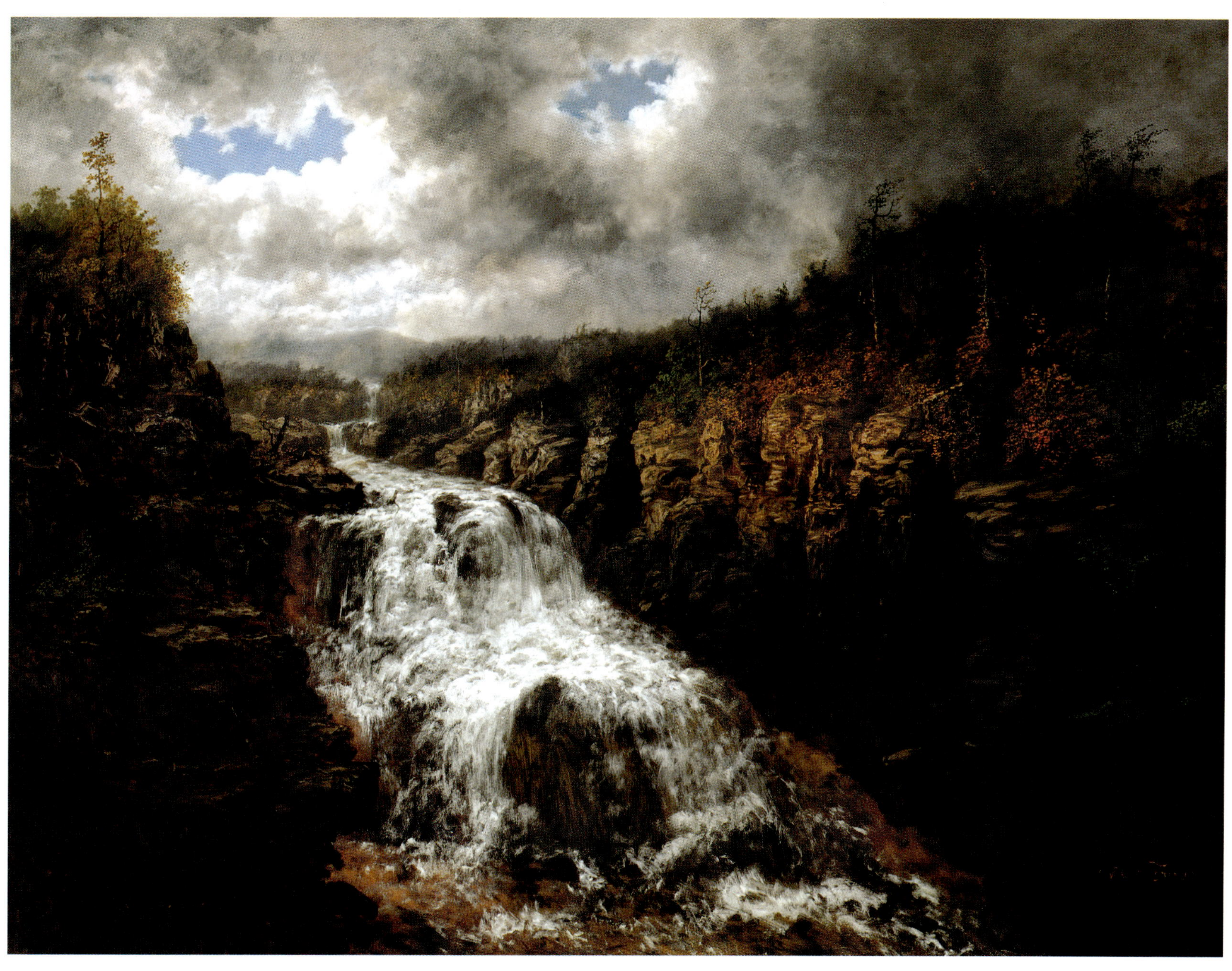

Caroline Davis Wilson

1810–1890

Mary of Bethany, 1860

marble, 36¼ × 28⅜ × 30½ inches
signed, on base: *Caroline Wilson, Cin., 1860*
Museum purchase with funds from the 1991 Museum Antiques Show, Elliott, Davis & Company, CPAs, sponsor; Corporate Benefactors: Barker Air and Hydraulics; Brunson and Associates, Inc.; Carolina First Bank; Eastern Trading Company, Inc.; FIBERWEB North America, Inc.; First Union National Bank of South Carolina; Greenville Hospital System; Greenville News–Piedmont Company; Hartness International; KEMET Electronics Corporation; Liberty Corporation; Pepsi-Cola Bottling Company of Greenville; United Embroidery, Inc.; Varat Enterprises

Neoclassicism, the revival of ancient forms, played a critical role in shaping both American architecture and sculpture. Initially, the popularity of Neoclassic themes reflected the ideological associations of youthful America with the values of democratic Greece and republican Rome. As American sculptors went to Italy for study they encountered an environment conducive to their work, and, as a result, many stayed, setting up studios in Florence and Rome. With the assistance of Italian stonecutters who did the actual carving, sculptors produced idealized figures, commemorative monuments, and portrait busts. Horatio Greenough and Hiram Powers led the way. The latter created a sensation with his *Greek Slave,* a full-length female nude. Puritan attitudes and Victorian prudery made the statue controversial—and overwhelmingly successful—on its national tour in 1847. Its subject matter was timely: Powers explained the young girl as not only the innocent victim of the recently concluded Greek-Turkish Wars but also the embodiment of the Christian virtues of chastity and humility. Moreover, the sculpture had special significance to a country embroiled in a dispute over slavery.

Of American cities, Cincinnati had a distinct role in the development of Neoclassical taste. Named for the Roman general Cincinnatus, it was hailed as the "Athens of the West." Powers grew up in Cincinnati, and at midcentury many sculptors, working mostly on portrait busts, gravitated there. In this environment the little-known sculptor Caroline Wilson emerged, also making portrait busts. Her signature work, however, is a life-size figure drawn from the New Testament. While her counterparts, Randolph Rogers and William Wetmore Story, portrayed idealized subjects from the classical era or from the Old Testament, Wilson's selection of a Christian theme is exceptional.

Several women named Mary may be found in the New Testament: Mary, the mother of Christ; Mary of Bethany, the sister of Martha and Lazarus; and Mary Magdalen, an infamous sinner. Over time the last two were melded together, in part because the attributes, or artistic conventions, associated with them are the same: long hair and an ointment jar. Wilson's Mary could be interpreted as either one, except for the inscription on the base: LET HER ALONE: AGAINST THE DAY OF MY BURYING HATH SHE KEPT THIS, which clearly refers to an episode involving Mary of Bethany. In the passage from John 12, Christ chides Judas for complaining about Mary's extravagant use of oil for wiping his feet and goes on to say: "For the poor ye shall always have with ye."

Little is known about Wilson's training, other sculpture by her, or her life in Cincinnati. According to contemporary sources, on a trip to Kentucky she spontaneously modeled a convincing likeness of Ralph Waldo Emerson. One account of the event reads:

> A gentleman acquainted with Mrs. Wilson mentioned an incident that occurred on a journey to the Mammoth Cave of Kentucky. Struck with the aspect of a distinguished person in the company—Mr. Emerson—the sculptress gave directions to stop near a bank of soft red clay, and, putting out one hand to grasp a sufficient portion of the material, with the other she signed to her subject to remain motionless. In a few moments she had modeled a very creditable likeness of the author.[1]

Wilson seems to have aroused the jealousy of a fellow artist, John Frankenstein, who in 1864 wrote a scathing satire on the state of American art, in which a reference to Wilson seems clear. In addition to attacking her for her sharp tongue and her scheming, he alludes to her as "venomous" and as an "unadulterated dunghill dame."[2] Exactly what Wilson had done in Victorian Cincinnati to deserve such vitriolic treatment is unclear. If the kneeling figure, atypical for its Christian theme, is read as a representation of Mary Magdalen, a reformed sinner, the statue might be seen as an autobiographical statement by Wilson. This interpretation is substantiated by Frankenstein's comment, "in chastened Magdalens concerns herself," and by the fact that her own daughter, Genevieve, served as the model. Her youthful, idealized features are not unlike those employed by Powers or Story for their depictions of maidens in humbled positions, and like them Wilson's *Mary of Bethany* was probably carved by stonecutters in Rome.[3]

---

1. Mrs. E. F. Ellett, *Women Artists in All Ages and Centuries* (New York: Harper & Row, 1859), 296–297.

2. John Frankenstein, *American Art: Its Awful Altitude: A Satire* (1864; reprint, ed. by William Coyle, Bowling Green, Ohio: Bowling Green University Popular Press, 1972), 19–20.

3. Charlotte Streifer Rubinstein, *American Women Sculptors* (Boston: G. K. Hall, 1990), 31, and curatorial files of the Cincinnati Art Museum.

Born, Cooperstown, New York, 1810; modeled head of Ralph Waldo Emerson, Mammoth Cave, Kentucky, circa 1855; died, Cincinnati, 1890.

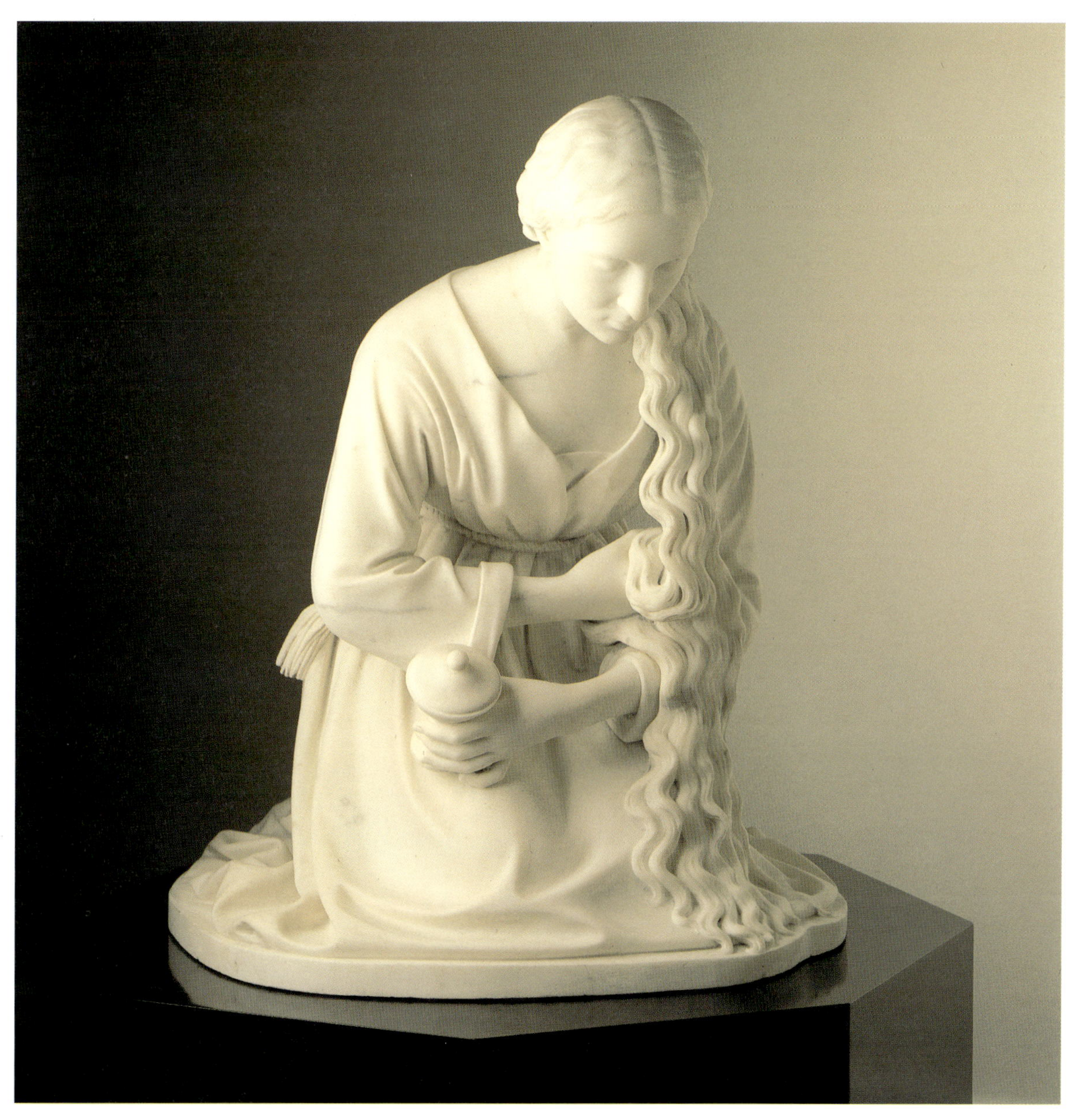

John Ross Key

1837–1920

Bombardment of Fort Sumter, Siege of Charleston Harbor, 1863, 1865

oil on canvas, 29 × 69 inches
Museum purchase with funds donated by Suzanne Cochrane Austell; Dorothy Hipp Gunter; Buck and Minor Mickel; Dorothy P. Peace; John I. Smith Charities; Ball Unimark Plastics; First Union National Bank of South Carolina; Michelin Tire Corporation; 1988 Museum Antiques Show, Elliott, Davis & Company, CPAs, sponsor; 1989 Collectors' Group

With the maturation of the Hudson River School and the increased acceptance of landscape painting, artists began to work on a grand scale, often selecting distant and dramatic sites. Frederic Edwin Church and Albert Bierstadt, in particular, emerged as masters of theatrical compositions. Bierstadt frequently painted breathtaking vistas of the West, a territory unknown to his eastern audience. The public's imagination was captivated by Bierstadt's monumental representations of the vast, unspoiled mountain ranges of California. These images and others like them led to the founding of the national park system and the preservation of extensive acreage.

Both Bierstadt and Church developed elaborate and lucrative techniques to showcase their work, using curtains, dramatic lighting, and press announcements to promote their spectacles. Bierstadt was known for large dramatic paintings, and his fame led to the misattribution to him of several paintings, including the Museum's *Bombardment of Fort Sumter, Siege of Charleston Harbor, 1863.* At one time this canvas even bore a forged Bierstadt signature. Although it is unclear when the signature was added, Bierstadt was troubled by forgeries even during his lifetime.

Although the painting shares certain qualities with works by Bierstadt, it was seen as an anomaly and explained as an early work. In the collection of the Union League Club in Philadelphia since the late 1930s, the painting has an impressive exhibition and publication history. Yet conclusive research has revealed that Bierstadt could not have done the Museum's painting, and that it is instead the masterwork of John Ross Key, an eyewitness to the 1863 bombardment of Fort Sumter.[1]

During the 1850s Key served as a draftsman and cartographer with the United States Coast Survey. With the onset of the Civil War, Key was commissioned a second lieutenant in the Confederate Engineers. He arrived in Charleston in August 1863 in time to participate in the second bombardment of Fort Sumter. As a draftsman, Key had the responsibility among other things to draw maps of Charleston harbor and record the placement of fortifications.

Less famous than the bombardment of April 1861, which ignited the Civil War, the engagement two years later demonstrated Confederate endurance against hopeless odds. Key's rendition is a dramatic amalgamation of the 1863 siege, and the bird's-eye perspective permits a panoramic sweep of the horizon and the harbor. During his time in Charleston, Key had probably surveyed the harbor from a hot-air balloon, a vantage point sympathetic to topographical views. Fort Sumter, which had come to symbolize the defiance of the South, is at the exact midpoint of the composition. Bathed in cool, crystalline light, appropriate to Charleston in the autumn, the painting reflects Key's concern for accuracy as well as his aesthetic sensibility. The encampment at Fort Johnson, with the remains of its martello tower, dominates the foreground, while two Confederate ironclads move out from Charleston toward the fort. To the right of the fort two Union monitors enter the harbor. Smoke rises from guns stationed on islands both to the right and in the far distance, adding action to an otherwise serene image.

Unlike Bierstadt, who idealized his landscapes, Key meticulously recorded everything, even wheel ruts in the foreground. The elevated viewpoint dramatizes the event, while allowing the viewer to remain aloof from the conflict. Citing a "venturesome originality in color-use" and "breadth and fidelity," a critic described the artist, "Young, ambitious, and but little educated in art, Mr. Key made up that lack in boldness of subject and treatment."[2]

---

1. See Alfred C. Harrison, Jr., "Bierstadt's *Bombardment of Fort Sumter* Reattributed," *The Magazine Antiques,* February 1986, 416–422.

2. T. C. DeLeon, *Four Years in Rebel Capitals* (Mobile, Ala., 1890), 301, as quoted in Harrison, "Bierstadt's *Bombardment,*" 421.

Born, Baltimore, Maryland, 1837; served as draftsman and map maker with United States Coast Survey, 1850s; studied at the National Academy of Design, New York, 1856, 1857; Confederate Army, Charleston, South Carolina, 1863–1865; to Baltimore, late 1860s; Boston, late 1870s; died, Baltimore, 1920.

David English Henderson

1832–1887

Drawing for *Halt of the Stonewall Brigade*, circa 1862

ink and wash on paper, 12 7/16 × 19 1/16 inches
Museum purchase with funds donated by John I. Smith Charities

Halt of the Stonewall Brigade, circa 1865

oil on canvas, 26 × 38 inches
signed, lower left: *D. E. Henderson*
Museum purchase with funds donated by the John I. Smith Charities

Documentation of the Civil War is found in official records as well as in letters and diaries recounting personal experiences. It was the first major military conflict to be recorded by the camera, as the photographer Mathew Brady, among others, conveyed the genuine horrors of war in graphic images. Winslow Homer's insightful behind-the-scenes drawings for *Harper's Weekly* revealed the boredom that plagued the Army of the Potomac. Other individuals responded to the war by rendering eyewitness accounts, either written or drawn.

Thus David English Henderson, a soldier with some background in art, chronicled a moment typical of the military campaign of Stonewall Jackson. From Jefferson County, Virginia, Henderson enlisted in the Confederate Army in April 1861. Because of his skill as a draftsman, he was made a lieutenant in the Topographical Engineers. He served as an aide to Jackson, whose retinue had gained a reputation for their stalwart loyalty at the notorious battles of Chancellorsville, Gettysburg, and Spotsylvania. The charismatic Jackson, a graduate of West Point and a career soldier, was a demanding leader who transformed a company of up-country farmers into an elite corps with an outstanding military record.

Rather than portray a major military event, Henderson elected to depict a recurring phenomenon: a rest stop on one of the brigade's marches. In a preparatory sketch Henderson noted the critical features of his composition: soldiers at rest on the banks of a stream, some bathing their feet, while a long column of infantrymen trails off into a distant, hilly landscape. Officers and horses stand at the center of the drawing. In the painting, which Henderson probably completed after the war, the artist made significant changes, not the least of which was the insertion of portraits of Jackson and five members of his staff. On the back of the canvas, Henderson titled the painting and listed: 1 Genr Stonewall Jackson; 2 Capt Sorilla ADC; 3 Col A. R. Botelar A.D.C.; 4 Col Sandy Pendleton A.AG; 5 Maj W. J. Hawks CS; 6 Maj H.K. Douglas J.G. Their likenesses appear to derive from *cartes des visites,* or photographic portraits mounted on stiff paper, that were popular and widely circulated at the time.[1] In addition, the painting's background is more defined. The house and farm buildings resemble in a very general way Chancellor House, the former federal headquarters near Chancellorsville, although not all of the participants shown were with the brigade there. Despite its eyewitness qualities, Henderson did not create a record of a specific time and place; instead he painted a kind of eulogy to Jackson. The landscape glows with an eerie golden light, perhaps foreshadowing the doom the brigade would face at the battle of Chancellorsville, where their beloved leader, Stonewall Jackson, was mistakenly shot by one of his own men.

1. The Valentine Museum, Richmond, owns several composite photographs; one by Vannerson & Jones depicts Jackson surrounded by nine of his staff members, including portraits of Douglas, Hawks, and Pendleton.

Born, Jefferson County, Virginia (now West Virginia), 1832; studied in Georgetown and New York; cartographer in the Confederate Army, 1861–1862; lived in Brooklyn, after the war, before returning to Jefferson County; died, Jefferson County, 1887.

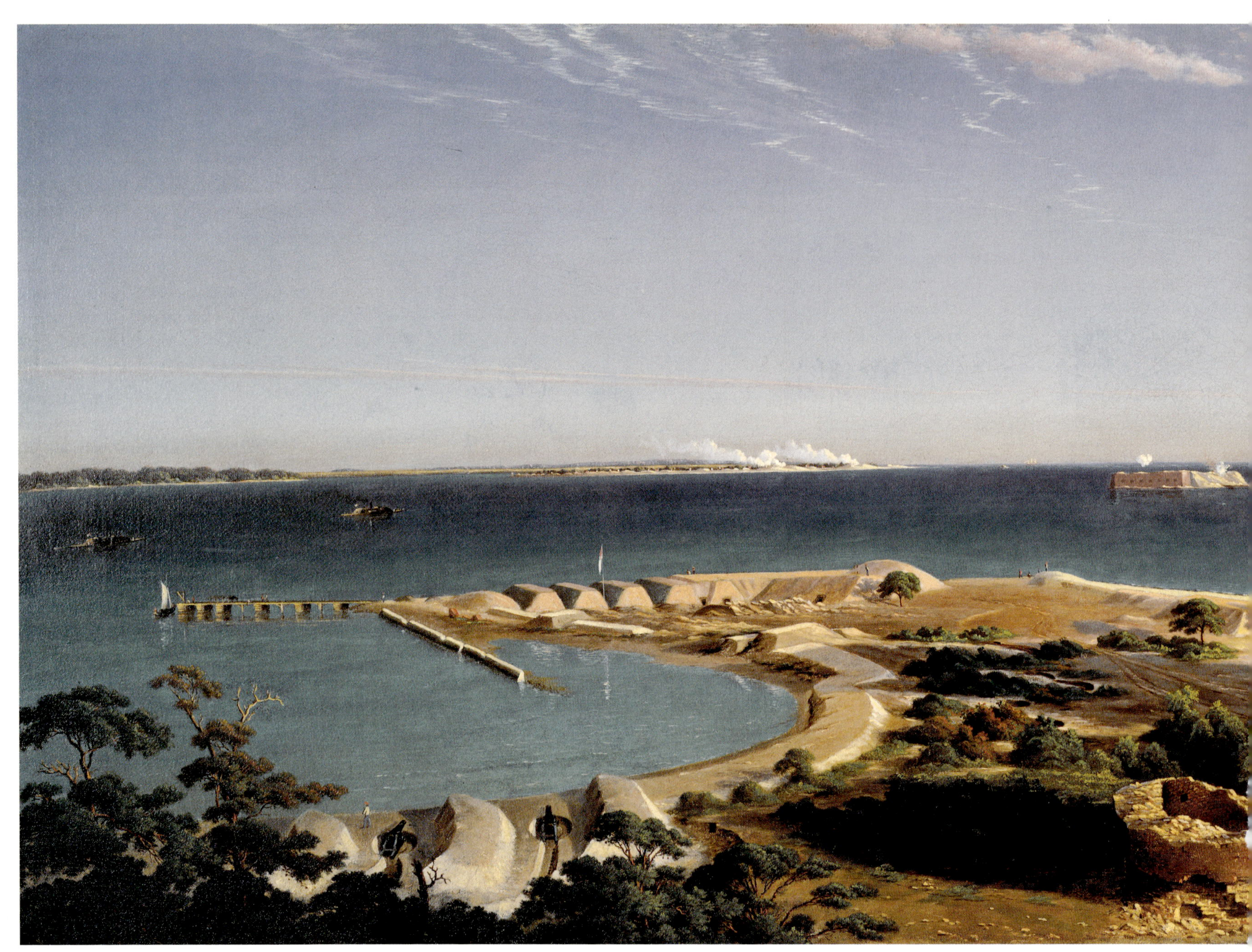

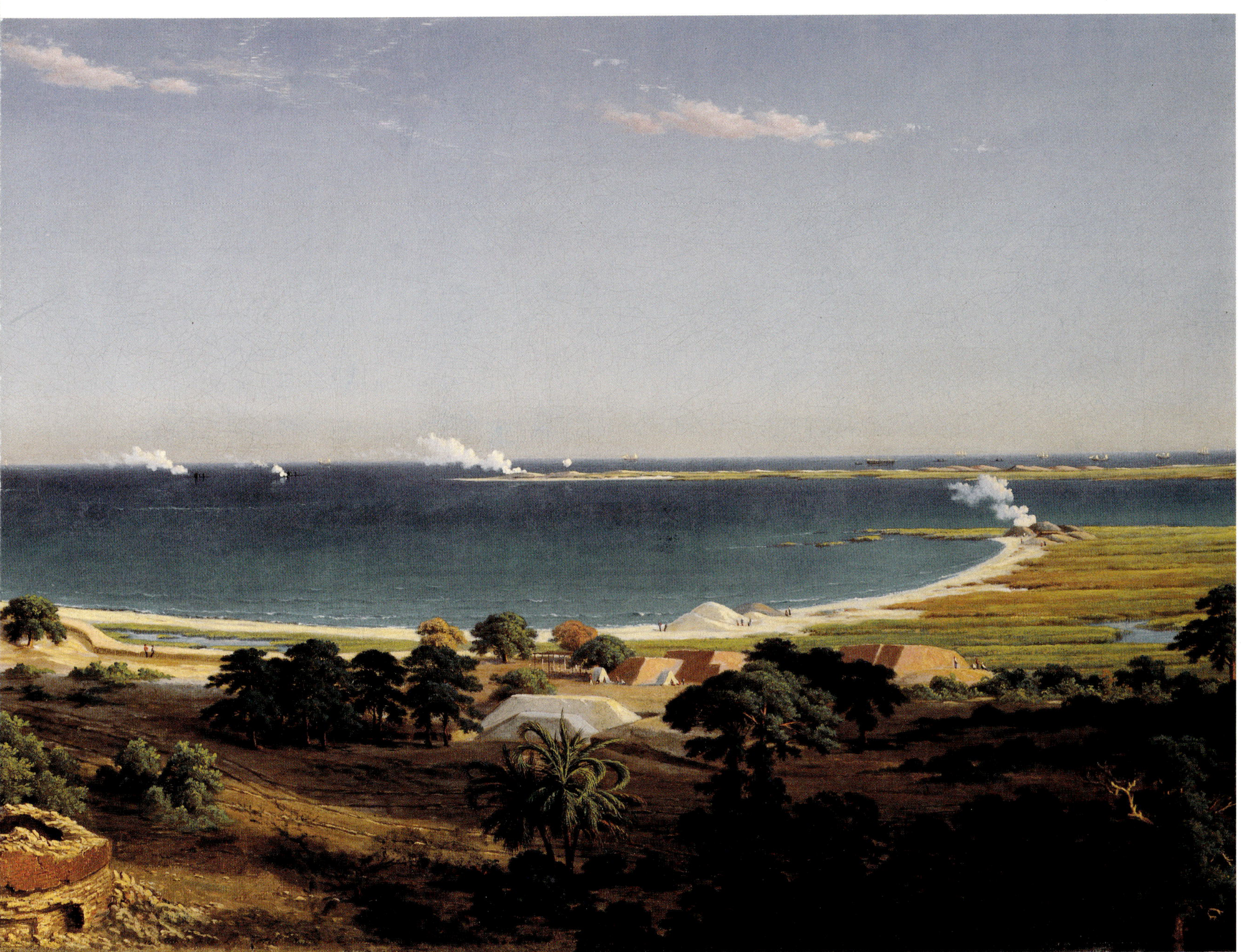

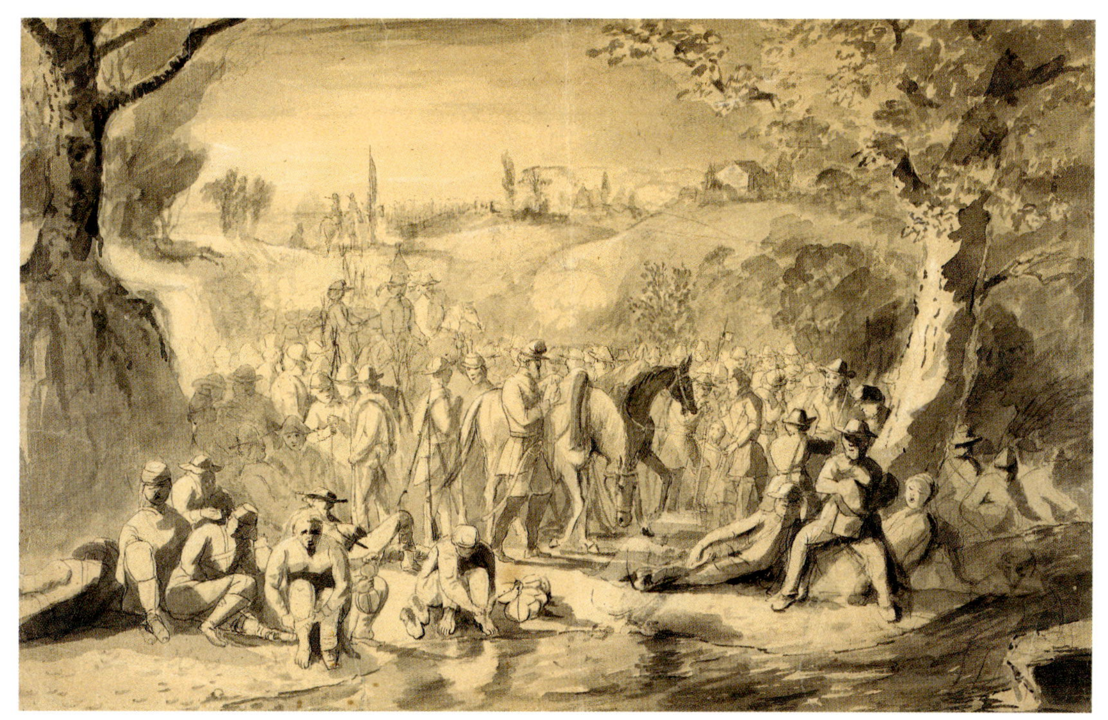

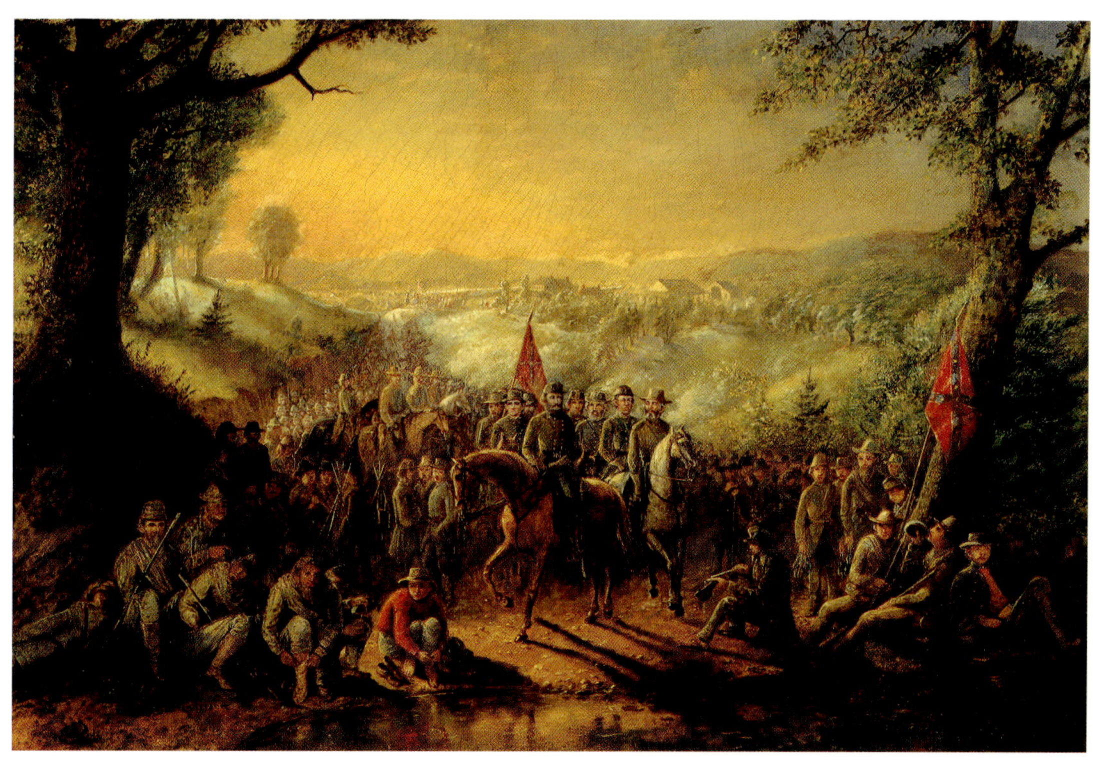

Alexander François Loemans

circa 1816–1898

Scene Presented in the Ditch and on the Southern Slope of Fort Wagner, Charleston Harbor, Assault of July 18, 1863, 1865

oil on canvas, 41 5/8 × 60 inches
signed, lower left: *A. F. Loemans, 1865*
Museum purchase with funds from the 1993 Museum Antiques Show, Elliott, Davis & Company, CPAs, sponsor; Corporate Benefactors: Alice Manufacturing Company, Inc.; Barker Air and Hydraulics, Inc.; BB&T; Carolina First Bank; The First Union Foundation; Greenville News–Piedmont Company; Hartness International; Insignia Financial Group, Inc.; KEMET Corporation; Liberty Life Insurance; Michelin North America; Odell Associates, Inc.; Pepsi-Cola Bottling Company of Greenville; Portman Marina, Inc.; Provence Printing, Inc.; Suitt Construction Company; Thoracic and Cardiovascular Associates

The experience of the Civil War fostered new forms of expression in the 1860s and 1870s. Portraits, both paintings and photographs, of heroic military and political figures were equally popular in the North and the South. Topographical views, marine paintings, and battle scenes such as those by Conrad Wise Chapman and John Ross Key recorded the actual sites and the main events of the war. The North not only celebrated its victory but also paid tribute to its war dead; in small towns throughout New England monuments of single soldiers commemorated the deceased. In the South numerous publications, including *The Lost Cause* and *The Confederate Soldier in the Civil War,* presented the Southern perspective, attempting to set the record straight and to provide some degree of solace.

Artists were aware of this continued fascination with the conflict that had torn the Union apart, and they sought to provide appropriate images. Although artists like David English Henderson offered eyewitness accounts, other artists, it seems, had not seen firsthand the events they depicted. Alexander Loemans, for example, cannot be placed at the engagement shown in his *Scene Presented in the Ditch and on the Southern Slope of Fort Wagner, Charleston Harbor, Assault of July 18, 1863.*

Born in Paris, Loemans came to the United States as a young man and spent most of his career in the North, first in upstate New York, and then in Minnesota. A contemporaneous newspaper account described him as eccentric, and it has also been suggested that his personal life was complicated by the fact that he had two wives living in different cities.[1]

Loemans specialized in landscape paintings. "Always a student of nature, yet often painting from remembrance, possessed of an extremely imaginative mind, he would produce picture after picture, days and weeks together, without having a sketch before him, while placing it upon the canvas."[2] He also consciously emulated the work of other artists, including Albert Bierstadt and Frederic Edwin Church. He was particularly attracted to the South American scenes of the latter, although it seems he did not travel there himself. Despite producing work at a feverish pace, Loemans was frequently in financial difficulty, a predicament that may have forced him to look at art from an entrepreneurial vantage point.

Perhaps sensing the popularity of images related to the Civil War, Loemans may have done the Museum's painting either on speculation or as the result of a direct commission. The choice of subject, however, is most unusual and raises the question as to who might have wanted to acquire the work, as the incident presented difficulties to both sides. It may have been destined for a European patron interested in the subject's racial undertones. The painting depicts the bloody aftermath of the engagement at Battery Wagner, Charleston Harbor, in which the Fifty-fourth Massachusetts Regiment was repulsed by the Confederates. Led by Colonel Robert Gould Shaw, this Union regiment was made up primarily of African-Americans, presenting a special kind of affront to Southerners. Even Confederate accounts recognized the horror:

> The carnage of the enemy in the confined space in front of Battery Wagner was extreme. The ditch and glacis were encumbered with the slain of all ranks and colors, for the enemy had put the poor negroes, whom they had forced into unnatural service, in front, to be, as they were, slaughtered indiscriminately. The white colonel who commanded them fell with many officers of the regiment (the Fifty-fourth Massachusetts), and the colors under which they were sent to butchery by hypocrisy and inhumanity, fell, draggled in blood and sand in the ditch, a mournful memorial of the waste of industry.[3]

Loemans appears to have used as his model an engraving that appeared in the *London News.* This illustration derives from an on-the-spot sketch by Frank Vizetelly, who also provided a chilling account on the reverse of his drawing: "In the ditch, they lay piled, negroes and whites, four and five deep on each other, there could not have been less than 250 in the moat, some partially submerged. . . . In the distance Charleston can be seen with a thunder cloud breaking over—heaven as it were casting loose its mighty artillery."[4] Loemans adapted the title of the engraving and wrote it almost verbatim across the bottom of the painting. In translating the image to a large canvas Loemans elevated the significance of the site by reducing the size of the figures, making them diminutive. This technique also distances the viewer from the bloody reality of the event. Curiously, the artist portrayed most of the dead as white, perhaps out of ignorance of the actual battle. In the foreground he replaced a group of soldiers and corpses with debris. He also broadened the horizon, added an ironclad, and embellished the skyline of Charleston by adding several more church spires. Although the original wood engraving has a bolt of lightning, Loemans has dramatized this motif in a more expansive sky and romanticized the composition with the glow of early morning light. Through these subtle modifications, Loemans moved the image from the pages of journalism to the realm of painting.

---

1. Colonel Terance J. Kennedy, "A Paper on Art and Professional Artists of Cayuga County," *Auburn Morning News,* 14–16 March 1878; Dr. Ross Fox to the author, 23 April 1993. Obituary, *Minneapolis Journal,* 18 November 1898, mentions that Loemans some years earlier had "left the town very suddenly," leaving his wife behind to fend for herself.

2. Kennedy, *Auburn News.*

3. Brigadier-General Roswell S. Ripley, "Charleston Harbor: Assault on Fort Wagner; Operations on Morris Island, etc., July 8 to 22, 1863," *The Confederate Soldier in the Civil War* (Louisville, Ky.: The Prentice Press, 1897), 181.

4. Drawing and inscription by Frank Vizetelly (shelf mark pfMS Am 1585), quoted by permission of the Houghton Library, Harvard University; it was engraved by F. J. Skill for the *Illustrated London News,* 26 September 1863, 317, and later reproduced in Ripley, "Charleston Harbor," 191.

Born, Paris, circa 1816; painted in Auburn, New York, 1854–1856, followed by an interval in Utica, New York; Minneapolis, Minnesota, 1875–1880; in Boston, 1880; in Toronto, Canada, 1882, Hamilton, 1884–1885, Montreal, 1887, and Vancouver, 1894; died, Minneapolis, 1898.

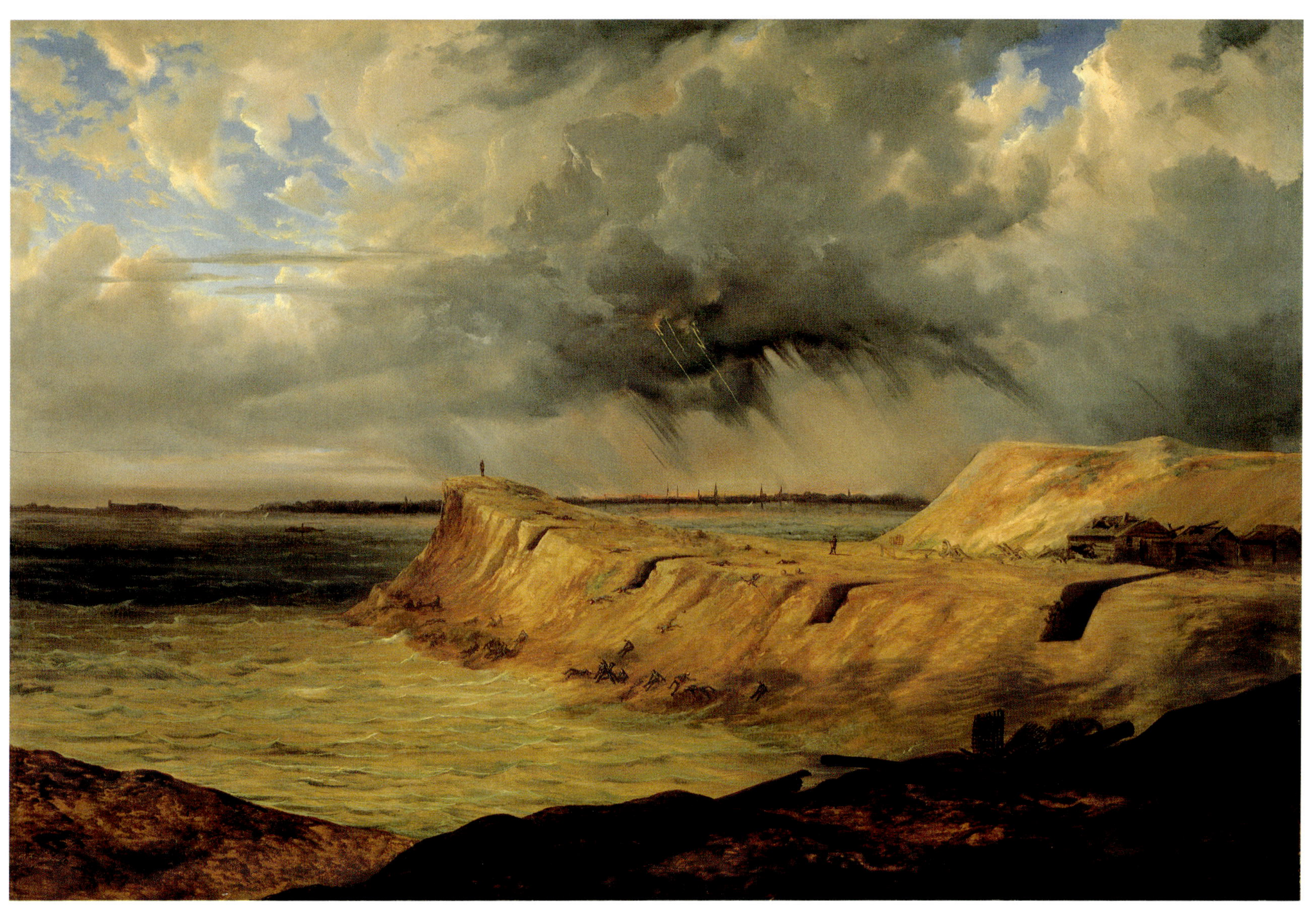

Thomas Satterwhite Noble

1835–1907

Fugitives in Flight, 1869

oil on canvas, 30⅛ × 40¼ inches
signed, lower left: *Noble. 1869*
Museum purchase with funds from the 1994 Museum Antiques Show, Elliott, Davis & Company, CPAs, sponsor; Corporate Benefactors: Alice Manufacturing Company, Inc.; Barker Air and Hydraulics, Inc.; Carolina First Bank; Dodge Group–Reliance Electric; Greenville News–Piedmont Company; Hartness International, Inc.; Insignia Financial Group, Inc.; KPMG Peat Marwick; KEMET Corporation; The Liberty Corporation; Michelin North America; Odell Associates, Inc.; Pepsi-Cola Bottling Company of Greenville; Phillips Staffing; Provence Printing, Inc.; Suitt Construction Company; and the Arthur and Holly Magill Purchase Fund

During the mid-nineteenth century, abolitionist sentiment found expression in the written word more readily than in visual art. Whether fictional novels or political essays, antislavery literature garnered large audiences, especially in the North. Nothing exceeded the widespread appeal of Harriet Beecher Stowe's *Uncle Tom's Cabin*; published in 1852, it sold three hundred thousand copies its first year. Stowe, who lived for eighteen years in Cincinnati just across the river from Kentucky, drew upon personal observations as well as published accounts for her novel. So intense was the public response that President Abraham Lincoln acknowledged the author's role: "So this is the little lady who started the great war."[1] Southerners blamed Stowe for the conflict, calling her a slave lover and disparaging her because of her gender. The reaction to *Uncle Tom's Cabin* was international; writing the year it was released, the French author George Sand described how "people devoured it, they covered it with tears."[2]

During the antebellum period few artists were as bold as Stowe, although the popular press contained numerous satirical illustrations presenting both sides of the slavery issue. Several artists, including William Sidney Mount, alluded obliquely to civil-rights issues in their genre paintings. The most notable and overt example of abolitionist art, however, was Hiram Powers's pure white marble sculpture, *Greek Slave,* which was controversial not only because it depicted a nude woman but also because it addressed the issue of slavery. Only European-born artists, like Christian Mayr, were comfortable portraying the lives of African-Americans without reference to the slaves' white masters.[3] After the Civil War, images of ex-slaves and preemancipation situations became the frequent subject matter for Eastman Johnson, Winslow Homer, and Thomas Noble.

Unlike Johnson and Homer, both New Englanders, Noble was a Kentuckian with firsthand knowledge of slavery. A native of Lexington, the center of that state's slave trade, Noble seems to have had ambivalent feelings about abolition, just as Kentucky, a border state, was divided politically, socially, and economically.[4] Growing up in Lexington and later Louisville, Noble was exposed to debates about emancipation and recolonization of Africa and witnessed African-Americans working for his father, a hemp producer. After some elemental training in Louisville, Noble went to Paris, where he entered the atelier of Thomas Couture in 1856. For three years Noble participated in a curriculum that was neither totally traditional nor completely innovative. It combined drawing from plaster casts of ancient sculpture with drawing of live models, both male and female. Couture served as an important influence, both as a teacher and as a politically involved painter.

Returning from Paris in 1859, Noble moved to St. Louis, Missouri, another slave state that, like Kentucky, did not secede. Despite his personal antislavery sentiments, Noble eventually enlisted in the Confederate Army and saw action in Arkansas and Louisiana. Shortly after his release he began a series of stirring canvases with proabolitionist content, perhaps as expiation for his apparent endorsement of slavery. Two in the series portray specific individuals, John Brown and Margaret Garner. Brown, a fanatic crusader for the abolitionist cause, is shown as he was led to his execution. Garner, a fugitive slave who had successfully fled to Ohio, is portrayed just as she is about to be recaptured; she attempts to kill her children in order that they may avoid the sufferings of slavery.

Less biographical are a group of paintings whose subjects reflect recurring themes found in *Uncle Tom's Cabin:* a slave auction, miscegenation, and escape from slavery. Painted in 1865, *The Last Sale of Slaves* brought Noble national recognition and was even exhibited in the rotunda of the United States Capitol. Perhaps Noble's most chilling image is *The Price of Blood,* which depicts a menacing white planter selling his mixed-race son into slavery.

Although the Museum's painting does not depict a specific event in *Uncle Tom's Cabin,* it envisions the goal of many of the novel's protagonists. Incidences of fugitive slaves attempting to cross the Ohio River would have been familiar to both Stowe and Noble, who lived on opposite sides of the river. The simple landscape scene is centrally lit by a rising sun, symbolic of a new day in the lives of the fugitives. The figures are motionless, except for the oarsman; two women clasp babies, reminders of the biblical flight into Egypt. For them, as for the female protagonist Eliza in *Uncle Tom's Cabin,* the river is both obstacle and opportunity: "It lay like Jordan, between her and the Canaan of liberty on the other side."[5]

Fugitives in Flight was the last of Noble's antislavery subjects, begun in St. Louis and continued in New York from 1866 to 1869. He may have painted these works for personal reasons or in response to Northern patrons desirous to own images that validated their stand against slavery. *Fugitives in Flight* also serves as the culmination of the series, which moves from specific, biographical narratives to generalized, oft-repeated themes. In the year of the painting's completion, Noble moved to Cincinnati to head the McMicken School of Art, and he abandoned his antislavery paintings.

---

1. As quoted in Elizabeth Ammons, ed., *Critical Essays on Harriet Beecher Stowe* (Boston: G. K. Hall, 1980), xi.
2. "Review of *Uncle Tom's Cabin,*" *La Presse,* 17 December 1852, in Ammons, *Stowe,* 3.
3. See Elizabeth Johns, *American Genre Painting: The Politics of Everyday Life* (New Haven: Yale University Press, 1991), 100–136.
4. Albert Boime, "Burgoo and Bourgeois: Thomas Noble's Images of Black People," *Thomas Satterwhite Noble, 1835–1907* (Lexington: University of Kentucky Art Museum, 1988), 30.
5. Stowe, *Uncle Tom's Cabin* (New York: The Library of America, 1982), 70.

Born, Lexington, Kentucky, 1835; studied in Paris with Thomas Couture, 1856–1859; returned to Louisville, served in the Confederate Army, 1861–1865; lived in New York, 1866–1869; appointed head of the McMicken School of Art, Cincinnati, 1869, until his retirement in 1904; died, New York, 1907.

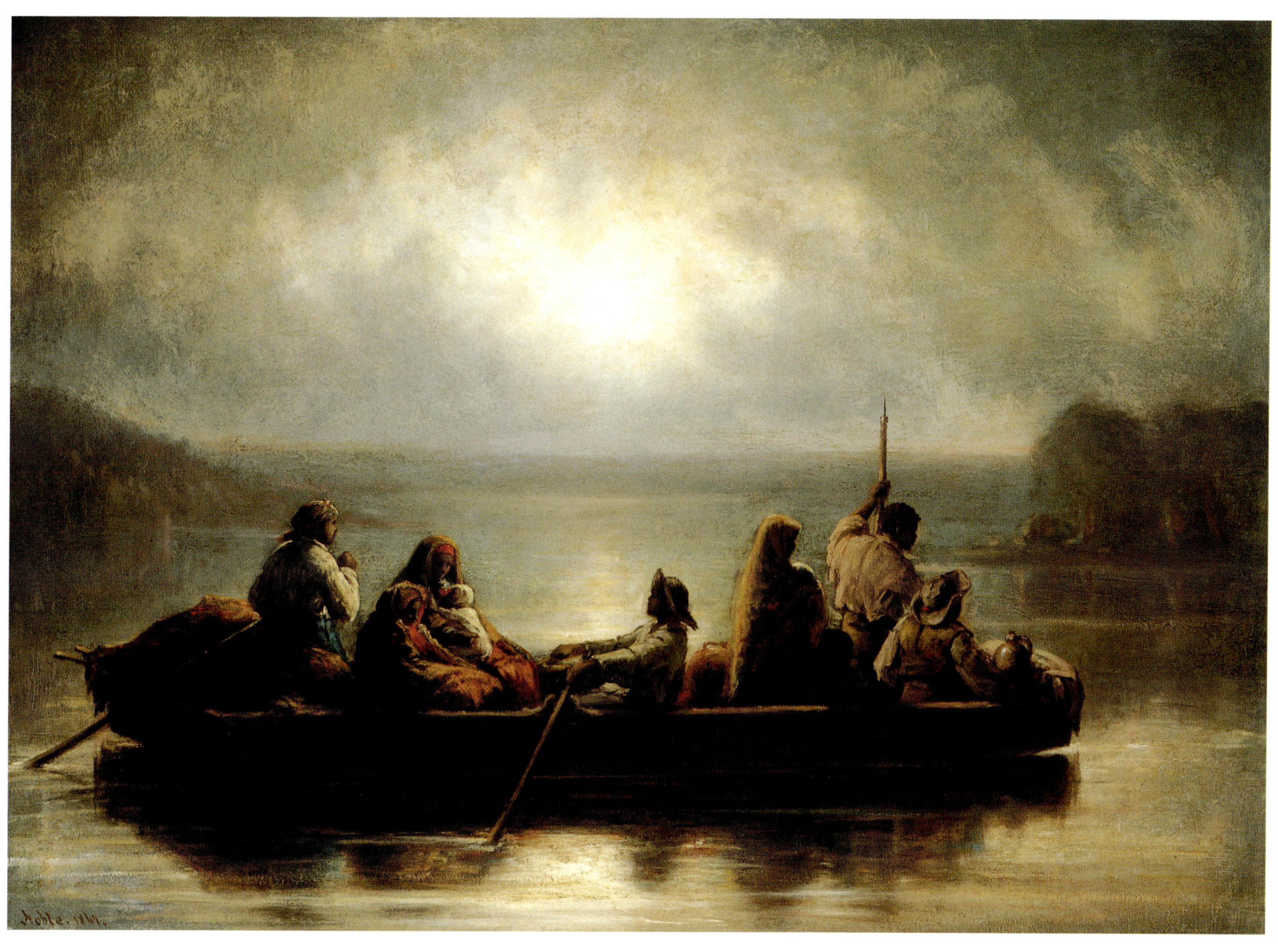
Noble.

Louis Rémy Mignot

1831–1870

Mount Chimborazo, circa 1865

oil on canvas, 38 5/8 × 63 1/8 inches
signed, lower right: *Mignot*
Museum purchase with funds donated by the Arthur and Holly Magill Foundation; The Museum Association's 1992 Collectors' Group; the 1992 Museum Antiques Show, Elliott, Davis & Company, CPAs, sponsor; Museum Corporate Partners: Carolina First Corporation; Greenville News–Piedmont Company; Director's Circle Members: Laura E. duPont; Mr. and Mrs. Alester G. Furman III; Stanton D. and Jessica S. Loring; Mr. and Mrs. John J. Sakas; W. Thomas Smith; Corporate Benefactors: Alice Manufacturing Company; Barker Air and Hydraulics, Inc.; Carolina First Bank; Eastern Trading Company, Inc.; Greenville News–Piedmont Company; Hartness International, Inc.; Insignia Financial Group, Inc.; KEMET Corporation; Liberty Life Insurance Company; Odell Associates, Inc.; Pepsi-Cola Bottling Company of Greenville; Portman Marina, Inc.; Ryan's Family Steak Houses, Inc.

By the late 1850s the second generation of Hudson River School painters undertook more ambitious projects, choosing dramatic sites and painting on a larger scale. This trend is exemplified by Frederic Edwin Church's *Niagara,* which boldly captured the spirit of Manifest Destiny. Exhibited widely at home and abroad, this monumental canvas became a sensation and a symbol of the American spirit.[1] Church's overwhelming success inspired Albert Bierstadt and Thomas Moran to paint equally theatrical vistas of western scenery at Yosemite and the Grand Canyon.

Church expanded his own horizons by traveling to South America, which had become more accessible with improved steamship and railroad service. South America was a destination for scientists and naturalists as well as for artists; great significance was attached to this other, largely unspoiled, American continent. With its tropical vegetation, imposing mountains, and suffused light, the southern hemisphere inspired romantic associations with the Garden of Eden, a concept that was challenged in 1859 when Charles Darwin published his *Origin of the Species.*[2]

Louis Rémy Mignot accompanied Church on his second trip to South America in 1857, and for ten weeks they explored the mountain ranges and lagoons of Ecuador, making quick pencil studies and oil sketches that they later developed into finished paintings in their studios. Whereas Church painted quasi-scientific canvases, Mignot created more evocative statements. Raised in coastal South Carolina, Mignot would have been familiar with the haze and plant life of the tropics. His sympathetic response was noted by the critic Henry Tuckerman, who commented on Mignot's "remarkable facility of catching the expression, often vague, but, therefore, more interesting. . . . He seizes upon the latent as well as the prominent effects. He is a master of color, and some of his atmospheric experiments are wonderful."[3] Rather than the grandiose schemes of his traveling companion, Mignot preferred more poetic and serene visions.

Mount Chimborazo is one of Mignot's most ambitious paintings; it entices the viewer to enter a luxuriant, exotic, and symbolic world. Hailed as the Queen of the Andes, Chimborazo rises 20,561 feet and is among the highest peaks in South America. Majestic in Mignot's depiction, the great snow-capped mountain looms magnificently above a high, rolling plain, where vegetation is sparse. In the right foreground carefully detailed palm trees and colorful birds invite examination, but these were probably added for artistic effect. The palm, for example, does not grow at such an elevated altitude. In the lower center two figures and their animals walk toward the viewer, an unusual motif; Mignot and other mid-nineteenth-century painters normally depicted figures from behind. In other, earlier paintings, Mignot regularly employed humans as indicators of scale. Frequently these were done by another hand; both Thomas Rossiter and Eastman Johnson are known to have painted figures in Mignot's landscapes.

Rather than the intense midday light often employed by Church, Mignot set his scene at sunrise, contributing to the dreamlike aspect of this painting. Particularly short-lived in the tropics, this fleeting moment is further enhanced by the rainbow encircling Chimborazo. A London newspaper described a painting by Mignot entitled *Table Lands of the Rio Bamba* in words that fit the Museum's canvas:

> The lofty plateau stretches away as far as the eye can reach, its sandy surface broken into countless mounded loaves crested with stunted vegetation. Above the horizontal mists of the table-land, rises at an immense distance the mountain range of the Andes. In the foreground are strange plants and grasses, with a vast earthquake chasm, its depth lost in thick vapour overhead, the sun is dissipating the morning exhalations of fantastic forms, and earth and sky are flush together in the fervid glow of the tropics.[4]

Mignot drew upon his Ecuadorian trip throughout the remainder of his life, often making composite paintings from his numerous sketches. Restless by nature, he left New York in 1862 when growing hostility made it uncomfortable for a Southerner to live in the North. His intention was to go to India, but he settled in England, where he exhibited at the Royal Academy. He also made occasional trips to Italy and Switzerland to paint Alpine scenery. More loosely painted than earlier works, the Museum's painting seems to have been completed during Mignot's English period. In its misty, visionary quality it suggests that Mount Chimborazo was also a fading memory from long ago and far away. In its lush attention to clouds and proto-Impressionist brushwork, the painting reflects the influence of two eminent British painters: John Constable, known for his billowing clouds; and Joseph Mallord William Turner, celebrated for his coloristic and atmospheric compositions.

1. Church's *Niagara,* collection of the Corcoran Gallery of Art, was painted in 1857. See John K. Howat et al., *American Paradise: The World of the Hudson River School* (New York: The Metropolitan Museum of Art, 1987).

2. See Katherine Emma Manthorne, *Tropical Renaissance: North American Artists Exploring Latin America, 1838–1878* (Washington, D.C.: Smithsonian Institution Press, 1989).

3. Henry T. Tuckerman, *Book of the Artists* (1867; reprint, New York: James F. Carr, 1966), 563.

4. *Illustrated London News,* quoted in Tom Taylor, "Sketch of the Life of Louis Rémy Mignot," *Catalogue of the Mignot Pictures* (London: 25 Bond Street; Brighton: The Pavilion, 1876), 3.

Born, Charleston, South Carolina, 1831; studied at The Hague, 1848–1855; in New York, 1855–1862; to Ecuador, 1857; London, 1862–1870, with trips to Italy and Switzerland; died, Brighton, England, 1870.

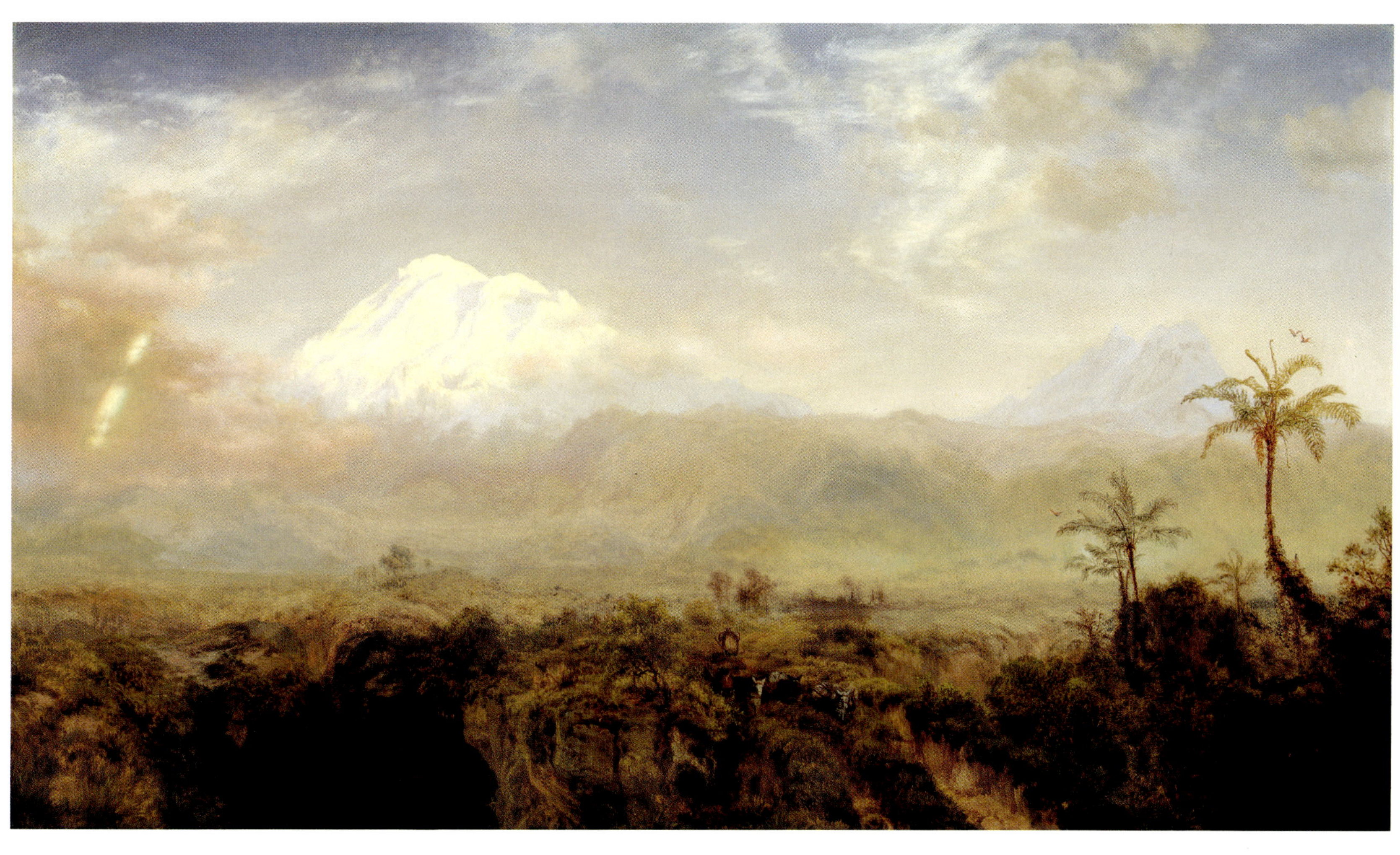

John Beaufain Irving, Jr.

1825–1877

Feeding Goldfish, 1873

oil on canvas, 20⅛ × 16⅛ inches
signed, lower right: *J. Beaufain Irving, 1873*
Gift of Director's Associates: Mr. and Mrs. Glenn Hilliard; Dr. and Mrs. Jeffrey G. Lawson; Alice and Hal Lonnecker; Mr. and Mrs. Thomas A. Roe; Mr. and Mrs. Robert Scott Small; Mr. and Mrs. Wilson C. Wearn

The economic climate during the Civil War was not conducive to art patronage, and, with few exceptions, opportunities to produce and exhibit art were limited. Artists on both sides enlisted in the military. Some Southern artists returned home; others, who had achieved success in New York, remained there; and still others, like Louis Rémy Mignot, went abroad. After the war the mood of the country changed; nationalistic pride gave way to disillusionment, and industry, so instrumental to the Union victory, became king. New fortunes had been made, cities in the North boomed with increased industrialization, and the immigration of large numbers of people from Ireland and Italy changed the cultural composition of cities.

For Southern artists who remained in the South during the war, like William Harrison Scarborough and John Beaufain Irving, the conflict caused serious financial difficulties. Writing from New York in 1875, Irving mused: "I should like very much to be with you all in Old Charleston once again, but Alas! . . . My life here is one of severe application to my profession, I scarcely have time to leave my Studio such is the necessity for money. My family now has increased to 8 children and I fear I have not seen the last one yet. And to provide for the wants of so large a number my brush must move briskly."[1] As a child from a well-to-do Charleston family, Irving had the advantage of instruction in his native city before attending the Düsseldorf Academy for six years. After returning to the United States in 1858, he painted both portrait and genre paintings.

One of the most prevalent themes following the war was that of the rural, barefoot boy.[2] Although young people were depicted before 1860 in genre paintings by William Sidney Mount, Henry Inman, and James Clonney, by the 1870s the numbers increased markedly. In popular literature and in children's books such quintessential characters as Tom Sawyer and Huck Finn quickly became favorites of the public. These youths came to symbolize the loss of innocence brought about by the war. Winslow Homer, who had seen the war firsthand as an art correspondent for *Harper's Weekly,* portrayed carefree days spent fishing, lolling in meadows, or playing snap-the-whip.

A similar mood of nostalgia pervades Irving's *Feeding Goldfish.* Whereas other artists depicted lighthearted farm boys, Irving shows an urbane and well-dressed young girl. While alluding to her childlike innocence, Irving also used her to symbolize the captive female of the Victorian period. Her environment is dominated not by open fields but by architectural forms; nature is present only in the formal garden on the other side of the wall. Weighed down by the monumental columns rising above her, she appears world-weary. Alone, she wistfully drops crumbs into the small pool at her feet. The fish, like the pensive girl, are confined to a spiritless setting, where they are dependent on their keeper.

Goldfish were not bred in this country until 1878, so Irving probably relied on book illustrations or his experiences in Germany to portray the ornamental species. Prized for their brilliant color, which develops only with maturity, goldfish have long served as decorative elements in the garden, especially in the Far East. Irving's model, with her crimson coat and embroidered dress and pantalets, also displays a great deal of finery. In all likelihood Irving used one of his daughters as his model and dressed her in clothes befitting a child of affluence, despite the family's modest means.

1. Irving to S. Prioleau Ravenel, as quoted in Anna Wells Rutledge, *Artists in the Life of Charleston* (1949; reprint, Columbia: University of South Carolina Press, 1980), 168.

2. Sarah Burns, "Barefoot Boy and Other Country Children: Sentiment and Ideology in Nineteenth-Century American Art," *The American Art Journal* 20, no. 1 (1988): 24–50.

Born, Charleston, South Carolina, 1825; studied at the Düsseldorf Academy 1851–1858; in Charleston during the war; moved to New York, circa 1865; died, New York, 1877.

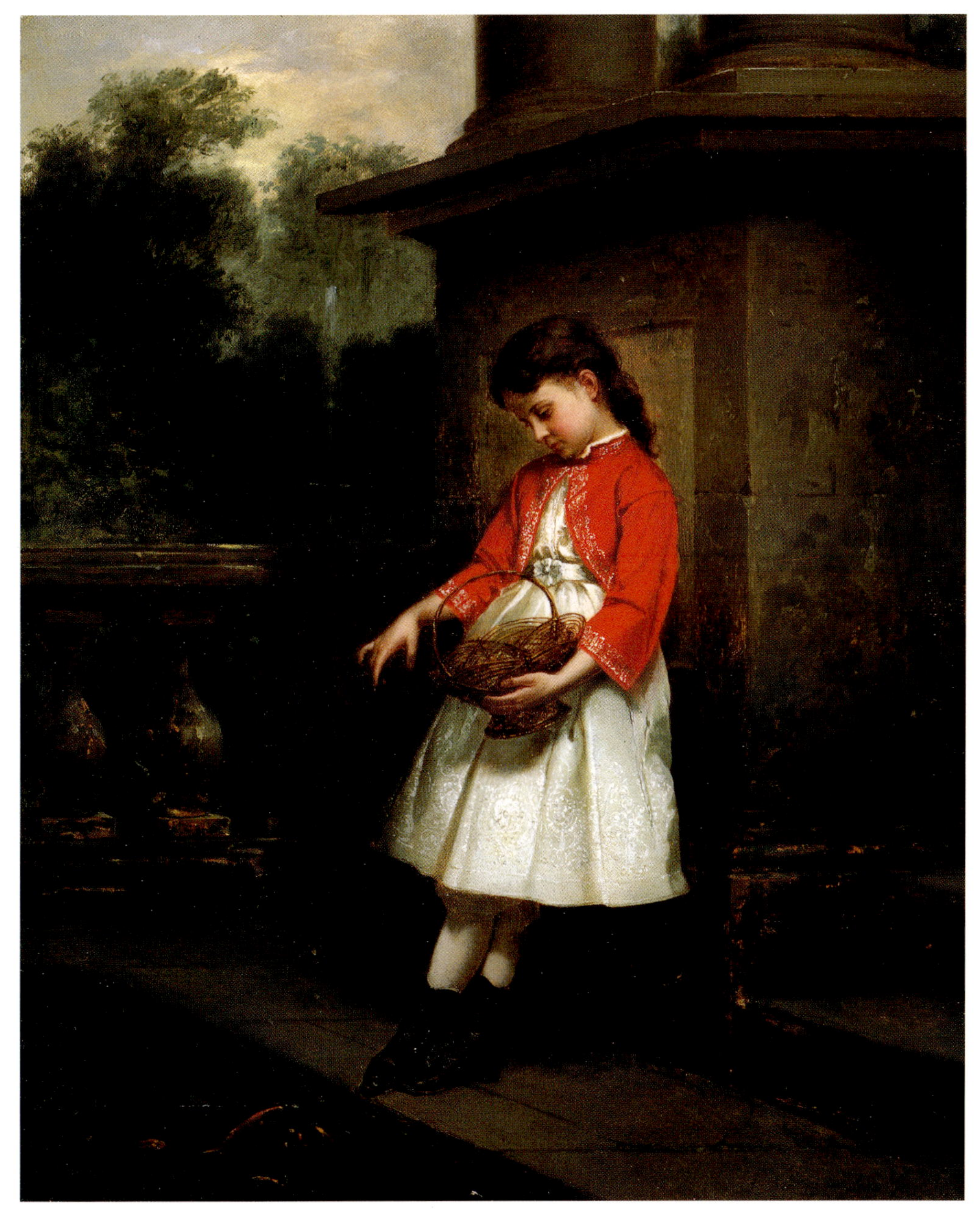

Edwin Lord Weeks

1849–1903

In the Everglades of Florida, 1872

oil on canvas, 25 × 32 inches
signed, lower right: *E. L. Weeks, 1872*
Museum purchase with funds donated by the estate of John F. Bannon, The Museum Association, Inc., and John S. Hard (by exchange)

Artists emerging in the decades after the Civil War were often frustrated by the limitations of art education in America. Both the National Academy of Design and the Pennsylvania Academy of the Fine Arts offered instruction, but there were few additional opportunities in this country. Throughout the nineteenth century American artists sought training in London, Florence, The Hague, Düsseldorf, Munich, and Paris. In addition to good teachers, European cities could supply models, studios, libraries, and a cosmopolitan environment conducive to the cultural development of young American artists. By the last quarter of the nineteenth century Paris was the destination most attractive to art students, and the state-supported Ecole des Beaux-Arts, whose policy of free tuition applied to students of all nationalities, was the preeminent art school in the world.

The rich European experience gained as a student often radically changed an artist's style as well as his outlook. In many instances, artists decided not to return to America but led lives as expatriates. James McNeill Whistler, Mary Cassatt, and John Singer Sargent are among the most famous examples of this phenomenon. Edwin Lord Weeks, who went to Paris to study, also became an expatriate. His work is exemplary of Orientalism, a painting style that derived its exotic motifs and subject matter from North Africa and the Middle East.

Weeks demonstrated his restless spirit and his fascination with distant locales at age twenty, when he made his first trip to the Florida Keys. The following year he traveled to Surinam. Two years later he returned to the Everglades to paint the lush vegetation and the modest living conditions. In the Museum's *In the Everglades of Florida,* Weeks emphasized the indigenous palm, just as Frederic Edwin Church and Louis Rémy Mignot had done in their South American scenes. The palm was seen as an emblem of paradise, and it was identified with the Tree of Life.[1] The foreground in the Museum's painting is cluttered with low, spiked varieties of the tree, while the upper right is dominated by a group of three palms majestically silhouetted against the sky.

Weeks's art underwent dramatic changes during his later years in Paris. His debt to the mood and subject matter of the Barbizon School as seen in the Museum's painting was replaced by an academic realism that emphasized clear light and attention to detail. His teacher, Léon Bonnat, and his mentor, Jean-Léon Gérôme, instilled in Weeks both an appreciation of and a thirst for foreign travel.[2] Weeks's peripatetic life-style took him to Morocco, Egypt, Persia, and India, although he maintained a studio in Paris. He exhibited regularly and successfully at the Paris Salons and at the Pennsylvania Academy of the Fine Arts.

---

1. See Katherine Manthorne, "The Quest for a Tropical Paradise: Palm Tree as Fact and Symbol in Latin American Landscape Imagery, 1850–1875," *Art Journal* 44, no. 4 (Winter 1984): 374–382.

2. See H. Barbara Weinberg, *The Lure of Paris: Nineteenth-Century American Painters and Their French Teachers* (New York: Abbeville Press, 1991), 107 and 176.

Born, Boston, 1849; traveled to Florida, 1869 and 1872; to Surinam, 1870; early 1870s to Syria, the Holy Lands, and Egypt; studied in Paris with Léon Bonnat, 1874; maintained a Paris studio and exhibited in the Salon for the remainder of his life; traveled to Spain, Morocco, and in 1883 and 1892 to India; died, Paris, 1903.

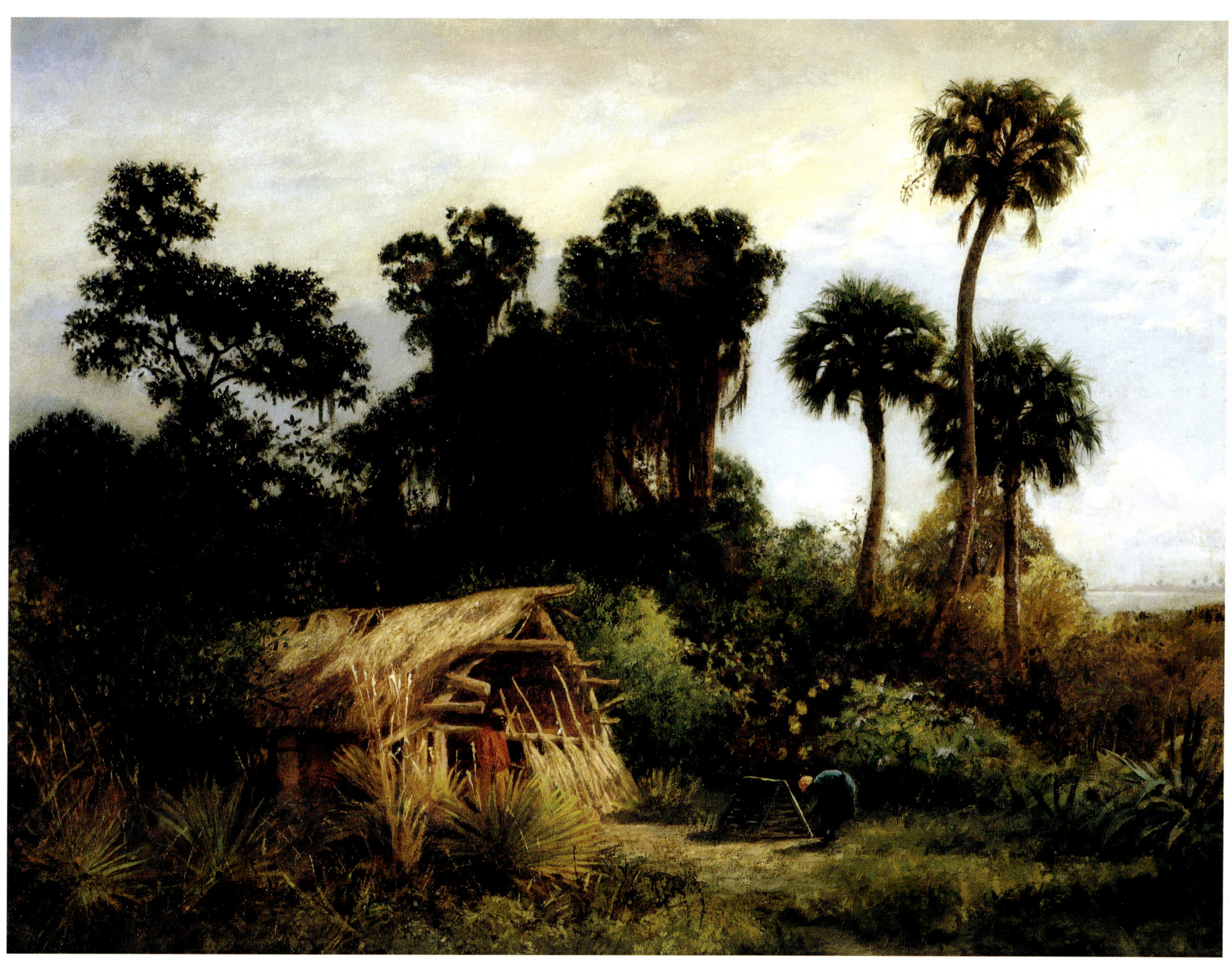

Martin Johnson Heade

1819–1904

On the San Sebastian, circa 1890

oil on canvas, 17¼ × 36 inches
signed, lower left: *M. J. Heade*
Museum purchase with funds donated by the Arthur and Holly Magill Foundation

The direction of landscape painting at midcentury seemed to diverge: on the one hand were the grandiose spectacles of Frederic Edwin Church and Albert Bierstadt; on the other were the more serene and contemplative canvases of the Luminists. The Luminists were not organized as a group or school, and, in fact, the term *Luminism* was not coined until 1954.[1] Nevertheless, the style is now seen as the natural culmination of the Hudson River School ideal. As the name suggests, Luminism was primarily concerned with the depiction of clear, still light. The typically modest, horizontal canvases are characterized by humble subjects without literary pretensions. Unlike other landscape painters, the Luminists did not emphasize the majesty of nature but rather celebrated the holistic harmony of the natural world.[2]

The two painters most closely associated with Luminism are Fitz Hugh Lane and Martin Johnson Heade. Lane specialized in light-filled harbor scenes, where reflections abound and time stands still. Heade made marsh scenes his specialty, painting more than one hundred during his lifetime.[3] These unspoiled areas midway between land and sea lent themselves to expansive and thoughtful interpretations. Heade often punctuated his emphatically horizontal canvases with haystacks, marks of human endeavor.

A friend and colleague of Church, with whom he shared a space in New York's Tenth Street Studio Building, Heade was restless by nature.[4] His training in art was modest, limited to guidance from Edward Hicks and Hicks's younger cousin Thomas. Perhaps inspired by Church's trips to South America, Heade made his own pilgrimage to Brazil and later to Nicaragua with the goal of illustrating a volume on hummingbirds. These intense studies resulted in a series of paintings depicting the radiant tropical birds and their native habitat, similar in concept to the work of the naturalist John James Audubon.

In 1883 Heade concluded his years of wanderlust by settling in St. Augustine, Florida. Attracted by its coastal setting, tropical climate, and good fishing, Heade also benefited from the patronage of Henry Morrison Flagler. A partner of John D. Rockefeller in the Standard Oil Company, Flagler was instrumental in Florida's development, expanding rail transportation and opening a series of hotels. At his Ponce de Leon Hotel in St. Augustine, Flagler erected studios for artists, hoping to enhance the cultural dimension of his endeavor.

With the hotel as his base, Heade painted fecund floral still lifes dominated by magnolias as well as serene interpretations of the marshlands and nearby river. Subdued in color, with the exception of the bright pink clouds, *On the San Sebastian* exhibits both Heade's characteristically low horizon line and his sense of quiet drama. The painting is permeated with anticipation as the distant storm moves along the horizon. The mood is underlined and prolonged by the physical proportions of the canvas, the width of which is double its height. Accenting the middle distance are the two small boats with their solitary figures, and in the far distance Heade painted the towers of Flagler's hotel and its power plant, both as a tribute to his patron and as an acknowledgment of industry's inevitable encroachment on his beloved marshland.

1. John Wilmerding et al., *American Light: The Luminist Movement* (Washington, D.C.: National Gallery of Art, 1980), 12.

2. See Wilmerding, *American Light.*

3. Theodore E. Stebbins, Jr., *The Life and Work of Martin Johnson Heade* (New Haven: Yale University Press, 1975), 42.

4. J. Gray Sweeney, "A 'Very Peculiar' Picture: Martin Johnson Heade's *Thunderstorm over Narragansett Bay,*" *Archives of American Art Journal* 28, no. 4 (1988): 6.

Born in Lumberville, Pennsylvania, 1819; circa 1838–1839, studied with Edward Hicks and Thomas Hicks, followed by European travel, 1840–1841; returned to New York area, until 1848 trip to Rome; 1851–1852 in St. Louis, then Chicago, 1854; Trenton, New Jersey, 1856; Providence, Rhode Island, 1857–1858; New York, 1859–1860; Boston, 1861–1863; 1864 trip to Brazil, then to London, 1865; in New York, 1866, with trip to Colombia and Nicaragua; based in New York, 1867–1882, with 1870 trip to Colombia; to Florida via Washington, 1883; in St. Augustine, 1884–1904; died, St. Augustine, 1904.

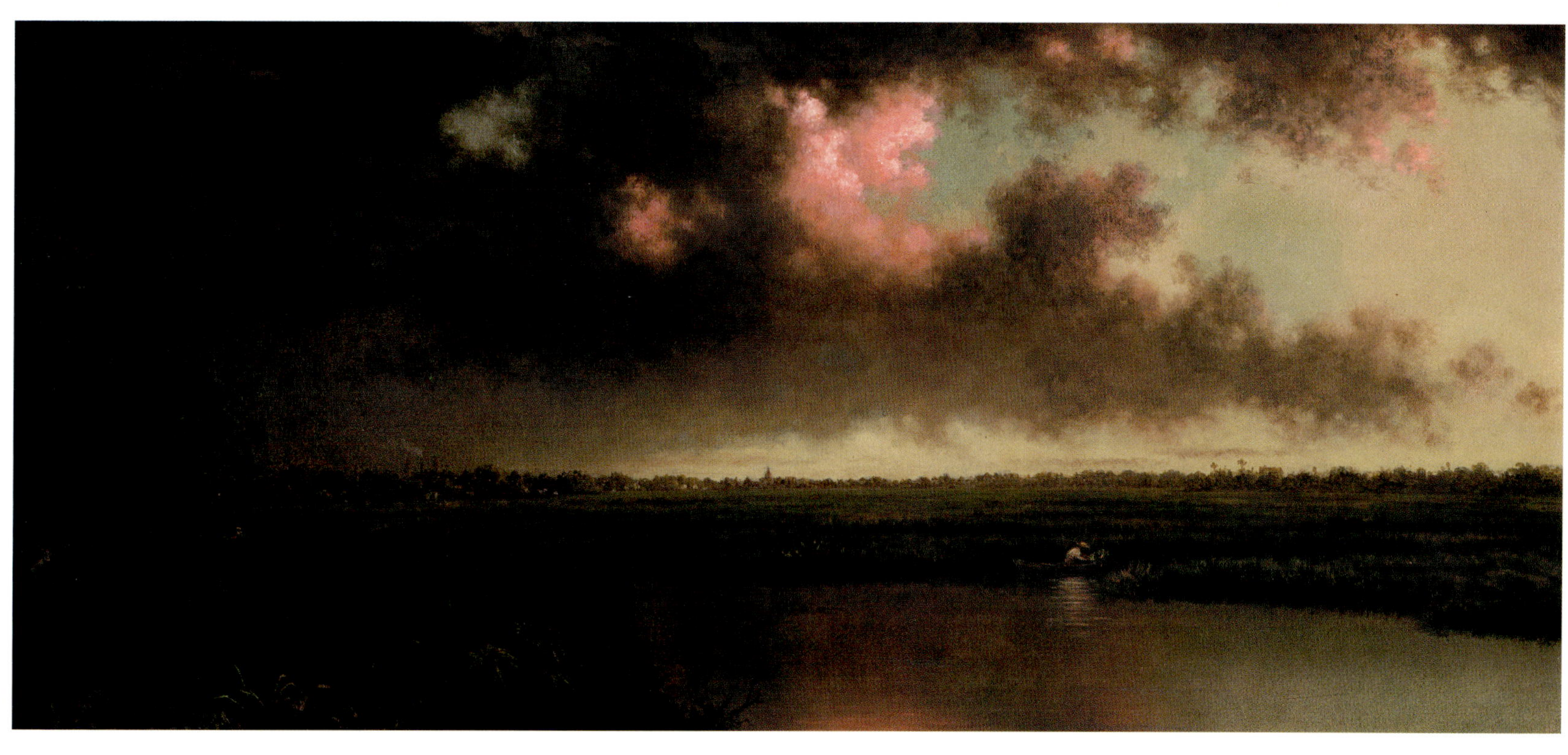

William Aiken Walker

1838–1921

Cabin by a Cornfield, circa 1885

oil on canvas, 10¼ × 16 inches
signed, lower left: *WAWalker*
Museum purchase with funds donated by First Union Bank and The Museum Association, Inc.

Before the Civil War, images of African-Americans were often exploited as political symbols, especially in the hands of Northern artists who found work illustrating the new weekly magazines. In their portrayals of slave auctions and abominable living conditions, these artists fueled the abolitionist cause. In other instances, in both art and literature, the representation of blacks is more difficult to interpret. For example, some would argue that Mark Twain was racist in his characterization of Jim, Huck Finn's friend and traveling companion. The original intent of writers and painters, all of whom would have been products of their milieu, is understandably hard for later audiences to ascertain.

William Aiken Walker painted engaging landscapes and still lifes, but he is best known for his depictions of former slaves. Although he employed the prevailing stereotypes of blacks, his own point of view seems to have been documentary rather than sentimental. Walker's choice of subject was probably commercially motivated, and he succeeded in earning a considerable livelihood. His output was prodigious, and evidently he was quite a salesman. While in Cuba in 1869 he sold 134 paintings in only sixty days.[1] His patrons, it seems, were of two types: visiting Northerners who wanted a memento of their days in the South, and Southerners who cherished depictions of a vanished way of life.

Like many antebellum portraitists, Walker maintained an itinerant lifestyle that initially took him to the South's major cities. A Charlestonian by birth, he often returned to his home to visit family and to sustain continuity with his roots. During the Civil War, Walker served briefly in the Confederate Army, and after his discharge he continued to aid the cause by drawing maps of Charleston harbor and its fortifications. Early in his career he made annual pilgrimages to Baltimore and New Orleans as well as visits to Galveston, Texas, and Augusta, Georgia. All were important urban centers, where he was able to develop a clientele and participate in exhibitions with other artists. He capitalized on New Orleans's many visitors, both tourists and business travelers, and at times sold his small paintings on street corners. Typically, these works presented single figures of cotton pickers painted on academy board. According to contemporary accounts, Walker mass-produced these souvenirs by painting the sky, the cotton field, and a row of figures on one large sheet that he then cut to yield a number of individual paintings, which he sold for a modest price.

Later in his life Walker gravitated away from cities to resort areas, where he joined other seasonal visitors. Thus in Arden, North Carolina, in the summer and in St. Augustine and Ponce Park, Florida, in the winter, he mingled with prospective patrons who enjoyed the company of the sociable artist. He gained national recognition in 1883 and 1884 when Currier & Ives reproduced two of his more ambitious cotton scenes as chromolithographs. The invention of chromolithography, a relatively inexpensive form of printmaking, made possible the color reproduction of paintings, which in turn led to the widespread distribution of popular images.

The Currier & Ives prints, coupled with the modest prices of his small paintings, made Walker's works accessible, in keeping with a lifelong goal of his: "I am like the machine; I paint and repaint these subjects so that many can share the feelings I have for this magnificent world of ours. Art is not only for the artist, it is for all and I shall do my best to see that all can afford it, to the extent that I shall paint and paint and paint until the brush runs dry."[2]

Although Walker regularly produced images that would sell quickly, he also painted tightly controlled compositions that reflected his studious interest in different locales. Although his numerous scenes of sharecropper cabins often include the same elements—the cabin, laundry hanging on a clothesline, livestock feeding, and family members performing everyday activities—each geographical region is differentiated. Cabins from the Louisiana bayou are distinct from those found in the Blue Ridge Mountains. Walker rendered these structures with a builder's eye, and he painted the appropriate flora with the mindfulness of a naturalist.

The Museum's *Cabin by a Cornfield,* probably painted in his room at the Arden Lodge, compresses an abundance of detail into a small format. Late summer crops, corn and tobacco, proliferate in the foreground against a diagonally rising tree-covered hill that obstructs any view into the surrounding countryside. The everyday activities of the chickens, the children, and the laboring sharecropper and his wife, who stands in the doorway matter-of-factly smoking her pipe, are presented objectively. Treating everything with clarity, Walker displays the intensive concern with minutiae that is typical of self-taught artists.

---

1. August P. Trovaioli and Roulhac B. Toledano, *William Aiken Walker* (Baton Rouge: Louisiana State University Press, 1972), 32.

2. Walker, interview with Ianthe Bond Hebel, as quoted in Trovaioli and Toledano, *Walker,* 3.

Born, Charleston, South Carolina, 1838; served in the Confederate Army, 1861; worked for the Confederate Corps of Engineers, Charleston, 1861–1863; in Baltimore, 1868, 1869, and 1872; to Cuba, 1869, and possible European trip, 1870; worked in New Orleans; Asheville, North Carolina; Augusta, Georgia; and Charleston, 1878–1900, and St. Augustine and Ponce Park, Florida, beginning in 1881; annual visits to Arden, North Carolina, Ponce Park, and Charleston; died, Charleston, 1921.

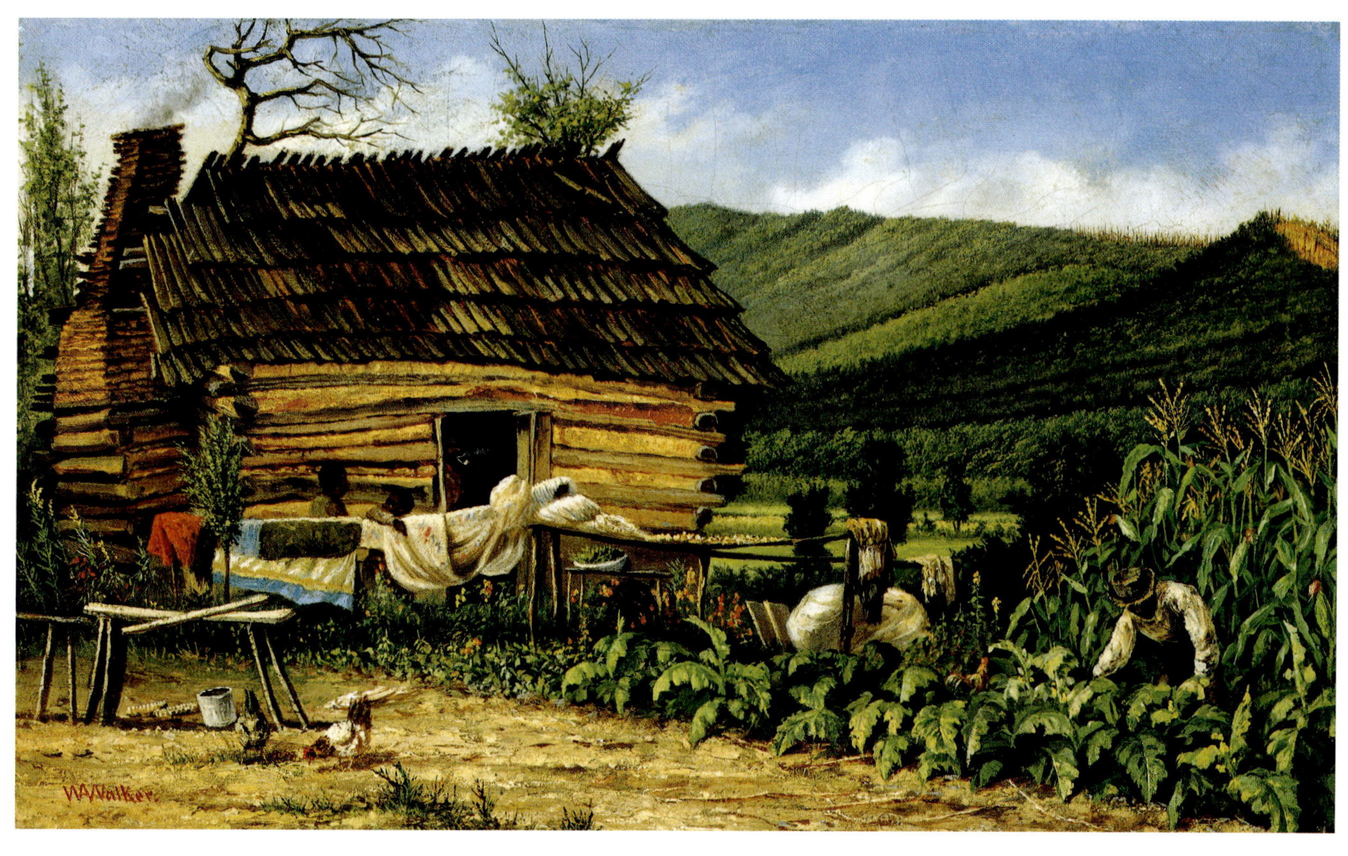
WAWalker.

Edward Lamson Henry

1841–1919

In East Tennessee, 1906

oil on canvas, 12 × 16 inches
signed, lower right: *E. L. Henry, 1906*
Gift of The Museum Association, Inc., with funds from the 1987 Museum Antiques Show, Elliott, Davis & Company, CPAs, sponsor

In 1876 the United States marked the anniversary of its independence from England. The celebration culminated in the Centennial Exhibition in Philadelphia, which included cultural displays and demonstrations of America's technological prowess. Recovering from the horrors of the Civil War and the shame of Reconstruction, the country indulged in a spirit of nostalgia. In response to the influx of immigrants and farmers seeking jobs, city dwellers romanticized rural life as charmed and idyllic.

Many artists illustrated this desire for a simpler life with wholesome, reassuring images, but none more than Edward Lamson Henry. A precocious and prolific painter, Henry exhibited at the National Academy of Design annually from 1859 until 1919, with the exception of only three years.[1] Over his entire career, his style and subject matter remained extraordinarily consistent. Resisting current fashions, Henry's imagery and his painting technique revert to an earlier era. His approach was studied and literal, and he even maintained an extensive collection of furniture, costumes, and carriages to use as props for his work. Ultimately, Henry's efforts were sentimental renderings of a lost way of life, and, in this respect, the artist was the embodiment of the Colonial Revival movement that swept the country at the end of the century.

For almost twenty years Henry rented space in New York's Tenth Street Studio Building alongside Frederic Edwin Church and Martin Johnson Heade. In 1883 he spent his first summer at Cragsmoor, eighty miles north of New York City. This small farming community provided inspiration for his work, and gradually Henry and Cragsmoor attracted other artists. The village evolved into a veritable art colony, and George Inness, Helen Turner, and Charles Courtney Curran each spent time there.

Henry's paintings are a synthesis of genre, historical, and narrative painting. He delighted in telling stories, not of momentous occasions but of everyday events from an earlier, unspecified time. He had a particular passion for subjects related to transportation, including carriages, canal barges, and eventually automobiles. Many of his paintings are composed around a rutted road, which, when placed at a right angle to the viewer, provides the illusion of distance as the lane recedes into the faraway hills.

In East Tennessee, a late painting, is typical of Henry's work. Based on studies Henry made while traveling through Tennessee in the 1880s, the painting portrays a neighborly encounter in the rural South. The work does not attempt to moralize; instead, it muses about a bygone day, when life was lived away from the hectic pace, noise, and insularity of the city.

---

1. Elizabeth McCausland, *The Life and Work of Edward Lamson Henry, N.A., 1841–1919* (1945; reprint, New York: Da Capo Press for Kennedy Graphics, 1970), 56.

Born, Charleston, South Carolina, 1841; attended the Pennsylvania Academy of the Fine Arts, circa 1858; studied in Paris and traveled abroad, 1860–1862; served in the Union Army, 1864–1865; elected associate, 1867, and full Academician, 1869, of the National Academy of Design, New York; studio in New York the remainder of his life; spent part of each year at Cragsmoor, New York, from 1883; traveled through Tennessee and South Carolina, 1888; died, Cragsmoor, 1919.

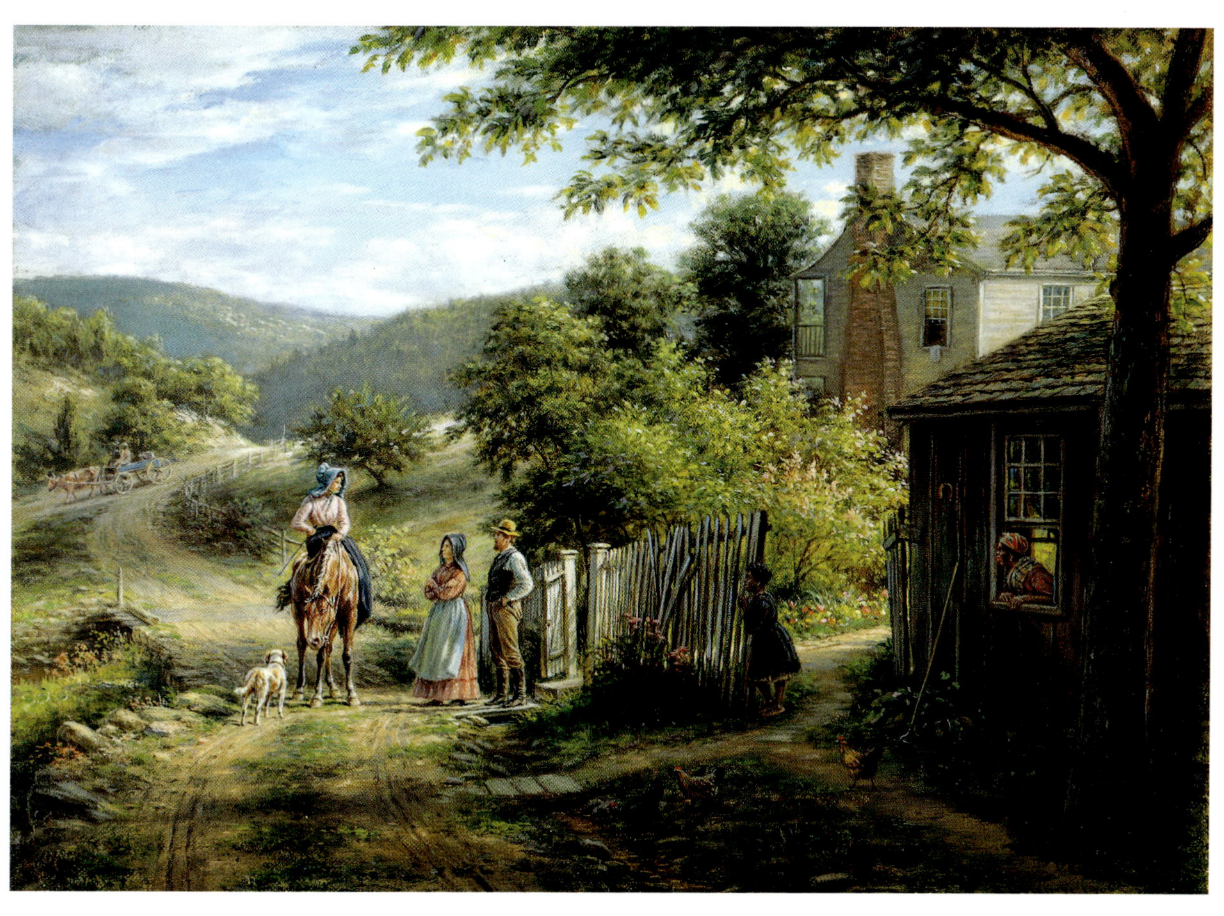

George de Forest Brush

1855–1941

In the Dark Forest, circa 1885

oil on canvas, 41⅝ × 31⅞ inches
signed, lower right: *Geo de Forest Brush*
Museum purchase with funds donated by the Arthur and Holly Magill Foundation

Variously called the Gilded Age, the Brown Decades, or the American Renaissance, the period between America's centennial and World War I was marked by sophistication. The expansionist spirit of Manifest Destiny came to an end as the country looked once again to Europe. Communications and transportation had vastly improved; the transatlantic cable was laid in 1866, and by the 1880s steamships traversed the Atlantic in only seven days. Cultural organizations, museums, libraries, and universities were founded across the country. The art world was characterized by the growth of educational and exhibition opportunities, the development of illustrated periodicals devoted to art, and the evolution of a network of dealers who mediated between artists and collectors. Wealthy patrons amassed impressive collections, which they housed in extravagantly decorated townhouses or in lavish country estates.[1]

The romantic ideal of the day was reflected in the recurring representation of beautiful women who were revered as wives, mothers, and seductresses. George de Forest Brush, who repeatedly painted his own wife and children in the guise of the Holy Family, was a proponent of this trend. Before settling on the Madonna theme, however, Brush studiously devoted himself to the portrayal of Native Americans in a style and treatment that were inspired by the Italian Mannerists of the sixteenth century.

After studying for three years at the National Academy of Design, Brush went to Paris, where he enrolled in the atelier of Jean-Léon Gérôme. Gérôme's emphasis on draftsmanship, firm outlines, and rich colors is evident in Brush's paintings throughout his long career. After almost seven years in France, Brush went to California, Wyoming, and Montana, living among the Arapahoe, Shoshone, and Crow, making studies and collecting tribal artifacts. Some of his drawings were published as illustrations in *Harper's Weekly,* and an account of his experiences appeared in *Century* in 1885.

Brush's paintings of Native American subjects, which were his specialty until 1890, were symptomatic of a national interest in ethnology. Natural history museums actively competed for ethnographic materials and regularly sent expeditions to the Northwest in pursuit of artifacts. At the World's Columbian Exposition in 1893 numerous tribal groups from around the world were enshrined in huts, teepees, and shacks along the Midway Plaisance, where they stood in striking contrast to the Neoclassical grandeur of the major exhibition spaces. Frederick Jackson Turner's warning in 1893 that the frontier was fading away only heightened the nation's nostalgia for the passing of "the old West," and, along with Brush, such artists as Frederic Remington, Charles Russell, and N. C. Wyeth took advantage of the public's perception that an era was ending.

Many of Brush's paintings record Native American artistic occupations like pottery making, weaving, and headdress making, as well as burial customs. The Museum's painting, *In the Dark Forest,* depicts a lone brave pulling a fish from a stream. Aspiring to be accurate in his portrayals, Brush used his own collection for source material. Later, in describing another painting of an Arapahoe chief, he wrote: "It was carefully studied from nature every bit of it. The costume was mine, also the pony. It has an increasing historical value, as that life has passed away, and very few artists have made very careful studies of the Indians."[2] Yet Brush's paintings should not be taken literally: he often combined objects from different tribes in one painting.

Furthermore, Brush often portrayed his subjects idealistically, almost as if they were classical sculpture. Brush wrote, "There are more superb and symmetrical men among [Native Americans] than I have ever seen elsewhere, their beardless faces reminding me always of the antique. . . . Their constant light exercise, frequent steam-baths, and freedom from overwork develop the body in a manner only equaled, I must believe, by the Greek."[3] In addition, Brush held Michelangelo in great regard; *In the Dark Forest*'s athletic figure resembles the *ignudi,* or restless nudes, on the Sistine Chapel ceiling. Also reminiscent of Michelangelo is Brush's use of drapery, especially the magenta fabric on which the brave sits. Although purporting to be authentic, the painting, with its dark, ambiguous setting, is a romantic statement about a vanishing way of life. The painter Elliott Daingerfield echoed this sentiment when he described a similar Brush painting as "a poem of American life that is epic in its grandeur."[4]

1. See Richard Guy Wilson et al., *The American Renaissance, 1876–1917* (Brooklyn: The Brooklyn Museum, 1979), and H. Barbara Weinberg, *The Lure of Paris: Nineteenth-Century American Painters and Their French Teachers* (New York: Abbeville Press, 1991).

2. Brush to Mr. Knoedler, Knoedler & Co., 10 February 1907. Archives, M. Knoedler, New York.

3. George de Forest Brush, "An Artist among the Indians," *Century* 30 (May 1885): 55, as quoted in Alex Nemerov, "Doing the 'Old America,'" in William H. Truettner, ed., *The West as America: Reinterpreting Images of the Frontier, 1876–1917* (Washington, D.C.: Smithsonian Institution Press, 1991), 323.

4. Elliott Daingerfield, "George de Forest Brush," *Art in America,* June 1930, 217.

Born, Shelbyville, Tennessee, 1855; attended National Academy of Design, New York, 1870–1873; studied in Paris under Jean-Léon Gérôme, 1873, and at the Ecole des Beaux-Arts, 1874–1876, and again with Gérôme, 1876–1878; remained in Paris until return to the United States, 1880; to the West, 1881; taught in New York, 1882–1886; to Canada, 1886–1887; studio in New York with summers in Cornish, New Hampshire, 1888–1890 and 1892–1898; to Paris, 1890–1892; in Florence, 1903–1905, 1907–1909, and 1913–1914; resided in New York and Dublin, New Hampshire, 1914–1941; died, Dublin, 1941.

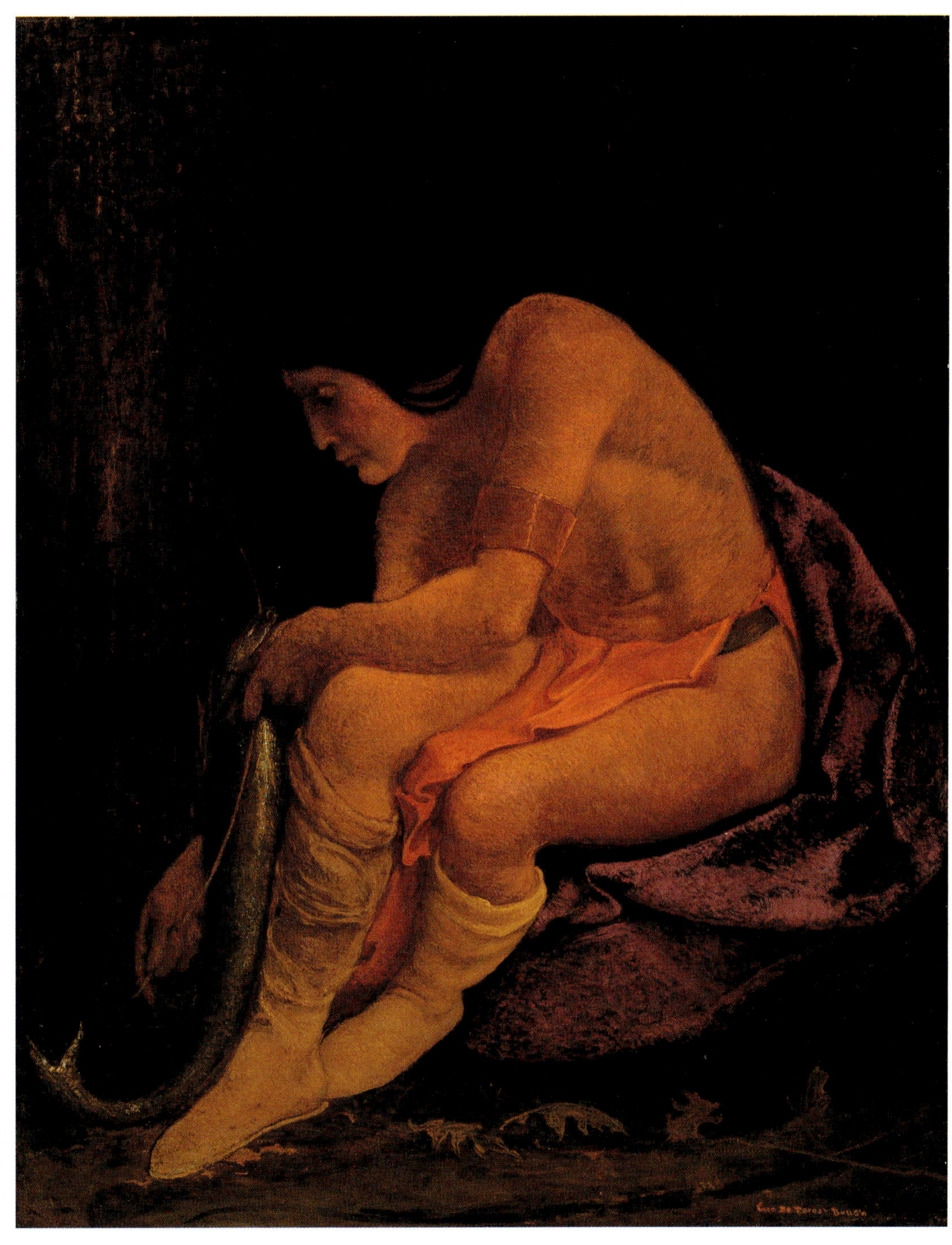

Elliott Daingerfield

1859–1932

Carolina Twilight, 1889

oil on canvas, 27 × 22⅛ inches
signed, lower right: *Elliott Daingerfield 1889*
Museum purchase with funds from the 1986 Museum Antiques Show and donated by The Museum Association, Inc.

Toward the end of the nineteenth century, when naturalistic, academic art was popular, painting with spiritual overtones found a limited audience. In these works, which focused on an internal and symbolic world, introspection replaced observation and study; factual reality gave way to imagination. A related movement, Symbolism, thrived in France in the work of Gustave Moreau and Odilon Redon. In America, which prized materialism and naturalism, few artists embraced Symbolism fully, although many incorporated the movement's emotive qualities in their paintings.[1]

In both his paintings and his writings Elliott Daingerfield was attracted to the spiritual, even promoting the religious mission of the artist. He defined art as "a principle flowing out of God through certain men and women by which they perceive and understand the beautiful. The office of the artist is to express the beautiful."[2] In their evocative and atmospheric qualities Daingerfield's paintings reflect his fondness for the ethereal; he often wrote poems to accompany his paintings, further enhancing their Symbolist quality.

As a youth in Fayetteville, North Carolina, Daingerfield served as an assistant to a photographer and learned to tint images. In 1880 he went to New York to pursue his training at the Art Students League, but he returned to North Carolina regularly, especially to the western mountains near Blowing Rock. The most crucial influence on his art was his friendship with the landscape painter George Inness. The two artists had adjoining studios in New York, and it was there that Daingerfield learned firsthand Inness's remarkable glazing technique, which was ultimately derived from such old masters as Titian. Inness, as well as Daingerfield, alternated layers of pigment and varnish, creating a surface that was simultaneously rich and deep. Two other artists who employed this elaborate glazing technique, Albert Pinkham Ryder and Albert Blakelock, also shared Daingerfield's spiritual interests.

The other great influence on Daingerfield was the work of the Barbizon painters. Although he did not go to Europe until midcareer, he earned the sobriquet "the American Millet." Daingerfield shared the Barbizon painters' fascination with peasants and pastoral scenery, but instead of the Forest of Fontainebleau he depicted the hardwoods of North Carolina.

Carolina Twilight illustrates his indebtedness to both Inness and the French painters. It is a moody evocation in which a shadowy figure moves forward under the weight of her bundle at the end of a long day of labor; the moon is on the rise. The painting is infused with the tonal softness of twilight. In a letter written about one of Inness's paintings, Daingerfield offered a description that could easily apply to the Museum's painting: "There are times when one is permitted to see in nature supremely beautiful moments; when the assembling of time, color, light and atmosphere produces a harmony that appeals to our deepest emotion. If the mystery of effect such as the rising of the moon, is added, how perfect the emotion and how intense the reverence in even the most sordid of us."[3]

---

1. See Charles C. Eldredge, *American Imagination and Symbolist Painting* (New York: Grey Art Gallery, New York University, 1979).

2. Daingerfield, "Sketch of His Life—Written by Elliott Daingerfield—in Response to a Request." Undated manuscript, Elliott Daingerfield Papers. Center for the Study of Southern Painting, Morris Museum of Art, Augusta, Georgia.

3. Daingerfield to William O'Brien, 6 May 1917. Daingerfield Papers, Archives of American Art, roll 89.

Born, Harper's Ferry, Virginia (now West Virginia), 1859; studied briefly in New York with Walter Satterlee and at the Art Students League; studio in New York next to George Inness, 1884–1894; frequent stays in North Carolina; toured Europe, 1897 and 1924; died, New York, 1932.

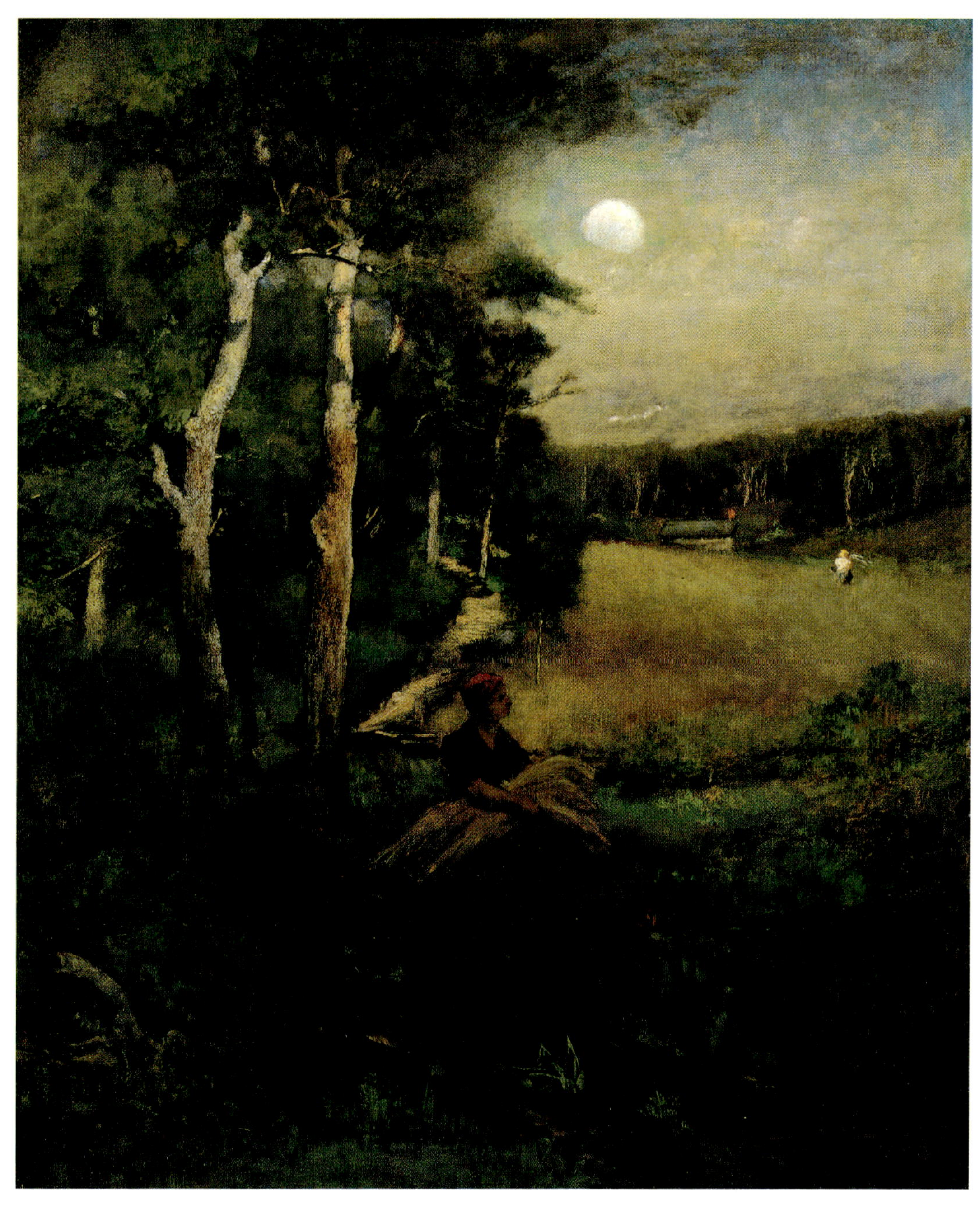

Robert Loftin Newman

1827–1912

Red Riding Hood, circa 1890

oil on canvas, 16¼ × 13¾ inches
signed, lower right: *R. L. Newman*
Museum purchase with funds donated by Mrs. E. A. Ramsaur and The Museum Association, Inc.

With the advent of industrialization and the expansion of cities, a back-to-nature movement celebrating landscape and rural life arose in the United States and Europe. In France, the small village of Barbizon became the artistic center for this return to simplicity. As early as the 1830s, Camille Corot and Théodore Rousseau frequented Barbizon, and in 1849 Jean-François Millet settled there permanently. By the next decade the town had become an art colony attractive not only to European painters but also to American artists. Equipped with cozy inns, an abundance of woodlands and small farms, and peasants willing to serve as models, Barbizon was an attractive alternative to Paris and Rome, which were constricted by lofty traditions and academic principles.

The Boston painter William Morris Hunt was responsible for establishing Millet's reputation in the United States. Hunt owned an early version of Millet's *Sower,* which, through countless reproductions, has become the international icon of peasant life.[1] Hunt also was pivotal in persuading Robert Loftin Newman to study in Paris rather than at the Düsseldorf Academy, where tightly controlled, brightly colored, and detailed canvases, similar to John Beaufain Irving's *Feeding Goldfish* were the norm. Instead, Newman took instruction in Thomas Couture's atelier, where he emulated the expressive brushwork of his teacher. In addition to learning from Couture, Newman profited from studying at the Louvre, where he admired the religious subject matter, glowing colors, and textural canvases of Titian and Eugène Delacroix. On a second trip to Paris in 1854 Newman spent time in Barbizon, where he was introduced to Millet.

A native Virginian, Newman served as an artillery lieutenant in the Confederate Army. During the 1870s he worked in New York as a designer of stained glass, which may have contributed to the rich colors and subtle radiance of his paintings. Never able to earn a living from painting, he was sustained by a small group of friends, including the artists Daniel Chester French and William Merritt Chase and the collector Thomas B. Clarke.

Newman's paintings typically are dark and small; both qualities enhance the intimacy and mystery of his work. Preferring religious and literary themes, Newman painted a number of subjects repeatedly, including the fairy tale "Little Red Riding Hood." His paintings usually portray one or two people in an outdoor setting in which the background is secondary to the figures. Nature, however, plays an important role in creating the mood of Newman's paintings. In the Museum's *Red Riding Hood* a faceless figure emerges from a shadowy netherworld. Seated at the center of the composition, she is motionless, weighed down by the heavy cloak and drapery that envelop her; a sense of foreboding permeates the scene.

Newman's work is stylistically similar to that of Albert Pinkham Ryder, a younger painter known for his mystical visions. Newman and Ryder knew each other; they lived in the same building in New York, were both influenced by Couture, and had several patrons in common. Both existed outside the conventional art world, painting esoteric themes for which there was little demand.[2]

In 1894 Newman's friends and supporters organized an exhibition of more than one hundred of his works, the only event of its kind during his lifetime. After writing about the analogy of Newman's work to that of Delacroix, Millet, John LaFarge, and George Inness, the reviewer for *The Critic* continued: "Mr. Newman's individuality is not eclipsed by his affiliations. . . . What one feels first is the sincerity and brilliance of his color on a poetic background of mysterious tones. He handles color not timidly, but with an almost spiritual perception of its pervasiveness in nature. He has nothing of the exactness of the topographical school that can map the very mist; but he adds to nature the subtle indefinable but indispensable ideality that makes it art."[3]

---

1. Michael Jacobs, *The Good and Simple Life: Artist Colonies in Europe and America* (Oxford: Phaidon, 1985), 21.

2. See Michael E. Landgren, *Robert Loftin Newman, 1827–1912* (Washington, D.C.: Smithsonian Institution Press, 1974).

3. "The Newman Exhibition at Knoedler's," *The Critic,* no. 629 (10 March 1894), as quoted in Landgren, *Newman,* 53.

Born, Richmond, Virginia, 1827; studied in Paris with Thomas Couture, 1850; to Clarksville, Tennessee; to France, 1854; Confederate Army, 1861–1864; probably in New York, 1865–1871; in Nashville, 1872–1873, before settling in New York permanently; trips to France, 1882, 1908, and 1909; died, New York, 1912.

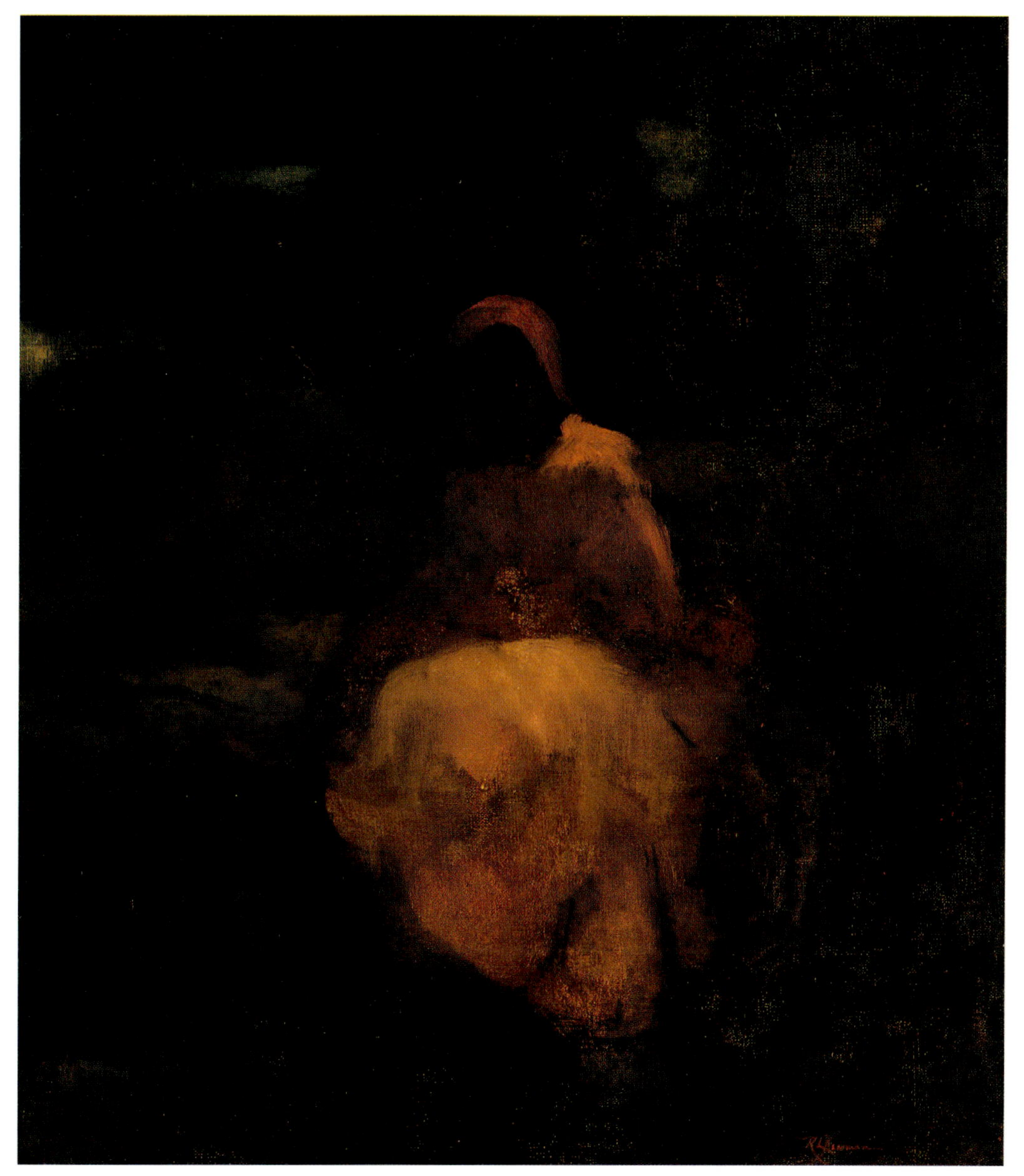

Thomas Satterwhite Noble

1835–1907

The Sibyl, 1896

oil on canvas, 50 × 41 inches
Museum purchase with funds donated by Mr. and Mrs. C. Guy Gunter

Of all of the mid-nineteenth-century Parisian painter-teachers, Thomas Couture was one of the most influential, counting among his students Edouard Manet as well as the Southerners Robert Loftin Newman and Thomas Noble. At age thirty-two Couture achieved fame with his entry in the Paris Salon, and that same year, 1847, he began his teaching career. At his peak he taught sixty students in two shifts a day.[1]

Noble's career mirrored that of his teacher. Like Couture, he attained early and quick success during the late 1860s with a series of narrative paintings about slavery. Shortly thereafter he became the head of Cincinnati's McMicken School of Art, a significant force in American art education. From Couture he learned the importance both of drawing, after casts and live models, and of the study of old-master paintings in the Louvre. Couture's emphasis was less on the crisp outline of the figures and more on the painted sketch and on chiaroscuro, the use of lights and darks, to create the illusion of volume. Couture was also interested in the technical aspects of painting, emphasizing pure colors and visible brushwork in his teaching, thus laying a foundation for the later Impressionists.[2] Noble implemented many of Couture's methods at the McMicken School.

Noble's career shifted dramatically in 1869. Recruited to become the first principal of the McMicken School, Noble moved to Cincinnati, where he administered the school and taught for the next thirty-five years. Cincinnati was a cosmopolitan economic center that was eager to support culture; the McMicken School spurred the founding of the University of Cincinnati and the formation of the Cincinnati Art Museum. Nevertheless, Noble's position in the community was often tenuous; viewed as an outsider, he was regularly subjected to the jealousy of local artists.

With its exotic decor and emphasis on colorful tapestries, *The Sibyl* reflects the influences of Orientalism, a style initially popularized in France by Eugène Delacroix. During the 1890s American artists like Edwin Lord Weeks and Frederic Arthur Bridgman exploited the taste for Orientalism, traveling and painting extensively throughout North Africa and the Middle East. Continuing to follow the advice of Couture, Noble painted the Museum's canvas freely, so that areas of impasto, or heavy paint, are visible, creating a lively, textured surface quality that contrasts with the mystical subject and dark tonalities.

The Sibyl displays Noble's continuing interest in African-American subjects, although it avoids the sensationalism of his earlier works. Instead, it is a haunting image of a provocative figure. In ancient times sibyls, priestesses with powers of prophesy, were regarded cautiously. In the Middle Ages and the Renaissance, sibyls were considered to be the female counterparts of the prophets who foretold the coming of Christ. The most famous representation of the sibyls can be found on Michelangelo's Sistine Chapel ceiling. The sculptor William Wetmore Story was one of the few other nineteenth-century American artists to undertake the subject. Recognizing the prophetic powers of his *Libyan Sibyl,* he described it in words that could apply to Noble's interpretation as well: "It is a very massive figure, big-shouldered, large bosomed, with nothing of the Venus in it, but, as far as I could make it, luxuriant and heroic. She is looking out of her black eyes into futurity and sees the terrible fate of her race. This is the theme of the figure—Slavery on the horizon, . . . it is thoroughly African."[3]

---

1. See Albert Boime, *Thomas Couture and the Eclectic Vision* (New Haven: Yale University Press, 1980).
2. Boime, *Couture,* 441–456.
3. William Wetmore Story to Charles Eliot Norton, August 1861, as quoted in Wayne Craven, *Sculpture in America* (Newark: University of Delaware Press, 1968), 279.

Born, Lexington, Kentucky, 1835; studied in Paris with Thomas Couture, 1856–1859; returned to Louisville, served in the Confederate Army, 1861–1865; lived in New York, 1866–1869; appointed head of the McMicken School of Art, Cincinnati, 1869, until his retirement in 1904; died, New York, 1907.

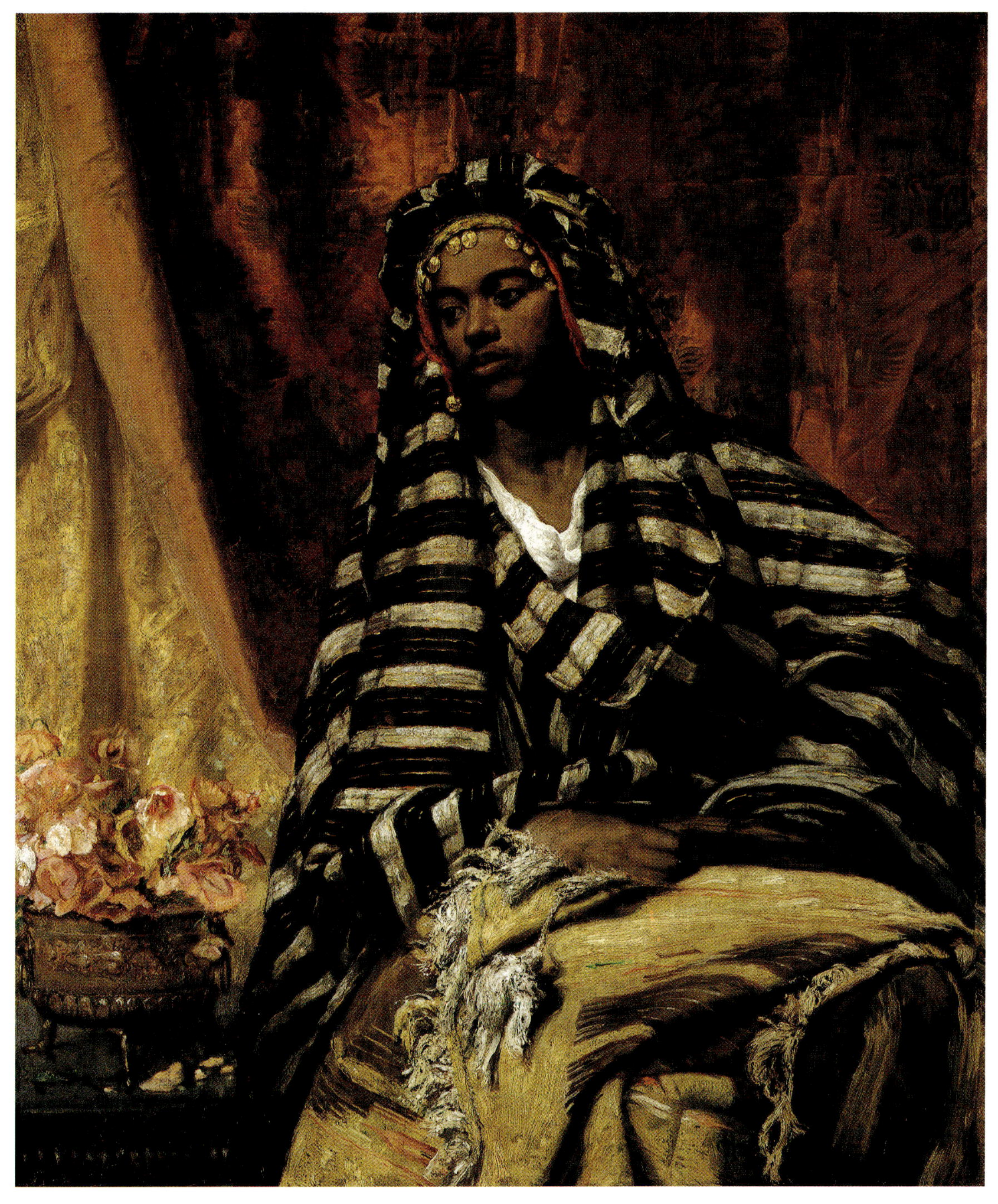

Frank Duveneck

1848–1919

Portrait of Miss Westlake, circa 1889

oil on panel, 22 × 15¾ inches
signed, center right: *FD*
Museum purchase with funds donated by the Arthur and Holly Magill Foundation

During the last three decades of the nineteenth century, figure painting gained popularity, especially among artists identified with Realism and Impressionism. A figure painting is neither a portrait nor the portrayal of a character in a narrative, but rather the representation of a type. The depiction of a single figure was not novel; it was popularized by the Dutch masters Frans Hals and Rembrandt van Rijn, whose influences were perpetuated in the figurative painting tradition of the Munich School. During the 1870s Munich, a thriving center of culture that attracted many American students, rivaled both the classical orientation of the Paris academies and the anecdotal emphasis of the Düsseldorf school.

Of the American artists affiliated with Munich, Frank Duveneck and William Merritt Chase did the most to promulgate the Munich figurative style through both their own work and that of their students. Profiting from instruction that emphasized the study of old masters and encouraged direct painting, Duveneck and Chase shared an interest in realism and in spontaneous brushwork.

For Duveneck, the selection of Munich was logical: his ancestors were from Germany; he was fluent in the language; and he had apprenticed with Munich-trained artists in his native Covington, Kentucky. In early 1870 he enrolled at the Bavarian Royal Academy, where his instructors included Wilhelm von Diez and Wilhelm Leibl. Duveneck's talents were soon recognized, and he was quickly promoted. His loosely painted figure studies rendered in bold contrasts of darks and lights parallel the early work of the French realist Edouard Manet.

Duveneck opened his own school in 1878 for English-speaking students and, after one year in Munich, moved the program to Italy. From this endeavor grew the "Duveneck Boys," a supportive group of fellow painters and students that included Chase, Joseph DeCamp, and John Twachtman. In Venice Duveneck encountered two expatriates, John Singer Sargent and James McNeill Whistler, and in 1880 he began to produce etchings akin to Whistler's. Returning to the United States in 1888, Duveneck supported himself with occasional portrait commissions and teaching jobs in Cincinnati, where he often conflicted with Thomas Noble, head of the McMicken School.

In its directness, the Museum's painting, *Portrait of Miss Westlake,* exemplifies the realist figurative style of the Munich School. Both the frontal pose and the neutral background make the figure foremost. The chiaroscuro, the strong juxtaposition of light areas with dark ones, as well as the placement of the figure close to the viewer intensify the immediacy of the painting. The theatrical lighting from the upper left casts shadows along the left side of the face, creating the illusion of three dimensionality. Although the name of the sitter is partially known, the painting is not a true portrait; Miss Westlake was probably an artist's model, or possibly one of Duveneck's students.

In the development of American art Duveneck served as an important conduit of European Realism. Robert Henri, a pivotal realist painter of the next generation, evaluated Duveneck in the following terms: "He is an extremely sensitive painter, a great draughtsman and every stroke of his brush manifests a consciousness of life, an intense conception of nature. His pictures are replete with life; no drawing of dead matter but rather a great refinement is evinced."[1]

---

1. Robert Henri, interview with Mary L. Alexander, *Cincinnati Enquirer,* 31 May 1936, as quoted in Robert Neuhaus, *Unsuspected Genius: The Art and Life of Frank Duveneck* (San Francisco: Bedford Press, 1987), 133.

Born, Covington, Kentucky, 1848; apprenticeship to church painters, 1866–1869; studied in Munich, 1870–1873; in Cincinnati, 1874–1875; returned to Munich, 1876–1879; trip to Venice, 1878, and resided there and Florence, 1880–1886; to Paris, 1887–1888; to Boston, 1888, then moved to Covington and Cincinnati, 1890–1919, with occasional trips to Italy; died, Cincinnati, 1919.

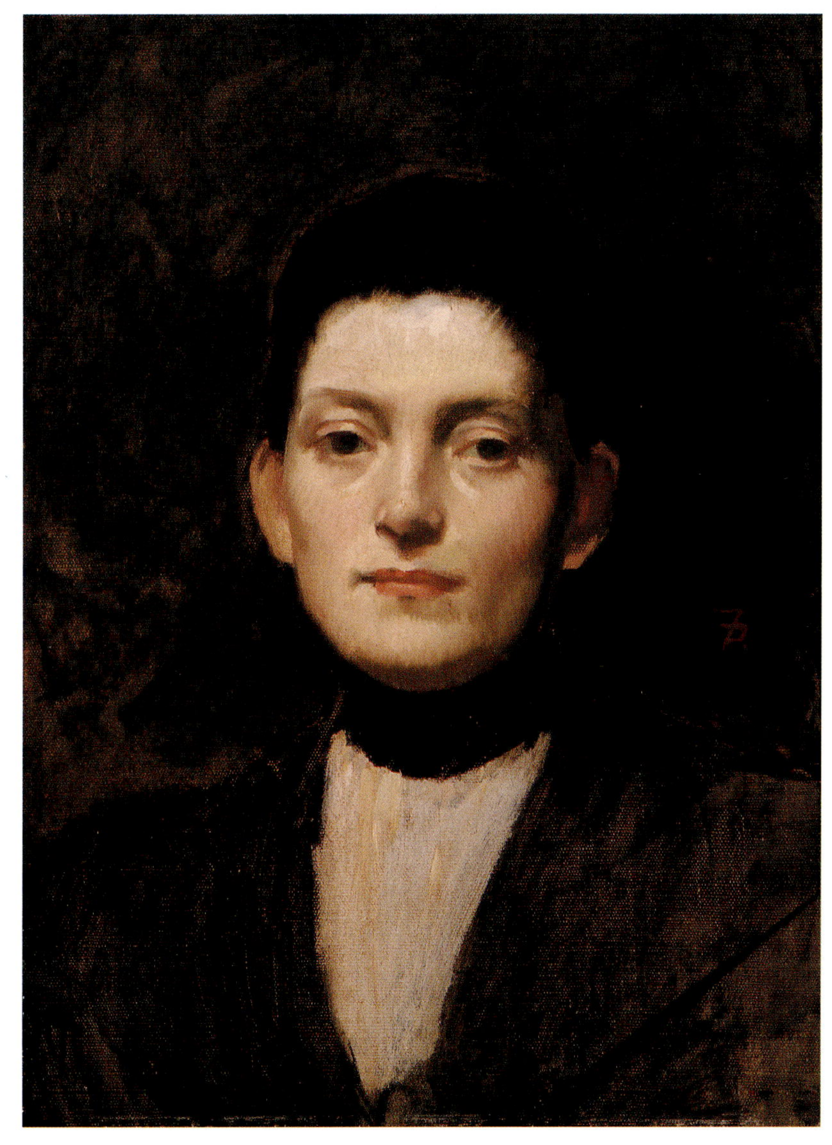

Thomas Pollock Anshutz

1851–1912

Mother and Child (Mrs. Anshutz and Her Son Edward), circa 1895

oil on canvas, 42¼ × 30⅛ inches
signed, upper right: *Thos. Anshutz*
Museum purchase with funds donated by the Arthur and Holly Magill Foundation

Toward the end of the nineteenth century the undisputed authority of the academic tradition began to be challenged. Inherently conservative, the academies were convinced that art could be taught through a strict regimen that emphasized life drawing and the study of casts of ancient sculpture. In France the annual exhibitions of the Salons reaffirmed this philosophy, and acceptance into the highly competitive Salon exhibitions validated the talents of thousands of aspiring artists. But by 1863 the power of the Salon began to erode, when a breakaway group of "refused" artists, led by Edouard Manet, mounted its own exhibition, the Salon des Refusés. In this country, the National Academy of Design was challenged in 1875 by the Art Students League, which was founded by and for artists who proposed to control the curriculum.

At the Pennsylvania Academy of the Fine Arts, Thomas Eakins revolutionized the study of anatomy by introducing actual dissection to his art classes. Eakins's sober realism was further enhanced by the use of photography; he assisted the noted photographer Eadweard Muybridge in pivotal studies of sequential movement. Eakins's scientific approach, which neglected landscape and the decorative arts, did not win him unqualified support. In 1886 he was forced to resign, making way for Thomas Anshutz, a former protégé who helped instigate Eakins's departure.[1]

A native of Kentucky, Anshutz had studied at the National Academy of Design but was attracted to the Pennsylvania Academy because of the prominence given life study. He became an assistant to Eakins, both in the anatomy laboratory and in the photographic experiments with Muybridge. Anshutz's style, especially in portraits, demonstrates his indebtedness to his master; like Eakins, he preferred earth tones, placed his sitters against a somber background, and was concerned with the anatomical correctness of his figures.

Anshutz's affiliation with the Pennsylvania Academy spanned thirty years. As a teacher he was exceptionally influential, serving as a mediator between the late-nineteenth-century scientific realism of Eakins and the urban realism of the next generation. Among his many students Anshutz counted such key proponents of the so-called Ash Can School as John Sloan, Robert Henri, Everett Shinn, and William Glackens. The Ash Can painters shared a revolutionary philosophy that espoused direct sketchlike depictions, often featuring the characters and activities of the urban scene.

A turning point for Anshutz came in 1892 when he married and traveled to Paris to study at the Académie Julian. His palette lightened and he turned to watercolor and pastel, possibly in response to the Impressionists. William Merritt Chase, who exhibited regularly and later taught at the Pennsylvania Academy, may also have been instrumental in effecting these new interests.[2] Despite its date in the mid-1890s, the Museum's painting demonstrates the somber color range associated with Eakins, as well as a painterly, or roughly brushed, application of paint. Radiating an intimacy and gentleness rarely found in Anshutz's work, his portrayal of his wife and young son partakes in the long tradition of the Madonna and Child theme that enjoyed a revival at the end of the century. Like other artists, Anshutz may have been reacting to patrons' interest in familiar Renaissance imagery, and he also may have been influenced by the artist most associated with the mother-and-child subject, Mary Cassatt, a Pennsylvanian and student at the Pennsylvania Academy in the 1860s.

---

1. William Innes Homer, *Thomas Eakins: His Life and Art* (New York: Abbeville Press, 1992), 155–182.

2. Sally Webster, "Thomas Anshutz: The Philadelphia Connection," *Arts Magazine,* November 1979, 139.

Born, Newport, Kentucky, 1851; studied in New York at the National Academy of Design, 1872–1875, and in Philadelphia with Thomas Eakins, 1875–1882; affiliated with the Pennsylvania Academy of the Fine Arts, 1880–1911; studied in Paris at the Académie Julian with Lucien Doucet and Adolphe-William Bouguereau, 1892–1893; died, Fort Washington, Pennsylvania, 1912.

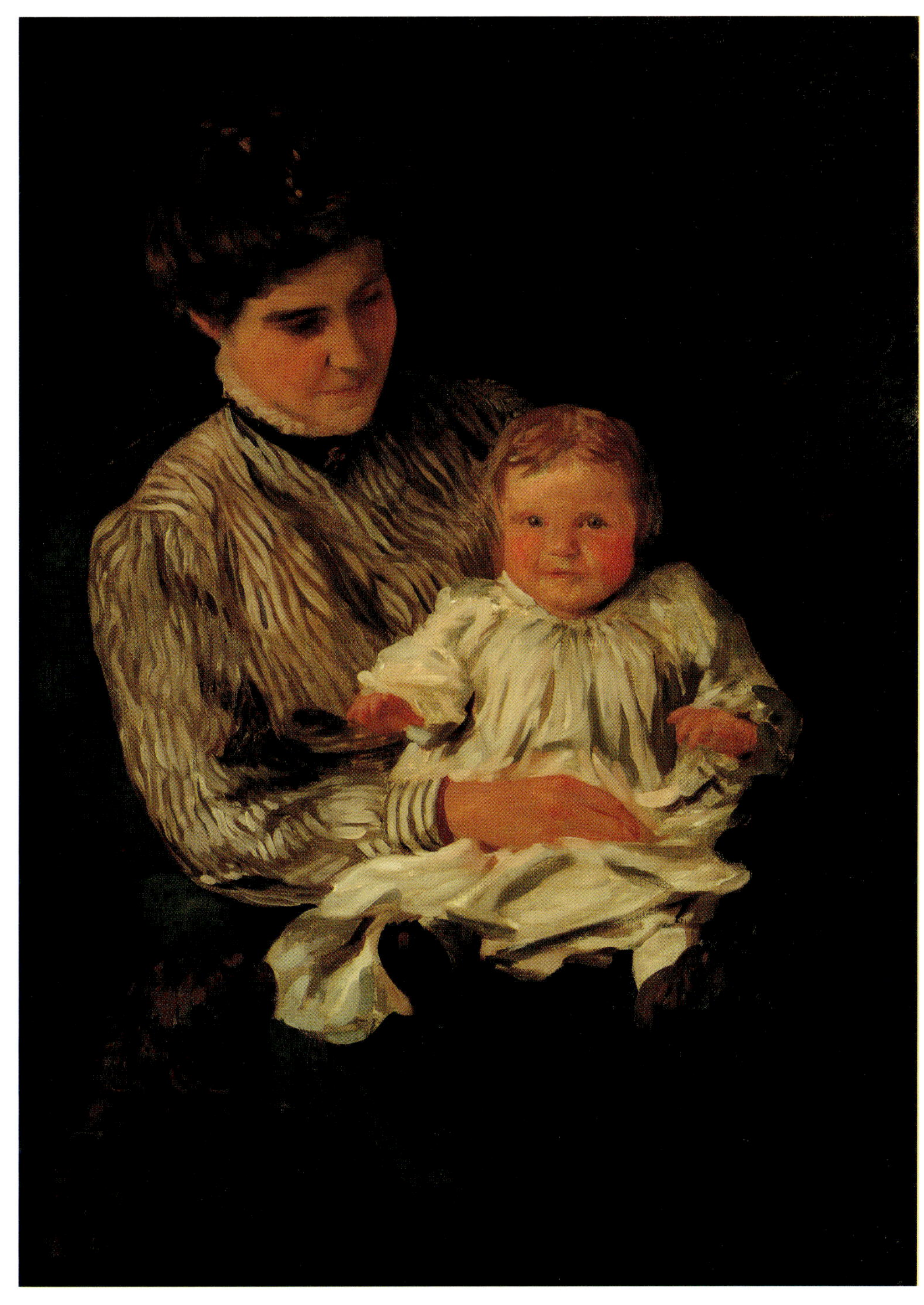

Gaines Ruger Donoho

1858–1916

Sheep, Late Afternoon, 1891

oil on canvas, 24 × 44 inches
signed, lower left: *Ruger Donoho / 1891*
Museum purchase with funds donated by Mr. and Mrs. Christie C. Prevost
(illustrated on page 19)

Storm over Loing Valley, 1902

oil on canvas, 45 × 67½ inches
signed, lower right: *G. Ruger Donoho / 1902*
Museum purchase with the assistance of (by exchange): Mr. and Mrs. Mason Alexander, in memory of Mr. Alexander's uncle, Mr. William H. Gardner; Mrs. William O. (Carolyn C.) Ballentine; Mr. and Mrs. Bernard Bertland; Burr Galleries; Mr. Thomas K. Connor; A. L. DePersio; Hugo Dreyfuss; Ferdinand Roten Galleries; Albert Fried, Jr.; John F. Hard; Mrs. J. M. Holmes; Dr. Melvin S. Horowitz; Mr. and Mrs. Arthur F. Magill; J. F. McCrindle; Leo McDonald; Dr. C. P. Meek; Kenneth D. Moskowitz; Mr. and Mrs. John L. Petty, Jr.; Richard B. Sarver; Michael Todd

Offering artists a respite from the rigors and drudgery of city life, the summer art colony had its beginnings in France in the mid-nineteenth century. Barbizon, forty miles from Paris, was the locale favored by painters; there they began to take their canvases *en plein air,* or out-of-doors, to capture the colors of nature and the quality of light. These ventures away from the studio were made possible by the invention in 1841 of the metal paint tube, which permitted artists to carry their materials more easily. Summer art colonies also prospered in this country, where American Barbizons flourished in unspoiled areas not too far from cities. Among the most vital communities were the ones at Old Lyme, Connecticut, and East Hampton, New York. The latter, located on the eastern end of Long Island, was discovered earlier and remained active longer than Old Lyme.[1] East Hampton provided numerous picturesque opportunities: windmills, colonial houses, even cows grazing on the town green. Near the ocean, saltwater bays and sand dunes heightened artists' perceptions of color and light.

The pastoral charms and creative stimulation that emanate from most art colonies were critical to the development of Ruger Donoho, who spent time at Barbizon and Grez-sur-Loing in France as well as at East Hampton. A native of Mississippi, Donoho was taken to Washington, D.C., as a child following his father's death during the Civil War. Interested in landscapes, he studied for a short while with Jervis McEntee, a follower of the Hudson River School. Donoho became a student at the newly formed Art Students League in 1878, the same year William Merritt Chase began there as an instructor of drawing and painting. Donoho's New York training was short; the following year he went to Paris, enrolling at the Académie Julian, where Childe Hassam also was studying. Like other art students in France in the 1880s Donoho escaped to the pastoral calm of the country during the summer months.

Although many of his counterparts preferred to depict peasants in their rustic environment, Donoho usually chose pure landscape, albeit cultivated. In *Sheep, Late Afternoon,* a diagonal lane cuts across the composition; a flock of sheep are dispersed throughout a shaded foreground of brush and trees. A few of the sheep, particularly the one to the far right, appear startled, as if responding to an intruder. The Museum's painting could very well be the canvas exhibited by Donoho at the World's Columbian Exposition of 1893 entitled *The Explorers.* It was described at the time: "A bit of thin woods is shown with the big leaves in a brown carpet among gray rocks and a pasture in the background. Sheep have strayed from the pasture to explore the piece of timber where one stunted and queerly branching tree forms a picturesque center for the rest of the bare woodland."[2] The painterly, or thickly brushed, texture of the surface, the uncomplicated composition, and the earthy coloration highlighted with the brilliant blue sky relate this painting to Donoho's plein air experiences at Barbizon.

Donoho's interest in light at different times of day and climatic effects are reflected in the two paintings owned by the Museum. *Sheep, Late Afternoon,* painted in 1891, is contemporary with Claude Monet's studies of grainstacks and Rouen Cathedral, both of which examine changing light. *Storm over Loing Valley* is a more ambitious and dramatic work, perhaps reflecting Donoho's desire to maintain a presence at the Paris Salon. The diminutive shepherd at the lower edge of the painting provides a narrative element and may have religious significance. The ominous and tumultuous sky overwhelms the man and his flock, calling to mind the Twenty-third Psalm: "The Lord is my shepherd. . . . Yea, though I walk through the valley of the shadow of death, I will fear no evil."

In 1891 Donoho moved to East Hampton, separating himself from New York, where he had achieved a modicum of success at various exhibitions. With the exception of an extended visit to France, he remained on Long Island, where he benefited from the support of fellow artists, the rustic setting, and the experience of painting his own garden *en plein air.* In response to painting flowers and the outdoors, Donoho's palette lightened.

Hassam, who was introduced to East Hampton by his former classmate, wrote in the catalogue of Donoho's memorial exhibition: "An artist is a person who pursues his calling in quiet and solitude and is only known by his own kind. Ruger Donoho had a great deal of this kind of recognition, and if he did not have as much of the world's recognition as many others, or as much as he deserved, all is well."[3]

---

1. See William H. Gerdts, "East Hampton, Old Lyme and the Art Colony Movement," in William H. Gerdts, Jeffrey W. Andersen, and Helen A. Harrison, *En Plein Air: The Art Colonies at East Hampton and Old Lyme, 1880–1930* (East Hampton, N. Y.: Guild Hall; Old Lyme, Conn.: Lyme Historical Society, 1989).

2. "Monthly Record of American Art," *Magazine of Art* (December 1891–November 1892): xxvi, as quoted in Carolyn Kinder Carr, *Revisiting the White City: American Art at the 1893 World's Fair* (Washington, D.C.: Smithsonian Institution Press, 1993), 236.

3. Childe Hassam, *Memorial Exhibition: Paintings by the Late Ruger Donoho* (New York: Macbeth Gallery, 1916), foreword.

Born, Church Hill, Mississippi, 1858; as a child lived in Washington, D.C.; studied in New York at the Art Students League, 1878; in Paris, studied at the Académie Julian, painted there and in Barbizon, 1879–1887; returned to New York, 1887–1891; moved to East Hampton, New York, 1891; in Europe, 1901–1902; died, New York, 1916.

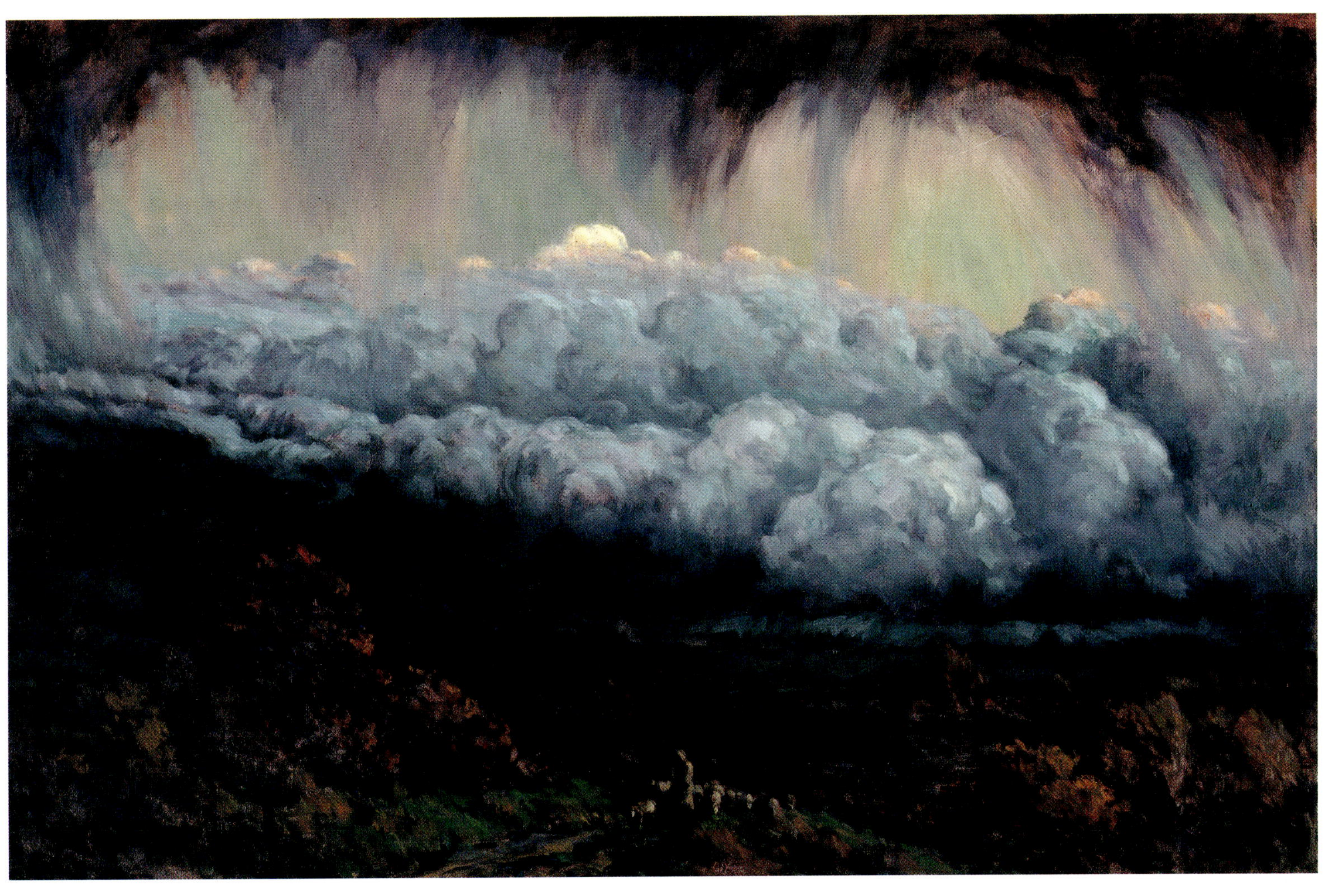

Mattie Dubé

born 1861–death date unknown

Pumpkins and Onions, 1891

oil on canvas, 34¼ × 45¼ inches
signed, lower left: *[ ]ttie Dubé / [ ]ris 91*
Gift of Mr. and Mrs. James M. Shoemaker, Jr.

Although American male artists were readily accepted at the academies of Europe, their female counterparts were not extended the same welcome. Women were not admitted to the Ecole des Beaux-Arts in Paris, a government-supported, tuition-free institution that was open to men of any nationality. In response to this prohibition, the privately funded Académie Julian began in 1873 to admit women. In addition to paying higher fees, the women were taught apart from the men. In this country, women were permitted to take classes at the Pennsylvania Academy of the Fine Arts, but they were segregated when drawing nude models. These and other restraints tended to restrict the ambitions and the accomplishments of women artists. Often women tended to paint on a smaller scale in watercolor and pastel, preferring simple still lifes and modest portraits. The visibility of women artists was also overshadowed by their relationships to men; they often married their instructors or fellow students, thus forfeiting their individual identities.

Among the many American women artists who studied at the Académie Julian were Cecilia Beaux, Elizabeth Jane Gardner, both of whom pursued figurative paintings, and Mattie Dubé, who specialized in still lifes. Their primary teachers in the standard academic curriculum were Tony Robert-Fleury and Adolphe-William Bouguereau. Both gained the admiration of their students, as evidenced in one woman's recollection: "Tony Robert-Fleury is the favourite master, extremely courteous and good natured: he seldom, if ever, utters a harsh criticism. . . . Bouguereau admires in others the very opposite qualities which distinguish his own work. '*Faire large et simple*' is his advice, and anything like imitation of his own style finds but little sympathy from him."[1]

Both the place and date of Dubé's birth, Florence, Alabama, 1861, are documented, but her maiden name and her date of death have yet to be discovered. Her parents, who were identified as English in an entry on Dubé in a Paris Salon catalogue, may have been connected with the cotton industry in Alabama. Dubé's husband, Louis-Théodore Dubé, was an artist in Montreal, and the couple may have met there or in Paris, where both were students. Dubé was more successful than her husband at the Paris Salon; she exhibited eight paintings between 1890 and 1898. None is recorded for Louis-Théodore Dubé.[2]

The Museum's painting gained Dubé recognition at the 1891 Salon, where the work was exhibited as *Nature Morte.* Two years later at the World's Columbian Exposition in Chicago, it was displayed as *Pumpkins and Onions.* Although subtle, this title change reflected one of the key agendas of the 1893 fair: after years of allegiance to French painting, the time had come to celebrate American art.

Pumpkins and Onions is an imposing composition, in part because of its large size but also because of the variety of bold forms and the range of surfaces and textures skillfully rendered. Dubé employed familiar conventions in the placement of the tabletop, the hanging fish, and the knife projecting over the table's edge. Stylistically, the painting, with its earthy colors, orderly composition, and choice of humble objects, resembles the work of the eighteenth-century French master Jean-Baptiste Chardin. The combination of pumpkin, onion, and fish, however, is unusual and creates a piquant medley. The painting's realism as well as its pungency were noted by one reviewer: "It is a picture you cannot look upon without crying—not because it is tragic, but because you seem to smell the onions, so natural are they."[3]

Throughout the nineteenth century, still-life painting was not well regarded. Nevertheless, a few artists like Dubé, William M. Harnett, and William Merritt Chase persisted in elevating ordinary household objects as worthy subjects. Ironically, the next generation of artists adopted still life as primary subject matter. Pablo Picasso, Georges Braque, and Juan Gris performed their Cubist experiments with bowls of fruit, guitars, and newspapers, and their American counterparts similarly found still-life compositions useful as frameworks for formal experimentation.

---

1. Marie Adelaide Belloc, "Lady Artists in Paris," *Murray's Magazine* (September 1890): 375–376, as quoted in H. Barbara Weinberg, *The Lure of Paris: Nineteenth-Century American Artists and Their French Teachers* (New York: Abbeville Press, 1991), 223.

2. For Louis-Théodore Dubé see David Karel, *Dictionnaire des artistes de langue française en Amérique du Nord* (Sainte-Foy, Québec, 1992), 249–250. For Dubé's Salon records see Lois Marie Fink, *American Art at the Nineteenth-Century Salons* (Washington, D.C.: Smithsonian Institution Press, 1990), 339.

3. Unnamed French critic quoted by the *Witness* (Montreal), 29 September 1899.

Born, Florence, Alabama, 1861; studied at the Académie Julian, Paris, with Tony Robert-Fleury and Adolphe-William Bouguereau; resided in Paris until 1919; date and place of death unknown.

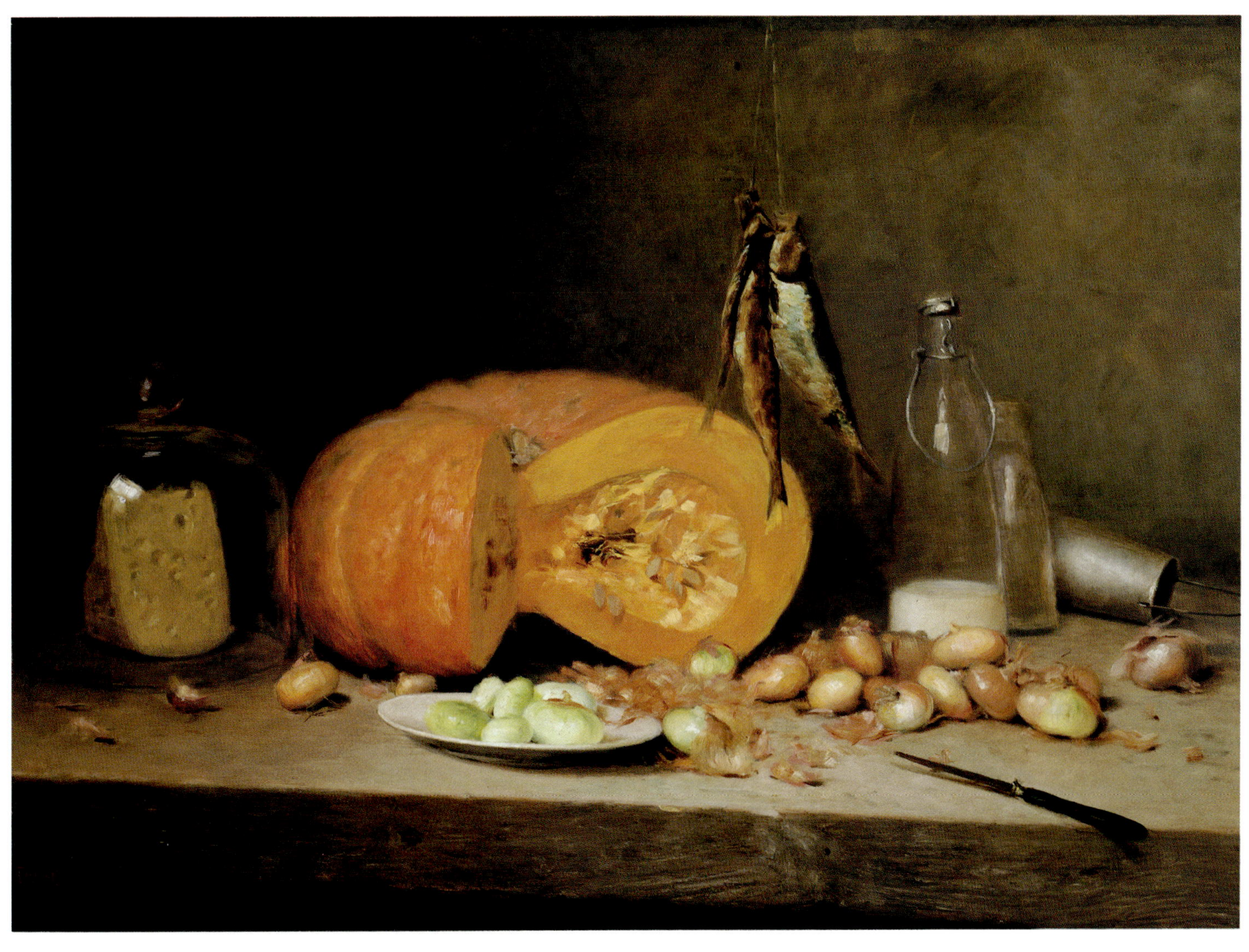

Maria Howard Weeden

1847–1905

Uncle Champ, circa 1895

watercolor on paper, 16⅛ × 13½ inches
signed, lower left: *Howard Weeden*
Museum purchase

Portrait of a Woman, circa 1895

watercolor on paper, 16¾ × 13½ inches
signed, lower left: *Howard Weeden*
Museum purchase

In the late Victorian period art entered many homes through magazine and book illustrations. Improvements in printing techniques and the manufacture of paper greatly enhanced the production of newspapers and fashion magazines as well as that of sheet music and children's literature. Countless artists started work professionally as illustrators, a demanding way to earn a living. In the South, tales about plantation life, freely employing illustrations and dialect, proliferated and were widely distributed. For example, for thirty years Joel Chandler Harris's tales of Uncle Remus and Br'er Rabbit disseminated stereotypes of African-Americans as backward and superstitious yarn spinners.

Many artists, however, did not indulge in these forms of caricature, preferring instead to render more dignified and uplifting images of former slaves. Such was the case with the reclusive Maria Howard Weeden. After visiting the World's Columbian Exposition in Chicago, where she encountered many of these caustic images of the Uncle Remus variety, she resolved to pursue a different direction with her portraits of African-Americans. Weeden later recalled: "Then and there I awoke to the realization that right around me was a subject of supremest artistic interest—the old ex-slave, who henceforth became theme for my muse and model for my brush."[1]

Living the sheltered existence of an impoverished, husbandless, and sickly Victorian woman, Weeden labored at her art in an attempt to supplement the family's income. Because she used her middle name, Howard, in her signature and correspondence, many people wanted to know more about "Mr. Howard Weeden." In response to a request for information about her background, Weeden wrote: "Happy women have no histories it is said—and perhaps it is because I have been so happy that I have nothing to tell you. I live in the old house in which I was born, here in the loveliest old town in the world, with my friends, my books and my pictures, and this is my history."[2] With little formal art training, she developed a distinctive style for which she gained a modicum of recognition in the environs of Huntsville, Alabama, and Nashville, Tennessee.

Using sepia-toned watercolors Weeden developed a style closely allied to, but more sensitive than, photography. Often selecting older African-Americans as her subjects, she usually posed them in profile or three-quarter views from behind. Thus the sitter does not confront the viewer but maintains a distance. The background and clothes are kept simple, allowing the facial features to dominate. Her subjects were generally members of her community who served as cooks, nannies, and gardeners to her peers. Weeden's delicate renderings are exceptional because they are formal portraits of African-Americans. One of the sitters in the Museum's pair, Uncle Champ, was a favorite subject whom she painted several times. Champ had served as a valet to Robert Miller Patton, governor of Alabama from 1865 to 1867. Weeden knew Champ personally, since he worked as a gardener for her nephew.

In addition to her portrait work Weeden illustrated small volumes of poetry, and when she could not find passages appropriate to her art, she began to write her own verse. Paralleling the vernacular simplicity of her watercolors, the poems are nostalgic paeans to the world she knew best. Weeden herself recognized this aspect of her work: "The books are but modest songs and verses snatched from the fading remnant of a people now nearly passed away, only valuable because the past is always precious, and only beautiful for being old and gone."[3]

---

1. As quoted in Mary Brabson Littleton, "Howard Weeden, Poetess and Artist," *Confederate Veteran* 14, no. 4 (April 1906): 162.

2. Weeden to Miss Arrington, 16 March 1904, as quoted in Sarah Huff Fisk, *The Alabama Review,* April 1861, 125.

3. Weeden, as quoted in F. P. Gamble, *Library of Southern Literature* (New Orleans: Martin & Hoyt, 1907), 13:5721.

Born, Huntsville, Alabama, 1847; art instruction as a child from William Frye, portraitist; attended the Tuskegee Female Methodist College, continuing her training in art, circa 1863–1865; died, Huntsville, 1905.

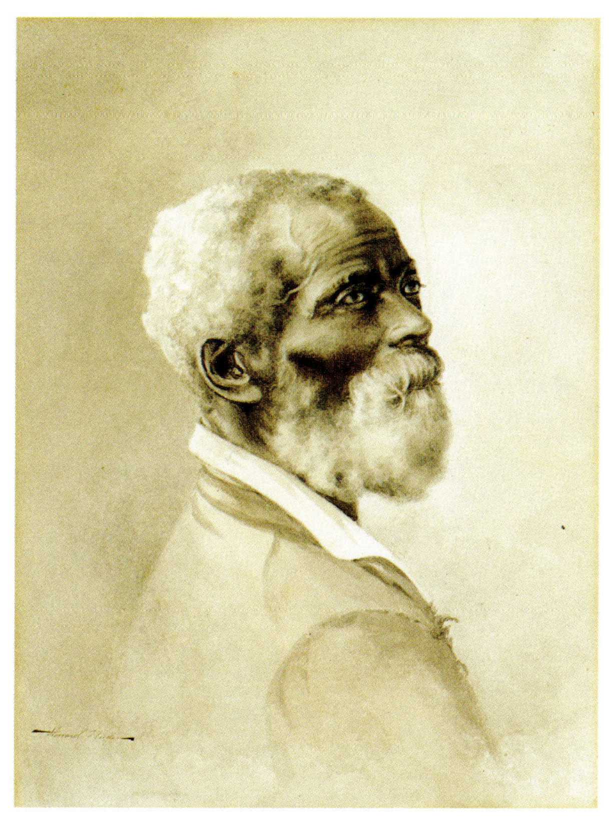

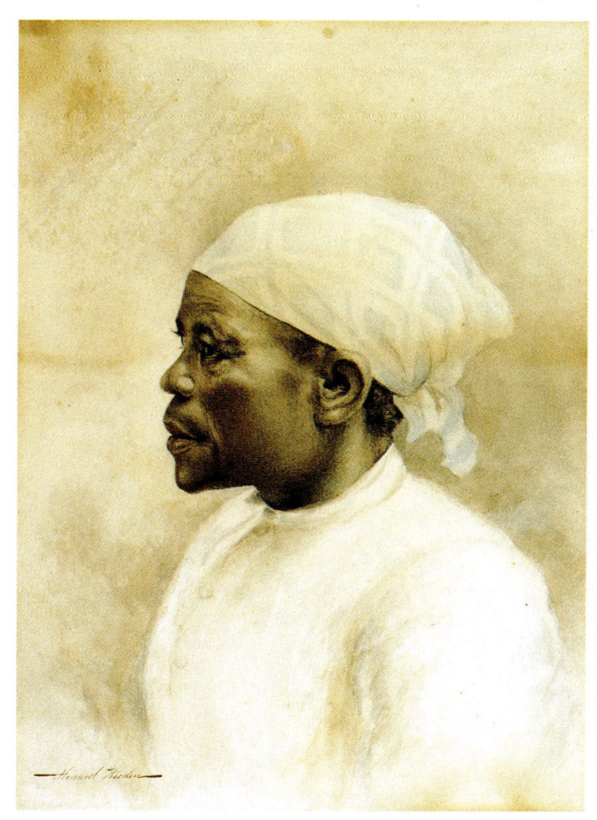

William Gilbert Gaul

1855–1919

Waiting for Turkeys (On the Turkey Stand), circa 1890

oil on academy board, 24½ × 18½ inches
signed, lower left: *Gilbert Gaul*
Museum purchase with funds donated by the Arthur and Holly Magill Foundation

Whereas genre painting often dealt with domestic scenes dominated by women, by the end of the century outdoor subjects relating to male pastimes became popular. As a counterpoint to Victorian sentimentality these masculine and virile depictions are closely related to military images where heroic feats were glamorized. Winslow Homer, for example, who served as a Civil War correspondent for *Harper's Weekly,* rendered hunters and fishermen whose self-reliance and independent spirit paralleled that of the soldiers he encountered during the war.

Although too young to witness the Civil War, Gilbert Gaul embraced many of the same heroic, masculine ideals as Homer. And like Homer, who retreated to Maine, Gaul absented himself from cosmopolitan New York and went to Tennessee regularly. At age seventeen Gaul began four years of study in New York at the National Academy of Design, which he supplemented with night classes at the newly founded Art Students League. In 1876 Gaul traveled west, where he saw some of the United States Army's campaigns against the Sioux, an experience that provided him with material for future paintings.

The mainstay of Gaul's career was military imagery that he developed as illustrations for *Century, Harper's Weekly,* and *Scribner's Monthly.* The lingering fascination with the Civil War in the popular press led Gaul to depict events that he had not actually seen. Working from verbal descriptions and possibly from illustrations, Gaul offered realistic interpretations of the release of prisoners at Andersonville, a Union drill, and lonely sentinels and army stragglers, among other subjects. When in 1907 he collaborated on an illustrated portfolio, *With Confederate Colors,* the public's passion for Civil War images had subsided, and the project was not the financial success he had hoped.

Waiting for Turkeys reflects a more privately conceived work, one designed not for reproduction in a national magazine but rather to convey Gaul's personal experiences. In 1881 Gaul had inherited land in Van Buren County, Tennessee, with the stipulation that he live there for at least four years. Rural Tennessee, both its landscape and its people, provided subject matter for the rest of his career. At the heart of the Museum's painting is the hunter's concentration. Accompanied by his dog, the hunter gazes at something beyond the limits of the image. The composition, however, is intensely focused on the figure who is positioned against lush vegetation. The dappled light, fresh green colors, and painterly brushwork suggest that Gaul was aware of the nascent popularity of Impressionism.

For his model, Gaul may have had in mind Homer's image of a Yankee sharpshooter who, precariously balanced in a pine tree, takes aim at an enemy soldier. Homer's work appeared as an illustration in *Harper's Weekly* in November 1862, and Gaul, also an illustrator of Civil War subjects for *Harper's,* would certainly have known Homer's chilling image. Both compositions are pared down to the essentials: the marksman in nature. Gaul's addition of the patient hunting dog and the verdant, sunlit surroundings combine with the hunter's homespun clothing and the nonthreatening position of the rifle in his lap to create an image of sport rather than of war.

Born, Jersey City, New Jersey, 1855; studied in New York at the National Academy of Design, 1872–1876, and at the Art Students League, 1875; traveled west, 1876; in Van Buren, Tennessee, 1881–1885; maintained a camp and studio there for most of his life; at age twenty-seven, became youngest Academician of the National Academy of Design, 1882; returned to Tennessee, 1904–1910; died, Jersey City, 1919.

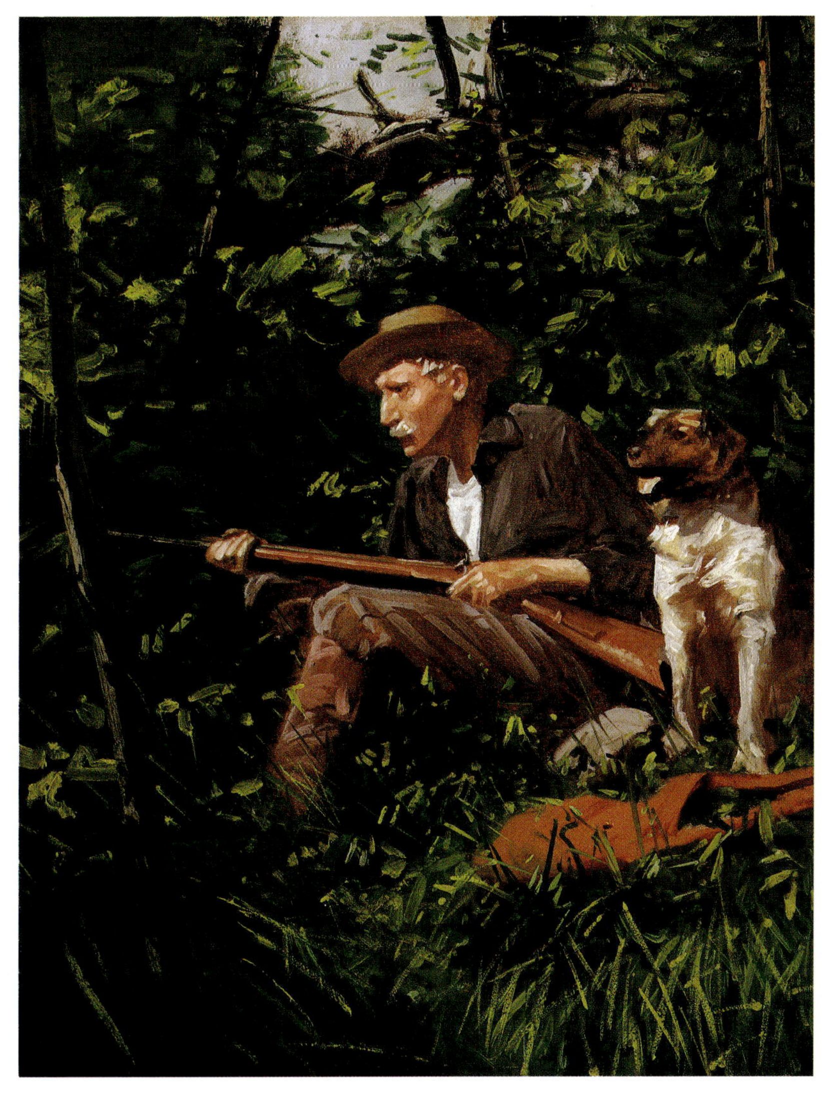

Louis Betts

1873–1961

Cows Watering, 1897

oil on canvas, 16 × 22 inches
signed, lower right: *Louis Betts 97*
Museum purchase with funds raised by the 1989 Museum Antiques Show, Elliott, Davis & Company, CPAs, sponsor, and donated by The Museum Association, Inc.

The overwhelming popularity of portraiture in America continued until the 1840s, when the public's taste shifted toward landscapes and genre paintings and when photographic portraits began to supplant the painted image. Portraits continued to be painted, however, especially of socialites and dignitaries. A prolific artist, George Healy painted notable figures until his death in 1894, but it was the work of John Singer Sargent that was the rage among the international aristocracy at the turn of the century. Employing broken brushstrokes and dramatic highlights, Sargent, with his fluid and flattering likenesses of the social elite, set a new standard for portraiture. Although he earned his considerable livelihood as a portraitist, Sargent indulged his own painterly interests with landscapes, often watercolors of the faraway places he visited on his extended travels.

Other painters similarly made significant incomes and gained impressive reputations by painting portraits, and Louis Betts learned not only from Sargent's example but also from that of William Merritt Chase. Betts studied with Chase both at his summer school on Long Island and at the Pennsylvania Academy of the Fine Arts. Born in Little Rock, Arkansas, Betts was the son of Edwin D. Betts, a painter, primarily of landscapes, who served as the younger Betts's first instructor. Although he demonstrated his talent early, Louis Betts was almost thirty before he went to Philadelphia for formal study. At the Academy, he was awarded a travel fellowship, which he used to go abroad to study the great seventeenth-century masters of portraiture, Frans Hals and Diego Velázquez.

While on his fellowship in Paris, because he found models to be expensive, he painted the parks and boulevards that the Impressionists had made famous. In a letter asking for funds, he complained: "my bills for materials, modelling, etc. are quite large & materials are more expensive than in America."[1] Over the next several decades Betts painted numerous important figures in the arts and letters, including the critic Royal Cortissoz and the authors Booth Tarkington and Hamlin Garland. Like legions of itinerant portraitists before him, Betts often went to his sitter's hometown to undertake the likeness. Thus, he traveled to Minnesota for his portraits of the Mayo brothers, William and Charles, founders of the Mayo Clinic, and to Rochester, New York, to paint the camera pioneer George Eastman. He painted stylish women as well, although he recognized that tastes had changed since Sargent painted portraits: "Painting a woman's portrait full length is not all of what it was in Sargent's time. Houses are not as large and magnificent, nor the gowns as handsome."[2] Accordingly, Betts's portraits were often bust length, but they still emulated Sargent in their broad brushwork and sensitive rendering of character.

Betts wrote a series of articles in which he advised artists on the proper techniques and approaches to portrait painting. Repeatedly he recommended stepping back from the canvas, so that details would not become all-consuming. He also urged: "Rapid, accurate seeing must be one of your gifts."[3] These skills, reflected in *Cows Watering,* were ones that Betts developed early in his career and were probably learned from his father. A pastoral landscape, *Cows Watering* is an extremely fresh canvas that foretells the immediacy that Betts later encouraged.

---

1. Betts to Harrison Morris, 20 January 1904, Paris. Archives, Pennsylvania Academy of the Fine Arts.
2. Louis Betts, "Experiences of a Portrait Painter," *Artist,* January–March 1957, 78.
3. Betts, "Experiences," 78.

Born, Little Rock, Arkansas, 1873; studied at home with his father, Edwin D. Betts, and with William Merritt Chase at the Shinnecock School and the Pennsylvania Academy of the Fine Arts, 1902–1903; traveled to Holland and to Paris, 1903–1904; Chicago, 1906–1912; moved to New York; died, Bronxville, New York, 1961.

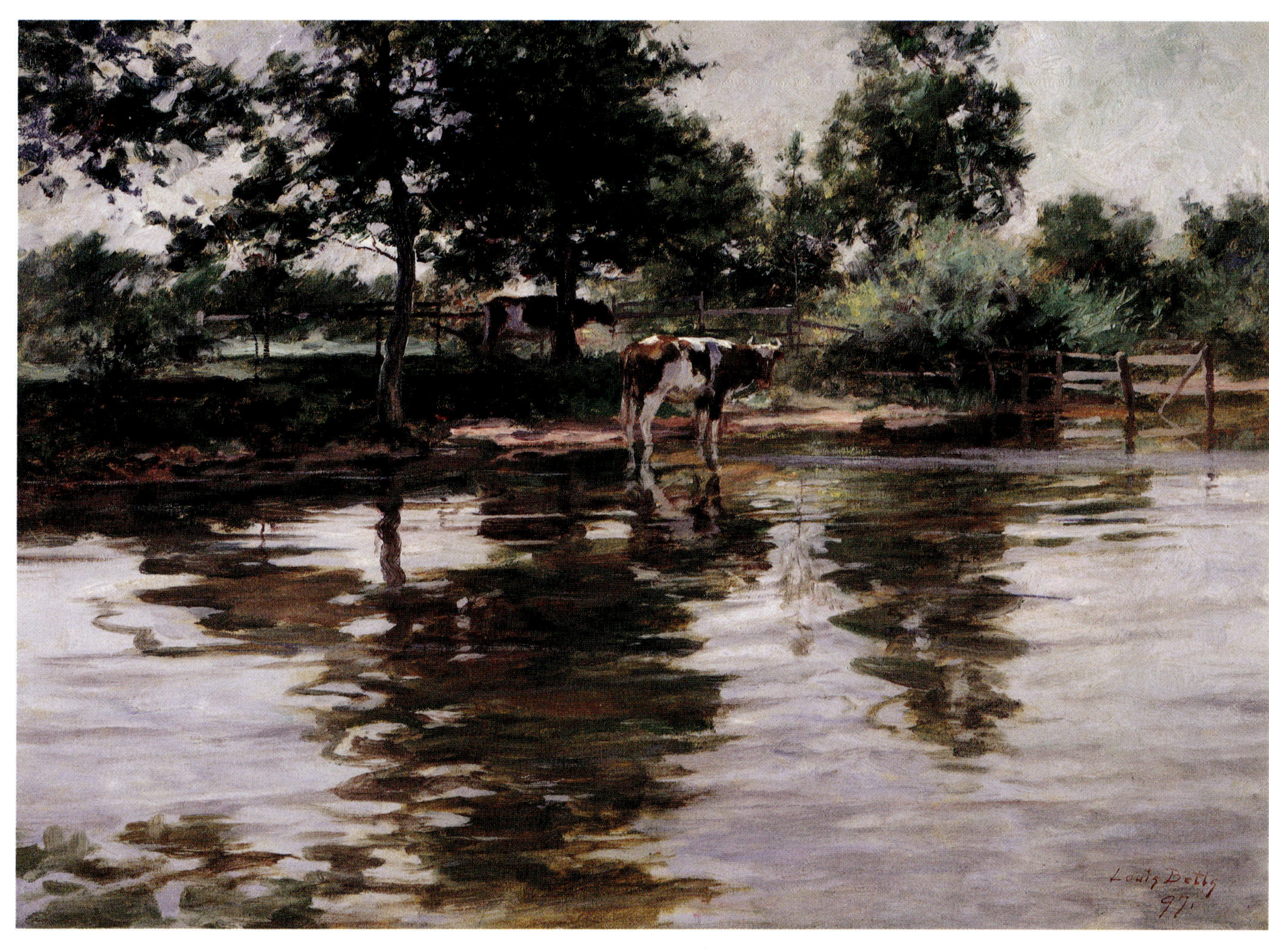

Enoch Wood Perry, Jr.

1831–1915

The Last Vision of Jeanne d'Arc, 1903

oil on canvas, 48 × 72 inches
signed, lower left: *E. Wood Perry Jr. NA / 1903*
Museum purchase with funds donated by Mr. and Mrs. Alester G. Furman III; Dorothy Hipp Gunter (Mrs. C. Guy Gunter); and The Museum Association, Inc.

The prevailing taste of the last quarter of the nineteenth century in America was Victorian. Eclectic in nature, the Victorian ideal permeated architecture and domestic interiors, social mores, and fashions; its effect on art, however, was not as pronounced. In grand family portraits, the artists Eastman Johnson and George H. Story depicted the sumptuous and cluttered surroundings of the elite without embracing a Victorian painting style. The Victorian penchant for sentimentality is reflected better in genre paintings that portray the simple life of peasants before industrialization.

In a series of genre paintings of the 1870s and 1880s Enoch Wood Perry extolled rural values and manual labor in a manner pleasing to Victorian sensibilities. Many of his works feature women, the center of Victorian existence, and bear titles that celebrate American domestic virtue, for example *Combing Flax by the Fireside* or *Preparing for Thanksgiving.* Others, like *The Grindstone* and *Young Ben Franklin at the Printing Press,* present themes relative to handicraft or male ingenuity. Perry, it seems, catered to a conservative clientele who favored familiar, slightly sentimental, and restorative images.

Perry spent his youth in New Orleans and then studied in Düsseldorf under Emanuel Leutze, who is best remembered for his retrospective portrayal *Washington Crossing the Delaware.* After two years in Germany Perry proceeded to Paris, where he studied with Thomas Couture. Upon his return to this country he stayed first in Philadelphia and then traveled to New Orleans, where he painted portraits until 1862, when he moved west. He spent almost two years in San Francisco, expanding his work to include landscape, possibly under the influence of Albert Bierstadt, a fellow Düsseldorf student, with whom he visited Yosemite Valley in 1863. From California Perry sailed to the Sandwich Islands, and there he painted portraits of Hawaiian royalty as well as landscapes of area ranches and sugar mills. Within a year he returned to California and traveled eastward via Salt Lake City, where he spent the winter months and painted likenesses of Brigham Young. Only when he finally settled in New York did he begin to pursue genre painting seriously.

The Last Vision of Jeanne d'Arc, a late painting, is unusual in Perry's oeuvre, or body of work. No documentation exists to explain Perry's choice of subject matter, which was a decided departure from his other work. He submitted the painting to the 1901 Annual exhibition of the Art Institute of Chicago and also copyrighted it, perhaps indicating either that he wished to retain his stature as an important academic painter or that he aspired to use the image as an illustration or both. Joan of Arc, the youthful heroine, had long been associated with French nationalism, and an interest in her plight, which peaked with her canonization as Saint Joan in 1920, was on the rise.

The composition of the painting is divided into two parts. The sleeping figure of Joan reclines across the bottom of the canvas, not unlike the recumbent saints placed at the foot of altars in numerous churches in Italy. Joan, dressed in armor with her arms folded across her chest, also resembles tomb figures typical of medieval knights. In the upper right, Joan's vision is painted in suffused light. Seven young peasant girls dance in a circle around the Fairy Tree, a reference not only to the carefree days of Joan's childhood but also to the future unity of France. Mark Twain, who assumed the role of the martyr's page in his biography *The Personal Recollections of Joan of Arc,* recounted the legend associated with the Fairy Tree: "I know that when the Children of the Tree die in a far land, then—if they be at peace with God—they turn their longing eyes toward home, and there, far-shining, as through a rift in a cloud that curtains heaven, they see the soft picture of the Fairy Tree, clothed in a dream of golden light."[1]

The painting is an ambitious one for Perry and displays his indebtedness to the academic tradition. The clarity of such details as the ceramic jug, the iron ring and chain, and even the straw reflects his studies in Düsseldorf. Emerging from the semidarkness is the fleur-de-lis, an emblem both of the French king for whom Joan had fought and of her family, who were issued a patent of nobility following her death. The radiant and beautiful face of the saint herself, surrounded by soft auburn hair, is reminiscent of English Pre-Raphaelite painting, an appropriate analogy for a work with such strong religious overtones and appeal to a Victorian audience.

---

1. Mark Twain, *Personal Recollections of Joan of Arc* (New York: Harper & Row, 1896), 11.

Born, Boston, 1831; lived in New Orleans, 1843–1852; attended the Düsseldorf Academy, 1852–1854, and studied in Paris with Thomas Couture, 1854; United States Consul in Venice, 1855–1856; settled in Philadelphia, 1858–1860; to New Orleans, 1860–1862; to San Francisco, 1862–1864; to the Sandwich Islands, 1864; Salt Lake City, 1864–1866; settled in New York, with occasional trips to San Francisco and Europe; died, New York, 1915.

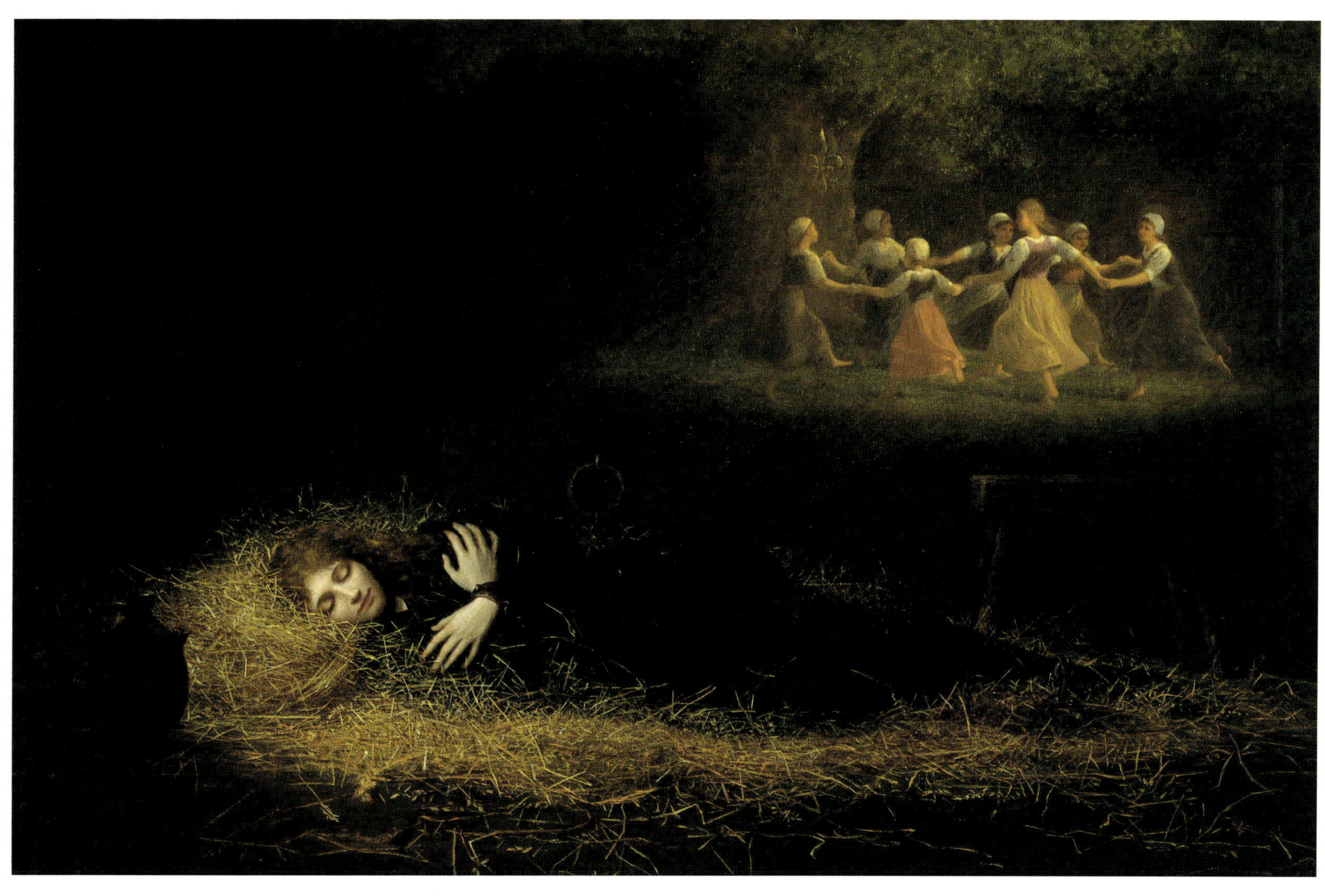

Anna Vaughn Hyatt Huntington

1876–1973

Colts Playing, 1904

bronze, edition of 3, 11½ × 18 × 7½ inches
signed, on base: *copyright Anna V. Hyatt / Roman Bronze Works, NY*
Museum purchase with funds donated by the Arthur and Holly Magill Foundation and gift of the artist (by exchange)

The end of the nineteenth century witnessed a heightened fascination with nature and animals that was manifested in the founding and growth of national parks, zoos, and natural-history museums. As America became more urban, a romantic interest in simpler, natural things developed. The allure of animals as subject matter was also fueled by the demand for small desktop sculptures in bronze. Antoine-Louis Barye, who worked in France as an animalier, did the most to promote this readily accessible medium that fostered the expressively realistic presentation of animals at rest, at play, and in mortal conflict. In a similar vein, Frederic Remington's bronzes of cowboys and their broncos appealed to a public still captivated by the glamour and excitement of the American frontier.

In this environment Anna Hyatt learned to model in clay and became internationally renowned for her small-scale depictions of animals as well as for a number of large equestrian monuments. It was only natural that she, the daughter of a zoologist and paleontologist who taught at the Massachusetts Institute of Technology, came to specialize in animal sculpture. Since she was an accomplished horsewoman, it is no surprise that horses were a recurring theme in her heroic sculptures and her more intimate pieces. Her work gained her both public and critical recognition: Lorado Taft, a sculptor and noted historian of American sculpture, commented, "Very exceptional it is to find a woman so completely master of her art as is Miss Anna Vaughn Hyatt, one of our foremost sculptors of animals. . . . There is not a sculptor in the land who does not pay homage to the able craftsmanship of Miss Hyatt's studies of wild life. You can invest in these bronzes of hers as confidently as you buy those of Barye, the French sculptor."[1]

Hyatt spent her adolescence in the Boston area, where her father provided her and her sister Harriet with a studio. Anna Hyatt took instruction from Henry Hudson Kitson, who was primarily a portraitist. She later commented on her early years: "I was brought up with clay in my mouth."[2] Domestic animals were her favorite subject matter, including dogs and horses, which she encountered on her brother's farm in Maryland. Dissatisfied with training opportunities in Boston, Hyatt moved to New York, where she studied with Hermon MacNeil at the Art Students League. She also had some contact with Gutzon Borglum, who would later carve the presidential heads on Mount Rushmore. Hyatt had the audacity to criticize Borglum's ambitious horse sculpture of 1904, the *Mares of Diomedes,* but despite this, the dynamism and energy of Borglum's *Mares* appear to have influenced her *Colts Playing,* which was conceived in the same year.

In contrast to other examples of animal sculpture that portray single figures at rest, *Colts Playing* is an ambitious and energetic rendering of three horses chasing one another. Furthermore, the work has no single viewpoint but must be viewed in the round, from several different perspectives. No one horse dominates, and the three are interwoven visually and rhythmically. Each horse touches the ground with only one hoof, a factor that adds movement as well as lightness to the piece. This is structurally possible on such an intimate scale and contrasts with Borglum's more massive treatment of six horses atop a heavy mound of earth. *Colts Playing* is further enhanced by the sheen of its surface, a quality that relates to the light-reflective surfaces of Auguste Rodin's bronzes.

The theme of horses continued to preoccupy Hyatt throughout her career, even as she expanded her knowledge of other animals. While residing in New York she frequented the Bronx Zoo, where she familiarized herself with lions, tigers, and elephants. In 1907 Hyatt went abroad and maintained studios in Auvers-sur-Oise and in Paris, interrupted only by a stay in Italy and a short visit home. While in France she embarked on her first major heroic study, an equestrian sculpture of Joan of Arc that was exhibited at the Paris Salon and resulted in the commission of a monument for New York. Dedicated in 1915, Hyatt's *Joan of Arc* reflects not only the pro-French feelings of Americans during World War I but also the tide of international sentiment that led to the French maiden's canonization in 1920. Because of its scale and commemorative function, Joan of Arc's horse is more static and dignified than the horses depicted in *Colts Playing.*

In 1923 Hyatt married Archer M. Huntington, a philanthropist with a particular interest in Spanish culture. For the Hispanic Society of New York, which Huntington founded, Hyatt made a replica of her *El Cid Campeador,* a militant equestrian figure originally made for Seville, Spain.

While exploring the South one winter the Huntingtons purchased several plantations near Murrells Inlet, South Carolina, including the ancestral home of Washington Allston. Here the Huntingtons lived part-time and established an outdoor sanctuary for the display of her sculpture and for the protection and study of nature and wildlife. Brookgreen Gardens, with more than nine thousand acres, became this country's first public sculpture garden, and the collection has expanded to include a comprehensive survey of American figurative sculpture. Like her counterpart Gloria Vanderbilt Whitney, who was both sculptor and founder of the Whitney Museum of American Art, Hyatt sustained a far-reaching and creative career in sculpture, while providing for the display of American art.

---

1. Taft, as quoted in J. Walker McSpadden, *Famous Sculptors of America* (1924; reprint, Freeport, N.Y.: Books for Libraries Press, 1968), 343–344.

2. Hyatt, as quoted in Beatrice Proske, "Anna Hyatt Huntington," *Brookgreen Gardens Bulletin,* Fall 1973, unpaginated.

Born, Cambridge, Massachusetts, 1876; studied with Henry Hudson Kitson, 1898; moved to New York, 1902; studied at the Art Students League with Hermon MacNeil, 1902; resided in Auvers-sur-Oise and Paris, 1907–1910, with a stay in Italy, 1908; acquired Brookgreen Gardens, 1930, resided there seasonally, and in Haverstraw, New York, then Bethel, Connecticut; died, Bethel, 1973.

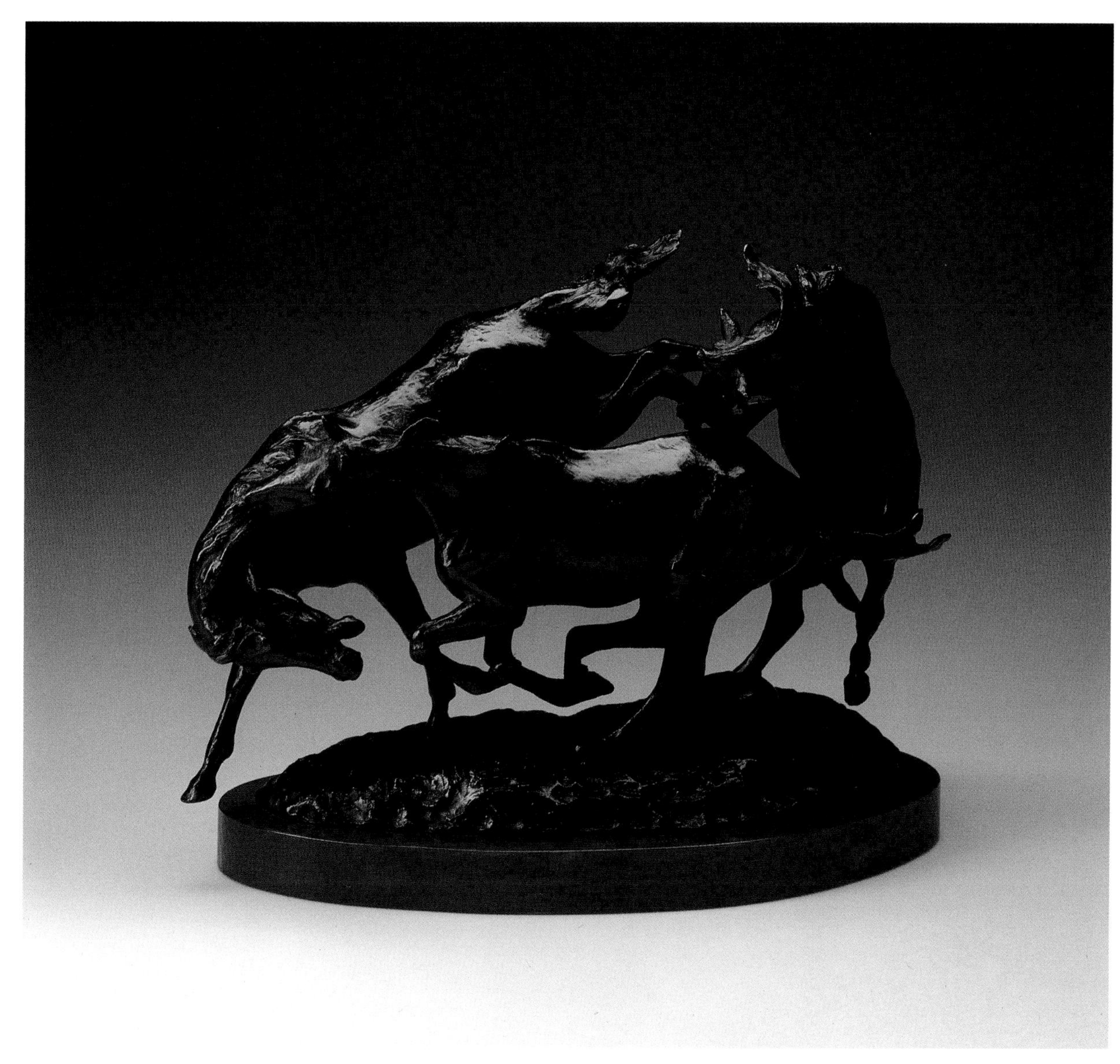

William de Leftwich Dodge

1867–1935

Summer Day under Spanish Moss, circa 1910

oil on canvas, 40 × 24 inches
signed, lower left: *Wm D. L. Dodge*
Museum purchase with funds donated by Alester G. Furman III; The Pellett Foundation; and The Museum Association, Inc.

In the second half of the nineteenth century the phenomenon of international expositions was a driving force that helped to shape art, architecture, and taste. Beginning with the 1851 Crystal Palace in London, these spectacles promoted the industrial accomplishments and cultural identities of participating countries. The largest and most vivid relic of such events is the Eiffel Tower, designed as the centerpiece of the 1889 Universal Exposition in Paris. In this country the most important fairs were held in Philadelphia, in 1876, and in Chicago, in 1893. The former marked the nation's centennial and initiated a wave of colonial revivalism, especially evident in the architecture of New England and the Midwest, as well as in the paintings of Edward Lamson Henry. The World's Columbian Exposition of 1893 commemorated the four-hundredth anniversary of the arrival of Christopher Columbus, while simultaneously proclaiming the arrival of Chicago on the cultural scene.

Typically these expositions devoted entire buildings or a suite of galleries to the display of American art. The 1889 Paris exhibition presented 572 works, featuring paintings, drawings, sculptures, and prints by American artists. Much more imposing, however, were the amount of space and the number of works at the Chicago Exposition: 10,000 works of art arranged in 145,000 square feet.[1] Nationally acclaimed artists such as Winslow Homer, Thomas Eakins, John Singer Sargent, and James McNeill Whistler, along with lesser-known figures like Mattie Dubé, were included. The impact on artists and the general public was considerable; nevertheless, European works outsold American ones by a ratio of ten to one.

The Chicago fair also fostered mural decoration in the vast spaces of its Beaux-Arts–style exhibition buildings. Idealistic and classical in nature, the murals mirrored the American Renaissance movement, which revived Italian prototypes in both theme and style. Competition for these large-scale commissions was fierce. A precocious and ambitious William de Leftwich Dodge persuaded the architect Richard Morris Hunt to allow him to undertake the decoration of the rotunda of the Administration Building. As the exposition's tallest structure, whose dome measured 315 feet in circumference and 50 feet deep, it presented a mammoth task for the young artist. The subject matter of the decoration, *The Glorification of the Arts and Sciences,* was equally lofty.[2]

Dodge was well suited to the project. He had spent his adolescence abroad and at age eighteen began studies with Jean-Léon Gérôme at the Ecole des Beaux-Arts in Paris. He achieved early success with several works at the 1888 Salon and at the 1889 Exposition. In addition to the Chicago mural he completed the decoration of the northwest pavilion of the Library of Congress, which featured an allegory called *Ambition,* and the Flag Room at the New York State Capitol in Albany, which was dominated by a twelve-foot-high personification of the state holding a sword and a shield. Dodge was clearly proud of his accomplishments as a muralist. In 1901 he wrote: "Somebody said, the other day, that I was essentially a decorator. This remark was meant to be rather uncomplimentary, but I don't feel the sting of it at all, unless the gentleman wanted to insinuate that I am a kalsominer. I hope my work is decorative. If it decorated a tenth as well as nature does, I should be completely satisfied."[3]

In addition to his large allegorical murals, Dodge painted portraits and landscapes. In the late 1890s while residing in Paris, Dodge spent the summers at Giverny, where the master Impressionist Claude Monet painted his gardens. Although more concrete than Monet's vaporous visions of water lilies, *Summer Day under Spanish Moss* reveals Dodge's interest in dappled sunlight and verdant gardens. Unlike many of his murals, which were often composed of iconic figures placed in a shallow space, the Museum's painting is naturalistically conceived and can be easily read from the languid dog in the foreground to the centrally dominant house in the background.

---

1. See Annette Blaugrund et al., *Paris 1889: American Artists at the Universal Exposition* (Philadelphia: Pennsylvania Academy of the Fine Arts, 1989), and Carolyn Kinder Carr, *Revisiting the White City: American Art at the 1893 World's Fair* (Washington, D.C.: Smithsonian Institution Press, 1993).

2. See Frederick Platt, "A Brief Autobiography of William de Leftwich Dodge," *The American Art Journal* 14 (Spring 1982): 55–63.

3. Dodge, *Truth* 20, no. 3 (March 1901). William de Leftwich Dodge Papers, Archives of American Art, roll 379.

Born at Liberty, now Bedford, Virginia, 1867; at age twelve went to Europe with his mother, a painter, and studied drawing beginning at age fifteen; student of Jean-Léon Gérôme; to New York, 1889–1891, Chicago, 1891–1893; returned to Paris, 1894–1896; New York, 1897, and then Paris, 1897–1900; New York and Setauket, Long Island, 1900–1935; to San Francisco, 1914; traveled to Italy and the Yucatán; died, New York, 1935.

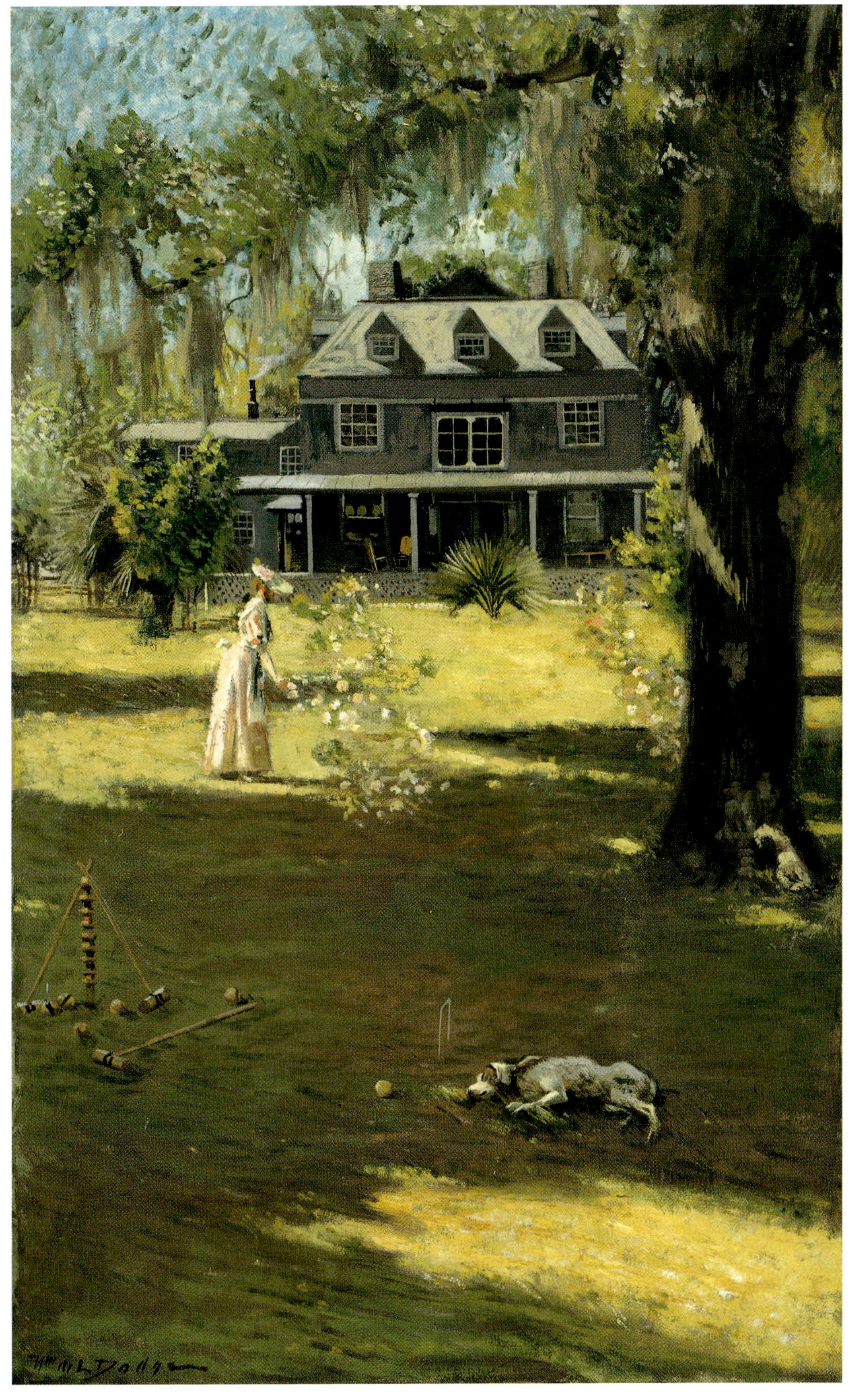

Clara Weaver Parrish

1861–1925

The Red Lily, circa 1914

oil on canvas, 29½ × 20 inches
signed, lower left: *Clara Weaver Parrish*
Museum purchase with funds donated by Lynne Thalheimer Nachman in memory of her father, Marcus Edwin Thalheimer

The goal of the American Aesthetic Movement was to infuse artistic values into the production of furniture and furnishings; its success depended upon the collaboration of architects, artists, and craftsmen. A majestic example of such aesthetic cooperation is Trinity Church in Boston, where H. H. Richardson and John LaFarge united to create a harmonious synthesis of color, light, structure, and religious imagery. In the South a comparably lavish endeavor took place when George Washington Vanderbilt brought together Richard Morris Hunt and Frederick Law Olmsted to erect his château, Biltmore, in the Great Smoky Mountains near Asheville, North Carolina. The paradigm for the union of art and craft was Louis Comfort Tiffany, who hired painters, sculptors, glass designers, and other artisans to create an American form of Art Nouveau. Closely linked to the Tiffany style, and an outgrowth of the Aesthetic Movement, Art Nouveau reveled in radiant, curving organic forms and is best exemplified by Tiffany-fabricated glass pieces.

Both the Aesthetic Movement and Art Nouveau placed increased emphasis on the role of women in determining taste, especially as it related to the home. As part of his legion of artisans Tiffany employed numerous women, including Clara Weaver Parrish. From a Selma, Alabama, family that included wood-carvers and writers, Parrish was predisposed to the aesthetic and collaborative ideal of Tiffany. In the early 1880s Parrish left Alabama to pursue the study of painting at the Art Students League in New York with William Merritt Chase and Kenyon Cox. Cox's Renaissance Revival mural work and his collaboration with the architect Stanford White served as models for Parrish's work.

The most potent influence on Parrish's painting was her experience in the Tiffany studios during the 1890s. While she was there the firm developed Favrile glass, a blown glass known for its iridescent colors and satiny surface. Specializing in stained glass, Parrish was part of a veritable industry devoted to the use of colored glass in private homes and public buildings. It has been estimated that by 1884 two thousand people were involved in the design and manufacture of stained glass in the New York area.[1]

Parrish's painting, *The Red Lily,* bears a striking resemblance to stained glass. The aquamarine tonality in the painting relates directly to the prevalent hue of opalescent glass. Akin to a window design with its transparency, the canvas creates its own luminescence.

In addition to its stylistic affinities to stained glass, the painting lends itself to a comparison in subject matter. The simple profile of a young woman is similar to the direct design of many stained-glass windows, which must be read from a considerable distance and under varying lighting conditions. Much of Parrish's work while at the Tiffany studios was for churches, and the iconography, or symbolic content, of *The Red Lily* relates to a lengthy tradition reverting both to the Middle Ages, the heyday of stained glass, and to the Renaissance. The lily was the attribute of several personages, including the angel of the Annunciation, who brought word of Christ's impending birth to the Virgin Mary. Both the profile pose and the hand gesture are typical of the angel of the Annunciation.

The lily is also the flower associated with Saint Clare, the female counterpart to Saint Francis and the namesake of the artist. In paintings lilies were typically white, suggesting purity; red flowers usually denote passion or death. Parrish may have been mixing symbols in some arcane autobiographical manner, possibly alluding to her own mortality or to the early deaths of her husband and young daughter.

---

1. "America's Stained Glass Interest," *American Architect and Building News* 15 (17 May 1884): 235, as cited in Alice Cooney Frelinghuysen, *In Pursuit of Beauty: Americans and the Aesthetic Movement* (New York: The Metropolitan Museum of Art, 1986), 177.

Born, near Selma, Alabama, 1861; studied in New York, at the Art Students League, with William Merritt Chase, Kenyon Cox, H. Siddons Mowbray, and J. Alden Weir during the 1880s; lived in Birmingham, Alabama, circa 1887–1889; employed at Tiffany Studios, New York, 1890s; traveled in Europe, and studied in Paris at the Académie Colarossi, 1910–1914; died, New York, 1925.

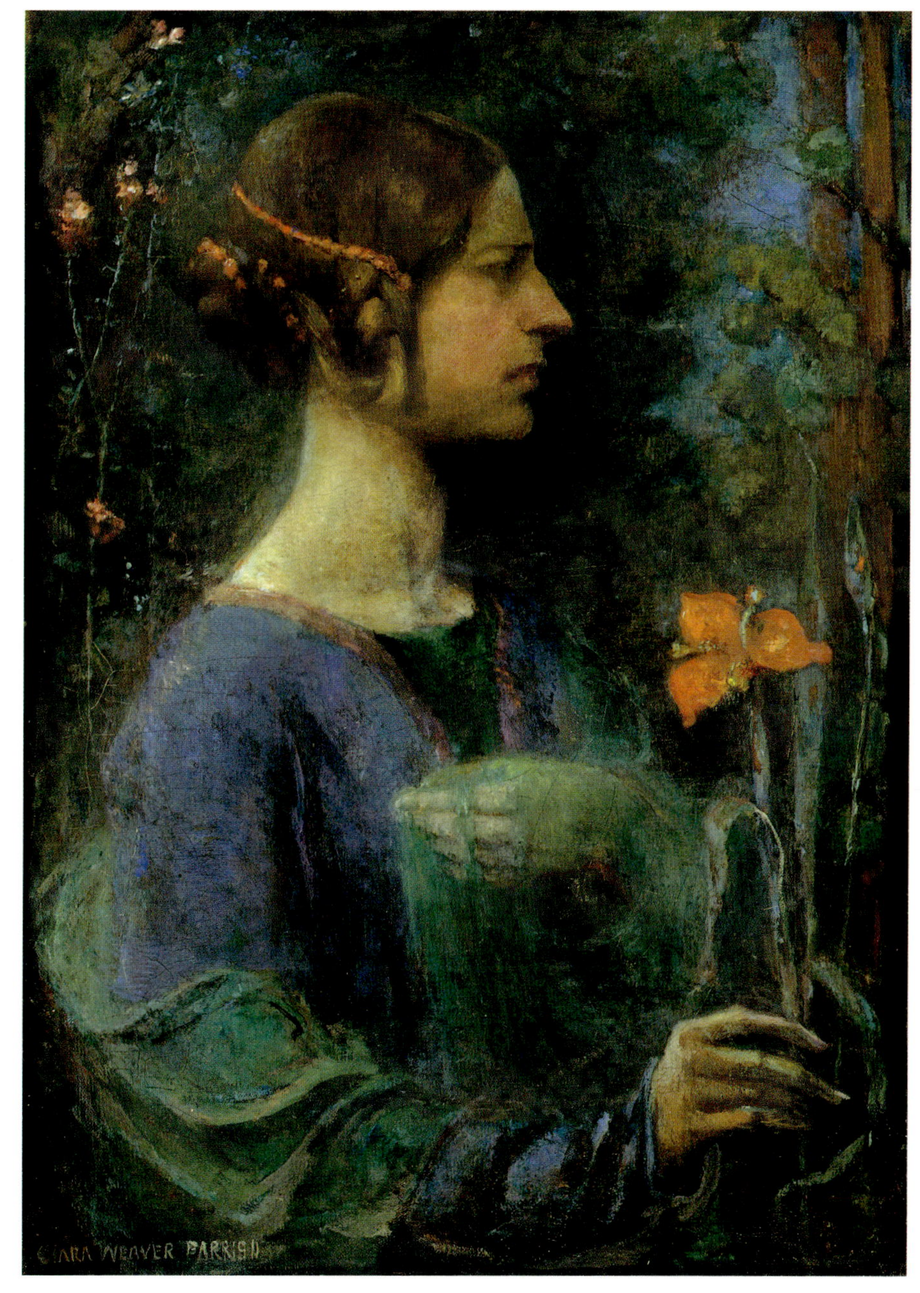
CLARA WEAVER PARRISH

Helen Maria Turner

1858–1958

Girl with Lantern, 1904

oil on canvas, 44 × 34 inches
signed, upper right: *Helen M. Turner / 1904*
Museum purchase with funds donated by The Friends of Helen Turner: Dorothy Hipp Gunter; Mr. and Mrs. R. Glenn Hilliard; Mr. and Mrs. William W. Kehl; Dr. and Mrs. Jeffrey G. Lawson; Mr. and Mrs. E. Erwin Maddrey II; Mr. and Mrs. Charles C. Mickel; Mr. and Mrs. G. Franklin Mims; Mr. and Mrs. Lawrence J. Nachman; Mary M. Pearce; Mr. and Mrs. John D. Pellett, Jr.; Mr. and Mrs. Thomas A. Roe; Mr. and Mrs. Robert Small; W. Thomas Smith; Mr. and Mrs. Thomas H. Suitt, Jr.; Mr. and Mrs. Robert T. Thompson, Jr.; Mr. and Mrs. Barton Tuck; Mr. and Mrs. Richard F. Watson, Jr.; Mr. and Mrs. Wilson C. Wearn; Mr. and Mrs. Irvine T. Welling III; anonymous donor

In the 1870s and the early 1880s, while American art students traveled abroad to attend the academies and compete for entry into the Paris Salon exhibitions, a revolution was underway: Impressionism. Although firmly grounded in nineteenth-century tenets that promoted plein air painting, the primacy of the sketch, and even "art for art's sake," Impressionism changed the way both nature and art were perceived. The stylistic principles advocated by the movement's proponents included informal subject matter, bright colors heightened with white, and conspicuous brushwork. The influences of photography and Japanese prints are reflected in asymmetrical and cropped compositions.

Impressionism coalesced in 1874 when Claude Monet, Pierre-Auguste Renoir, Edgar Degas, and others began to exhibit together independently from the Salon. The group was neither cohesive nor consistent; nor was their art warmly received. Impressionism was viewed as an artistic scandal; the public found the work outrageous, and some critics complained about the unfinished nature of the canvases.

Americans, even those in Paris, were slow to notice the advent of Impressionism, despite its extensive coverage in the press. Mary Cassatt was an exception: she not only became a close friend of Degas, but she also exhibited in four of the Impressionist exhibitions. In addition, she persuaded a few of her American friends to acquire examples of the new painting style for their collections. Childe Hassam, who encountered the movement in Paris in the late 1880s, and William Merritt Chase, the influential teacher, did even more than Cassatt for the spread of Impressionism in America.

By the early years of the twentieth century the influence of Impressionism in America had become pervasive. The American version was as diversified and individualistic as its French counterpart, and, just as the French gravitated toward certain locales like Argenteuil and Giverny, painters in this country found coastal and rural areas inspirational for their new aesthetic. While Hassam worked at Appledore, New Hampshire, and Chase at Shinnecock, New York, the painters Helen Turner and Charles Curran found inspiration at Cragsmoor, New York.

Turner, whose longtime home was New Orleans, moved in 1895 to New York, where she began four years of study at the Art Students League. She studied with Chase both at the League and during his summer programs abroad, and, in the manner of her teacher, Turner remained a realist at heart who indulged in sun-filled scenes painted with highly textured brushwork. Her imagery typically consisted of a single female figure pausing in thought or performing a simple task.

In its painterly surface, vivid colors, and quiet demeanor, *Girl with Lantern* demonstrates Turner's espousal of Impressionism. The main subject, dappled with sunlight, delicately adjusts a Japanese lantern. Placed slightly to the right of center, the young woman is positioned against a background that is completely dissolved into flecks of color. The cropping of the figure, the lantern, and the diagonal placement of the white fence reveal the influence of Japanese art. The lantern has a more practical explanation as well: it was a common device used at Cragsmoor to light the pathway home on a summer evening.[1]

1. Barbara Buff, "Cragsmoor, an Early American Art Colony," *The Magazine Antiques,* November 1978, 1073.

Born, Louisville, Kentucky, 1858; resided in New Orleans, 1866–1893; lessons with Andres Molinary and Bors Wickstrom, early 1890s; taught school in Dallas, 1893–1895; attended the Art Students League in New York, studying with William Merritt Chase and Kenyon Cox, 1895–1899; studied abroad with Chase, 1904, 1905, 1911; summered Cragsmoor, New York, 1906–1941; elected full Academician of the National Academy of Design, 1921; returned to New Orleans, 1926; died, New Orleans, 1958.

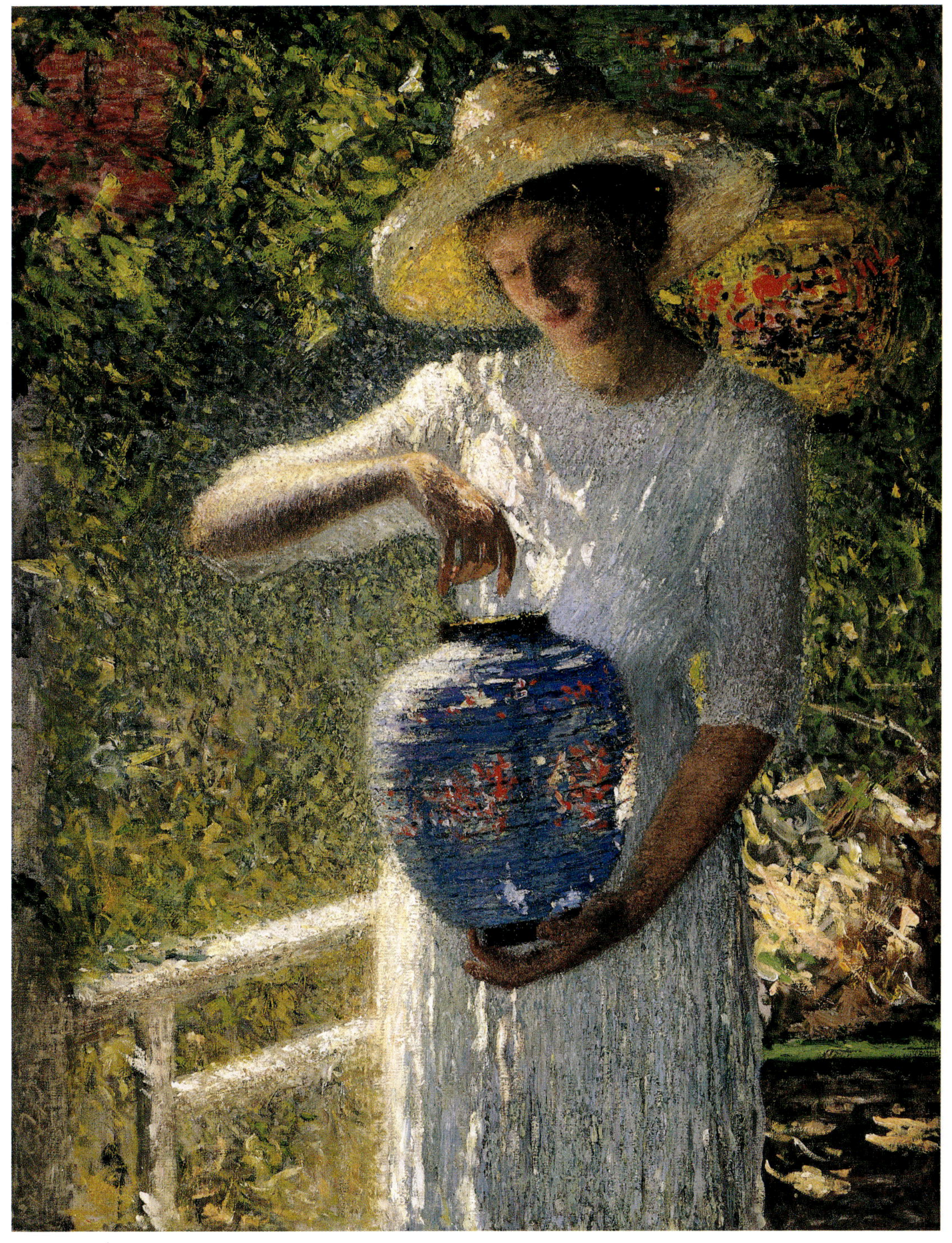

Julius Garibaldi Melchers

1860–1932

Woman Reading by a Window, circa 1905

oil on canvas, 25½ × 30 inches
signed, lower right: *G. Melchers*
Gift of The Museum Association, Inc., with funds donated by: Mr. and Mrs. Alester G. Furman III; Mr. and Mrs. M. Dexter Hagy; Mr. and Mrs. William W. Kehl; Dr. and Mrs. Jeffrey G. Lawson; Mr. and Mrs. Hurdle Lea; Stanton D. and Jessica S. Loring; Mr. and Mrs. E. Erwin Maddrey II; Mr. and Mrs. Buck Mickel; Dorothy P. Peace; Mary Burnet M. Pearce; Mr. and Mrs. James M. Shoemaker, Jr.; Mr. and Mrs. Robert Scott Small; W. Thomas Smith; Mr. and Mrs. Richard F. Watson, Jr.; Millie and Wilson Wearn

The changes initiated by the Impressionists, although dramatic, did not take hold immediately or universally. Many artists, whether established in the academic tradition or committed to their personal styles, were reluctant to embrace the new fashion. Certain aspects of Impressionism, namely its bright colors and informal subject matter, were often applied to existing stylistic armatures. William Merritt Chase, for example, achieved early success, especially in portraiture, with his version of the dark tonalities inspired by the old masters and stressed at the Munich school. By the late 1880s Chase revised his approach, painting more plein air landscapes with a lighter palette, although like most American Impressionists he always remained grounded in realism.

Gari Melchers, an expatriate for almost three decades, is another artist whose style evolved into Impressionism in midcareer. By 1900 he had earned an international reputation for a naturalistic approach firmly rooted in academic principles. His work was narrative in content, at times with a religious or moralistic overtone, and his subjects derived from the remote and rural life of Dutch peasants.

Melchers's earliest artistic training was as a casual student of his father, a Detroit, Michigan, sculptor. In 1877 Melchers began four years of study at the Düsseldorf Academy, where he learned the importance of bright colors and anecdotal subject matter. His student experience in Düsseldorf had a more lasting effect on his development than his subsequent schooling at the Académie Julian and the Ecole des Beaux-Arts in Paris. This mix of American, German, and French study parallels the international scope of Melchers's success.

In pursuit of rustic, unspoiled peasant imagery, Melchers settled in the Egmond area of Holland, on the North Sea. Even when he traveled to this country for mural commissions at the World's Columbian Exposition and the Library of Congress as well as to other parts of Europe, the Egmond region was his home for a quarter of a century. Beginning in 1906 he rented a studio in New York, where he worked intermittently until his death. He taught in Germany for six years, but as the war in Europe escalated, Melchers returned to America permanently, dividing his time between New York and his rural retreat, Belmont, near Fredericksburg, Virginia. During this period he assisted the Telfair Academy in Savannah, Georgia, with the formation of its collection.

By the 1890s Melchers had begun to move in the direction of Impressionism. His subjects became less weighty, and he gravitated toward more intimate images. This shift was accompanied by a looser painting technique marked by visible brushstrokes. His palette, which had always tended toward intense and highly saturated hues, was well suited to these fresh depictions. *Woman Reading by a Window,* painted at Egmond aan den Hoef, also reflects his newfound domestic happiness; after his marriage in 1903 Melchers often portrayed his wife reading or engaged in simple, everyday activities.

Despite its obvious Impressionist qualities, *Woman Reading by a Window* remains a highly structured painting and mirrors the reluctance of many American painters to dissolve their compositions into purely coloristic effects. The geometry of both the door and the windowpanes prevents the total disintegration of the composition. The darkened foreground casts the figure in shadow, inviting the viewer to examine the brightly lit garden beyond. This device of looking from indoors out was used by such seventeenth-century Dutch painters as Pieter de Hooch, whose work Melchers would have known. This motif can also be found in contemporaneous canvases by Pierre Bonnard and Henri Matisse. Like Bonnard, who considered himself "the last of the Impressionists," Melchers presents an engaging interior that directs the viewer's gaze to the main focus of the painting. The brightly speckled flowers recall the Fauvist color and technique of Matisse's paintings.

Born, Detroit, Michigan, 1860; studied at Düsseldorf Academy, 1877–1881, and at the Académie Julian and the Ecole des Beaux-Arts, Paris, 1881–1884; to Egmond area of Holland, 1884, owning property there until 1922; regular trips to New York, Paris, and Brussels; murals at the World's Columbian Exposition, 1893, and the Library of Congress, 1895; taught at the Ducal Academy of Fine Arts in Weimar, Germany, 1909–1915; returned to the United States, 1915, maintaining a studio in New York with main residence at Belmont, Fredericksburg, Virginia; died, Belmont, 1932.

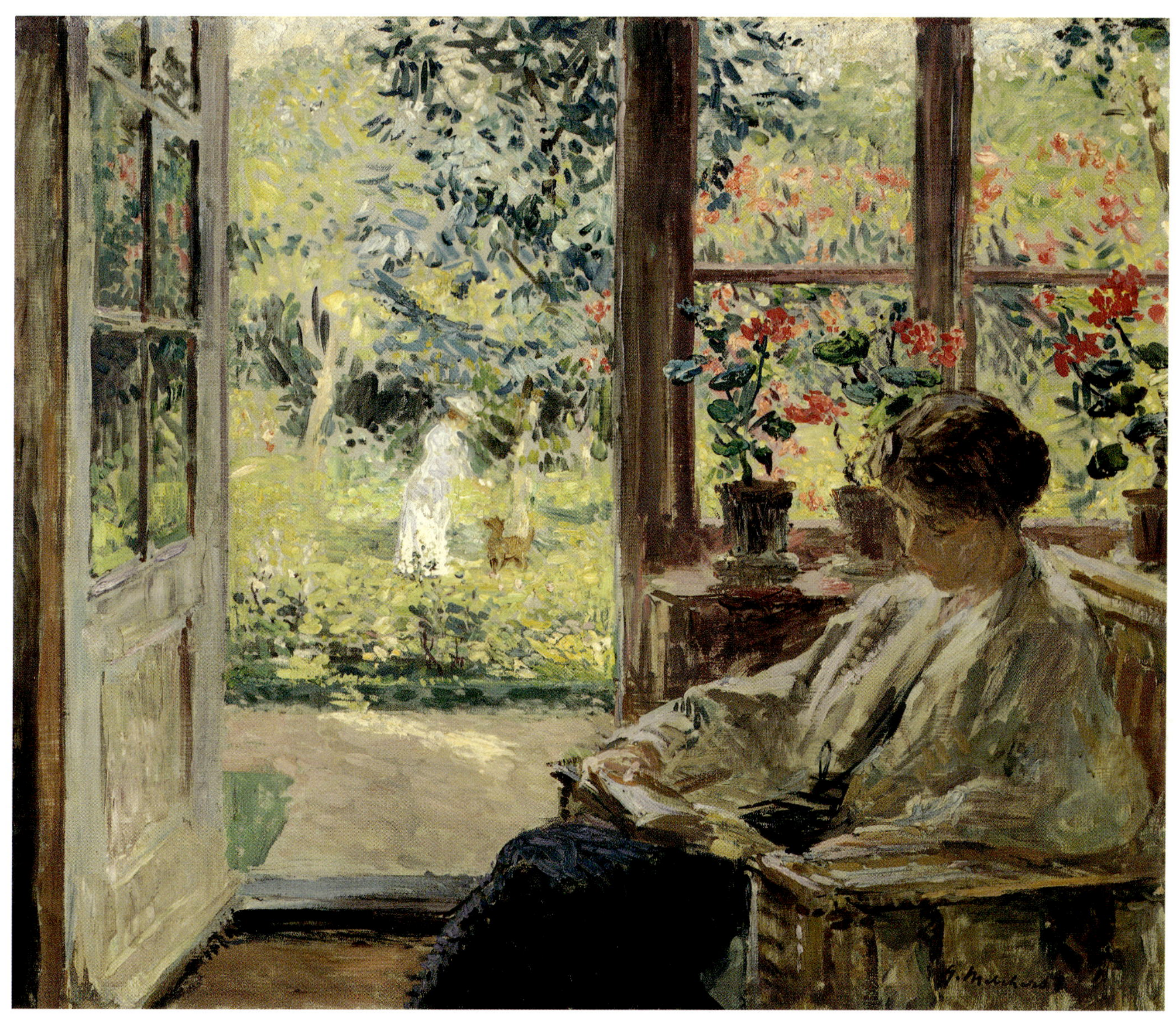

Charles Courtney Curran

1861–1942

Lavender and Old Lace, 1914

oil on canvas, 18 1/8 × 22 inches
Museum purchase with funds from the 1993 Museum Antiques Show, Elliott, Davis & Company, CPAs, sponsor; Corporate Benefactors: Alice Manufacturing Company, Inc.; Barker Air and Hydraulics, Inc.; BB&T; Carolina First Bank; The First Union Foundation; Greenville News–Piedmont Company; Hartness International; Insignia Financial Group, Inc.; KEMET Corporation; Liberty Life Insurance; Michelin North America; Odell Associates, Inc.; Pepsi-Cola Bottling Company of Greenville; Portman Marina, Inc.; Provence Printing, Inc.; Suitt Construction Company; Thoracic and Cardiovascular Associates

Once established, American Impressionism was adapted to a variety of subjects. Landscape, intrinsically associated with the American ethos, maintained its popularity, and, in the hands of the Impressionists, views of intimate gardens and sunlit shorelines proliferated. Many aspiring American painters gravitated to Giverny, outside Paris, where the French master Claude Monet and his carefully cultivated gardens were sources of inspiration. The city also became a subject of interest for the Impressionists, especially Childe Hassam, whose ebullient streetscapes captured the vitality of the urban scene. Another favorite setting was the cozy interior. In sitting rooms and parlors, one or two women, often members of the artist's family, sat reading, sewing, or musing. Arranged for beauty and harmony, the women, who are rarely mentioned by name in the title of the work, are merely decorative entities akin to James McNeill Whistler's portrayal of his mother in *Arrangement: Gray and Black*.[1]

The first major United States exhibition of French Impressionist works took place in Boston in 1883; the city emerged as a center of Impressionist activity, and painters working there had a penchant for domestic scenes. When the group known as The Ten assembled in late 1897, half were artists with ties to Boston. A loosely knit clique of established painters, The Ten shared a dissatisfaction with the limited exhibition opportunities available to them. The key founding members of the group were Hassam, J. Alden Weir, John Twachtman, Frank Benson, and Edmund Tarbell. Benson and Tarbell, both faculty members of the School of the Museum of Fine Arts, Boston, devoted numerous canvases to the depiction of women.

Another American artist, Charles Curran, painted imagery similar to that of Benson and Tarbell. All three shared a similar educational experience in Paris, where they studied under Jules Lefebvre at the Académie Julian. Curran, a native of Hartford, Kentucky, attended the Cincinnati School of Design and the Art Students League, before he left for Paris in 1889. Upon his return he settled in New York, where he taught at the Pratt Institute and the Art Students League. Beginning in 1903 he became a pivotal figure in the art colony at Cragsmoor, New York, where he maintained a summer studio. It was Curran who introduced Helen Turner to the rural beauty and quiet of Cragsmoor.

Curran's favorite subjects were affluent women engaged in a variety of genteel activities. He frequently painted them in gardens, surrounded by flowers. Interpreted both as an affirmation of the ornamental and passive position of women and as an attempt to keep women in their place as the suffrage movement gained momentum, these works portray women as symbols of beauty and fertility.[2] However, Curran in his late work, like Benson, also painted vigorous women standing on windy bluffs, their postures evoking their strength and reflecting their growing independence. Curran, who like Benson and Tarbell taught many women students, may have begun to recognize the emerging role of women in the art world as well as their contribution to his livelihood.

Nonetheless, the woman in *Lavender and Old Lace* is painted as a beautiful, decorative object. As she fingers her old, but still beautiful, lace, she may be contemplating the fragility of youth and beauty. Unlike similar works by Benson or Tarbell in which the woman industriously sews, Curran's figure carefully weighs her finery. In this respect and in its cool serenity, the painting is reminiscent of the works of Jan Vermeer, the seventeenth-century Dutch master who painted at least one intimate scene where a woman is shown weighing gold. Vermeer's paintings, which had been ignored for almost two centuries, had been rediscovered in the 1860s, and their influence on interior paintings was potent. In the Museum's painting, the strong light and the highlighting of such objects as the chair and the vessel behind the woman also refer to Vermeer. The placement of the figure at a slightly awkward angle against a dark, ambiguous background adds to the immediacy of the work and may reflect the impact of photography on Curran's work.

The title, *Lavender and Old Lace,* which was given by the artist, at first appears to be purely descriptive: the scene is bathed in a deep lavender light, and the sitter holds lace.[3] However, there may be a deeper, underlying meaning: lavender is a plant well known for its perfume, but it is also believed to have preservative properties. It was commonly used when lace and linen were put away. Lace, in turn, may also have the added meaning of a net, an object designed to ensnare. As the unidentified woman contemplates her lace she may be wondering how to preserve her own beauty, or she may be devising ways to entrap a member of the opposite sex.

---

1. Bailey Van Hook, "Decorative Images of American Women: The Aristocratic Aesthetic of the Late Nineteenth Century," *Smithsonian Studies in American Art* 4, no. 1 (Winter 1990): 51–52.

2. Annette Stott, "Floral Femininity: A Pictorial Definition," *Smithsonian Studies in American Art* 6, no. 2 (Spring 1992): 60–77.

3. A small photograph of the painting is inscribed on the reverse by the artist: "This is to certify that this is a photograph of my painting entitled *Lavender and Old Lace.* Charles C. Curran. July 20, 1920." Archives, Greenville County Museum of Art.

Born, Hartford, Kentucky, 1861; studied at the Cincinnati School of Design and in New York at the Art Students League; studied at the Académie Julian, Paris, 1889–1891; returned to New York; taught at the Pratt Institute and the Art Students League; died, New York, 1942.

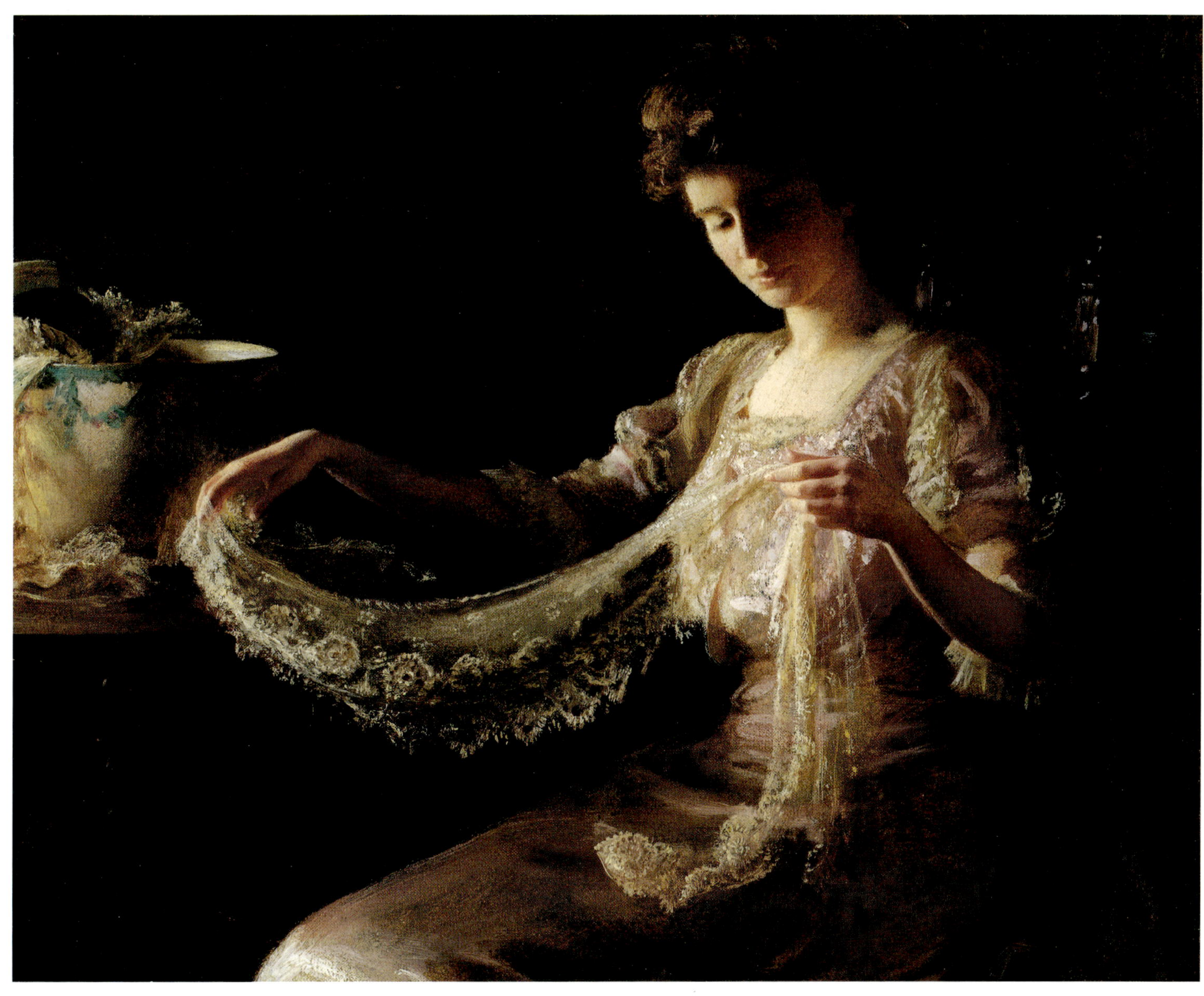

Anna Catherine Wiley

1879–1958

A Sunlit Afternoon, circa 1915

oil on canvas, 36 × 40 inches
Purchased with funds donated by Dorothy Hipp Gunter (Mrs. C. Guy Gunter)

Although Impressionism ultimately achieved widespread critical success in the early 1900s, its commercial appeal was still limited, and many American Impressionists supplemented their income by painting portraits. Of the artists working at the end of the century William Merritt Chase, James McNeill Whistler, and John Singer Sargent were the most successful and popular portraitists. Chase, who worked in New York, along with Edmund Tarbell and Frank Benson, in Boston, earned additional income as teachers at two of the country's most respected art schools, the Art Students League and the School of the Museum of Fine Arts, Boston.

By the turn of the century the number of aspiring women artists had greatly increased, and these artists often had a difficult time supporting themselves. Many became teachers, not in the prestigious art schools but in art programs at liberal arts colleges and state universities. Catherine Wiley, who studied for two years at the Art Students League, returned to her alma mater, the University of Tennessee, as an Instructor in Art in the School of Home Economics.

As a student Wiley pursued an early interest in illustration, and even took a course taught by Howard Pyle, one of the key figures in American illustration. At the University of Tennessee Wiley often produced drawings for various publications and annuals. These black-and-white images were usually stylized renderings of women in which line and pattern are emphasized. They resemble the then-popular fashion of Art Nouveau design, where sinuous curves predominate.

In sharp contrast to her illustration work, Wiley's painting style reflects the popularity of Impressionism. Although her subjects continue to be women, the figures are moved to outdoor settings, where the sunlight creates a dappled effect on their hair, faces, and clothing. Her decision to position her figures in natural settings may have been the result of Wiley's study with Robert Reid during the summer of 1912 at Cos Cob, Connecticut. His curriculum emphasized figures *en plein air,* and the surrounding countryside provided abundant picturesque scenery. Reid was one of the founding members of The Ten, the group of American artists who exhibited Impressionist canvases together for twenty years.

A Sunlit Afternoon relates to Reid's and Benson's paintings of wholesome women as active subjects in the outdoors. A lively and engaging depiction of a woman with three young girls, the painting is compositionally connected by a fluid rhythm that is sustained across the canvas. The most captivating aspect of the Museum's painting, however, is the sunlight: it falls on the girls' backs, casting their faces in shadow and bathing the central, largest figure in glowing color. The painting is further enhanced by a bold impasto, truly a loaded brush, which at times uses shorthand to lend the impression of a hand, a foot, or a tree. In her use of such ample pigment, especially toward the bottom of the canvas, Wiley transcended even the most painterly of her Impressionist counterparts.

As an extension of her teaching responsibilities Wiley published lectures on modern painting. Obviously well informed, she peppered her lectures with quotes by scholars, philosophers, and artists from throughout the history of art. Her comments also reveal her own artistic preferences: "The exhibitions of today are as though flooded with atmosphere—landscapes of vibrating sunlight; . . . [paintings] in which the light of day has crept in, silvering the tops of trees, lighting women's gowns, touching and revivifying all." Acknowledging the significance of Impressionism, she also questions, rather prophetically, where it will lead and "whether it shall develop a type of abstract art, in which the arrangement of the spots and dashes of color will afford aesthetic pleasure without any ulterior meaning to the picture."[1]

---

1. Wiley, "Lecture XVIII: II—The Mind in Art; Modern Painting," *Woman's Athenaeum* 10 (1912): 178 and 179.

Born, Coal Creek, now Lake City, Tennessee, 1879; studied at the University of Tennessee, 1895–1897, and at the Art Students League, New York, 1903–1905; Instructor in Art, School of Home Economics at the University of Tennessee, Knoxville, 1905–1918; summer study with Martha Walter and Robert Reid, Cos Cob, Connecticut, 1912; hospitalized in a Philadelphia mental institution, 1926–1958; died, Philadelphia, 1958.

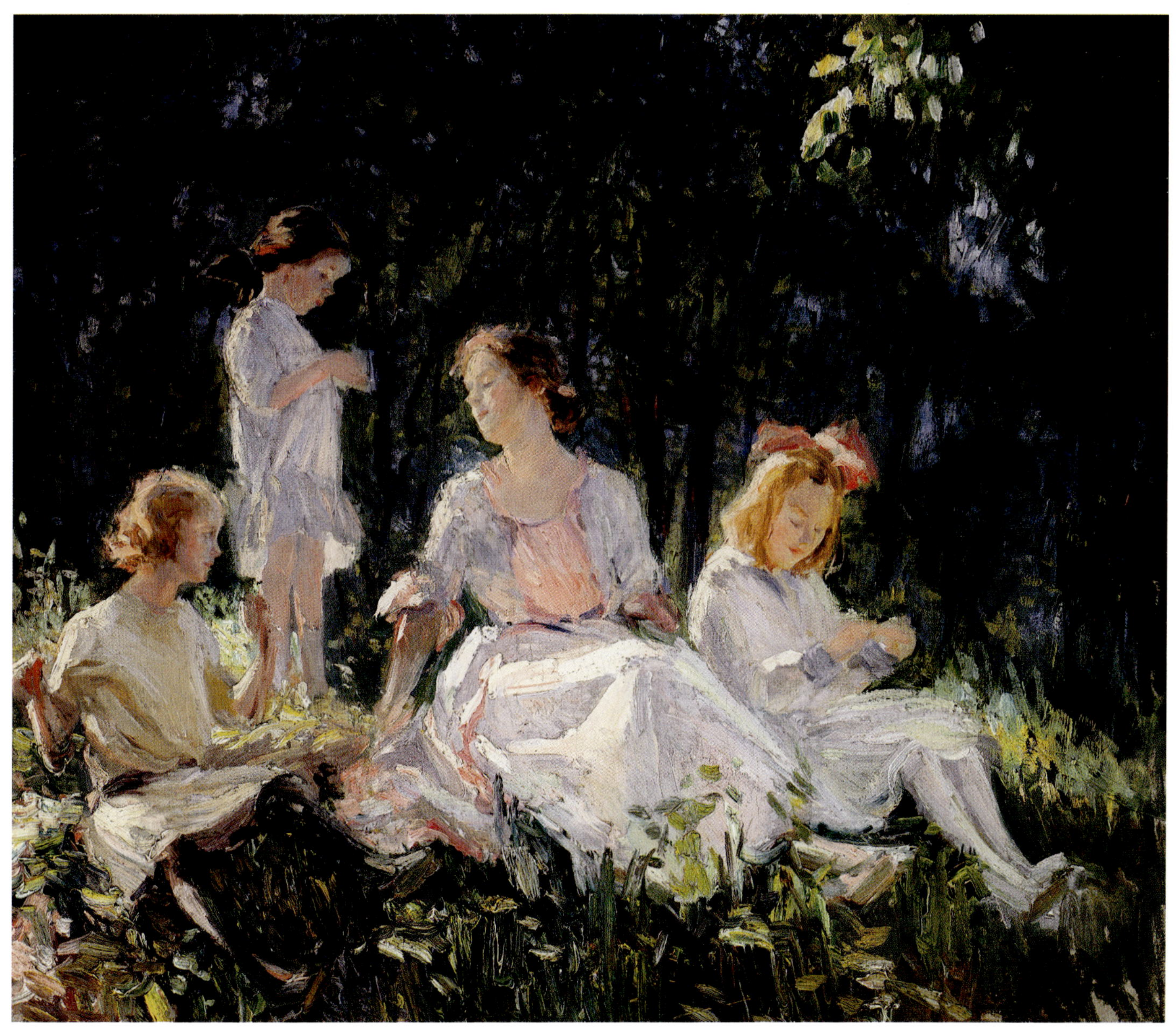

William Partridge

1858–1938

Garden Flowers, 1927

oil on canvas, 25 × 30 inches
signed, lower right: *W. H. Partridge / 1927*
Museum purchase with funds donated by the Arthur and Holly Magill Foundation

The history of art primarily records major shifts in style. Occasionally this emphasis on the avant-garde does a serious disservice to artists who continue working in a conservative mode that is still viable, although no longer innovative.

One such painter was William H. Partridge, whose *Garden Flowers* exemplifies a manner of painting made popular a generation earlier. The conservative nature of this work may be best explained by an examination of Partridge, his artistic community, and his primary occupation. The artist spent his early childhood in his birthplace of Wheeling, West Virginia, before moving to the Boston area. He studied at the School of the Museum of Fine Arts, Boston, but never devoted himself full-time to painting.

Partridge's father owned several commercial photography studios, and Partridge and two brothers continued in the same field. The family was known for their innovative use of photographic technology. Partridge and his brother Edward went to Portland, Oregon, in the 1880s, where they did both portrait and landscape work. Mirroring the Western paintings of Albert Bierstadt and the dramatic photographs of William Henry Jackson, Partridge spent the summer of 1886 in Alaska. He used the newly available dry-plate technique which allowed greater flexibility; plates could be exposed, then stored, to be developed in a studio rather than on site. Returning to Boston, Partridge operated several successful photography studios until his retirement in 1915. Technologically inventive, Partridge was also a shrewd businessman, as indicated by his advice to fellow photographers: "Anything new and novel in the line of photography is sure to be talked of by your patrons, and when backed by good, careful work, is the best possible advertisement for the maker."[1]

In his painting, however, Partridge was neither adventuresome nor concerned for commercial acclaim. Almost seventy when he painted *Garden Flowers,* Partridge reverted to his school days when Boston, with its new museum, busy network of galleries, and active collectors, was a lively center for the arts. The city had enthusiastically embraced Impressionism, to which Partridge's painting closely relates, and Boston patrons continued to prefer conservative paintings in that style, especially of interiors, well into the twentieth century. Not a traditional still life, *Garden Flowers* presents an array of luxuriant flowers depicted *en plein air* in full sunlight at close proximity. The near-at-hand placement of the flowers may relate to Partridge's work as a photographer but was also an approach popularized by the American Impressionists John Twatchman and Abbott Fuller Graves. Typical of Impressionism, Partridge's handling of paint is abundant and lush, not unlike the flowers themselves.

---

1. Partridge, "A Novelty for Cabinet Photographs," *Photographic Mosaics* (Philadelphia: Philadelphia Photographer, 1881), 144.

Born, Wheeling, Virginia (now West Virginia), 1858; studied painting at the School of the Museum of Fine Arts, Boston; photographer in Portland, Oregon, 1883–1885; summer in Alaska, 1886; returned to the Boston area, 1886; died, Wellesley Hills, Massachusetts, 1938.

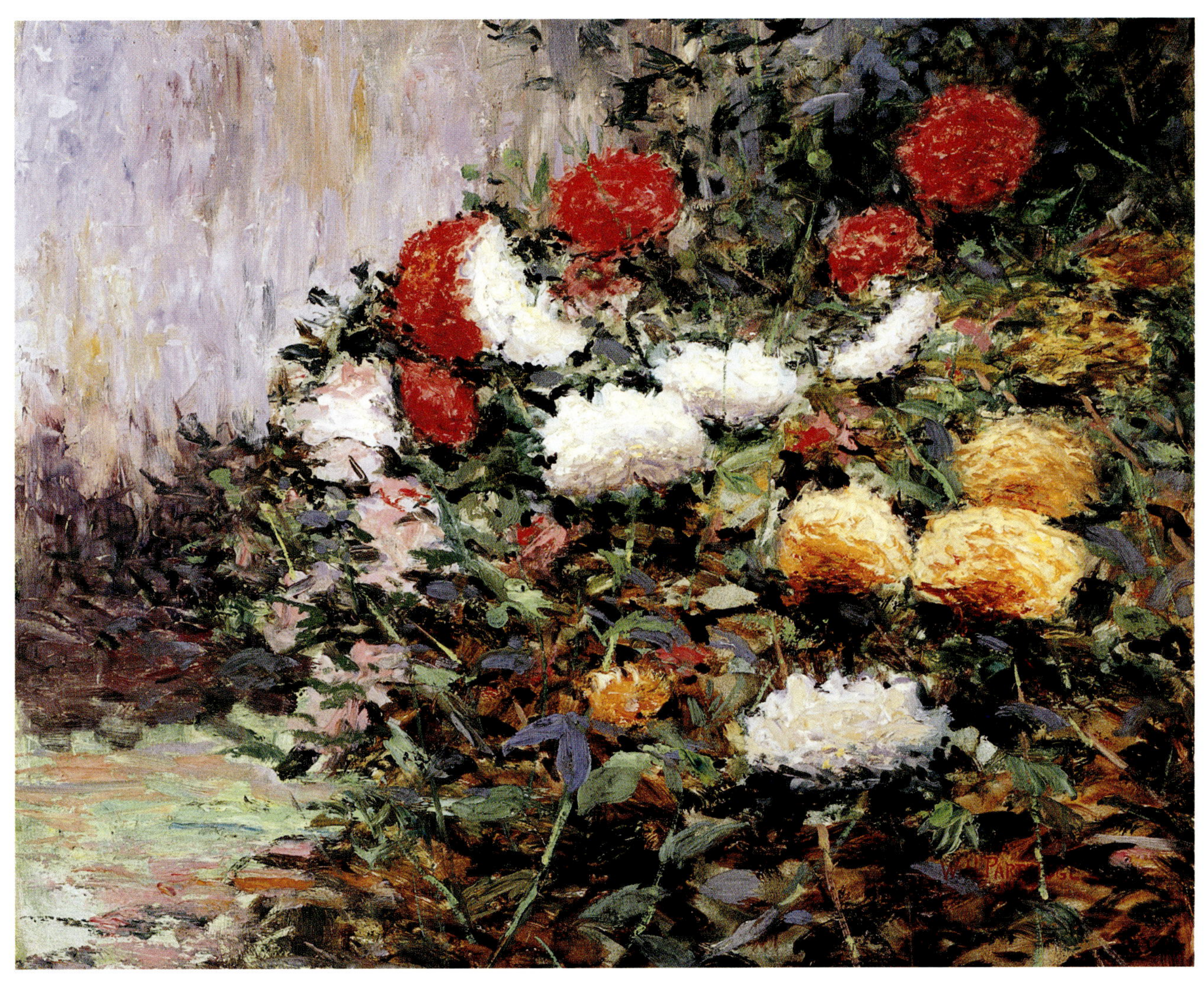

Jerome Myers

1867–1940

The End of the Walk, 1907

oil on canvas, 25 × 30 inches
signed, lower left: *Jerome Myers / N.Y. 1907*
Museum purchase with funds donated by The Museum Association, Inc., and (by exchange): Mrs. S. M. Beattie; Mrs. Robert S. Conahay III; Paul Doll; Ronald Green, Jr.; Mr. and Mrs. Maxine Hermanos; Sigmund Rothschild

The evolution of art is often accelerated by younger artists who rebel against the norms established by older generations. Emerging artists struggle to find exhibition opportunities that entrenched artists are unwilling to share. The group of artists known as The Eight was born out of rebellion; they strongly objected to the status quo, in particular to the juried exhibitions of the National Academy of Design. Robert Henri, an accomplished figure painter and influential teacher, was the acknowledged leader and spokesman for The Eight, which included John Sloan, Everett Shinn, and George Luks. The group, who initially exhibited together at the Macbeth Gallery in 1908, painted unsentimental, realistic images of everyday life, usually of the city and its residents. Sloan, Shinn, and Luks were former newspaper artists whose painting was a natural outgrowth of their journalistic work. The members of The Eight were hailed as the "apostles of ugliness," and later the term *Ash Can School* was used to describe these painters, who preferred somber back alleys to sunny boulevards.

In 1910 Henri and Sloan spearheaded the Independent Artists Exhibition. The response to this nonjuried, invitational exhibition was overwhelming: several hundred works were submitted and hung in alphabetical order; police were called to manage the crowds at the opening. A jubilant Henri proclaimed: "Freedom to think and to show what you are thinking about, that is what the exhibition stands for."[1] The stars of the exhibition were Henri and other members of The Eight, who were joined by two other notable realists: George Bellows and Jerome Myers. Their work, which emphasized dark, heavily painted figure groups, was sympathetic to the Ash Can ideal.

Perhaps because of the modest circumstances of his early years, Myers empathized with city dwellers and recent immigrants who frequently lived in poverty. Born in Petersburg, Virginia, Myers spent his childhood in Philadelphia, Baltimore, and finally New York. This great, thriving metropolis was to become his passion and the primary subject of his work. Performing odd jobs, as well as acting and doing stage sets, Myers began his formal art studies first at the Cooper Union Art School and then at the Art Students League, where he took classes for more than ten years. New York City itself, however, provided his real education: "Directly, I ventured out to interpret life for myself, to render the impression of the city and the people that I really cared for. With a pencil, at first timid and faltering, I adapted my line to what I saw. . . . In this instinctive way, I set myself in opposition to the authority that had governed my art instruction."[2] Myers, in fact, was so enamored with New York that his two trips to Paris left him unimpressed.

New York provided Myers with a broad range of images, including concerts in the park, ethnic street festivals, bustling markets, and solitary figures. The Museum's painting is unusually pessimistic for Myers, who said of it, "the picture signifies my reaction to sorrow, the sorrow of resignation." An early title for the painting was *Their Life.* The present title, *The End of the Walk,* may be intentionally ambiguous: it could either allude to an actual location, perhaps the end of a pier, or refer to a rest after physical exertion. The figures sit isolated from one another, each thoughtfully in his or her own world; even the children do not interact. The entire setting is shrouded in darkness and gloom, "the unrelieved sky is but a curtain for a few figures one sees dimly, as though they were outward bound."[3] Shadowy outlines of other figures appear to the right of the main group and are probably pentimenti, or changes made by the artist which have become more visible over time.

The painting was one of two oils, along with fifteen drawings, Myers exhibited in the pivotal Armory Show of 1913. Myers, one of four artists at the first gathering of the Association of American Painters and Sculptors, had been an active participant from the show's inception. The four discussed "organizing a society for the purpose of exhibiting the works of progressive and live painters, both American and foreign—favoring such work usually neglected by current shows and especially interesting and instructive to the public."[4] Myers, who served on the executive committee, proposed Bellows and three members of The Eight: Sloan, Shinn, and Maurice Prendergast, for inclusion in the exhibition. Although fully involved in the Association, even serving as chairman of the committee charged with the exhibition, Myers was not in complete sympathy with the European direction of the Armory Show; his initial hope had been for an exhibition that would promote modern American art. He viewed the Armory Show as a critical turning point: "Our land of opportunity was thrown wide open to foreign art, unrestricted and triumphant; more than ever before, our great country had become a colony; more than ever before we had become provincials."[5]

---

1. Robert Henri, "Insurgency in Art," *The Literary Digest* 40 (23 April 1910): 814, as quoted in Bennard B. Perlman, *The Immortal Eight: American Painting from Eakins to the Armory Show, 1870–1913* (Westport, Conn., 1979), 195.
2. Jerome Myers, *Artist in Manhattan* (New York: American Artists Group, 1940), 18.
3. Myers, *Artist in Manhattan,* 131.
4. Association minutes, 14 December 1911, as quoted in Milton W. Brown, *The Story of the Armory Show* (Greenwich, Conn.: New York Graphic Society, 1963), 30.
5. Myers, *Artist in Manhattan,* 36.

Born, Petersburg, Virginia, 1867; classes in New York at the Cooper Union Art School followed by ten years of classes at the Art Students League; traveled to Paris, 1896 and 1914; died, New York, 1940.

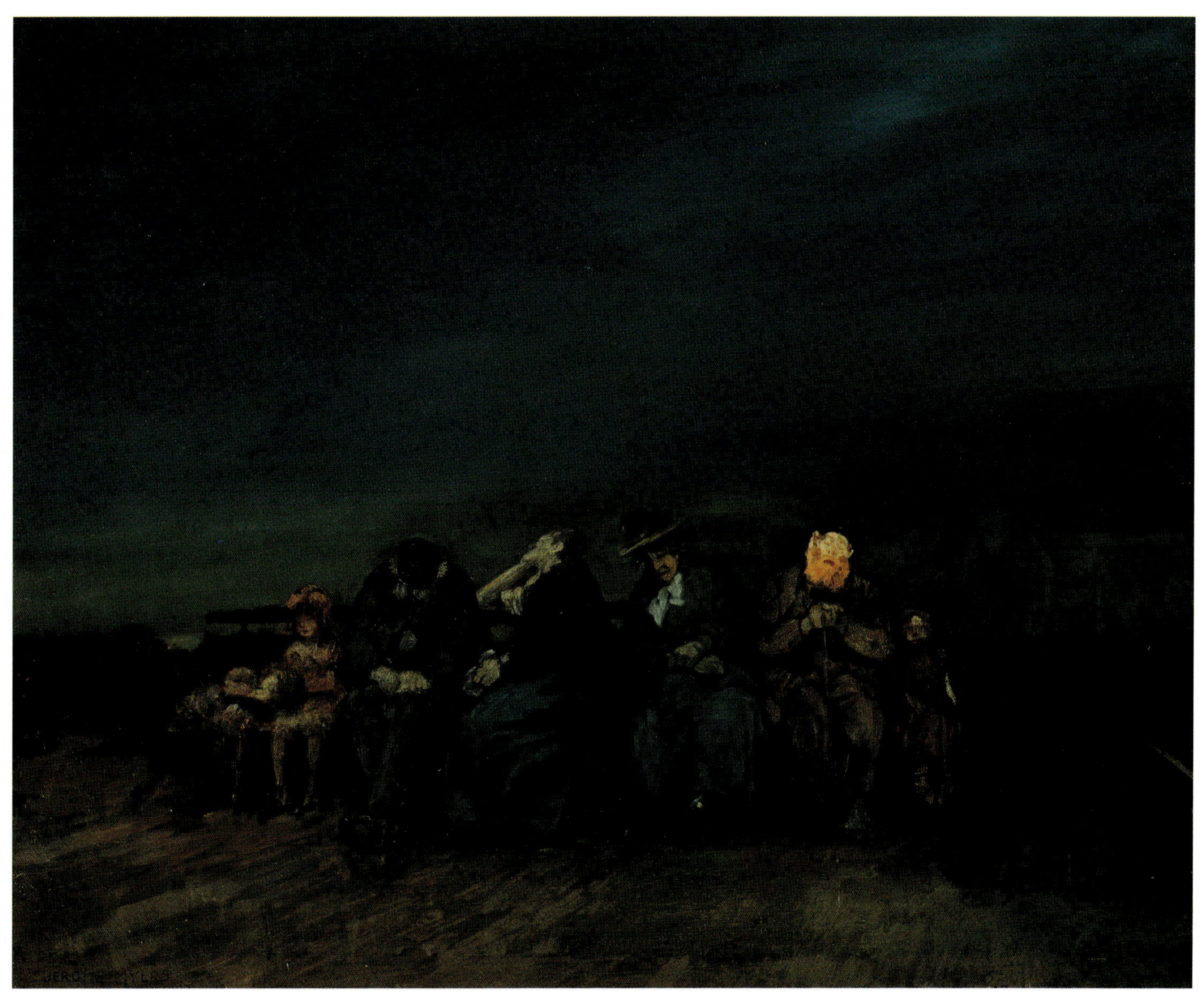

Max Weber

1881–1961

Meditation, 1910

charcoal and graphite on paper, 24½ × 17 inches
signed, lower right: *Max Weber 1910*
Museum purchase with funds donated by
The Museum Association, Inc.

Modernism, a collective term that embraces such diverse artistic movements as Post-Impressionism, Cubism, and Futurism, promoted an analytical approach to art. Instead of emphasizing the perception of nature as the Impressionists did with studies of light and color, the modernists stressed the formal elements underlying the work of art. In this country early modernism is associated both with Alfred Stieglitz and his vanguard gallery at 291 Fifth Avenue and with the Armory Show of 1913, which introduced modernism to large audiences in America. Significantly, works by European as well as American artists were exhibited at both places.

At this time large numbers of artists and patrons gravitated to Paris, the avowed international capital of modernism. Among them was Max Weber, who after studying at the Pratt Institute in New York and two years' teaching in Lynchburg, Virginia, went to Paris in the fall of 1905. There he saw the work of Paul Cézanne and Paul Gauguin, and he met Henri Matisse, Pablo Picasso, and Henri Rousseau, with whom he developed a close friendship. He encountered other American painters there as well, including John Marin and Patrick Henry Bruce. The informal soirée hosted by a collector replaced the academies and the salons as the place for artists to meet patrons and one another. The gatherings organized by the members of the Stein family, themselves collectors of Matisse and Picasso, were among the most popular, and Weber was often present at these intellectually stimulating events.

Weber's Parisian sojourn shaped his artistic vision. In addition to conventional study at both the Académie Julian and the Académie Colarossi, Weber benefited from the numerous exhibitions mounted at the Petit Palais, at independent salons, and at commercial galleries. He also frequented the Louvre and the ethnographic collections of other museums, where he studied African and Oceanic objects. In addition, he helped to organize a class conducted by Matisse in which Bruce also participated. Weber recalled: "Matisse's criticism was generous and very searching, at times very severe and admonishing, but always constructive, enlightening, and sympathetic. His warm interest in our technical problems and difficulties gave us confidence and courage."[1]

Meditation, done after Weber's return to New York, is reflective of Matisse's tutelage. Although lacking color, one of the hallmarks of Matisse's painting, the drawing retains a strong linear emphasis akin to the sinuous curves associated with the French master. Using the female nude in a nontraditional pose, *Meditation* is an analysis of form rather than the study of musculature or movement. The many sources of modernism are also evident in the drawing. In addition to the bold line of Matisse, the compressed positioning of the cropped figure recalls Cézanne's spatial explorations, and the masklike face is reminiscent of Picasso's interest in African sculpture.

Once settled in New York, Weber turned more toward Cubism, the movement pioneered by Picasso and Georges Braque. After analyzing the component parts of an object from multiple viewpoints, the Cubists often rendered the fragmented forms as a series of interpenetrating planes. Struck by the dynamism of New York, Weber began to convey his response through Cubist images of the cityscape. He developed a short-lived relationship with Stieglitz, whose photographs of the New York skyline from numerous perspectives may have influenced Weber. He was included in Stieglitz's famed 1910 exhibition, *Younger American Painters,* but he and Stieglitz later parted after disagreeing about the prices of his works.[2]

Viewed as an artist ahead of his time, Weber was not only one of the first Americans to espouse Cubism, but he was also a theorist. To support himself he wrote for Stieglitz's *Camera Work,* which published his poetry and his treatise, "The Fourth Dimension from a Plastic Point of View." Weber's manifesto sheds light on one of the underlying concepts of Cubism. For him the fourth dimension "is real, and can be perceived and felt. It exists outside and in the presence of objects, and is the space that envelops a tree, a tower, a mountain, or any solid, or the intervals between objects or volumes of matter if receptively beheld."[3]

---

1. Weber, The Museum of Modern Art, Symposium on Matisse, 1951. Courtesy of Forum Gallery, New York.

2. See Percy North, "Turmoil at 291," *Archives of American Art Journal* 24, no. 1 (1984): 12–20.

3. Weber, "The Fourth Dimension from a Plastic Point of View," *Camera Work,* no. 31 (July 1910), as quoted in Percy North and Susan Krane, *Max Weber: The Cubist Decade, 1910–1920* (Atlanta, Ga.: High Museum of Art, 1991), 97.

Born in Bialystok, Russia (now Poland), 1881; immigrated to the United States and settled in Brooklyn, 1891; studied at the Pratt Institute with Arthur Wesley Dow, 1897–1900; taught construction drawing and manual training in Lynchburg, Virginia, 1901–1903; taught at State Teachers College in Duluth, Minnesota, 1903–1905; studied in Paris at the academies Julian, Colarossi, and de la Grand Chaumière, and with Matisse, 1905–1909; trips to Spain and Italy; returned to New York, taught at the Clarence White School of Photography, 1914–1918, and the Art Students League, 1920–1921 and 1926; died, New York, 1961.

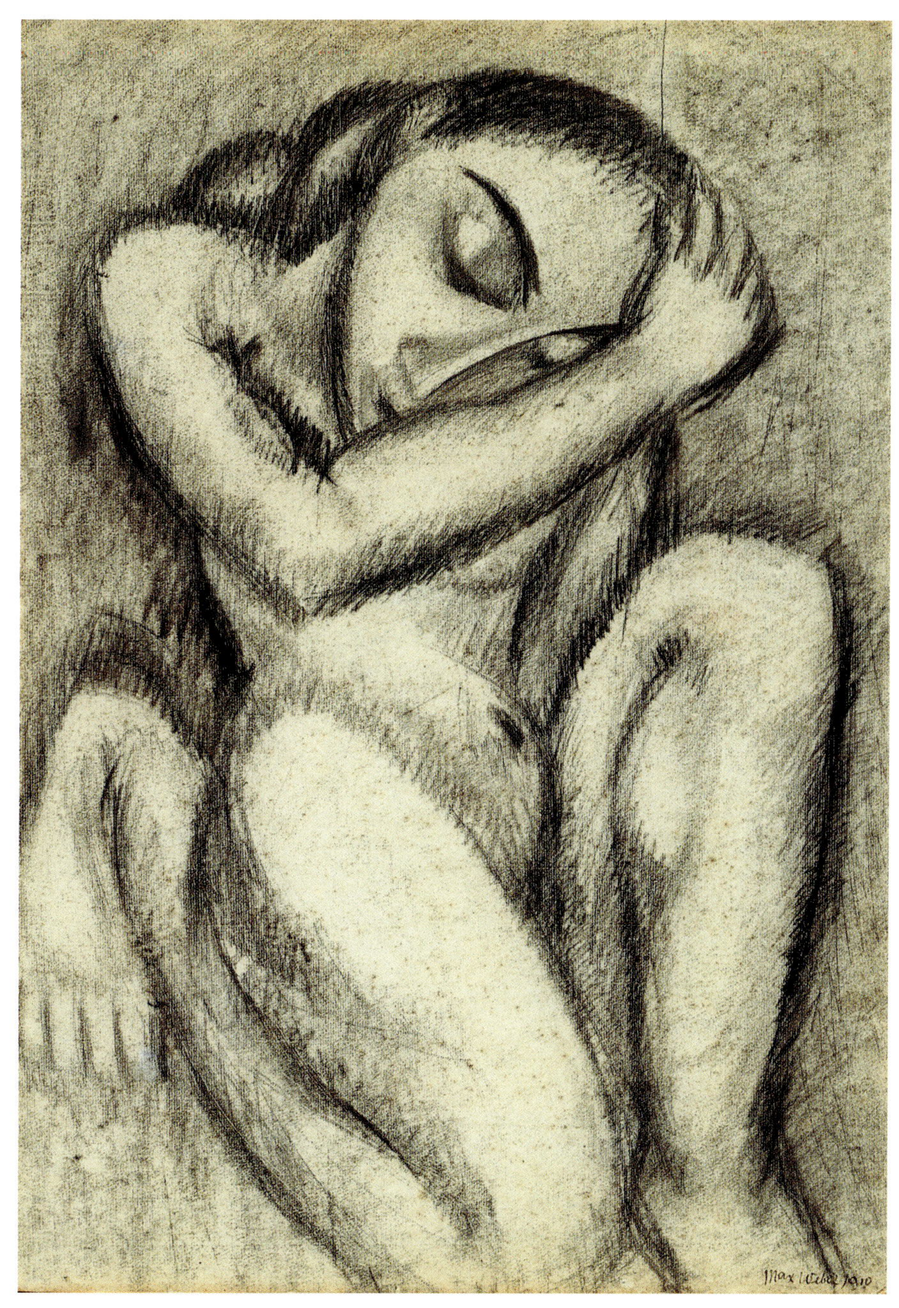
Max Weber 1910

Patrick Henry Bruce

1881–1936

Still Life (with Dish of Fruit), 1911

oil on canvas, 12½ × 16 inches
signed, lower right: *Bruce*
Museum purchase with funds donated by the Arthur and Holly Magill Foundation

The Armory Show of 1913 was a watershed event in the history of American art. Its proper name was the International Exhibition of Modern Art, organized by the Association of American Painters and Sculptors; its simpler designation evolved naturally from its location in New York's Sixty-ninth Regiment Armory. A massive undertaking, the Armory Show exhibited more than 1,300 paintings, sculptures, prints, and drawings gathered from a variety of sources here and abroad. Artists, dealers, and collectors lent works that ranged from conventional and historical examples by Eugène Delacroix and Gustave Courbet to avant-garde works by Paul Cézanne, Henri Matisse, and Pablo Picasso. Odilon Redon, whose individualistic and Symbolist images were virtually unknown in this country, was represented by the largest selection. The single most controversial work was Marcel Duchamp's *Nude Descending the Staircase.* Alongside these European works many of the American examples seemed traditional and tame by comparison. The caustic and sensational coverage by the press resulted in remarkable crowds and, in a few instances, some purchases.

The primary organizers of this pivotal endeavor were the artists Arthur B. Davies and Walt Kuhn, and the critic Walter Pach. Although they worked with a governing board and a variety of committees, their personal tastes shaped the exhibition. Their goal was to introduce modern European art to American audiences, and many American artists, including Jerome Myers, felt slighted and overshadowed, having hoped American art would be promoted. Max Weber, who was offended that only two of his works had been accepted, refused to participate. Other controversies included Robert Delaunay's insistence that his works be removed from the exhibition because Davies had neglected to hang his newly completed monumental canvas, *City of Paris.* Sympathizing with Delaunay, Patrick Henry Bruce requested that his paintings also be withdrawn, but the organizers did not acquiesce.

A close friend of Delaunay and other French artists, Bruce was an expatriate who lived in Paris most of his career. Born on a Virginia plantation, Bruce took evening classes at the Art Club of Richmond. He also received instruction in mechanical drawing and drafting, training that would be reflected in his late work. In 1902 he went to New York, where he studied with William Merritt Chase, Robert Henri, and Kenneth Hayes Miller. In his proclivity for still-life compositions Bruce was following Chase's example, but his real mentor was Henri. By late 1903 or early 1904 Bruce was in Paris, where he met American and French artists as well as the collectors Gertrude and Leo Stein and where, with Weber, he helped to organize the Matisse School. Bruce, who remained in France until 1936, did not even see the Armory Show, which exhibited four of his canvases.

Bruce's immersion in modernist European art was complete and is exemplified by the Museum's *Still Life (with Dish of Fruit),* which was in the Armory Show. Bruce's study with Matisse is evident in the bright palette, but the strongest influence on Bruce's work was Cézanne, whose reputation was at its apogee following his death in 1906. Cézanne's accomplishments were celebrated in a major retrospective at the Salon d'Automne in 1907. Unlike Matisse whose passion was color, Cézanne's interests were structure and perception. In several series he systematically examined the same objects again and again. Similarly, Bruce, in a lifelong series of still-life paintings, investigated the shapes and volumes of fruits, plates, and tabletops and their interrelationships.

Still Life (with Dish of Fruit) is reminiscent of Cézanne's work in many ways. In addition to the simple subject matter, the clustered arrangement of the fruit and the tilted tabletop are devices found in the French master's work. By bringing the triangular point of the table to the front plane of the picture Bruce also emulated Cézanne's tendency to pull objects forward, thus flattening the composition. The manner in which the canvas is painted, with short, choppy brushstrokes and with primed, unpainted canvas showing, also resembles works by Cézanne.

The influence of Cézanne was strongest in Bruce's early Parisian work. His midcareer was characterized by abstract and dynamically colorful compositions that relate to Delaunay's Orphic Cubism. At the end of World War I Bruce returned to his beloved still lifes, which become more geometric and pure. Many of the shapes resemble furniture moldings and other furniture components, perhaps because Bruce supported himself by repairing and selling antiques.

Born, either at Long Island, in Campbell County, Virginia, or near South Boston, Halifax County, Virginia, 1881; instruction at the Art Club of Richmond, 1898–1902, and at the Virginia Mechanics Institute, 1900–1901; studied at the New York School of Art with William Merritt Chase, Robert Henri, and Kenneth Hayes Miller, 1902–1903; early 1903 or late 1904 to Paris, permanently until 1936, except for trip to New York, 1905; studied with Henri Matisse, 1908–1909; returned to New York, 1936; died, New York, 1936.

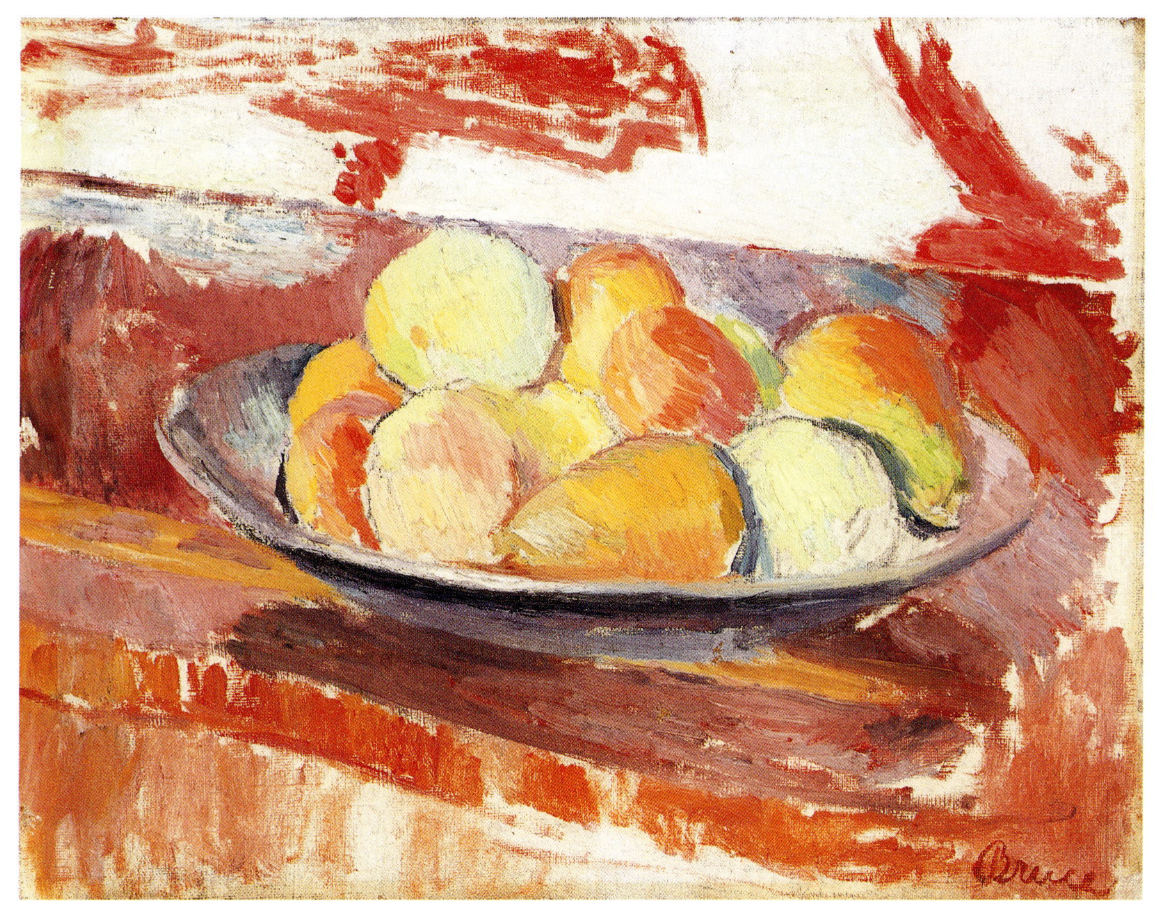
Bruce

Henry Lee McFee

1886–1953

Still Life, circa 1916

oil on canvas, 20⅛ × 16¼ inches
signed, lower right: *McFee*
Museum purchase with funds donated by the First Union Bank and The Museum Association, Inc.

With the advent of modernism, still-life painting was transformed into the ideal vehicle for the analysis of form and structure. Except for *vanitas* examples that included skulls and half-eaten fruit as symbols of the transience of life, most early still-life paintings were done chiefly for the visual pleasure they offered. Although a painter might include any object lying about the studio, fruit and flowers were favored not only for their appealing colors and sensuous qualities but also for their ready availability. Lacking both the transitory effects of landscape and the emotional involvement of portraits and figure studies, still-life compositions permitted repeated and extended study. Working in series similar in process to Claude Monet's grainstacks and water lilies, Paul Cézanne alternated between a landscape subject, Mont Sainte-Victoire, and tables laden with apples and other items. Cézanne's systematic study of form and volume along with his analysis of space were fundamental to the evolution of Cubism. For Pablo Picasso and Georges Braque, credited with the invention of Cubism, the still life, often composed of a tabletop littered with newspapers and a bottle of wine, was a major theme for their visual investigations.

American modernist painters, following the example of Cézanne, Picasso, and Braque, also turned to still life as a viable subject. Patrick Henry Bruce and Henry Lee McFee made still-life painting their specialty. Their work was rooted in that of Cézanne and the Cubists, but whereas Bruce, in his mature work, developed colorful, mechanistic arrays of familiar shapes, McFee moved in the direction of a strictly controlled realism.

After receiving some formal training in his native St. Louis at the School of Fine Arts, McFee intended to study in New York. He was diverted, however, by summer classes conducted by the Art Students League in Woodstock, New York. When McFee finally went abroad in 1921, he made a pilgrimage to Arles, the home of Cézanne in the south of France. He returned to Woodstock in the late 1920s and spent his winters at Bellevue Plantation in Bedford County, Virginia.

McFee recounted his rather methodical procedure for a still life: "For the set-ups, I gather on a studio table things that will make an interesting group to paint. Being careful not to get too much illumination on the table, I adjust the curtains. . . . I arrange and rearrange objects and draperies, always endeavoring to find the organic rhythm that will give me a lead into the endlessly complicated thrusts and pulls of the organization. . . . I plan the canvas well and proceed little by little to build it up."[1]

The Museum's *Still Life* exemplifies McFee's systematic approach to his compositions. In its retention of recognizable objects the painting is more akin to Cézanne than to Cubism. Of this painting McFee stated: "I am endeavoring, by analysis, to find the essential planes of the emotional form of my motifs, and to realize these planes by right placing of color and line, and by such a just relation of shape to shape, that the canvas will be, when completed, not a representation of many objects interesting in themselves, but a plastic unit expressive of my understanding of the form-life of the collection of objects."[2]

Still Life was included in the noteworthy 1916 Forum exhibition, an attempt to redress some of the criticism leveled at the Armory Show. Although the Armory Show showcased almost twice as many American works as European, public and press attention largely focused on the more sensational and controversial European examples. Numbering almost two hundred works, the Forum exhibition, according to the catalogue's preface, sought "to put before the American public in a large and complete manner the very best examples of the more modern American art; to stimulate interest in the really good native work of this movement; . . . to turn public attention for the moment from European art and concentrate it on the excellent work being done in America."[3] At a time when Europe was embroiled in war, this call for American art coincided with emergent nationalist tendencies, yet, ironically, modernist American art was highly dependent on European prototypes.

McFee continued painting still lifes for the remainder of his life, claiming, "still life I have always with me."[4] His style changed from his Cézanne- and Cubist-oriented work to more concrete representations. For these works he has been called a Formalist-Realist, a term coined to suggest continuity with, not opposition to, the abstracting, formalist inclinations of his earlier work. The rekindled interest in realism was not restricted to McFee or even to America, and by the 1930s realism would again become the dominant style.

---

1. McFee, as quoted in Ernest W. Watson, "Still Life Paintings by Henry Lee McFee," *American Artist*, February 1948, 21.
2. McFee, in the catalogue *The Forum Exhibition of Modern Painters* (1916; reprint, New York: Arno Press, 1968), unpaginated.
3. *Forum Exhibition*, 5.
4. McFee, as quoted in Watson, "Still Life Paintings," 20.

Born, St. Louis, Missouri, 1886; attended the School of Fine Arts, St. Louis, before 1907; attended Stevenson Art School, Pittsburgh, 1907–1908; summer program of the Art Students League, Woodstock, New York, 1909; resided in Woodstock, with winters spent in Virginia from the late 1920s to about 1936; to France, 1921; New Mexico, 1926; taught in San Antonio, 1937–1940, with summer teaching in Savannah, Georgia, 1939; moved to Los Angeles area, 1940; taught at Scripps College, Claremont, California, 1943–1953; died, Altadena, California, 1953.

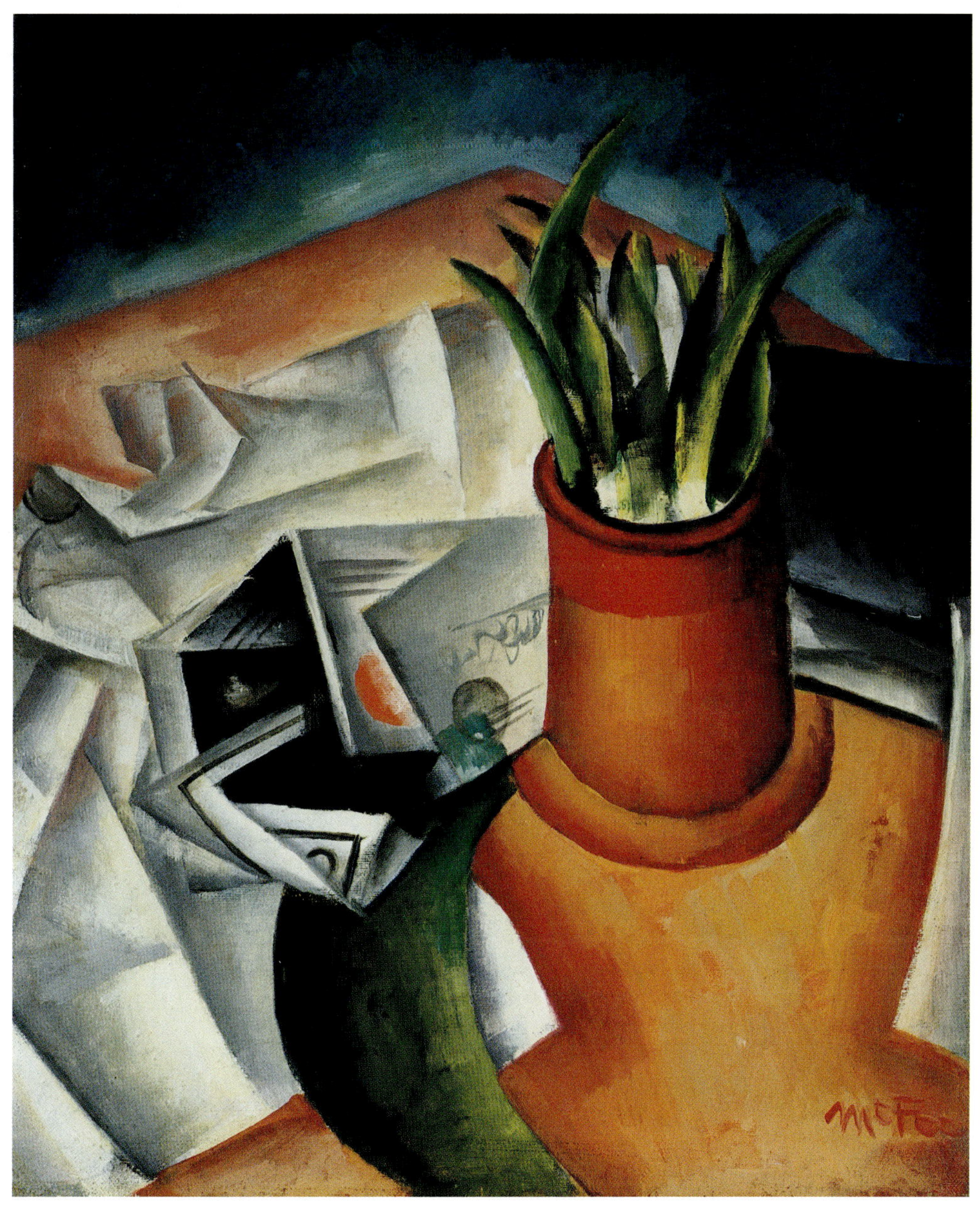

John Bernhard Alberts

1886–1931

War, 1917

oil on canvas, 35½ × 53¼ inches
signed, lower right: *J. B. Alberts –17*
Museum purchase with funds donated by the Arthur and Holly Magill Foundation

During the Civil War such artists as John Ross Key and William Aiken Walker provided important logistical support to the Confederates through their maps and drawings of fortifications. Other artists supplied firsthand accounts of the action both behind the lines and at the front. Later, during World War I, camouflage was developed as a military strategy, and painters assisted in the disguise of ships, airplanes, and tanks. Charles Burchfield, for example, was assigned to a camouflage unit at Fort Jackson, South Carolina, during his short stint in the army. Not all artists, however, so willingly contributed to military efforts; many, including George Bellows, objected to the atrocities committed in wartime.

Somewhat contradictory in nature was John Bernhard Alberts, who volunteered for duty, yet his painting in the Museum's collection reflects a strong antiwar sentiment. A native of Louisville, Kentucky, Alberts enlisted for service in World War I, hoping to join a camouflage unit. Instead, he was assigned to a hospital, where his task was scientific drawing. Like thousands of other soldiers he underwent the required series of preventive inoculations, but before the war's end, Alberts was stricken with a muscular disorder that left him bedridden. The actual diagnosis for his disability was multiple sclerosis, which his obituary attributed to a "rare infection laid to serum injections while in the service."[1]

Alberts studied with distinguished artists, including Frank Duveneck at the Cincinnati Art Academy and Frank Benson and Edmund C. Tarbell at the School of the Museum of Fine Arts, Boston. He traveled to Europe in 1913 but returned to Louisville to work in stained glass and painting. His accomplishments were described in the newspaper: "Mr. Alberts was preeminently a painter of decorative allegories. He had the happy facility of seeing the fairies in the bending bough of the pine and the fairy queen's throne in the dew-pearled center of the early morning spider web. While the clean imagery of the fictitious was his lodestone, he also devoted much time to painting portraits."[2] His portraits of Louisville's elite were painted in the manner of Duveneck and presumably were the cornerstone of his livelihood.

The Museum's painting, *War,* painted in 1917, is Alberts's magnum opus. A biting allegory about the treachery of war, the painting is reminiscent of both Renaissance Revival murals and the work of the Symbolist painter Elihu Vedder. The three key elements of the painting are arranged simply across the front plane: an attentive young boy; a tormented, naked woman; and a menacing bird. Filled with clouds, the background may refer to the explosion of a bomb. The visual intensity of the painting is compounded by both the blood red tonalities that pervade the canvas and the insistently stippled or dotted brushstroke that recalls the technique of the French Pointillists. Its mood is further heightened by contrasting emotions: the boy appears captivated and eager as his gaze meets that of the bird. Although the woman's face is almost completely hidden, her anguish is evident in the way her hands tear at her hair.

The bird, beckoning toward the innocent youth, has a dual personality. In reality, Alberts has represented the Egyptian vulture that swarmed the battlefields of Europe during World War I. Emblematically, with its large size and bald head, the bird resembles an eagle, that long-standing symbol of America. The boy's mother, represented by the nude, is distraught, recognizing her powerlessness in the face of both death and patriotism. The image may have been Alberts's invention, but more likely, it derives from a literary source. Alberts is known to have depicted figures from *The Pied Piper of Hamlin,* and he illustrated a poem entitled *Salamander* by his friend Madison Julius Cawein. The local press commented: "About his picture, as about these verses, there is something rather luxurious and hard; something both sumptuous and rigid . . . and it reminds us, not a little, of the exotic quality of Gustave Moreau, whose effect is that of a jewelled immobility."[3]

1. "J. Bernhard Alberts, Jr., Dies of Illness Due to World War," *Louisville Courier Journal,* 25 August 1931.

2. "Alberts . . . Dies."

3. "Mr. Albert's Painting," *Louisville Post,* 18 August 1917.

Born, Louisville, Kentucky, 1886; attended the Cincinnati Art Academy for three years, studied with Frank Duveneck, and for three years at the School of the Museum of Fine Arts, Boston, with Frank Benson and Edmund C. Tarbell; spent one year in New York, followed by a European year of study, 1913; enlisted 1917; died, Louisville, 1931.

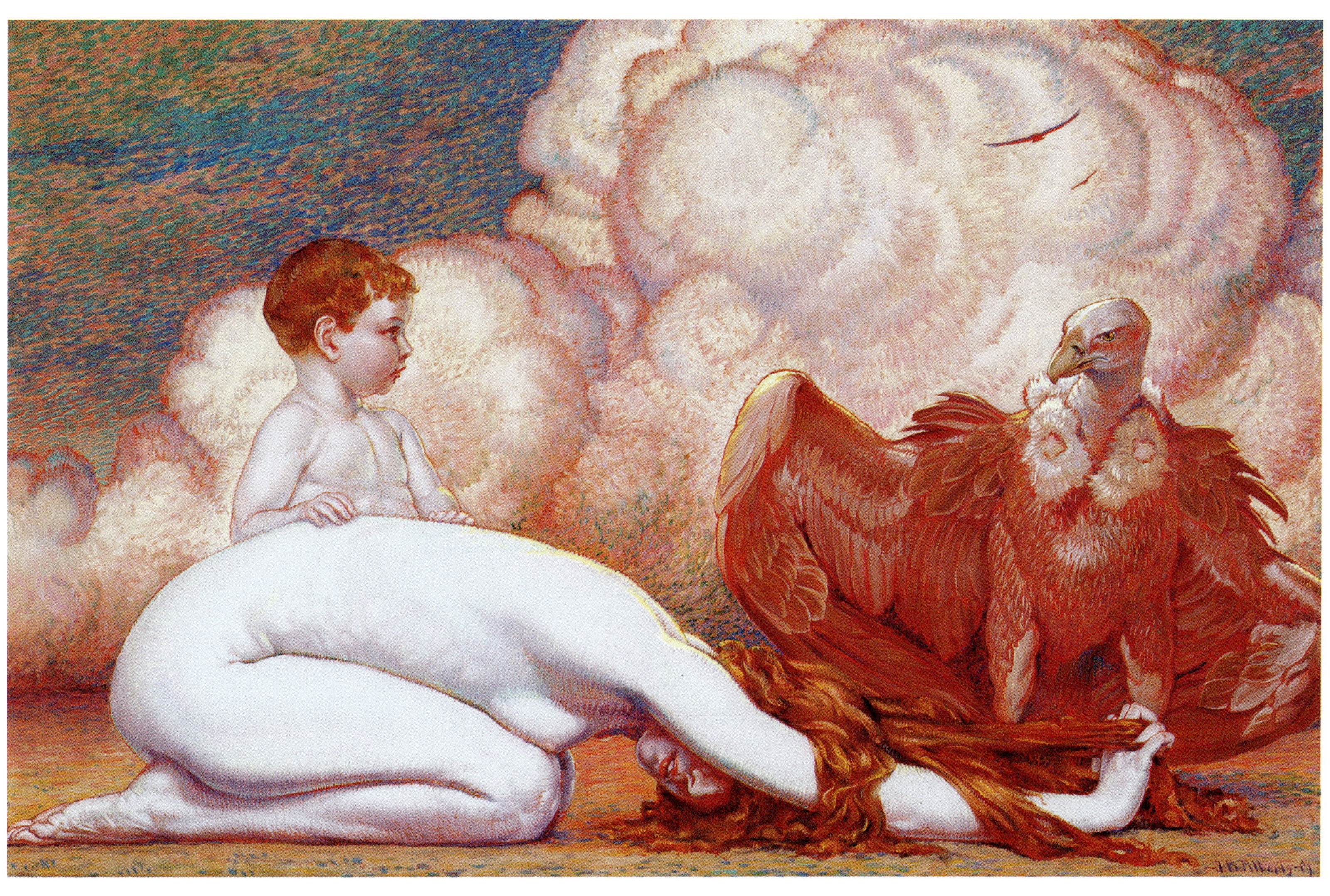

George Wesley Bellows

1882–1925

Massacre at Dinant, 1918

oil on canvas, 49½ × 83 inches
signed, bottom center: *Geo. Bellows*
Gift of Minor M. Shaw, Buck A. Mickel, and Charles C. Mickel; and Arthur and Holly Magill Purchase Fund

Artists have often served as the conscience of society. In retrospect these artists are regarded reverently, despite the fact that in their lifetimes they may have never won favor for their views. Francisco Goya's *The Third of May, 1808* stands as an eternal indictment of Napoleon's troops as they slaughter defenseless Spanish peasants. In his series of etchings *Los Desastres de la Guerra* Goya bitingly portrayed the savagery and stupidity of war. In the twentieth century another Spaniard, Pablo Picasso, dramatically addressed the horror of the bombing of the ancient center of Basque culture in his monumental work *Guernica.*

Toward the end of World War I, during an intensely creative period of fewer than nine months, George Bellows devoted his energies to the depiction of horrible events that had occurred in Belgium. As a realist who eschewed the abstracting tendencies of the emerging modernists, Bellows was ideally suited to create a series that, like Goya's, dealt forcefully with specific events, while simultaneously making a timeless statement about the victims of military conflict. Bellows commented: "In presenting these pictures of the tragedies of war, I wish to disclaim any intention of attacking a race or a people. Guilt is personal, not racial. Against that guilty clique and all its tools, who let loose upon innocence every diabolical device and insane instinct, my hatred goes forth, together with my profound reverence for the victims."[1]

Bellows was the unusual mix of athlete and artist; at Ohio State University, which he attended for three years, his success at baseball led to an invitation to play professional ball with the Cincinnati Reds. However, art interested him as well, and in 1904 he enrolled as a student of Robert Henri at the New York School of Art. A highly respected teacher, Henri instilled in his students an appreciation for the immediacy of a subject, encouraging them not to belabor their compositions. Bellows became immersed in the activity of New York, capturing on canvas its street life and painting a series of prizefights that brought him national attention. Bellows also taught, first at the University of Virginia in 1908, and later at the Art Students League. In 1911 he discovered the rugged beauty of the coast of Maine and painted numerous landscapes and seascapes that reveal the pervasive influence of Winslow Homer.

Bellows's meteoric career was cut short by his death from a ruptured appendix at age forty-three. He painted a broad cross section of subjects, including insightful portraits and intriguing allegories. His series documenting the atrocities of Germany's invasion of neutral Belgium, a contemporary event with political overtones, is indicative of the strong passions that fueled Bellows's work. Although a pacifist by nature, Bellows volunteered for duty upon the United States' entry into the war. He was assigned to the Tank Corps, but he remained in this country, separated from the actual conflict. His knowledge of the events that transpired in Belgium came through newspaper reports, and he convincingly translated them into a powerful series of thirty drawings, twenty lithographs, and five oil paintings. The signing of the armistice brought the series to an abrupt conclusion.

Massacre at Dinant portrays the senseless slaughter of noncombatants, as recounted in excruciating detail in the Bryce Report that investigated the alleged atrocities.[2] Although the painting does not present a particular event, it represents a situation repeated again and again as the Germans swept into Belgium. When the lithograph of the same subject was published in *Vanity Fair,* it bore a chilling caption: "This lithograph represents an episode which was of frequent occurrence during the advance of the German hordes through Belgium and France. Arrived at a village, the Hun soldiers—if they encountered the slightest opposition from the civilian population—rounded up groups of them, stood them before the guard and shot them, their excuse being that in the next village people would be a bit more reasonable."[3]

In its raw directness *Massacre at Dinant* transcends the specificity of actual events and becomes a universal statement about the horrors of war. Bellows, however, was criticized for his lack of accuracy in some of the details. Responding to criticism from fellow artist Joseph Pennell, Bellows retorted: "I've never heard that Leonardo da Vinci had a ticket of admission to the Last Supper."[4]

By the time Bellows concluded the series in November 1918, the fervor of the war was fading, and Germany had signed the armistice pact with the Allies. Although his war series would have no commercial viability, Bellows had succeeded in creating the most powerful and challenging antiwar statement in American art history.

---

1. Bellows, preface to exhibition at Keppel & Co., November 1918, as quoted in Glenn C. Peck and Gordon K. Allison, *George Bellows and the War Series of 1918* (New York: Hirschl & Adler Galleries, 1983), 10.

2. Printed in its entirety, *The New York Times,* 13 May 1915.

3. *Vanity Fair,* November 1918, 37.

4. Bellows to Pennell, as quoted in Krystyna Wasserman, "George Bellows' War Lithographs and Paintings of 1918" (master's thesis, University of Maryland, 1981), 67.

Born, Columbus, Ohio, 1882; attended Ohio State University, 1901–1904; studied with Robert Henri at the New York School of Art, New York, 1904; lived in New York, 1904–1925; taught at the University of Virginia, Charlottesville, 1908; summers in Maine, 1911 and 1913–1916; California, 1917, and Woodstock, New York, 1920–1924; taught at the Art Students League, New York, 1910–1911 and 1917–1919; died, New York, 1925.

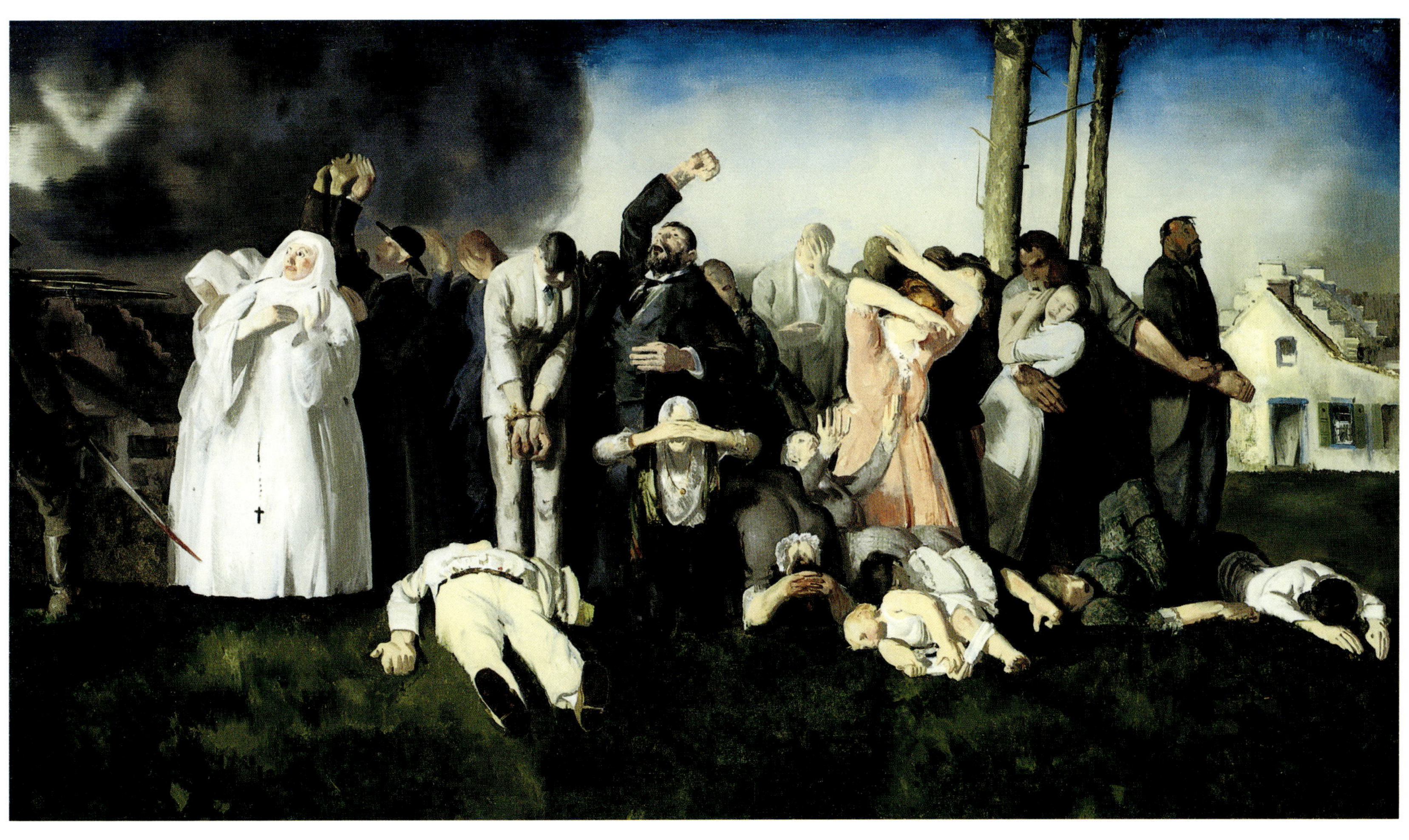

Georgia O'Keeffe

1887–1986

Abstraction, 1916

charcoal and wash on paper, 24¼ × 18⅞ inches
Museum purchase with funds donated by The Museum Association, Inc.; Mr. and Mrs. Thomas Howard Suitt, Jr.; Rich's; and Mr. and Mrs. C. H. Abbe (by exchange)

Fifty years after its defeat on Civil War battlefields, the South was still considered by Northerners to be a wasteland. H. L. Mencken summarized the feelings of many with his deprecating 1917 assessment of the entire South as "The Sahara of the Beaux Arts." Yet for some the region provided a respite from the mainstream, a chance to be reflective and creative.

Georgia O'Keeffe's short period in South Carolina was just such an experience and, in retrospect, was a turning point in her career. From September 1915 to March 1916 she taught art at Columbia College, a women's college in the state capital. O'Keeffe viewed the city as a cultural backwater, and the lack of artistic stimulation forced her to look to herself. In a letter to Alfred Stieglitz in February she described her situation: "Hibernating in South Carolina is an experience I would not advise anyone to miss—The place is of so little consequence—except for the outdoors—that one has a chance to give one's mind, time and attention to anything one wishes."[1]

O'Keeffe later acknowledged the importance of this Southern sojourn: "I didn't start until I was down in South Carolina—alone—thinking things out for myself."[2] But as with many artists, her achievements were the culmination of a variety of learning experiences. Several years earlier she had studied at the School of the Art Institute of Chicago with John Vanderpoel, who stressed the beauty of nature and the human body. Soon after, O'Keeffe virtually abandoned her art for two years and earned her living designing embroidery and lace. A course in the summer of 1912 at the University of Virginia rekindled her creative instinct, in part because of the teaching of Alon Bement, a student of Arthur Wesley Dow. Dow, a critical figure in the evolution of modernism, had promulgated the importance of organic design, basing many of his tenets upon the art of the Japanese. O'Keeffe pursued Dow and took a course with him at Teachers College, Columbia University, in New York. Her work from her South Carolina period is a synthesis of these influences in her life and represents her first mature attempts at her own personal vision.

The results of O'Keeffe's cultural exile were a series of abstractions, some of which she labeled *Specials.* In these primarily ink-and-charcoal drawings, one of the hallmarks of her style is already evident: a sinuous, curving, organic line. This line relates as much to figures and natural forms as to the fashion of Art Nouveau, the turn-of-the-century movement that embraced the decorative arts and emphasized natural forms. *Abstraction,* like other works in the series, pushes the image to the paper's edge. The resulting assertive two dimensionality became one of O'Keeffe's most compelling compositional devices, used to thrust flowers and cow skulls toward the viewer.

The South Carolina series of abstractions was also pivotal in bringing O'Keeffe's work to the attention of Stieglitz. An artist in his own right, Stieglitz, through his gallery, did more than anyone to nurture a small group of emerging modernists that included O'Keeffe, John Marin, Marsden Hartley, and, for a short time, Max Weber. When Stieglitz saw a group of O'Keeffe's drawings, his response was immediate and positive, and, without her permission, he placed ten on exhibition. From this somewhat contentious beginning a dynamic relationship between O'Keeffe and Stieglitz developed, resulting in their eventual marriage and one of this country's most creative partnerships. Not only did Stieglitz exhibit and promote her work, but he also used O'Keeffe as his model in photographs that reflect his aesthetic response to her work.

Beginning in 1921 Stieglitz exhibited his evocative nude photographs of O'Keeffe, and the alignment of his work with her paintings culminated in a controversial joint exhibition three years later. Many viewers saw implicit sexual imagery in O'Keeffe's work, but she vociferously denied the allegations. "The things they write sound so strange and far removed from what I feel of myself."[3] Although many critics continued to find sexual innuendo in her floral compositions, O'Keeffe maintained that her primary motivation was to get people's attention: "I began painting my very large flowers thinking not only that it provided a unique perspective on a familiar object, but frankly, that it would make New York take notice."[4] It did.

---

1. O'Keeffe to Alfred Stieglitz, 1 February 1916, as quoted in Jack Cowart, Juan Hamilton, and Sarah Greenough, *Georgia O'Keeffe: Art and Letters* (Washington, D.C.: National Gallery of Art, 1988), 150.

2. O'Keeffe, *Georgia O'Keeffe* (1976; New York: Penguin Books, 1985), opposite plate 12, quoted in Charles C. Eldredge, *Georgia O'Keeffe: American and Modern* (New Haven: Yale University Press, 1993), 161.

3. O'Keeffe to Mitchell Kennerly, Fall 1922, in Cowart, *O'Keeffe,* 170.

4. O'Keeffe, in Leo Janos, "Georgia O'Keeffe at Eighty-Four," *Atlantic,* December 1971, 116, as quoted in Barbara Buhler Lynes, "Georgia O'Keeffe and Feminism: A Problem of Position," *The Expanding Discourse: Feminism and Art History* (New York: Harper Collins, 1992), 445.

Born, near Sun Prairie, Wisconsin, 1887; studied at the School of the Art Institute of Chicago, 1905–1906; attended the Art Students League, New York, 1907–1908; worked in Chicago as commercial artist, 1908–1910; taught at Chatham, Virginia, 1911; summer class at University of Virginia, Charlottesville, 1912; taught in Amarillo, Texas, 1912–1914; studied at Teachers College, Columbia University, New York, 1914–1915; taught at Columbia College, Columbia, South Carolina, 1915–1916; taught at West Texas State Normal School College, Canyon, 1916–1918; moved to New York, 1918, until 1945, making regular trips to Lake George, New York, and York, Maine; first extended trip to New Mexico, 1929; settled in Abiquiu, New Mexico, 1945; moved to Santa Fe, New Mexico, 1984; died, Santa Fe, 1986.

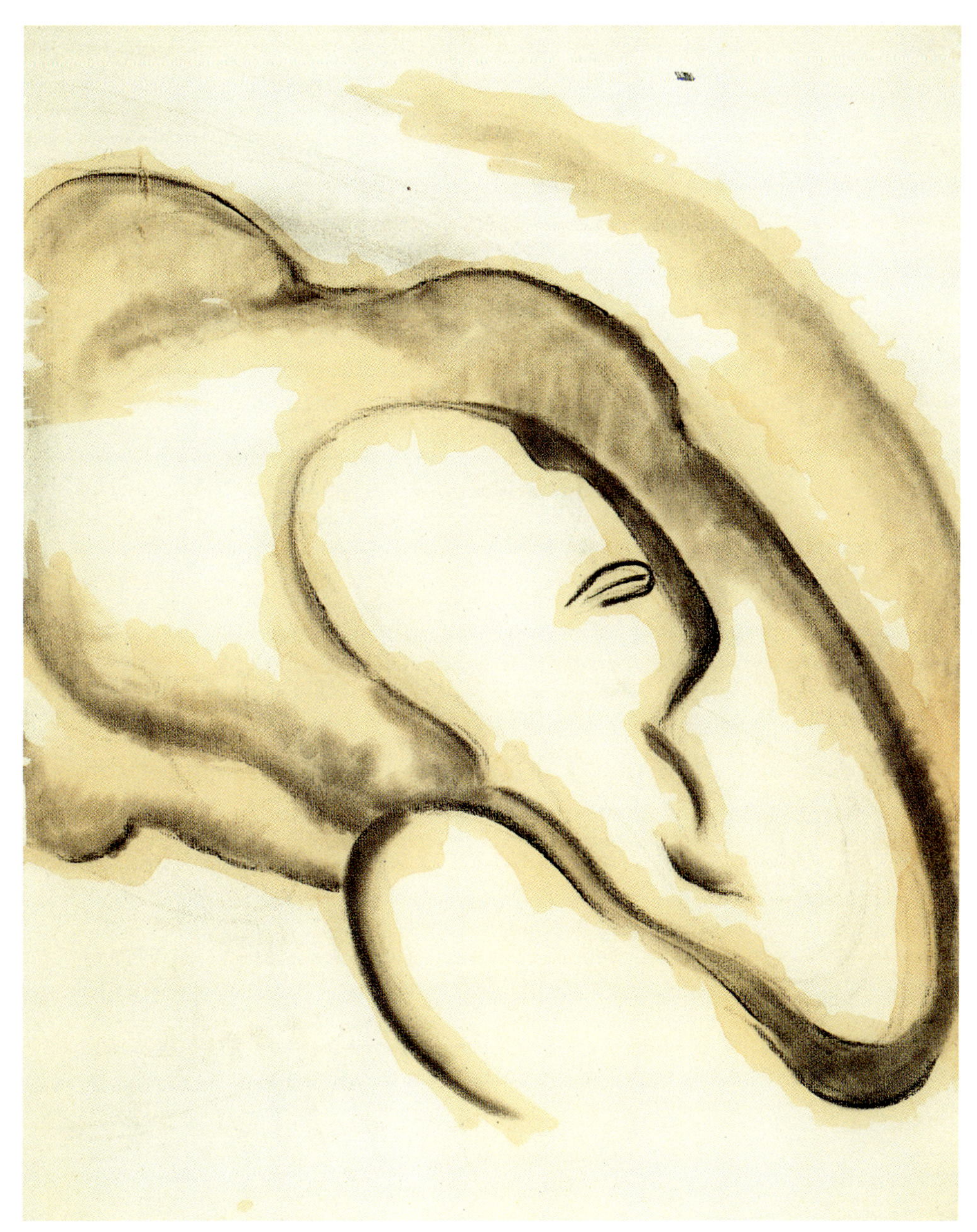

Charles E. Burchfield

1893–1967

Ravine in Summer Rain, 1917

watercolor on paper, 22 × 17½ inches
signed, lower left: *Chas Burchfield / 1917*
Gift of Mr. and Mrs. Arthur F. Magill

Until the 1880s the watercolor medium was used in America primarily for preparatory sketches, for studies for larger works, or for quick notations made outdoors. Because watercolors were usually done on a small scale and on paper, the materials and equipment were easy to transport and conducive to working *en plein air.* Impressionism, which emphasized light and spontaneous effects, brought watercolor wider acceptance. Two Americans, John Singer Sargent and Winslow Homer, were masters of watercolor and used it whenever they were away from their home studios, whether traveling through Italy and North Africa or fishing in the Adirondacks and the Caribbean.

John Marin and Charles Burchfield understood the particular properties of watercolor, and they learned to capitalize upon them in different ways. While Marin also explored etching and oil, Burchfield, with the exception of a trial period with oils in the early 1930s, devoted himself almost exclusively to watercolor. Late in his career he increased the scale of his watercolors by pasting sheets of paper together.

Burchfield grew up in Salem, Ohio, a small midwestern town that would serve as a reservoir of imagery throughout his life. A precocious artist, he gave his high-school valedictory address, "The Evolution of Art," in which he proclaimed: "Nature is better understood today than formerly, for in attempting to interpret her moods, the artist and the poet cast aside all reserve and give themselves up to her entirely."[1] For four years he attended the Cleveland School of Art (now the Cleveland Institute of Art), where initially his interest was in illustration and, later, design. He was awarded a scholarship at the National Academy of Design but withdrew after only one day in the life-drawing class. Two months later he returned to Salem. He never traveled abroad, and perhaps the most unsettling experience in his life was the seven months of army duty in South Carolina, where he was assigned to a camouflage unit. Of his army stint he wrote: "The new life threw my mind into utter chaos, so that I was like unto a primitive man."[2] In 1921 Burchfield moved permanently to the Buffalo, New York, area, where he worked as a wallpaper designer for eight years. Isolated in western New York, Burchfield was removed from modernist European influences and from the work of his contemporaries.

From 1909 to 1965 Burchfield kept a journal in which he recorded his activities, impressions, and artistic philosophy. He looked upon 1917, the year he completed the Museum's painting, as his golden year, filled with "halcyon days without a single worry." This bright outlook was partly the result not only of great productivity but also of the fact that things had begun to coalesce for him as an artist.[3] Nature had always been Burchfield's preoccupation, but his work also abounds with analogies to music and sound. Trees, for example, became critical emblems for his personal expression. At times they are depicted as dead and rotting, contorted and suffering; at other times they are verdant and lush, as in *Ravine in Summer Rain.* Ravines, dark and mysterious, were among the artist's favorite subjects during this period. In 1917 Burchfield developed *Conventions for Abstract Thoughts,* a sketchbook in which his motifs, a kind of graphic shorthand, were assigned such qualities as fear, insanity, melancholy, loneliness, and nostalgia. Variations on many of these can be found in *Ravine in Summer Rain.*

Burchfield's early work has been described as visionary, but it contains a sinister note as well. He ascribed to both nature and the man-made environment moods and personalities, a device that became most evident when he painted houses that appear to have faces. Burchfield pushed his early work toward abstraction, borrowing from his experience as a camouflage and wallpaper designer. The work of his midcareer, from 1921 to 1943, reveals a more measured realism, in which he depicted the farms and factories of middle America. He still used watercolors for these more sober images, but his technique is more controlled and geometric. These paintings align him with Edward Hopper and other Regionalist painters, although Burchfield chafed at his designation as a painter of the American Scene: "I am not an Ohio, or western New York artist, but an American artist—or should I say an artist who happens to be born, living, painting in America. . . . 'Regionalism'—It makes me sick!"[4]

---

1. *The Salem News,* 16 June 1911, as quoted in John I. H. Baur, *Life and Work of Charles Burchfield* (Newark: University of Delaware Press, 1982), 24.

2. *Charles Burchfield's Journals: The Poetry of Place,* ed. J. Benjamin Townsend (Buffalo: State University of New York Press, 1993), 112.

3. See Baur, *Burchfield,* 58 and 252, and *Charles Burchfield, His Golden Year* (Tucson: University of Arizona Art Gallery, 1965).

4. Burchfield to Frank Rehn, 11 October 1938, as quoted in Baur, *Burchfield,* 168–169.

Born, Ashtabula Harbor, Ohio, 1893; attended the Cleveland School of Art (now the Cleveland Institute of Art), 1912–1916; attended one day at the National Academy of Design but remained in New York for two months, 1916; in Salem, Ohio, 1916–1918; United States Army, Fort Jackson, South Carolina, 1918–1919; returned to Salem, until his move to Buffalo, New York, 1921; Gardenville, suburb of Buffalo, 1925–1967; died, West Seneca, New York, 1967.

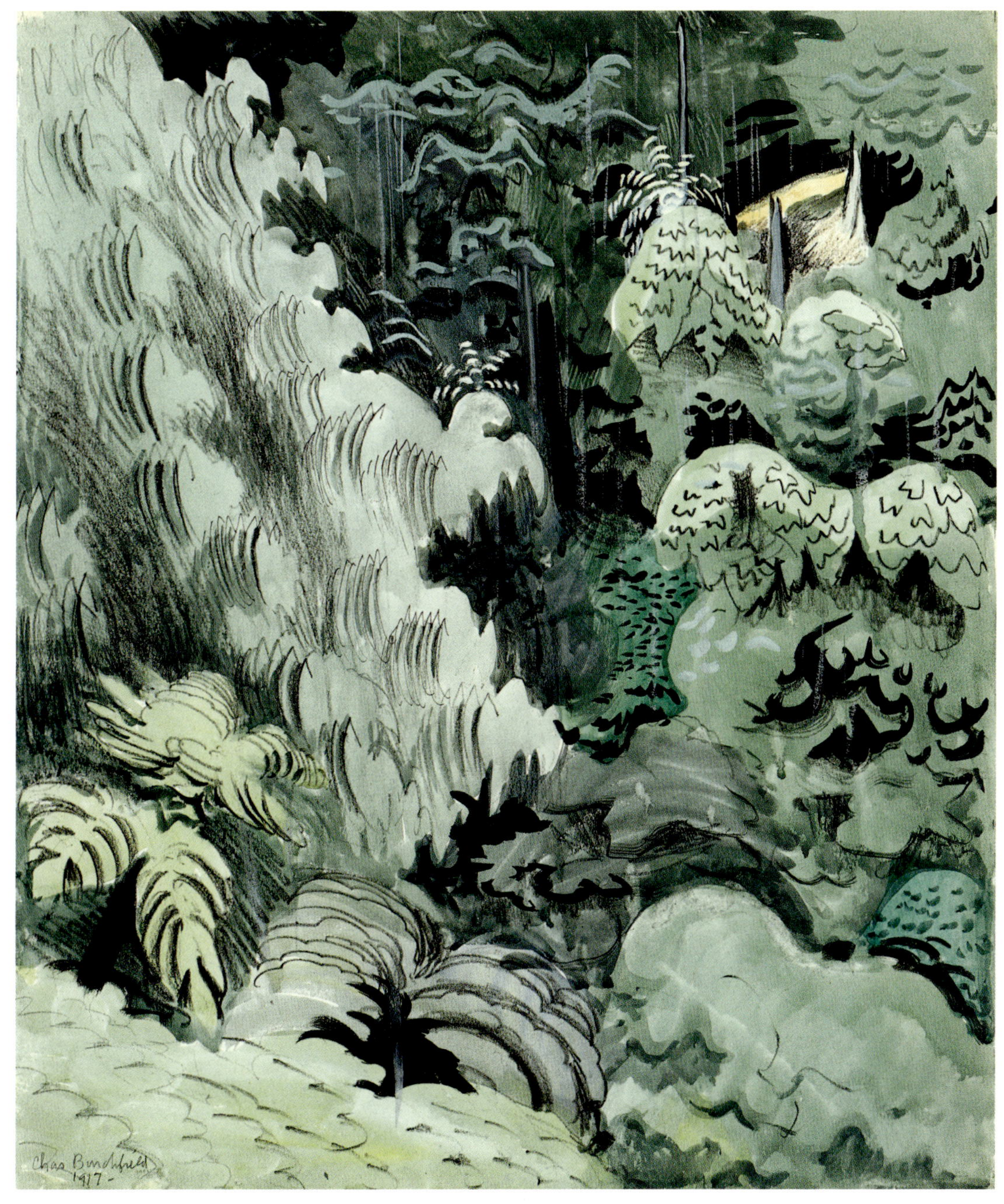

Ellen Ravenscroft

1876–1949

Still Life (Print #2), 1918

color wood-block print: image, 14½ × 9⅜ inches;
paper, 16¾ × 12¹⁄₁₆ inches
signed, lower left: *Ellen Ravenscroft*
Museum purchase with funds donated by
Liberty Life Insurance Company and
The Museum Association, Inc.

World War I marked a turning point for American artists, especially those working abroad. With the exception of Patrick Henry Bruce who remained in France, most artists returned to the United States. The halcyon days of soirées at the Steins and stimulating exhibitions at the Salon d'Automne were over. Artists as well as writers had to reestablish themselves in this country, and, as part of their effort to forge new identities and nurture their creativity, many collected together to live in small European-like communities for at least part of each year.

Provincetown, Massachusetts, a fishing village on Cape Cod with the flavor of old Portugal, became the center for artists fleeing Paris. Primarily printmakers, many of these artists had been exposed to European modernism, to Paul Cézanne and Cubism, as well as to Japonisme, the strong influence of Japanese style and techniques. They became part-time residents of Provincetown and, beginning in 1915, devoted themselves to making wood-block prints. Initially they produced their prints in the traditional Japanese way, using a series of individually cut blocks, one for each color. While in Provincetown the painter B. J. O. Nordfeldt, who had studied Japanese prints in England, devised the technological innovation that revolutionized the printmaking process. Frustrated by the tedium of cutting and registering the printing of several different blocks, Nordfeldt invented a technique using only one block, in which deep grooves separated one color area from another. In the resulting print these grooves appear as slightly raised or embossed white outlines around each shape. Stylistically, these white lines define contours and control colors, creating simplified two-dimensional designs.

In the next few years Provincetown attracted other printmakers who embraced Nordfeldt's single-block, white-line woodcut method. Among the first to arrive was Blanche Lazzell, who would evolve as the most prolific of all the artists who worked there. Lazzell was followed two years later by Ellen Ravenscroft, a native of Jackson, Mississippi. That same summer, 1918, saw the founding of the Provincetown Printers, the first wood-block printmaking society in America. This closely knit group actively promoted the merits of wood-block prints, an ambitious undertaking given the fact that few schools offered courses in printmaking, and those that did taught only etching.[1]

Ravenscroft, a student of both William Merritt Chase and Robert Henri in New York, had, like many of her colleagues, studied in Paris before the war. Her arrival in Provincetown coincided with the heyday of the wood-block print movement, and she clearly benefited from the collegial spirit of experimentation. As Lazzell later recalled, "Creative energy was in the air we breathed. It was in this quaint setting that the Provincetown Print came into being."[2] Unlike etching or lithography, wood-block prints do not require a press, an expensive and heavy piece of equipment that usually generated collaboration among artists. In wood-block prints the artist drew directly on a plank of wood, working the design in reverse. Then v-shaped grooves were cut around each shape. After moist, thin paper was attached to the edge of the woodblock, watercolor was brushed onto the uncut area of the block, the paper was folded over and pressed down, either with the artist's hand, a pad, or even a wooden spoon. This pressure transferred the color onto the paper and pushed the paper into the grooves, resulting in an embossed effect. The process was repeated for each individual color used. Judging from the number of different colors in *Still Life (Print #2),* Ravenscroft probably inked her block about ten different times.

Although technically a process that leads to multiple impressions, single-block prints have so many variables that in many respects each print is one of a kind. The hand-exerted pressure, for example, does not have the consistency of a mechanical press, and therefore the potential for color variation among prints taken from a single block is great. For this reason, single-block woodcut prints tend not to be issued in numbered editions. The Museum's print, labeled number *2,* may refer either to the second print pulled from the block, the second still-life image, or the second print undertaken by Ravenscroft.

Still Life (Print #2) demonstrates the simplification and coloration typical of Provincetown prints. The design is stylized, with each color contained by a white line, and the composition, without any shading, is two dimensional. However, the predominance of round shapes repeated in the flowers, the vase, and the tabletop conveys a rhythmic, organic quality that contrasts with the more geometric work of Ravenscroft's cohorts.

Ravenscroft remained a summer resident of Provincetown most of her life, often designing stage sets for the theatrical performances popular there. In the mid-1920s she became active in the New York Society of Women Artists, founded to provide support for women artists working in a modernist vein. As part of an outgrowth of the suffragette movement, this professionally oriented group was also organized in response to the National Association of Women Painters and Sculptors, which catered primarily to society women.[3]

---

1. See David Acton et al., *A Spectrum of Innovation: Color in American Printmaking, 1890–1960* (Worcester, Mass.: Worcester Art Museum, 1990), 15–16, and Janet Altic Flint, *Provincetown Printers* (Washington, D.C.: Smithsonian Institution Press, 1983), 22.

2. Lazzell, "The Provincetown Print," undated manuscript, collection of James and Janet Reed, Morgantown, W.Va., as quoted in Flint, *Provincetown Printers,* 14.

3. Amy J. Wolf, *New York Society of Women Artists 1925* (New York: ACA Galleries, 1987), 9.

Born, Jackson, Mississippi, 1876; studied with William Merritt Chase and Robert Henri in New York, and with Claudio Castelucho in Paris; summer resident in Provincetown, Massachusetts, 1918–1947; lived in St. Louis, Missouri, early 1920s; moved to New York by 1926; died, New York, 1949.

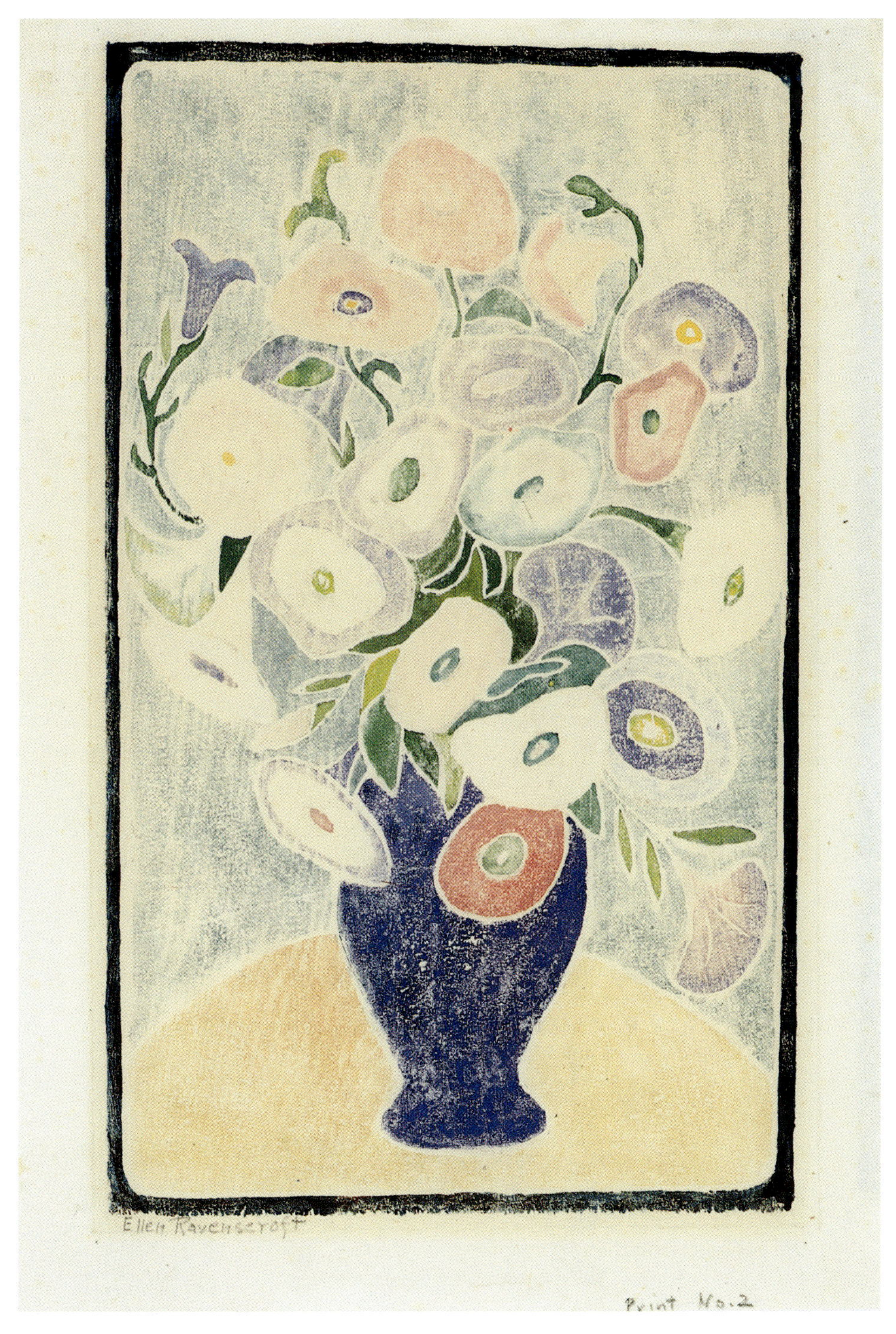
Ellen Ravenscroft
Print No. 2

Nettie Blanche Lazzell

1878–1956

untitled, 1924

mixed media on paper, 10½ × 8 inches
signed, lower right: *Blanche Lazzell, Paris, 1924*
Museum purchase with funds provided by The Liberty Corporation Foundation and The Museum Association, Inc.

The "Roaring Twenties" was the era of Art Deco. This elegant and reductive style informed the architecture and decorative arts of the time, which witnessed the elevation of machine design to a high aesthetic. Shiny metallic surfaces proliferated alongside exotic woods highlighted with lacquer or silver leaf. The ocean liner and the automobile emerged as the symbols of a society preoccupied with speed and obsessed with the latest fashion. France dominated this international taste, hosting the 1925 Exposition des Arts Décoratifs; the work of some French painters and their students mirrored the Art Deco taste.

In the 1920s French painters were not only recovering from World War I but were also absorbing the analytical conclusions of Cubism and the invention of collage, the arrangement on a flat surface of scraps of paper, cloth, and other materials pasted together to form a composition. Both Fernand Léger and Albert Gleizes matured in this environment, revising and purifying Cubism. They worked with large, bold shapes, often curved, and Léger reintroduced the primary colors of red, yellow, and blue.

Although many American artists fled Europe during the war, several later returned to renew their studies. Thus Blanche Lazzell, who had been abroad between 1912 and 1914, went back in 1923 to work with Léger and Gleizes. Lazzell, a native of West Virginia, was an inveterate student throughout her life, graduating from West Virginia University with three degrees. She pursued art as a student of William Merritt Chase at the Art Students League, and at age fifty she joined Hans Hofmann's classes in Provincetown, Massachusetts.

Lazzell went to Provincetown in 1915, just as white-line, single-block prints became the rage. Like Ellen Ravenscroft who arrived two years later, Lazzell became intrigued with the newly invented technique and quickly excelled at it, cutting 138 images during her lifetime. The Provincetown Print, with its clearly separated color areas, induced the artist to think both in terms of shapes and their interrelationships and in terms of color. This approach was sympathetic with Lazzell's artistic philosophy, which was inclined toward abstraction. "Abstract art does not represent anything seen by the eye. It is made up of tones, and planes or shapes of color. These shapes must be so related as to give harmony and rhythm, must be balanced."[1]

In the Museum's untitled work, Lazzell follows her own dictum as well as the example of her instructors, Léger and Gleizes. As a nonobjective painting, or one without any overtly recognizable objects, it is a carefully composed network of shapes and colors. Organized around a strong central vertical axis, the shapes alternate between curving Art Deco–like forms and geometric ones. The visual vocabulary, which resembles a keyhole and a guitar, derives from Cubism and relates specifically to Léger. The severity of the flat, untextured, and opaque surface is alleviated by the rhythmic addition of dots and the bright colors. Just as Léger accented his canvases with lively primary colors, so Lazzell used color for contrast, as a means of separating one contour from another in a manner similar to her prints. However, in her use of the secondary colors of green, orange, and purple, she differed from Léger's example. In 1927 she wrote her sister: "At present I am just finishing up a still life, in which I have used my usual color scheme, red violet, blue green and yellow orange. I have used this same color scheme in my Cubist compositions, but there are never two alike in color or composition."[2]

More than likely the Museum's painting is a thoughtfully arranged preparatory study for a larger oil painting. The reverse of the work bears the following inscription in the hand of her teacher Gleizes, in which he offers advice for her final painting: "Si vous le faite, sur une toile vous devez donner un interêt plus grands à certains endroits. Ce que j'ai fait n'a aucune importance. Si vous trouvez qque choses de mieux faites le" (If you do it on canvas, you ought to give greater interest [emphasis] to certain places. That which I have done is of no importance. If you find something better, do it.)

---

1. Lazzell to her sister, from Provincetown, Massachusetts, 15 April 1927. Blanche Lazzell Papers, Archives of American Art, roll 2990.

2. Lazzell to her sister, from Provincetown, Massachusetts, 4 April 1927. Blanche Lazzell Papers, Archives of American Art, roll 2990.

Born, near Maidsville, West Virginia, 1878; graduated from West Virginia University, 1905; studied in New York at the Art Students League with William Merritt Chase, 1908, and in Paris at the Académie Moderne, 1912–1914; summered in Provincetown, Massachusetts, 1915–1956; returned to Paris and studied with Fernand Léger and Albert Gleizes, 1923–1924; employed by the Works Progress Administration, 1933–1934; died, Morgantown, West Virginia, 1956.

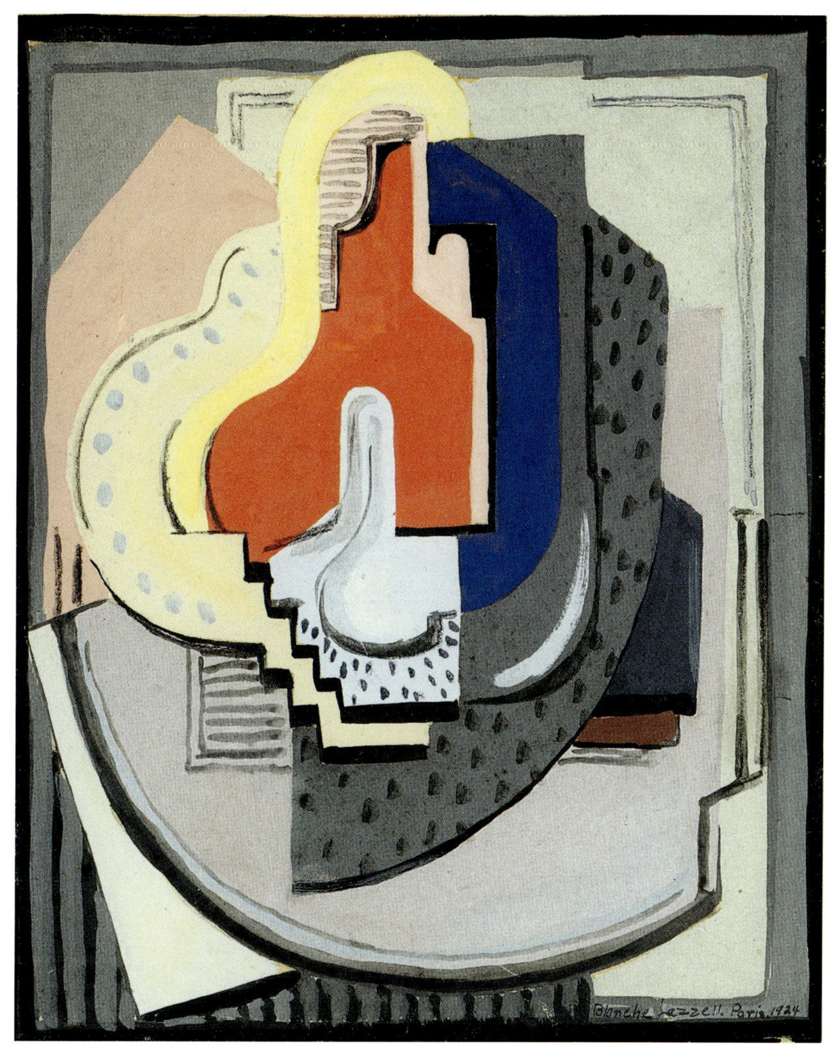
Blanche Lazzell. Paris. 1924

Mary Harvey Tannahill

1863–1951

Sisters, circa 1920

oil on canvas, 32 × 24 inches
signed, lower right: *Mary H. Tannahill*
Gift of Paul Doll (by exchange)

The rediscovery of early American folk art was largely made by artists living in New England. In Europe a similar development had already occurred: artists discovered the merits of indigenous peasant art and tribal objects from Africa and incorporated some of the qualities of those traditions into their work. In America artists working in a modernist vein saw stylistic affinities between their own work and that of American primitives, individuals who created without exposure to formal training.

During the 1920s, collectors and patrons began to recognize the appeal of folk art, and in 1932 the correspondence between modern and folk art was embraced by the Museum of Modern Art with its landmark exhibition of American folk art. The exhibition's curator, Holger Cahill, a specialist in modern art, concluded: "Public interest in American folk art is a development of the past few years. The discoverers of its aesthetic quality were the pioneers of modern art . . . [who] were in revolt against the naturalistic and impressionistic tendencies of the nineteenth century."[1] In its emphasis on simplicity and flattened compositions, the work of Mary Harvey Tannahill clearly demonstrates the interrelationship between folk art and the modernist aesthetic.

Tannahill, a native of North Carolina, was not a naive, untrained artist. She took instruction in New York at the Art Students League as a student of Kenyon Cox, H. Siddons Mowbray, and John Twachtman; she also studied under Arthur Wesley Dow. Her earliest success came with miniature portraits, an art form revived at the turn of the century. Miniatures had experienced their heyday in the middle of the nineteenth century and were often produced by painters outside the mainstream. Tannahill was adept in other media; she was an accomplished embroiderer as well as a printmaker, and throughout her long career she explored a variety of styles.

Like several other Southern-born women artists, including Blanche Lazzell and Ellen Ravenscroft, Tannahill produced most of her prints at Provincetown, where she spent her summers and regularly participated in exhibitions between 1916 and 1938. The single-block, white-line print seems to have been ideally suited to Tannahill's proclivity toward simplified and flattened compositions. Similarly, her paintings tend to be straightforward, often symmetrically arranged, and two dimensional.

In *Sisters* the theme of innocence is reinforced by the painting's style. Two young girls, dressed simply and identically, are posed frontally with alert facial expressions, recalling American folk portraiture. Their contours are crisply defined, almost in the tradition of early limners. The girls are accompanied by two doves, typically symbols of peace and purity, and a cat and a dog, who could denote domesticity and loyalty. Folk portraiture frequently employed animals as symbols for the innocence of children. The trees and flowers are carefully balanced, emerging as decorative elements akin to the designs found on painted furniture. The outdoor setting is stylized, with the pinkish mountains rising behind the figures in a form of flattened perspective resembling folk art.

Sisters has an air of mystery similar to the work of the great French master Henri Rousseau, whose work Tannahill may have seen while abroad. However, there is nothing sinister in her painting, as there often is in Rousseau's jungles, where lions lurk behind lush foliage. Instead, Tannahill evokes a childlike world filled with sisterly affection, bathed in soft, warm mauves and pinks.

1. Holger Cahill, *American Folk Art: The Art of the Common Man in America, 1750–1900* (1932; reprint, New York: The Museum of Modern Art, 1969), 26–27.

Born, Kinderhook Plantation, Warrenton County, North Carolina, 1863; studied in New York at the Art Students League with Kenyon Cox, J. Alden Weir, John Twachtman, and H. Siddons Mowbray, and under Arthur Wesley Dow, 1893–1898; visited Europe, circa 1913 and 1923; summered in Provincetown, Massachusetts, 1916–1938; died, Warrenton, North Carolina, 1951.

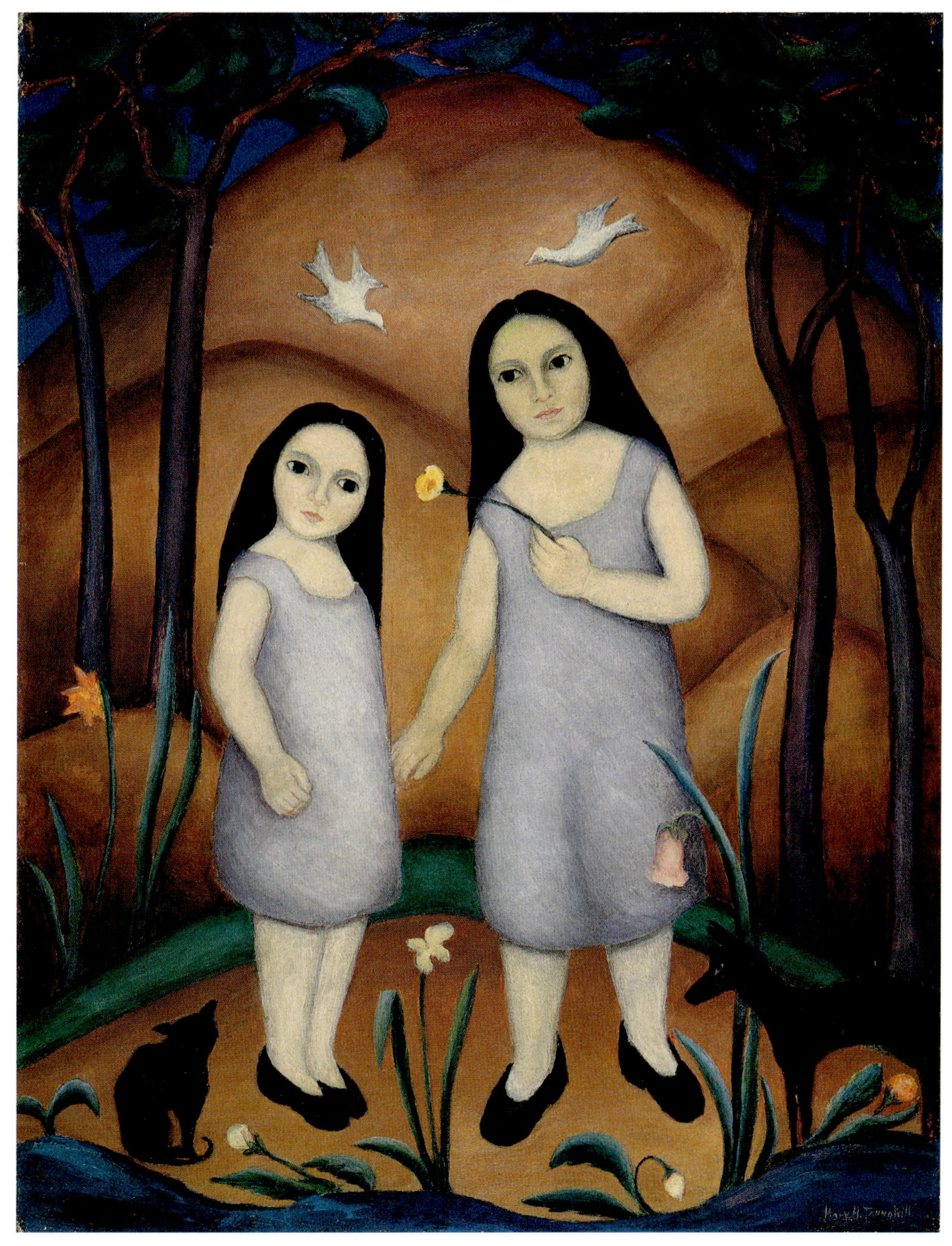
Mary H. Tannahill

Anna Heyward Taylor

1879–1956

Gaden on he Head! circa 1925

color wood-block print: image, 11 × 8 inches; paper, 14¾ × 11 inches
signed, lower right: *Anna Heyward Taylor*
Museum purchase

Artists have often played a pivotal role in shaping their communities. For areas that evolved into art colonies like Old Lyme in Connecticut, East Hampton in New York, and Taos in New Mexico, the cultural and economic impact made by artists has been considerable. Certain locales have undergone revitalization as a result of artistic activity. Charleston, South Carolina, which had fostered a distinguished art and architectural heritage during the colonial and antebellum periods, remained dormant following Reconstruction. Beginning in the second decade of this century, the city experienced a renewal that was largely generated by artists whose depictions instilled pride in local residents and brought national attention to this "ancient, beautiful city that time had forgotten before it destroyed."[1] A coterie of three South Carolina women and one Northern man produced evocative images of the city and its environs that led ultimately to the country's first historic preservation ordinance and to a flourishing tourism industry.

Alice Ravenel Huger Smith, Elizabeth O'Neill Verner, Alfred Hutty, and Anna Heyward Taylor formed the core of the group responsible for the Charleston Renaissance that also included authors, architects, and preservationists. Using watercolors, prints, and illustrated volumes, the artists created work that was aesthetically pleasing and easily disseminated. Smith and Verner were native Charlestonians; Hutty and Taylor consciously selected Charleston as their residence. The four artists lived and worked within three blocks of one another in one of the city's historic sections, a neighborhood that DuBose Heyward immortalized in *Porgy and Bess.*

Taylor was born in the state capital, Columbia, and graduated from college in her hometown before spending a term as a graduate student at Radcliffe College. She studied with William Merritt Chase in England and Holland and went to Provincetown during the summer of 1916 just as B. J. O. Nordfeldt and the other printmakers were inventing and exhibiting the Provincetown Print. That year she joined a four-month expedition to British Guiana, where she did the floral studies she later translated into wood-block prints and batik designs. With brilliant, contrasting colors and bold forms she created dense, compact prints that exude an exotic flavor.

More narrative and more closely related to the work of her Charleston colleagues is *Gaden on he Head!* The print combines two traditional images of Charleston: the gates, decorated with pineapples, of a celebrated federal-period mansion and African-American women selling vegetables. The title, too, is evocative, deriving from the Gullah language, a melodious mix of African, Creole, and English that the street vendors spoke freely among themselves and used to peddle their wares. Both the site and the women exemplify the city's growing preservation sentiment and awareness of its potential as a tourist attraction.

The Museum's wood-block print demonstrates Taylor's familiarity and facility with the Provincetown Print: white lines separate each color area, allowing the artist to use one block in the printing process. Taylor used a limited number of intense colors as well as a strong black. Unlike many of the Provincetown Prints, Taylor's image is pictorial with an emphatic perspective dramatically offset by the heavy vertical form of the dark tree. Another difference is Taylor's extensive use of unprinted paper, a phenomenon that relates well to her purely black-and-white prints. Inscribed *No. 5,* the Museum's print may be either the fifth impression printed by Taylor or the fifth in a series about Charleston.

As one of the artists of the Charleston Renaissance, Taylor did a great deal to promote the city's charms, both through her individual prints and through the publication *This Our Land,* which featured twenty of her incisive linoleum-block prints. Steeped in the history and aura of the Carolina Low Country, it is unclear how aware Taylor and the other Charleston artists were of international art movements. When a critic made analogies between her work and that of Henri Matisse, Taylor denied any connection. The reviewer persevered: "Many of [her prints] were so strongly reminiscent of the Matisse manner and method. I remember that I never quite understood Matisse until some one pointed out his debt and relationship to the Persian color print. It was particularly enlightening to hear Miss Taylor say that she was always fascinated by Persian prints."[2]

---

1. DuBose Heyward, *Porgy* (1925; reprint, Charleston, S.C.: The Tradd Street Press, 1985), 11.

2. Henry Bellaman, "The Work of Anna Heyward Taylor," *The State,* 21 December 1930.

Born, Columbia, South Carolina, 1879; graduated from the South Carolina Presbyterian Institute for Young Ladies, Columbia, 1897; student of William Merritt Chase in Holland, 1903, and London, 1904; traveled to England, Switzerland, and Italy, 1908–1909, and Tokyo, 1914; graduate student at Radcliffe College, 1915; to Provincetown, Massachusetts, 1916; to British Guiana, 1916 and 1920; moved to Charleston, South Carolina, 1929; traveled to Mexico, 1930; died, Charleston, 1956.

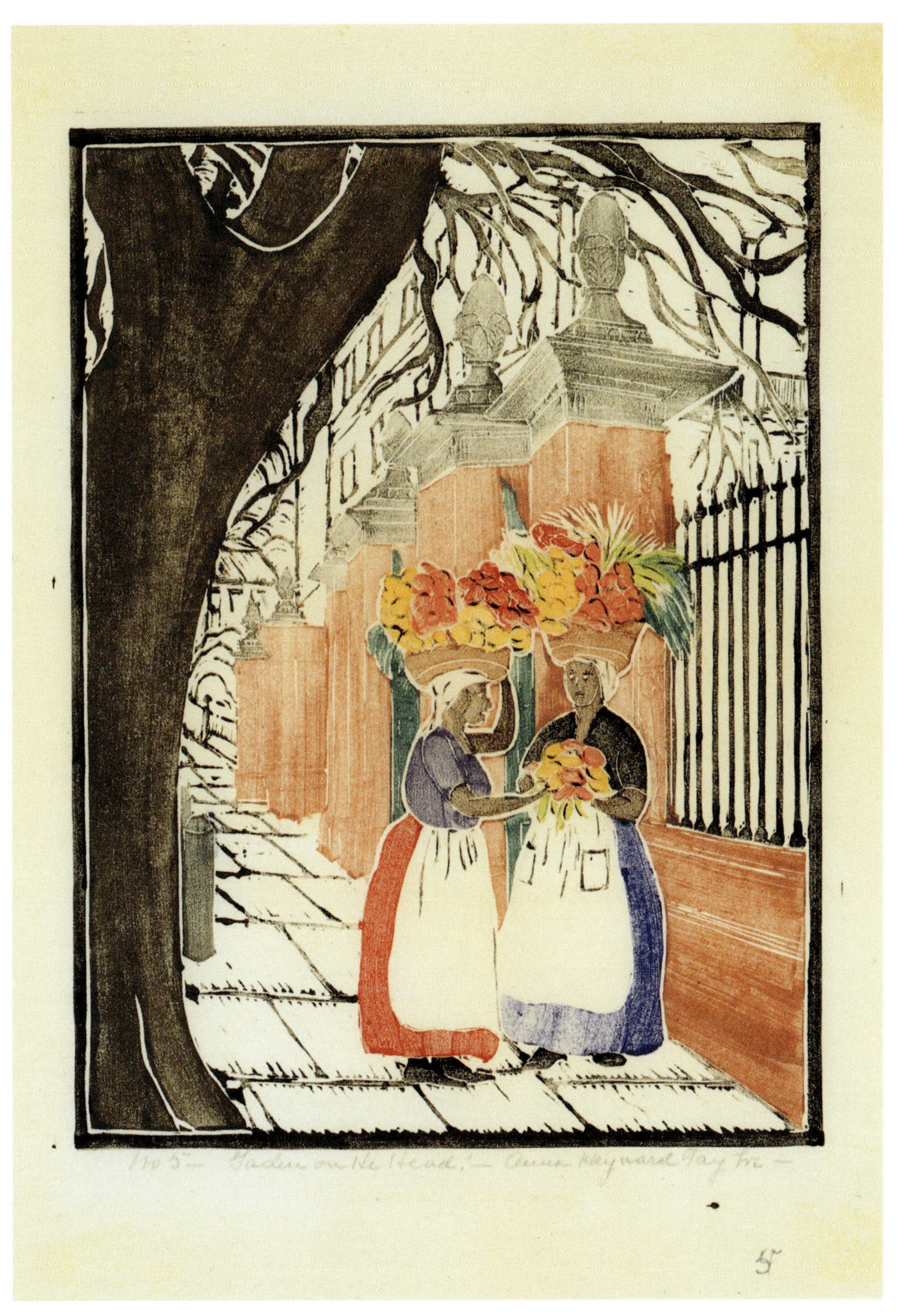

Anne Goldthwaite

1869–1944

New York Skyline, circa 1923

oil on canvas mounted on board, 20 × 24 inches
signed, lower left: *Anne Goldthwaite*
Gift of Richard Goldthwaite in memory of Anne Goldthwaite

"The tall building is the landmark of our age," wrote the architectural critic Ada Louise Huxtable.[1] The buildings themselves provide significant testimony to this assertion along with the numerous cityscapes created by American artists. Although Chicago was the first city to profit from the new technology that made tall buildings possible, it was New York that quickly capitalized upon its potential. By 1920 New Yorkers were working and living dozens of stories higher than ever before, gaining new vistas on the city's great urban expanse. Such notable structures as the Flatiron and Woolworth buildings were rendered in all kinds of weather conditions and at various times of day by some of the era's most progressive artists, including John Marin, Georgia O'Keeffe, Alfred Stieglitz, and Edward Steichen.

After seven years abroad Anne Goldthwaite left Paris to visit her family in Montgomery, Alabama, stopping in New York to see the Armory Show, which included one of her paintings. She finally settled in New York, a place she was familiar with from her student days at the National Academy of Design. In Paris Goldthwaite had helped to organize the Académie Moderne, where a group of students benefited from the criticism of Charles Guérin, a disciple of Paul Cézanne, who sought to clarify for the young artists the "countless theories and preachments, so strange, novel and exciting, that confusion was natural and inevitable."[2]

Goldthwaite taught at the Art Students League for more than twenty years, supplementing her income with portraits on canvas and in prints. Her subject matter was broad, encompassing graceful depictions of Isadora Duncan and other dancers, engaging family pets, architectural views of New York and New Orleans, and rural figures derived from her annual summer visits to Montgomery. She found that "the South was, and is now, a strange mixture of luxury and poverty."[3] For her native state she did two post-office murals, for Atmore and Tuskegee, under the auspices of the federal government's Depression-era Section of Fine Arts.

New York Skyline reveals Goldthwaite's response to her adopted city. From an elevated perspective, probably from her studio on East Tenth Street, she portrayed the evolution of urban density as lower tenements give way to taller structures. Visually linking the buildings across the top of the canvas is the Queensboro Bridge, one of several connecting Manhattan to the other boroughs. From her chosen viewpoint no human activity is visible, symptomatic of the isolation often felt in cities. Goldthwaite's palette, dominated by somber grays and browns, does little to refute the artist's sense of detachment from the scene below her. With its insistent repetition of square shapes, bare canvas, and visible brushwork, the painting recalls Cézanne, whose work Goldthwaite admired. Throughout her life, the artist rejected the modernist label: "Whenever I had shown my work I had been called a modernist. This was a great surprise to me, for I knew I was painting, not according to any school, but according to the way I saw my subject. Perhaps I *was* modern, but if it were true, I was so innately and not by conscious effort."[4]

Goldthwaite was an active member of the National Association of Women Painters and Sculptors. She was also outspoken about art created by women. In a 1934 radio interview she acknowledged the increased visibility women artists had been receiving: "The best praise that women have been able to command until now is to have it said that she paints like a man. . . . We want more—to speak to eyes and ears wide open and without prejudice—an audience that asks simply—is it good, not—was it done by a woman."[5]

---

1. Ada Louise Huxtable, *The Tall Building Artistically Reconsidered* (New York: Pantheon Books, 1984), 7.

2. Martin Birnbaum, *Catalogue of an Exhibition of Paintings, Water Colors and Etchings by Anne Goldthwaite* (New York: Berlin Photographic Company, 1915), 4.

3. Goldthwaite memoirs, 1935, as excerpted in Adelyn Dohme Breeskin, *Anne Goldthwaite: A Catalogue Raisonné of the Graphic Work* (Montgomery, Ala.: Montgomery Museum of Fine Arts, 1982), 14.

4. Goldthwaite memoirs, in Breeskin, *Goldthwaite*, 30.

5. Radio interview, 1934, as quoted in Adelyn Breeskin, *Anne Goldthwaite, 1869–1944* (Montgomery, Ala.: Montgomery Museum of Art, 1977), 9.

Born, Montgomery, Alabama, 1869; studied in New York at the National Academy of Design and with Walter Shirlaw, 1898–1904, and in Paris, 1906–1913, at the Académie Moderne; resided in New York, with annual summer visits to Montgomery, 1913–1944; faculty of Art Students League, 1922–1944; died, New York, 1944.

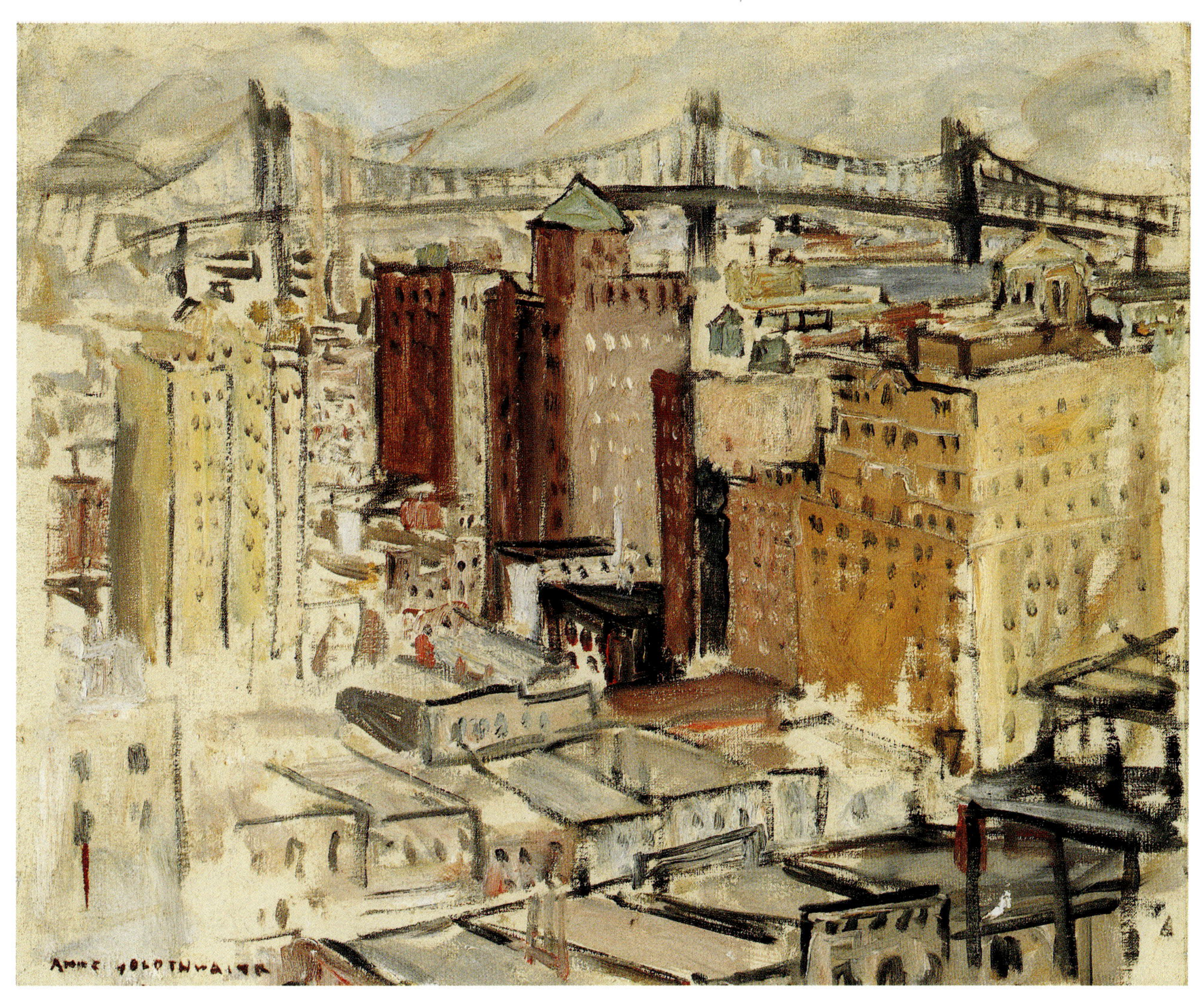
ANNE GOLDTHWAITE

Hugh Henry Breckenridge

1870–1937

Landscape #1, 1925

oil on canvas, 25 × 30 inches
signed, lower right: *Hugh H. Breckenridge*
Museum purchase with funds donated by The Museum Association, Inc., and Friends of the Museum (by exchange)

The scientific and aesthetic qualities of color were a major concern of theorists and artists from the late nineteenth century onward. The revolution instigated by the Impressionists brought new attention to the physical properties of colors, which resulted in the publication of numerous treatises. Simultaneously, more stable paints and brighter hues had become available, and painters responded in innovative ways. Henri Matisse was the leader of a group labeled the Fauves, or "wild beasts," because of their raw and bold use of vivid color. Both Vincent van Gogh and Wassily Kandinsky capitalized on the expressive potential of color and its ability to elicit emotional reactions in viewers. Van Gogh, in particular, is recognized for his use of high-intensity colors, such as the radiant yellows in his paintings of sunflowers.

American artists, who were not as preoccupied with color, were concerned primarily with formal problems. Paul Cézanne, who sought to introduce structure to Impressionism, exerted more influence on American artists than did Van Gogh. Hugh Henry Breckenridge, because of his interest in intense color, was an exception. Nonetheless, his objective seems to have been to create visual impact rather than to convey emotional content.

Breckenridge, who demonstrated a precocious talent for art while growing up in Leesburg, Virginia, was an influential and beloved teacher. Of his students he wrote: "I have given them my best thoughts, both as to life as well as to art. In return, they have given me their affection, which I prize."[1] He began his fifty-year affiliation with the Pennsylvania Academy of the Fine Arts, Philadelphia, in 1887 when he enrolled as a student. He furthered his education under Adolphe-William Bouguereau in Paris, where he was stirred by contemporary French art in the commercial galleries. He returned to Philadelphia in 1894 and joined the faculty of the Academy. Later he taught with Thomas Anshutz at the Darby Summer School of Painting in rural Pennsylvania, and in 1920 he established his own summer school in East Gloucester, Massachusetts.

Throughout his career Breckenridge was a successful and popular portraitist, and during his lifetime he embraced a number of styles, including a form of Post-Impressionism derived from Cézanne and a Pointillist landscape idiom similar to Georges Seurat's technique of applying paint in clusters of short strokes. Instead of styles, Breckenridge considered these variations "methods," believing that "some methods are probably better than others to express certain ideas. . . . You can't expect any one to talk in the same tone of voice or walk with the same step all the time; yet that is exactly what so many people expect of a painter."[2]

Between 1917 and 1935 Breckenridge completed a series of small abstractions, many untitled. These powerfully painted works may have derived from landscapes or still lifes, but they eschew recognizable imagery and are instead essays in color, texture, and form. Like Kandinsky's *Improvisations,* these works have a dynamic visual energy, which is also exemplified in the Museum's *Landscape #1.*

Landscape #1 consists of a series of boldly colored, kaleidoscopic forms. Not only did Breckenridge leave visible traces of his own gestures, but he also left areas of the canvas unpainted, exposing his underdrawing. The final work is extemporaneous, prefiguring the emotive techniques of the later Abstract Expressionists. According to Breckenridge's theory of painting, *Landscape #1* is more than a painting to be looked at; it demands contemplation as well: "There are two different enjoyments of art, one purely sensuous, an enjoyment open to everyone, and the other intellectual, a pleasure only to those who realize that an intellectual performance has gone on in expressing the emotion."[3]

---

1. Breckenridge to Margaret Breckenridge Skinner, circa 1933, as quoted in Margaret Vogel, *The Paintings of Hugh H. Breckenridge (1870–1937)* (Dallas: Valley House Gallery, 1967), 13.

2. Breckenridge, interview with Dorothy Grafly, *The North American,* 12 March 1922, as quoted in Vogel, *Breckenridge,* 19.

3. Breckenridge interview, as quoted in Vogel, *Breckenridge,* 20.

Born, Leesburg, Virginia, 1870; entered the Pennsylvania Academy of the Fine Arts, Philadelphia, 1887; to Paris to study with Adolphe-William Bouguereau, William Gabriel Ferrier, and Lucien Doucet, 1892–1893; taught at the Pennsylvania Academy of the Fine Arts, 1894–1937; at the Darby Summer School of Painting, 1900–1908 and 1913–1918, and the Breckenridge School of Art, East Gloucester, Massachusetts, 1920–1937; to Europe, 1909; died, Philadelphia, 1937.

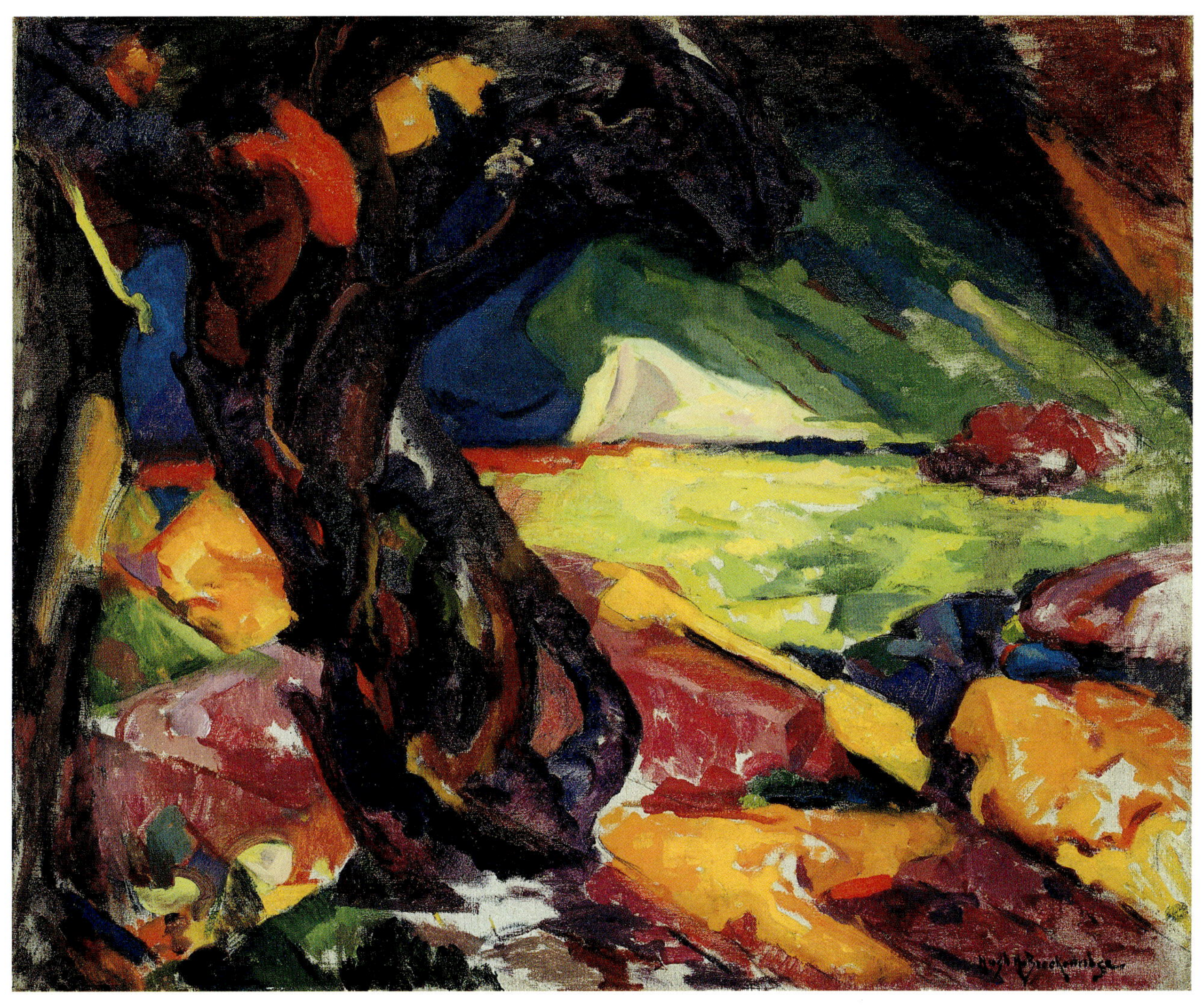

Hale Aspacio Woodruff

1900–1980

Landscape near Vence, France, between 1928 and 1931

oil on canvas, 18 × 22 inches
signed, lower left: *Hale Woodruff*
Museum purchase with funds donated by the Arthur and Holly Magill Foundation

Despite their emancipation, African-Americans faced numerous challenges during the first half of this century. Although all Americans endured two world wars and the Depression, African-Americans also suffered discrimination and segregation. Exhibition opportunities and financial resources for all artists were extremely limited, and many painters, including the African-Americans William H. Johnson and Palmer Hayden, worked as janitors to support themselves. With few exceptions, art education for African-Americans was nonexistent in this country, and, as a result, many gravitated to France.

A friend of both Johnson and Hayden, Hale Woodruff followed them to France, but after four years there he returned to America, where he established in Atlanta one of the strongest art programs available for African-Americans. Woodruff presided over a far-reaching curriculum that served young students, educators, accomplished artists, and the general public. In a thoroughly Southern city Woodruff persevered; he even persuaded the segregated Atlanta Museum to open for his students. While at Atlanta University he organized national exhibitions of works by African-American artists that served to shape and promote their work, and as a successful artist in his own right, Woodruff was an important role model for countless aspiring artists. After a summer spent with the great Mexican muralist Diego Rivera, Woodruff completed several murals dealing with African-American history for Southern colleges. In a 1942 *Time* magazine article Atlanta University's art department was equated with the Ecole des Beaux-Arts in Paris, and Woodruff was credited with this accomplishment. Woodruff spoke of his goal to the reporter: "We are interested in expressing the South as a field, a territory, its peculiar run-down landscape, its social and economic problems, and its Negro people."[1]

Early in life Woodruff determined that he wanted to be a painter. After high school in Nashville, Woodruff went to Indianapolis, where he did odd jobs to put himself through the John Herron Art Institute. His education was conventional and conservative, with a heavy emphasis on landscape painting. Interested in learning more about European modernism, Woodruff gathered his limited resources and went to Paris in 1927. He took classes at the Académie Scandinave and the Académie Moderne, but his real passion was for the art he saw in museums. Before leaving the Midwest he had arranged to write a travelogue for the *Indianapolis Star,* which documents his enthusiastic response to the French capital. "In its studios, ateliers, schools and, let us not forget, its cafés, artists from every corner of the globe can be found. . . . The coming student rubs elbows with the already arrived and there is found a genial spirit of 'live and let live.'"[2]

Although enthralled with Paris, Woodruff found it expensive, and as a foreigner he could not find employment. At Johnson's urging Woodruff went to the south of France, following in the footsteps of Vincent van Gogh, Paul Cézanne, and Chaim Soutine. He settled in Cagnes-sur-Mer, a small village near Vence, and, after claiming to be North African, was able to get work. He turned his attention to painting expressionist landscapes, revealing the potent influence of the artists who had preceded him. The spell of Soutine, whose house he rented for a while, was especially strong and is clearly visible in *Landscape near Vence, France.* Like Soutine, Woodruff used a rich, deep palette, with a limited tonal range. The landscape appears to erupt with bushes and buildings piled upon one another. Like Cézanne, Woodruff used blocky, textured brushstrokes that simultaneously define forms and create a visual rhythm on the surface of the canvas. With the curving shape of a hill as a backdrop, the illusion of depth is constricted, making the landscape more immediate.

One of Woodruff's express purposes in going to France was to encounter modernism. His response was somewhat equivocal. "Although most of the modernists fail to impress me, I would not be justified in condemning any of them. I feel it is every artist's privilege to create whatever he desires in the manner that pleases him most. And who can say what works of art now being produced are worthy or unworthy. Only the test of time and elimination are capable of making such a decision."[3] This attitude of open-mindedness no doubt served Woodruff well in his later role as teacher and exhibition organizer. Following twelve years at Atlanta University, Woodruff taught for more than two decades at New York University, and until his death he continued to be active as a champion of African-American artists.

---

1. "Black Beaux Arts," *Time,* 21 September 1942, 74.
2. Woodruff, "Paris Montparnasse," *Indianapolis Star,* 17 February 1929, as quoted in Winifred Stoelting, "Hale Woodruff, Artist and Teacher: Through the Atlanta Years" (Ph.D. diss., Emory University, 1978), 19.
3. Woodruff, "Local Negro Artist Finds Painters Hard to Classify," *Indianapolis Star,* 18 March 1928, as quoted in Stoelting, "Woodruff," 27.

Born, Cairo, Illinois, 1900; studied at the John Herron Art Institute, Indianapolis, 1920–circa 1922, at the School of the Art Institute of Chicago, and the Académie Scandinave and the Académie Moderne, Paris, 1927–1928; lived in Cagnes-sur-Mer, France, 1928–1931; taught at Atlanta University, 1931–1943 and 1945, and New York University, 1946–1967; died, New York, 1980.

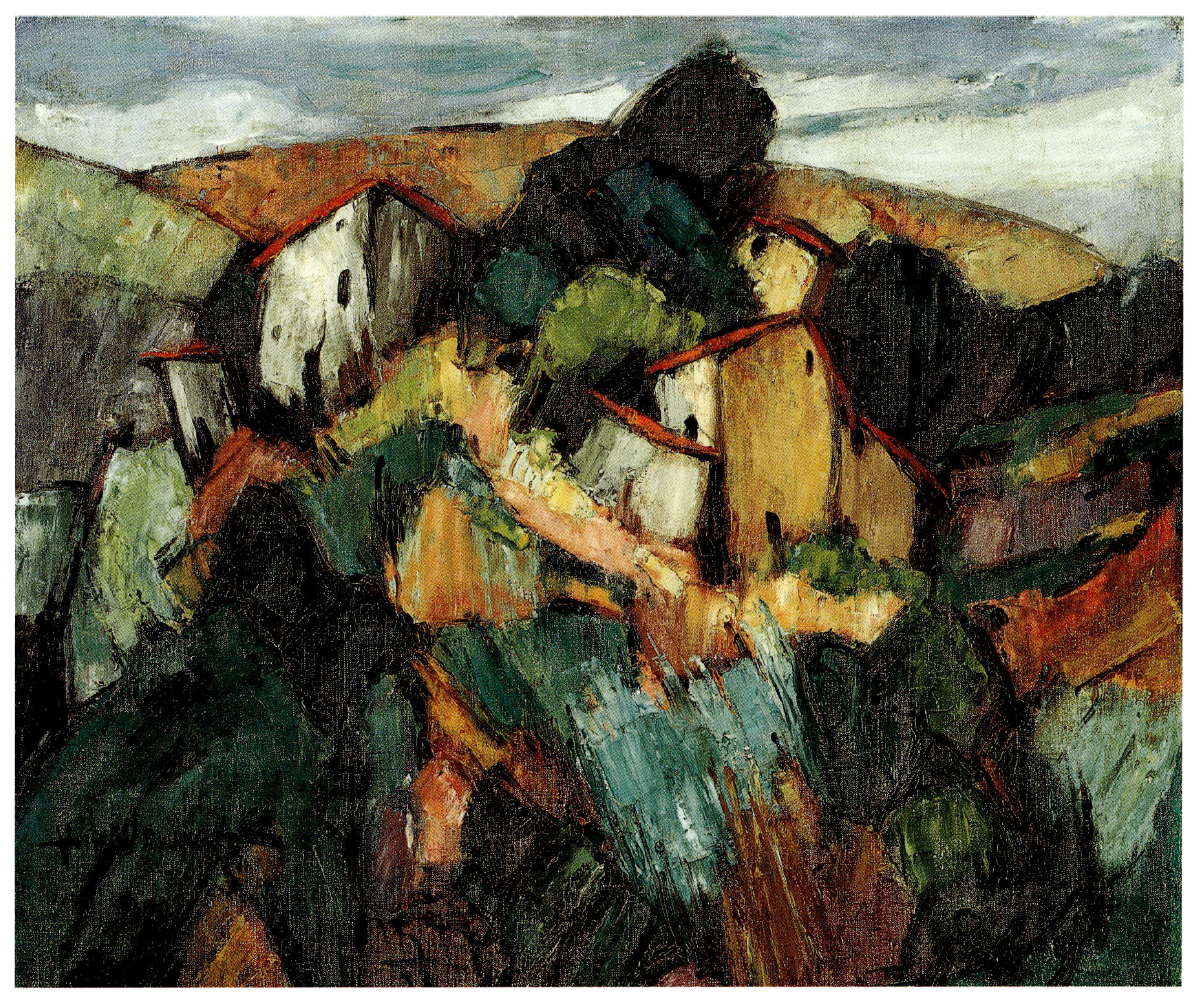

William Henry Johnson

1901–1970

Port in Gray Weather, Kerteminde, circa 1934

oil on canvas, 21 × 26 inches
signed, lower right: *W. H. Johnson*
Museum purchase with funds donated by the Arthur and Holly Magill Foundation

Little Talk, circa 1935

hand-colored wood-block print: paper, 15¼ × 18½ inches
Museum purchase with funds donated by the Arthur and Holly Magill Foundation
(illustrated on page 24)

African-American artists, especially those who grew up in the rural South, often faced overwhelming challenges in the pursuit of their careers. Inadequately funded segregated schools scarcely taught the fundamentals; classes in the arts were nonexistent. Musical talent was nurtured through churches, but instruction in painting and sculpture was not available to African-Americans in the early twentieth century.

As a child coming of age in the small farming community of Florence, South Carolina, William H. Johnson copied and drew cartoons. His native town was a railroad hub through which white Northern tourists passed on their way to Florida; it was also an exit point for Southern blacks migrating North in pursuit of a better life. At seventeen, Johnson left South Carolina for New York, where he worked odd jobs to help pay for his classes at the National Academy of Design. More conservative and less expensive than the Art Students League, the National Academy gave Johnson a sound academic background in drawing. Among his teachers were Charles Curran and Charles Hawthorne, who not only taught him but also encouraged him to spend several summers at the art colony in Provincetown, Massachusetts. In New York, Johnson met the Ash Can School painter George Luks, who hired the fledgling artist to assist him in his studio. Hawthorne and Luks helped to raise the funds that enabled Johnson to study abroad.

Paris in the late 1920s was the cultural capital of the world, a mecca for writers and artists; unlike America, France provided an environment where such talented African-Americans as Henry Ossawa Tanner, Josephine Baker, and Johnson were accepted and even nurtured. Johnson studied briefly in Paris before traveling to the south of France, where he came under the spell of Paul Cézanne, Vincent van Gogh, and Chaim Soutine. Here Johnson began a series of expressionist paintings that featured intense colors and heavy brushwork.

In 1930 Johnson settled in Kerteminde, Denmark, a small, picturesque fishing village, where he shared studio space with his Danish wife, Holcha Krake, a textile artist. He spent most of the next eight years in Scandinavia, with excursions to Germany, France, and North Africa. He averaged about two exhibitions a year, but his sales were modest. During an interview with a Danish newspaper, Johnson was asked how he, as an African-American outsider, could paint Danish subjects. He replied: "Why not? On the contrary, I say that I have never worked as well in any place as Kerteminde. In no place have I had greater peace to work, nor better motifs than right here in Denmark."[1]

Johnson's energized landscapes, with their heavily textured surfaces, reflect the emotional intensity of the expressionists Oskar Kokoschka and Edvard Munch. His familiarity with the former may have come through his wife, who had pursued art in Dresden during the 1920s.[2] Although *Port in Gray Weather, Kerteminde* lacks the agitated Van Gogh–like perspective of much of his Danish work, it is enlivened by a wavering and nervous application of paint similar to Kokoschka's. Much of the pigment, especially that denoting the masts and their reflections, was applied directly from the tube, while other areas were put on with a palette knife. A local resident recalled the response of an older fisherman upon seeing Johnson at work: "Well, now we can throw our brushes away! Now [when we paint our boats] we have to put the paint on with a knife!"[3]

The influence of the Norwegian expressionist Munch is vividly demonstrated in the hand-colored woodcut print *Little Talk,* an intimate portrait of Johnson and his wife. The image is one in a long series of self-portraits that Johnson, like Van Gogh, did throughout his life, revealing his shifts in style and mood. In the juxtaposition of his profile with her full face the artist hints at the discrepancies in the couple's race and age; the artist and Holcha are united by a tension-filled design consisting of solid blacks and harshly gouged lines. In its raw, sharp-edged lines and the expressive exaggeration of features the print resembles Munch's work in the same medium, but instead of loneliness and isolation Johnson portrays a harmony of spirit.

---

1. Johnson interview with An-dre, "Stor Kunstner fra lille By," *Aarhus Stiftstidende,* 26 November 1934, as quoted in Richard J. Powell, *Homecoming: The Art and Life of William H. Johnson* (Washington, D.C.: Smithsonian Institution Press, 1991), 62.
2. Powell, *Homecoming,* 69.
3. Niels Hansen, as quoted in Powell, *Homecoming,* 61.

Born, Florence, South Carolina, 1901; lived in New York, 1918–1926, attended the National Academy of Design, 1921–1926; to Paris, 1926–1927, and Cagnes-sur-Mer, 1928–1929; short visits to New York and Florence, 1929 and 1930; resided in Kerteminde, Denmark, 1930–1938, with excursions to Tunisia, 1932, via Hamburg, Amsterdam, Cologne, returning via Paris; to Copenhagen and Oslo, 1935; to Sweden, 1937; returned to Oslo, 1938; left Kerteminde for New York, 1938; lived in New York, 1938–1948, with a trip to Denmark, 1946–1947; institutionalized at Central Islip State Hospital, 1948–1970; died, Central Islip, New York, 1970.

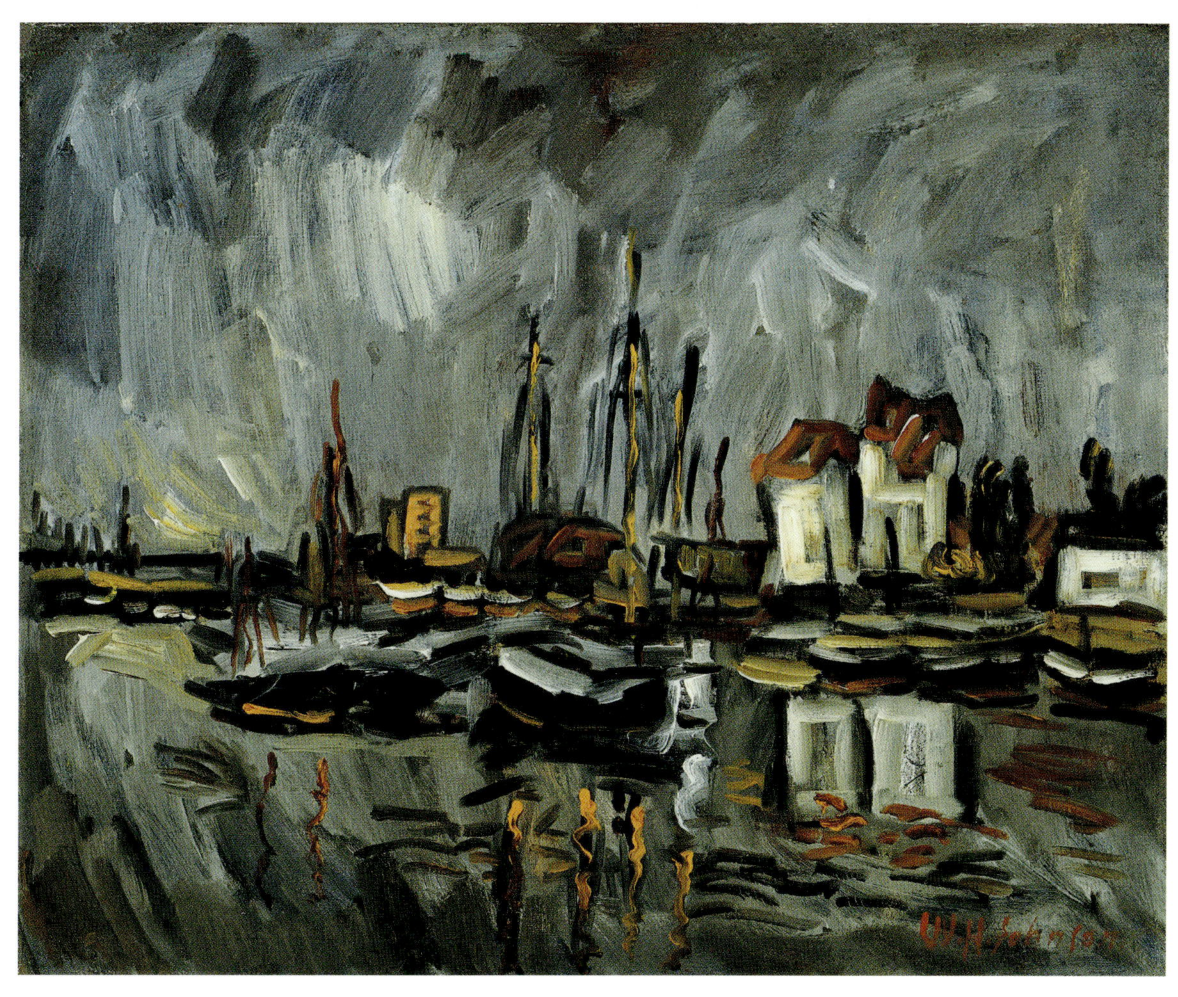

José de Creeft

1884–1982

Femme au Chignon, 1932

walnut, 24½ × 9¼ × 9 inches
signed, vertically on neck: *J. de Creeft*
Museum purchase with funds donated by the Arthur and Holly Magill Foundation

In the nineteenth century the process for making sculpture typically began with the artist's conceiving of the work and subsequently rendering a model of it in clay, wax, or plaster. Supervised by the sculptor, artisans, often Italian stonecutters or foundry workers, then translated the model into marble or bronze. With the advent of modernism, however, the sculptor became more intimately involved with his creation at every stage of development. In addition, modern sculptors carved directly, responding to the particular properties of their materials. The emphasis was most often placed on cutting, a subtractive process, rather than on modeling, an additive one. Constantin Brancusi, Robert Laurent, William Zorach, and José de Creeft were the key figures who promoted and practiced what came to be called "direct carving."

De Creeft's early training and background provided the ideal preparation for his versatility in a variety of media. A Catalan by birth, de Creeft moved to Barcelona as a child, and by his early teens had become an apprentice to a maker of religious images. He then worked at a bronze foundry before moving to Madrid, where he apprenticed with the Spanish government's official sculptor. From 1911 to 1914 he was employed in Paris and became acquainted with the work of Brancusi and Amedeo Modigliani. Working as a traditional stonecutter, he re-created clay or plaster models in stone through the use of a mechanical pointing machine. Frustrated by the restrictions of this long-standing method, he began to carve his own works directly in 1915.

The noted Southern writer Eudora Welty, selected by de Creeft to write an article about him, explained his creative processes. "Material is important to him for its own sake in a very deep sense: fundamentally it directs what he does with it. It has taught him the great craftsmanship which is implicit in his work—it is an inspirer itself, a piece out of the earth, with the whole of life implicit in itself, and its earthly shape, grain, color, weight, warmth, and the undefinable qualities, which he by study calls forth, and by physically working upon it brings into full spirit and life."[1]

Femme au Chignon, with its heavily chiseled surface, exemplifies direct wood carving and de Creeft's sensitivity to the unique properties of the medium. The artist's marks, in the form of insistent gouges, create a dynamic visual rhythm across the entire work. Because of their angle and shape these gouges catch and deflect light, achieving a dappled surface not unlike an Impressionist painting. In subject matter *Femme au Chignon* is sister to Brancusi's *Mlle Pogany;* both are stylish females enhanced by elegant proportions, Asian features, and sleek coiffures. With its aggressively carved surface *Femme au Chignon* also relates to African tribal art, a quality further hinted at by the subject's masklike expression.

De Creeft's versatility with materials embraced a wide variety of different woods and metals, which he cast, carved, and assembled. Perhaps his most novel use of metal came in his construction of *Le Picador,* a Don Quixote–like horseman, from a stove pipe and other scrap pieces. It shares certain attributes with the assemblages fabricated by his fellow countrymen Pablo Picasso and Julio Gonzalez. It also displays de Creeft's sense of humor, a quality that served him well at Black Mountain College near Asheville, North Carolina. Teaching there during the summer of 1944, a term filled with shortages and internal strife, de Creeft provided some comic relief by staging a mock bullfight replete with matadors, toreadors, and beautiful Spanish ladies.[2]

---

1. Eudora Welty, "José de Creeft," *Magazine of Art,* February 1944, 44.
2. Mary Emma Harris, *The Arts at Black Mountain College* (Cambridge, Mass.: MIT Press, 1987), 96.

Born, Guadalajara, Spain, 1884; Madrid, apprentice to Don Agustin Querol, 1900; moved to Paris, 1905; studied at the Académie Julian, 1905–1907, and worked at La Maison Greber, 1911–1914; Majorca, 1927–1929; immigrated to the United States, settling in New York, 1929; taught at Black Mountain College, near Asheville, North Carolina, 1944, and the New School for Social Research and Art Students League, New York, 1932–1978; died, New York, 1982.

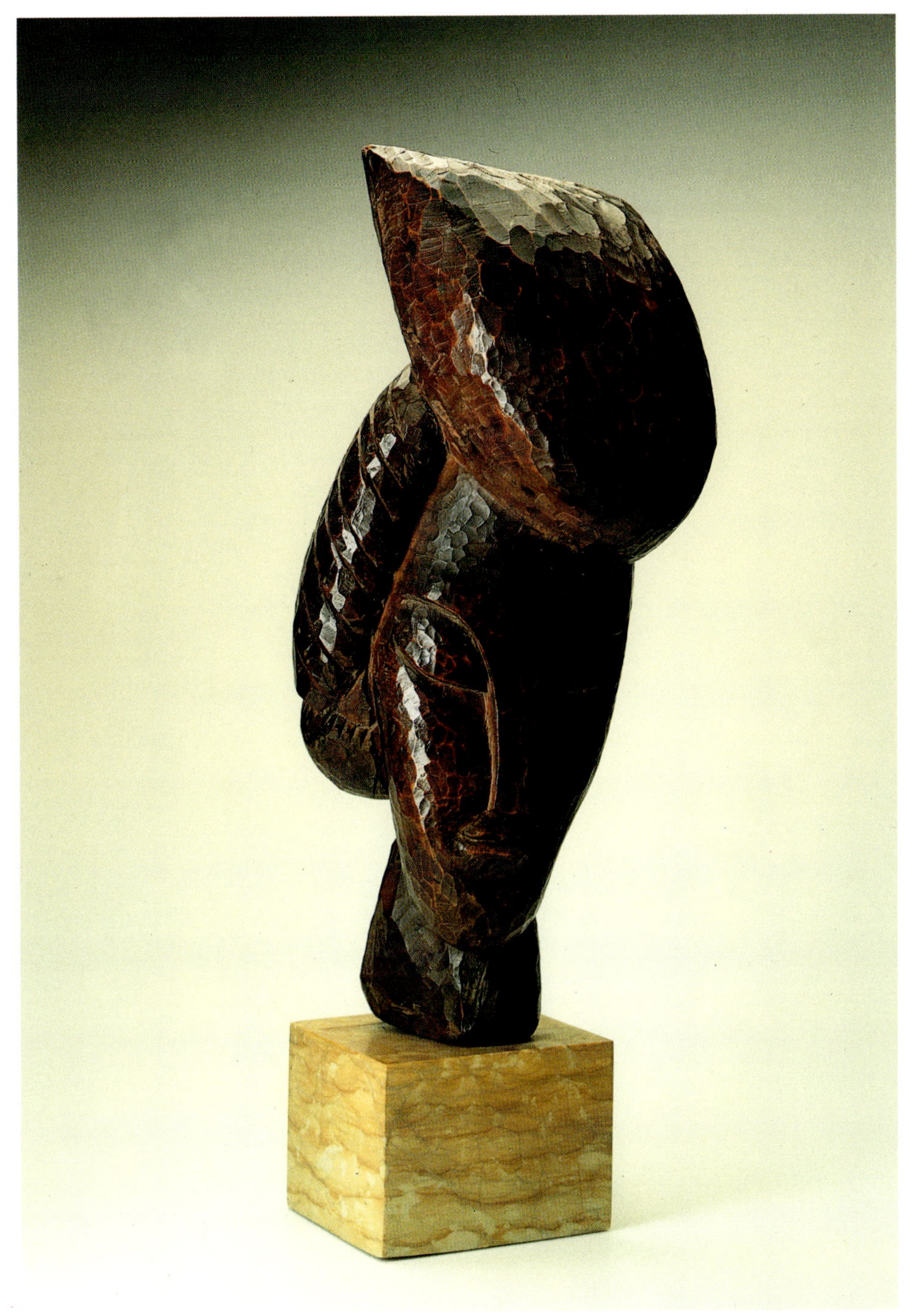

George Biddle

1885–1973

Fruit Market, Charleston, 1930

oil on canvas, 36 × 36 inches
signed, lower left: *Biddle*
Museum purchase with funds donated by
The John F. Bannon Trust; Mr. and Mrs. Alester G. Furman III; and The Museum Association, Inc.

In the midst of the Depression, Franklin Delano Roosevelt's New Deal instituted two programs that provided direct assistance for artists. The massive Works Progress Administration identified needy individuals, put them on relief, and assigned them to various tasks, including teaching, building roads, and creating artwork for public buildings. The Federal Art Project, which later evolved into the Treasury Department's Section of Fine Arts, was specifically structured to provide opportunities for artists, regardless of their financial situation. During its nine-year history the Section supervised the completion of almost 1,400 projects, most of which were murals for new federal buildings, primarily post offices and courthouses. Artists, who competed anonymously for the assignments, were encouraged to develop subject matter with local significance.

Although Roosevelt is generally credited with the invention of the New Deal, the art programs were actually the inspiration of his schoolmate, the painter George Biddle. In 1933 Biddle wrote to the president, commending him on his achievements and stating, "I am really proud to have known you at college and school." Biddle proceeded to suggest a government-sponsored mural program, modeled on one he had seen in Mexico. Biddle maintained that artists "would be contributing to and expressing in living monuments the social ideals that you are struggling to achieve and I am convinced that our mural art with a little impetus, can soon result, for the first time in our history, in a vital national expression."[1]

Before his involvement with the federal art programs, Biddle led a somewhat peripatetic existence. Although he graduated from Harvard Law School in 1911, he decided to pursue art. He studied at the Pennsylvania Academy of the Fine Arts and in Paris at the Académie Julian. While he was in France, he spent two summers in Giverny. After serving in the army during World War I, Biddle, modeling himself on Paul Gauguin, spent two years in Tahiti, where he executed a number of prints. In 1928 he joined Diego Rivera on an extensive sketching trip through Mexico. Two years later he paid an extended visit to Charleston, South Carolina, before leaving for Rome, where he lived for two years. For the remainder of the 1930s and 1940s Biddle was actively involved in government-sponsored art programs. He completed several murals and taught in Colorado and California as well as in Italy.

In its eclectic style and subject matter, Biddle's art reflects the variety of his training and experiences. A graphic artist as well as a painter, he created work that is energized by restless contours, an element that may reflect the influence of his French friend, the painter Jules Pascin. In *Fruit Market, Charleston,* for example, the forms are defined by a meandering line that lightens the otherwise ponderous figures. Shimmering colors further enliven the figures, which appear to be randomly scattered in the verdant landscape. The composition's unusually compressed perspective also contributes to the vigor with which Biddle's style animates the mundane scene.

The rhythmic, excited nature of the Museum's painting may reflect Biddle's response to the ambiance of Charleston, a city that was beginning to awaken, slowly, from a deep and long slumber. Others, too, were inspired by the city's vitality, colors, and racial heritage. Biddle may have gone to Charleston at the suggestion of either the composer George Gershwin or the novelist DuBose Heyward, the collaborators on the folk opera *Porgy and Bess.* At different times both Biddle and Gershwin visited Heyward at Folly Beach, near Charleston. While there Gershwin visited local churches, where he was inspired not only by the Negro spirituals but also by the "double clap [with its] electric effect."[2] Similarly, Biddle would have seen African-Americans tending gardens and selling produce, much as he represented them in *Fruit Market, Charleston.*

---

1. Biddle to Roosevelt, 7 May 1933, diary copy. George Biddle Papers, Archives of American Art, roll D 127.

2. Dorothy Heyward, unpublished autobiography, chapter 15. DuBose Heyward Papers, South Carolina Historical Society, Charleston, South Carolina.

Born, Philadelphia, 1885; graduated from Harvard Law School, 1911; studied at the Académie Julian, Paris, 1911–1912, and at the Pennsylvania Academy of the Fine Arts, 1912–1914; to Tahiti, 1920–1922, except for the winter of 1921, in New York; in Paris, 1924–1926, with travels to Tahiti, Puerto Rico, and Cuba; settled in Croton-on-Hudson, New York, 1927; trip to Mexico with Diego Rivera, 1928; to Charleston, South Carolina, 1930; to Rome, 1931–1932; resided at Croton-on-Hudson, except for teaching positions, at Colorado College, 1936–1937, in Pacific Palisades, California, 1941, and Rome, 1951–1952; spent six months in North Africa and Tunisia with American forces, 1943–1944; traveled to the Far East, 1959; died, Croton-on-Hudson, 1973.

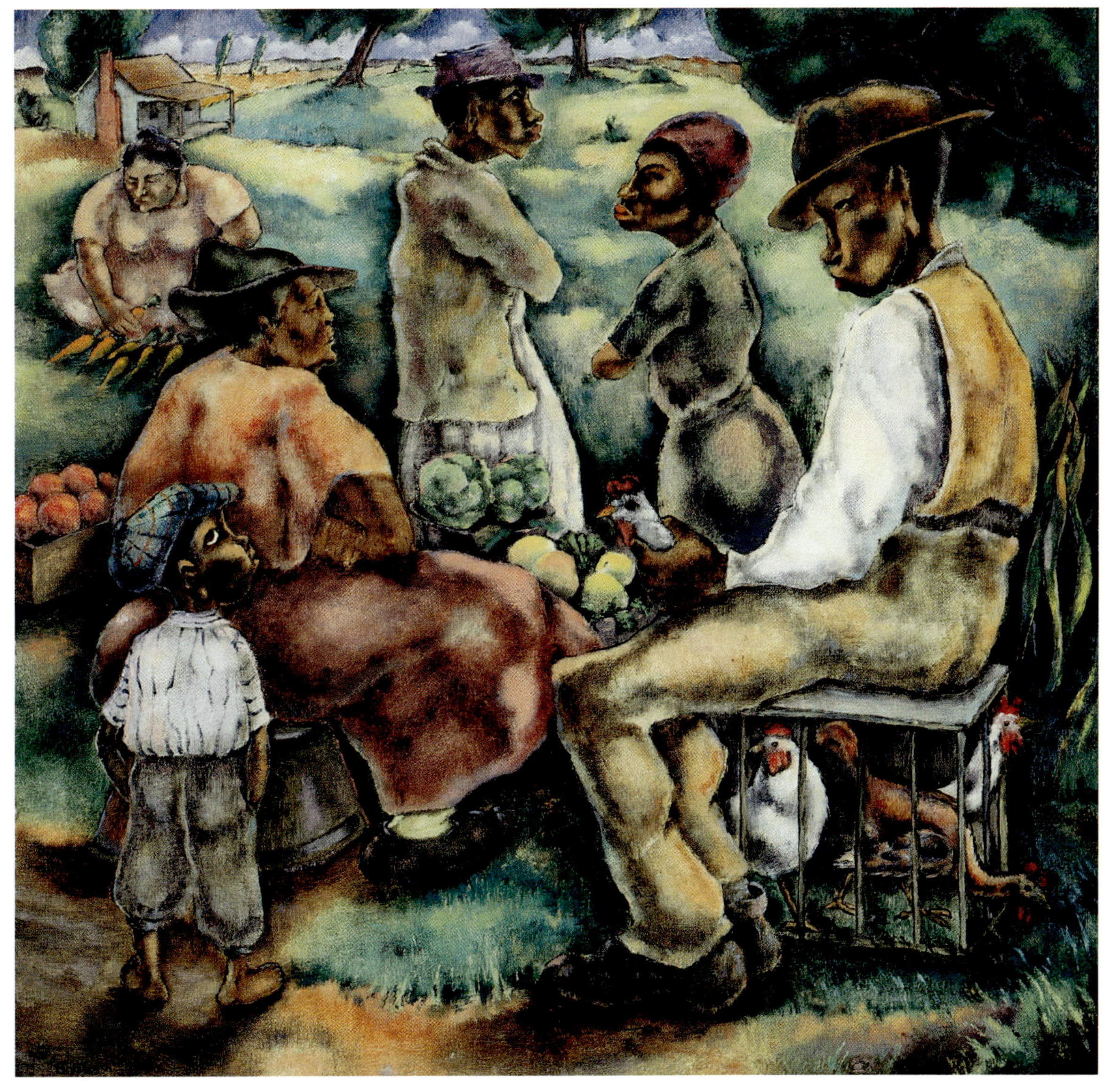

Simka Simkhovitch

1893–1949

Study for a Mural, circa 1936

oil on canvas, 23¾ × 30¾ inches
Museum purchase with funds donated by the estate of Caroline Foster

Each mural created under the auspices of the federal government was the result of a collaboration among the artist, the staff in Washington, the community, and often the building's architect. Although every commission was different, the Treasury Department's Section of Fine Arts had certain guidelines. Artists were chosen through national and regional competitions, with artistic merit a higher criterion than financial need, and whenever feasible, artists were selected to work in the areas where they lived. They were encouraged to visit the community where the commission was to be executed, to conduct research, and to communicate with local citizens. Nevertheless, the expense and inconvenience of long-distance travel often prevented artists from making these initial visits, and many went only for the installation of their work. The extent of involvement by community members varied, depending on the individual personalities of the respective postmaster, judge, or civic leader. In some instances the community vociferously objected to what it felt was an extravagant and frivolous expenditure during the Depression.[1]

In the South, where there were more projects than artists, mural commissions for post offices and courthouses were occasionally fraught with problems. Northern artists, not fully understanding Southern sensibilities, created works that either were subjected to major revision or were not warmly received. The fate of Simka Simkhovitch's mural for the Jackson, Mississippi, Federal Courthouse is an illuminating example of divergent artistic and civic perceptions.

At the time of the commission, 1936, Simkhovitch was residing in Connecticut and it is doubtful that, as a recent émigré from Russia, he went south before the installation of his mural in Jackson. As a teenager, he had attended an art school in Odessa and then pursued further training at the Royal Academy in St. Petersburg. Following the 1917 Revolution he was awarded a prize by the new regime, and several of his paintings were purchased by the Modern Museum in Petrograd. He immigrated to the United States in 1924.

As a relatively new citizen, Simkhovitch may have been overly idealistic about America and the South. The Museum's *Study for a Mural* was probably Simkhovitch's submission to one of the competitions conducted by the Section of Fine Arts. In a tripartite format the artist portrayed a harmonious, integrated society in which both races live and work together. In the center panel the main figure, to whom the others appear to listen, is a heroically muscular African-American, nude to the waist. Equally remarkable, the right panel depicts, albeit in a less idealized manner, an older couple, with the woman in a wheelchair. The overall setting is a compromise between a natural landscape and industrial elements. The prominence given to utility poles and construction workers conveys an optimism about the future of the country and may refer to the success of the Tennessee Valley Authority, a New Deal project that brought cheap electricity to northern Mississippi.

It was probably on the basis of the Museum's painting that Simkhovitch was selected to paint the mural in the Jackson courthouse. Several motifs, including the woman holding the child and the seated workman looking at drawings, do recur in the finished work. The study also fits the artist's written description, "The subject matter consists of family life, past and present. . . . The characters in the mural are of every-day life, with a typical note of their social position."[2] However, as installed, the central focus and tenor of the work have been dramatically altered. Neighborly racial harmony has been replaced by a more authoritarian reiteration of African-Americans as cotton-picking and banjo-strumming laborers, while white men distribute justice under a rigidly symmetrical classical pediment. Whether it was the Section staff in Washington or the authorities in Jackson who instigated these changes may never be known. What is clear is that the final mural, entitled *Pursuits of Life in Mississippi,* is more in keeping with the state's self-image, as reflected in the contemporaneous *Mississippi: A Guide to the Magnolia State.* Compiled and written by the Federal Writers' Project, this volume reflects the sentiment that "it is a place where everybody grows cotton on land which only a few of them own." And as a guidebook, the text in general disregards or patronizes the role of African-Americans, just as Simkhovitch did in the final mural.[3]

The initial response to the mural was reasonably positive. But subsequent generations have taken offense at the demeaning portrayal of African-Americans; since the civil-rights movement the mural has endured extended periods hidden behind a curtain while court is in session. Ironically, had Simkhovitch's original proposal been painted behind the judge's platform, it might serve as a fitting backdrop for the dispensation of justice.

---

1. The New Deal programs for the support of artists are often confused because their names and objectives frequently changed. Public Works of Art Project, 1933–1934, was the pilot program, which was administered regionally; the Section of Painting and Sculpture, later of Fine Arts, supervised murals for new federal buildings, 1934–1943; the Treasury Relief Project oversaw the decoration of existing federal buildings; and the Works Progress Administration/Federal Art Project provided economic assistance, 1935–1943. See Karen Ann Marling, *Wall to Wall America* (Minneapolis: University of Minnesota Press, 1982); Marlene Park and Gerald Markowitz, *Democratic Vistas* (Philadelphia: Temple University Press, 1984); Sue Bridwell Beckham, *Depression Post Office Murals and Southern Culture* (Baton Rouge: Louisiana State University Press, 1989); and Barbara Melosh, *Engendering Culture* (Washington, D.C.: Smithsonian Institution Press, 1991).

2. Word account for the Jackson, Mississippi, Court House, addressed to Forbes Watson, 16 July 1939. Files of the Section of Fine Arts, National Archives.

3. Federal Writers Project, *Mississippi: A Guide to the Magnolia State* (New York: Hastings House Publishers, 1938), 3.

Born, near Kiev, Ukraine, 1893; attended art school in Odessa, 1907–1912; student at the Royal Academy, St. Petersburg, 1913–1915; taught at the Academy of Fine Arts, and at the Architectural Institute for Women, until 1924; immigrated to New York, 1924; moved to Greenwich, Connecticut, 1931; died, Greenwich, 1949.

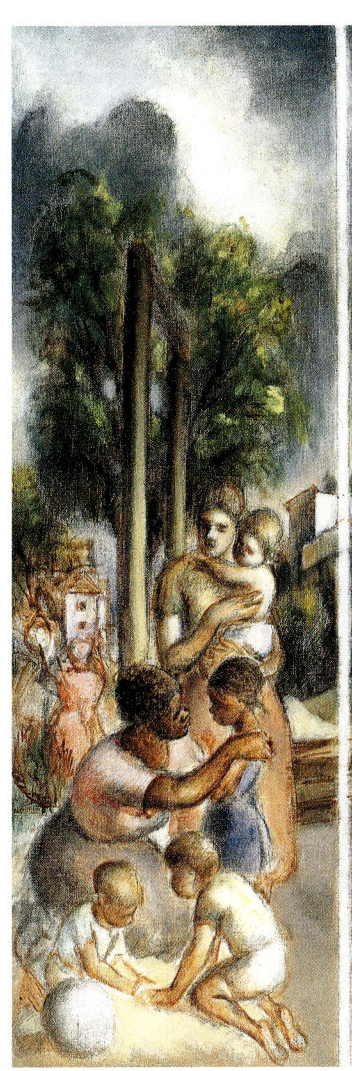

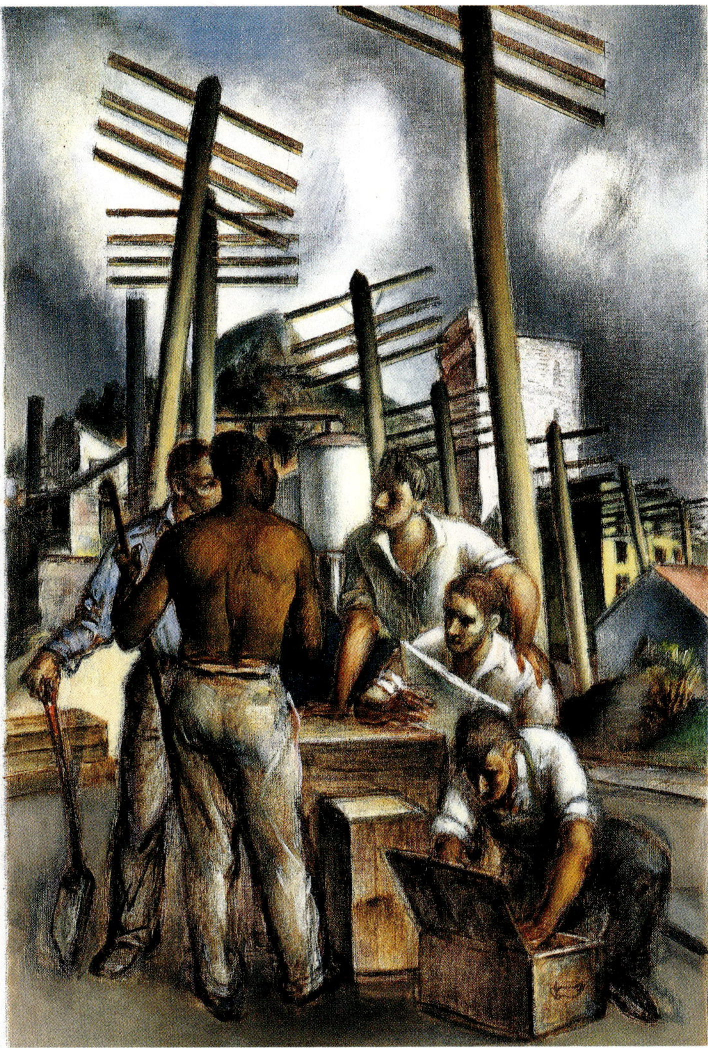

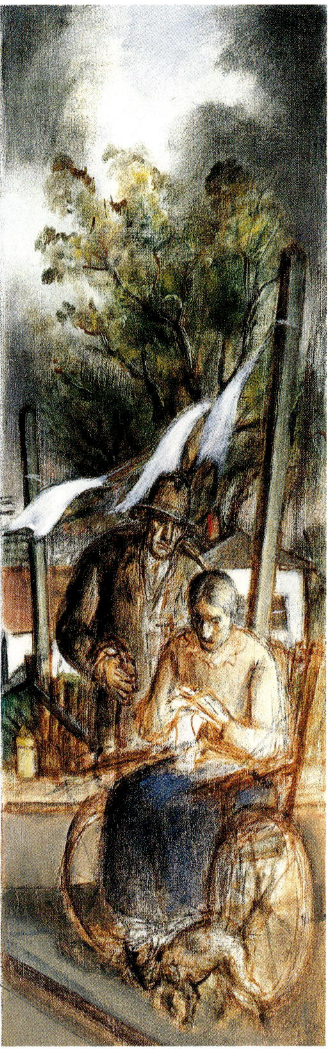

Frederick Stallknecht Wight

1902–1986

Mr. Allgood, Augusta, 1934

oil on canvas, 30 × 36 inches
signed, bottom center: *F. Wight*
Museum purchase

During the Depression American art was characterized by a rejection of abstraction and a return to realism. In 1939 the abstract painter Stuart Davis bemoaned this shift, saying, "domestic naturalism, the chicken yard, the pussycat, the farmer's wife, the artist's model, Route 16A, natural beauties of the home town, etc., became the order of the day in painting."[1] For others the depiction of the American Scene renewed confidence in the American way and reaffirmed the vitality of the country. Three midwestern painters—Thomas Hart Benton, John Steuart Curry, and Grant Wood—are the artists most closely associated with this celebratory Regionalism, but in actuality the spirit of the American Scene pervaded other regions as well, including the South.

Raised in New England, Frederick S. Wight attended the University of Virginia and then, for health reasons, spent two winters in the warmer climate of Augusta, Georgia. There he became sufficiently familiar with the cultural environment to author an insightful novel about the mores and escapades of a Southern mill town during the Depression. In addition, he completed a remarkable series of figure paintings.

A thinly veiled autobiography of a young Northern painter who travels south to the fictional town of Millington, *South* tells the story of Frederick Winslow, a portrait painter who becomes fascinated by the mill hands. Wight's novel is a picture of a depressed South, just as his compelling likeness of Mr. Allgood in the Museum's painting captures "not only a crushing universal poverty, but a desolateness that looked out from another time."[2]

For most of its history Augusta has been dominated by textile mills. In *Mr. Allgood, Augusta,* the gaunt profile of the Augusta Cotton Factory stands starkly behind Allgood and evokes Wight's description: "Hideous in slate and red brick, doubtless. The stacks of the cotton mills loom from the heavier vapors of the River. And the huge cathedral-penitentiary, hulks of the mills themselves. Silently onerous."[3] Like the fictional Winslow in his novel, Wight sought out mill hands to sit for portraits. William Allgood, a retired worker who lived across the street from the factory, is the subject of this painting. In a spare, hard-edged manner and with a limited palette Wight successfully portrayed the spirit of the Depression. Carefully balanced by the architectural mass of the mill, the immobile figure is placed uncomfortably close to the viewer. Just as Grant Wood's *American Gothic,* painted four years before, has emerged as the icon of midwestern agriculture, *Mr. Allgood, Augusta* could stand for the Depression-ravaged South.

Wight's later career encompassed painting, teaching, and museum administration. After obtaining his master's degree in museology at Harvard University on the G.I. Bill in 1946, Wight worked at the Institute of Contemporary Art in Boston, before becoming the director of the Art Gallery at the University of California, Los Angeles. Recognized for his monographic exhibitions of such artists as John Marin and Charles Sheeler, Wight explained his enthusiasm for in-depth exhibitions by saying, "the critical, biographic, written portrait has been . . . basic for me. . . . The one-man show, late enough in life so that you have a biography, . . . has been characteristic of me. I have been a biographer in the field of art."[4]

---

1. Stuart Davis, "Abstract Painting Today," Francis V. O'Connor, ed., *Art for the Millions* (Greenwich, Conn.: New York Graphic Society, 1973), 122.

2. Frederick S. Wight, *South* (New York: Farrar & Rinehart, 1935), 8.

3. Wight, *South,* 5.

4. Frederick S. Wight, "Of Art and Exhibitions," oral history, 1972–1973, as quoted in Elizabeth Shepherd and Stephen S. Prokopoff, *Sudden Nature: The Art of Frederick S. Wight, 1902–1986* (Los Angeles: Wight Art Gallery, University of California, 1991), 8.

Born, New York, 1902; graduated from the University of Virginia, 1923; studied at the Académie Julian, Paris, 1923–1925; resided in Cape Cod, Massachusetts, with winters in Virginia, Georgia, and Louisiana, 1925–1937; served in the Navy during World War II; master's degree from Harvard University, 1946; director of education and associate director at the Institute of Contemporary Art, Boston, 1946–1953; director, University of California, Los Angeles, Art Gallery, 1953–1973; died, Los Angeles, 1986.

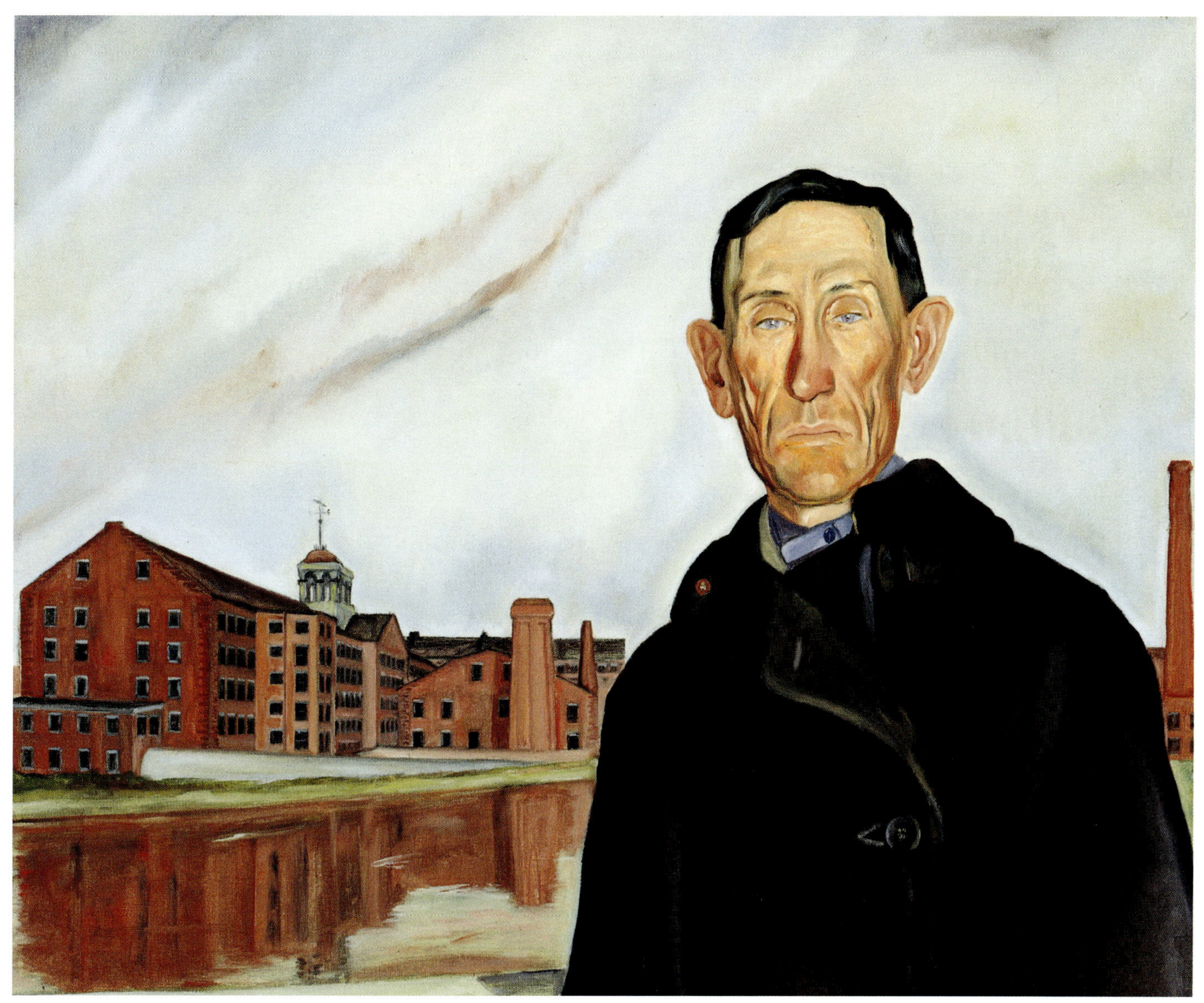

Morris Cole Graves

born 1910

Kid Goat in an Abandoned Garden, 1934–1935

oil on canvas, 53 × 46¼ inches
Museum purchase with funds donated by the Arthur and Holly Magill Foundation and funds from the National Endowment for the Arts and the Foundation for Contemporary Performance Arts, Inc. (by exchange)

The American Northwest has become the region most associated with artists concerned with the spiritual aspects of art. Perhaps because of its perceived proximity to the Far East, the Northwest has been receptive to Eastern mystical thought and, in particular, to Zen Buddhism. The presence of the Northwest Coast Indians, who believe in the spiritual essence of animals, reinforced this predilection. The artists who responded most positively to this inclination toward spirituality are Mark Tobey, John Cage, and Morris Graves.

Graves's search for the spiritual in art has been a lifelong pursuit, beginning with a sickly childhood that led him to channel his energies into art and gardening. His formal training was modest, and it is the art and thought of the Far East that have had the greatest impact on Graves's creative development. Working on a merchant ship at age seventeen, he made his first trip to Tokyo, Shanghai, and Hong Kong; for the rest of his life he yearned for the East, and he succeeded in making several visits. While finishing high school he spent two summers in New Orleans, an experience that would affect his earliest mature work of the 1930s. In Louisiana he stayed with the family of the future painter Fritz Bultman. Although he felt "happy and fortunate to be in such a home, . . . [New Orleans] did not work out for me. The city brought me up against my upbringing. The Bohemian life, the sensuality, the endless talk, the lounging and postponements turned me away with a sense of contamination."[1]

While in New Orleans Graves frequented the zoo with the young Bultman; there Graves studied animals and birds, which provided him with a reservoir of imagery. He became acquainted with classical art and architecture as represented in the city's Garden District. In addition, *Kid Goat in an Abandoned Garden* suggests that Graves visited the city's above-ground cemeteries, known for their elaborately embellished monuments. The painting's preponderance of urns relates to the artist's lifelong interest in vessels, ranging from classically inspired marbles to three-legged Chinese ceremonial objects to simple glazed flowerpots. For Graves these vessels were associated with ritual; in *Kid Goat in an Abandoned Garden* the presumed use of the urns is funerary, to hold either ashes of the deceased or funeral bouquets. Another vessel reference may be the analogy of the human body as the receptacle of the soul, alluded to by the classical torso. The use of such symbols, including even the goat that appears placed on an altar as if for sacrifice, became a hallmark of Graves's visual language.

In Graves's early work he painted on canvas, often applying his oils directly with a palette knife. His colors tend to be somber and dense, and, as in the Museum's painting, the works are often composed from many disparate parts. In his later years Graves chose to work on paper, usually in watercolor or pastel. His touch became lighter and more calligraphic, similar to Chinese scroll paintings. Likewise, his compositions became more understated.

Throughout his long and productive career Graves has remained apart from the mainstream, with a carefully focused interest in mysticism. His later work, which at times is gently humorous, deals with profound issues that have a timeless quality. Graves has described his objective in the following terms: "I paint to evolve a changing language of symbols, a language with which to remark upon the qualities of our mysterious capacities which direct us toward ultimate reality. I paint to rest from the phenomena of the external world—to pronounce it—and to make notations of its essences with which to verify the inner eye."[2]

---

1. Graves, as quoted in Frederick S. Wight et al., *Morris Graves* (Los Angeles: Wight Art Gallery, Universtiy of California, 1956), 8.

2. Graves, as quoted in Dorothy Miller, ed., *Americans 1942: 18 Artists from 9 States* (New York: The Museum of Modern Art, 1942), 51.

Born, Fox Valley, Oregon, 1910; sailed to the Far East, summers of 1928, 1929, and 1930; attended high school, Beaumont, Texas, 1931–1932, with summers spent in New Orleans; in the Seattle and Puget Sound area, 1933–1941, with extended stays in Los Angeles, 1934, and New York, 1937; detained in California by United States Army, 1942; returned to Puget Sound, 1943–1946; to Hawaii, 1946; Edmonds, Washington, 1947–1954, with trips to Europe, 1948, Mexico, 1950, and Japan, 1954; lived in County Cork, Ireland, 1954–1956 and 1959–1960; to Seattle, 1956–1958; traveled around the world including India and Japan, 1961–1963; settled in Loleta, California; traveled to Asia, 1971, Africa and South America, 1972, and the Far East, 1973; resides in California.

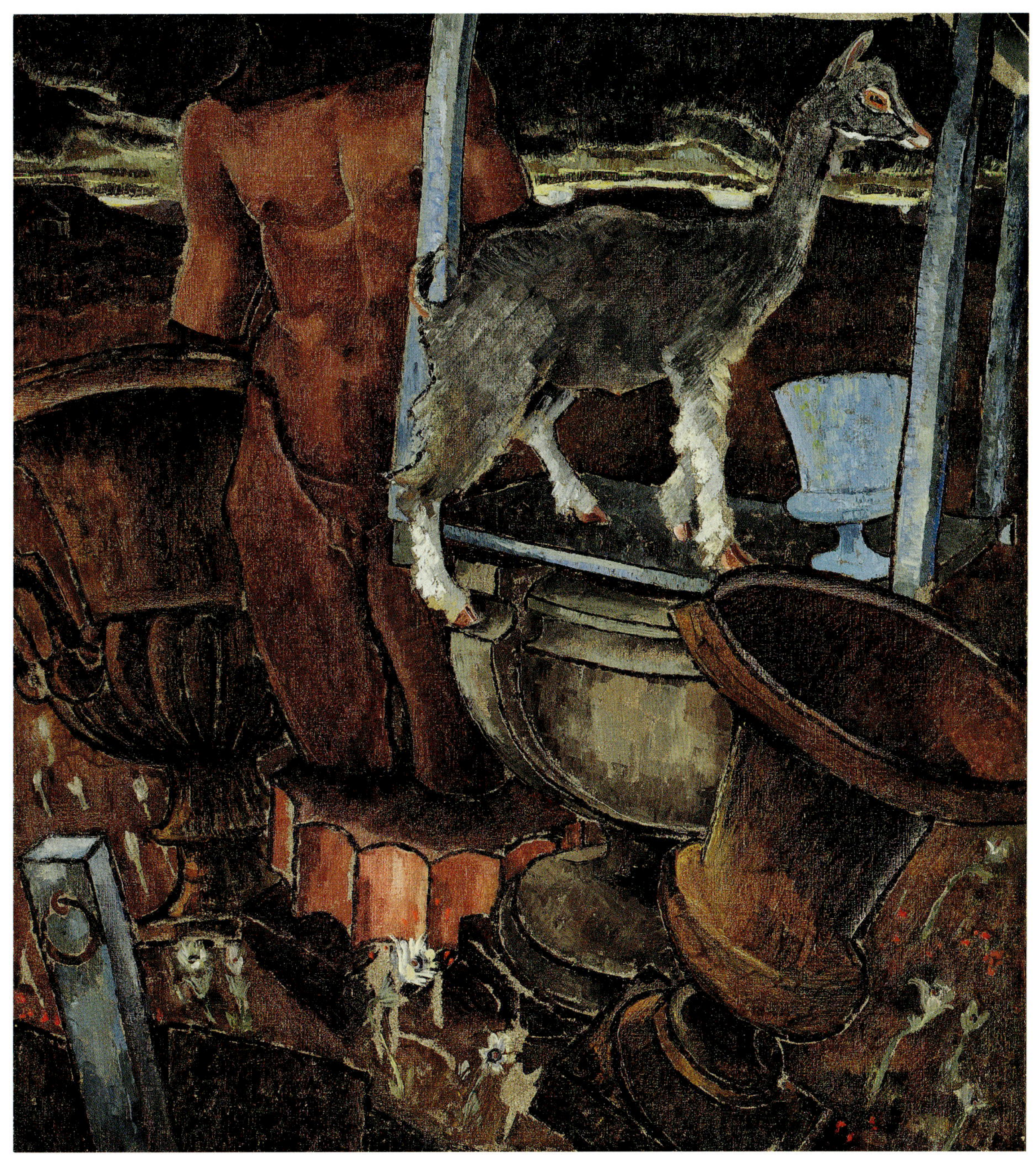

Jacques van Aalten

born 1907

Repent, You Sinners, 1938

oil on canvas, 28 5/8 × 31 3/8 inches
signed, lower right: *van Aalten / NYC 38*
Museum purchase with funds donated by the Arthur and Holly Magill Foundation

The art of Social Realism paralleled the evolution of American Scene painting and Regionalism; however, the tenor of Social Realism differs dramatically. The American Scene and Regionalist artists celebrated the virtues of this country and often portrayed the beleaguered as heroic survivors. Conversely, the Social Realists criticized abominable living conditions, glorified the proletariat, and often expressed grievances against the establishment as seen in the caustic and politically driven imagery of such artists as Ben Shahn and Philip Evergood. Shahn's subjects in particular related to controversial contemporary events. For example, his series representing *The Passion of Sacco and Vanzetti* examines the miscarriage of justice and ethnic prejudice, both universal topics. *The New Republic* summarized the essence of Shahn's success: "By being 'hard-boiled,' by making his 'anarchist bastards' pathetically funny, sallow martyrs—though reverent all the while—Mr. Shahn has been able to let himself go rippingly on the subject of Judge Thayer . . . fishy, green-eyed, bony-faced, lantern-jawed."[1]

Part of the success of Shahn's imagery is the immediacy of the work: the figures are positioned close to the viewer and are painted with a sure hand that occasionally indulges in caricature. These qualities can be found in Jacques van Aalten's painting *Repent, You Sinners,* in which a compressed space is crowded with social stereotypes.

Like Shahn, van Aalten was born abroad and immigrated to this country as a child. He received training at both the National Academy of Design and the Art Students League and worked on murals under the auspices of the Works Progress Administration's Federal Art Project. During World War II he worked at the Brooklyn Navy Yard before going to Detroit, where he established his own school. In the late 1940s he moved to New Orleans, where he remained active for three decades.

In *Repent, You Sinners* van Aalten painted the scene of a street evangelist, a middle-aged African-American woman dressed in clerical garb. She exhorts a crowd of onlookers that consists mostly of working-class whites. The figures in the foreground listen with rapt attention, while two men at the center stare directly out of the canvas, engaging the viewer. Separate from the group is the stylishly dressed woman to the far right who wears a condescending smirk on her face. Behind the preaching woman, aping both her expression and gesture, is a man attempting to sell a Communist-oriented newspaper, the *Daily Worker.*

In this urban setting van Aalten has portrayed a variety of individuals who, although focused on one event, remain isolated from one another. The workers, the newspaper seller, the evangelist, the businessman, and the society matron have come together accidentally, a frequent occurrence in such large cities as New York, where van Aalten lived at the time.

---

1. Matthew Josephson, "The Passion of Sacco-Vanzetti," *The New Republic,* 20 April 1932, 275, in David Shapiro, ed., *Social Realism: Art as a Weapon* (New York: Frederick Ungar, 1973), 291.

Born, Antwerp, Belgium, 1907; immigrated to the United States, 1917; studied in New York at the National Academy of Design, 1926–1930, and Art Students League, 1932–1934; taught at the Nassau Conservatory of Art, Rockville Center, New York, 1940, and the Van Aalten Studio School, Detroit, Michigan, 1944–1947; lived in New Orleans, circa 1947–1975; resides in Deerfield Beach, Florida.

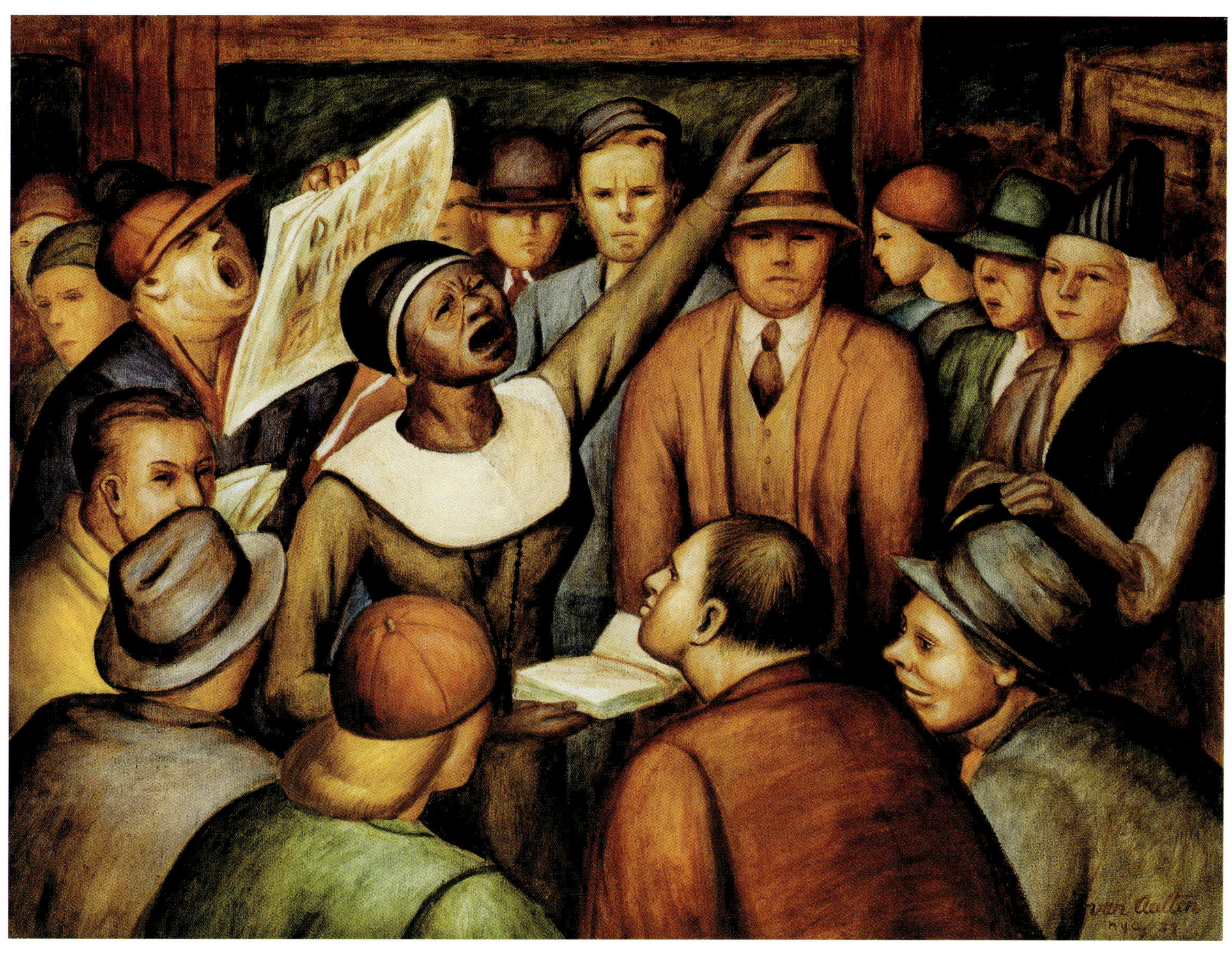

Francis Speight

1896–1989

Eleventh and Pine, 1938

oil on canvas, 40 3/8 × 30 3/8 inches
signed, lower right: *Francis Speight*
Museum purchase with funds donated by the Arthur and Holly Magill Foundation

When the Ash Can School painters abandoned the sun-filled landscapes of the Impressionists for dingy city life, the urban scene was elevated to the status of viable subject matter, where it would remain for half a century. Several Regionalists adopted cityscapes as an alternative to the farms and the cultivated landscapes immortalized by Thomas Hart Benton and Grant Wood. After all, urban populations had increased markedly since the end of the previous century, as farm families, some displaced by automation and some seeking new opportunities, moved to the cities. With the advent of the Depression, however, cities, the locus of bread lines and relief agencies, became symbols of hopelessness and desperation. The themes of loneliness in a crowd and the emptiness of a city street are fundamental to the mature work of Edward Hopper and Charles Burchfield. The depiction of solitary figures, or figures who do not interact, was a standard motif for Hopper, who also used stark lighting to reinforce the harshness of his settings.

This same feeling of solitude and isolation recurs in the paintings of Francis Speight. A native of rural North Carolina, he lived his early life on a farm; however, for most of his career he resided in Philadelphia, painting urban subjects and teaching. After two years at Wake Forest College in Winston-Salem, North Carolina, Speight joined the United States Army. Following his short tour of duty, he attended the Corcoran School of Art in Washington, D.C., for one term, before enrolling at the Pennsylvania Academy of the Fine Arts. Like Thomas Anshutz and Hugh Breckenridge before him, Speight moved from the status of student to faculty member, a position he held for thirty-five years. His affiliation with the Academy was critical to his development; with his dark tonalities, free brushwork, and realistic bent, he followed in the footsteps of Thomas Eakins and Anshutz. His choice of urban subject matter reflects the influences of John Sloan and Everett Shinn, both of whom had been newspaper artists in Philadelphia.

In *Eleventh and Pine* Speight depicted a view from his Philadelphia studio, about ten blocks from the Academy. At the time the neighborhood was a mix of residential buildings and small shops specializing in books, antiques, and used objects. The steep angle of the sun, the smoke emanating from chimneys in the background, and the hunched posture of the lone pedestrian combine to give the painting a forlorn, wintry aspect. Speight's limited palette of somber and cool tones reiterates the chilliness of the image. The precipitous perspective and elevated viewpoint create a sense of remoteness, an emotional quality typical of Speight's work. The elongated shadows of the two automobiles propel the viewer's eye to the lower right, while the strong contrapuntal verticals of the street lights and the buildings hold the painting in a delicate balance.

Like Hopper, Speight evokes the loneliness of the city, the austerity of which is alleviated only slightly by a solitary, anonymous figure. Painted in 1938, *Eleventh and Pine* mirrors the gloom of the Depression. Although Speight produced murals under the New Deal programs for artists, his income derived primarily from his teaching salary, which must have been meager. In later years, he recalled, he "didn't even know there was a Depression," reflecting a phenomenon felt by many artists accustomed to a modest lifestyle.[1]

---

1. Speight, as quoted in David Sellin, *Francis Speight: A Retrospective* (Washington, D.C.: Taggart, Jorgensen and Putnam, 1986), 3.

Born near Windsor, North Carolina, 1896; attended Wake Forest College, Winston-Salem, North Carolina, 1915–1917; United States Army, 1917–1919; studied one term at the Corcoran School of Art, Washington, D.C., 1920; studied at the Pennsylvania Academy of the Fine Arts, 1920–1925; instructor at the Academy, 1925–1961; retired to North Carolina, 1961, and taught at East Carolina University, Greenville, North Carolina; died, Greenville, 1989.

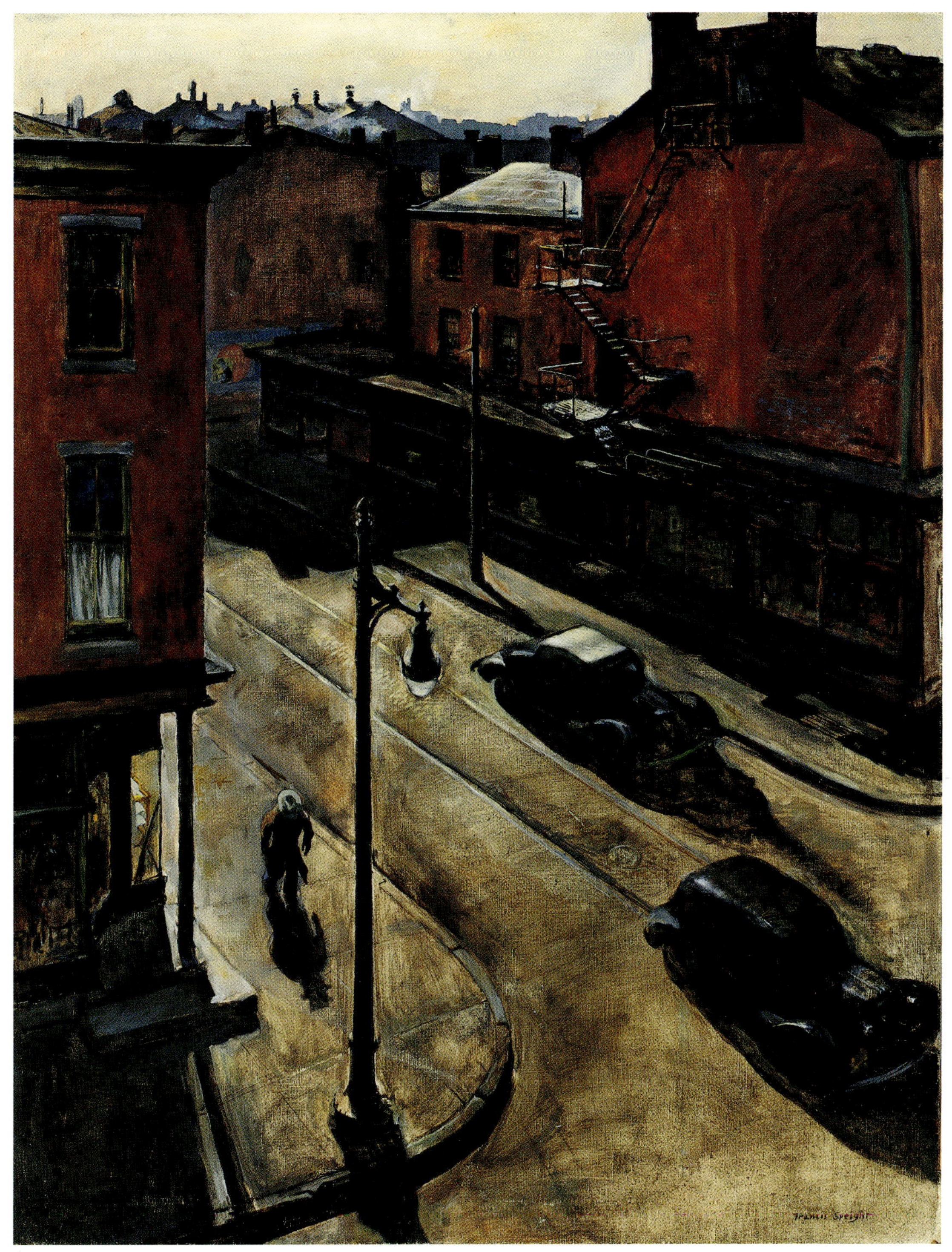
Francis Speight

Josef Albers

1888–1976

Construction (On Yellow), 1938

oil on Masonite, 23⅛ × 26¹⁄₁₆ inches
signed, lower right: *A 38*
Museum purchase with funds donated by the Arthur and Holly Magill Foundation

Upon Adolf Hitler's rise to power, many artists, architects, musicians, and writers fled Europe for the United States, where they helped to shape America's cultural destiny. Despite the language barrier they faced, many became influential teachers, and their legacy continues through their students. At Harvard University, Walter Gropius and Marcel Breuer, along with Ludwig Mies van der Rohe in Chicago, created a truly international style of architecture by transplanting the ideology of the Bauhaus to American soil. The Bauhaus had been founded by Gropius with the express purpose of uniting art and design aesthetics with modern industrial technology. Gropius's and Mies's glass-and-steel boxes became the hallmark of the International Style.

Josef Albers, both a former student and faculty member at the Bauhaus, brought his design expertise to this country and emerged as a pivotal figure in American art education. Albers's background and training emphasized craftsmanship and teaching, qualities the artist combined at the Bauhaus, at Black Mountain College, and at Yale University. He grew up in Germany's heavily industrialized Ruhr district in a family that stressed handicraft. He was educated as a teacher and taught public school for many years. In 1920 he attended the newly founded Bauhaus at Weimar, where he worked in glass. Two years later he joined the faculty and set up the school's glass workshop. He went on to design furniture and typography and other functional objects in metal, glass, and wood. His affiliation with the Bauhaus lasted thirteen years, longer than that of anyone else.[1]

With the rise of Nazism the Bauhaus was closed, forcing many of its faculty and students to disperse, not only Gropius, Mies, and Breuer but also Wassily Kandinsky and Paul Klee. Albers and his wife, Anni, a Bauhaus-trained textile artist, were invited to Black Mountain College, an experimental institution in rural North Carolina near Asheville, to establish visual art at the core of the curriculum. Albers was recommended by Philip Johnson, Director of Architecture and Design at the Museum of Modern Art in New York, who knew of the Alberses' plight and their need to leave Germany. The college's leaders were not deterred by the fact that Albers spoke no English, and for fifteen years Albers remained at Black Mountain College, where his philosophy and teaching style dominated the entire program. Like the Bauhaus when Albers first went there, Black Mountain was a young and idealistic institution. Initially occupying quarters used for church summer camps, the college was a utopian commune operating on a modest budget. Despite the Depression, enrollment hovered around fifty students, who benefited from Albers's credo "to teach the student to see in the widest sense: to open his eyes to the phenomena about him and, most important of all, to open his own living, being, and doing."[2]

Albers's primary teaching tools were the simplest of materials: paper and pencil. Having little faith in the traditional, academic study of drawing, he had his students fold and manipulate the paper to enhance their imagination and manual skills. This process is directly mirrored in his work, including both the Museum's painting and his landmark series, *Homage to the Square.* Albers's approach was studied and intellectual. Unlike many of his contemporaries who reveled in spontaneity and the materiality of paint, Albers denied its textural qualities and methodically applied colors in flat, clearly delineated areas.

In an article for *Art News* Elaine de Kooning, who sat in on his classes during the summer of 1948, called Albers "a master of optical illusion." She quoted him as stating: "The concern of the artist is with the discrepancy between physical fact and psychological effect."[3] In *Construction (On Yellow),* for example, there are conflicting illusions: the white square at the painting's center, a harbinger of the *Homage to the Square* series, both recedes and projects. Similarly, the longest black diagonal line can be read as either the element closest to or farthest from the picture plane. Relying on his early experience with glass, Albers manipulated transparent and opaque colors, creating the effects of overlapping shapes. *Construction* is typical of Albers's work: it was painted on Masonite, a firmer surface than canvas, and it is simply presented in a metal-and-wood frame designed by the artist.

In 1949 Albers left North Carolina and the following year became chairman of the design department at Yale University. It was there that he began his square series in earnest, demonstrating that "color is the most relative medium in art."[4] In carefully apportioned formats Albers analyzed color perception and the interrelationships of colors. His art was not unlike his teaching: a series of exercises designed to encourage people to see. His reputation as a teacher is also celebrated. Robert Rauschenberg paid him the following tribute: "Years later, though, I'm still learning what he taught me, because what he taught had to do with the entire visual world. . . . I consider Albers the most important teacher I've ever had."[5]

---

1. Nicholas Fox Weber, "The Artist as Alchemist," in Nicholas Fox Weber et al., *Josef Albers: A Retrospective* (New York: The Solomon R. Guggenheim Foundation, 1988), 21.
2. Albers, as quoted in George Heard Hamilton, *Josef Albers—Paintings, Prints, Projects* (New Haven: Yale University Art Gallery, 1956), 13, in Weber, *Albers: A Retrospective,* 11.
3. Elaine de Kooning, "Albers Paints a Picture," *Art News,* November 1950, 41.
4. Albers, as quoted in Weber, "Artist as Alchemist," 53.
5. Rauschenberg, as quoted in Calvin Tomkins, *The Bride & the Bachelors: Five Masters of the Avant-Garde* (New York: Viking Press, 1968), 199, in Weber, "Artist as Alchemist," 55.

Born, Bottrop, Germany, 1888; attended Lehrerseminar (Teacher's College), Burren, 1905–1908; taught public school, 1908–1913 and 1916–1919; studied at the School for Applied Arts, Essen, 1916–1919, the Royal Bavarian Academy of Pictorial Art, 1919, and the Bauhaus, 1920–1922; faculty member, Bauhaus, 1923–1933, Black Mountain College, 1933–1949, and Yale University, 1950–1960; died, New Haven, 1976.

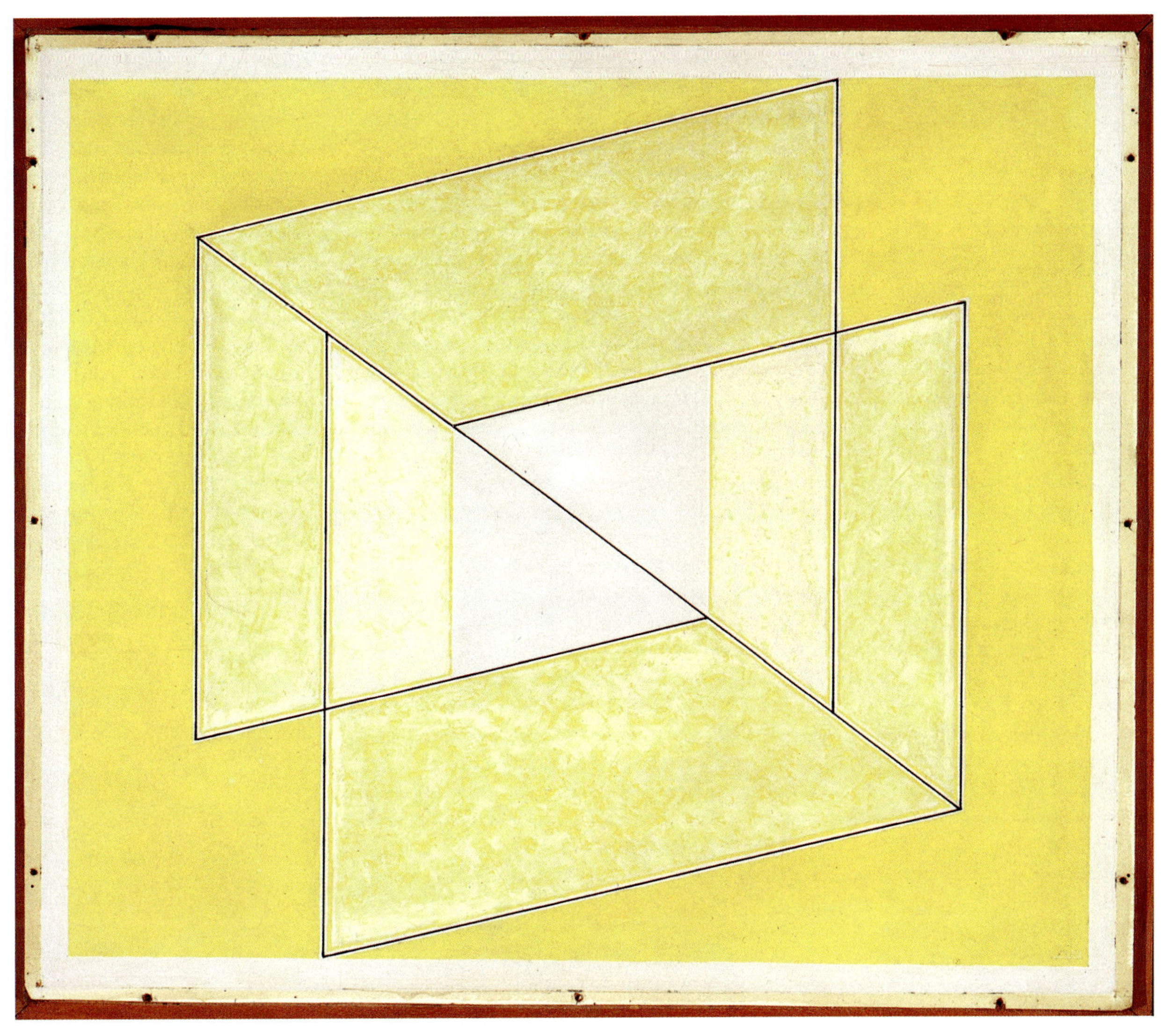

Will Henry Stevens

1881–1949

Green Leaves, 1938

mixed media on paper, 26 × 22 inches
signed, lower right: *Stevens 38*
Museum purchase with funds donated by
The Museum Association, Inc.

Nonobjective painting is often divided into two schools of thought, each with a master: Piet Mondrian, whose work is characterized by pure geometry; and Wassily Kandinsky, whose early painting is loose and expressive. Of the two, Kandinsky was the first to exert his influence through his writings, which were partially published in English by Alfred Stieglitz in 1912.[1] In *On the Spiritual in Art* Kandinsky made a strong case for the analogies between art and music, suggesting that colors and forms have corresponding sounds. He believed in the emotive power of painting, expressed through formal means, without reference to external reality. Kandinsky thus emphasized the inner feelings of the artist. Several American artists responded to Kandinsky, each in a distinctive way. Arthur G. Dove, for example, played upon musical themes, creating painted versions of symphonies and sonatas. Marsden Hartley, in his work from the 1910s, developed a style that in its colorful explosiveness seems cacophonous.

Will Henry Stevens, employing materials inventively, developed a personal vision that was closely allied to Kandinsky's premises. In 1944 an exhibition of Stevens's work was held at Black Mountain College, where Josef Albers headed the art program. Toward the end of the exhibition Albers wrote Stevens: "I am impressed with your sensitive musicality for color and your ability to handle a multitude of forms and to combine them [in]to an organic whole."[2] Albers sensed a kinship between Stevens's work and that of Kandinsky, a former colleague at the Bauhaus. Perhaps Albers was unaware that Stevens was a musician and had admired the work of Kandinsky since the mid-1920s. Although Stevens never went to Europe, he made regular visits to New York throughout his life. Many works by Kandinsky were owned by Solomon R. Guggenheim who, before opening his museum, made his collection available by appointment. Kandinsky's work, both written and visual, would also have been available in a variety of publications.

A midwesterner, Stevens studied initially at the Cincinnati Art Academy, and for a short while worked at Rookwood Pottery, noted for its Arts-and-Crafts approach to ceramics. In 1906 he became a student at the Art Students League in New York, where he found William Merritt Chase's teaching style to be somewhat pompous. Stevens spent most of his life as a teacher, first in Louisville, Kentucky, and then in New Orleans. In 1921 Stevens joined the faculty of Sophie Newcomb College, where he remained until his retirement twenty-seven years later. Newcomb was renowned for its pottery, a distinctive ceramic type that employed iridescent colors and translucent glazes to depict motifs derived from nature.

Stevens's connection with the Rookwood and Newcomb potteries is reflected in his mature work, in which organic and graceful shapes proliferate. The dominant hue of his palette is an elegant blue-green, and many of his paintings appear to glow from within, partly as a result of his innovative use of pastel. Working with an associate at Newcomb and relying upon knowledge gained as a youth assisting his father in an apothecary shop, Stevens developed a technique that combined pastel and tempera with alcohol and turpentine, which he applied with a brush. He preferred a small format, and his more intimate compositions allowed the artist a degree of mobility.

In its sonorous and glowing colors, *Green Leaves* reveals Stevens's mastery of materials, as well as the "sensitive musicality" to which Albers alluded. The Museum's painting is a harmonious symphony; against a muted gray backdrop a variety of organic forms appear to float. Although they resemble seeds, leaves, and pods, none of the forms is definitively recognizable, and each hovers independently, scarcely touching the surrounding shapes. Stevens responded to the variety and lushness, as well as to the decay, of Southern vegetation. Through this work and similar images Stevens invited the viewer into his world, where introspection, poetry, and nature dominate. For Stevens, "Art is based on emotional understanding . . . and on the creative power to reconstruct in visual or audible terms the artist's feelings and moods. There is always the desire to express the harmonious interconnection of each and every element, and to create a feeling of wholeness more satisfying than our ordinary experience in time."[3]

At the same time Stevens painted nonobjective compositions, he continued to paint evocative landscapes. Although the more abstract examples seem to have been produced in his studio, the landscapes were done outdoors, mostly in the Blue Ridge Mountains, which he frequented every summer. Linked by a similar palette, technique, and musicality, the two bodies of work did not conflict in Stevens's mind: "I do not draw a line between objective and nonobjective and have painted in the former way this winter and will continue to do so when I feel I have something to say in that way. What I have linked in nonobjective is, for me, the new experience in design I am permitted when I do not have to tie everything to a base, as in objective painting. Anyway, I am doing both and will continue to, so long as either seems vital to me."[4]

---

1. See Gail Levin and Marianne Lorenz, *Theme and Improvisation: Kandinsky and the American Avant-Garde, 1912–1950* (Boston: Bulfinch Press, 1992).

2. Albers to Stevens, 16 February 1944. The McDowell Collection, Asheville, N.C., as quoted in Jessie Poesch and Thomas W. Styron, *Will Henry Stevens* (Greenville, S.C.: Greenville County Museum of Art, 1987), 53.

3. Stevens to W. G. Constable, 7 May 1941. The McDowell Collection, as quoted in Poesch and Styron, *Stevens,* 69.

4. Stevens to Bernard Lemann, circa 1940, in Lemann, "Will Henry's Nature, The Pictorial Ideas of W. H. Stevens," unpublished typescript, 1947–1948. Files, Greenville County Museum of Art.

Born, Vevay, Indiana, 1881; studied at the Cincinnati Academy of Art, 1901–1904; employed by Rookwood Potteries, Cincinnati, 1904–1905; studied in New York at the Art Students League, 1906; remained in New York before returning to Vevay, 1912; taught classes in Louisville, Kentucky, 1912–1921; began to summer in Blue Ridge Mountains of North Carolina, 1916; faculty member, Sophie Newcomb College, New Orleans, 1921–1948; director, Natchitoches, Louisiana, summer program, 1922–mid-1930s; moved to Vevay, 1948; died, Madison, Indiana, 1949.

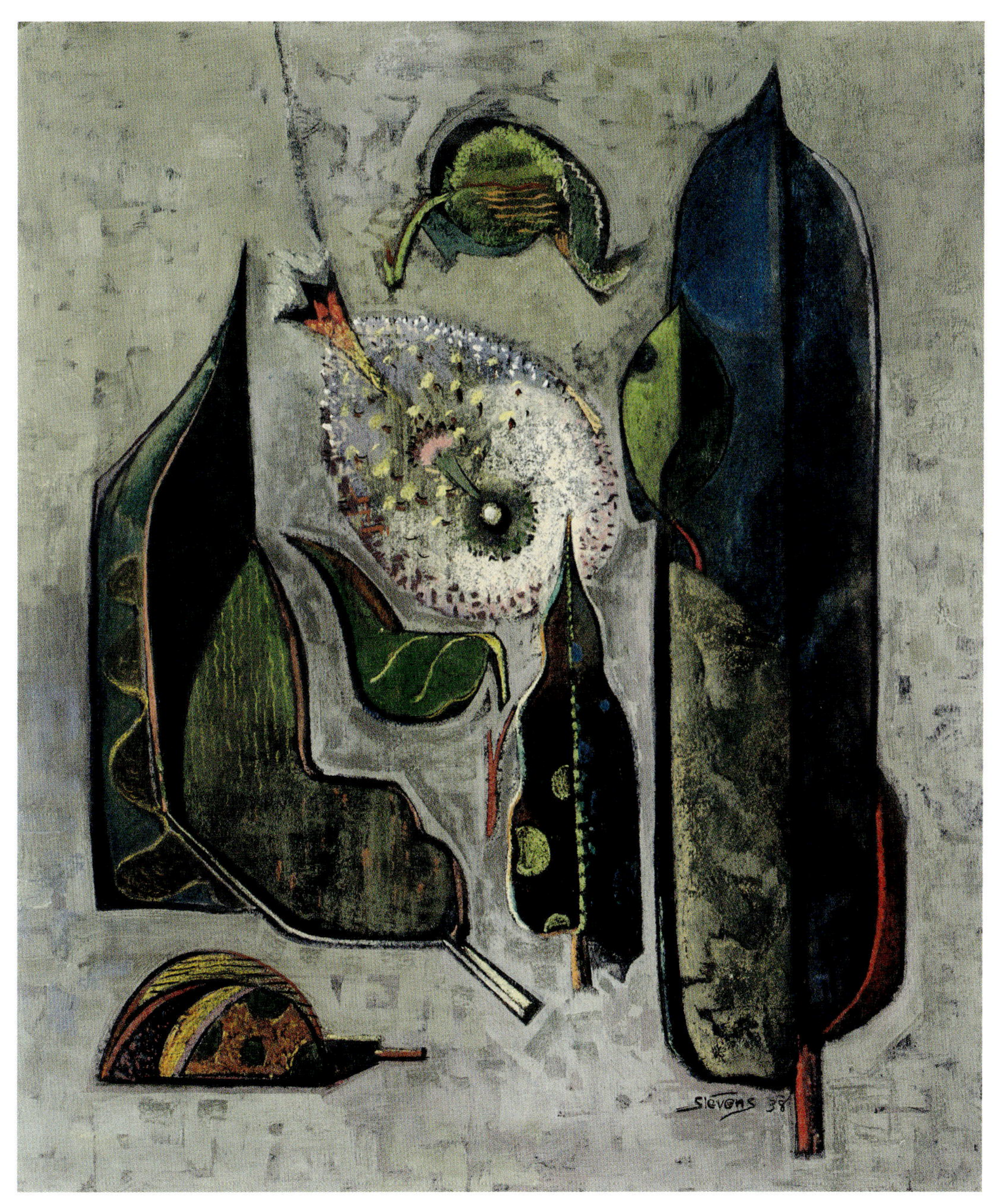
Stevens 38

Frank London

1876–1945

Time, 1940

oil on canvas, 50¼ × 32⅛ inches
signed, right of center: *Frank London, 1940*
Museum purchase with funds donated by the Arthur and Holly Magill Foundation

Surrealism, a diversified movement that espoused nonrational visions, dreamlike images, and automatic painting techniques, was first introduced to the United States in the early 1930s. Painters and sculptors, as well as writers and filmmakers, created work that, despite its fantastic elements, was also often disquietingly realistic. Unlike other trends, Surrealism did not emerge from a cohesive group of like-thinking artists; instead, such painters as René Magritte, Max Ernst, Salvador Dalí, and Giorgio de Chirico practiced their personal idioms. Although at times playful, Surrealism sprang from the post–World War I malaise and the world's anxiety about Adolf Hitler's rise to power.

The American reaction to Surrealism was mixed; few artists embraced it wholeheartedly. Several painters, including Jackson Pollock and Arshile Gorky, used it as a springboard for the development of their mature work. Frank London was one of the few artists to create work in tune with the Surrealist ideology. A North Carolina native, London attended the University of North Carolina at Chapel Hill before going to New York. There he enrolled at the Pratt Institute and studied later at the William Merritt Chase School of Art. London remained in New York, designing stained glass and other ecclesiastical objects until the early 1920s, when he left for France. His residence in Paris coincided with the heyday of Surrealism.

Electing to specialize in still lifes, London worked within a traditional art form, one that had flourished in seventeenth-century Holland. Despite his use of such conventional items as tabletops, draperies, and fruits, his combinations are unique. His bizarre subject matter is complemented by an overall somber palette and emphatic shadows. In the Museum's painting, *Time,* the arrangement is along a vertical axis that ascends from the simple legs of the table through the littered surface of the tilted tabletop to the raven and the calendar. The clock, curiously turned upside down, is the focus of the composition.

With its emphasis on the passage of time, the Museum's painting partakes of a long tradition of still lifes whose theme is the malleability of all things. Called *vanitas* depictions, these still lifes often include skulls, overripe fruit, and other indications of the fleeting nature of life and beauty. London, whose ecclesiastical work had involved religious imagery, must have consciously selected each object for its symbolic or portentous quality. In addition to the clock, the raven, a dark silhouette against a white background, marks time and conjures up associations with Edgar Allan Poe's "quoth the raven, 'Never More.'"

In addition to the general theme of transience, the painting alludes to June 1940, the date indicated on the calendar, and the period of Hitler's advance on France, Holland, and England. A convincing explanation is offered by the artist's son, Marsden London, who claims that the painting's original title was *Arts of Europe Interrupted.* He suggests that the change in title was made by the painter Bradley Walker Tomlin when he organized a memorial exhibition for London, his friend and mentor. Marsden London explains the iconography of the Museum's painting:

> The Raven or Crow which is sitting on the overturned Dutch clock represents Hitler who in 1940 was overpowering surrounding European countries; running over Holland and the low countries and conquering France. The Germans were looting the Louvre and art treasures of France and taking them back to Germany. Destruction was everywhere and decay was setting in. Creativity and the arts were tied up and taking second place to destruction and survival. Vineyards were destroyed and the pitcher is empty. Time is running out, all is confusion and the Crow is responsible for it all. Europe has been humbled. America is drunk with pacifism.[1]

For a Surrealist painting to have more than one meaning is not unusual. Magritte and Dalí in particular indulged in double entendres and visual puns. London simultaneously presented the traditional *vanitas* theme, while alluding to contemporary events. For the artist, who had lived in Paris for an extended period, Hitler's siege of the city must have been devastating. Rather poignantly, London's son concludes his letter with the following statement: "Frank London never lived to see the Crow destroyed and the clock and the arts righted and restored."[2]

---

1. Marsden London to Franklin Riehlman, H. V. Allison Galleries, New York, 8 November 1990. Files, Greenville County Museum of Art.

2. London to Riehlman.

Born, Pittsboro, North Carolina, 1876; attended the University of North Carolina, Chapel Hill, 1893–1895, and Pratt Institute, New York, 1895–1897; studied with William Merritt Chase in New York, 1900; resided in New York, 1895–1923; in Paris, 1923–1925 and 1927; New York, circa 1929–1945, with summers in Woodstock, New York; died, New York, 1945.

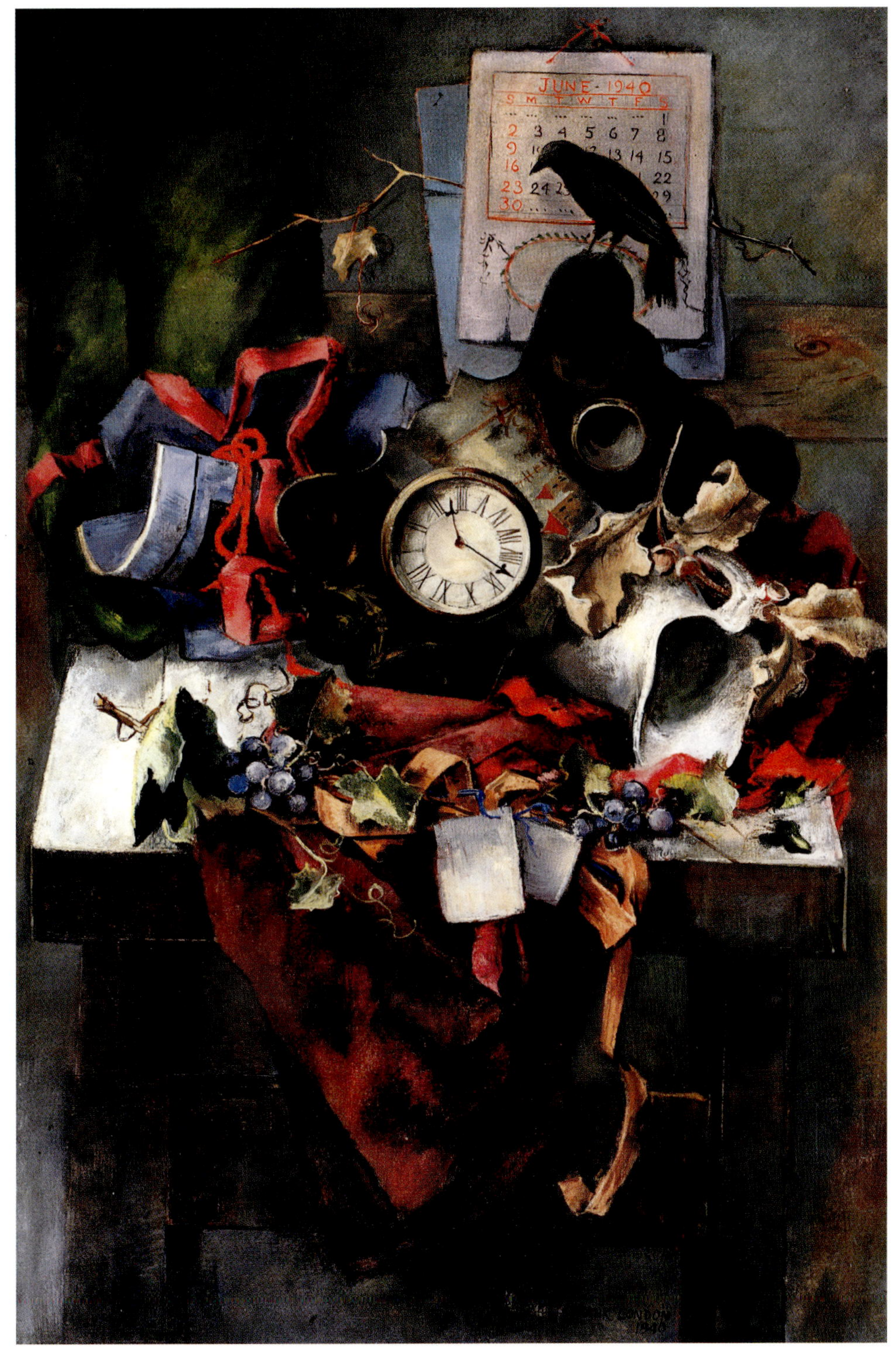
JUNE · 1940
S M T W T F S

John McCrady

1911–1968

Heaven Bound, 1940

tempera and oil on canvas, 48½ × 48½ inches
signed, right center: *John McCrady, 1940*
Museum purchase with funds donated by the Arthur and Holly Magill Foundation

American Scene painters and artists working in the government-sponsored mural programs tended to depict their subjects realistically. Realism was not only appropriate to the populist themes of the period, but it was also sympathetic to the public function of the art created under the auspices of the New Deal. Artists looked to the art of the Italian Renaissance as prototypes for their own wall decorations and for stylistic references. Italian painters of the fifteenth century had covered vast surfaces with religious subjects in frescoes painted directly on the wall. Most Depression-era muralists, however, preferred secular content and the convenience of painting monumental canvases in their studios.

Renaissance examples were particularly important to John McCrady, an American Scene painter who undertook several projects for the Works Progress Administration. Depicting clearly delineated figures reminiscent of Luca Signorelli's fifteenth-century frescoes, McCrady worked in a technique that ultimately derived from Renaissance masters. Using a foundation of tempera paint, an opaque medium mixed with egg, he completed his painting in stages using a series of oil glazes. Light passes through the transparent glazes and is reflected off the white ground. This technique allowed McCrady to develop a brilliant palette, in which the colors are bright and resonant. McCrady learned this approach while a student at the Art Students League under Kenneth Hayes Miller. Although McCrady was responsive to Miller's teaching and even studied at the League with Thomas Hart Benton for a month, he hated New York and was eager to return to his native South.

In addition to using a technique similar to that found in Renaissance panel paintings, McCrady rendered religious images deeply rooted in Southern traditions. Instead of selecting standard Judeo-Christian iconography, McCrady invented images derived from African-American religious practices. As the son of an Episcopal minister, McCrady's early life had been filled with church gatherings and hymn singing, and the spirituals were what ignited his imagination. "The music that surrounded me all my young life, and which was as natural to my environment as any other element of nature, was that which I experienced in the songs that came from the Negro, an expression of a religious philosophy crossed with the legends and myths that would startle and alarm, a philosophy acquired from the white man combined with a metaphysical heritage from the darkness of Africa."[1]

The Museum's painting, *Heaven Bound,* is a pictorial translation of a religious pageant that combined music, drama, and verse. Individuals representing newly released souls are confronted by Satan who tempts them with jewels, liquor, and other earthly delights, while St. Peter stands at the altar waiting to open the gates of heaven. During the performance some souls get into heaven, while others do not.

McCrady captures some of the frenetic tension of the drama; he portrays the climactic moment when the soul, in the form of a nude woman, turns from the devil and chooses salvation, symbolized by the oversized hand of God reaching down from above. Satan and the soul are posed against a stormy sky and a severely eroded landscape, where a subplot unfolds, explaining the nature of her death. In a beam of light from the farmhouse a woman lies dead, presumably murdered by the man fleeing directly into a bolt of lightning. Paralleling the hand of God in both shape and direction, the lightning indicates that justice may follow.

McCrady's acrid color scheme of mustard tones and flaming pinks conveys an unreality, heightened by the immediacy of the two large figures looming in the foreground. The artist intensified the painting further by compacting the composition into a tondo, a circular format popular during the Renaissance. Designed by the artist, the hand-carved frame with doves, symbols of peace, in each corner, reiterates the theme of salvation.

In *Heaven Bound* and many other contemporary paintings McCrady portrayed African-Americans nude, a device that was often justified by the subject matter. In 1946 when a group of his paintings was exhibited in New York, he received a scathing review, and the exhibition was called "a flagrant example of racial chauvinism."[2] Deeply hurt by these allegations, McCrady faced an artistic crisis, and soon thereafter he discontinued his depictions of African-American angels.

---

1. McCrady letter, as quoted in Keith Marshall, *John McCrady, 1911–1968* (New Orleans: New Orleans Museum of Art, 1975), 43.

2. Marion Summers, "Studies in Contrasts: Chauvinism and Truth," *Daily Worker,* 29 May 1946, as quoted in Marshall, *McCrady,* 21 and 29.

Born, Canton, Mississippi, 1911; attended University of Mississippi, Oxford, 1930–1932; studied at the Pennsylvania Academy of the Fine Arts, summers of 1931 and 1932, at the New Orleans Art School, 1932, and at the Art Students League in New York under Kenneth Hayes Miller and Thomas Hart Benton, 1933–1934; settled in New Orleans, 1934; participant in federal mural program, 1936–1942; died, New Orleans, 1968.

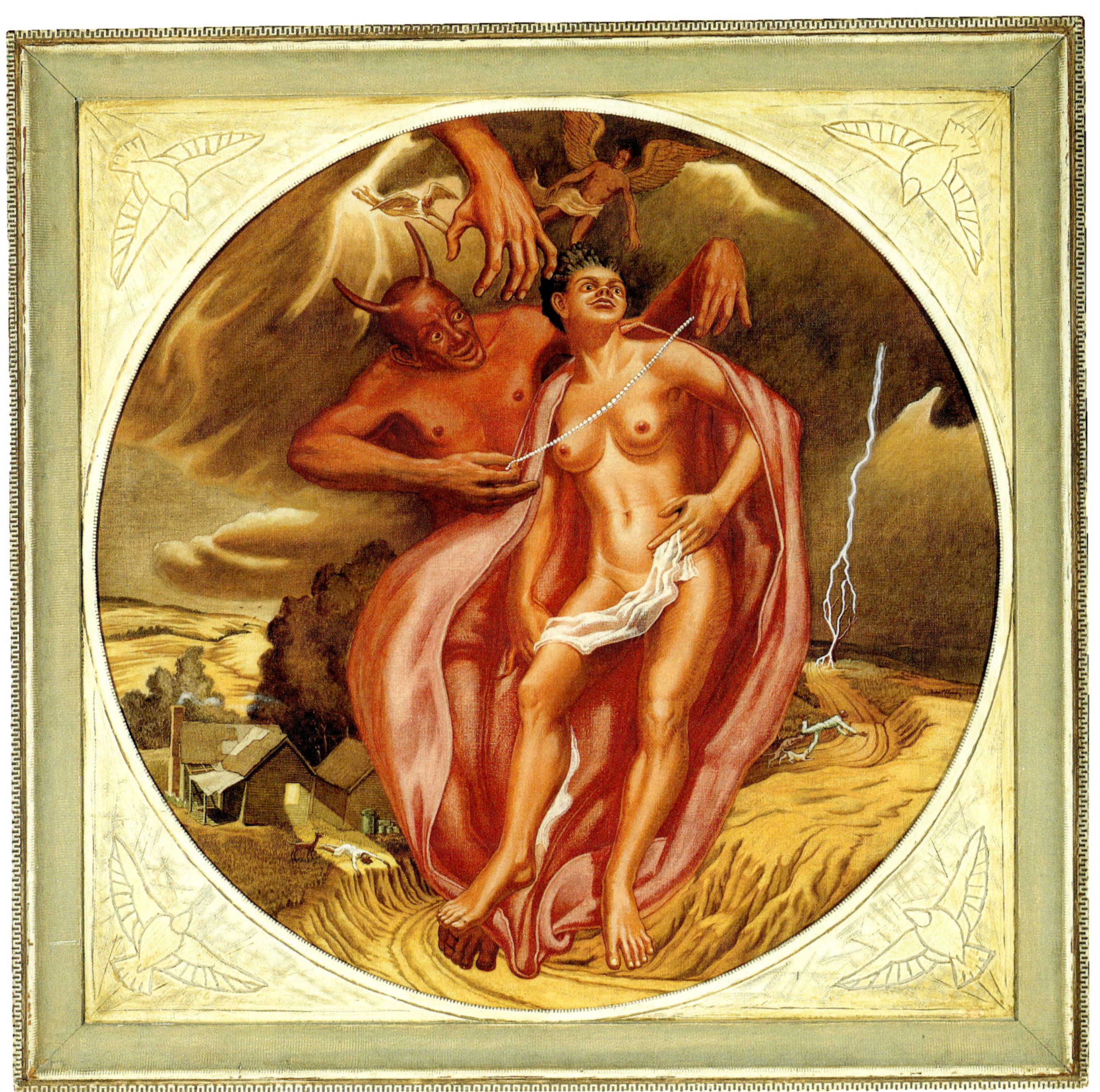

Selma Hortense Burke

born 1901

Dancers, circa 1940

ebony, 35½ × 12½ × 8½ inches
signed, lower left: *SHB*
Museum purchase with funds donated by the Arthur and Holly Magill Foundation

The plight of African-American women artists, especially those working in sculpture, was even more formidable than the challenges faced by their male counterparts. Nevertheless, a small number of African-American female sculptors have emerged and have made a significant contribution to the history of American art. Shortly after the Civil War Edmonia Lewis struggled against considerable prejudices to achieve recognition both here and abroad. Like the African-American painter Henry Ossawa Tanner who worked in France, as well as numerous other women sculptors, Lewis found Europe conducive to her work. In Rome she modeled her signature piece, *Forever Free,* which relates the joyous and incredulous reaction of a slave couple to the Emancipation Proclamation. Stylistically a synthesis of realism with Neoclassicism, the statue is also incongruous: the figures are carved from pure white marble.

Twentieth-century African-American sculptors, instead of accommodating the strictures of the academic tradition, eagerly embraced the principles of direct carving, which had particular appeal because it provided a link to their own cultural heritage. As promulgated by José de Creeft, Robert Laurent, and William Zorach, direct carving encouraged the artist to work with the expressive potential of the material. Instead of classical Greek and Roman examples, African, Mayan, and Aztec prototypes provided inspiration. The direct carvers admired the work of Pablo Picasso and the sculpture of Paul Gauguin and Constantin Brancusi, whose elemental forms were indebted to prehistoric, primitive, and tribal art.

Despite many obstacles Selma Burke achieved her ambition to be a successful sculptor: "I made up my mind that I would do something with my life."[1] Growing up in rural North Carolina, Burke found few creative opportunities and met resistance to her pursuit of a career in art. At her mother's insistence she studied nursing, which she practiced in New York while earning her master's degree in fine arts from Columbia University. In 1938 she traveled to Europe, studying for a period with the French sculptor Aristide Maillol. Although a classicist who used traditional processes, Maillol created powerful and sensuous nudes that clearly influenced Burke's figurative work. Unlike this French master who worked chiefly in bronze, Burke preferred direct carving.

In *Dancers* Burke subscribed to the concept that the role of the sculptor is to liberate the form inherent in the block of material. In the Museum's piece the figures are compressed within the tree-trunk contours of the ebony, an exotic wood known for its hardness and darkness. Although it is not indigenous to Africa, ebony, because of its color and luster, has a long-standing association with tribal Africa. Not finished in the round, *Dancers* is designed to be viewed from the front, reinforcing its columnar quality. The bodies glisten with a highly polished patina, or surface quality, while chisel marks give textural definition to the hair. The angularity of legs and arms is reminiscent of African sculptures, which Burke is known to have collected.

Like both Maillol and the African carvers, the bulk of Burke's work is figurative. She is also an accomplished portraitist. Her most famous subject was President Franklin Delano Roosevelt, whose likeness she was commissioned to do shortly before his death in 1945. Burke's portrait plaque of Roosevelt not only immortalized him but also became widely familiar as the image reproduced on the U.S. dime.

---

1. Burke, as quoted in gallery brochure, Winston-Salem State University, circa 1982.

Born, Mooresville, North Carolina, 1901; graduated from Slater Normal and Industrial School (now Winston-Salem State University), 1920; degree from St. Agnes School of Nursing, Raleigh, North Carolina, 1924; to New York, 1935; master of fine arts degree from Columbia University, 1941; traveled in Europe and studied with Aristide Maillol, 1938; conducted Selma Burke School of Sculpture, New York, 1942–1948; resides, New Hope, Pennsylvania.

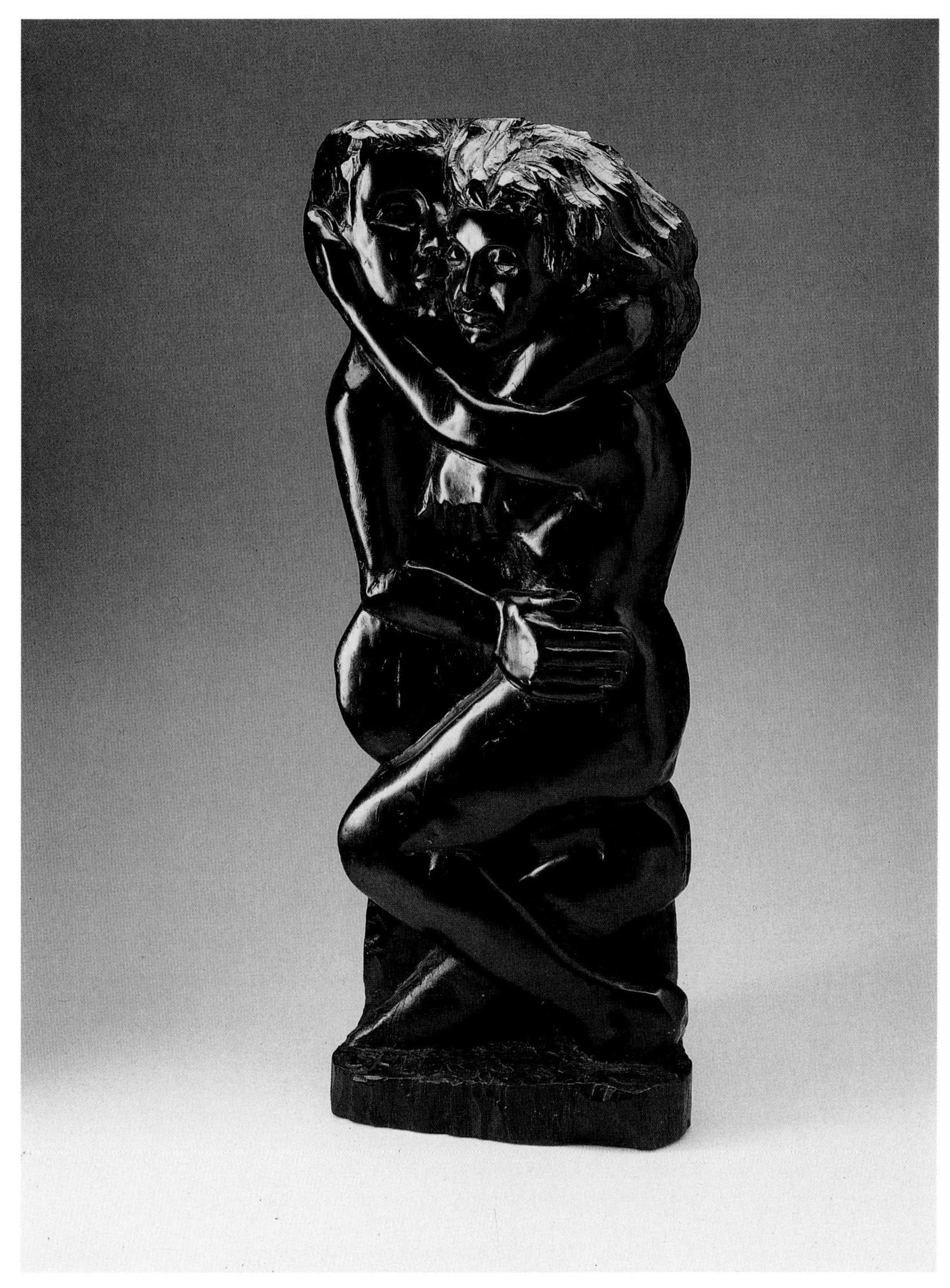

Jacob Lawrence

born 1917

The Plowman, 1942

tempera on board, 19½ × 23¾ inches
signed, upper right: *J. Lawrence 42*
Museum purchase with funds donated by the Arthur and Holly Magill Foundation

The Harlem Renaissance and the Depression were the most potent forces affecting the development of African-American artists emerging in the 1930s. During and following World War I African-Americans migrated from the rural South to Northern cities, especially to New York's Harlem. Throughout the next decade Harlem became the focal point of a cultural awakening best known for its jazz bands, which attracted large crowds to the Savoy Hotel and the Cotton Club. When the Depression came, Harlem, economically weak and overpopulated, was ill prepared, but from adversity grew several programs that would help to shape the future of American art.

The Federal Art Project of the Works Progress Administration was the largest of several endeavors designed to assist individuals in dire need. In addition to the direct support given to artists for mural and sculptural decorations, painters were enlisted in the easel program, which, by providing materials and a salary, equated art with more traditional employment. The WPA also established community centers for art instruction that benefited both instructors and young Harlem residents who learned the fundamentals of art. Charles Alston and William H. Johnson were among the instructors; Jacob Lawrence became the program's outstanding pupil.

Lawrence's innate talent was recognized early; as a precocious fifteen year old he began classes under the sponsorship of the College Art Association with Alston, who provided encouraging support rather than rigid instruction. Lawrence's early work was with poster paints, or water-based temperas, on brown paper, and throughout his life he has worked in the related media of tempera and gouache. For content, he drew upon the world about him, the life of Harlem, and the African-American history he studied at the neighborhood library and at an after-school history club.

Under the auspices of the WPA Lawrence took more classes with Alston at the Harlem Art Workshop between 1934 and 1937 before he earned a scholarship to the American Artists School. When he was old enough, he joined the easel program of the WPA. During this time he devoted himself to three major series, each a moving narrative about African-American history. In both the *Toussaint L'Ouverture* and the *Harriet Tubman* series the protagonist assumes heroic proportions, gains freedom, and helps to liberate others. The theme of the *Migration* series was derived from a more recent phenomenon, the exodus of thousands of African-Americans from the rural South. The subject was also more personal to Lawrence, whose own parents had moved north from Virginia and South Carolina.

Lawrence's nontraditional style evolved from his student work, which ignored the formulas of conventional academic training. Living in Harlem he was, on the one hand, isolated from the commercial-art world that was dominated by whites. On the other hand, he could avail himself of museums, including both the Metropolitan Museum of Art, where he was fascinated by Egyptian art, and the Museum of Modern Art, where in 1935 he saw an exhibition of art from West Africa. Typically, Lawrence's paintings revolve around stylized, two-dimensional figures whose sharp angles denote Egyptian as well as Cubist influences. Pictorial space is often compressed, resulting in immediate, forceful compositions. Colors are used expressively, ranging from hot, intense colors to gloomy, somber tones.

Although his parents were from the South, Lawrence apparently did not visit the region until 1941, when he spent six months in New Orleans working on a series about John Brown, one of his few projects to focus on a white protaganist. On his return North the following spring, Lawrence lingered for several weeks with his in-laws in Lenexa, Virginia; this was his first extended contact with the rural South. The Museum's painting, *The Plowman,* dates to this period and reflects Lawrence's response to the harsh conditions faced by African-Americans. Just as the *L'Ouverture, Tubman,* and *Migration* series dealt with the theme of struggle, so the diminutive farmer in the Museum's painting pushes against his plow, against formidable odds. Even the larger-than-life mules bend their bodies forward, against the earth. The tilted perspective exaggerates the curvilinear pattern of the furrows, which may allude to Depression-era propaganda favoring contour plowing.

The Plowman is an evocative rendering of the drudgery and difficulty of farm labor, which in the South had been done by African-Americans for generations. Although the image is a somber one, Lawrence may also be sensitive to the long-standing association of the plowman and the sower as figures of dignity and hope. "Behold, the days come, saith the Lord, that the plowman shall overtake the reaper" (Amos 9:13).

After serving in the United States Coast Guard during World War II, Lawrence returned to the South, this time to Black Mountain College in North Carolina. Finding the campus an integrated oasis in the midst of segregation, Lawrence taught alongside Josef Albers. Although the two artists differed dramatically in their approach to representation, Lawrence found his contact with Albers the color theorist stimulating and affirming. Lawrence later commented on this summer: "This was a milestone for me, as it initiated me into the ranks of teacher. It was an experience for all of us concerned, for it was the South. Most of all, through Albers, I came to know something of the Bauhaus concept of art, which simply put, stresses design—the theory and dynamics of the picture plane."[1]

---

1. Lawrence, in Carroll Greene, Jr., "Interview with Jacob Lawrence," 25 October 1968, as quoted in Ellen Harkins Wheat, *Jacob Lawrence: American Painter* (Seattle: University of Washington Press, 1986), 73.

Born, Atlantic City, New Jersey, 1917; moved to Harlem, 1930; studied with Charles Alston, in classes sponsored by the College Art Association, 1932, and by the Works Progress Administration at Harlem Art Workshop, 1934–1937; studied at American Artists School, 1937–1939; to New Orleans, six months, 1941–1942, returning by way of Virginia; served with United States Coast Guard, 1943–1945; taught at Black Mountain College, near Asheville, North Carolina, 1946; lived in Nigeria, 1964; teaching positions at Pratt Institute, New York, 1955–1970, Brandeis University, Waltham, Massachusetts, 1965, New School for Social Research, New York, 1966–1969, Art Students League, New York, 1967–1969, California State College, Hayward, 1969–1970, and University of Washington, from 1970; resides in Seattle.

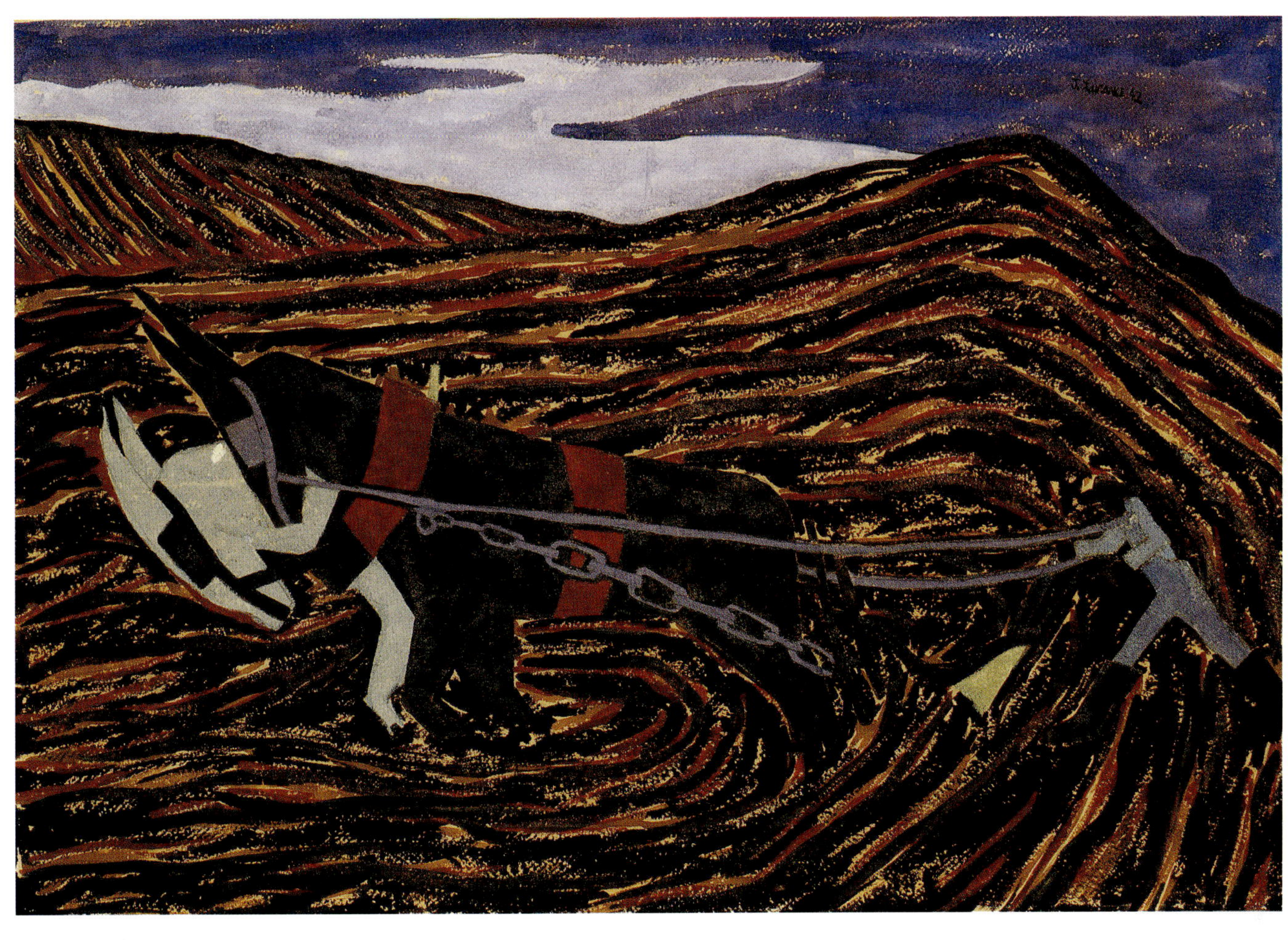

William Henry Johnson

1901–1970

Lift Up Thy Voice and Sing, circa 1942–1943

gouache, pen and ink on paper, 15 × 12 inches
signed, lower right: *W. H. Johnson*
Museum purchase with funds donated by the Arthur and Holly Magill Foundation

In the decade before the stock-market crash of 1929, "Harlem was in vogue."[1] This succinct statement by Langston Hughes, poet and spokesman for the Harlem Renaissance, summarizes the cultural awakening that transpired in that densely populated area of northern Manhattan. In a variety of artistic expressions, including painting, sculpture, and literature, but most of all music, African-Americans asserted their cultural identity and looked to their own experiences for inspiration. The overwhelming popularity of jazz and the emergence of dance palaces brought whites to Harlem to absorb the sounds and rhythms of Duke Ellington, Cab Calloway, and Fats Waller. It was the place to be, and the place to be seen.

It was to this environment that William H. Johnson, motivated by the threat of advancing Nazism, returned in 1938, after having lived abroad since 1926. While Johnson was overseas a great deal had changed for African-American artists in America: most important was the Harlem Renaissance, but the Depression and the establishment of federal art programs were also significant. Shortly after his arrival, Johnson was hired by the Works Progress Administration to teach art to schoolchildren in Harlem.

Inspired by the cultural renewal that was taking place, Johnson shifted both his subject matter and style dramatically, from his European expressionist landscapes and still lifes to scenes of fashionably dressed African-Americans in city cafés and nightclubs. Flattened forms rendered in bright colors and often heightened by bold stripes and patterns dominate his compositions. The brassy, strident, and upbeat sounds of the Jazz Age along with its melancholy undertones find their visual counterpart in Johnson's work. His subjects included Harlem, the rural South remembered from his childhood, portraits of his family in South Carolina, and the segregated army of World War II. All of these images are closely tied to Johnson's heritage and cultural milieu, and he invented a uniquely personal style to present them.

Johnson did not abandon his European experience entirely; rather, he assimilated it in his later work. His style is inconceivable without the dynamic vision of Cubism and the vibrant palette of Fauvism. Equally important, however, was Johnson's own discovery of African art. His interest in tribal sculpture, fostered by Picasso's example, was nourished in the museums and galleries of New York. His attraction to the brightly woven textile designs of Africa was probably inspired in part by his wife, a textile artist.

The Museum's *Lift Up Thy Voice and Sing* embodies many of the qualities of Johnson's late work, including exaggerated gestures, a fundamental two dimensionality, and the bold patterning of stripes. The scene may reflect his teaching experience in Harlem or memories of his own schooling in South Carolina. The upside-down American flag, a signal of distress, refers to the struggle that African-Americans faced in this country but is also an encouraging symbol of their resolve to rejoice in their Americanness. The painting celebrates the communal strength that fortified and united African-Americans to combat the adversity that surrounded them.

Johnson was no stranger to the challenges that African-Americans, especially artists, encountered in segregated America. He achieved a modicum of critical success on the eve of World War II, but the entry of the United States into the conflict thwarted any financial success—few patrons were interested in his subject matter. Johnson was beset by personal troubles as well as by a debilitating mental illness, and his painting career ended in 1947 when, at age forty-six, he was hospitalized for the remainder of his life.

---

1. As quoted in Mary Schmidt Campbell, *Harlem Renaissance: Art of Black America* (New York: Harry N. Abrams, 1987), 11.

Born, Florence, South Carolina, 1901; lived in New York, 1918–1926, attended the National Academy of Design, 1921–1926; to Paris, 1926–1927, and Cagnes-sur-Mer, 1928–1929; short visits to New York and Florence, 1929 and 1930; resided in Kerteminde, Denmark, 1930–1938, with excursions to Tunisia, 1932, via Hamburg, Amsterdam, Cologne, returning via Paris; to Copenhagen and Oslo, 1935; to Sweden, 1937; returned to Oslo, 1938; left Kerteminde for New York, 1938; lived in New York, 1938–1948, with a trip to Denmark, 1946–1947; institutionalized at Central Islip State Hospital, 1948–1970; died, Central Islip, New York, 1970.

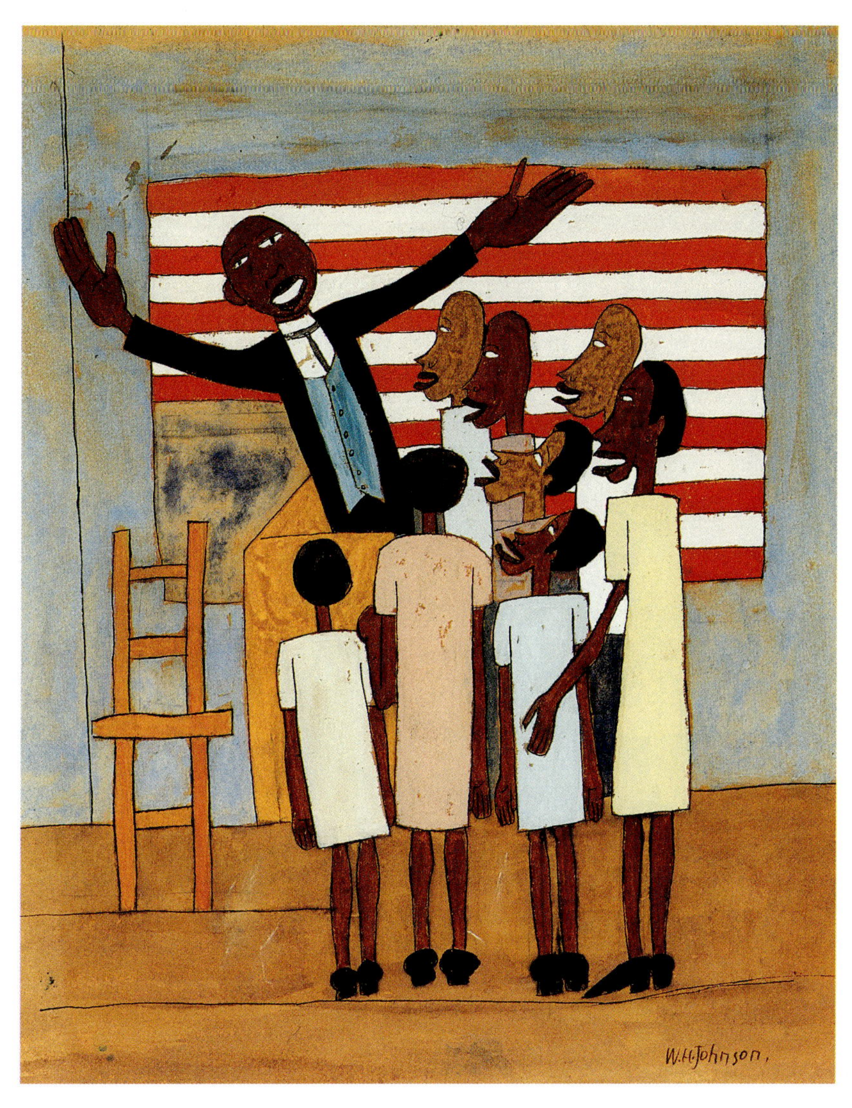
W.H.Johnson.

Robert Gwathmey

1903–1988

Shelling Peas, circa 1945
oil on canvas, 36¼ × 20 inches
signed, lower left: *Gwathmey*
Museum purchase with funds donated by the Arthur and Holly Magill Foundation

Artists, especially in the highly politicized 1930s and 1940s, were often ostracized because others viewed them as radical. When George Biddle proposed a mural program to President Roosevelt in 1933, he drew inspiration from the Mexican muralists, in particular, Diego Rivera. Rivera believed in art as propaganda: "At present art has a very definite and important role to play in the class struggle. It is definitely useful to the proletariat. . . . Art has the advantage of speaking a language that can easily be understood by the workers and the peasants of all lands. . . . A revolutionary painting takes far less time and it says far more than a lecture does."[1] Rivera became a cause célèbre in the press when his mural for Rockefeller Center was destroyed because it was seen by some to be anticapitalist and pro-socialist. At the center of the controversy was Rivera's portrait of Lenin joining the hand of an African-American worker with that of a white. Rivera was just one of many artists during the Depression and the years following who attempted to raise the social consciousness of viewers.

In his numerous renderings of African-American sharecroppers, Robert Gwathmey reiterated the themes of poverty, prejudice, and the stratification of society. Gwathmey developed imagery drawn from his native South, which he combined with a distinctive visual language to create potent, often biting statements about social conditions. Because of this subject matter and his involvement with the Artists Union, a group that sought a living wage for artists through collective bargaining, Gwathmey was monitored by the Federal Bureau of Investigation on the suspicion that he was a Communist.[2]

Born in Richmond, Virginia, Gwathmey first studied art at the Maryland Institute, followed by four years at the Pennsylvania Academy of the Fine Arts. With two summer fellowships from the Academy he was introduced to European art. To ensure a regular income Gwathmey taught, first at Beaver College near Philadelphia, then at the Carnegie Institute of Technology in Pittsburgh and the Cooper Union Art School in New York. Gwathmey, who returned to Virginia on regular summer visits, recalled: "When I got home, I was shocked by the poverty. The most shocking thing was the Negroes, the oppressed segment. If I had never gone back home, perhaps I would never have painted the Negro. I was shocked at the red clay, at the *redness* of the clay. The green pine trees and red clay were everywhere. The Negro seemed to be everywhere, too, omnipresent. But he was a thing apart, so segregated."[3]

The theme of segregation pervades Gwathmey's work from the late 1930s until his death. At times he directly satirized the role of white politicians and Ku Klux Klan members. His handling of oppressed African-Americans is both sensitive and perceptive; his style is as incisive as his content. Painted in flat, searing colors, the figures are angularly composed, suggesting a Cubist ancestry and underscoring the dehumanizing conditions suffered by his subjects.

In *Shelling Peas* Gwathmey creates a powerful image of resignation and dignity. Attention is focused on the figure; the setting is spare and reduced, a careful balance of horizontal and vertical elements. The colors, however, of mustard yellow and magenta purple harshly contrast one another, creating a cheerless tension. The withered body of the old woman, with her downcast eyes, sagging shoulders, and drooping breasts, epitomizes the tedium of manual labor. Nevertheless, her singleness of purpose and her resolve transform her into an icon of hope and endurance.

Throughout a long and productive career Gwathmey employed similar figures to communicate his concerns about society, and as the issues shifted toward civil rights and the antiwar movement, the artist continued to take a stand. Despite the rising popularity of abstraction, Gwathmey never wavered from his chosen subject matter. "I believe that in painting the use of limited imagery is the best method of presentation of your content. I believe that if the symbols are strong enough, they can transcend the literary in painting."[4]

---

1. Diego Rivera, "The Revolutionary Spirit in Modern Art," *Modern Quarterly* 6, no. 3 (Autumn 1932), as quoted in David Shapiro, ed., *Social Realism: Art as a Weapon* (New York: Frederick Ungar, 1973), 55.
2. Charles K. Piehl, "Robert Gwathmey: The Social and Historical Context of a Southerner's Art in the Mid-Twentieth Century," *Arts in Virginia* 29, no. 1 (1989): 9.
3. Gwathmey, interview with Elizabeth McCausland, "Robert Gwathmey," *Magazine of Art*, April 1946, 149.
4. Gwathmey, in McCausland, "Gwathmey," 151.

Born, Richmond, Virginia, 1903; attended the Maryland Institute of Design, 1925–1926; studied at the Pennsylvania Academy of the Fine Arts, 1926–1930; traveled to Europe, summers of 1929 and 1930; taught at Beaver College, Glenside, Pennsylvania, 1930–1938, at the Carnegie Institute of Technology (now Carnegie-Mellon University), Pittsburgh, 1939–1942, the Cooper Union Art School, New York, 1942–1966; moved to Amagansett, New York, 1966; died, Southampton, New York, 1988.

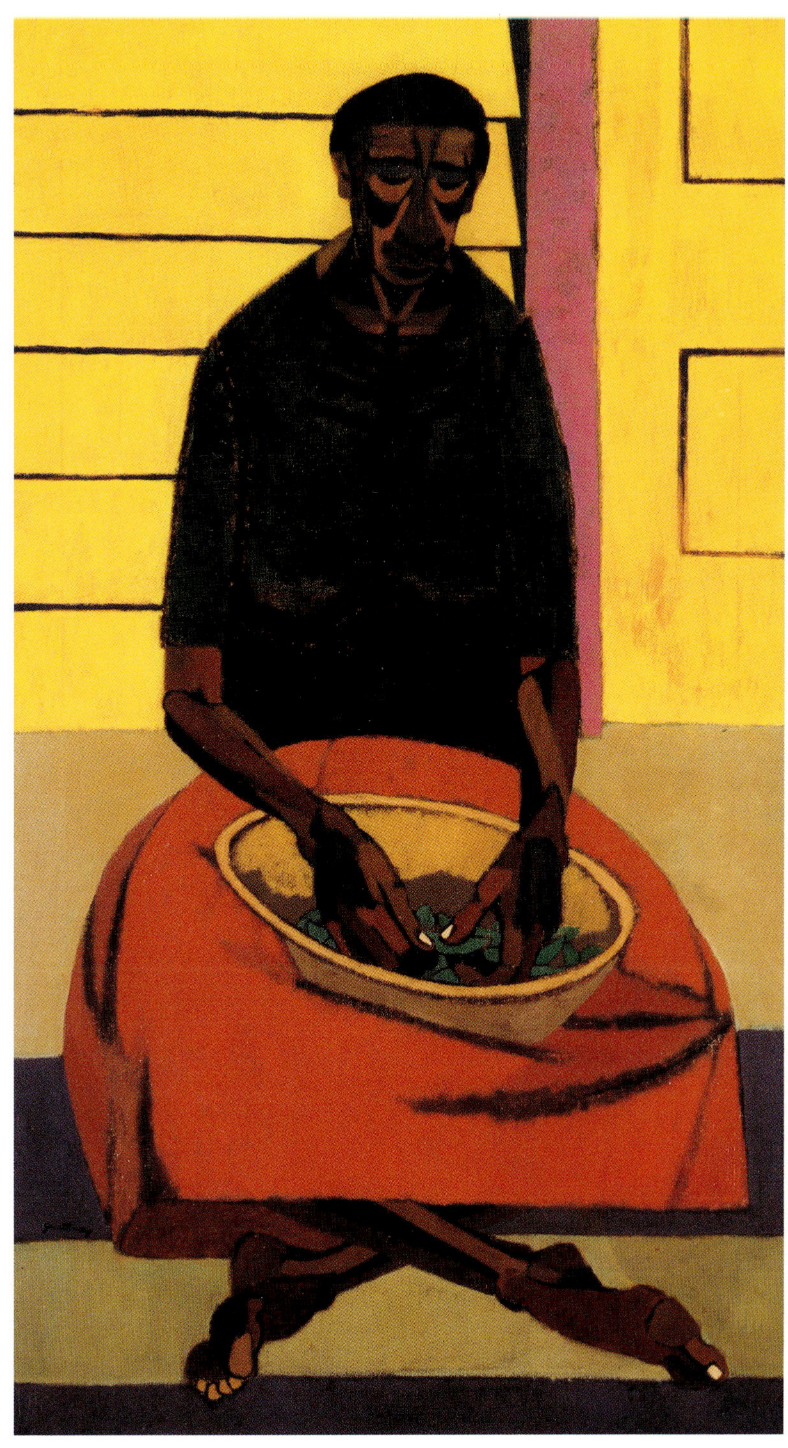

Walter Inglis Anderson

1903–1965

Garden, circa 1942–1944
watercolor and graphite on paper,
24⅞ × 37¾ inches
Museum purchase with funds donated by
The Museum Association, Inc.

Abstract painting can take a variety of forms, including one dependent on an organic, nature-oriented vocabulary. Organic abstraction implies a reduction from nature with an emphasis on the salient features of a particular object. Both Joan Miró and Wassily Kandinsky pursued this approach in their work, Miró preferring human and animal forms, and Kandinsky landscape. Kandinsky's work relates as well to expressionist interpretations in which the emotional qualities of color, shape, and brushwork play an important role in the artist's statement.

Walter Anderson, a Mississippi artist, was clearly aligned with the organic form of abstraction. He worked directly from nature, reducing its forms to a kind of visual shorthand. His association with nature was extremely intimate and he had an almost mystical appreciation of the natural world. Anderson spent much of each year on a barrier island off the coast of Mississippi. Here the artist was his own master, and he could commune with nature, creating fluid watercolors and recording his experiences in an extraordinary set of journals. Just as Vincent van Gogh, the famous artist-outcast of the nineteenth century, had little success during his lifetime, Anderson rarely showed or sold his work, but at his death left behind a legacy of more than five thousand works, mostly watercolors and drawings on small sheets of paper.

Anderson was born in New Orleans, and as a teenager attended the Manual Training School there. His education in art consisted of a year at the Parsons School of Design in New York and the full program at the Pennsylvania Academy of the Fine Arts. During his last year there he traveled to Europe, primarily to France, where he seems to have been more impressed by prehistoric cave paintings than by the cosmopolitanism of Paris. He returned to coastal Mississippi, near Ocean Springs, which would remain his home for the rest of his life. There members of his family had established a pottery in which Anderson would periodically work as a designer. He also did a number of murals in the area under the auspices of the Works Progress Administration.

Anderson suffered from severe bouts of mental illness, was hospitalized on several occasions, and was finally diagnosed as a schizophrenic. Nevertheless, he continued to paint, and his extended periods as an island recluse provided him the time, space, and imagery that allowed his art to be a form of therapy for him.

From the time of his mature work in the mid-1930s, Anderson displayed a keen fascination with patterns. Like Charles Burchfield, he even associated certain emotions with particular shapes.[1] The design elements that recur in his paintings also relate to his work in the family pottery business. In the early 1940s Anderson was reading about the history of art and was evidently influenced by the numerous patterns found in Egyptian, Persian, Greek, and Mayan cultures.[2]

Working with images of nature derived from the Mississippi coast, Anderson developed a patterning technique, reminiscent of tapestry, that hovered between the concrete and the abstract. Landscape, trees, animals, and insects are subjected to a rigid stylization that is reiterated to create a dynamic, pulsating rhythm. In the Museum's work, *Garden,* the repeated forms of trees, bushes, and hillocks are linked with one another in a systematic arrangement. This visual rhythm is further enhanced by Anderson's use of the complementary colors yellow and purple. By virtually duplicating the pattern in a diptych format of two sheets of paper, Anderson presented an emphatic, two-dimensional design.

That Anderson sought a psychic harmony in nature is evident in his paintings, drawings, and voluminous writings. From 1950 onward he alternated time on Horn Island with stays of the same length on the mainland. Living a Robinson Crusoe–like existence, Anderson had to fend for himself in fog, storms, chilling cold, and blazing heat. His self-reliant life-style resulted in an intimate relationship with nature and, in particular, with the other inhabitants on the island—the pelicans, crabs, frogs, and, of course, the mosquitoes. With little reference to the creation of his art, his logs record day-to-day concerns, as well as some of the exuberance he derived from his island existence:

> I left the boat and carried my bedding and a can of sauerkraut and salmon to the top of the dune and ate by the light of the moon without the runcible spoon—I used my fingers. After supper I renewed my youth and went swimming. The foam made beautiful patterns on the surface of the wave after it had struck, and I went until I could barely touch sand with one foot between each wave and danced by the light of the moon. But slept with mosquitoes.[3]

---

1. Redding S. Sugg, Jr., ed., *The Horn Island Logs of Walter Inglis Anderson* (Jackson: University Press of Mississippi, 1985), 15.

2. John Paul Driscoll, *Walter Anderson: Realizations of the Islander* (Ocean Springs, Miss.: Estate of Walter Anderson, 1985), unpaginated.

3. Anderson, as quoted in Sugg, *Anderson,* 51.

Born, New Orleans, 1903; attended Manual Training School, New Orleans, 1919–1922; studied at the Parsons School of Design, New York, 1923, and the Pennsylvania Academy of the Fine Arts, 1924–1929; to France, 1928; returned to Ocean Springs, Mississippi, 1929; hospitalized, 1937–1940; resided, Gautier, Mississippi, 1940–1946, then Ocean Springs with trips to Horn Island; died, New Orleans, 1965.

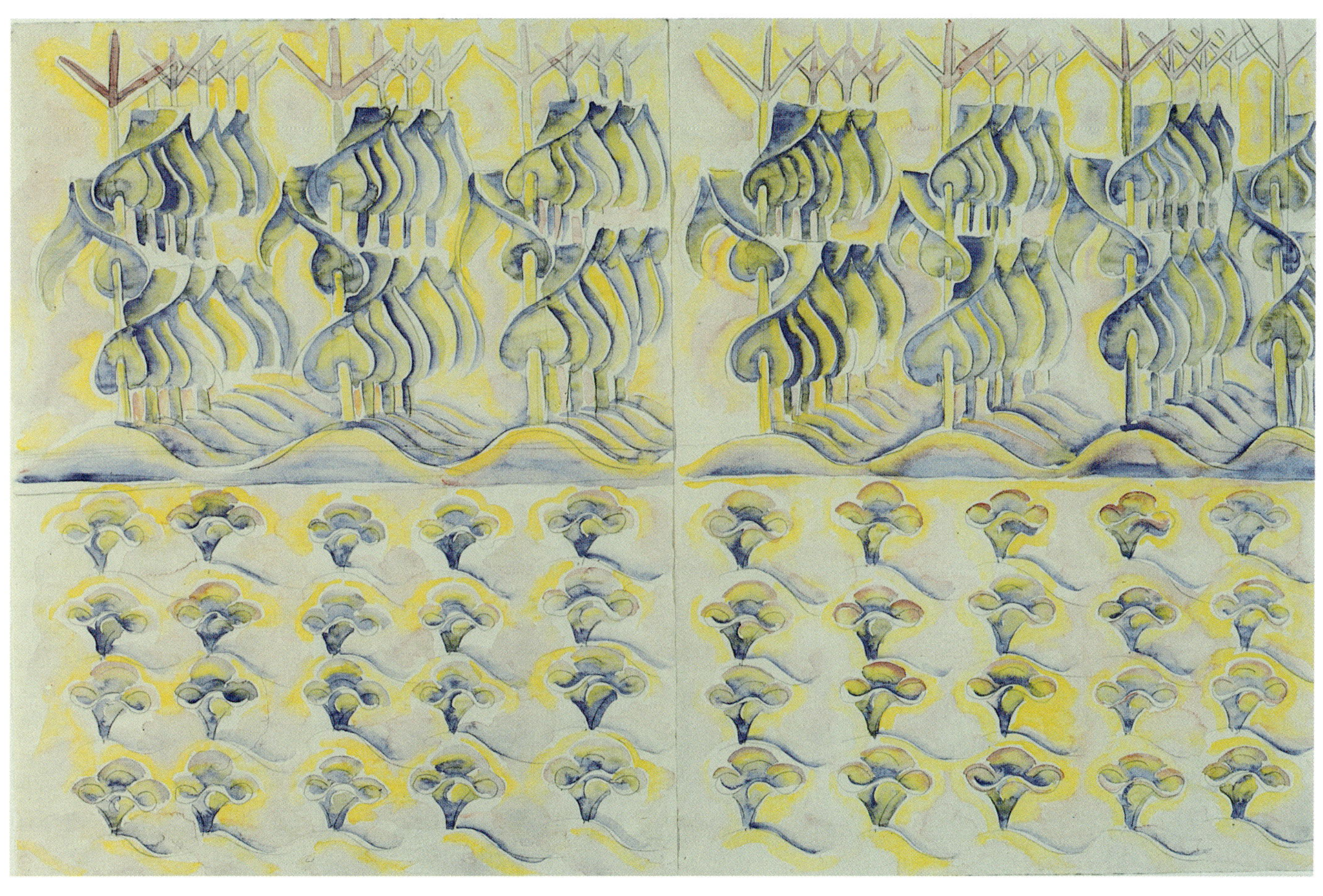

Edmund D. Lewandowski

born 1914

Chemical Plant, 1946

watercolor and gouache on paper, 19½ × 16 inches
signed, lower left: *Edmund D. Lewandowski 1946*
Museum purchase with funds donated by the Arthur and Holly Magill Foundation

Americans view machines with ambivalence; although they recognize that industrialization has brought great wealth, efficiency, and convenience, they also admit that it has dramatically altered a once-virgin landscape, forever upsetting a delicate ecological balance. The American fascination with industry culminated in the twentieth century in the work of the Precisionists, painters whose Machine-Age aesthetic informs their geometrically serene depictions. Ultimately, their work is related to the analytical formulations of Purism and Futurism, European offshoots of Cubism. In this country the Precisionist vision was tempered by realism and an overriding interest in geometry. Black-and-white photography, with its high contrasts of light and dark, also played a role in shaping Precisionism.

Among the leading Precisionist painters were Charles Sheeler and Charles Demuth, but at times the works of Georgia O'Keeffe, Stuart Davis, and Edward Hopper also correspond to their aesthetic. The photographs of Paul Strand, Edward Weston, and Berenice Abbott present a similar vision. Although Precisionism had peaked by the mid-1930s at the height of the Depression, a few artists, including Sheeler, Ralston Crawford, and Edmund Lewandowski, continued to render crisp images of machines, harbors, and landscapes well into the ensuing decades.

Much of the initial attention of the Precisionists was focused on the Midwest and its automobile assembly lines. Sheeler, for example, devoted a series of photographs and paintings to the Ford Motor Company's River Rouge plant, where more than fifteen million Model T's had been manufactured. And it was in this environment that Lewandowski matured; for four years he attended the Layton School of Art in his native Milwaukee, a major industrial center. Later, under the auspices of the federal government, he painted murals for three midwestern post offices. During World War II he served in the military, an experience that may have heightened his appreciation of machines.

Completed the same year he was discharged, *Chemical Plant* reflects Lewandowski's preoccupation with the formal qualities of machines. The painting was one of three done by the artist to secure a commission from *Fortune* magazine. Working with photographs for certain details, Lewandowski developed a variety of composite images. Rendered in a tightly controlled style that corresponds to the insistent regularity of its composition, *Chemical Plant* is dominated by a large funnel-shaped machine used to dehumidify chemicals. The sharply raking light from the left illuminates and elevates the funnel while it casts deep shadows in the right foreground. Here the viewer is given a clue to the scale of the machine: a very palpable handle is the element placed closest to the viewer. The scene is devoid of human presence; an awesome, clinical calm prevails.

Like the other Precisionists, Lewandowski elevated machine parts to objects of power. About his subject matter he has commented: "From as far back as I can recall, the cityscapes, farms, and the depiction of industrial power and technological efficiency has had a great attraction for me. . . . Rather than present reality I try to treat these observations with personal honesty and distill these impressions to visual order."[1] Now retired in Rock Hill, South Carolina, where he taught for more than a decade at Winthrop College, Lewandowski acknowledges that the move South has altered his painting; brilliant blues have replaced the grays that dominated his midwestern work. "If you look at the work of artists throughout history and identify their location you're going to find that geography has had its influences. I find that I'm responding more enthusiastically to the quality of light—sunlight and airiness."[2]

---

1. Lewandowski to author, 5 March 1994.
2. Lewandowksi to author, 4 January 1994.

Born, Milwaukee, 1914; attended the Layton School of Art, Milwaukee, 1931–1935; United States Army Air Force, 1942–1946; taught at the Layton School of Art, Milwaukee, 1947–1949, and served as its president, 1954–1972; taught at Florida State University, Tallahassee, 1949–1954, and at Winthrop College, Rock Hill, South Carolina, 1973–1983; resides, Rock Hill.

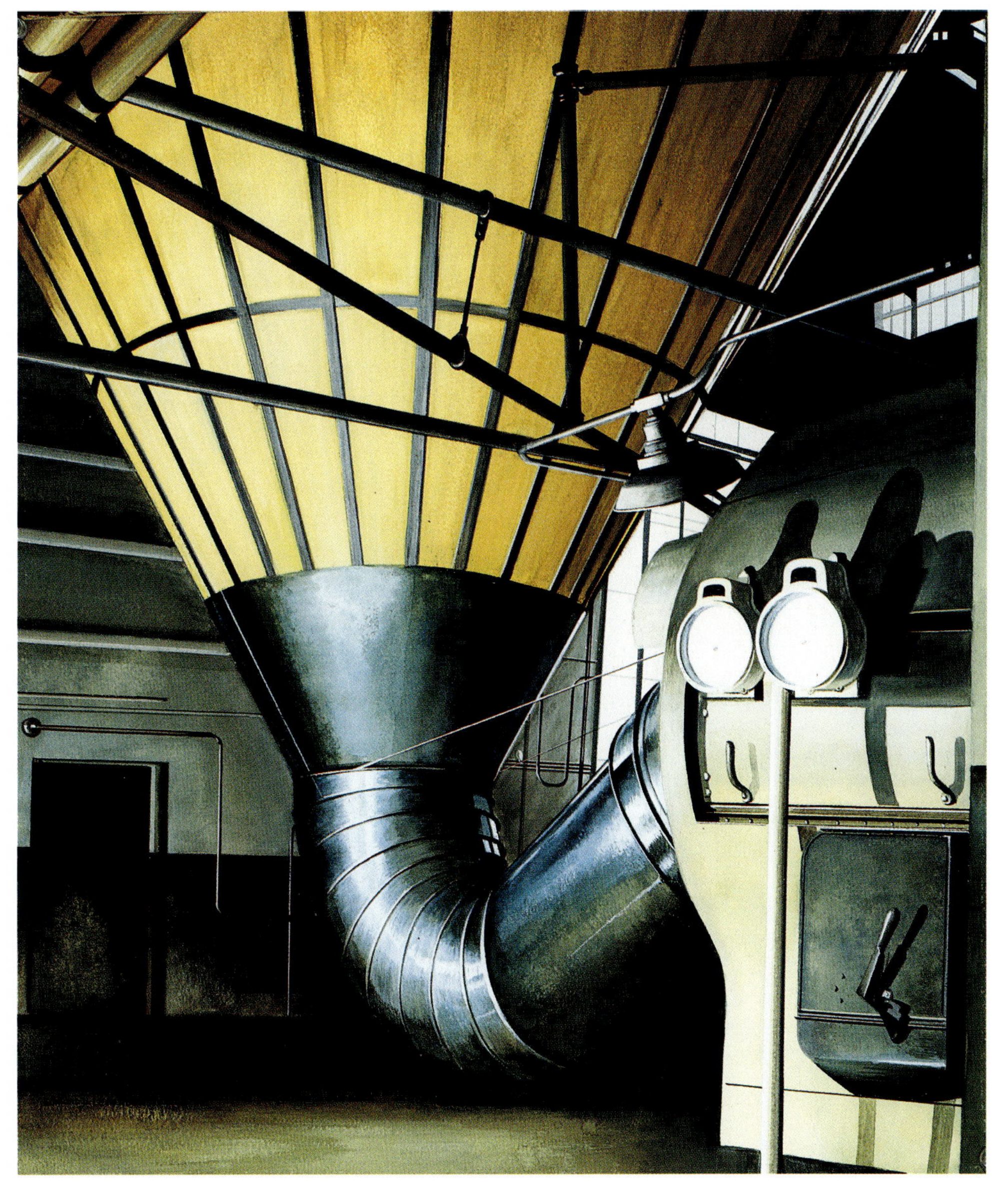

Arshile Gorky

1904–1948

untitled, between 1943 and 1945

graphite and crayon on paper, 18 × 24 inches
Gift of Mr. and Mrs. C. Guy Gunter; Mrs. Minor H. Mickel; Richard B. Sarver, M.D. (by exchange)

The decade of the 1940s witnessed the advent of Abstract Expressionism, the first international movement in the history of art centered in this country and dominated by American artists. Abstract Expressionism grew out of the experimental works of various European artists, including Pablo Picasso, Wassily Kandinsky, and Joan Miró. The ideology of Surrealism, however, exerted the greatest influence; its reliance on the role of the subconscious and of automatism, the spontaneous and random creation of an object with little conscious intervention from the artist, was seminal to the evolution of Abstract Expressionism.

Of the painters associated with early Abstract Expressionism, Arshile Gorky did the most to synthesize European sources into a uniquely personal vision. Born Vosdanik Manuk Adoian in Armenia, Gorky had a troubled childhood; he and his family were victims of ethnic persecution. In his midteens, he fled to America, where he remained an outsider who romanticized his lost heritage. His formal art training was modest; he studied at the New School of Design in Boston for two years, then at the National Academy of Design, New York, where he lasted only a month in the life-drawing class. He voraciously studied the works of other artists in books and periodicals and at museums and galleries. Despite his limited background, Gorky became a drawing instructor at the Grand Central School of Art in New York, and in 1937 he was selected for the Works Progress Administration's Federal Art Project. Under this program he created murals for Newark Airport, which sparked a controversy because of their abstract nature.

In its use of formulaic anatomical shapes, Gorky's work from the 1930s openly demonstrates the influence of Picasso. Akin to Miró, however, is the buoyant quality of Gorky's compositions, in which objects appear to float in limitless space. This feeling of suspension is enhanced in later works by Gorky's use of thin, transparent pigment, which he often allowed to drip down the canvas. Organic shapes prevail, and these are often interconnected by thin lines that resemble wire armatures.

Within the context of automatism, drawings are deemed important because they reveal the artist's initial inspiration, usually an uninhibited creative act. Drawing was always Gorky's forte, and his output was prodigious. His drawing technique ranged from dense, heavily cross-hatched work in pen and ink to lyrical and fluid expressions in pencil. Gorky seems to have enjoyed both the spontaneity and suggestive quality of drawing. For him drawing was alive and immediate.

The Museum's drawing relates to one of the few periods of contentment in Gorky's professional and personal life. Beginning in 1942 he began to rediscover nature, a breakthrough that culminated in an extensive series of light and airy drawings and paintings that he completed at Crooked Run Farm, Virginia. After more than twenty years in New York, Gorky immersed himself in landscape, an experience that brought back memories of his beloved homeland. Writing to his sister, he explained: "It is as if some ancient Armenian spirit within me moves my hand to create so far from our homeland the shapes of nature we loved in the gardens, wheatfields, and orchards of our Adoian family in Khorkom. Our beautiful Armenia which we lost and which I will repossess in my art."[1]

As in so much of Gorky's mature work, the Museum's drawing is filled with organic shapes suggestive of pelvic forms, thigh bones, and bladders. This imagery, initially derived from Picasso, is given new meaning and form through Gorky's intense study of nature on the farm in Virginia.

Gorky's view of the landscape was close-up, involving the intimate scrutiny of flowers, leaves, insects, and weeds. For Gorky shapes could have a variety of interchangeable meanings. The painter Elaine de Kooning, writing three years after the artist's death, perceived his visual transmutations. "Poignantly graceful, Gorky's gardens at first flutter with light and witty loquacity, but in their overpowering flux of successive and simultaneous images, forms change, as you look, into a cruel and opulent sexual imagery. . . . [P]lant forms change into human organs and a riotous pageant is transformed into a desolate landscape strewn with viscera."[2] In the Museum's drawing references to a spreading tree and soft petals can be discerned, along with suggestions of organlike shapes. Relating to Gorky's nostalgia for his homeland, the small touch of orange at the center may allude to an apricot, one of the special things he recalled from childhood. That viewers might not understand exactly what he did was of little concern to Gorky, who was confident that they would intuitively sense his purpose. He commented: "Though the various forms all had meanings to me, it is the spectator's privilege to look for and find his own meaning here. I feel they will relate to or parallel mine."[3]

---

1. Gorky to Vartoosh Mooradian, April 1944, as quoted in Jim M. Jordan, "Arshile Gorky at Crooked Run Farm," *Arts Magazine*, March 1976, 99.

2. Elaine de Kooning, "Gorky: Painter of His Own Legend," *Art News*, January 1951, 64.

3. Gorky, as quoted in Malcolm Johnson, "Café Life in New York," *New York Sun*, 22 August 1941, in Diane Karp, "Arshile Gorky's Iconography," *Arts Magazine*, March 1976, 82.

Born, Khorkom, Armenia, 1904; immigrated to the United States, 1920; studied and taught at New School of Design, Boston, 1922–1924; moved to New York, attended one month at the National Academy of Design, 1925; taught at Grand Central School of Art, New York 1925–1931; joined Works Progress Administration, 1935–1941; three weeks in Connecticut, 1942; summers of 1943 and 1946 and nine months, 1944, at Crooked Run Farm, Hamilton, Virginia; moved to Sherman, Connecticut, 1945; died, Sherman, 1948.

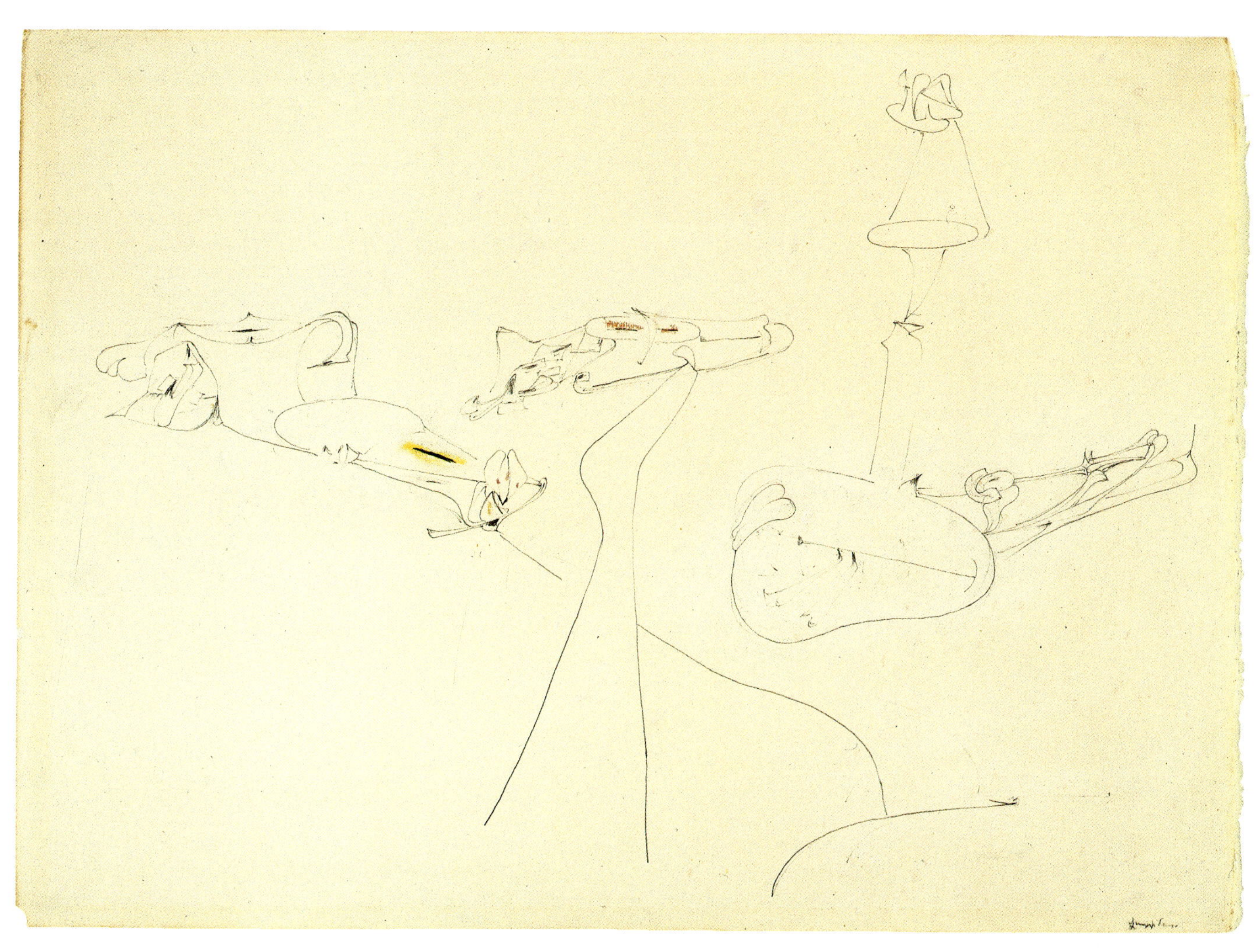

Anthony Fred (Fritz) Bultman

1919–1985

Still Life, 1942

oil on canvas, 30 × 25 inches
Museum purchase with funds donated by the Arthur and Holly Magill Foundation

The year 1950 marked a critical moment for Abstract Expressionism. In the aftermath of World War II, attention decidedly shifted from Paris to New York, where most of the key figures in the art world were living and exhibiting. The controversy revolving around the lack of interest evinced by the Metropolitan Museum of Art toward contemporary art brought many of these artists together and generated publicity in the popular press. An article on the group in *Life* magazine was accompanied by a photograph captioned the "Irascibles," which has led some, incorrectly, to think that the eighteen artists pictured were part of a cohesive movement. In retrospect, the photograph is misleading; it includes painters who did not embrace Abstract Expressionist ideals, and it excludes others who rightfully belonged to the movement.[1]

One of the original protestors, or Irascibles, Fritz Bultman was not in the *Life* photograph because at the time it was taken he was on a fellowship in Italy. His absence from New York at this momentous time precluded his sharing in and benefiting from the spotlight focused on the emerging Abstract Expressionists. His good friend and fellow painter Robert Motherwell had his own explanation for why Bultman has been overlooked:

> After forty years of acquaintanceship with Fritz Bultman and his work, I am still convinced that he is one of the most splendid, radiant and inspired painters of my generation, and of them all, the one drastically and shockingly underrated. I do not know why this is so. Perhaps, with his explosive temperament, he was not very adept at playing the New York gallery game. But whatever the reason for the neglect of his work I still find it as radiant as ever, after all these years.[2]

In his native New Orleans Bultman demonstrated an early interest in art. When Bultman was thirteen the young artist Morris Graves spent the summer with the Bultman family, and together they went on sketching trips to the zoo. Later, Bultman went to Germany, hoping to attend the Bauhaus, the school noted for its advanced curriculum that combined the arts and architecture, but was disappointed to find that it had been closed by Adolf Hitler. He studied for a while at the Munich Preparatory School and was befriended by Miz Hofmann, the wife of the noted painter Hans Hofmann. Upon his return to the United States, Bultman attended the New Bauhaus in Chicago for a short period before studying with Hofmann for three years.

Bultman revered his teacher as a pivotal figure, stating: "Hofmann's presence did so much to set American painting in motion. No one else gave it the courage for multiple developments."[3] Although Hofmann labored to keep his students from imitating him, his influence on Bultman is evident. Hofmann painted highly textured canvases, with bold brushstrokes and heavy impasto. Bultman likewise considered the surface of the canvas to be critical, although his paint application was more restrained than that of his teacher. Hofmann emphasized duality and subscribed to the "push-pull" theory of color, stating that some colors visually recede while others project forward. In like manner, Bultman manipulated colors to create the illusion of space, and, even when he worked in black and white, spatial tensions were paramount.

The Museum's painting, *Still Life,* not only reveals Bultman's allegiance to his teacher but also places him squarely among his peers. The painting presents in embryonic form some of the visual language that would recur in Bultman's later work. The geometry and diagrammatic scheme may ultimately relate to the desire of the painter's father that his son become an architect, but it also refers to Bultman's preoccupation with mazes. Along the grid are a series of circles or dots, a motif that persisted into Bultman's late collages; almost like footprints, these give direction to the composition. Other elements in the painting appear as pictograms—a pictorial shorthand that, for example, renders a human being as a stick figure. Under the influence of Native American designs and Japanese calligraphy such artists as Adolph Gottlieb invented similar pictograms. Unlike some of Bultman's other paintings that bear titles derived from classical myths, *Still Life* is simply designated, perhaps paying oblique homage to Pablo Picasso.

In later years Bultman's versatility with material and form was manifested in his large-scale collages, which resemble the late cutouts of Henri Matisse. Bultman also became an accomplished sculptor in bronze, making him one of the few artists to translate the Abstract Expressionist aesthetic into three dimensions.

---

1. See April Kingsley, *The Turning Point* (New York: Simon & Schuster, 1992).
2. Motherwell, "A Tribute to Fritz Bultman," as quoted in April Kingsley, *Fritz Bultman* (New Orleans: New Orleans Museum of Art, 1993), 9.
3. Bultman, "The Achievement of Hans Hofmann," *Art News,* September 1963, 45.

Born, New Orleans, 1919; drew with Morris Graves, 1931; attended Munich Preparatory School and traveled in Europe, 1935–1937; studied at the New Bauhaus, Chicago, 1937–1938, and with Hans Hofmann in New York and Provincetown, Massachusetts, 1938–1941; studied bronze casting in Italy, 1950–1951; taught at the Pratt Institute, New York, 1958 and 1962–1963, Hunter College, New York, 1959–1963, Tulane University, New Orleans, 1978–1979; Fulbright fellowship in France, 1964–1965; died, Provincetown, Massachusetts, 1985.

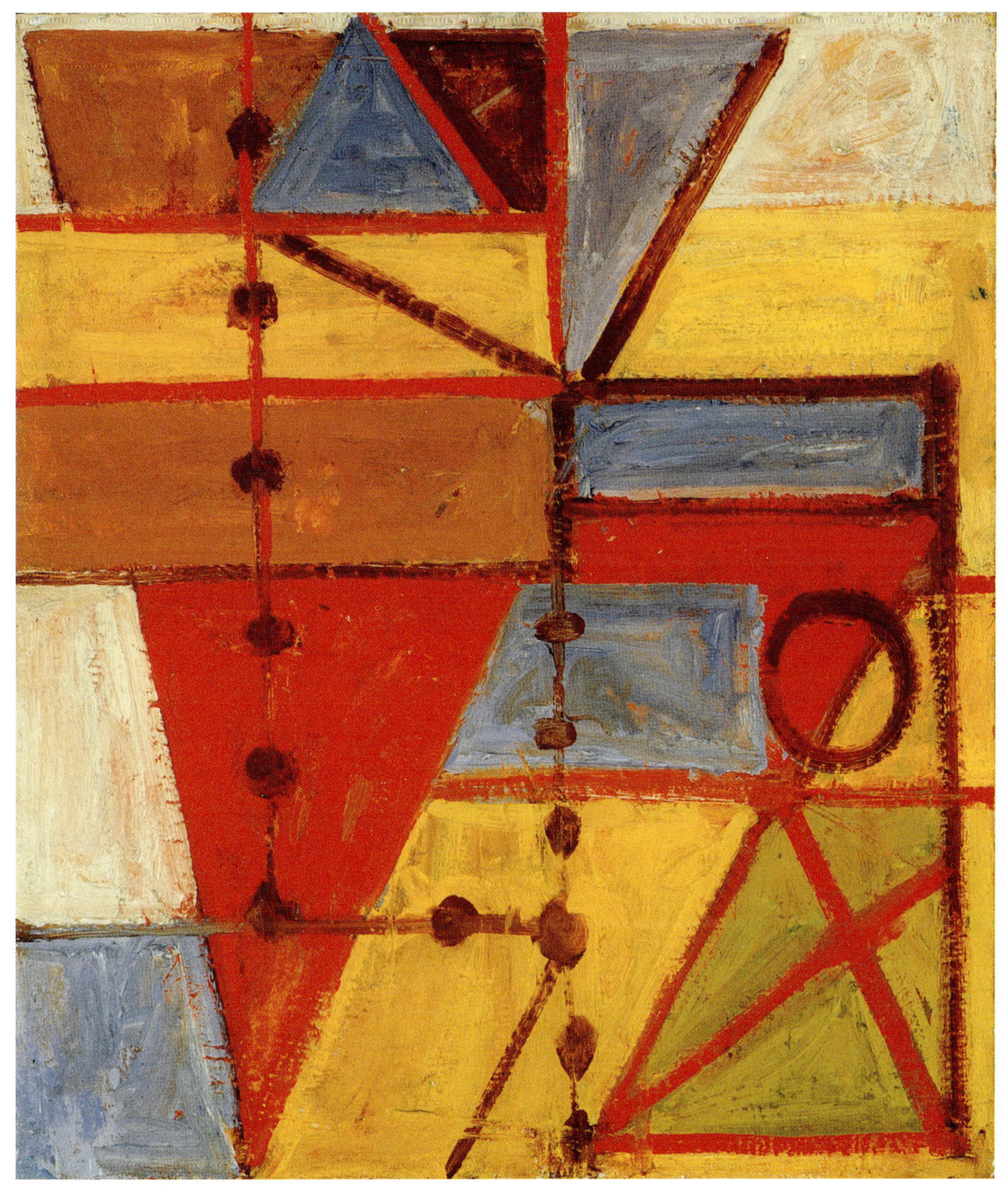

Nell Blaine

born 1922

***The Mechanical Warrior*, 1946**

charcoal, ink, paint, and shellac on paper, 25¼ × 19½ inches
signed, lower left: *N. Blaine, 1946*
Gift of Elaine de Kooning

Just as during the seventeenth, eighteenth, and early nineteenth centuries painting was separated into the categories of *colore* and *disegno,* or the distinguishing characteristics, respectively, of Peter Paul Rubens and Nicolas Poussin, the art of the twentieth century has been subdivided between the colorism of Henri Matisse and the intellectual approach of Pablo Picasso. Matisse, the Fauve, was considered the greater colorist of the two; Picasso's primary concern in his Cubist works was the dynamic of form.

Hans Hofmann, who was in Paris in the cataclysmic decade from 1904 to 1914 when Fauvism and Cubism were in ascendancy, succeeded in combining the divergent forces in both his work and his teachings. Hofmann's synthesis of color and design became the foundation of his concept of "push-pull" that characterized his later work, in which brightly colored rectangles can be viewed as either advancing or receding.[1] As an eminent teacher, Hofmann influenced the thinking of many students, including Fritz Bultman, Nell Blaine, and Judith Godwin.

One of Hofmann's favorite students, Blaine was born in Richmond, Virginia, and displayed a precocious interest in art. She studied for three years at the Richmond School of Art (now Virginia Commonwealth University), where the curriculum was conventional and academic. Blaine's view of painting conflicted with the Southern view: "There was a certain notion in Virginia about 'culture': that art was a genteel thing, prissy, and somewhat bland. That was the kind of 'proper taste' I absorbed from the 'art lovers,' and in a way it was a hindrance, an inhibiting thing."[2] To support herself she did commercial artwork, which eventually allowed her to go to New York to study with Hofmann. Her response to Hofmann was positive: "I thought him a kind of jovial, intellectual Santa Claus. He demanded you regard him as a master, and I gave him what he wanted in that way because I was a real disciple. I had feared his teaching would be scary and obscure; but that was not so. I never found him hard to understand. To me he was clear."[3]

In addition to absorbing the potent influence of Hofmann, Blaine became intimately involved in the music world, and her work before 1950 reflects the energy and vitality of the Jazz Age. In 1944, at age twenty-two, she became the youngest member of American Abstract Artists, the group that had formed to promote the acceptance of abstract art. Employing an analytical approach to abstraction, Blaine created images that emulate the formal properties of collage. In *The Mechanical Warrior* Picasso's legacy is evident in the stylized forms, except that Blaine has made them larger and simpler. In keeping with the emerging Abstract Expressionist aesthetic, the artist's gesture, or act of painting, can be tracked across the paper. The dominance of rectangular forms relates to Hofmann's work. In its boldness and intensity, the work is not unlike the jazz sounds that were played in Blaine's studio-loft, which she shared with her musician husband.

A dramatic shift in Blaine's work occurred after a trip to France in 1950. There she encountered Impressionism. After a transitional period during which she worked as a commercial designer and teacher, she devoted herself to lush, painterly landscapes and still lifes that appear as late flowerings of Fauvism. Despite her frustration with the critical writings of Clement Greenberg, an outspoken art critic largely responsible for the promulgation of Abstract Expressionism, she persists. "Critics like Clement Greenberg have preached novelty to a point where people are suspicious of art that seems to bear a connection with the past. That's had a bad effect on the public and therefore on artists in terms—simply—of bread. And it seems to me it has shut the door on what I think of as genuine creativity. A freely creative person ought to be able to move out in any direction."[4]

1. Irving Sandler, "Hans Hofmann: The Dialectical Master," in Cynthia Goodman, *Hans Hofmann* (New York: Whitney Museum of American Art, 1990), 81.

2. Blaine, as quoted in Eleanor Munro, *American Women Artists* (New York: Simon & Schuster, 1979), 263.

3. Blaine, in Munro, *American Women,* 265.

4. Blaine, in Munro, *American Women,* 271.

Born, Richmond, Virginia, 1922; studied at the Richmond School of Art (now Virginia Commonwealth University), 1939–1942; studied with Hans Hofmann in New York, 1942–1944; traveled to France and Italy, 1950, and to Italy, Egypt, Turkey, and Greece, 1959; resides in New York, with summers at Gloucester, Massachusetts.

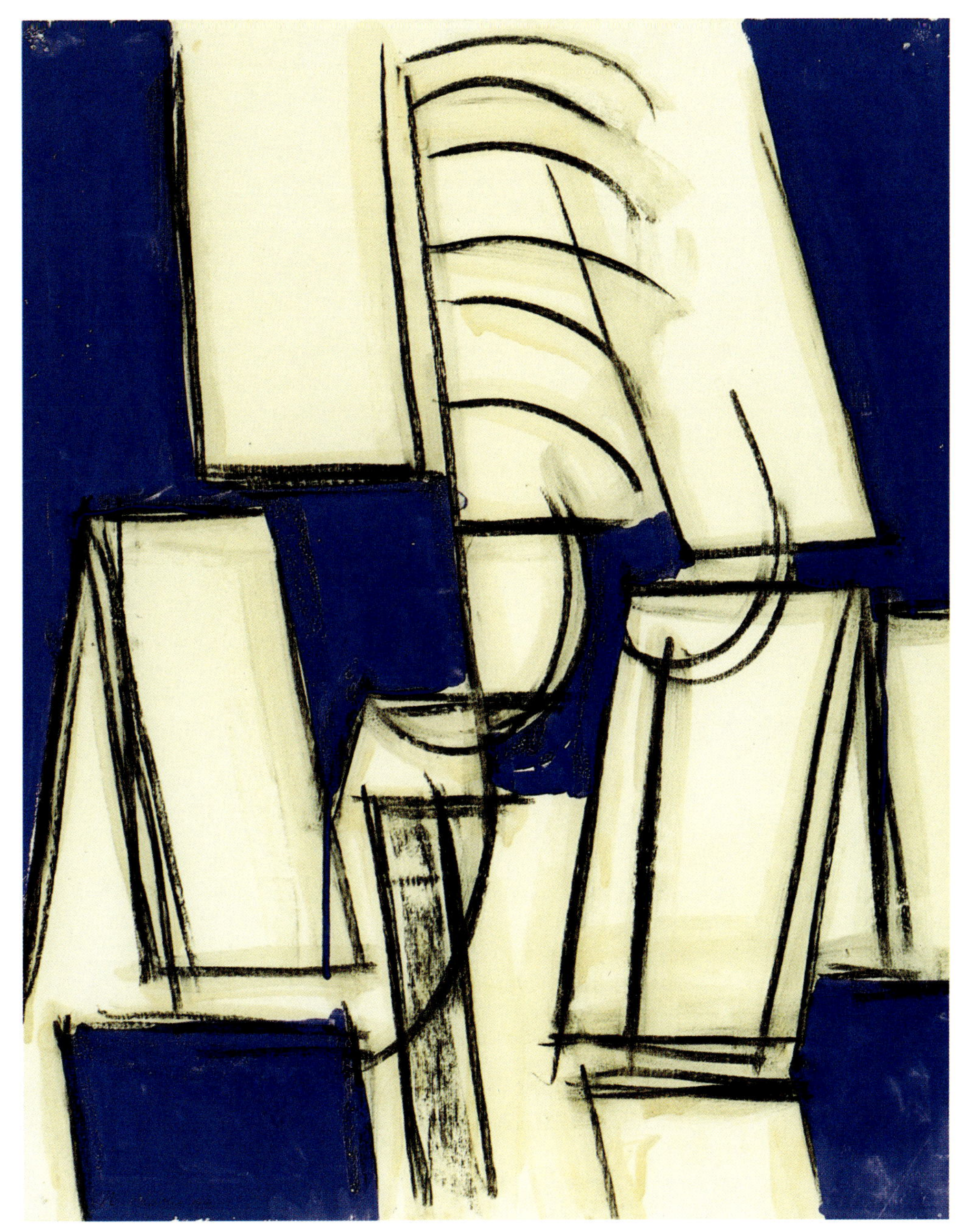

Elaine Fried de Kooning

1918–1989

untitled #10, 1948

enamel on paper mounted on canvas,
25¼ × 32½ inches
Museum purchase with funds donated by the
Arthur and Holly Magill Foundation

The term *Abstract Expressionism,* not coined until 1951, became a convenient designation for the first art movement dominated by Americans. The label has some merit because most of the work is nonrepresentational and contains an emotive and personal quality. Although painters of the New York School retained their particular identities, the work was categorized by critics under two rubrics: Action Painting and Color Field Painting. The most notorious practitioner of the former group was Jackson Pollock, who involved his entire body in the act of creation by throwing, splattering, and dripping paint onto canvas. Mark Rothko's serene expanses of color, often soaked into the canvas, best exemplify the Color Field aesthetic.

Pollock and Willem de Kooning, considered two of the major "Action Painters" because of their loose and energetic application of paint, contributed greatly to the myth of the painter as a larger-than-life, inebriated genius. Both were married to artists, Lee Krasner and Elaine Fried de Kooning, who went to great lengths to foster and promote their husbands' careers. Although both women were initially overshadowed by their spouses, they also created significant bodies of work that reflect the diversity and vitality of Abstract Expressionism.

Growing up in Brooklyn, Elaine Fried demonstrated an early interest in art that was fueled by study at the Leonardo da Vinci Art School, the American Artists School, and regular visits to museums. The turning point in her art education occurred when she began to study with Willem de Kooning in his studio in 1938. From him she learned to analyze the shapes of objects as well as to assess the intervals of space between them, and she came to admire the work of Arshile Gorky, whose emphasis on contours influenced her own development. De Kooning, however, set herself apart by undertaking two roles in which her husband had no interest or facility: writing reviews for *Art News* and painting portraits. As a critic de Kooning not only came into close contact with the major figures of the art world, but she also helped to shape contemporary art. As a portraitist she successfully applied the Abstract Expressionist idiom to the representation of people, which was anathema to her peers. Most of her sitters were her friends, which, because of her personal insights into their characters, allowed her great freedom in her portrayals. Her most important commission was a portrait of President John F. Kennedy. The project continued for more than a year and remained unfinished at the time of his assassination.

In 1948 Josef Albers invited Willem de Kooning to participate in the summer program at Black Mountain College, a critical opportunity for the de Koonings that provided a modest income and a break from routine. The experience of living in a sheltered, creative environment in the hills of western North Carolina had a greater impact on Elaine de Kooning than on her husband. Removed from New York and thrust among students and faculty, she participated fully in the summer's offerings. She attended Albers's color-theory classes and dance sessions with Merce Cunningham, and she was the only woman in the course taught by the visionary architect Buckminster Fuller. Her evenings were divided between attending John Cage's avant-garde concerts and rehearsing for a theatrical performance in which she starred. As she later recalled, "The school activities engulfed us like a warm breeze."[1]

While at Black Mountain College de Kooning also found time to produce a series of paintings. "Despite all of the unaccustomed student and social activity, I still managed to come away with a roll of enamel paintings on wrapping paper—a testimonial to the durability of paint, if nothing more."[2] In these seventeen paintings, which include the Museum's, de Kooning addressed aesthetic issues relating to shape, depth, and density of composition. With a limited palette dominated by pinks, the artist focused on a variety of organic, biomorphic shapes distantly reminiscent of Gorky's work. Rounded contours are constricted by outlines, and the illusion of three dimensions is strictly suppressed. The result is an overall network of undulating forms that resembles some of the fabric collages of Conrad Marca-Relli, one of her teachers at the Leonardo da Vinci Art School.

For de Kooning the Black Mountain series represented a resolution to problems that she had been exploring for some time. But upon her return to New York, the paintings were placed in storage, where they remained until 1985. They were never exhibited during her lifetime. While she continued to produce Abstract Expressionist works, de Kooning simultaneously maintained her interest in figurative art, including portraits and images of athletes in action. In 1957 she left her husband, and the following year she taught at the University of New Mexico, an experience that turned her toward landscapes painted in bold colors. Other travels, to the cave paintings at Lascaux, to the gardens of Paris, and to the Far East, provided additional inspiration and resulted in various thematic series not unlike those from her summer at Black Mountain College.

---

1. Elaine de Kooning, "De Kooning Memories," *Vogue,* December 1983, 394.

2. De Kooning, "Memories," 394.

Born, Brooklyn, 1918; attended Hunter College, New York, 1936; classes at the Leonardo da Vinci Art School and the American Artists School, 1937; instruction from Willem de Kooning, beginning 1938; summer at Black Mountain College, 1948; visiting professor, University of New Mexico, 1958, Pennsylvania State University, 1960, and University of California, Davis, 1964; taught at Yale University, Pratt Institute, Carnegie Mellon University, University of Pennsylvania, Parsons School of Design, Brandeis University, University of Georgia, and Bard College, 1967–1982; traveled to Paris, 1974, to Cortona, Italy, 1977, to Lascaux, France, 1983, to Spain and Kenya, 1984, to China and Japan, 1986; died, Southampton, New York, 1989.

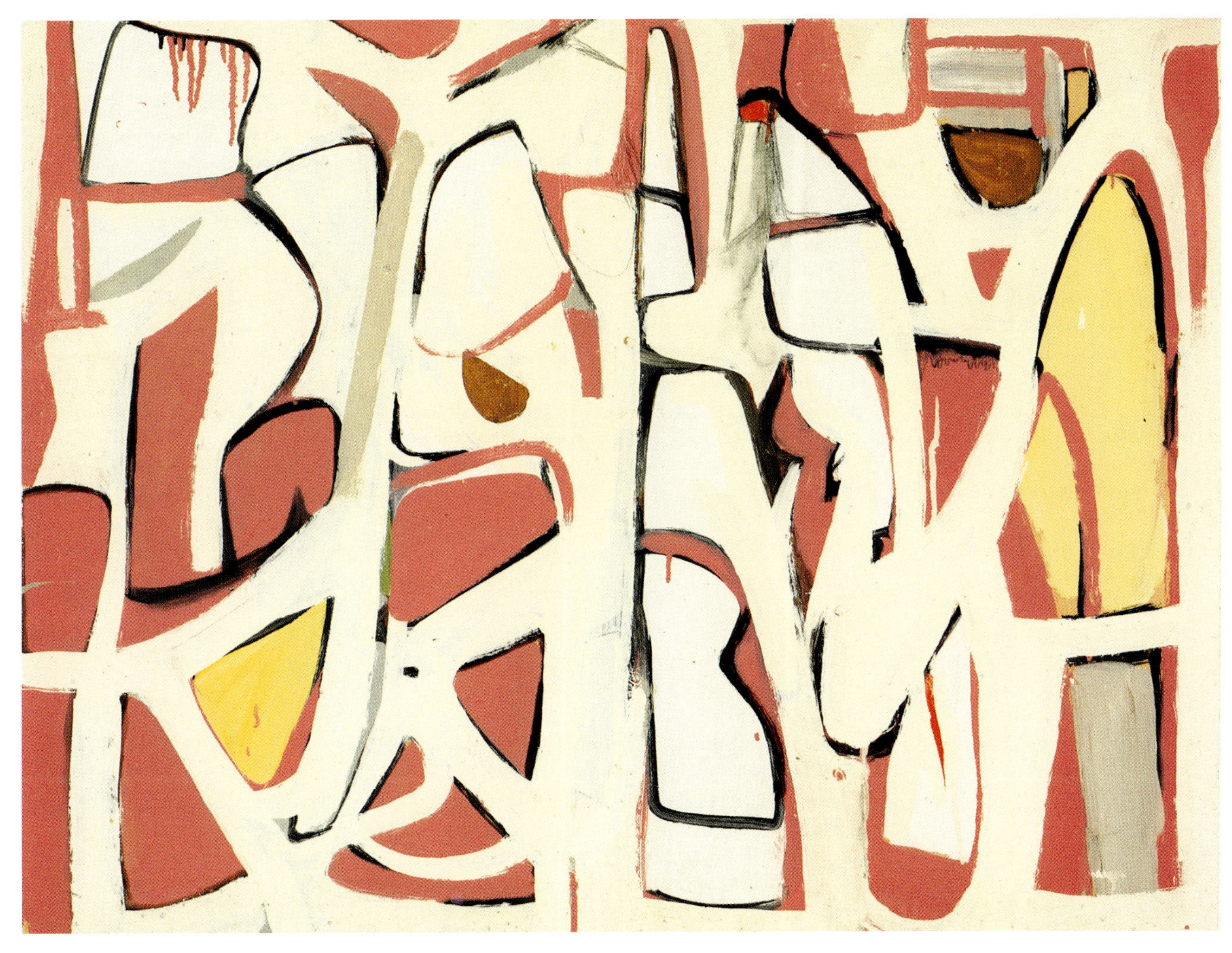

Judith Godwin

born 1930

Red Planes, 1954

oil on canvas, 60 × 38 inches
signed, lower right: *Godwin*
Anonymous gift

Abstract Expressionism, an extremely diverse and complicated movement, has been subdivided chronologically. Most of the artists of the first generation were born before the United States entered World War I. Many had worked on mural projects sponsored by the federal government during the Depression, a factor that contributed to the large scale of their paintings. Primarily men with strong, sometimes outlandish personalities, the first-generation painters promoted individualism and raw genius; few were successful teachers, with the exception of Hans Hofmann who excelled in this role. The second generation of Abstract Expressionists included many women, a few of whom were married to members of the first generation. Several studied with Hofmann, and all were unabashedly indebted to those who went before. While resolving their own stylistic challenges, they persisted with the expressionist idiom at a time when other movements were emerging in opposition to their ideology.

In 1950 a group of the first-generation painters began to get national attention in the popular press; that same year Judith Godwin turned twenty. Godwin was born and raised in Suffolk, Virginia. She went to Virginia schools, first Mary Baldwin College, then the Richmond Professional Institute (now Virginia Commonwealth University). At both institutions she was fortunate to study with forward-looking instructors familiar with European modernism and current American trends. By 1950 she was painting emphatically abstract works. After a short period of study at the Art Students League in New York, she joined Hofmann's summer classes in Provincetown and later studied with him in New York.

Hofmann was working on his bold abstractions with heavily textured surfaces. Unlike some Abstract Expressionists who preferred to work in black and white, Hofmann delighted in the expressive potential of color. In addition, he maintained that viewers did more than see paintings, they also related to them through touch and smell. At the same time that Godwin became his student, Hofmann began to paint his hallmark series of "push-pull" paintings, in which crisply defined, brightly colored rectangles swim in an impasto-laden sea of paint.

The Museum's painting demonstrates the strength of Hofmann's teaching, an influence Godwin willingly acknowledges: "From Hofmann I learned freedom of color, and how to release myself from more conventional thinking and feeling. I began using color as a movement with a definite direction. Color established distinct planes in my work."[1] Aptly titled *Red Planes,* the Museum's painting is virtually an exegesis of Hofmann's instruction: the painting must originate in nature, whether figure, landscape, or still life; color should be used spatially; and the painting should create a sense of empathy. Godwin's composition revolves around a figure, defined by the dominant red planes, which, as Hofmann taught, tantalizingly touch the edge of the canvas. Other geometric shapes, defined by strong outlines, overlap the figure but remain transparent, allowing the viewer's gaze to penetrate the painting.[2] Contrasting with this is another Hofmannesque quality: the tactile nature of the paint, which projects forward, but in a more restrained fashion than Hofmann's contemporaneous works. Color is vigorous and intense; complementary colors—red and green, yellow and purple—are used abundantly.

When Godwin arrived in New York, she cultivated her interest in modern dance, especially the work of Martha Graham. Whereas William H. Johnson, Nell Blaine, and Romare Bearden responded to the rhythms of the Jazz Age, Godwin reacted and absorbed many of the energetic movements made famous by Graham.[3] Wearing long heavy skirts instead of gauzy ballet costumes, Graham was frequently captured in photographs in her most characteristic pose, a lithe arc. In the Museum's painting the figure appears as a gracefully bowing dancer who elegantly places her left foot forward.

As Godwin matured she began to distance herself from Hofmann and to respond to other sources, namely the work of Franz Kline and the philosophy of Zen Buddhism. Kline, the Abstract Expressionist known for his calligraphic, large-scale strokes of black on white surfaces, became especially important to Godwin after she moved into his Greenwich Village house in 1964. Still retaining her own powerful palette, under Kline's influence Godwin painted more expansive compositions with broader, more emphatic gestures. In her discovery of Zen, Godwin embraced its meditative approach as well as its emphasis on intuition and harmony with self. Movement, whether the painter's gesture or the dancer's graceful lift, has remained important throughout and has become a leitmotif of her work. "I often feel as I stand before a canvas what I felt when I put my arms around a tree a long time ago and felt its strength—it is the feeling of exerting force without moving. Painting is often a great physical force."[4]

---

1. Godwin to Robert Hobbs, 15 June 1992, as quoted in Robert Hobbs, "Judith Godwin: Aesthetic Mediations between East and West," *Woman's Art Journal* 14, no. 1 (Spring–Summer 1993): unpaginated.
2. Hobbs, "Judith Godwin."
3. Hobbs, "Judith Godwin."
4. Godwin, interview with Joyce E. Davis, 1977, quoted in Hobbs, "Judith Godwin."

Born, Suffolk, Virginia, 1930; attended Mary Baldwin College, Staunton, Virginia, 1948–1950, and Richmond Professional Institute (now Virginia Commonwealth University), 1951–1953; studied in New York at the Art Students League, 1953, and with Hans Hofmann, in Provincetown, Massachusetts, and New York, 1953–1954; traveled around the world, 1964; studied interior design, 1964, and historic restoration, 1970; resides, Warren, Connecticut.

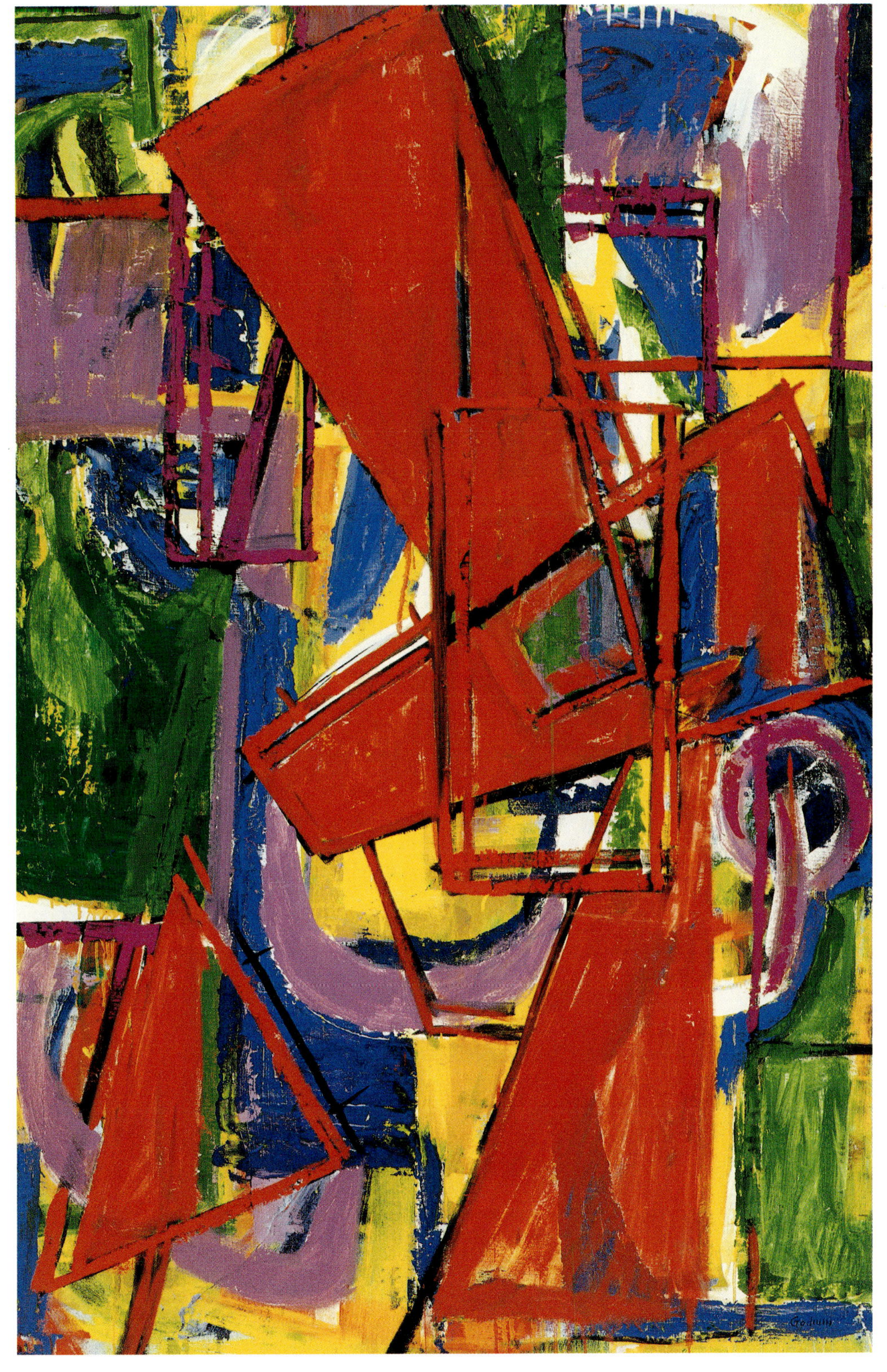

Ida Rittenberg Kohlmeyer

born 1912

Activated, 1965

oil on canvas, 62 × 49 3/4 inches
signed, lower left: *Kohlmeyer*
Museum purchase

One of the hallmarks of Abstract Expressionism was the emphasis placed on the physical act of making art. This was an outgrowth of automatism, an aspect of Surrealism in which the artist either responded spontaneously to materials or let things happen automatically. Jackson Pollock's dripping and throwing of paint is the best-known example of this approach, but his peers Franz Kline, Robert Motherwell, and Adolph Gottlieb also employed large-scale gestures as they painted their canvases. Kline and Motherwell initially painted imposing calligraphic works in black and white, while Gottlieb typically divided his surface into compartments, variously filled with color and gestural brushstrokes. Gottlieb's paintings call to mind Oriental handwriting and prehistoric wall paintings that contain their own esoteric visual language.

Living and working in New Orleans, Ida Kohlmeyer has pursued a painting style that, like Gottlieb's, is a marriage between color and the gestural act of painting. Only when she was in her mid-thirties did Kohlmeyer determine to become a painter; she obtained a master's degree in art from Sophie Newcomb College, but the decisive moment came in 1956 when she studied with Hans Hofmann in Provincetown, Massachusetts. Hofmann's teaching and his own painting emphasized the sensuous properties of paint and the spatial role of color on a two-dimensional surface. The other potent influence on her development was Mark Rothko, a visiting artist at Sophie Newcomb College in 1957 who stayed with the Kohlmeyers. Rothko was less interested in individual strokes than he was in painting expansive areas of color.

In 1963 Kohlmeyer came to a crossroads; she had to choose between New Orleans and New York, the avowed capital of the art world. Determining that New York might be too overwhelming, she persevered in her native environment, and she began to emerge from Rothko's spell. A few years earlier the noted sculptor George Rickey had written to encourage her to find herself: "I think you need Ida. You need to find your own style, the one that exploits the very maximum of your capacities. You are really too independent, too ambitious, and too strong a personality to be content with eclecticism."[1] Only in New Orleans, away from the madding crowd, could Kohlmeyer find her own identity.

The Museum's painting, *Activated,* was completed while Kohlmeyer was exploring her own potential. Softly muted in color, it displays the influence of Rothko in its floating, airy quality that becomes more dense toward the top of the canvas. Suspended in this harmonious field of tinted browns are numerous pictorial elements. The touch or gesture of these ranges from a heavy, dark pair of parallel black forms to more delicate, merely suggested shapes. In its illusion of unlimited space and tentative markings the painting is reminiscent of the work of Arshile Gorky. However, where Gorky employed organic forms derived from nature, Kohlmeyer works with handwritten formulas of her own invention. Many of these are inscribed within a circle or a square, foreshadowing work to come.

In her more recent work Kohlmeyer has capitalized on these individualistic marks. Giving more structure to her painting, she has employed a grid system to contain her visual vocabulary, which encompasses x shapes and circles, dashes and chevrons, squiggles and letterlike forms. Great variety exists within each work, and her palette has brightened to include pastels as well as intense, Day-Glo colors. Yet Kohlmeyer does not reject her roots or her earlier work: "The evolution of an artist's style takes many turns—some more apparent than others. This may happen voluntarily or involuntarily. . . . The past is never annihilated and keeps seeping back in, and in so doing reaffirms grass roots. There is no progress in an artist's work once it has reached maturity—only different ways of saying the same thing."[2]

---

1. Rickey to Kohlmeyer, 25 November 1958, as quoted in Jane Kessler and Whitney J. Engeran, *Ida Kohlmeyer: Thirty Years* (Charlotte, N.C.: Mint Museum of Art, 1983), 103.

2. Kohlmeyer, *Crux Series, 1967–1969* (Birmingham, Ala.: Dick Jemison Gallery, 1978), introduction.

Born, New Orleans, 1912; graduated from Sophie Newcomb College, New Orleans, major in English, 1933; master of fine arts degree, Sophie Newcomb College, 1950–1956; studied with Hans Hofmann, summer 1956; lived in Paris, three months, 1956; taught at Sophie Newcomb College, 1956–1964, and Louisiana State University, Baton Rouge, 1973–1975; resides, Metairie, Louisiana.

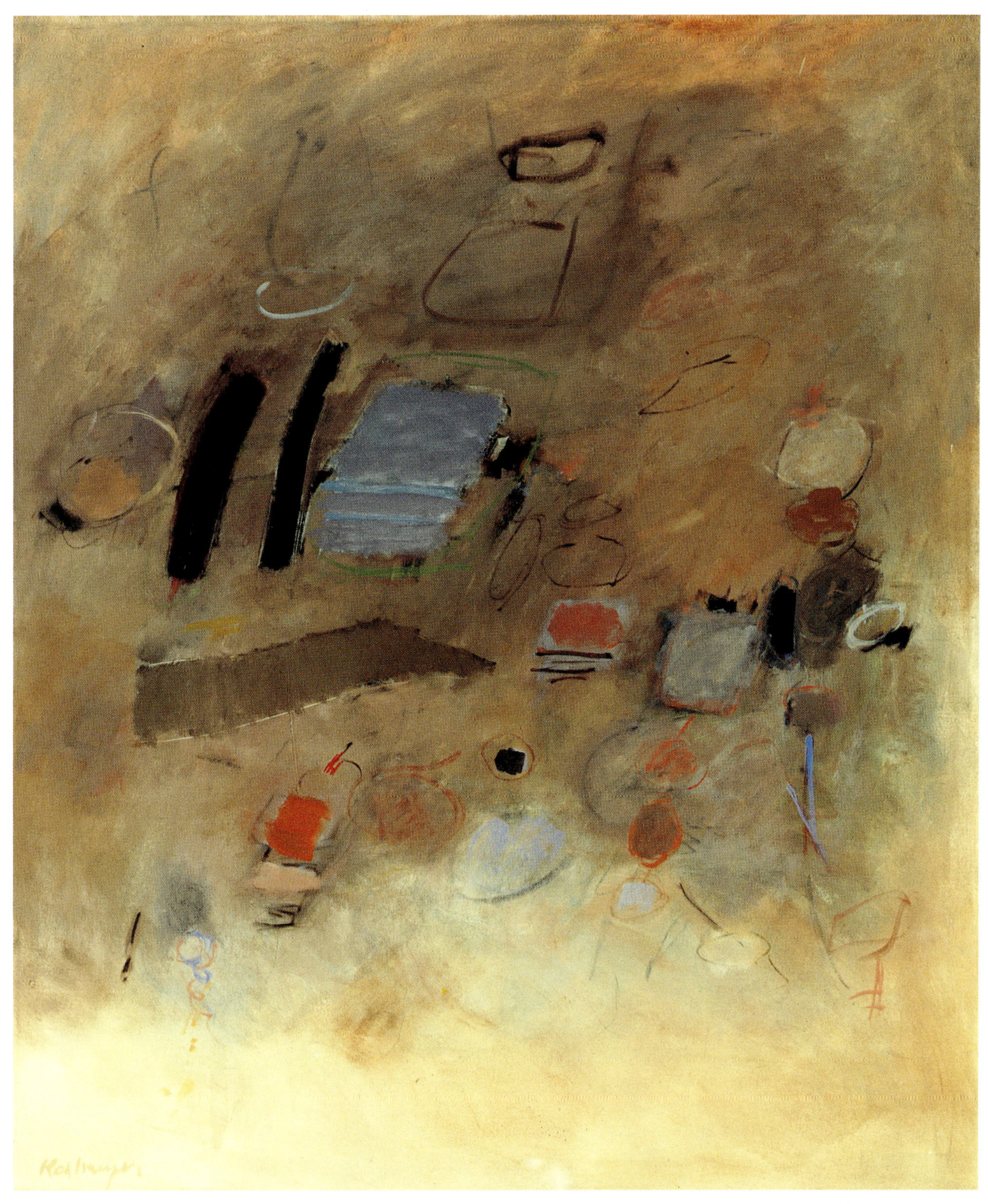

José de Rivera

1904–1985

Construction, 1951

bronze, 21 × 40 × 2¼ inches
stamped, underneath: *Jose de Rivera, 1951*
Museum purchase with funds donated by the Arthur and Holly Magill Foundation

One goal of the artists at the Bauhaus was to use modern technology to express contemporary ideas. Along with the Russian Constructivists Naum Gabo and Anton Pevsner, the artists affiliated with the Bauhaus created spatially dynamic sculptures using steel, wire, and plastic. Simultaneously with these industrially oriented explorations, Constantin Brancusi placed a renewed emphasis on the primacy of materials. Although he used such traditional media as marble, wood, and bronze, he shaped them to form modernist interpretations of the female form and movement in space. His most noted work, *Bird in Space,* is a streamlined evocation of motion. Its sleek, highly polished, gently arcing contour alludes to the flight path rather than to the bird.

The American artist who came closest to Brancusi's elemental and sophisticated approach was José de Rivera. A proficient machinist and superb craftsman, de Rivera, who was comfortable with industrial materials, transcended Brancusi, whose works remained stationary and somewhat static. De Rivera not only abstracted and implied motion in his work, but he actually incorporated movement in many of his works.

De Rivera was born José A. Ruiz in West Baton Rouge, Louisiana, and from his father, a sugar-plantation engineer, he learned about machines at an early age. Determining not to follow in his father's footsteps, de Rivera went to Chicago, where he took jobs as a pipe fitter and machinist. His only formal art education consisted of evening classes, primarily in calligraphy and figure drawing, at the School of the Art Institute of Chicago. In 1930 he exhibited his first sculpture, a cylindrical owl crafted from a solid brass rod. A turning point for de Rivera came a year later when he traveled abroad and saw at firsthand examples of Egyptian and Greek sculpture. After that experience he committed himself to creating sculpture.

Like many of his contemporaries, de Rivera worked under the auspices of the Works Progress Administration. For Newark Airport, where Arshile Gorky installed his virtually abstract murals, de Rivera conceived *Flight,* a stylized image of a bird's wingspan, which also resembles an airplane. Carved from aluminum rods, the piece was intentionally installed above eye level in a position where its surface would catch light. Almost thirty years later de Rivera finished another federal commission to be placed in front of the Smithsonian's Museum of History and Technology. *Infinity* actually moves, catching sunlight and creating ever-changing patterns as it revolves through space and revolutionizes the experience of sculpture.

After 1940 de Rivera worked exclusively with abstracted imagery, proclaiming, "What I make represents nothing but itself."[1] In sympathy with this idea, de Rivera's works are usually innocuously titled *Construction* followed by a number. Not only does this indicate that the work has been fabricated rather than carved, but it also adds to the technological quality of his work. In the time elapsed since the Museum's piece was made in 1951 its specific numerical designation has been lost. It is a transitional example between de Rivera's series of tabletop works of large, curving shapes and his later, thinner, tubular pieces that calligraphically curve into themselves. In its resemblance to a stylized and streamlined bird, along with its sleek profile and highly polished bronze surface, the Museum's piece clearly reveals de Rivera's debt to Brancusi.

De Rivera achieved success and recognition at the same time that the Abstract Expressionists dominated painting, yet their respective aesthetics were worlds apart. De Rivera's craftsmanship, use of modern materials, clean lines, and polished surfaces are more akin to the ideology of International Style architects who were contemporaneously erecting glass-and-steel skyscrapers. Many of de Rivera's public commissions were for these architects, and his gleaming, curving, and moving sculptures offer a pleasant digression from the strict geometry of their architecture. He saw the marriage of his sculpture with architecture as synergistic: "While architecture can stand alone as a functional form as a space experience it can be aided by the proper painting and sculpture. Painting, sculpture, and architecture are in themselves complete experiences; yet if brought together they can produce a total experience beyond that which they express alone."[2]

---

1. De Rivera, as quoted in Dore Ashton, "The Sculpture of José de Rivera," *Arts,* April 1956, 38.
2. De Rivera, as quoted in Ashton, "De Rivera," 41.

Born, West Baton Rouge, Louisiana, 1904; moved to New Orleans as a child, and to Chicago, 1924; studied at night at the School of the Art Institute of Chicago, 1926–1930; traveled through Spain, France, Italy, Greece, Egypt, and North Africa, 1932; settled in New York, 1932; private, United States Army, 1942–1945; taught at Brooklyn College, 1953, Yale University, 1953–1955, and at North Carolina School of Design, Raleigh, 1957–1960; died, New York, 1985.

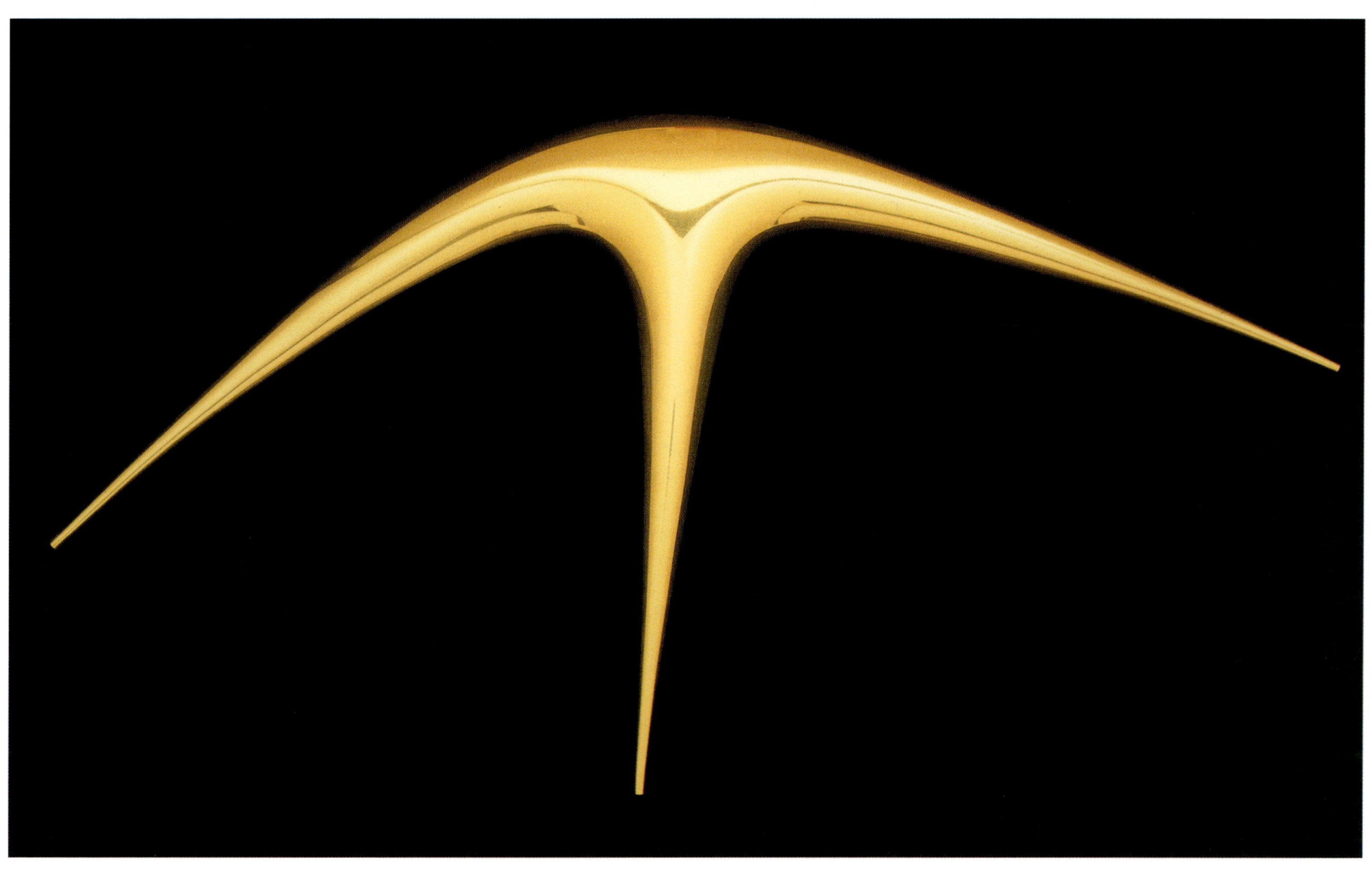

Leo Amino

1911–1989

Landscape I, 1956

stained poplar, 8 3/4 × 31 × 4 inches
signed, underneath: *Leo Amino, 1956*
Museum purchase with funds from the
Arthur and Holly Magill Purchase Fund

Modern American and European sculpture is dominated by a preoccupation with the formal properties of materials. Adherents of direct carving responded to the evocative potential of wood and stone and explored new varieties that included substances as exotic as ebony and as mundane as cement. Complementing this subtractive approach to sculpture were experiments with technologically advanced metals and plastics. Under the aegis of the Bauhaus, artists investigated the expressive and structural possibilities of manufactured materials.

Among American sculptors, David Smith and Leo Amino led the way in their use of steel and plastic, respectively. Stylistically, both integrated the inventive application of materials with a personal form of organic surrealism. The spatial interaction of positives and negatives, solids and voids, was critical to their work. Their careers coincided with the evolution of Abstract Expressionist painting, an offshoot of Surrealism that stressed the materiality of paint.

Amino, born in Taiwan to Japanese parents, first came to the United States in 1929. His earliest art training consisted of carving in a Tokyo school. He studied liberal arts in California before he became a student of Chaim Gross. Although Amino's relationship with Gross was contentious, the older artist instilled in his student a deep appreciation for materials. The other potent influence on Amino was the sculptor Henry Moore, whose work Amino encountered on a trip to England in 1938. Like the British master, Amino exploited the yin-yang–like interplay between voids contained within exterior contours.

Landscape I relates to the work of Smith, Gross, and Moore, yet emerges as an individualistic statement. The interaction between voids and solids is reminiscent of Moore and early Smith and is critical for both content and form. In the history of art the majority of sculpture is devoted to the human figure; landscape per se is unusual. In the Museum's *Landscape I* the attenuated horizontal format frames the scene in which are arranged objects suggesting trees, figures, and a body of water. Using a visual language derived from Surrealism, Amino created an environment in which significant spatial relationships are repeated throughout the composition. For example, on the left, the quasi-lozenge-shaped opening is mirrored in reverse in the horizontal element suspended within this void. The rounded headlike form to the right is echoed by the round perforation near the bottom center.

Amino, who initially supported himself by working at an ebony-importing firm in New York, taught sculpture for two summers at Black Mountain College, near Asheville, North Carolina. Although he taught in wood, he was beginning to experiment with plastic in his own work. His exploration of the expressive potential of plastic was thoroughly in keeping with the Bauhaus-influenced curriculum of the college, but the school's lack of facilities prevented him from working in plastic while in North Carolina. Subsequently, while teaching at the Cooper Union and residing in New York, Amino pioneered uses of plastic that embraced carved, cast, and embedded processes. Just as *Landscape I* has see-through passages, the later plastic works incorporate transparency as a fundamental aspect of Amino's aesthetic.

Born, Taiwan, 1911; childhood in Tokyo; immigrated to the United States, 1929; attended San Mateo (California) Junior College, 1929–circa 1931; studied with Chaim Gross at the American Artists School, New York, 1937; taught summer sessions at Black Mountain College, 1946 and 1950, and at the Cooper Union School, 1952–1977; died, New York, 1989.

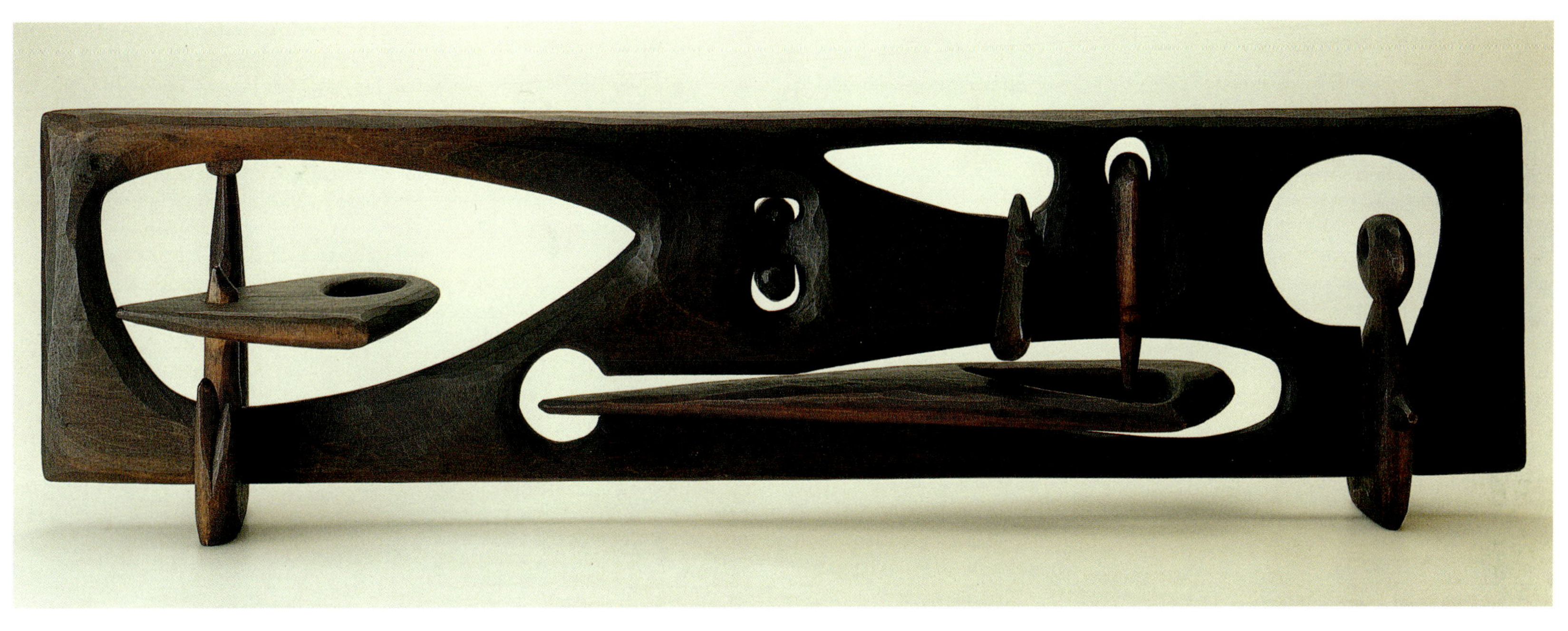

Osvaldo Louis Guglielmi

1906–1956

Vertical Suspension, 1952

oil on canvas, 52 × 34 inches
Museum purchase with funds donated by the Arthur and Holly Magill Foundation

Although the American reaction to Surrealism was reserved, a small group of artists employed aspects of it, sometimes synthesizing its dreamlike qualities with other forms of expression. Thus such trends as Magic Realism evolved, which emphasized the fantasy elements of Surrealism with a sinister undertone. Magic Realism, because of its tendency to editorialize, was also allied to Social Realism.

Throughout the 1930s, the heyday of Magic Realism, O. Louis Guglielmi embraced a highly personalized style that displayed the strong influence of Giorgio de Chirico in its repeated use of stark urban settings, exaggerated perspectives, and high-contrast lighting. Reflecting upon that period, Guglielmi commented: "The early 1930s were coldly sobering years. The artist, a highly sensitive person, found himself helplessly a part of a devastated world. Faced with the terror of the realities of the day, he could no longer justify the shaky theory of individualism and the role of the spectator."[1] Guglielmi's paintings at the time often portrayed destitute city dwellers in quasi-surrealistic settings that reveal the passion and depth of the artist's feelings. After the conclusion of World War II, Guglielmi, who was a slow and methodical painter, developed a more optimistic outlook and moved toward more abstract, design-oriented painting. Chafing in response to a catalogue entry that labeled him an imaginary realist as late as 1950, Guglielmi wrote: "In recent years I have been increasingly concerned with the idea that a painting is in itself an aesthetic object. This very basic conception and the combination of whatever expressive images my fancy releases motivates a visual experience of creative drawing of space, precise shapes and resonant color."[2]

Guglielmi, who was addressed as "Gu" by his friends, was born in Cairo, Egypt, and was raised in northern Italy until 1914, when his family moved to New York. Initially he studied sculpture before becoming a full-time student at the National Academy of Design. During the Depression he joined the easel program of the Works Progress Administration, which required that he submit a certain number of paintings each year. He achieved a degree of success and recognition and was included in several notable exhibitions on Surrealism and related styles organized by the Museum of Modern Art. During World War II he served in a camouflage unit of the armed forces, and by 1950 Guglielmi started to explore teaching as a means to ensure a regular income.

In the summer of 1950 and again two years later he taught at Louisiana State University in Baton Rouge. Perhaps recognizing that Guglielmi's art was firmly rooted in his New York environment, the Baton Rouge *State-Times* announced his appointment with the explanation that "he plans to paint one painting while on campus this summer, but because of the nature of his work, he'll not reproduce any Southern scenery."[3] However, it was just at this time that his art was undergoing a transformation, and *Vertical Suspension* exemplifies the dramatic shift in his style.

The Museum's painting can also be seen as the culmination of one of Guglielmi's favorite images, the bridge. In the earlier Magic Realist paintings, the bridge is usually a de Chiricoesque structure that looms forbiddingly in the background while some tragic human drama unfolds in the foreground. One of Guglielmi's most compelling works, *Mental Geography,* bears a title reminiscent of Salvador Dalí. In it the bridge, shown after an explosion, is the main subject; its towers are crumbling, the cables are twisted, and the roadway falls into the river—a genuine image of horror to any island-bound New Yorker.

Vertical Suspension is instead a lyrical, airy, and almost musical arrangement of decorative color. "My attitude towards painting today is to be clear, saturated with hope, to give people a reason to live out of the debris of our years." The painting relates as well to the work of Joseph Stella, the Italian-American Futurist, who elevated the Brooklyn Bridge as the supreme symbol of steel construction. Whereas Stella evoked a sense of speed through prismatically conceived space, Guglielmi offered a delicately controlled harmony of colors, lines, and shapes. In this respect his work is close to that of the Precisionists who celebrated American vigor through the clean geometry of machines. Guglielmi acknowledged the importance of the leading Precisionists, saying, "There have been many influences in my work, both traditional and contemporary. A debt and kinship to slightly older Americans, Demuth, Dickinson, Davis, Sheeler, for they created a style out of the native experience."[4]

In addition to the Surrealist-Futurist-Precisionist image of the bridge, *Vertical Suspension* may contain a more personal allusion to music. Not only does the painting refer to a musical score, but the thin lines may also be read as the strings of a musical instrument. Guglielmi's father played the violin professionally, and when speaking of an earlier painting, the artist makes the analogy between bridge and violin: "I am directly under a bridge spanning a wide river. Great waves of muted sound rumble off in space. My mind's eye sees the tower as a musical instrument. . . . A violin rests mute below the cables."[5] *Vertical Suspension* is an updated, less concrete, and more optimistic interpretation of this same theme.

---

1. Guglielmi, "After the Locusts," in Francis V. O'Connor, ed., *Art for the Millions* (Greenwich, Conn.: New York Graphic Society, 1973), 113.

2. Guglielmi to Edwin C. Rae, 3 December 1950. O. Luigi Guglielmi Papers, Archives of American Art, roll N 69/119.

3. "Louis Guglielmi to Conduct Art Classes at LSU," *State-Times,* undated clipping, early June 1950. O. Louis Guglielmi scrapbook, Archives of American Art, roll N 69/119.

4. Guglielmi, artist's statement, *American Realists and Magic Realists* (New York: The Museum of Modern Art, 1943), 38.

5. Guglielmi, "I Hope to Sing Again," *Magazine of Art,* January 1944, 174.

Born, Cairo, Egypt, 1906; immigrated to the United States, 1914; attended evening classes at the National Academy of Design, New York, 1920–1922; studied sculpture at the Beaux Arts Institute, New York, 1921–1923; full-time at the National Academy of Design, 1923–1927; summer fellowships at the McDowell Colony, Peterborough, New Hampshire, 1932–1942; easel program, Works Progress Administration, 1935–1939; United States armed forces, 1943–1945; taught at Louisiana State University, Baton Rouge, summers of 1950 and 1952–1953; died, Amagansett, New York, 1956.

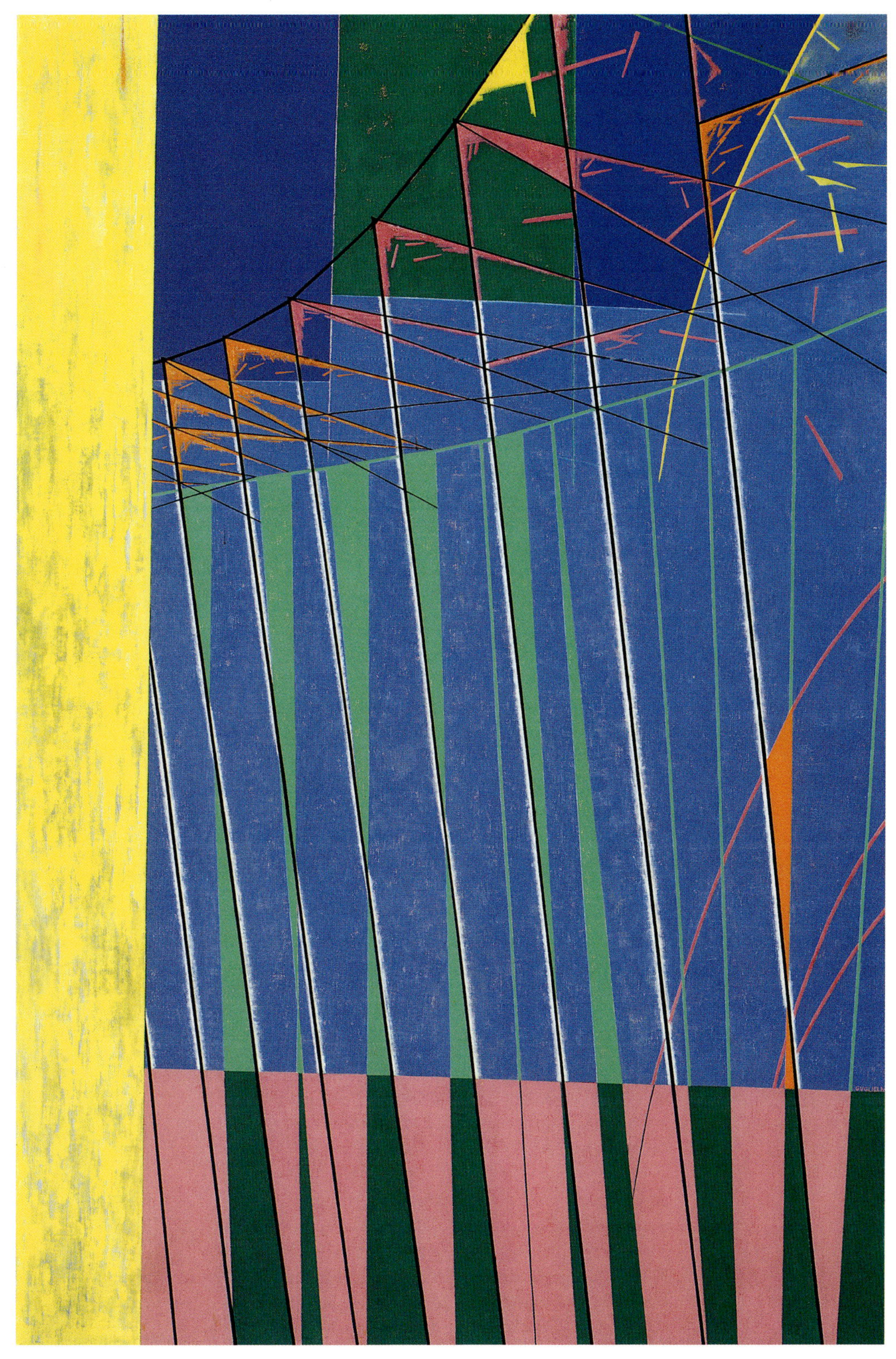

Ilya Bolotowsky

1907–1981

Variation in Blue, 1958

oil on canvas, 33 × 23 inches
signed, lower right: *Ilya Bolotowsky 58*
Museum purchase with funds donated by the Arthur and Holly Magill Foundation

In the mid-1930s, at the height of realism, abstract artists banded together to form American Abstract Artists, a group devoted to the promotion and acceptance of abstract visual art. Unable to secure many of the New Deal commissions because of governmental and public antipathy to non-representational art, these artists found support from one another. The organization mounted exhibitions and attempted to define abstract art. "Our purpose is to unite abstract artists residing in the United States, to bring before the public their individual works, and in every way possible to foster public appreciation for this direction in painting and sculpture."[1] By 1940, when Fernand Léger and Piet Mondrian, both highly respected European abstract artists, arrived in the United States, the environment had improved only slightly.

Ilya Bolotowsky, a founding member of American Abstract Artists, and Arshile Gorky were among a small minority of painters whose abstract designs for murals were accepted by the federal government for public buildings. Of the two, Bolotowsky's mural was the more abstract. He, along with Philip Guston, was responsible for large-scale decorations at the 1939 World's Fair, and once again Bolotowsky was the more aggressively abstract. He later commented with some bitterness: "The art establishment was not ready for American abstraction until the mid-forties. By that time, it was more convenient to discover new talent, the artists of the forties, instead of correcting the omissions and recognizing the artists of the thirties."[2]

Like Gorky, Bolotowsky immigrated to this country as a teenager. He followed a traditional course of study at the conservative National Academy of Design, and his early work was figurative. In 1932 he traveled abroad, and his painting underwent a change in style. "In Europe I became rather more of an Expressionist. As a matter of fact, it was not so much the influence of the Germans, but more the influence of Soutine by way of a certain black artist who was at that time living in Denmark. His name was William Henry Johnson and he had been a remarkably gifted student in the National Academy in New York, and a fantastic colorist."[3] Upon Bolotowsky's return to this country, he worked as a designer with a textile firm, and then he took part in both the easel and the mural programs of the Works Progress Administration.

In response to two exhibitions of European art, Bolotowsky gradually began to explore abstraction. In 1933 works by Mondrian from the Albert E. Gallatin collection were exhibited at New York University, and shortly afterward paintings by Joan Miró were on view at the Pierre Matisse Gallery. Mondrian espoused a clean and pure form of abstraction that ultimately resulted in gridlike arrangements of primary colors on a field of white marked off by black lines. Miró's work consisted of brightly colored, floating biomorphic shapes. Initially, Bolotowksy attempted to synthesize both trends, but in the end Mondrian had a more lasting impact. Another source of inspiration for Bolotowsky was the work of the Russian Suprematists, whose subtle white-on-white paintings reminded Bolotowsky of "bird's eye views of tremendous snowy landscapes with houses."[4]

Bolotowsky allied his work with Neoplasticism, which he defined as totally void of representational associations and spatial illusion. He distinguished it also from geometric, Minimal, and Op art. Unlike Mondrian, the preeminent Neoplasticist, he generally found little need for black lines to separate color areas, substituting white instead. He also reintroduced nonprimary colors, including the violets and pale blues in the Museum's painting. Often compared to Josef Albers, who delighted in the spatial tensions of color, Bolotowsky's objective was a totally two-dimensional surface. The careers of Albers and Bolotowsky intersected during 1946–1948 when the latter joined the faculty at Black Mountain College during Albers's sabbatical leave. Their art was different, and so were their teaching styles. As a product of the National Academy, Bolotowsky was the more conventional of the two, encouraging the examination and copying of other artists; he also believed in the merits of student exhibitions. Furthermore, he, unlike Albers who tended to remain aloof, was gregarious and enjoyed the companionship of students.[5] Bolotowsky, however, did not fully sympathize with the utopian aspect of the college. "It was interesting at first but it got to be a self-centered and closed community, since on the outside it was the old South, you know. It was different from the present day [1974] South. It feels almost a century away."[6]

Part of the success of Bolotowsky's abstraction was his use of nonsuggestive, generic titles. *Variation in Blue* distinguishes the canvas from other paintings and, at the same time, gives the viewer some parameters for understanding the work. As indicated, it is a carefully orchestrated arrangement of various violet-blues, subtly divided by clean, white lines and highlighted by an intense fuchsia at the center and, on the left edge, thin strips of yellow, the color complementary to purple. Little optical illusion or visual movement is created. It is compact and neatly fits within a well-proportioned vertical canvas. To Bolotowsky the format of the canvas was as important as the colors he selected; he experimented with diamonds, ellipses, and tondos, acknowledging that each shape creates a different challenge to the pure Neoplasticist.

---

1. *American Abstract Artists 1938* (1938; reprint, New York: Arno Press, 1969), 6.

2. Bolotowsky, "On Neoplasticism and My Own Work: A Memoir," *Leonardo* 2 (1969), 222.

3. Bolotowsky, interview with Louise Averill Svendsen and Mimi Poser, quoted in *Ilya Bolotowsky* (New York: Solomon R. Guggenheim Foundation, 1974), 15.

4. Bolotowsky, "On Neoplasticism," 222.

5. Mary Emma Harris, *The Arts at Black Mountain College* (Cambridge, Mass.: The MIT Press, 1987), 120–122.

6. Bolotowsky, Svendsen and Poser interview, 21.

Born, Petrograd, Russia, 1907; immigrated to the United States, 1923; studied at the National Academy of Design, New York, 1924–1930; traveled in Europe, 1932; member, Works Progress Administration, circa 1935–circa 1939; military service, Alaska, 1942–circa 1946; Acting Head of Art Department, Black Mountain College, near Asheville, North Carolina, 1946–1948; taught at University of Wyoming, 1948–1957, Brooklyn College, 1954–1956, State Teachers' College, New Paltz, New York, 1957–1965, Hunter College, New York, 1963–1964, and University of Wisconsin, 1965–1971; died, New York, 1981.

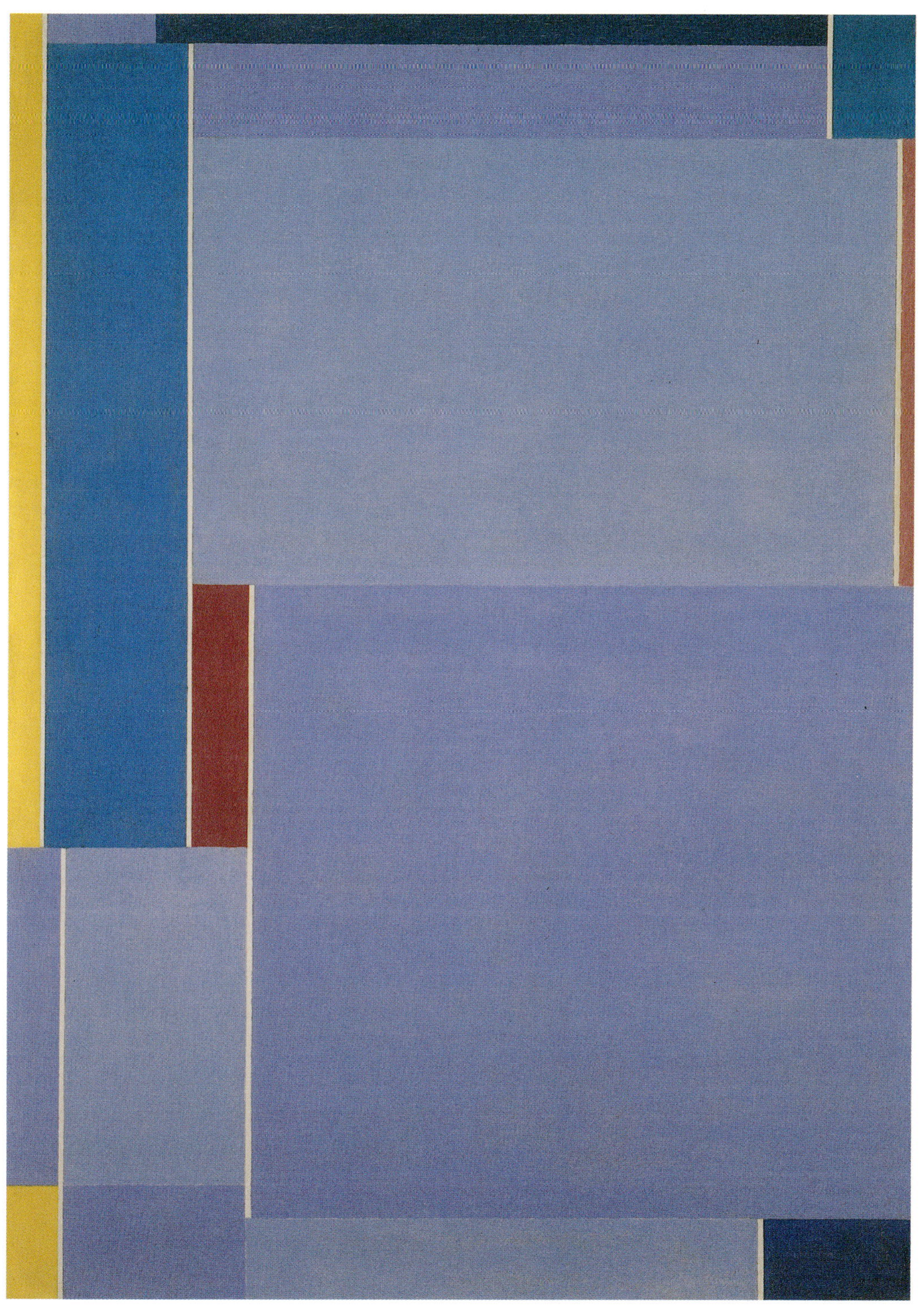

Houghton Cranford Smith

1887–1983

South Carolina Bay, Pawley's Island, circa 1950

oil on canvas, 19¼ × 28½ inches
signed, lower right: *Houghton Cranford-Smith*
Museum purchase with funds donated by the Arthur and Holly Magill Foundation

Although much Precisionist imagery was geometric and focused on machines and industrial plants, other artists applied a similar aesthetic to nature. In her magnified visions of flowers and cattle skulls, Georgia O'Keeffe displayed a comparable penchant for cleanly delineated forms, while at the same time retaining her love for organic and curvilinear shapes.

Houghton Cranford Smith, a landscape painter who absented himself from the competitiveness of the New York art scene, evoked an equivalent world of quietude and clear light. The painter he most admired was the Impressionist Claude Monet, whom Smith saluted as "the greatest painter of all times, and I felt he saw nature as I myself did."[1] In his early work Smith clearly emulated Monet's plein air style and talent for transitory effects. By the end of his career, however, Smith worked indoors from numerous sketches to create subtly distilled landscape images. In many respects both Smith's emphasis on light and his cerebral approach to landscape mirror Rockwell Kent's luminous paintings.

Smith's earliest study of art was in New York at the Art Students League, followed by two summers working with Charles W. Hawthorne in Provincetown, Massachusetts. Hawthorne, a demanding teacher, emphasized working outdoors, and it was from him that Smith learned an appreciation for rendering the effects of changing light. Just before World War I, Smith went to Paris, where he encountered the work of Monet and studied at the Académie Julian. After five years in South America, primarily in Chile, and several years teaching at the University of Kansas, Smith returned to Paris, where he studied with the Purist painter Amedée Ozenfant and the Cubist André L'Hôte. Their rational and intellectual approach caused Smith to refine further his landscape vision. In 1933 Smith settled in New York but continued to travel both abroad and in this country, making frequent trips to South Carolina, the home state of his second wife. With the advent of Abstract Expressionism he abandoned the public aspect of his career, choosing neither to exhibit nor to promote his work.

George Elmer Browne, a good friend and Smith's traveling companion on a bicycle tour of France, advised Smith to change his name to something more provocative. As Smith wrote to his family, "He says most people like to buy a picture from a man with a fancy name."[2] The familiarity and simplicity of Smith's name, however, match the unpretentiousness of his art. His landscapes, often stylized into crisp forms, are of a universal nature. Seen with a precise vision, his locales are broadly familiar and comforting.

In *South Carolina Bay, Pawley's Island,* Smith employed a slightly elevated viewpoint, which serves to distance the viewer from the scene. Similarly, human elements are diminutive, albeit central to the composition. Smith has allocated equal importance to the clouds, the water, and the sand, making the painting as much a skyscape as a land- or seascape. All are bathed in a clear light that barely casts shadows. Movement—of people, waves, and clouds—is held in abeyance, contributing a timelessness to the depiction. Tonal modulations are minimized, and unlike younger artists who were exploring the tactile properties of paint, Smith has covered his surface with regular, disciplined brushstrokes. Like much of his mature work, the Museum's painting is an intimate portrayal of the equilibrium of nature.

Saluting Smith as a true discovery, the art critic Hilton Kramer recognized his talent as well as his relationship to the mainstream:

> In these paintings he is a master of a certain kind of light—a pale, pearly light that seems almost unearthly in its origin. Every image—of clouds, mountains, the sea, ships or skyscrapers—is turned into a kind of archetype. . . . In the later painting everything is stripped of accident, removed from the realm of time and weather, and distilled in a structure of pure painting. Without being abstract in the literal sense, these are paintings that nonetheless address the eye as virtual abstractions.[3]

---

1. Smith to Georgette Passadoit, 28 July 1944, as quoted in Karen Wilkin, *Houghton Cranford Smith, 1887–1983: Early Landscape Studies* (New York: Grace Borgenicht Gallery, 1990), unpaginated.

2. Smith, as quoted in Tony Vevers, *Houghton Cranford Smith: The Provincetown Paintings* (Provincetown, Mass.: Provincetown Art Association and Museum, 1991), 11–12.

3. Hilton Kramer, "Art by 2 Americans With 'Artistic' Concerns," *The New York Observer,* 2 April 1990.

Born, Arlington, New Jersey, 1887; attended Art Students League, New York, 1907; participated in Charles W. Hawthorne's summer classes, Provincetown, Massachusetts, 1909 and 1910; to Bermuda, Cuba, and Jamaica, 1912; studied at the Académie Julian, Paris, and traveled in France, 1913–1914; in Provincetown, 1915–1916, in Chile, 1916–1920; taught at University of Kansas, Lawrence, 1920–1925; divided time between New York and Paris, where he studied with Amedée Ozenfant and André L'Hôte, 1925–1933; settled in New York, 1933, and continued to travel, to Guatemala, New England, and South Carolina; summered on the New Jersey coast; died, New York, 1983.

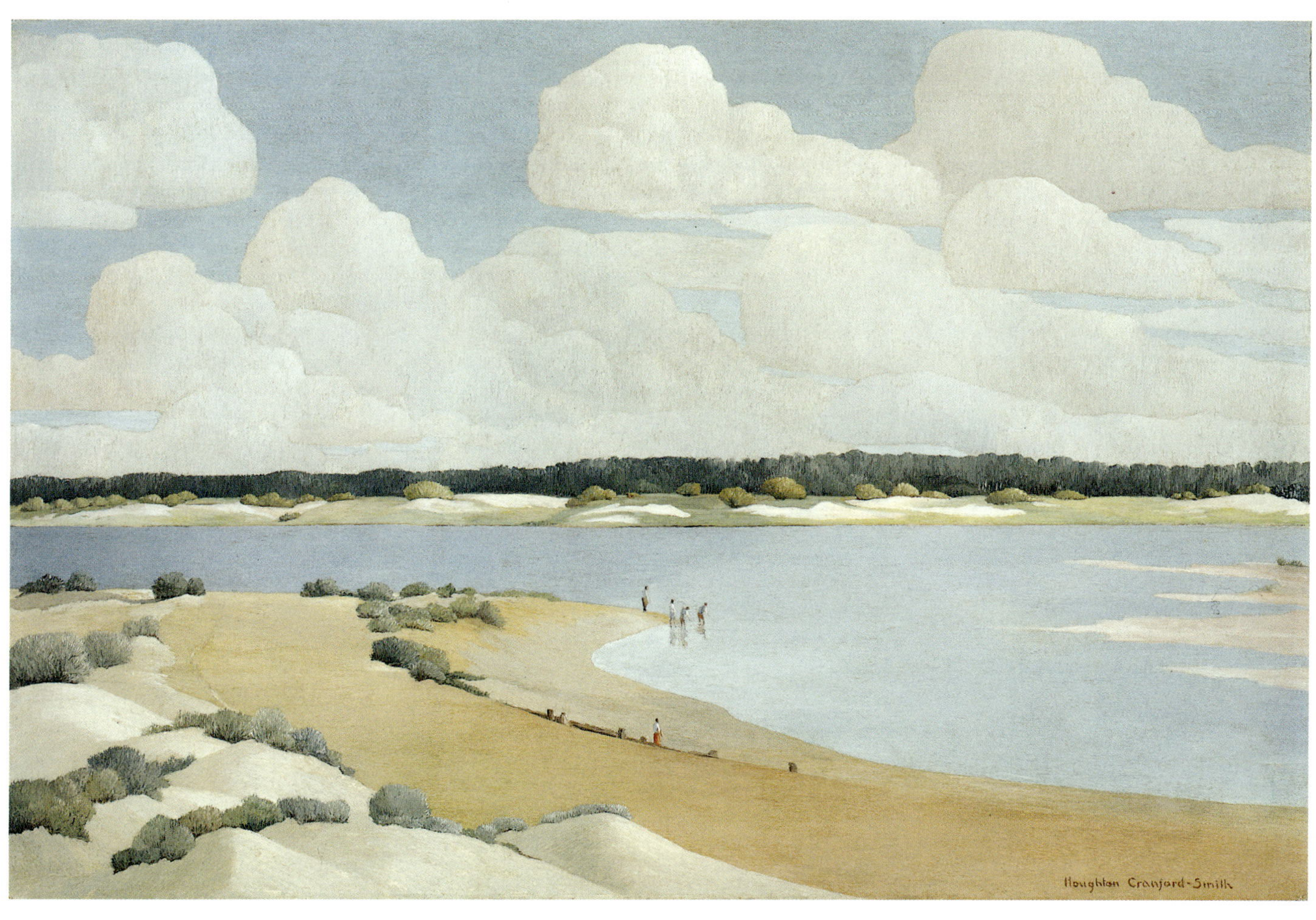
Houghton Cranford-Smith

Doris Emrick Lee

1905–1983

Grey Day, circa 1950

oil on canvas, 50 × 38 inches
Museum purchase with funds donated by the Arthur and Holly Magill Foundation

Sophisticated naiveté is a phrase that might aptly describe a number of artists whose work simultaneously relates to American Scene painting, folk art, and modernism. Simplification, of both form and subject matter, was an abiding quality of these artists, who often tinged their work with a sense of humor. They ran counter to the trends of the day that emphasized deep psychological significance and spontaneity as embodied in the work of the emerging Abstract Expressionists. Difficult to categorize, these artists please and amuse, making their point through satire rather than confrontation. Elie Nadelman's stylized and stylish walking figures not only relate to folk art but also comment on contemporary fashion. Milton Avery's understated narratives and landscapes display a consistent, antiheroic vision as well as a sophisticated awareness of modernist painting, specifically the work of Henri Matisse.

Similarly, the work of Doris Lee presents a focused vision of a fairly modest world. A friend and admirer of Avery, Lee, in her late work, shared with him a wry wit, a tendency toward reductive shapes, and flat color areas. For both Lee and Avery, less was more; knowing when to stop was as important as setting and content. In her typically understated fashion she once said: "A painting is a thing in itself, like a musical composition. It has a life of its own."[1]

Lee was a native of northern Illinois who at the end of her life spent extended periods in Florida. She initially studied at the Kansas City Art Institute with the American Impressionist Ernest Lawson, from whom she may have developed her lively and, at times, delicate color sense. She went to Paris and took instruction from André L'Hôte, a Cubist painter, and then studied further in California. Lee's murals painted under the auspices of the Works Progress Administration are charming anecdotes about the pleasures and rewards of rural life. In preparation for her commission in Summerville, Georgia, Lee visited the site and traveled in the region. Despite an endorsement from the local community, her designs ran into trouble with the program's administrator who required several revisions, because, as he explained: "all the figures have the same stem-like necks and skinny arms and there is a danger that the people of Summerville will regard this as your personal characterization of them and will, no doubt, resent being presented as though they were half fed regardless of the poetry you have achieved with this mannerism. I am sure you are aware of how sensitive the people of the South are about such matters and it would be well for you to make the changes."[2]

During the 1940s Lee's ability to characterize people and situations was capitalized on by *Life* magazine for whom she did several series, including two on the quintessentially American musicals *Show Boat* and *Oklahoma.* In connection with other *Life* projects she traveled to Hollywood, the South, the tropics, and North Africa. Her humor shines throughout her works from this period, and in the accompanying text for the views of Hollywood, Lee herself is equated to Tinsel Town. "Few painters are so well-equipped to capture its peculiar exuberance and its splendid extroversions of color as the exuberant, extroverted artist Doris Lee, whom *Life* commissioned to watch, work, and generally enjoy herself there." The caption to one seascape that shows seagulls scattered about reads as follows: "Laguna Beach and Balboa are favorite weekend spots for people from Hollywood. There is also an artists' colony and an energetic birds' colony on the rocks which jut offshore. With their flutter of colors decorating their brackish roost, the birds seemed to Miss Lee 'more impressive than the artists.'"[3]

From her experiences in Key West, Florida, Lee developed a body of work that incorporates serene landscapes and decorative, whimsical figurative paintings. Narrative elements are deemphasized, and shapes and flat areas of color dominate. Details are often generalized or merely suggested in a manner reminiscent of Avery, who also spent several winters in Key West. Horizon lines are usually placed high, which adds to the flattened aspect of the canvases. *Grey Day* is a stylized and satirical portrayal of two diametrically opposed female figures, one clothed, one not. They exist as separate entities, with no interaction, and may be Lee's commentary on the disparate natures of Key West's two constituencies: tourist and native. The nude, representing sun-seeking tourists, frolics in the outdoors and joyously bathes despite the inclement weather, while the other figure timidly seeks the shelter of her umbrella. Stylistically the nude, with her back turned, recalls in its utter simplification some of Matisse's figures and his penchant for forms expressive of the joy of life. The colors in *Grey Day* share a similar tonal value; no single hue appears more intense than another. The paint in turn is applied in a somewhat thin and dry manner.

In their persistence of figurative painting and their lack of heavy impasto, both Lee and Avery thwarted the popular trend pursued by the majority of New York painters. Although apart from the mainstream, they were not totally isolated either; the use of discrete horizontal bands of color with their softly differentiated textures mirrors the color symphonies of Mark Rothko, while their mundane subject matter anticipates Pop Art.

---

1. Lee, as quoted in her obituary, *The New York Times,* 16 June 1983.

2. Edward Rowan to Lee, 27 March 1939. Summerville, Georgia, file, National Archives, as quoted in Sue Bridwell Beckham, *Depression Post Office Murals and Southern Culture* (Baton Rouge: Louisiana State University Press, 1989), 43.

3. *Life,* 15 October 1945, 85 and 89.

Born, Aledo, Illinois, 1905; graduated from Rockford College, Rockford, Illinois, 1927; studied at the Kansas City Art Institute with Ernest Lawson, 1928–1929, in Paris with André L'Hôte, and at the California School of Fine Arts, San Francisco, with Arnold Blanch, 1930; moved to Woodstock, New York, 1931; traveled to Cuba and Mexico, 1946, to North Africa, 1950; spent winters in Key West, Florida; died, Clearwater, Florida, 1983.

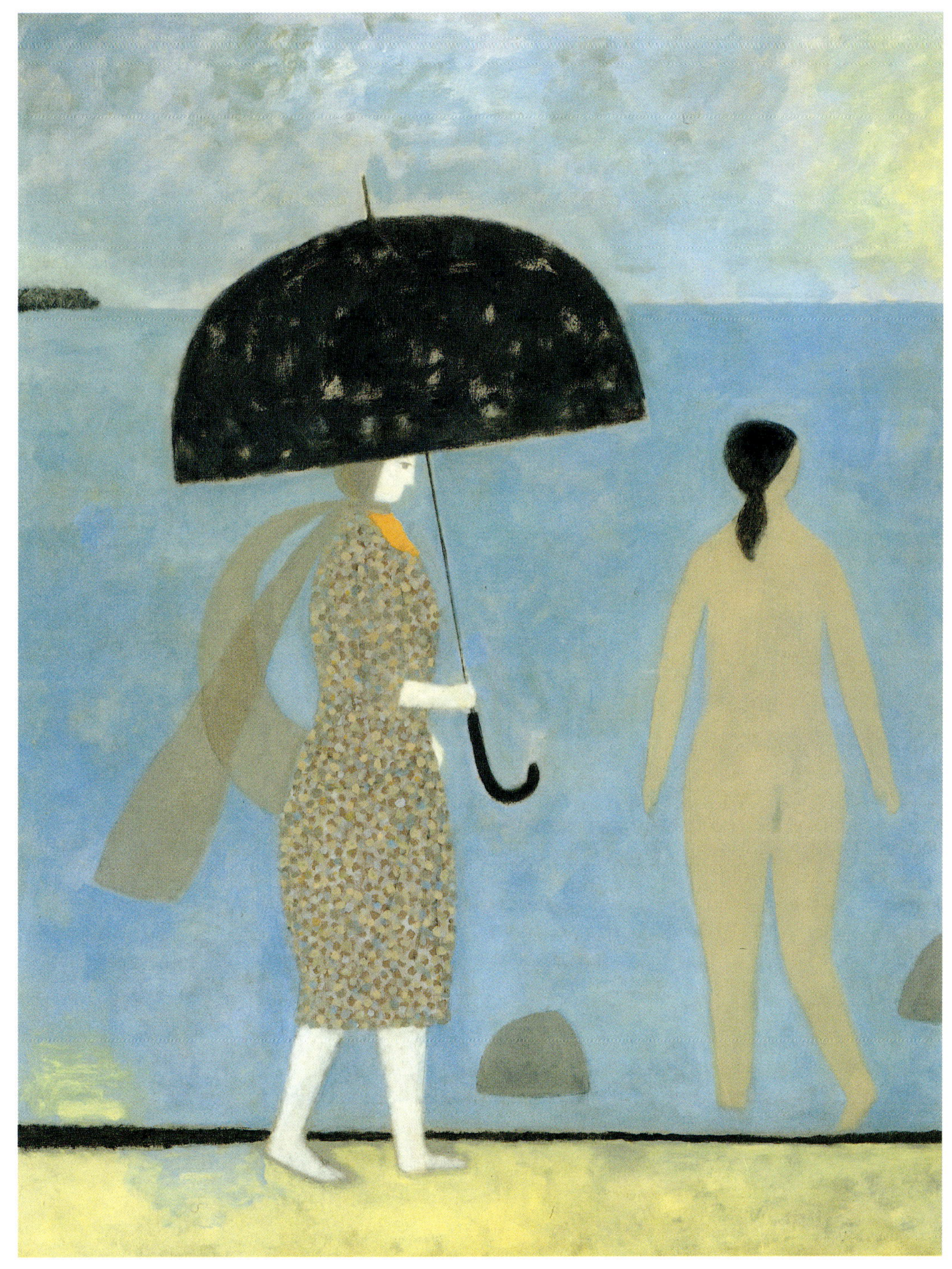

Charles Henry Alston

1907–1977

Woman with Shopping Bag, circa 1955

oil on canvas, 50 × 28 inches
signed, lower right: *Alston*
Museum purchase with funds donated by the Arthur and Holly Magill Foundation

African-American artists have spent much of this century struggling for recognition. The successful efforts of Hale Woodruff, who organized exhibitions in the early 1940s in Atlanta, were joined by other smaller endeavors, many in the Northeast. Publications specifically on African-Americans were issued, including James A. Porter's landmark study of 1943, *Modern Negro Art.* Gradually, African-American artists were seen in mainstream exhibitions and publications. The work of Jacob Lawrence and Romare Bearden, in particular, gained widespread attention among the public as well as in museum circles. But some artists wanted more—full-scale participation without regard to color.

Among the most outspoken in this respect was Charles Alston, whose objective was to be viewed as an American artist, not only as an African-American one. "Being told I have to paint African rhythms exclusively because I am a Negro artist is like telling me that I can't play Beethoven or Mozart or that I should start to learn the Gold Coast chants. A lot of me comes out of America, New York City, and North Carolina, too."[1] In his obituary, *The New York Times* reiterated his contention: "I don't believe there's such a thing as 'black art' though there's certainly a black experience. I lived it. But it's also an American experience."[2]

Born in Charlotte, North Carolina, Alston, like many African-Americans at the time, migrated North to Harlem as a child. His family were successful members of the middle class, and Alston had the advantage of taking Saturday classes at the National Academy of Design. Later he attended Columbia University, where he obtained his master's degree from Teachers College in 1931. During the 1930s he was active in organizations for the education of young people, including Utopia House, where one of his students was Lawrence. He helped to establish the Harlem Artists Guild in 1935 and spearheaded a group known simply as 306, which provided a forum for African-American artists. In the late 1930s he toured the South with a Rosenwald Fellowship, taking photographs that resemble those by Walker Evans and Dorothea Lange done under the auspices of the Farm Security Administration. In 1950 Alston became the first African-American to be appointed an instructor at the Art Students League, where he conducted classes for more than twenty years. He also taught at the City College of New York for sixteen years. In a eulogy delivered at his memorial service it was estimated that in his classes Alston came into contact with more than five thousand "incipient artists."[3]

Despite his great desire for integration, Alston's own work reflects his heritage, in both style and content. To support himself he worked as an illustrator for such popular magazines as *Collier's, The New Yorker,* and *Mademoiselle.* In 1936 he joined the Works Progress Administration and painted murals for Harlem Hospital, which created a great controversy because they dealt specifically with African-American subject matter. Hospital administrators felt they should serve a broader cross section of the community. The most racially oriented work by Alston, however, was done while he was a member of the Office of War Information, when he created inspirational images to be used by the African-American press. Overtly propagandistic, they celebrated the role of African-Americans in the war effort. Typical of these images was one devoted to "Sgt. Joe Louis, Champion of Champions."

Alston was both painter and sculptor, and in each medium there is a reflection of his interest in African art. "African art is the common heritage of mankind, and all artists, not only Negro, draw from its genius as only one source. . . . We must recognize and become more aware of its power, its beauty and nobility."[4] But just as he felt all artists owed a debt to African art, he also believed there were other artistic resources as well. In *Woman with Shopping Bag,* the frontal placement of the figure, slightly bent, is mildly reminiscent of tribal figures whose knees and elbows project. Yet Alston has shown her in modernist terms, isolated against flat areas of color that recall the work of Henri Matisse. Only the figure is developed, and the background serves as a geometric framework for her. In this respect the painting resembles the work of Alston's contemporary, the California painter Richard Diebenkorn.

Although at times Alston attempted abstraction, his work in both painting and sculpture tended to be figurative, often highly stylized. His subject matter derived from the world around him; the woman with her shopping bag, possibly a domestic, was presumably an image Alston saw in his neighborhood. "Most of my subject matter was the local scene. I don't think I was consciously aware that I was doing a social job. . . . Practically all of my subject matter was related to the community, not in an aggressive, protest way, but just a statement of 'this is it and this is the beauty of it.'"[5]

---

1. Alston, as quoted in A. C. Sterling, "Art Is Our Common Heritage," *Courier Magazine,* undated, circa 1952. Charles Alston Papers, Archives of American Art, roll N70-23.

2. Alston, as quoted in his obituary, *The New York Times,* 28 April 1977.

3. George Gregory, "Eulogy to Charles Alston," published in *Crisis,* August–September 1977, 351. Alston Papers, Archives of American Art, roll N70-23.

4. Alston, as quoted in Sterling, "Heritage."

5. Alston, interview with Harlan Phillips, 25 September 1965. Oral History Collection, Archives of American Art, roll 4210.

Born, Charlotte, North Carolina, 1907; moved to New York, circa 1913; graduated from Columbia University, 1929, followed by a master's degree from Teachers College, 1931; involved in various community organizations: Utopia House, Harlem Artists Guild, 306, 1930s; affiliated with Office of War Information, 1940–1942; attended Pratt Institute, 1944–1945, and worked as commercial artist; instructor at the Art Students League, 1950–1975, and faculty member at City College of the City University of New York, 1962–1977; died, New York, 1977.

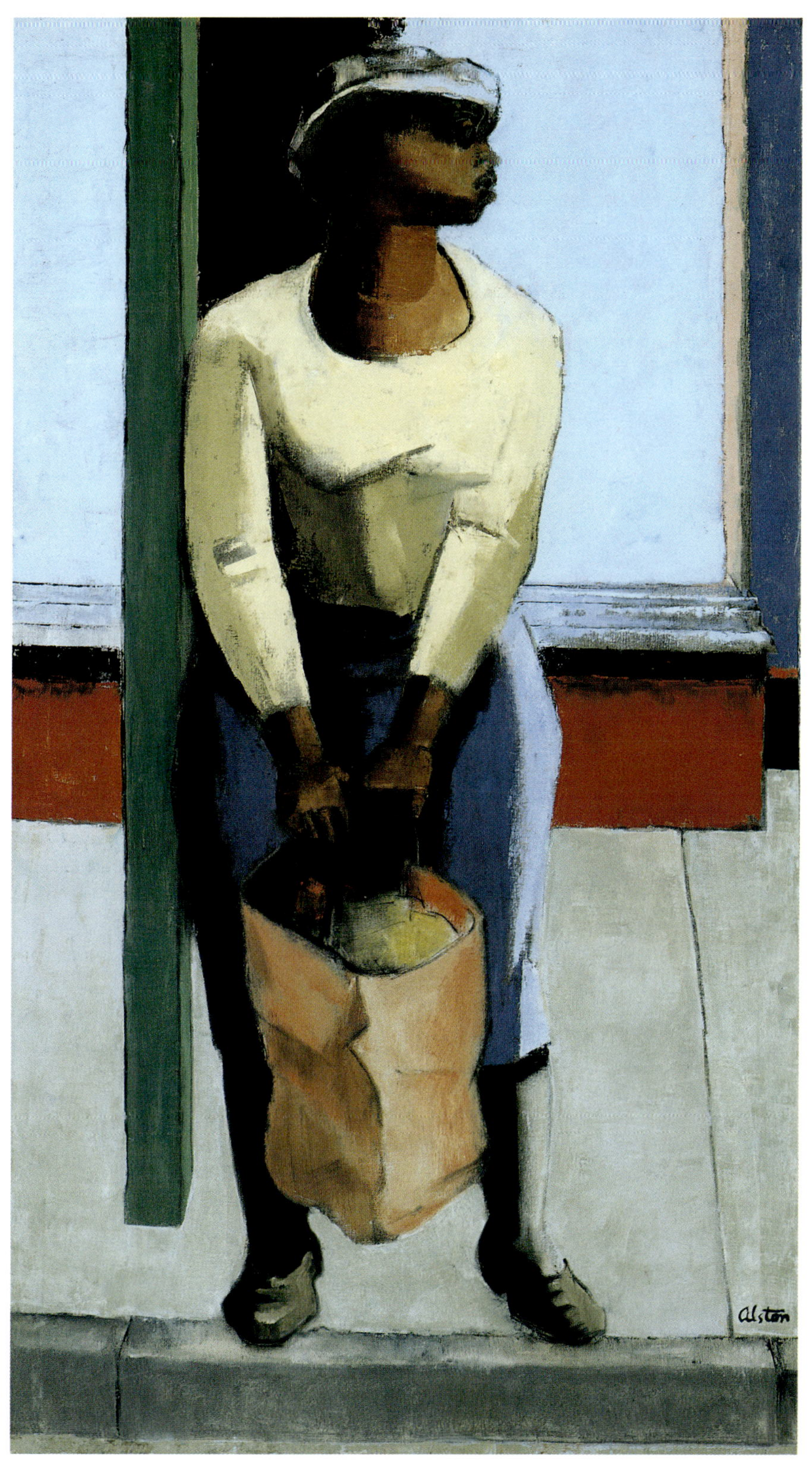
Alston

Morris Louis

1912–1962

Roseate, 1960

acrylic on canvas, 82½ × 105¼ inches
signed, on reverse, bottom center: *M. Louis*
Acquired in memory of Betsy Dew Ashley with funds provided by her friends, The Liberty Corporation, and a donation by Dr. Marcella Brenner

Jackson Pollock, considered by some to be the paradigmatic artist of Abstract Expressionism, revolutionized the act of painting. When he dripped and threw paint on his canvases and stained the actual fabric with pigment, he was not only responding to the automatism of Surrealism but was also opening the way for subsequent generations of artists. Simultaneously, innovations in the manufacture of paint, specifically the development of quick-drying acrylics, corresponded to the creative needs of artists. At times equated in importance with the invention of oil painting in the fifteenth century, the availability of acrylic made possible the watercolorlike application of paint that was impossible with oils.[1]

In the nation's capital in the late 1950s and early 1960s a small group of painters began to emerge who owed a considerable debt to Abstract Expressionism. The Color Field painters Morris Louis, Kenneth Noland, Gene Davis, and Sam Gilliam embraced certain of the movement's attributes, especially its large canvases and nonrepresentational imagery. Using the new acrylics, they avoided heavily encrusted surfaces and placed new emphasis on color, often using it to create optical effects. Louis, who was born Morris Bernstein in Baltimore, Maryland, pointedly absented himself from New York, then the mecca of the art world. Preferring the relative isolation of Washington, Louis created paintings that owed an initial debt to Abstract Expressionism but, in their lyrical simplicity, transcended it.

An exact contemporary of Pollock, Louis studied at the Maryland Institute before going to New York in the late 1930s to join the easel program of the Works Progress Administration. He returned to his native Baltimore in 1940, and later that decade moved to the nation's capital. Unlike Pollock, who was photographed and filmed while painting his canvases, Louis worked in seclusion in a small studio, where he was secretive about his technique, not wishing people to become preoccupied with the process of his painting. Throughout his career Louis carefully pruned his output, often destroying many of his works.

Two events helped to shape Louis's development: the rediscovery and exhibition of Claude Monet's late water-lily paintings and a visit to New York. Monet's late works, which were atmospheric and virtually abstract, had been painted on a monumental scale with broad gestures, and they served as a historic antecedent for many of the Abstract Expressionists. What seems to have affected Louis most, however, was the expansive and spatial nature of Monet's compositions. In 1953 Louis, along with Noland and Clement Greenberg, the art critic who championed Abstract Expressionism, visited the New York studio of Helen Frankenthaler. A second-generation Abstract Expressionist, Frankenthaler had just begun to capitalize upon Pollock's technique of staining raw, unsized canvas; for Louis and Noland her method was a revelation. Noland stated: "We were interested in Pollock but could gain no lead from him. He was too personal. But Frankenthaler showed us a way—a way to think about, and use, color."[2]

For the next eight years Louis combined what he learned from Frankenthaler with his knowledge of acrylic paints, which he had been among the first to use. Louis maneuvered the paint onto unstretched canvas; he appears to have poured and pushed the paint while folding, pleating, and tilting the fabric. The paintings that resulted are often poetic evocations, expansive and fluid. His initial series, called *Veils,* consists of layers of staining, one color upon another, usually in tapering symmetrical and vertical arrangements. Like the veils of modern dancers, these transparent color areas move gracefully and organically across the surface. Louis's method of layering infused these paintings with a deep, rich tonality, which he clarified in his later work.

The Museum's painting, *Roseate,* is a transitional work that demonstrates Louis's attempt to purify his colors. Working within a limited color range of rosy hues and restricting himself to the central axis of the composition, Louis created a simple declarative visual statement. The pigment is fully absorbed into raw, unprimed canvas, leaving a tentative, feathered edge. Movement is upward, probably in contradiction to the way the painting was produced; Louis in all likelihood positioned the top of *Roseate* higher than the bottom, allowing the paint to flow downward naturally. To achieve the regular width and density of the colors, Louis carefully controlled the orientation of the canvas; unpainted areas were as important as the stained ones, as the whiteness of the paper is to a watercolorist. Offering further evidence that *Roseate* is a transitional work is the fact that Louis brushed on sizing in the nonpigmented areas; in later works these sections would be left bare.

Roseate anticipated Louis's two other series: *Unfurleds,* begun that same year, and the later *Stripes.* From this point forward Louis's colors are bright and lively. Instead of the verticality and centrality of *Veils* and *Roseate,* the *Unfurleds* are based on diagonals cutting across the lower corners and leaving the center blank. These paintings appear as a visual antidote to the compulsive horror vacuii of the Abstract Expressionists. Like *Veils,* the *Unfurleds* created the illusion of motion, as Sam Gilliam recognized: "One day in the Metropolitan [Museum] I realized that the relativeness of Louis's *Unfurled* to the term *unfurled* means the unfurled flag and the approach to stripes."[3] Having captured the sense of a flag billowing in the breeze in the *Unfurleds,* Louis concluded his painting career with a series of multicolored flat stripe paintings that ultimately have their origin in *Roseate.*

---

1. William C. Seitz, *Art in the Age of Aquarius, 1955–1970* (Washington, D.C.: Smithsonian Institution Press, 1992), 16.

2. Noland, as quoted in James M. Truitt, "Art—Arid D.C. Harbors Touted 'New' Painters," *Washington Post,* 21 December 1961.

3. Gilliam, as quoted in Donald Miller, "Hanging Loose: An Interview with Sam Gilliam," *Art News,* January 1973, 43.

Born, Baltimore, Maryland, 1912; studied at the Maryland Institute of the Fine and Applied Arts, 1927–1932; in New York, 1936–1943; worked for the Works Progress Administration, 1939–1940; in Baltimore, 1943–1947, and Silver Spring, Maryland, 1947–1952; settled in Washington, D.C., 1952; died, Washington, 1962.

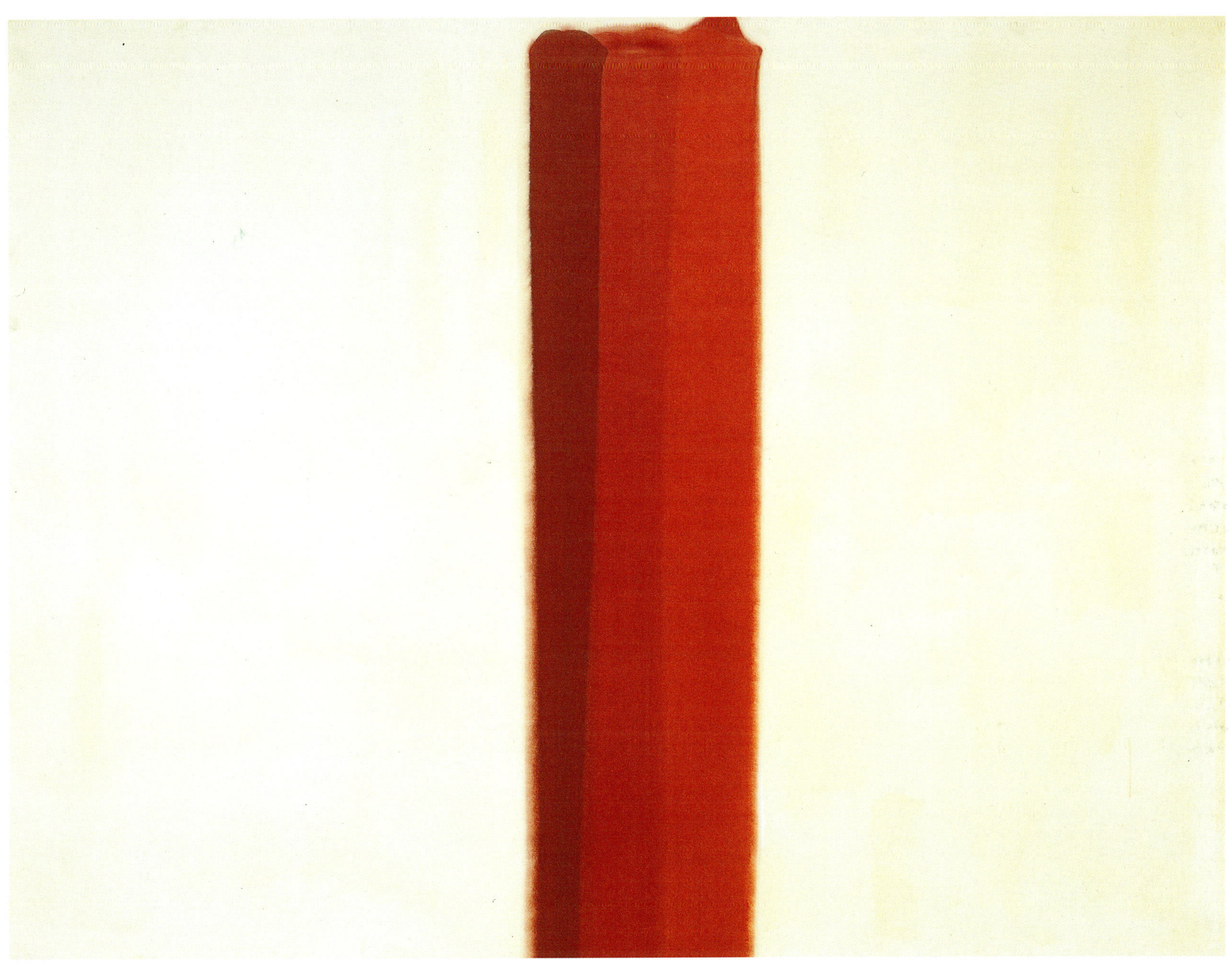

Kenneth Noland

born 1924

Quiet Night, 1960–1961

acrylic on canvas, 69 3/4 × 69 7/8 inches
signed, on overlap: *Kenneth Noland*
Museum purchase with funds donated by the Arthur and Holly Magill Foundation

In some circles American nonobjective painting at mid-twentieth century has been called "painterly abstraction." Thus, it became convenient to call the subsequent wave of work "post-painterly abstraction," a term that conveys chronology and acknowledges the debt to Abstract Expressionism. Like Post-Impressionism, post-painterly abstraction was both an outgrowth from and a reaction against the principles of the previous dominant movement. Mirroring the aesthetic of such painters as Mark Rothko, many of the painters of the 1960s dealt with broad expanses of color on large canvases, and as a result earned the designation Color Field painters. Some, like Morris Louis, pursued the expressive application of paint while others were more minimal or geometric in their compositions.

Of the latter group Barnett Newman and Ad Reinhardt developed highly structured works that ranged from radiant fields of red with single stripes to subtly orchestrated essays in black. Both Newman and Reinhardt were members of the first generation of Abstract Expressionists, and although as individuals they were socially and politically aligned with this group, their art remained distinct from it. They, along with the Washington painters Louis and Kenneth Noland, were the beneficiaries of the attention of Clement Greenberg, critic, exhibition organizer, and trendsetter.

Noland emerged as an articulate Color Field painter who, like Newman and Reinhardt, relied on geometric substructure. One of the few natives of Asheville, North Carolina, to attend and prosper at nearby Black Mountain College, Noland was thoroughly steeped in the abstract idiom, one of the first major painters to be so trained. Through his teachers Ilya Bolotowsky and Josef Albers he learned the importance of geometrical relationships and color theory. Under Bolotowsky, with whom he had a great personal affinity, he was forced to reckon with Neoplasticism and the heritage of Piet Mondrian; from Albers, Noland acquired problem-solving skills and a predilection for working in series.[1]

Following service in the Air Force during World War II, Noland went to Paris in 1948 on the G.I. Bill. Having already attended Black Mountain College for two years, Noland was familiar with the major American figures, as well as with many Europeans who had connections with the campus. He realized that the former art capital of the world had been passed by: "We already knew that there was work being done by another generation of artists such as Pollock or even, say, the American Abstract Artists that somehow had absorbed a lot that had developed in Europe. So we weren't even interested in, let's say, Picasso. . . . The tradition . . . of avant-garde art had been broken in Europe."[2]

Upon his return, Noland settled in Washington, D.C., and became good friends with Louis, whose technical facility with acrylic paint influenced him. Of the two, Noland was the more gregarious, enjoying annual visits to New York and regular contact with the mainstream. After a pivotal visit to Helen Frankenthaler's studio in 1953, Noland and Louis had an intense period of collaboration, one that has been equated to a jam session of jazz musicians. Together they experimented with the new acrylic paints, particularly in regard to staining. Whereas Louis consistently retained the spontaneity of Abstract Expressionism in his staining and soaking of raw canvas, Noland in his early work focused upon familiar geometric shapes that he enlivened with loosely applied flourishes of paint. Noland also employed pure colors. Like Louis and, earlier, Albers, Noland worked in discrete series ranging from targets to chevrons and stripes and, more recently, to diamonds and plaids.

The Museum's painting, *Quiet Night,* not only relates to Noland's numerous targets but also reveals the artist's move away from freely applied pigment. Instead of surrounding concentric circles with visible brushwork and blank canvas, in *Quiet Night* he has filled the field with a medium-value gray. He has also replaced the circle with an elliptical shape that is directional and active. Gray, pink, and black paint are seamlessly soaked into the raw canvas, becoming one with the fabric. The cream-colored ring remains unpainted, forming a bright contrast to the color areas. Through shape and color Noland has created an optical effect as well as a dynamic dialogue. The surface is flat and unmodulated, yet it is pierced through the center with a floating black ellipse.

Noland's approach is thoroughly formalist, and since the early 1960s he has worked with a bright palette on a large scale. He experimented with various formats, including diamonds, tondos, and lozenges. Perhaps his interest in unorthodox shapes derived from his teacher Bolotowsky. At the same time, such painters as Frank Stella and Ellsworth Kelly were also challenging the traditional concept of the canvas as a rectangle. For Noland, the canvas remained a field, regardless of its shape. "I do open paintings. I like lightness, airiness, and the way color pulsates. The presence of the painting is all that's important."[3]

---

1. See Kenworth Moffett, *Kenneth Noland* (New York: Harry N. Abrams, 1976).

2. Noland, interview with Paul Cummings, 1971, Archives of American Art, as quoted in Moffett, *Noland,* 18.

3. Noland, as quoted in "Peacock Duo," *Time,* 8 January 1965, 44.

Born, Asheville, North Carolina, 1924; studied at Black Mountain College, near Asheville, 1946–1948 and 1950, and in Paris with Ossip Zadkine, 1948–1949; moved to Washington, D.C., 1949; taught at the Institute of Contemporary Art, Washington, 1949–1951, Catholic University, 1951–1960, and Washington Workshop Center of the Arts, 1952–1956; to New York, 1961; taught at Bard College, Annandale-on-Hudson, New York, 1985; resides, South Salem, New York.

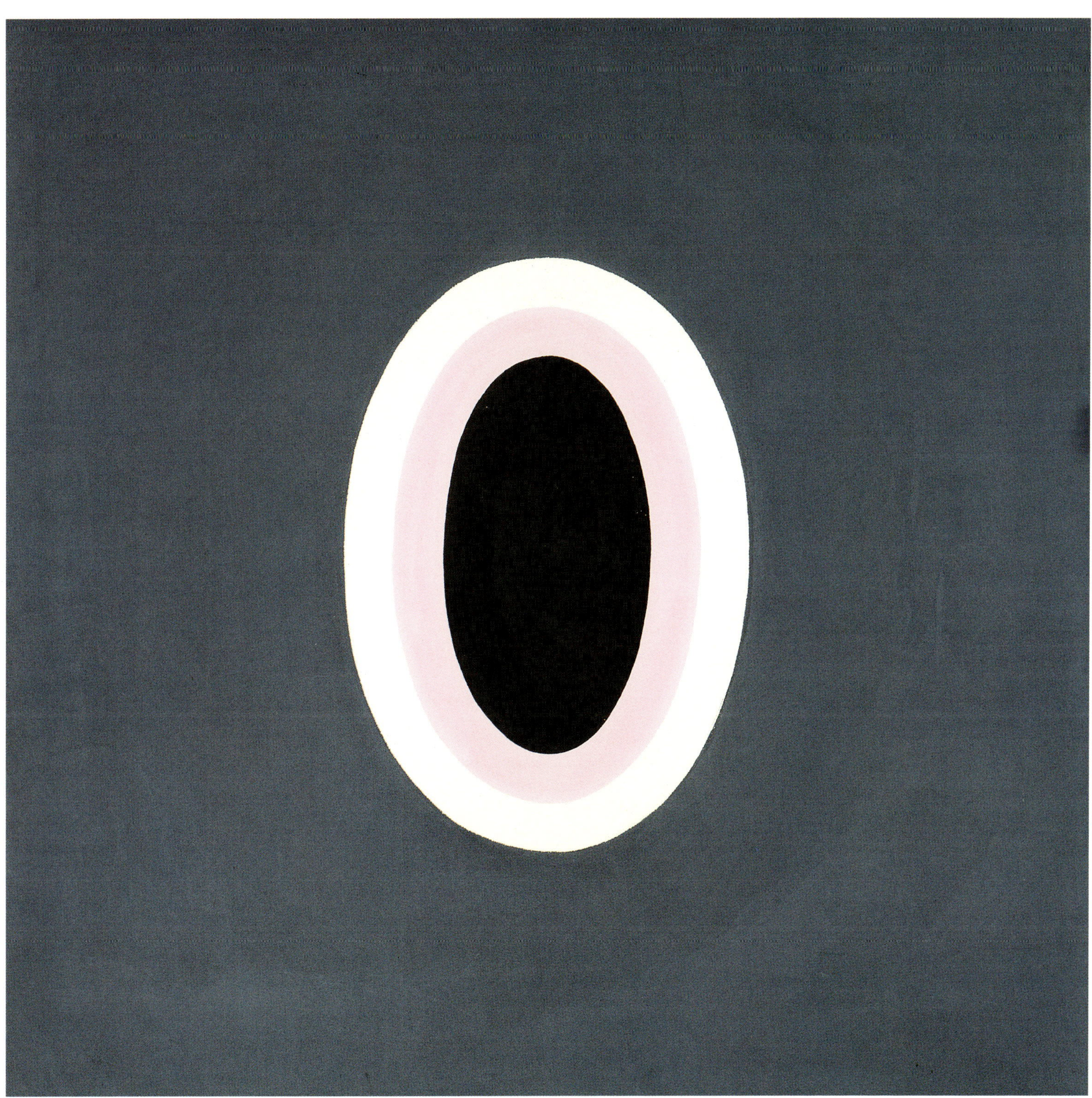

Sam Gilliam

born 1933

Carousel Merge 4, 1971

acrylic on canvas, 118 × 900½ inches
signed, on reverse: *Sam Gilliam / 1971*
Gift of the artist

Abstract Expressionism led to new attitudes about paint, its application, and even the disposition of canvas. Jackson Pollock, for instance, painted with his canvas on the floor. By the 1960s painters no longer felt confined to the limitations of easel paintings, and their canvases expanded to mural-size proportions. Natural outgrowths of the Abstract Expressionists' experiments were the large, unsized canvases of Morris Louis and Helen Frankenthaler and the shaped canvases of Frank Stella and Ellsworth Kelly.

Through a distinctively personal innovation Sam Gilliam further dismantled the traditional painting by removing the canvas from its stretcher or underlying support. He then painted the loose material, by direct application, by pouring, and by staining. For display these paintings are draped and hung, often suspended in space rather than placed against a wall. Their arrangements are flexible and can be accommodated to a variety of spaces, allowing for greater spontaneity and a three-dimensional presence.

Gilliam, a native of Tupelo, Mississippi, grew up in Louisville, Kentucky. He attended the University of Louisville, where he earned bachelor's and master's degrees. In 1962 he moved to Washington, D.C., and shortly afterward he became identified with the emerging Color Field group. Along with Kenneth Noland, Gene Davis, and Louis, Gilliam experimented with new uses of the basic elements of painting: pigment and canvas. Whereas the others continued to display their work in traditional wall-hung formats, Gilliam invented more environmentally oriented pieces. Unlike Davis and Noland, who retained a geometric order in their work, Gilliam's conceptions are organic and fluid. Reflecting upon his evolution, Gilliam told an interviewer: "I'd been painting stripes and doing this very, very hard-edged thing—getting into Albers's interaction and working very logically with masking tape and striping. But I realized that the ideas I was dealing with were mostly someone else's."[1]

Beginning in the spring of 1968 Gilliam began to work directly with unstretched canvas. Inspired by clotheslines stretched between poles and weighed down with clothes, Gilliam worked with fabric, pouring paint onto it, letting the paint fall and form blotches and rivulets, and then folding the material to let it dry. When asked, "How much serendipity is there in the way folds fall?" Gilliam answered, "There's a hell of a lot."[2] For Gilliam, like the Abstract Expressionists before him, process is all-important. The titles of these suspended paintings, however, do not relate to their creation, but rather are evocative of movement: *Baroque Cascade* and *Wave* allude to a dynamic rush of water, and the frequently recurring title *Carousel* refers to the up-down and forward motion of merry-go-rounds as well as to the directional nature of Gilliam's pieces once installed.

The Museum's *Carousel Merge 4* is typical of Gilliam's draped paintings of the period. Throughout its entire surface the work reflects a variety of paint applications, from pouring and splattering to raking and brushing. Gilliam donated *Carousel Merge 4* to the Museum following an exploratory trip to Greenville. Spending a week in the area, the artist visited a number of textile mills, gave a slide presentation about his work, and went to Clemson University. Searching for fabric in large quantities, Gilliam discovered polypropylene and was given five hundred yards of it by a local firm. Recalling his trip, the artist commented: "Everybody was trying to find new resources, and new things. [My trip] was very significant—a significant break. I never really used canvas again until recently."[3]

By the mid-1970s Gilliam returned to flat, wall-hung compositions, but his inventiveness continued in the manipulation of vivid colors and heavily encrusted surfaces. Much of his energy has been devoted to large-scale mural productions in public places, where his forms and colors enliven the space. These usually project from the wall, causing some to comment on the sculptural nature of Gilliam's work. The artist disagrees: "I don't consider it sculpture. I know it's painting."[4]

---

1. Gilliam, as quoted in Donald Miller, "Hanging Loose: An Interview with Sam Gilliam," *Art News*, January 1973, 42.

2. Gilliam, as quoted in Miller, "Hanging Loose," 43.

3. Gilliam, telephone interview with author, March 1994.

4. Gilliam, as quoted in Miller, "Hanging Loose," 42.

Born, Tupelo, Mississippi, 1933; bachelor's and master's degrees from the University of Louisville, 1955 and 1961; moved to Washington, D.C., 1962; taught at Corcoran School of Art, Washington, 1964–1967, Maryland Institute of Art, Baltimore, 1967–1982, University of Maryland, 1982–1985, and Carnegie Mellon University, 1985–1989; resides, Washington.

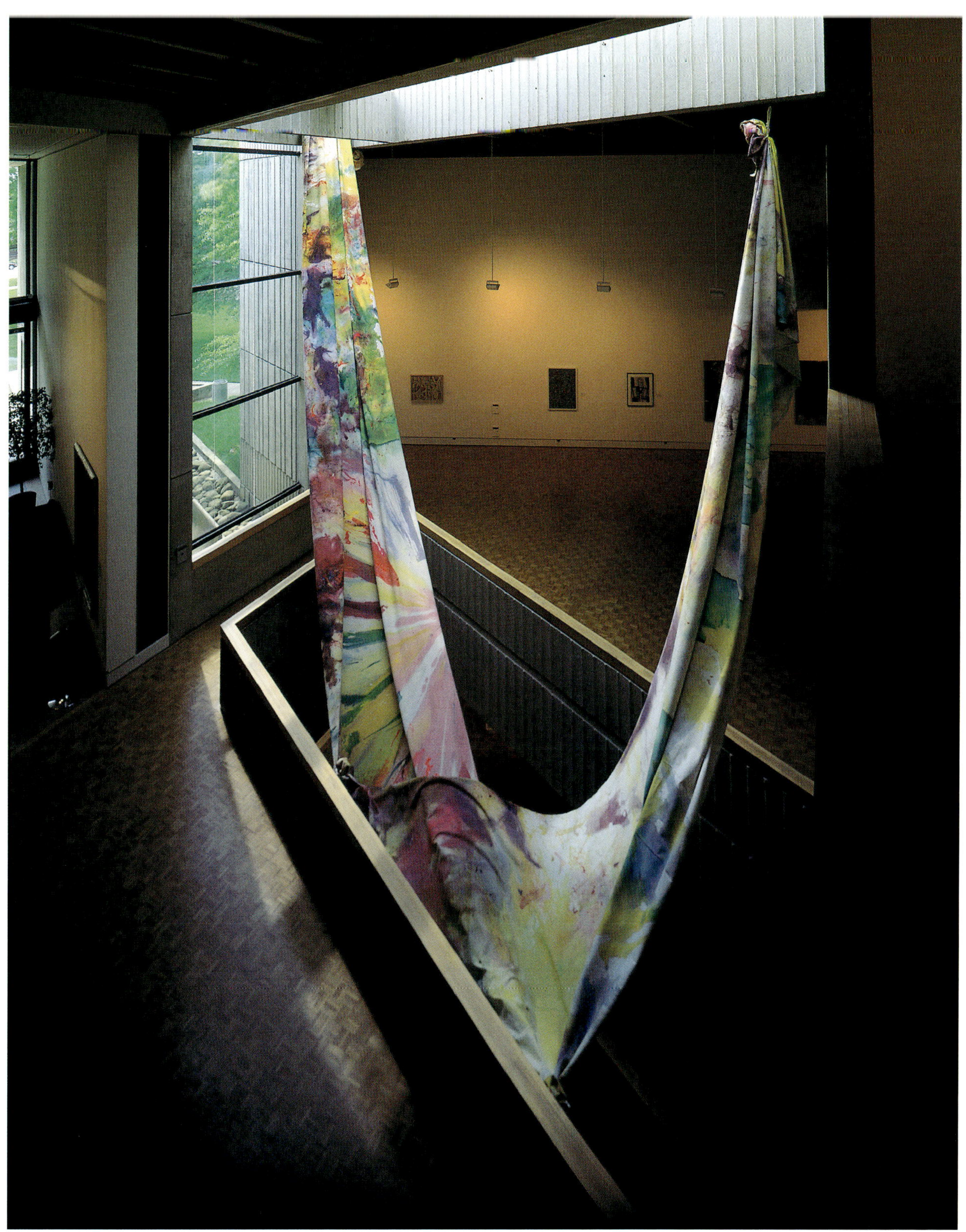

Robert Beauchamp

born 1923

untitled, 1960

oil on canvas, 48 × 57½ inches
signed, at left: *Robt / Beauchamp*
Gift of Allan Stone

Just as Abstract Expressionism coalesced and became the focal point of American art criticism, a revolution took place within the movement's ranks. Willem de Kooning, one of the leading exponents of the New York School, reintroduced in his paintings the depiction of human figures. As a cornerstone of the academic tradition, the female nude was virtually anathema to the Abstract Expressionists, who delighted in aggressively painted, nonrepresentational canvases. Mystifying both critics and historians, de Kooning's paintings on the theme of woman have been variously interpreted as references to his mother and his wife, as essays on primitive goddesses and Hollywood stars, and simply as the reintroduction of structure and narrative.[1]

Although de Kooning may have been the most visible painter to return to the figure, he was not alone. Other painters, including second-generation Abstract Expressionists and even a few students of the paragon of abstraction, Hans Hofmann, found the human figure a rewarding subject for their expressionistic painting. The most noted were Elaine de Kooning, Jan Müller, Grace Hartigan, and Robert Beauchamp. Beauchamp may have summarized the sentiments of his colleagues when he announced: "I do not paint abstractly because it leaves too much out."[2]

Beauchamp was born in Denver, Colorado, and studied at the Colorado Springs Fine Arts Center both before and after serving in the Navy during World War II. He then earned his bachelor of fine arts degree at Cranbrook Art Academy in Bloomfield Hills, Michigan. In 1950 he moved East and studied with Hofmann for three years. Beauchamp acknowledged that this experience was critical to his development, especially in understanding the expressive potential of pictorial elements. Beauchamp, however, remained unsatisfied with the purely abstract direction that Hofmann encouraged: "Figurative painting has more expressive possibilities than only formal considerations of abstract painting. To paint a head means more than to paint a circle—a nude, more than a plane of color. But why not have your cake and eat it too? Be formally strong but open the painting to many associative possibilities."[3]

Beginning in the late 1950s, Beauchamp began a series of expressionistically painted canvases dominated by long-limbed, long-haired nude women. In contrast to de Kooning's robust and fleshy females, Beauchamp's women are haunting creatures displayed in awkward positions: they crouch, squat, loll, and wait. They usually appear bored, even as they partake in mysterious rituals. Many of the paintings bear such provocative titles as *Initiation* or *White Witch/Black Witch,* suggestive of some demonic happening. Although the Museum's painting remains untitled, its two women are sisters to these witches. In their inexplicable nakedness, lack of self-consciousness, and outdoor placement, they relate to two icons in the history of art: Giorgione's *Fête Champêtre* and Edouard Manet's *Le Déjeuner sur l'Herbe.* Beauchamp's women are neither seductive nor sensual but are animallike, in both their poses and their clawlike hands and feet. In mood they are more akin to the women of the German Expressionists Emil Nolde and Max Beckmann.

Beauchamp's painting style complements the apparent bestiality of the figures. Paint strokes are not only visible, they are raw; drips and splatters cover the lower left side of the painting's surface. Except for the blood red thick slash of pigment, colors are impure and bleak, and the ashen flesh tones stand out in sharp contrast to the dark background. By placing the knees of the upper nude at the edge of the canvas and by cropping the other figure, the artist has created an image as forceful and immediate as de Kooning's aggressive and overpowering women.

Painting provides an outlet for Beauchamp's personal feelings; for ten years, including the period he taught art at the University of Georgia, he repeatedly painted his self-portrait and that of his brother, a wheelchair-bound polio victim. In these works the colors become progressively more radiant and intense, and the impasto is dense with swirling brushstrokes. In contrast to the earlier female nudes, in these later paintings male figures are placed frontally, hovering between comic and tragic images. Beauchamp says: "I can't say what my paintings mean. They mean something to me and I paint them in a particular way to make them mean a particular thing to me. . . . The more you can submerge yourself in the painting and act intuitively the more things solve themselves."[4]

---

1. See Paul Schimmel, "The Women," in *The Figurative Fifties: New York Figurative Expressionism* (Newport Beach, Calif.: Newport Harbor Art Museum, 1988), 53–56.

2. Beauchamp, Ohio State University Fine Arts Gallery, December 1978, as quoted in Joan Marter, "Robert Beauchamp: Haunting Images," *Arts Magazine,* February 1979, 147.

3. Beauchamp, "Self-Interview," in Ronald A. Kuchta, April Kingsley, and Robert Beauchamp, *Robert Beauchamp: An American Expressionist* (Syracuse, N.Y.: Everson Museum of Art, 1984), 19.

4. Beauchamp, "Self-Interview," 21.

Born, Denver, Colorado, 1923; studied at the Colorado Springs Fine Arts Center, 1942 and 1946; Cranbrook Academy of Fine Arts, Bloomfield Hills, Michigan, bachelor of fine arts degree, 1949; studied in Provincetown, Massachusetts, and New York with Hans Hofmann, 1950–1953; taught at Cooper Union Art School, New York, 1969–1971, University of Louisiana, Baton Rouge, 1971, Brooklyn College, 1973, and School of the Visual Arts, New York, 1974–1976; Lamar Dodd Chair, University of Georgia, Athens, 1981–1984; teaches at the Art Students League; resides, New York.

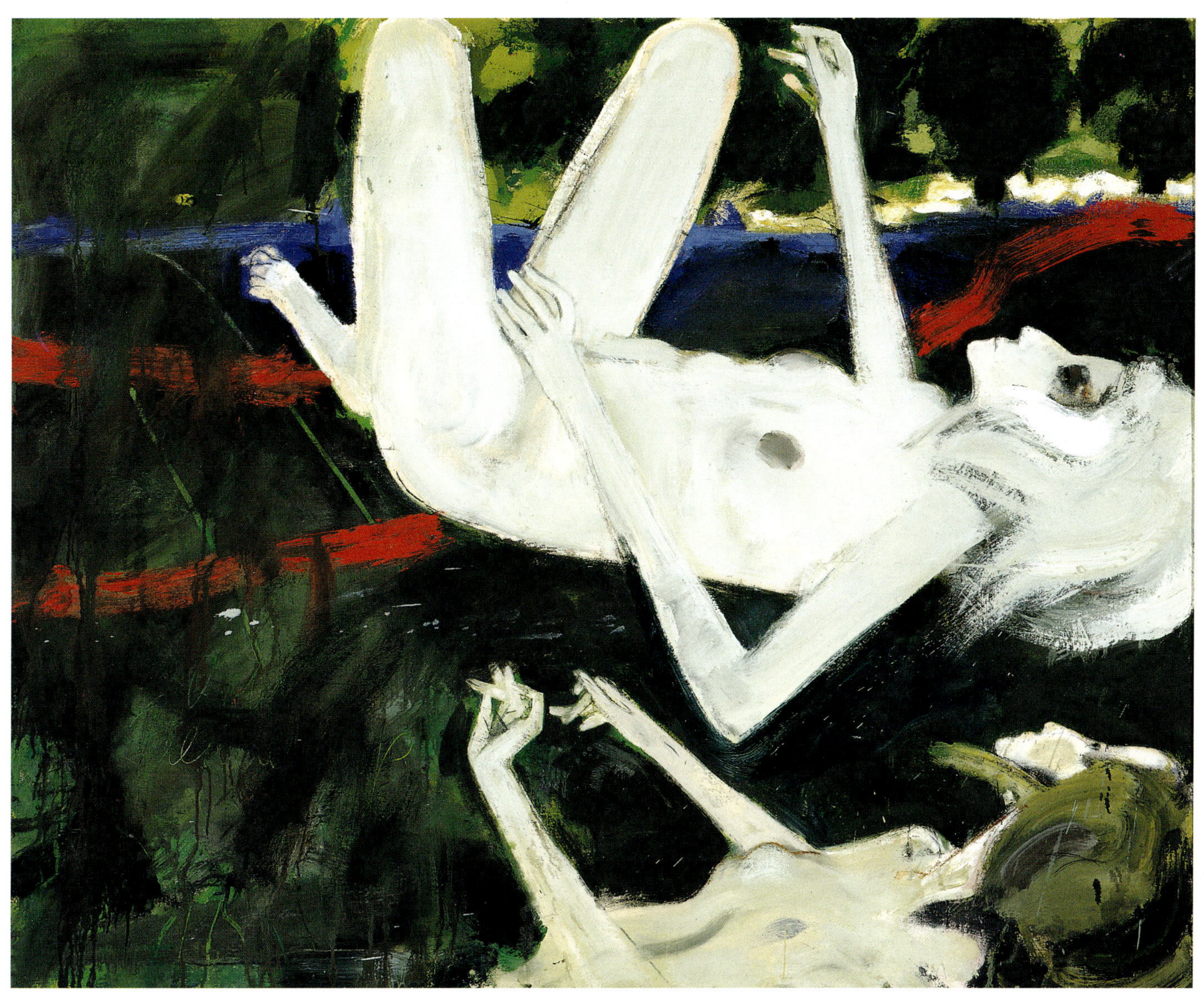

Robert Louis Thompson

1937–1966

Family Portrait, 1963

oil on canvas, 63⅛ × 86¾ inches
signed, lower left: *B. Thompson '63*
Museum purchase with funds from the Arthur and Holly Magill Purchase Fund

By the mid-1950s, Abstract Expressionism, sustained by the formalist theories of the influential critic Clement Greenberg, had become a monolithic presence in the avant-garde of the New York School. A growing number of artists, however, began to return to the figure, treating the traditional subject with the vigorous brushwork of Abstract Expressionism. These artists included the reigning masters of abstraction, Jackson Pollock and Willem de Kooning, as well as a new wave of young New York–based painters led by Robert Beauchamp, Lester Johnson, and Bob Thompson. To compete with the mythic ambitions of the Abstract Expressionists and to reinvigorate the figurative genre, Thompson, for one, chose to adapt the subjects of the old masters to a modern style.

A native of Louisville, Kentucky, Thompson attended the University of Louisville, where German Expressionism was highly regarded. While he was a student, the J. B. Speed Museum hosted a pair of exhibitions that featured the work of the contemporary California figurative painters David Park and Richard Diebenkorn.[1] In 1958 Thompson went to Provincetown, Massachusetts, where he took classes offered by the Seong Moy School, an alternative to Hans Hofmann's well-established program. More important than the instruction he received, however, was the presence of Hofmann and his disciples as well as that of other young figurative artists, specifically Red Grooms and Jan Müller. His friendship with Grooms was solidified the following year when Thompson moved to New York and participated in several of Grooms's Happenings.

Thompson avidly enjoyed the opportunities that the city offered which, in addition to the art world, extended to include friendships with such blues musicians as Ornette Coleman and Thelonius Monk. The art found in museums was also important to Thompson's painting. In 1961 he moved to France, where he became further enamored with the richness of art history: "The museums were driving me crazy. I was seeing so much art. . . . I was reading Kenneth Clark's book on the nude. . . . I began to think, God, I look at Poussin and he's got it all there. Why are all of these people running around trying to be original when they should just go ahead and be themselves and that's the originality of it all, just be yourself."[2] Thompson, it seems, was trying to reconcile the Abstract Expressionist emphasis on the individual creator with the stimulation he found in the work of such artists as Titian, Masaccio, and Goya.

In its broad, flat areas of strong color and its figures with masklike faces, the Museum's painting, *Family Portrait,* is typical of Thompson's work. The composition is based upon a dynamic duality, a quality found in several of Masaccio's frescoes which Thompson is known to have admired. The narrative is divided between a tightly clustered group in the left foreground, identified as Thompson's mother and sisters, juxtaposed with the single, nude figure of his wife. She firmly stands in the shadow of a bird's wing, a device frequently repeated by the artist. In the lower foreground, bearing the most haunted expression of all, is Thompson himself, making *Family Portrait* an autobiographical statement on the racial tensions evident in his family.[3] Thompson's own heritage was part African-American and part Native American; his wife was Caucasian.

Thompson derived much of his imagery from the world of dreams and from old-master paintings. *Family Portrait* relates directly to one of Goya's *Caprichos.*[4] At the time the painting was done, Thompson was living in Spain, and the influence of Goya, a visionary artist as well as a caustic social critic, was potent. Entitled *And they pluck her!,* Goya's image portrays three sinister-looking characters who defeather and devour a winged being whose counterpart is found in Thompson's batlike self-image in the Museum's painting. Whereas Goya satirized male lust and the tendency of prostitutes to fleece and be fleeced, Thompson personalized the image by including himself and members of his family. In addition, by borrowing from Goya's vitriolic image, Thompson added a sexual component to the Museum's painting. *Family Portrait* also resembles Paul Gauguin's paintings from Brittany and Tahiti, in which visions, more mystical and less horrific than Goya's, dominate a colorful, two-dimensional landscape.

In a poignant letter to his sister—who presumably is portrayed in the *Family Portrait*—written shortly before his untimely death, Thompson explained his artistic compulsion, writing,

> I paint many paintings that tell me slowly that I have something inside of me that is just bursting, twisting, sticking, spilling over to get out. Out into souls & mouths and eyes that have never been seen before. The Monsters are present now on my canvas as in my dreams. The horses are there, the dancing nudes, the little man with the pie-shaped hat and the earth, the earth sometimes green, purple, blue, violet—the trees, orange, yellow-green, red everything my imagination tells me. I feel free—can you hear me—free![5]

1. Judith Wilson, "Bob Thompson," in Paul Schimmel and Judith Stein, *The Figurative Fifties: New York Figurative Expressionism* (Newport Beach, Calif.: Newport Harbor Art Museum, 1988), 156.

2. Thompson, as quoted in Mary Schmidt Campbell, *The World of Bob Thompson* (New York: The Studio Museum in Harlem, 1978), 19.

3. Campbell, *Thompson,* 20.

4. Campbell, *Thompson,* 20.

5. Thompson, as quoted in *Bob Thompson,* University Art Gallery, University of Massachusetts at Amherst, 1974, unpaginated.

Born, Louisville, Kentucky, 1937; studied at Boston University, 1955, and University of Louisville, 1956–1958; studied with Seong Moy, Provincetown, Massachusetts, summer 1958; moved to New York, 1958; lived in France, 1961–1962, and Spain, 1962–1963, New York, 1963–1965; lived in Italy, 1963–1966; died, Rome, 1966.

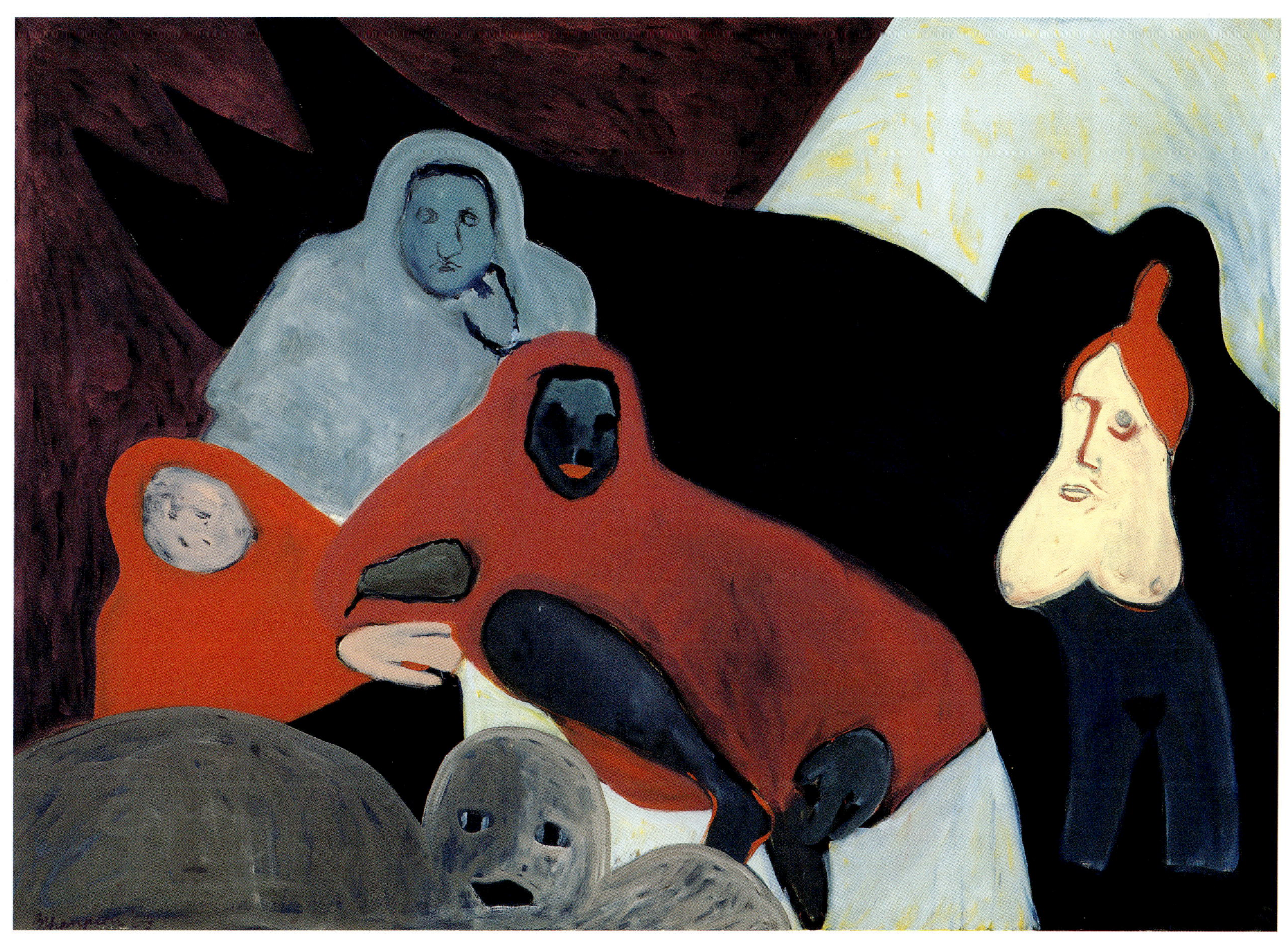

Charles Rogers (Red) Grooms

born 1937

Painting from "A Play Called Fire," 1958

oil and enamel on canvas, 53 × 90 inches
Museum purchase with funds from the Arthur and Holly Magill Purchase Fund

The Happenings of the early 1960s, a visual art form that incorporated painting, sculpture, and theater, were a protracted outgrowth of the Abstract Expressionist movement. By emphasizing the artist's centrality and the process of art making, Happenings became the paradigm of spontaneity. Performance oriented, these events included dialogue, music, group interaction, and the use of an extensive variety of mundane materials. Allan Kaprow, who was responsible for coining the term *Happenings,* was the movement's prime theorist as well as one of its most devoted practitioners. Addressing the perennial issue of the relationship between art and life, he maintained: "The line between art and life should be kept as fluid, and perhaps as indistinct, as possible." He further believed that Happenings should take place in several locales, be variously paced, and never be repeated.[1]

Red Grooms, who has been active in Happenings and filmmaking, has translated the theatrical, collaborative, and eclectic nature of both forms into his own work. Creating art that blurs the categorical division of painting and sculpture, Grooms makes three-dimensional paintings and painterly environments. His subjects revolve around contemporary life, especially the frenetic pace of cities, celebrity, and his own personal life. Urban, but hardly urbane, Grooms's work is upbeat, in contrast to the mythic seriousness of the Abstract Expressionists he admires and whose painterliness he emulates.

A native of Nashville, Tennessee, Grooms began to make art in his teens. Later, he reflected upon his decision to become an artist: "Growing up in Nashville in the 1950s I felt cooped up, locked into every kind of straitjacket you can imagine. But, like every family, mine had its share of eccentrics and nuts, so it wasn't all that bizarre not to fit in. . . . I was pretty clear that I was going to be an artist, which is a fairly regular variety of oddball."[2] Grooms studied for a short while at the School of the Art Institute of Chicago, and then at the New School in New York, before returning to Nashville for a year at the George Peabody College for Teachers. A turning point came in the summer of 1957, which he spent in Provincetown, Massachusetts, working as a monitor for Hans Hofmann. In Provincetown he met other young artists, including Kaprow; that winter Grooms settled in New York.

The Museum's *Painting from "A Play Called Fire"* is an artifact from one of Grooms's early Happenings, a performance that was to a large extent a satire of Abstract Expressionism. Appearing on stage at the Sun Gallery in Provincetown, the artist confronted a canvas over seven feet wide; in the manner of the Action Painters, Grooms attacked the surface with broad, sweeping brushstrokes in red, orange, and black paint. Slowly, from the myriad gestures emerged the image of firemen frantically fighting a conflagration. Within the Abstract Expressionist idiom Grooms reasserted the importance of figures, one of whom mirrors his own distinctive profile with its prominent nose and shock of red hair. Another pointed motif is the oversize hand in the foreground—an allusion to the primacy of gesture for the Abstract Expressionists.

Both Grooms and his critics have been troubled by the humorous element in his work. In the mid-1960s the critic Ted Berrigan confronted the issue: "Red's paintings are definitely not funny, at least not often. Which is not strange for they (the paintings) often resemble the Sunday funnies, which also are rarely funny. . . . I like Red's paintings even better than the funnies, mostly because they are so much richer. There is more detail, less story, more mystery and less art as art."[3] Fifteen years later Grooms was still wrestling with this dilemma: "Actually, for some time I've had feelings of wanting to do 'psychological' work, more mature sentiments and life situations, though I think some of it gets into the funny stuff I do. But it is probably better to have a unified front. It's almost subversive if I do something that isn't jokey."[4]

An essential part of Grooms's methodology is collaboration, ranging from early participatory Happenings to the involvement of other artists, including his first wife, Mimi Gross, as well as student and paid assistants. Many of his works reflect his colorful existence, which he has re-created in a variety of tableaux. Among Grooms's most ambitious projects was the large-scale environment called *Ruckus Manhattan,* which parodies such famed landmarks as the Statue of Liberty, the World Trade Center, the subway, and the Brooklyn Bridge. Fabricated from lumber, canvas, fiberglass, and found objects, its surfaces are crude, flashy, and reminiscent of the city's glitzy atmosphere. The success and vitality of *Ruckus Manhattan* led to similar regional manifestations in Philadelphia, Cleveland, Fort Worth, and Minneapolis. Underlying these works, and the Museum's *Painting from "A Play Called Fire,"* is Grooms's freewheeling sense for the burlesque, and a willingness to satirize his world, his art, and himself.

---

1. See Allan Kaprow, *Assemblage, Environments, and Happenings* (New York: Harry N. Abrams, 1966), 188–194.

2. Grooms, interview with Carter Ratcliff, 1981–1984, in Ratcliff, *Red Grooms* (New York: Abbeville Press, 1984), 233.

3. Ted Berrigan, "Red Power," *Art News,* December 1966, 45.

4. Grooms, as quoted in Grace Glueck, "Red Grooms Reshapes His Loony World," *The New York Times,* 29 March 1981.

Born, Nashville, Tennessee, 1937; studied at the School of the Art Institute of Chicago, 1955, the New School, New York, 1956, and the George Peabody College for Teachers, Nashville, 1957; studied with Hans Hofmann, Provincetown, Massachusetts, summers, 1957 and 1958; moved to New York, 1958; travel abroad, British Isles, Switzerland, Italy, Israel, 1960–1961; returned to New York; began summers in Maine, 1964; resides, New York.

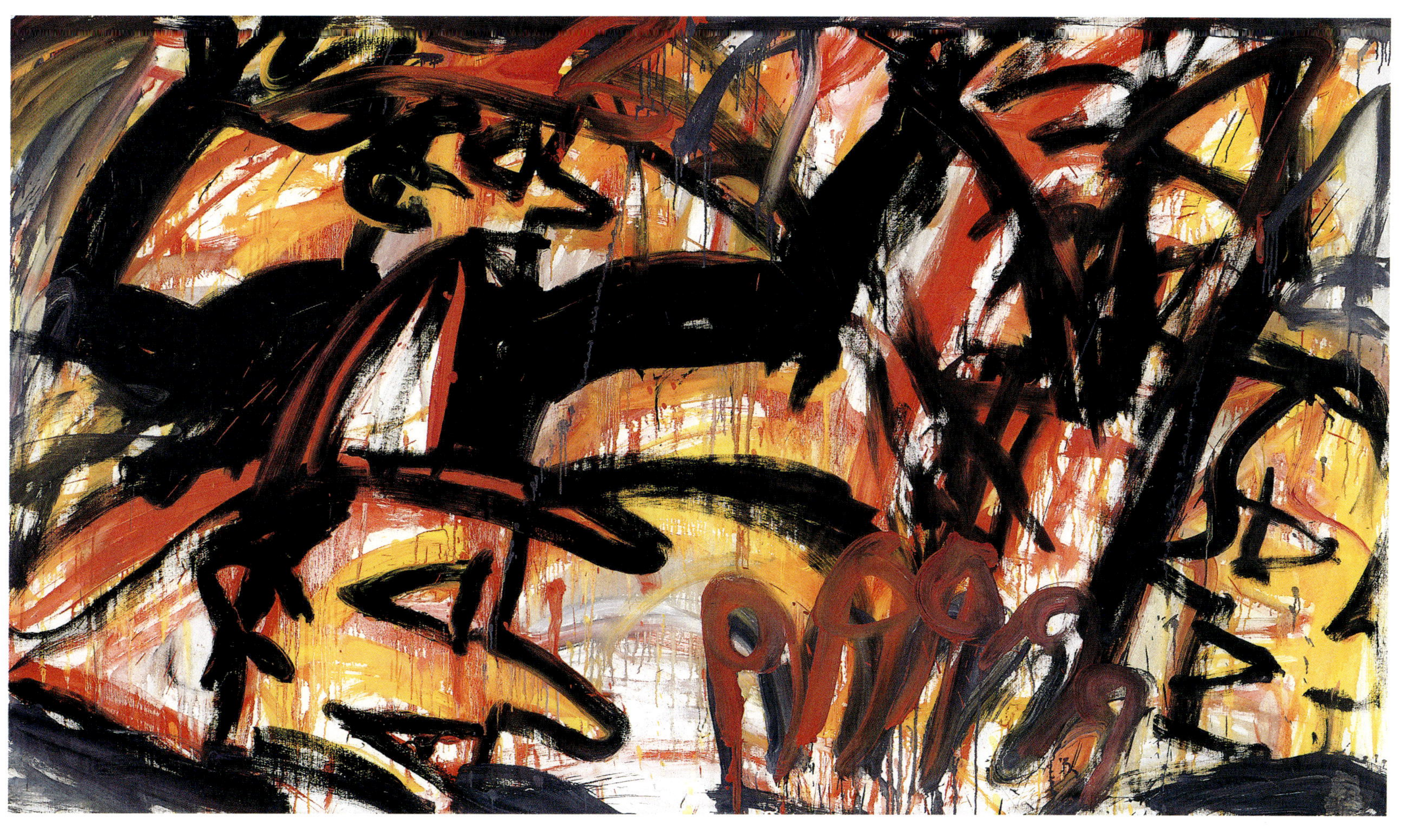

Walter Henry (Jack) Beal, Jr.

born 1931

Sondra on a Sofa, 1968

oil on canvas, 66 × 78 inches
signed, upper left: *Jack Beal*
Museum purchase with funds donated by the Arthur and Holly Magill Foundation

Contemporary art, dominated for nearly two decades by Abstract Expressionism, began to change when a trend toward realism developed within Abstract Expressionism itself. Several painters, including Willem de Kooning, Philip Guston, and Robert Beauchamp, reasserted the importance of concrete imagery and exploited the expressive potential of the human figure. Disenchanted with Abstract Expressionism, a number of artists elected to depict the figure in clear, cool, realistic styles. This realistic impulse was simultaneously manifested in Pop Art, which elevated ordinary and familiar objects to the level of art.

In the 1960s both Philip Pearlstein and Jack Beal chose the classic form of the female nude as their primary subject matter. In addition to their realist direction, they shared an interest in patterns, and both frequently employed oblique and dramatic perspectives. Light was important to both of them; for Pearlstein it revealed form and contour, while for Beal it enlivened his compositions with dynamic contrasts. Whereas Pearlstein's nudes are impersonal, muscular, and hard, Beal's paintings of his only model, his wife, the painter Sondra Freckelton, are ebullient and often sensual.

Beal's earliest work was within the Abstract Expressionist mode, but after study at the School of the Art Institute of Chicago and a subsequent move to New York, he rejected this direction, feeling it was derivative. A native of Richmond, Virginia, Beal had attended the Norfolk campus of the College of William and Mary, where he majored in biology. It was his experience in Chicago, however, that laid the foundation for his mature work. Encouraged to use the Institute's fine collection, he analyzed and scrutinized various works, honing his observation skills. Recalling his student days, Beal commented: "After all, I had studied biology, and I wanted art to be as forceful, challenging, and intelligent an occupation as that. Until I saw pictures of real quality, I had tended to think of painting as just so much self-indulgent smearing around, but when I saw masterpieces by Cézanne and Matisse, and other painters of similar stature, I was bowled over; suddenly I realized the force of art."[1]

Like Arshile Gorky, whom Beal greatly admired, he shifted his direction after spending a summer immersed in nature. Initially painting landscapes, Beal then turned toward interiors, many littered with boots, fishing gear, and old chairs—all objects that related to him personally. It was not until 1964 that Beal began to portray Freckelton nude or partially dressed in a series of large canvases. Several related to Greek myth, and many of the works employed mirrored reflections and strong patterns. Beal and Freckelton avidly shop at flea markets, and many of their purchases, such as large, overstuffed sofas and wooden chairs, find their way into his paintings.

Clearly, Beal was personally involved in what he painted, a factor that eventually led to his abandonment of the life-size nude depictions of his wife. One day in New York he was loading a painting of his wife onto a truck, and three workers walked by and started to fondle the canvas. Beal recounted the ambiguity of his reaction: "This incident shook me—I was enraged at the assault on the picture, but at the same time I was thrilled that the realism of the painting had provoked the attack."[2] Following this implied violation of his wife, he painted her either dressed or, if nude, with her face averted, hidden, or cast in shadow. The Museum's painting shows Freckelton semiclothed, looking unabashedly out toward the viewer in a confident, almost confrontational manner.

In *Sondra on a Sofa* Beal has placed the figure toward the upper right corner; her legs and the sofa are dramatically foreshortened, or contracted, to give the illusion of depth. In addition, the diagonal placement of the sofa and the tilted perspective of the floorboards make the image compelling, forcefully engaging the viewer. The immediacy of the composition is further enhanced by the way such forms as the corner and the foot of the sofa almost touch the edge of the canvas. A high-contrast light, with its source above the figure, casts deep shadows, hinting perhaps at a setting sun. This use of chiaroscuro, along with the intense perspective, reveals Beal's admiration for Renaissance masters. Relating to the sunset, the colors are warm and vaguely unnatural, especially in the couch, where slightly acrid hues rival one another. Renouncing the painterly application of the expressionists, Beal created a flat composition where color areas are crisply delineated with few modulations in hue.

Throughout the 1960s and early 1970s Beal's work was dominated by images of Freckelton. He undertook a number of portrait commissions but was most stimulated when the sitters were good friends. In the mid-1970s two narrative series preoccupied him: one was devoted to the history of labor and consisted of four large, complicated murals for the United States Department of Labor; the other set was a contemporary allegory about virtue and vice. This not only represented a new direction for Beal but also anticipated a later trend in American art.

> I felt that America [had] been going through a profound moral crisis, and I wanted to deal with that. . . . I thought that examining moral issues was eminently worthwhile. The world needs leadership. Few of us get it at home; we don't get it at school. Few of us go to church. So we don't get it there either; and although painting is not necessarily the best vehicle for moralizing, nonetheless it can be a moral vehicle for people who don't attend church or read philosophy.[3]

In keeping with this new sentiment Beal committed himself to teaching. As a visiting lecturer, artist in residence, and workshop leader, Beal has reached a broad audience throughout the country. He willingly shares his philosophy with his students: "Study life, study nature, study art, and try to bring them together in your work. There is no greater reward in art than the wedding of this trinity."[4]

---

1. Beal, interview, 1991, as quoted in Eric Shanes, *Jack Beal* (New York: Hudson Hills Press, 1993), 12.
2. Beal, interview, in Shanes, *Beal,* 36.
3. Beal, interview, in Shanes, *Beal,* 64.
4. Beal, "Sight and Sense: Studying Pictorial Composition," *American Artist,* February 1968, 97.

Born, Richmond, Virginia, 1931; attended Norfolk Division, College of William and Mary (now Old Dominion University), Norfolk, Virginia, 1950–1953; studied at the School of the Art Institute of Chicago, 1953–1956, and the University of Chicago, 1955–1956; moved to New York, 1956; divides time between New York and Oneonta, New York.

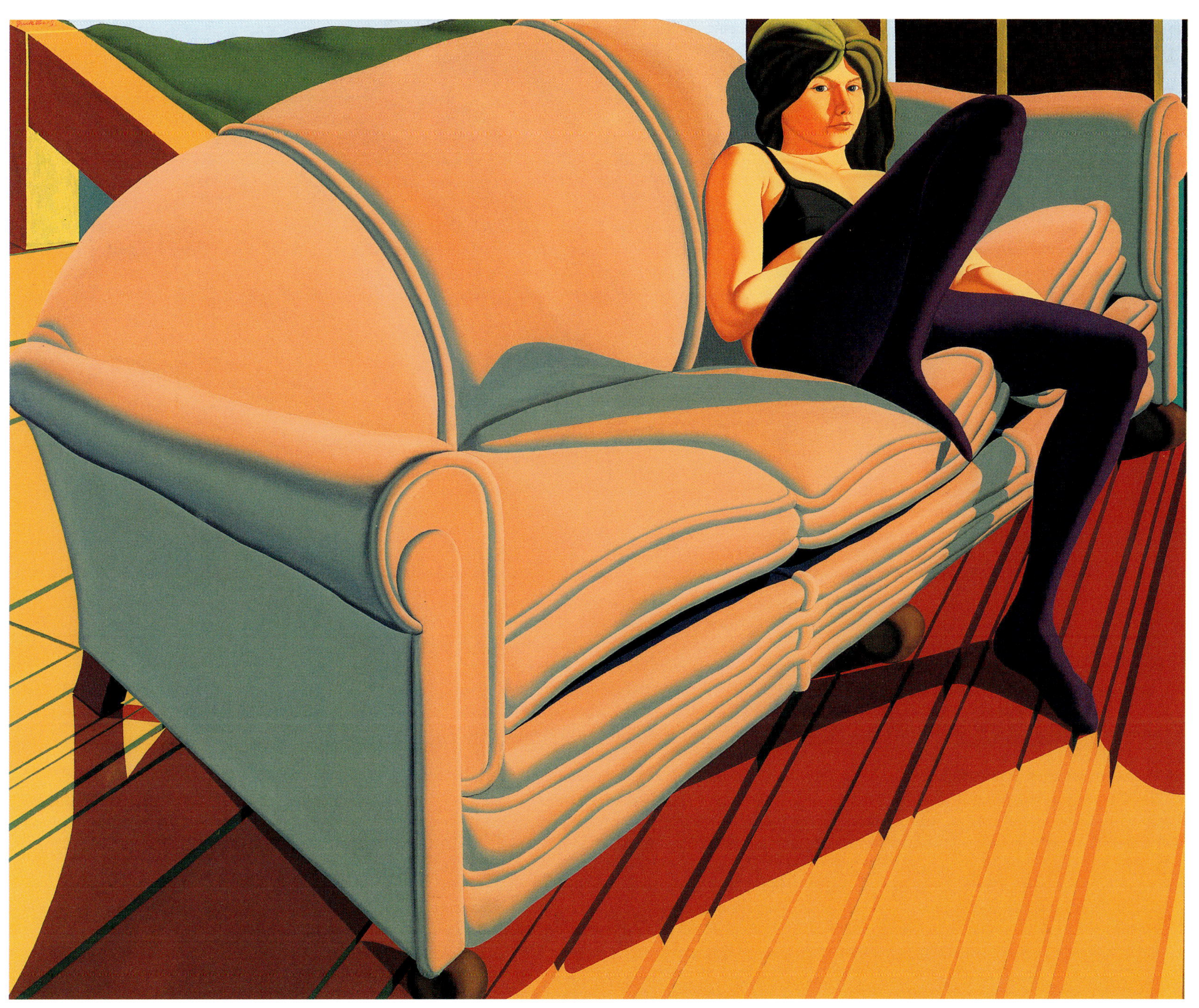

Philip Guston

1913–1980

untitled, 1971

oil on paper mounted on canvas, 29 × 39 inches
signed, lower right: *Philip Guston '71*
Gift of Elaine de Kooning (by exchange)

The painterliness of Abstract Expressionism has a long lineage, reaching back to Impressionism or, as some maintain, to Rembrandt, Diego Velázquez, and Frans Hals. All of these artists exploited the expressive potential of paint—the earlier ones to suggest textures and to create highlights, and the Impressionists to approximate the optical effects of sunlight. The Abstract Expressionists, however, were the ones to excel at paint manipulation; their facility at paint handling unites them as a group while simultaneously distinguishing each one. Jackson Pollock dripped and threw his paint, Franz Kline used house-painting brushes in broad sweeping strokes, and Clyfford Still created ragged edges by building up a heavy impasto with a palette knife.

In his Abstract Expressionist work Philip Guston allied himself with Pollock and Kline, emphasizing the primacy of gesture. With fairly short, discrete, blocky brushstrokes Guston applied paint to canvas, usually concentrating on the center and working outward. Like his longtime friend Pollock, Guston did not paint according to a predetermined plan but instead responded to the physicality of his materials. Both artists also limited the number and variety of colors on their palettes. In 1965 Guston made a simple declaration: "I expect other people to look at painting the way I look at painting, just as painting."[1] Five years later he shocked the art world by exhibiting a radically different type of work that revolved around concrete images and a personal iconography.

Guston grew up in California and, along with Pollock, attended and was expelled from the Manual Arts High School in Los Angeles, more for mischief making than for academic reasons. Guston held a scholarship at the Otis Art Institute, Los Angeles, in 1930, but dropped out, preferring to study art, especially Renaissance masters, independently. Impressed by the Mexican muralists, he watched Diego Rivera at Pomona College and then traveled to Mexico to work with David Alfaro Siqueiros. In 1935 he moved to New York, and while there he became a member of the mural division of the Federal Art Project. Experienced with content-oriented art, Guston produced a mural for the Commerce, Georgia, post office, which portrays the construction of the railroad and the arrival of mail service to the area in realistic, narrative terms. He remained in New York until the outbreak of World War II, after which he taught at the University of Iowa, Iowa City. After two decades of painting figuratively, Guston returned to New York in 1950 and initiated work that is closely identified with Abstract Expressionism. His analogies to landscape and the overall painterliness of his work led critics to dub Guston an Abstract Impressionist, an appellation he abhorred.

A hallmark of Guston's style was the color red, which he used liberally in heavy strokes on the surface as well as buried under multiple layers of paint. A fellow Abstract Expressionist, Robert Motherwell, explained the potency of the color: "The 'pure' red of which certain abstractionists speak does not exist no matter how one shifts its physical contexts. Any red is rooted in blood, glass, wine, hunter's caps, and a thousand other concrete phenomena. Otherwise we should have no feeling toward red or its relations, and it would be useless as an artistic element."[2] Variants on red, usually vivid, fleshy pinks, became a leitmotif in Guston's figurative style after 1970. His dramatic break with Abstract Expressionism was motivated by personal crisis, and initially it befuddled New York's art world. As a way of explaining himself he said, simply: "I got sick and tired of all that Purity! I wanted to tell Stories!"[3] Instead of quasi-lyrical essays on the quality of paint, savage autobiographical and politically oriented content proliferated. The self-portrait references consist of cigarette-smoking eyeballs and the soles of shoes accompanied by bottles and palettes.

Guston's sinister portrayals of the Ku Klux Klan, represented simply by cone-shaped hoods, recall motifs common in his preabstract paintings in which figures are often masked or wear pointed hats. Although neither a Southerner nor an African-American, Guston found the Klan imagery to be particularly compelling, reflecting unsettling memories from his childhood. Raised Philip Goldstein, the son of Russian Jewish refugees, Guston may have been the target of persecution by such groups as the Klan. Klansmen, with their hoods providing anonymity, were notorious for lynching, which Guston may have related to his father's suicide by hanging. Before he was twenty, Guston painted murals showing Klansmen whipping African-Americans; the works were destroyed by members of the American Legion in concert with the "Red Squad" police.

The caricaturelike quality of Guston's late paintings is similar to some of his earliest artwork, which was influenced by a correspondence course in cartooning he took at age thirteen. The Museum's painting displays the cartoonist's ability to simplify: a solitary Klansman is represented by the looming conical shape that symbolizes the hood but that also suggests a bullet or even a type of tank with gun turrets. The ambiguous red form to the right may be interpreted as a brick, a basic unit of building, or as an instrument of destruction in the hands of the hooded figure. The red and pinkish tones, the painterly brushwork, and the illusion of limited space are, despite their forceful personal iconography, links to Guston's early abstract work. Guston's ironically ambivalent, sinister, and self-deprecating late work not only rejected abstraction, but, in its biting and satirical use of mundane items, it also addressed the shallowness of Pop Art in which everyday objects exist for their own sake and are bereft of deeper meaning.

---

1. Guston, interview with Gladys Shafran Kashdin, 1965, as quoted in Robert Storr, *Philip Guston* (New York: Abbeville Press, 1986), 108.

2. Motherwell, "Beyond Aesthetic," *Design* 47 (1946), 14–15, as quoted in April Kingsley, *The Turning Point* (New York: Simon and Schuster, 1992), 323.

3. Guston, as quoted in Hilton Kramer, "A Mandarin Pretending to Be a Stumblebum," *The New York Times*, 25 October 1970.

Born, Montreal, Canada, 1913; attended Manual Arts High School, Los Angeles, 1927–1928; studied three months at Otis Art Institute, Los Angeles, 1930; traveled to Mexico, 1934; moved to New York, 1935; joined Federal Art Project, 1935–1940; taught at University of Iowa, 1941–1945, and St. Louis School of Fine Arts, Washington University, 1945–1947; moved to Woodstock, New York, 1947; traveled in Italy, 1948–1949; visiting artist, University of Minnesota, spring, 1950; settled in New York State, 1950–1980; taught at New York University, 1951–1958, and Pratt Institute, New York, 1953–1958; to Italy, 1960 and 1970–1971; moved to Woodstock, 1967; taught at Boston University, 1973–1978; died, Woodstock, 1980.

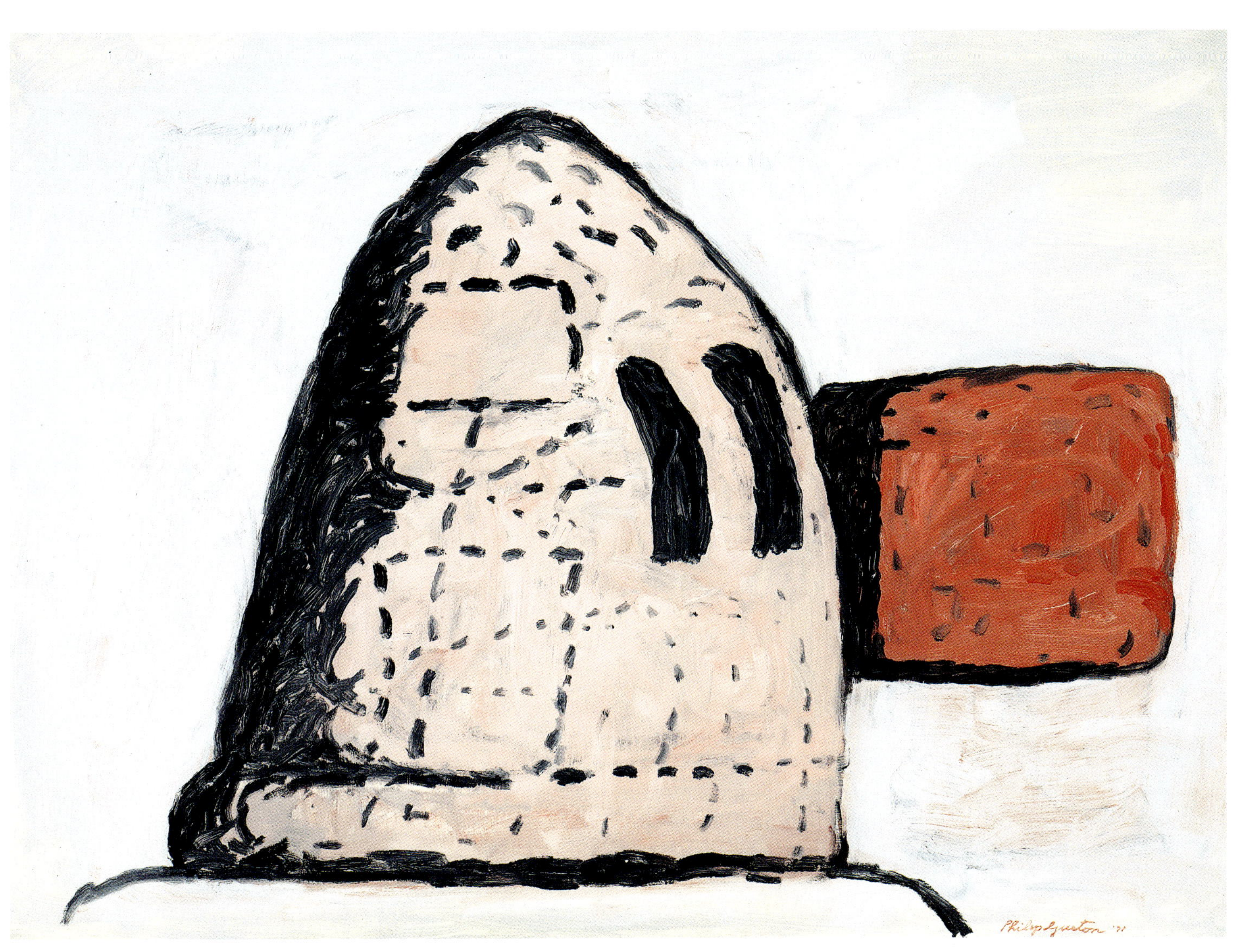

Jasper Johns

born 1930

0, 1966

liquid graphite, graphite, and colored pencils on paper: image, 5 1/8 × 4 inches; paper, 8 1/2 × 6 5/8 inches
signed, lower right: *J. Johns / '66*
Museum purchase with funds donated by the Arthur and Holly Magill Foundation
(Illustrated on page 23)

Flags I, 1973

serigraph, printed in color: image, 26 7/8 × 33 5/8 inches; paper: 27 1/2 × 35 inches
edition: 39/65, Simca Print Artists, New York and Tokyo
signed, lower left: *I 39 / 65*; lower right: *J. Johns / '73*
Gift of the artist

Emerging between Cubism and Surrealism, Dada was a modern movement officially begun in 1916. Its randomly selected name was an adaptation of the French word for "hobby horse." Characterized by the use of chance and mundane objects in art making, Dada was closely identified with Marcel Duchamp, whose paintings and sculptures were often unorthodox and anti-aesthetic. An iconoclast, Duchamp was frequently the center of controversy, beginning in this country in 1913 with the exhibition of his *Nude Descending a Staircase No. 2* at the Armory Show. Having an even greater impact on the history of art was his use of "ready-mades," ordinary objects he elevated to the realm of art. This phenomenon is best exemplified by the urinal he placed on its back, signed, and exhibited as *Fountain*.

In their use of banal imagery and found objects, Robert Rauschenberg and Jasper Johns emerged in the 1950s as Duchamp's rightful heirs. Often blurring the distinction between painting and sculpture, both created "combines," in which such ordinary objects as brooms, coat hangers, and beds were united with painting. As good friends who worked in the same studio building, they reinforced each other in a world dominated by Abstract Expressionism. Together they served as the bridge between Abstract Expressionism and the prevalent trends of the 1960s, Pop Art and Minimalism.

Virtually self-taught, Johns spent his childhood in South Carolina. At twenty, he went to New York and enrolled in commercial art classes. After military service Johns returned to New York, where he explored various combinations of collage, encaustic painting, and other media. The image that launched the young artist into the international spotlight was his 1955 painting based on the American flag. It was controversial not only because it employed a patriotic symbol but also because of its ambiguity and inscrutable irony.[1] Created during the heyday of abstract art, the work was an affront to the avant-garde because it was such a familiar object. Of the flag Johns commented, "It was something I could do that would be mine,"[2] a statement that anticipated his repeated use of the image and his identification with it.

By restricting himself to depicting the commonplace, Johns liberated himself from the burden of mythic content, a characteristic of Abstract Expressionist ideology. Instead of anguishing over subject matter, he devoted himself to the experimental and often innovative use of different media. Johns simultaneously explored such traditional processes as drawing, lithography, and etching, as well as the more contemporary process of serigraphy. "I like to repeat an image in another medium. . . . In a sense, one does the same thing two ways and can observe differences and sameness—the stress the image takes in different media. . . . I can understand that someone else might find that boring and repetitious, but that's not the way I see it."[3]

In one of his first attempts at lithography Johns worked with numbers: the simple, familiar numerals zero through nine, rendered in imitation of the stencil patterns he had used to make posters while he was in the army. He returned to numerals frequently, in series and individually, as in the Museum's drawing. Numbers have an inherent duality: they are universal and recognizable, yet they are simultaneously abstract. Zero is the most mysterious of numbers because, in a sense, it is the most abstract, the least quantifiable. It is the beginning, the starting point, but it is also nothing. It has the most purely geometric structure of all numerals and, as a design, recalls another of Johns's beloved subjects, the target. The Museum's drawing reveals the artist's adept manipulation of graphite, merging its linear and liquid characteristics with great intensity on a modest scale. By eliminating potentially distracting color, Johns focuses severely on the elemental; he explained the presence of many grisaille works in his oeuvre by declaring, "Gray is my favorite color."[4]

In contrast, the serigraph *Flags I* is a riot of color. With its painterliness and drip marks, the print betrays the artist's stylistic debt to the Abstract Expressionists; in its gestural quality, *Flags I* challenged the accepted concept of serigraphy, or silkscreening, a printmaking technique that had been used extensively for commercial purposes and that was, before Johns, usually hard-edged and static. Capitalizing on the skill of his printmaking collaborators at Simca Print Artists, Johns created a uniformly energetic design that required thirty-one separate screens, each inked to emulate Johns's individualistic brushwork. By doubling the flag and making the composition a diptych, Johns introduced duality and enhanced the retinal dynamics, as the eye naturally jumps from one flag to the other. Johns further indulged in visual trickery both by placing the flag vertically rather than horizontally and by showing the flag backward, with the field of blue in the upper right.

Johns has remained partial, and loyal, to the image of the American flag in his work, employing it repeatedly for more than thirty years. His curiously detached obsessiveness is revealed in an often-quoted notation in one of his sketchbooks: "Take a canvas / Put a mark on it. / Put another mark on it. . . . One thing working one way / Another thing working another way. / . . . Take an object. / Do something to it. / Do something else to it."[5]

---

1. See Roberta Bernstein, *Jasper Johns' Paintings and Sculptures, 1954–1974* (Ann Arbor, Mich.: UMI Research Press, 1975), 1–15.

2. Johns, as quoted in Michael Crichton, *Jasper Johns* (New York: Harry N. Abrams, 1977), 28.

3. Johns, as quoted in Christian Gellhaar, *Jasper Johns: Working Proofs* (Basel: Kunstmuseum Basel, 1979), 39.

4. Johns, as quoted in Crichton, *Johns*, 16.

5. Johns, sketchbook, in Riva Castleman, *Jasper Johns: A Print Retrospective* (New York: The Museum of Modern Art, 1986), 22–23.

Born, Augusta, Georgia, 1930; attended the University of South Carolina, 1947–1948, and commercial art school in New York, 1949–1950; United States Army, Fort Jackson, South Carolina, and Japan, 1950–1952; settled in New York, 1952; part-time resident, Edisto Island, South Carolina, 1961–1966; resides, upstate New York.

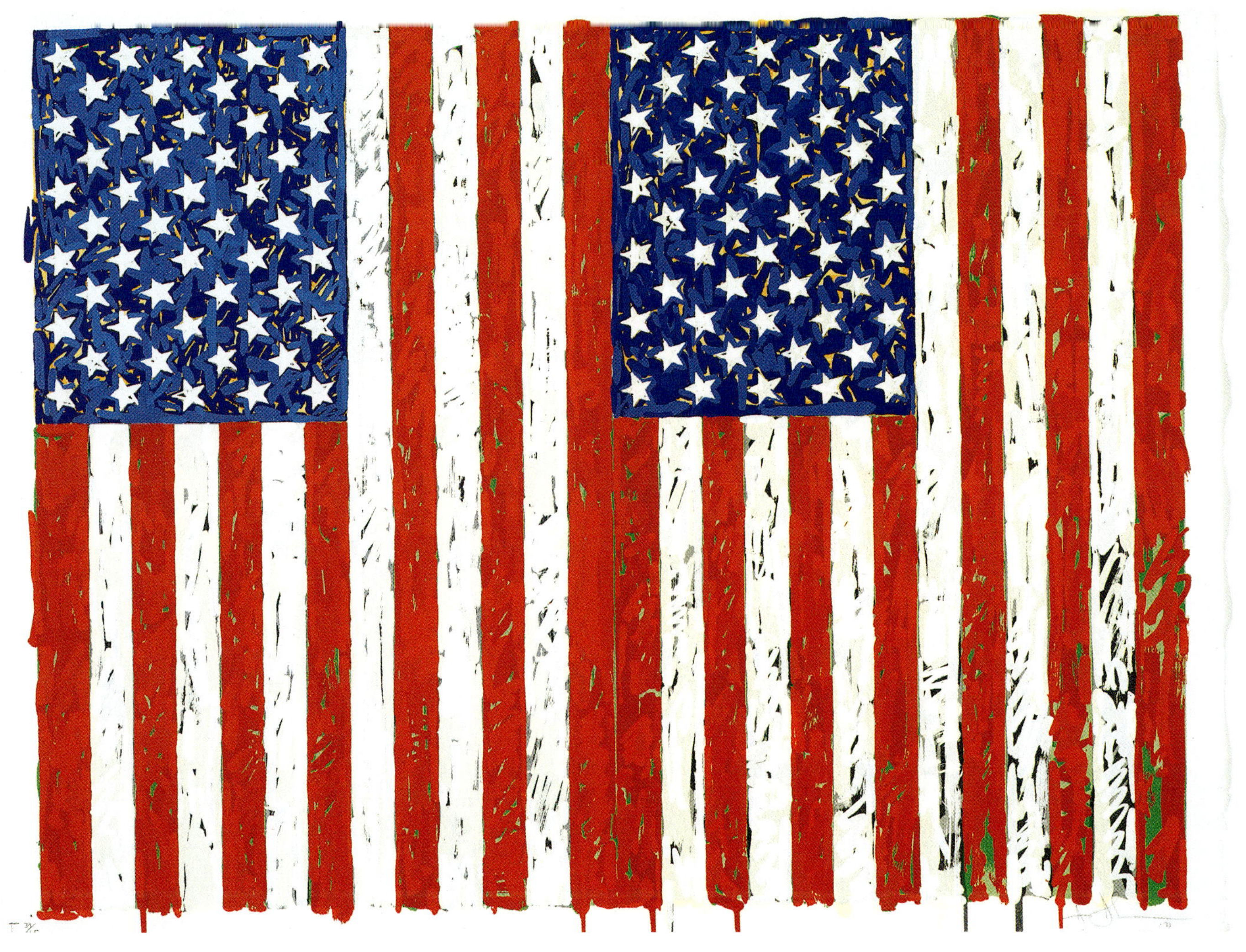

James Rosenquist

born 1933

***Paint Brush*, 1964**

oil on canvas, painted, molded plastic, and metal chain, 59 3/4 × 35 3/8 inches
signed, on reverse: *James Rosenquist / Paint Brush / 1964*
Museum purchase with funds donated by the Arthur and Holly Magill Foundation

Although Pop Art, which became the rage in the early 1960s, seems like a quintessentially American movement, it actually originated in England during the previous decade. Unlike the British Pop artists who aspired to pointed social comment, their American counterparts were less blatant. Through their depictions of the mundane, however, they did succeed in exposing the crass consumerism of American life by drawing attention to the public's obsessions with food, celebrities, sensationalism, and comic-strip culture. The two artists who epitomize American Pop are Andy Warhol and Roy Lichtenstein, both of whom featured ordinary, mass-produced images from the shelves of the supermarket and the pages of the newspaper. Rendered mechanically and bearing little trace of the artist's hand or psyche, their images were enlarged and persistently repeated.

Considered one of the pioneers of Pop Art, James Rosenquist resents that label as "a word invented by somebody to describe some sort of situation, a handy term that has nothing to do with the art."[1] His work is distinguished from that of Warhol and Lichtenstein in its visual disjunctiveness and its occasional political overtones. Rosenquist began his career as a sign painter, executing gargantuan commercial billboards, some as large as sixty by seventy feet, in New York's Times Square. This experience was manifested in his works on canvas. His images often derive from those found in advertising; his scale is monumental, and his colors are flat and weathered looking.

Rosenquist grew up in Minnesota, where as a teenager he had his first training at the Minneapolis School of Art. He later studied painting at the University of Minnesota, and during the summer he supported himself by painting highway advertisements. This skill served him well in New York, where he worked as a billboard painter after attending the Art Students League on a scholarship. Only two years after abandoning this commercial work, Rosenquist's art was internationally acclaimed and his first solo exhibition was sold out. New York was the focal point of his activities until 1971, when he moved to Florida for extended periods each year.

Like so many of Rosenquist's paintings, *Paint Brush* is an oversized fragment presented out of context. Enlarged and cropped nearly to the point of abstraction, *Paint Brush* refers both to the artist's roots as a billboard painter and to his stature as a fine artist. The added-on plastic strip that hangs below the canvas emulates two rows of brick already painted by the brush. The dichotomy established between the tool and its work is reinforced by the dramatic shift in colors, from the bleached photographlike rendering of the brush to the bright, primary intensity of the red and yellow bricks. In its two-part construction, *Paint Brush* acknowledges an immediate debt to the combines of Jasper Johns and Robert Rauschenberg and extends their Cubist, Surrealist, and Dada sources into the classic Pop movement.

In its utter simplicity, symmetry, and singularity, *Paint Brush* is exceptional in Rosenquist's oeuvre. It speaks directly to the artist's attempts to distill the myriad visual stimuli assaulting humanity: "I'm interested in contemporary vision—the flicker of chrome, reflections, rapid associations, quick flashes of light. Bing—bang! I don't do anecdotes. I accumulate experiences."[2]

---

1. Rosenquist, interview with Marcia Tucker, as quoted in *James Rosenquist* (New York: Whitney Museum of American Art, 1972), 11.

2. Rosenquist, as quoted in Judith Goldman, *James Rosenquist* (New York: Viking Penguin, 1985), 46.

Born, Grand Forks, North Dakota, 1933; classes at the Minneapolis School of Art, Minneapolis Society of Fine Arts, 1948; attended University of Minnesota, 1952–1954; studied at the Art Students League, New York, 1955; settled in New York, 1956; employed as billboard painter, 1957–1960; spent part of year in Tampa, Florida, 1971, in Ybor City, Florida, 1973; built a studio in Aripeka, Florida, 1976; divides time between Florida and New York.

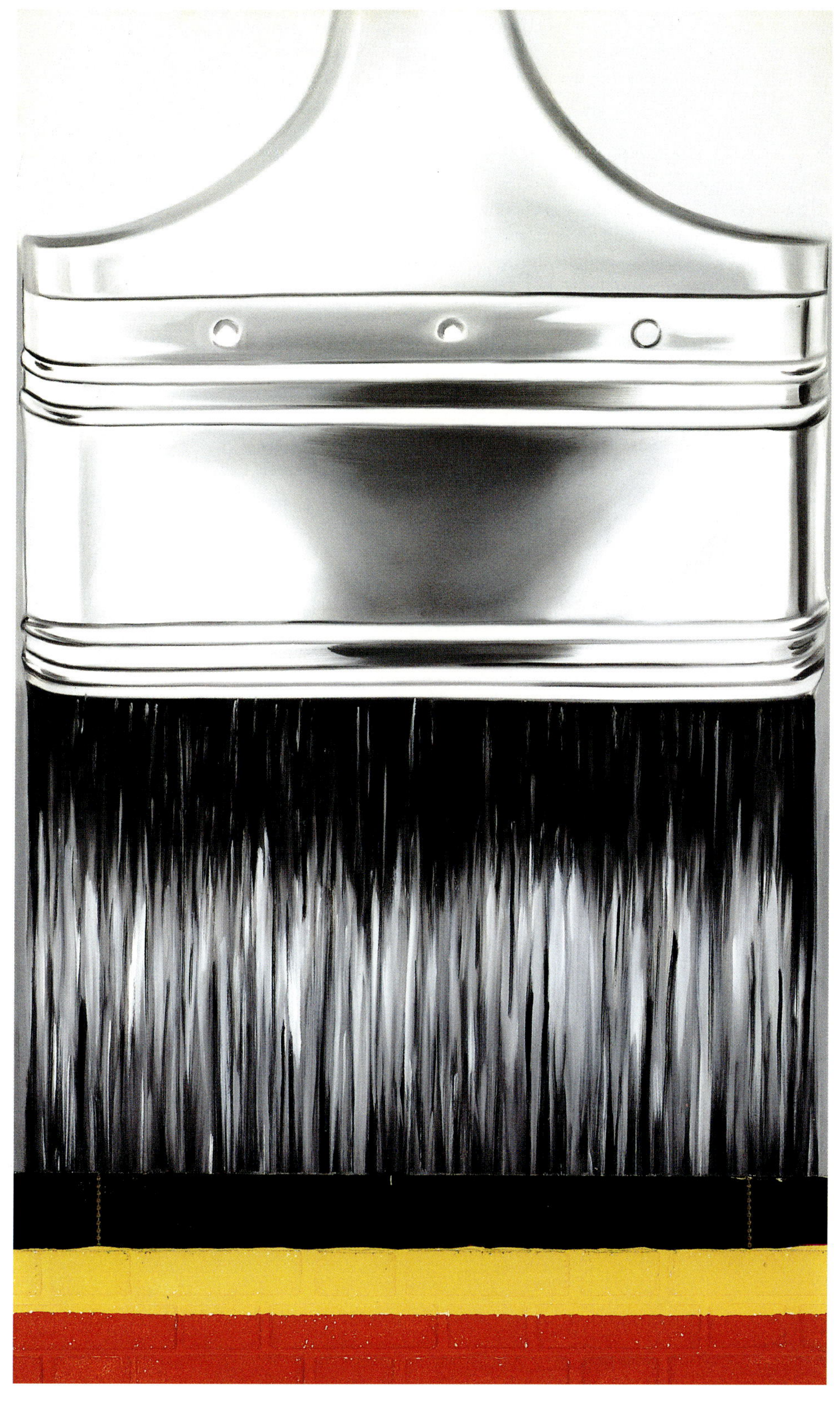

Robert Stanley

born 1932

George and John, 1965

acrylic on canvas, 38 × 45 inches
signed, on reverse: *Bob Stanley / 2 April 1965*
Gift of Buck A. Mickel in memory of Jeannie Williams Styron

Op Art, like its contemporary Pop Art, gained widespread and immediate fame, fueled by the popular press. Such headlines as *Time* magazine's "Op: Pictures That Attack the Eye" captured the attention of a public that relished the visual dynamics of Op Art. When Pop Art proffered familiar images from supermarket shelves and magazines, many people were provoked to question its validity as art. In contrast, Op Art, with its clever visual tricks, engaged viewers and demonstrated to them both skill and craftsmanship.

Working in the 1960s Bob Stanley explored the potential of both Pop and Op by synthesizing them into one aesthetic. Utilizing a basic premise of Op Art, the dramatic juxtaposition of colors, Stanley often obliterated or sublimated his Pop-derived images. So distinctive was Stanley's iconography at the time that he earned the sobriquet "pirate of the Pop Art movement."[1]

The Museum's painting is part of a series about rock-and-roll music. Although such stars as the Rolling Stones, the Everly Brothers, Chuck Berry, and the Beatles are featured, the paintings are not so much about the performers as they are about the cultural phenomenon that they represent, with specific reference to teenage fans. Stanley has explained his preoccupation with these celebrities as part of a "personal concern with teenage angst; I feel the paintings were an ideal way of dealing with it." Throughout the series Stanley employed intensely contrasting colors "to convey the jazziness, and the silliness of teenage emotions."[2]

In *George and John* the blatant rivalry of the complementary red and green nearly obscures the image, reducing it to jagged cutout shapes of dynamically opposed colors, resulting in an eye popping optical effect. Upon closer examination the likenesses of two Beatles emerge: George Harrison and John Lennon. Just as the colors make a brash visual statement, many critics, bystanders, and parents in the 1960s looked upon the Beatles as a crass, provocative intrusion into American popular culture. A similar tension is reflected in Stanley's synthesis of Pop Art, with its satirical critique of popular culture, and Op Art, with its noncritical, nonobjective illusory effects.

Just as the mania for the Beatles passed, so too did Pop and Op Art, to be replaced in the 1970s with a rich eclecticism. Stanley's evolution took a similar direction, with much of his work based on an individualistic, quirky combination of diverse images and references. While he was a visiting artist at Louisiana State University in 1976 he undertook a mammoth painting, measuring ninety-nine feet wide, which used disparate, if not clashing, styles. In addition to several Pop-related images of a motorcycle, a sunbather, and an ice cream roll, *Louisiana Sweet* consists of an oversized male nude torso, painting grids, and a pair of color diagrams. Whereas the color wheels refer backward to his palette in the rock-and-roll series of the mid-1960s, the expressionistically drawn nude projects forward to large-scale female nudes of the 1980s that challenge traditional, preconceived ideas about beauty and fine art.

---

1. Mario Amayo, as quoted in Michael Florescu, "Bob Stanley," *Arts Magazine,* November 1980, 6.

2. Interview with the author, 25 July 1994.

Born, Yonkers, New York, 1932; bachelor of arts degree from Oglethorpe University, Atlanta, Georgia, 1953; studied at the High Museum of Art, 1951–1952, Columbia University, 1951 and 1953, and Brooklyn Museum Art School, 1954–1956; visiting artist, Louisiana State University, Baton Rouge, 1976, Syracuse University, 1978, and Princeton University, 1979–1980; taught at the School of Visual Arts, New York, 1970–1972 and from 1984 to the present; resides, New York.

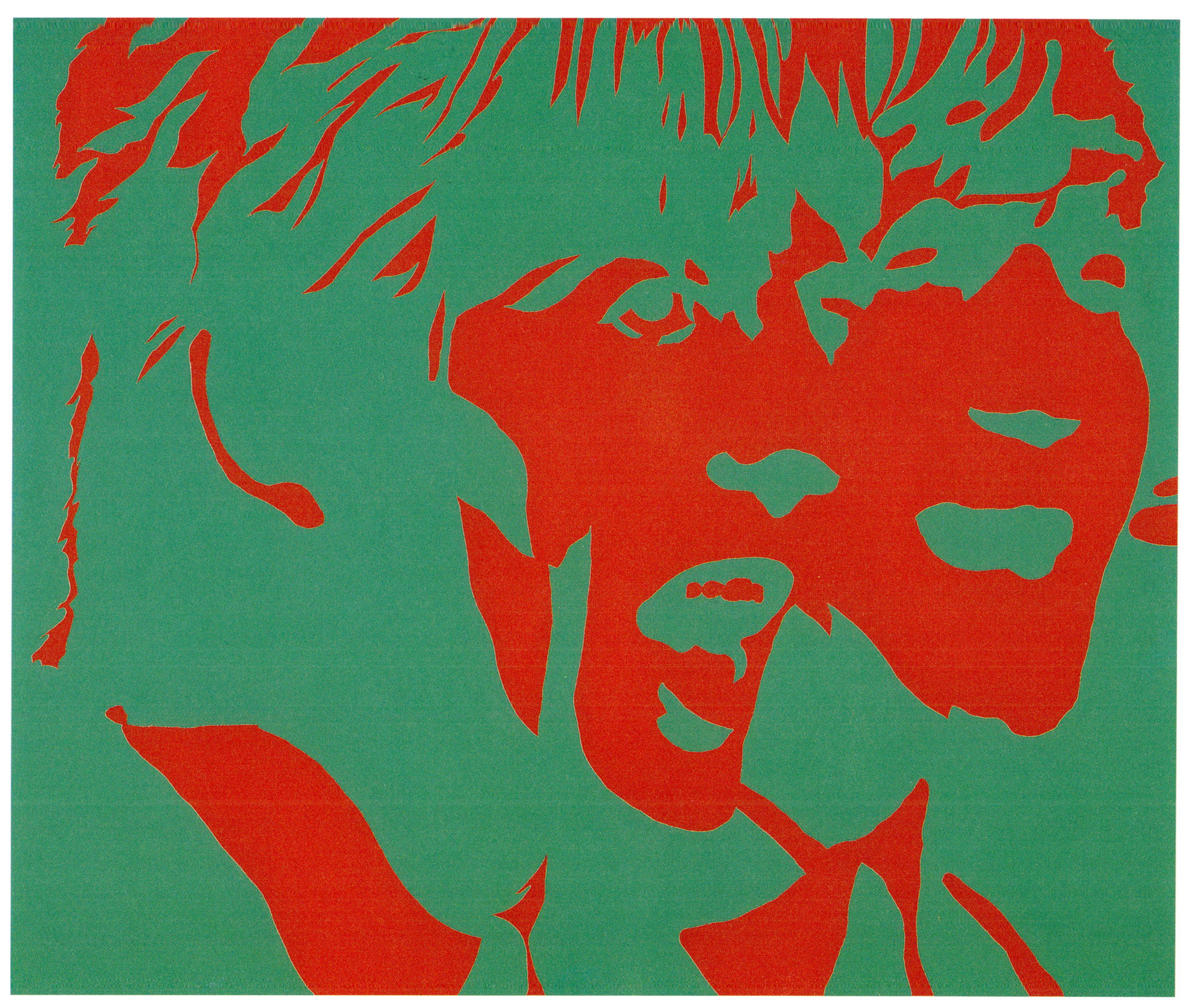

Romare Howard Bearden

1914–1988

Salome, 1973

acrylic and collage on Masonite, 40 × 50 inches
signed, upper left: *Romare / Bearden*
Gift of Elaine de Kooning (by exchange)

Pablo Picasso's invention of collage, an arrangement of paper, fabric, and other ordinary materials glued to a flat surface, revolutionized the concept of a work of art. Collage was a natural outgrowth of Picasso's study of African art, which often fragmented forms into essential components and used natural, found materials. Picasso's contemporary Henri Matisse reveled in the decorative potential of collage, using brightly colored paper for his celebrated series of cutouts.

Equating the improvisational aspects of collage to jazz music, Romare Bearden adapted it as the medium best suited to his temperament. Recognizing its ultimate origin in African art, Bearden devoted himself almost exclusively to collage from the mid-1960s, when, at the height of the civil-rights movement, he began to make photomontages, or collages composed from cut-up photographs, a type of art that relates to motion pictures. Although many of his images and stories are personal and relate to his African-American heritage, Bearden aspired to broader interpretations. His goal was to "bring Afro-American experience into art and give it a universal dimension."[1]

Bearden was born in Charlotte, North Carolina, but, as part of the African-American migration North, he was raised in Pittsburgh and Harlem. He studied at the Art Students League under George Grosz, the German émigré known for his caustic and satirical caricatures. Initially, Bearden did not dedicate himself totally to his art: in 1938 he joined the New York City Department of Social Services as a case worker, a position he held intermittently for almost thirty years.

During the 1950s Bearden worked in an abstract vein, a mode he later abandoned upon his discovery of collage's potential. Despite his obvious use of recognizable imagery, and the presence of razor-cut fragments of photographs, Bearden always maintained that the structure, not the subject, of a work of art is paramount. In *The Painter's Mind,* a treatise on art coauthored with Carl Holty, Bearden claimed: "But whatever the image, the only visual reality present is structure. There is no real face, no real ship, no real landscape, no real depth. These are illusions; the structure that supports them is not."[2] Yet the repertoire of Bearden's imagery—his childhood memories, his experiences in Harlem, his religious beliefs, and his thoughts on issues of the day—is compelling.

The Museum's collage, *Salome,* relates to a number of themes in Bearden's work and exemplifies an image with universal implications. Both the Old and New Testaments provided the artist with source material, often through the intermediary of Renaissance painters whom Bearden is known to have admired. Another recurring theme in Bearden's work is his depiction of family meals as ceremonial occurrences. Ritual pervades Bearden's work and was acknowledged by the artist in a series entitled *The Prevalence of Ritual,* to which the Museum's collage belongs. The rite of baptism was one of the artist's favorite themes, one that transcended a specific time and place. "In my work, if anything, I seek connections so that my paintings can't be only what they appear to represent. People in a baptism in a Virginia stream are linked to John the Baptist, to ancient purification, and to their African heritage."[3]

In the Bible, Salome was the protagonist in the story known as the Feast of Herod. Possibly intrigued by the timelessness of the episode's human passions, Bearden also may have been influenced by such early Italian Renaissance masters as Giotto. As told by the evangelists Matthew and Mark, the chilling tale of John the Baptist's death incorporates murder, seduction, treachery, fear, luxury, jealousy, slander, greed, and lust for power. Salome was a beautiful princess who danced at Herod's birthday celebration. Impressed by her charms, Herod vowed to give her anything she wanted, and, after consulting with her mother, Salome requested the head of John the Baptist, who was already captive in Herod's prison for making insinuating comments about the king's illicit relationship with Salome's mother. Reluctantly, Herod granted the wish, and John was decapitated.

Bearden artfully employed the collage technique to suggest some of the sumptuousness of Herod's court. Using actual fabric for Herod's cloak and hat, Bearden provided both visual and tactile interest to identify this character. Further distinguishing the king are the throne and the swath of royal fuchsia behind him. His bold gesture, with his fingers raised in mock horror at the saint's severed head, may be a reference to the later washing of hands, when Pilate attempted to absolve himself from any blame for the crucifixion of Christ. The masklike faces, reminiscent of African sculpture and Byzantine Madonnas, aptly display the dispassionate interest of the partici-pants. Silhouetted against a bright white background and highlighted by foil, a modern version of a gold-leaf halo, is John's head on a platter, the standard motif emblematic of his martyrdom. In an abrupt change of scale, a device frequently used by Bearden, the diminutive and mutilated body of the saint lies in the lower right corner. Also placed apart and to the right, a contrivance common in narrative paintings of the Renaissance, are the two henchmen completing the story of John's murder.

By the time Bearden began the Museum's collage he had abandoned photomontage. Instead of many fragmented and subdivided figures, his later work, like *Salome,* is dominated by a few key characters. Forms and shapes are larger and bolder, and the compositions are less complicated. Backgrounds typically consist of broad areas of bright color, either flat or sponged on, recalling some of the strident and improvisational qualities of the jazz that Bearden loved and knew so well. In his responsiveness to jazz and his use of bright colors and collagelike effects, Bearden resembled Stuart Davis, his friend and mentor. Bearden was inspired by eclectic sources, collecting ideas much as he collected papers, photographs, and fabrics for his collages. "Art is valuable, because for one reason we have direct access to it. Cézanne, the Africans, Matisse they put it *all* out there—their art, themselves."[4]

---

1. Bearden, as quoted in Michael Brenson, "A Collagist's Mosaic of God, Literature, and His People," *The New York Times,* 11 January 1987.

2. Romare Bearden and Carl Holty, *The Painter's Mind* (New York: Crown Publishers, 1969), 20.

3. Bearden, as quoted in Alexandra Anderson-Spivy, "Romare Bearden: A Modern Classicist," *Romare Bearden: The Human Condition* (New York: ACA Galleries, 1991), unpaginated.

4. Bearden to André Thibault, circa September 1987. Collection of André Thibault.

Born, Charlotte, North Carolina, 1914; attended Boston University, circa 1930–1932; graduated from New York University, 1935; studied with George Grosz at the Art Students League, New York, 1936–1937; worked as cartoonist, mid-1930s; employed as case worker, New York City Department of Social Services, 1938–1942, 1946–1949, and 1952–1966; military service, 1942–1945; to Paris and Italy, 1950 and 1961; taught at Williams College, Williamstown, Massachusetts, 1970; summered on St. Martin, the Caribbean, 1974–1987; died, New York, 1988.

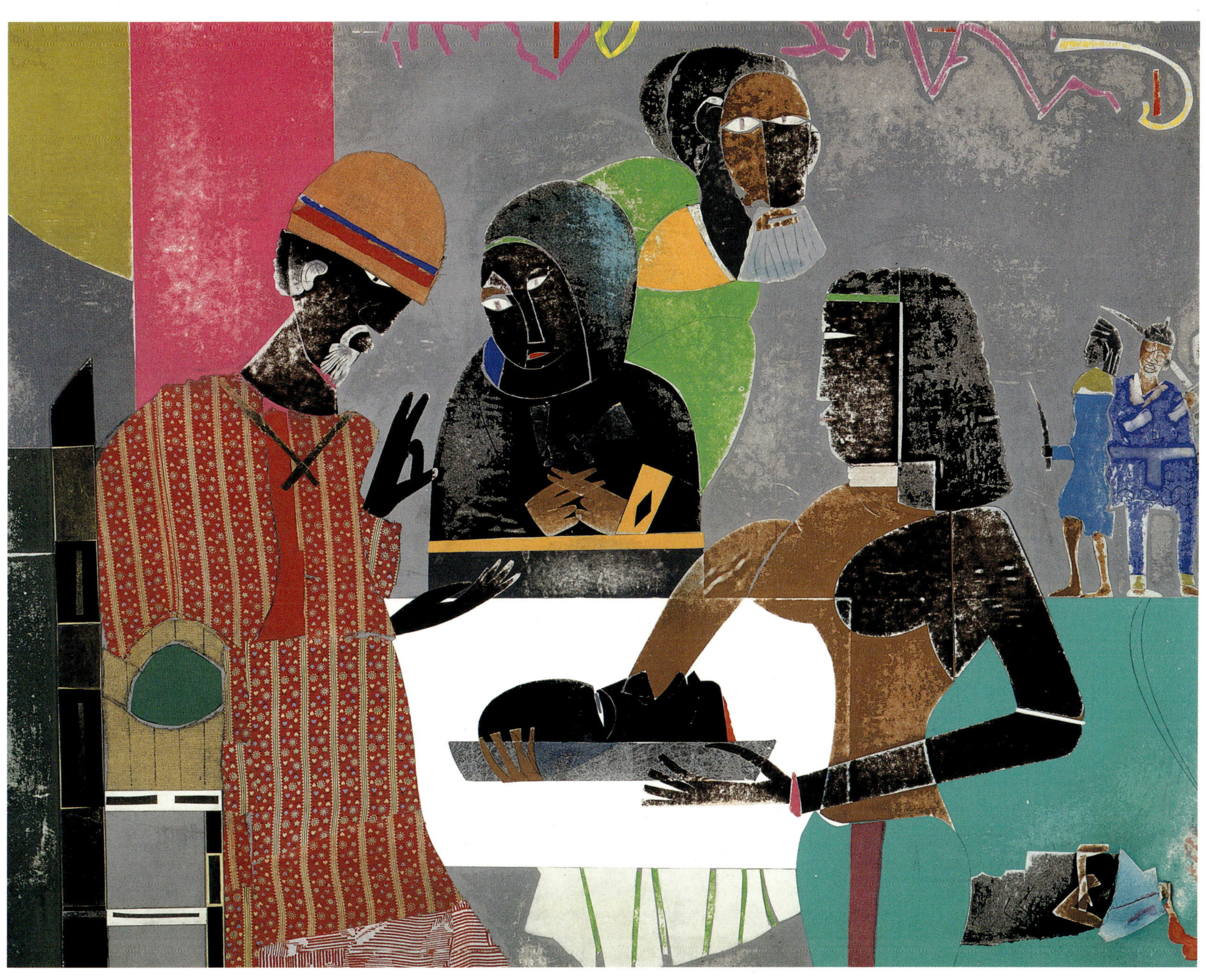

David Buchanan Parrish

born 1939

Hodaka, 1974

oil on canvas, 54 × 54 inches
signed, lower right: *D. Parrish '74*
Museum purchase with funds provided by The Museum Association, Inc., and the National Endowment for the Arts, 1988

Photorealism, which first emerged on the heels of the Pop movement in the late 1960s, unabashedly relies upon photography for both its production and its content. As a movement it has been viewed as a regressive fad in direct opposition to previous trends. Others argue that it is a natural outgrowth of Abstract Expressionism, Pop Art, and even Minimalism.[1] Photorealists use photography, typically in the form of projected slides, as a tool in the creation of their paintings. Although Photorealists share Pop artists' emphasis on imagery, they are generally less concerned with ironic commentaries on the decadence of popular culture.

While they employ similar working methods and share certain aesthetic ideals, the Photorealists rely on a broad variety of subject matter, ranging from the expansive and obsessively detailed cityscapes of Richard Estes to the monumental portrait heads of Chuck Close to the confrontational close-ups of David Parrish's motorcycles. Not unlike other contemporary artists, the Photorealists typically restrict themselves to everyday subjects. Nevertheless, they are adept at finding an infinite variety of visual opportunities within these limitations.

Parrish, for instance, appears preoccupied with motorcycles and, in his later work, with kitsch porcelain figurines of such celebrities as Elvis Presley and Marilyn Monroe. Like most Photorealist work, his paintings lack a clear focal point; instead, they offer a rich panoply of color and reflected light weighted equally throughout his compositions. This allover approach shares an essential aesthetic quality with Abstract Expressionism.

A longtime resident of Huntsville, Alabama, Parrish may have developed his interest in mechanistic imagery and slick metallic forms in a city whose contemporary identity is tied to high technology and missile and rocket research. After receiving his bachelor of fine arts degree from the University of Alabama, Parrish was employed for almost a decade making technical drawings, developing visual concepts, and designing exhibits for the aerospace industry, including the National Aeronautics and Space Administration. Although initially he aspired to be a magazine illustrator, Parrish seems to have benefited greatly from the demands of his design work, honing skills that serve him well as a Photorealist painter.

For his motorcycle series, Parrish made extensive photographic forays to motorcycle dealerships, often shooting as many as five or six rolls of color slides at a time. He was interested not only in the machines themselves but also in the showroom windows, lights, and reflections. Like photographs, Parrish's compositions are tightly cropped, with the image enlarged and close to the picture plane. The Museum's painting, *Hodaka,* is dominated by a single bike, but its iconlike singularity is almost consumed by the abundance of visual information that defines it. Parrish sees *Hodaka,* in which the emphasis is clearly on the multiple layering of reflections, as a departure from his earlier, more straightforward work. In the Museum's painting and in others like it, he recognizes that "the layering became ultimately so fractured and distorted that the machine is virtually disintegrated, and the paintings resemble abstractions."[2]

Although the image is frozen, movement is implicit. The motorcycle, a powerful and fast machine, suggests speed, and its highly reflective surfaces capture the dance of light that enlivens chrome, glass, and steel. Deep spatial illusion is strictly controlled, if not denied, even as the reflections incorporate disparate elements outside the painting's view, including the artist capturing himself in the act of photographing motorcycles, to be seen just to the right of center. This detail, which has a distinguished tradition in the art of Jan van Eyck and Diego Velázquez, adds another complex and personalizing dimension.

As late as 1972 Parrish himself had never ridden a motorcycle, even after painting them for several years. His treatment of motorcycle subjects is frequently linked to his father, who as a young adult traveled around the country on a motorcycle, at times with the circus and later with his wife. Regarding his intention to humanize his machines, Parrish has commented, "I associate them with the people who ride them; they're always somewhere in the background. They're invisible, but their influence is still there."[3]

---

1. See Louis K. Meisel, *Photo-Realism* (New York: Harry N. Abrams, 1985).

2. Parrish, interview with Nancy Foote, "The Photo-Realists: 12 Interviews," *Art in America,* November–December 1972, 83.

3. Parrish, interview with Foote, "The Photo-Realists," 84.

Born, Birmingham, Alabama, 1939; attended Washington and Lee University, Lexington, Virginia, 1957–1958, and the University of Alabama, Tuscaloosa, 1958–1961, graduating with a bachelor of fine arts degree; moved to Huntsville, Alabama; employed in aerospace industry, 1962– early 1970s; resides, Huntsville.

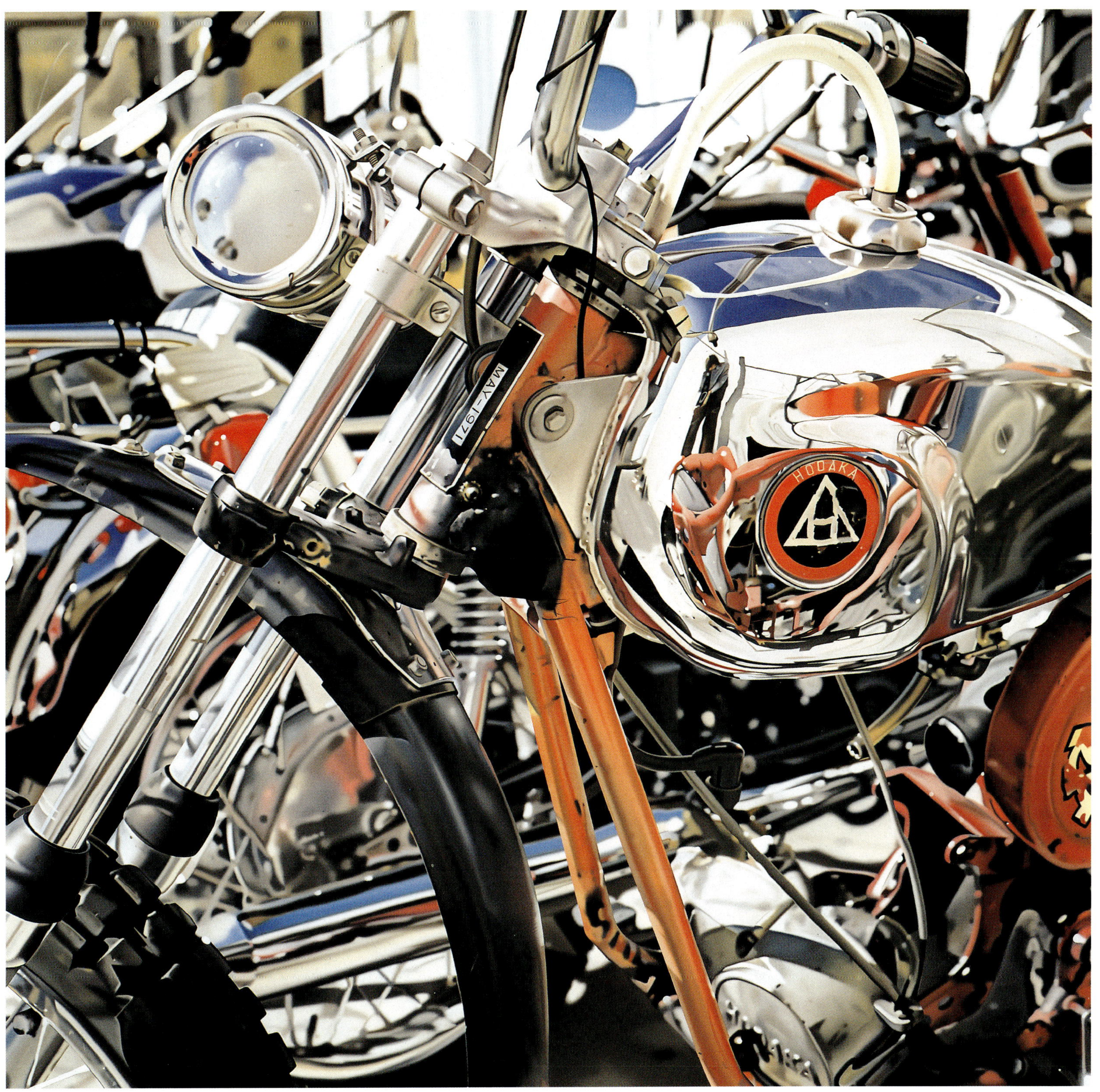
MAY-1971
HODAKA

Christo Javacheff

born 1935

Running Fence (Project for Sonoma County and Marin County, State of California) **and** ***Map of Running Fence*****, 1976**

pastel and charcoal on paper, 42 × 96 inches
signed, lower right: *Christo, 1976*
printed map and crayon on paper, 15 × 96 inches
Gift of Mr. and Mrs. Arthur Magill

Conceptual Art represents a dramatic redirection away from formal concerns toward more intellectual ones. As the term indicates, the idea of the work of art takes precedence over its physical manifestation; many conceptual works never make it beyond the proposal stage. A related art form, Earthworks, generally occurs outside of museums and galleries. Built outdoors and on a large scale, these works often raise questions about man's impact on the environment. Both Dennis Oppenheim and Robert Smithson attempted to reconfigure nature in a manner related to primeval peoples. The former's *Maze* created a laboratorylike labyrinth on a field in northern Wisconsin using corn and bales of hay; Smithson's *Spiral Jetty,* consisting of rocks and mud projected into the Great Salt Lake, Utah, cogently raised ecological issues pertaining to humankind's relation to nature.

The work of Christo is a unique marriage between Conceptual Art and Earthworks. Employing huge quantities of fabric, he reshapes both nature and the man-made environment. His typical method is to wrap buildings or elements of landscape in thousands of yards of fabric. In some instances, the actual project is thwarted by politics or lack of funding; the success of Christo's ambitious feats depends upon a partnership with his wife, Jeanne-Claude, and the coordinated efforts of engineers, fabric handlers, government authorities, and volunteers. In addition to the draped landscape or wrapped object, Christo makes drawings, prints, photographs, and films that document the various phases of each project. Unlike the inherently impermanent projects themselves, these items can be retained and collected, allowing the artist to raise income to support himself and his work.

Born Christo Javacheff in Gabrovo, Bulgaria, the artist received conventional academic training in Sofia before he fled the Communists. After six years in Paris, he moved to New York in 1964. His reputation is international, and his projects range worldwide from Colorado to Florida and from France to Australia. With some degree of hubris, Christo aspires to greatness: "I want to present something that is not an image, but a real thing—like the pyramids in Egypt or the Great Wall of China."[1] His choice of these two structures is apt: his wrapped monuments in their inchoate mass resemble the weighty solidity of the pyramids, and his fences, in their linear ambling through nature, relate to the Great Wall of China.

Running Fence, a four-year-long project in Sonoma and Marin counties in California, conceptually paralleled the Great Wall as it rose and fell along the rolling hillsides north of San Francisco, finally intersecting with the Pacific Ocean. An impressively large undertaking, it extended twenty-four and a half miles across the property of fifty-nine ranch owners from whom Christo had to gain permission to erect his curtain. Unlike the solidity, durability, and permanence of the Chinese wall, *Running Fence* was delicate, fluid, and temporary. Constructed of white nylon fabric suspended from steel cables, Christo's fence was flexible enough to waver in the breeze and was penetrable by cattle, wildlife, and passenger cars. Christo states, "It is my job to enhance the environment, not damage it."[2] To this end he commissions environmental-impact studies for his projects. Their relatively short duration does not seem to perturb the artist, who eagerly embraces the process and the challenges of his art form: "For me aesthetics is everything involved in the process—the workers, the politics, the negotiations, the construction difficulties, the dealing with hundreds of people. The whole process becomes an aesthetic—that's what I am interested in, discovering the process. I put myself in dialogue with other people."[3]

As part of any project, Christo makes numerous visual proposals that employ drawings, maps, and photographs. Most projects are also documented in photography and film; many are published as books. The Museum's piece combines two interrelated and complementary components: a topographical map outlined by the artist and a site drawing with construction specifics. The left-hand portion of the map remains blank, mirroring the white expanse of the fence on the left-hand side of the drawing. As a site rendering, the drawing provides for both a close-up view of the fence and a vista as it trails off into the distance. Drawn in earth-colored pastels and charcoal, the work reveals the dialectic tension between Christo's fence and nature.

For *Running Fence* Christo used white nylon that not only stood in contrast to the dark earth but also reflected light, glowing warm at sunset and shining brightly at noon. For his later project in Biscayne Bay, Florida, color selection was again an important consideration. He chose an intense flamingo color, one with both aesthetic and symbolic connotations. The pink polypropylene was designed to enshroud a series of eleven islands near Miami; the flaming artificiality of the fabric stood in stark contrast to the deep green of the island vegetation and the sea. Christo may have chosen flamingo as the color emblematic of Florida bird life, further canonized by plastic lawn ornaments. Because the location of *Surrounded Islands* was aquatic, it offered additional challenges as well as visual opportunities. The vista on *Surrounded Islands* was gained from land, sea, and air. From these perspectives *Surrounded Islands* was compelling but, like many of Christo's projects, also controversial. The artist labors to defuse critics who worry about delicate environments, the expense, and the fleeting nature of his work. Christo defends his approach: "Even though a work of art has great physical presence, it also must be very fragile. It must disappear. Art doesn't exist forever."[4]

---

1. Christo, as quoted in William C. Seitz, *Art in the Age of Aquarius, 1955–1970* (Washington, D.C.: Smithsonian Institution Press, 1992), 144.
2. Christo, "Artist in Exile," *Horizon,* July–August 1983, 24.
3. Christo, as quoted in Grace Glueck, "The Gap That Wouldn't Stay Closed," *The New York Times,* 20 August 1972.
4. Christo, in "The Artist Raps about Wrapping," *Newsweek,* 22 June 1981, 14.

Born, Gabrovo, Bulgaria, 1935; studied at the Fine Arts Academy, Sofia, 1952–1956, and at the Vienna Fine Arts Academy, 1957; moved to Paris, 1958, and New York, 1964; resides, New York.

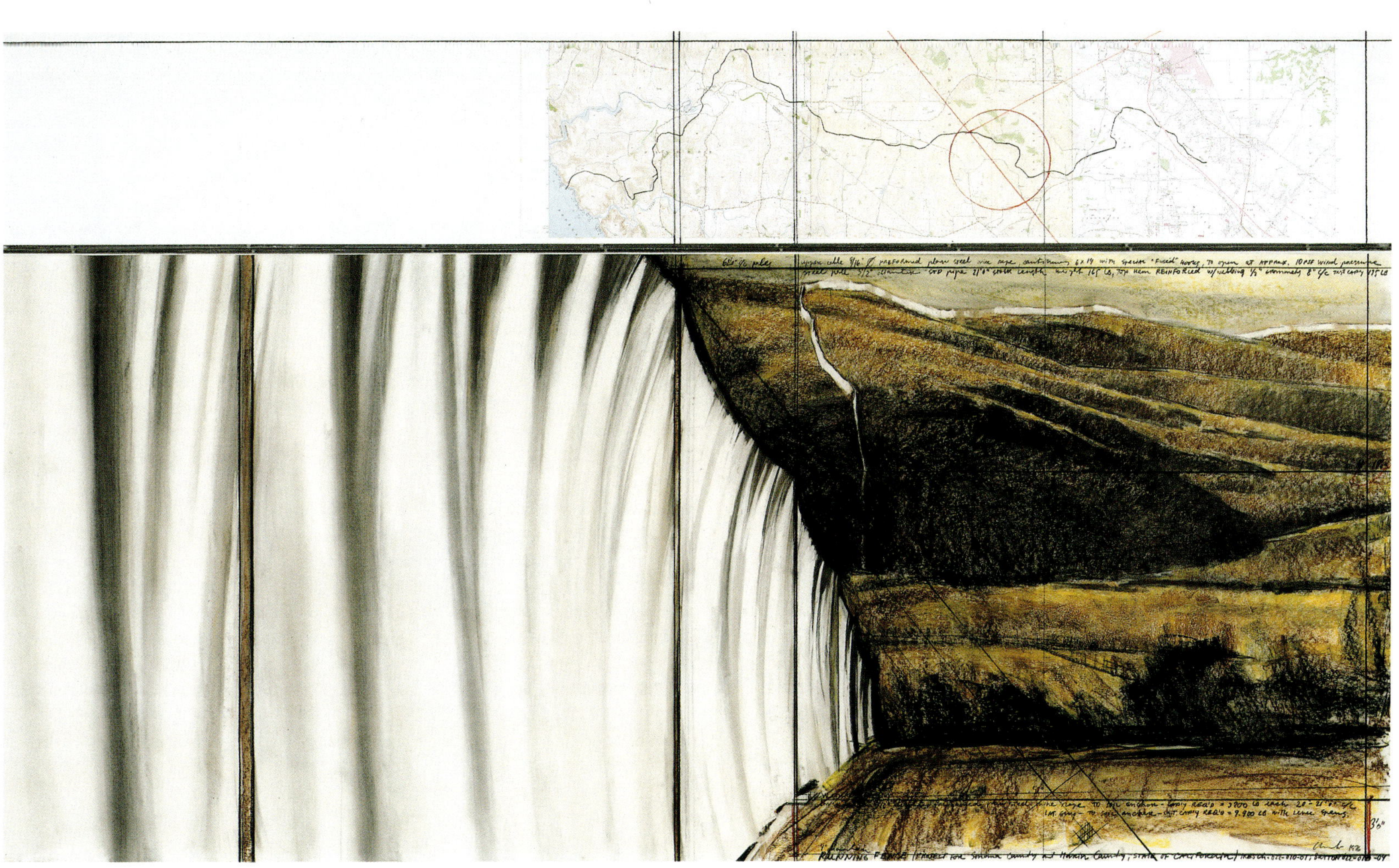

Lynda Marie Benglis

born 1941

Peter, 1974

enamel, acrylic resin, and hot glue on aluminum foil, 60 × 17 × 11 inches
Museum purchase with funds donated by the Arthur and Holly Magill Foundation

The Happenings of the early 1960s relied upon spontaneity and innovation. One-time events, they were not collectible, although they were regularly documented in photography and film. Over time, Happenings artists like Allan Kaprow pursued purely conceptual work, while others, including Jim Dine, Claes Oldenburg, and Red Grooms, moved from theatrical expressionism toward the creation of tangible objects. Oldenburg and Grooms challenged viewer expectations, altering the scale, media, and composition of common objects and scenes through the use of cheap materials and caricature. The art of Lynda Benglis shares many of these traits. In her inventive and spontaneous use of a vast range of materials, she often creates ephemeral or installation-oriented works. She is overtly self-promotional, in a manner similar to the theatrical aspect of Happenings.

A native of Lake Charles, Louisiana, Benglis studied art at Sophie Newcomb College, New Orleans, with Ida Kohlmeyer. In 1964 she moved to New York and for a short while continued her studies at the Brooklyn Museum Art School. She quickly moved away from conventional painting on canvas and explored new substances and processes. She learned to make her own latex paint and to work with pigmented polyurethane foam, which she poured around shaped armatures attached to the wall. The resulting forms are organic and molten, suggestive of strange prehistoric behemoths. They are simultaneously attractive and repulsive.

That Benglis embraced dichotomy is evident in her work and in her life. Frustrated by the machismo of the New York art world, Benglis drew attention to herself by provocatively posing nude as both pin-up queen and pornographic film star. Rather than join her feminist counterparts in their attempts to gain recognition and equality on the merits of their work, she exploited the stereotype of woman as sex object to disrupt the status quo. These antics succeeded in bringing Benglis controversy as well as notoriety.

Concerned about the fleeting nature of her elaborate temporary installations, Benglis began to gravitate toward individual objects that function either alone or in sets. The *Knot* series, exemplified by *Peter,* was one of her first attempts and involved wall-hung constructions inventively fabricated. Benglis considered them akin to frozen gestures.[1] The *Knots* challenge the demarcation line between painting and sculpture and can be read as three-dimensional gestures similar to the sweeping calligraphy of the Abstract Expressionist painter Franz Kline, whom Benglis admires. Variously titled with Greek letters, the names of male friends, or in emulation of the military's phonetic alphabet, the *Knots* twist and turn inside out, like pretzels. The earliest examples, including *Peter,* are brightly colored and, at times, are highlighted with glitter and enamel paint. In their scale and in their contours many of the *Knots* take on anthropomorphic qualities, appearing as animated human ciphers. Benglis also identified the *Knots* as quick symbols of emotional states.[2]

In addition to creating her installation pieces and wall-bound sculptures, Benglis was an active videographer throughout the 1970s. In this medium, Benglis released her frozen gestures and indulged in the recording of events as they freely evolved. She explained her involvement with video as an expression of her feminism: "I saw it as a big macho game, a big heroic, Abstract Expressionist macho sexist game. It's about territory."[3] One of her major collaborators was Robert Morris, whose artistic idiom paralleled Benglis's. Both indulged in self-parodying sexist imagery to promote their work and made wall-hung objects of distinctive materials: thick, dark felt for Morris and lightweight, metallic surfaces for Benglis. The theme that consistently dominates Benglis's video work is the dynamic between male and female. "I feel that art is an intellectual process which both questions and affirms the very nature of being. My concerns of identity within and outside the confines of my studio or working situation have everything to do with my experience. And my experience is primarily that of an artist and I am a female."[4]

---

1. Robert Pincus-Witten, "Lynda Benglis: The Frozen Gesture," *Artforum,* November 1974, 56.
2. Susan Krane, *Lynda Benglis* (Atlanta, Ga.: High Museum of Art, 1991), 35.
3. Benglis, as quoted in Pincus-Witten, "Frozen Gesture," 58.
4. Benglis, as quoted in "Eight Artists Reply: Why Have There Been No Great Women Artists?" *Art News,* January 1971, 43.

Born, Lake Charles, Louisiana, 1941; graduated from Sophie Newcomb College, New Orleans, bachelor of fine arts degree, 1964; moved to New York, 1964; attended Brooklyn Museum Art School, 1964; taught at the University of Rochester, 1970–1972, Hunter College, New York, 1972 and 1980, and California Institute of the Arts, Valencia, 1973, 1974, and 1976; resides, New York and East Hampton, New York.

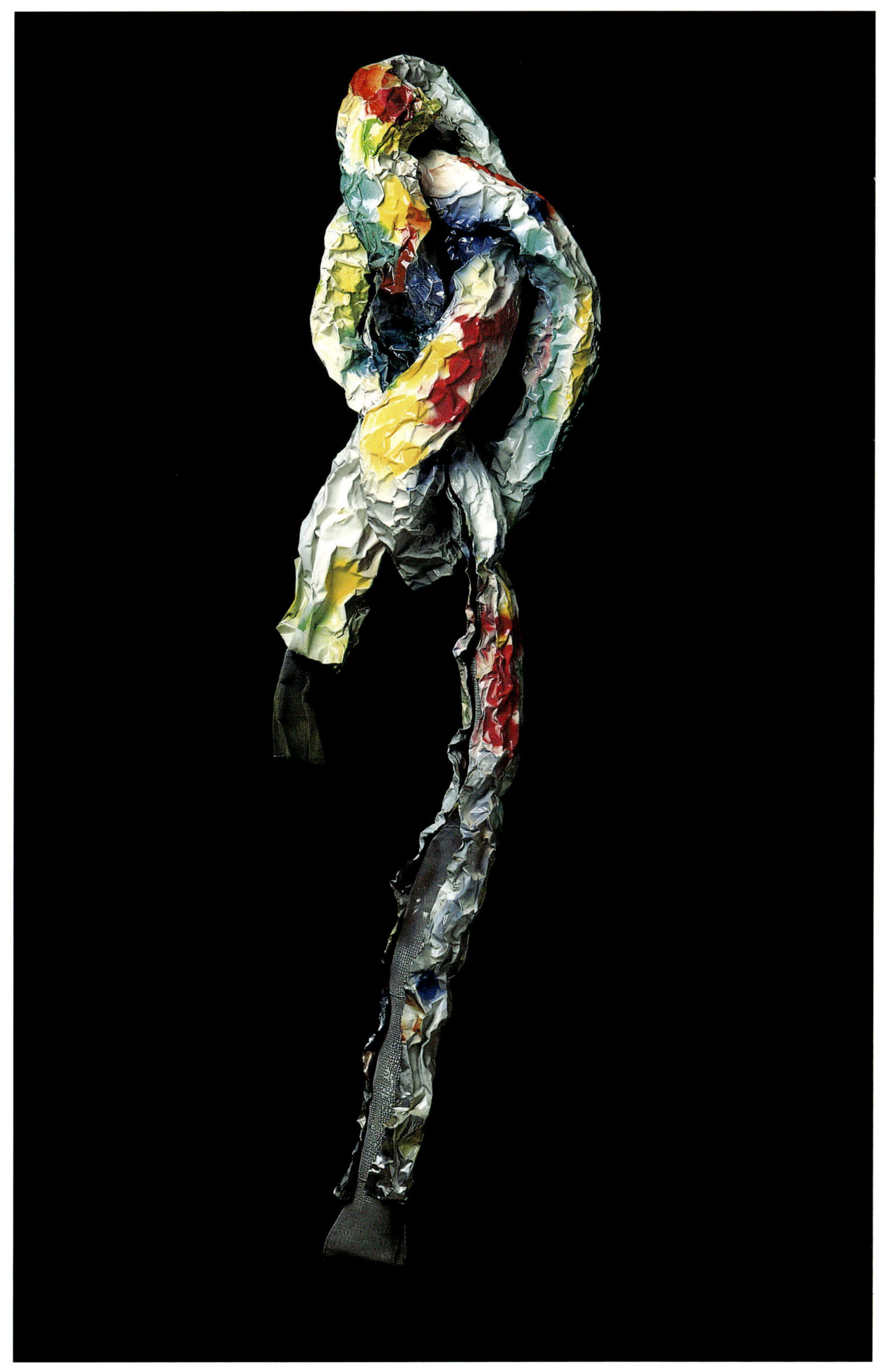

Valerie Jaudon

born 1945

Egypt River, 1980

oil and metallic pigment on canvas, 90 × 98 inches
signed, on reverse: *Valerie Jaudon 1980*
Museum purchase with funds donated by
the Arthur and Holly Magill Foundation

At midcentury many American painters were more concerned with the methods and philosophies of art making than with subject matter. While many experimented with new materials and innovative techniques, others were preoccupied with color and design. Josef Albers's investigations, which culminated in the publication *The Interaction of Color,* established the premise that visual perception is affected by the relationships of colors to one another as well as by each color's hue, value, and intensity. Similarly, line and shape alter perception and, when combined with color, can create certain illusions. In the 1960s, while numerous artists indulged in the optical illusions of Op Art, others were selective in their choice of visual effects. Both Ellsworth Kelly and Frank Stella eliminated the lighthearted, illusionary aspect of Op Art in favor of sober, geometric color compositions, often on unconventionally shaped canvases.

In the mid-1970s a close-knit group of painters built upon the visual complexities of Op Art by emphasizing its decorative potential. Featuring repetitive design motifs, their work earned the designation *Pattern and Decoration,* a term that, like Pop and Op, has some pejorative connotations. One of the leaders of the Pattern and Decoration movement is Valerie Jaudon. Rather than rely on purely optical formulae, Jaudon often emulates designs found in Celtic and Islamic art.

Jaudon was born in Greenville, Mississippi, and attended the Mississippi State University for Women in Columbus. She pursued her interest in art at the Memphis Academy of Art and at the University of the Americas in Mexico City, and subsequently in London.

The focus of Jaudon's work has been large-format symmetrical compositions devoted to allover patterns. In the early 1970s she was affiliated with an architectural firm, and although she did not serve as a draftsman, Jaudon's process of planning each painting reflects her experience working with architects. In *Egypt River* Jaudon's imagery recalls both Persian textile designs and medieval architecture. Salient arches, both pointed and curved, are arranged around a central axis, reminiscent of the structural diagram of a Gothic cathedral. Angles intersect with arcs, and diagonals weave in and out among verticals in a network of decorative arabesques. The title of the painting derives from Jaudon's background in Mississippi; for fifteen years she named her work after places in her home state.

Enhancing the exotic quality of the painting and its analogies to Celtic metalwork is the forceful contrast of bronze-toned bands and solid black. The metallic and tactile natures of the bands make them appear to project forward, away from the black background. The interstices between the bands also assume geometric and quasi-geometric shapes.

As pure painting, the work of Jaudon and some of the other Pattern and Decoration artists appears to have no message, but, in the context of the political activism of the 1970s, this was not the case. Jaudon, along with Joyce Kozloff, authored a polemic on why the label "decorative" was found offensive. They explained: "The prejudice against the decorative has a long history and is based on hierarchies—fine art above decorative art, Western art above non-Western art, men's art above women's art."[1] That there was a clear connection of Pattern and Decoration artists, not all of whom were women, and the feminist movement was further articulated by Kozloff:

> We used to get together and talk, and among ourselves there was a feeling of total equality with the men. The art world was not so marketplace-driven in the 1970s as it is now—there wasn't so much money around. We really did help each other. Some of the critics even got interested in the issues of the women's movement. And there were a lot of women curators in the museums by this time. We really created a sort of old-girl's network.[2]

---

1. Jaudon and Joyce Kozloff, "Art Hysterical Notions of Progress and Culture," *Heresies* 4 (Winter 1977–1978), 38.

2. Kozloff, as quoted in Calvin Tomkins, "Righting the Balance," in Randy Rosen and Catherine C. Brawer, eds., *Making Their Mark: Women Artists Move into the Mainstream* (New York: Abbeville Press, 1989), 46.

Born, Greenville, Mississippi, 1945; studied at the Mississippi State College for Women, Columbus, 1963–1965, the Memphis Academy of Art, Memphis, Tennessee, 1965, University of the Americas, Mexico City, 1966–1967, and St. Martin's School of Art, London, 1968–1969; resides in New York and teaches at Hunter College.

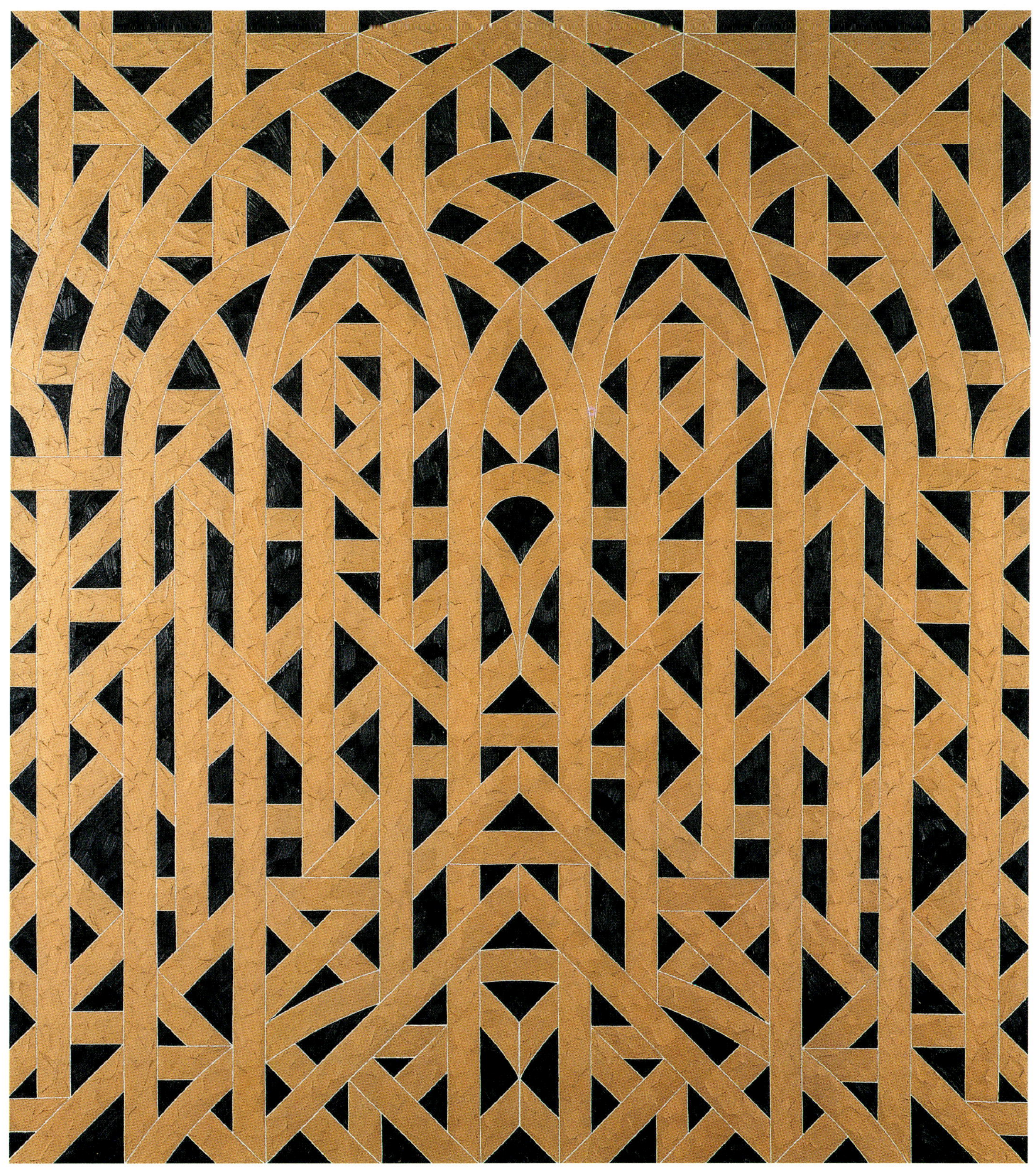

Robert H. Colescott

born 1925

Les Demoiselles d'Alabama (Des Nudas), 1985

acrylic on canvas, 94 × 90 inches
signed, lower right: *R. Colescott '85*
Museum purchase

Throughout history artists have responded to the examples of their predecessors, seeking either to build on the tradition of art making or to challenge its assumptions. Many are simply influenced by the handling of media or by the imagery, but in this century artists consciously appropriated, almost to the point of plagiarism, elements from the work of others. Impressed with the expressive potential of tribal sculpture, Pablo Picasso, in such paintings as *Les Demoiselles d'Avignon,* employed the dark brooding coloration, angular shapes, and stylized design of African masks. More blatant in his appropriations, Marcel Duchamp took a reproduction of the famed *Mona Lisa* and violated it by adding a mustache and a provocative caption. Following Duchamp's lead, Jasper Johns borrowed from the everyday world such familiar symbols as flags, targets, and numerals, while the Pop artists, Andy Warhol and Roy Lichtenstein in particular, appropriated vacuous commercial images from the mass media.

By the 1980s appropriation was a legitimate tactic that fed a proliferation of hybrid styles. This eclecticism is exemplified in a series of paintings by Robert Colescott in which the artist pointedly adapted the style and modified the imagery of well-known masterpieces. Colescott's purpose was to question the authenticity of traditional Western art and to comment upon racial and gender prejudice. To understand completely his particular bias, it is important to be familiar with the appropriated original.

Colescott was born in Oakland, California, and earned both his bachelor's and master's degrees from the University of California at Berkeley, where his primary interest was abstraction. He went to Paris in 1949 to study with Fernand Léger who, despite the fact that his own work inclined toward abstraction, encouraged Colescott to explore the human figure. Another important stimulus for Colescott's appreciation both for the figure and for art history were several years spent in Cairo, where he was a faculty member at the American Research Center and American University.

In 1975 Colescott began to revise classic paintings. In these parodies he typically substituted African-American figures for white ones, mining the richness of the original and adding his own ironic ethnic twist. In his version of *The Arnolfini Wedding* by Jan van Eyck, the bride is African-American and the groom is white, a situation that raises the issue of miscegenation. In his revision of Willem de Kooning's *Woman,* Colescott transposed the familiar face of Aunt Jemima onto de Kooning's frenzied female archetype; the result is a disturbing image that disrupts the stereotype of Jemima as a warm and loving earth mother. Employing a popular icon of American history, *George Washington Crossing the Delaware* by Emanuel Leutze, Colescott replaced the father of this country with his namesake, George Washington Carver, a clever assault on textbook American history that often overlooks the contributions of slaves and their descendants.

In the Museum's painting, *Les Demoiselles d'Alabama,* Colescott appropriated Picasso's seminal painting *Les Demoiselles d'Avignon.* Painted in 1907, Picasso's canvas generated controversy, in part for its depiction of five nude women in a bordello, but also for its fractured conception of space and its overt references to African sculpture, especially in the two figures on the right. Giving the modern masterpiece its comeuppance, Colescott paints contemporary women, three of whom are clearly descendants of African slaves, a fact alluded to by the title *d'Alabama.*

Colescott has contemporized, Americanized, and Southernized one of this century's most pivotal paintings. As he explained: "I wanted to turn it into an American painting, not a French or Spanish one. Like Picasso's, mine is set in a brothel, but this brothel is in Phenix City, Alabama, the wickedest city in America. . . . Picasso took live models and abstracted them according to his interpretation of the geometry in African art. I thought I would turn his process around and express the reality of the lusty women he painted. I hoped to possess his images, take them over, make them different."[1]

Overall, Colescott remains faithful to the original, at least in the arrangement and poses of the five women. Even the dimensions of the canvas approximate those of the original, making the figures slightly larger than life size. But his substitution of dark skin in the two central figures is a striking example of role reversal. Their darkness is further contrasted with the lightness and blondness of the figure in the lower right. Colescott also remarks punningly on the "painted lady" aspect of the women with their garish lips and fingernails. With tongue in cheek, the artist alters another telling and symbolic detail in the lower foreground; the still life now contains a slice of watermelon, a long-standing stereotypical attribute of Southern African-Americans.

Colescott's intent is both to amuse and to provoke by debunking deep-seated biases. He once remarked about his aspirations: "I want to paint ideas of freedom of expression which are so important to a democracy. And art can transcend bigotry. I had a show in Greenville, South Carolina. People saw the work as art and were very supportive. It's the kind of place where I'm sure people had strong prejudices. . . . It challenges people when you start painting about race."[2] In fact some of the most outspoken criticism has come from fellow African-Americans who claim that Colescott is only reinforcing the old stereotypes.

In many ways, Colescott's art-historical series is instructive about the viability, relevance, and resilience of the history of art. As *New York Times* critic John Russell stated: "What he proves is that great images retain their potency, no matter how roughly the world treats them."[3]

---

1. Colescott, as quoted in Matthew Diehl, "Picasso Was Here," *Art & Antiques,* February 1989, 38.
2. Colescott, as quoted in Marsha Miro, "Satiric Works Tell the Tale about Racial Relations," *Detroit Free Press,* 25 October 1992.
3. John Russell, *New York Times,* 9 January 1981.

Born, Oakland, California, 1925; received bachelor's and master's degrees from University of California, Berkeley, 1949 and 1952; studied in Paris with Fernand Léger, 1949–1950; taught at Portland State University, Oregon, 1957–1966, in Cairo, Egypt, at American Research Center, 1964–1965, and the American University, 1966–1967, California State College, Stanislaus, 1970–1974, University of California at Berkeley, 1974–1979, San Francisco Art Institute, 1979–1985; teaches University of Arizona, 1983 to the present; resides in Tucson.

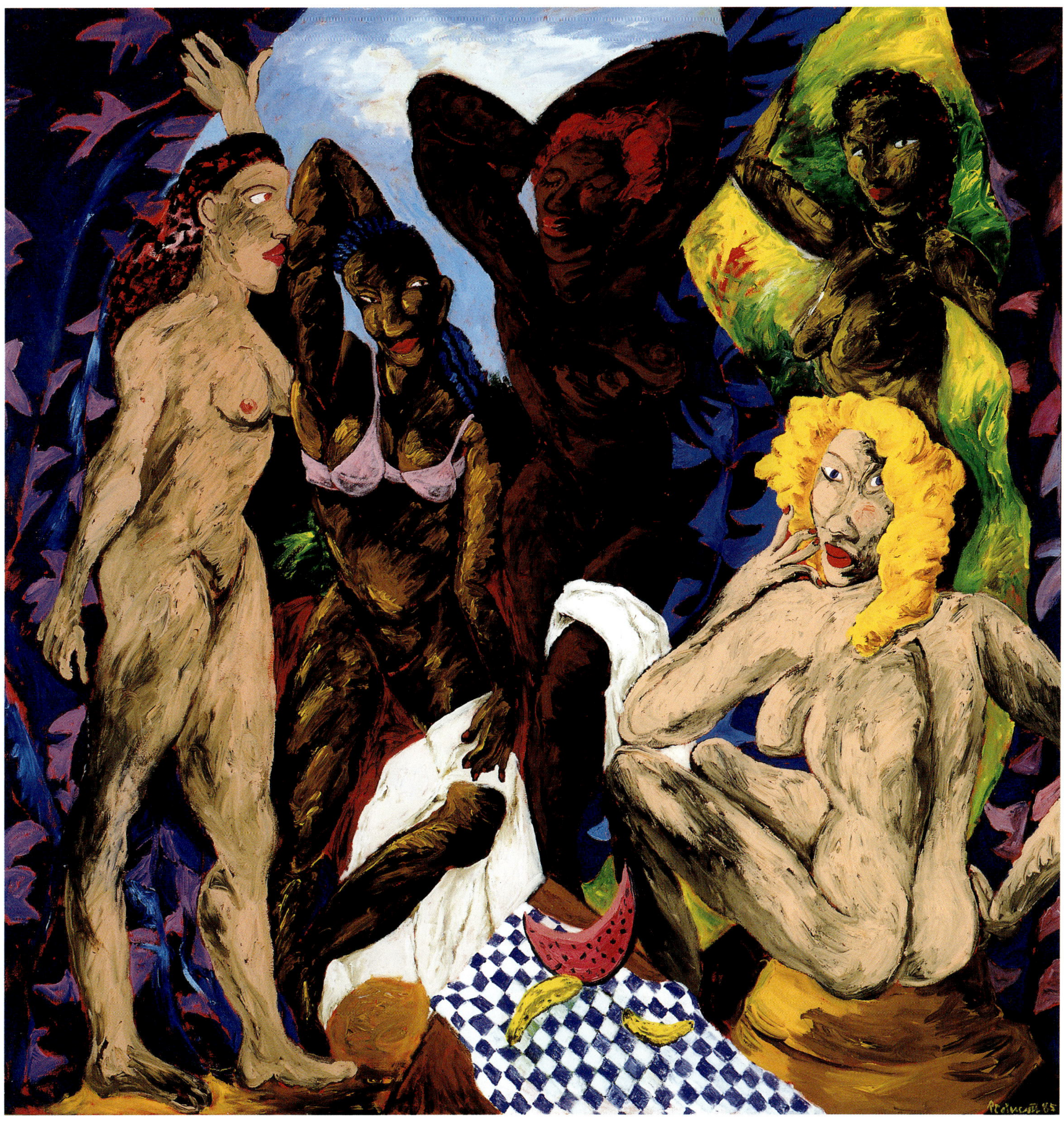

Frederick James Brown

born 1945

Billie's Blues, 1986

oil on linen, 90¼ × 78¼ inches
signed, on verso, upper right: *F. J. Brown, 1986*
Museum purchase

Frustrated by the emotional detachment of Pop Art, several artists in the 1970s and 1980s revitalized the expressionist tradition. Having attained a highly respected position as an Abstract Expressionist, Philip Guston led the return to a form of figurative expressionism; his self-deprecating depictions and haunting images of Ku Klux Klansmen are potent and unsettling statements. A group of younger and brasher artists, including Julian Schnabel and Jean-Michel Basquiat, reintroduced spontaneous brushwork that evoked the spirit of aboriginal cultures as well as urban graffiti writers. Their so-called Neo-Expressionism was mirrored beyond the confines of New York by numerous artists working abroad, especially in Italy and Germany, which have a long-standing expressionist heritage.

Frederick Brown, by focusing on intensely religious subjects as well as contemporary jazz figures, also participated in this trend toward exuberant style and emotional content. A native of Greensboro, Georgia, Brown grew up on the south side of Chicago, an area renowned for its blues music. Encountering a pair of Chicago blues performers at a concert in Denmark, Brown discovered that they were better known in Europe than in their own country; they also expressed concern that after their deaths they would be quickly forgotten. Both died shortly thereafter, and Brown resolved not to let them, and others like them, slip into oblivion.

Although there was little danger that the notorious and tragic Billie Holiday, the famed Duke Ellington, or the popular trumpeter Louis Armstrong would fade from memory, Brown has painted all three in his series of approximately fifty paintings devoted to jazz and blues musicians. Working from photographs and film images Brown captures salient characteristics of each performer, often exaggerating eyes, mouths, and hands. Most of the portrayals are close-up head shots depicted larger-than-life, referring to the celebrity status of each subject.

The Museum's painting, *Billie's Blues,* differs from the others in its narrative and emblematic quality. Brown also admits that this painting has an agenda: "Of course that's about Billie Holiday and the tragedy she went through, her final end, the drugs—it's sort of a graphic story of Billie Holiday with an anti-drug message to it—more than anything, though, just the story of Billie Holiday."[1] In this context Brown blatantly depicts a demonic, needle-wielding figure on the singer's shoulder, an allusion to drug addiction as "a monkey on the back." Nearby is a grave marked by a cross with Holiday's dates, 1915–1959, clear testimony to her death from substance abuse. Holiday, represented in her trademark fur coat, dominates the painting; she looms over a skeleton, whose mouth she covers with her right hand, a suffocating act that connects with her own self-destruction. In the left background, in front of the New York skyline, is a haunting lynching scene, an unmitigated reference to the song "Strange Fruit." With lyrics and music written specifically for Holiday, it became a chilling reminder of her own Southern roots and the discrimination she endured. Brown's image relates specifically to the first refrain: "Southern trees bear a strange fruit / Blood on the leaves and blood on the root / Black bodies swinging in the southern breeze / Strange fruit hanging from the poplar trees."[2]

Significantly, Brown has painted mostly blue tonalities, the color literally associated with Holiday's musical style. The palette also relates to an early phase of Pablo Picasso's career in which he depicted gaunt, depressed individuals, especially performers. *Billie's Blues* recalls Picasso's Blue Period depiction of a guitarist, whose emaciated figure and bent posture suggest utter hopelessness.[3] Brown has alleviated the monochrome of his canvas with a bright touch of red at Holiday's lips, bringing attention to the singer's mouth, the primary vehicle of her art. Arrayed across the bottom in a series resembling piano keys are the names of Holiday's fellow musicians. At right the words *Paris New York* connect her to the cities where she gained her reputation. Like the bluesmen who initially inspired Brown's series and like many other creative African-Americans, including painters and writers, Holiday was better received in France than in her own country.

---

1. Brown, as quoted in Marty Berry, "Artist's Paintings Brighten Museum," *The Greenville News,* 4 January 1988.

2. "Strange Fruit," words by Lewis Allan, copyright 1939, Edward B. Marks Music Company; copyright renewed. Used with permission. All rights reserved.

3. Ruth Bass, *Frederick Brown* (New York: Marlborough Gallery, 1987), 3.

Born, Greensboro, Georgia, 1945; bachelor of arts degree, Southern Illinois University, Carbondale, 1968; resides, New York.

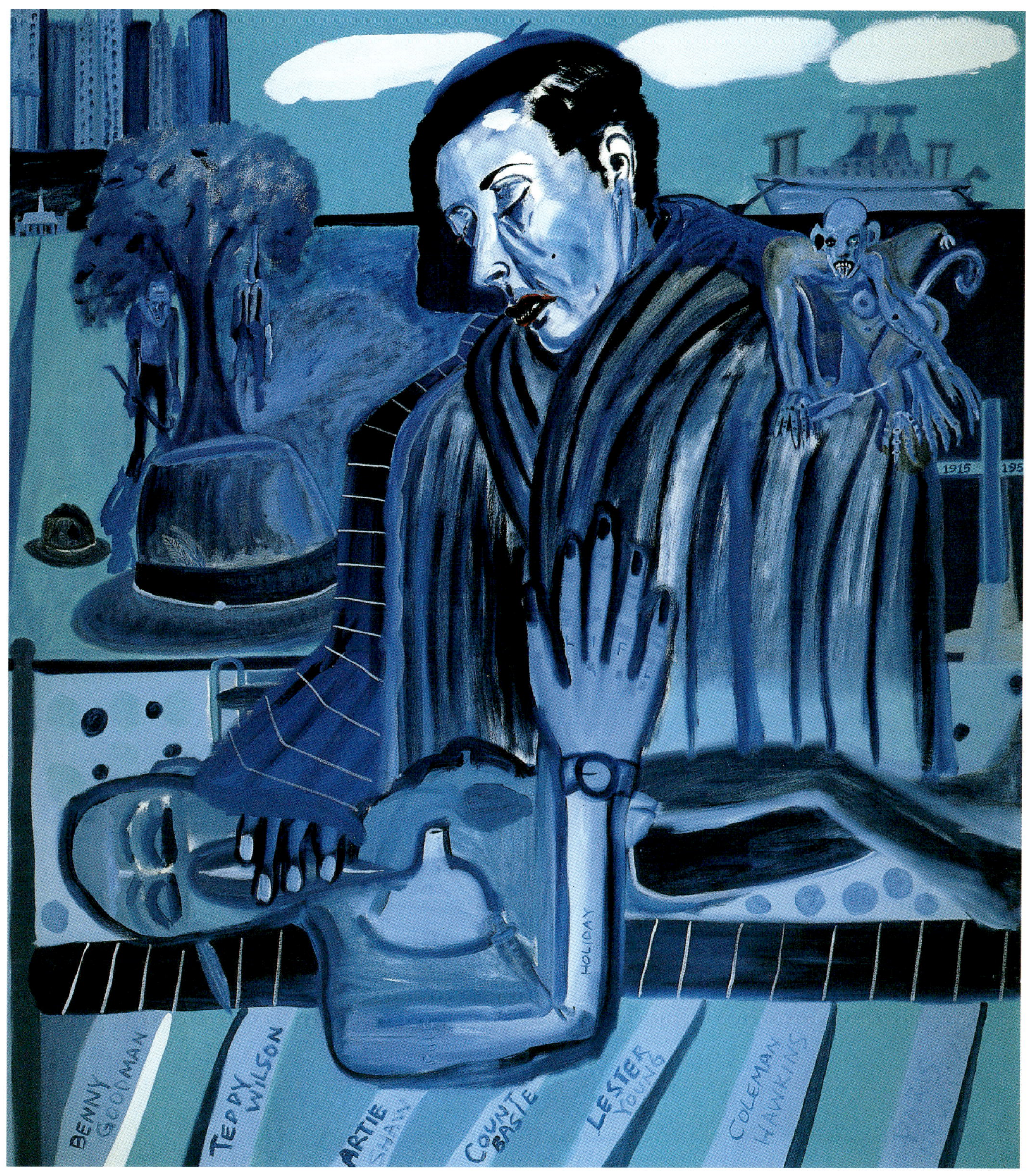
1915
HOLIDAY
BENNY GOODMAN
TEDDY WILSON
ARTIE SHAW
COUNT BASIE
LESTER YOUNG
COLEMAN HAWKINS
PARIS

James Roger Brown

born 1941

Don't Be Cruel, 1989

oil on canvas, 72 × 48 inches
Museum purchase with funds donated by
the Arthur and Holly Magill Foundation

The relationship between popular culture and art in the late twentieth century is a dynamic one. In architecture the appreciation of kitsch was spearheaded by Robert Venturi, whose book *Learning from Las Vegas* stimulated readers to acknowledge the aesthetic richness of neon highway signs as well as diners and drive-ins. In his postmodern designs Venturi artfully and self-consciously mines this wealth of vernacular forms. Similarly, a group of artists working in Chicago, like the Pop artists before them, embraced familiar imagery derived from the mass media. Labeled the Chicago Imagists, these painters indulged in humorous statements about the complexity of modern life and filled their work with emotionally charged and pointed references to popular culture.[1]

Both Jim Nutt and Roger Brown personify this preoccupation with the vernacular, each adding his own particular style and perceptions. Nutt's slightly sinister and sardonic use of comic strip–derived forms is ultimately an extension of Pop Art. Brown, in many respects, is an heir to Surrealism, which enjoyed continuing popularity in Chicago, and he laments the tendency of critics to pigeonhole him and the others generically and regionally as Chicago Imagists.

After a childhood in Alabama and a short period in Nashville, Brown arrived in Chicago in 1962. Vacillating as a student between the commercially oriented American Academy of Art and the School of the Art Institute of Chicago, he graduated from the latter with a bachelor of fine arts degree in 1968. Brown created a distinctive painting style that synthesizes his rural background with his urban experiences and his commercial training with his interest in Surrealism. He claims to have found little of interest in the collection at the Art Institute, except for the paintings of Giorgio de Chirico and René Magritte, who was a particular stimulus: "Magritte, all those weird things—the man that's a stone, the stone that's a lion, the things in the sky, big giant apple in the room, the train coming out of the fireplace."[2]

Brown is known for his depictions of city scenes in which silhouettes of men and women populate the windows of tall buildings. The streets are antiseptically clean and brightly lit; all movement is frozen. An eerie sense of foreboding is pervasive. His landscapes, derived from many cross-country adventures, are panoramas of stylized vegetation arranged in regular patterns. Again, all is still and curiously illuminated, as if from the backlit flicker of a television screen. Brown has also developed a penchant for disasters. He has painted avalanches, tornadoes, and fires, as well as the nuclear accident at Three Mile Island and Hurricane Hugo.

Icons of American history and culture have provided Brown with another reservoir of imagery. One series incorporates stereotypical representations of George Washington, Ronald and Nancy Reagan, and Elvis Presley, all of whom Brown portrays with a sardonic twist. Bust-length portraits of the Reagans, for instance, are enshrined in billowing clouds and hover above a suburban street lined with six identical Monopoly-style houses that allude to the ideal of a homogeneous American lifestyle. The Museum's painting of Elvis satirizes a certifiable symbol of the American myth: his rags-to-riches story, his bad-boy reputation, his success at the box office, his seductive music, and his obsessive lifestyle with its tragic ending all combined to make Elvis a legendary figure of this century. *Don't Be Cruel* also lampoons the fanaticism of Elvis's fans who maintain that the King will never die. As Brown explains, "I am a fan of Elvis's music and *Don't Be Cruel* was painted as my personal response to the 'sightings' of Elvis that won't allow him to rest in peace."[3] In Brown's view, the rock-and-roll idol withers away to cliché and nothingness because his admirers are unwilling to release him.

Brown portrayed Elvis with a super-realistic, grinning face mounted atop a skeleton, an ironic reference to the star's preoccupation with his wardrobe and physique. The skeleton's pose is characteristic: knees bent, hand grasping the microphone, and hips ready to gyrate and swivel. The contrast of the skeleton and the fleshed-out head is unsettling; equally disturbing are the singer's penetrating eyes. His fixed gaze simultaneously recalls the obsession of his fans and Presley's own addictions. The unreality of the scene is further enhanced by the ambiguity of the backdrop, which can be variously interpreted as a stagelike curtain or as clouds. Similarly patterned clouds appear in Brown's work as early as the mid-1970s, often in paintings of impending disaster.

Don't Be Cruel is emblematic of the American fascination with fame and celebrity. Brown's direct appropriation, or literal borrowing, of a publicity photograph reflects the pervasiveness and influence of the mass media in contemporary society. Brown's selection of Elvis Presley, however, may be more personal; Brown believes that he is distantly related to the rock-and-roll idol. Brown's interest in Elvis flourished at an early age; when he was fourteen he painted a skeleton singing *Hound Dog* for a Halloween window-decorating contest in his hometown. In his late teens Brown went to Nashville, the avowed capital of country music. At the time Presley was at the pinnacle of his career: his records shattered all previous sales figures, he starred in phenomenally popular teen movies, and in his sold-out performances he synthesized rhythm and blues and country music. More recently, Brown, who owns a life-size bust of Elvis, has analyzed his relationship to this aspect of American culture: "I can identify with country music. . . . It's satire, it's about vernacular, it always tells simple stories. I realized how much it is like what I am doing."[4]

---

1. See Russell Bowman, "Roger Brown: Style and Emblem," in Mitchell Douglas Kahan, Dennis Adrian, and Russell Bowman, *Roger Brown* (Montgomery, Ala.: Montgomery Museum of Fine Arts, 1980), 19–29.

2. Brown, "A Talking Profile of the Artist," in Sidney Lawrence and John Yau, *Roger Brown* (New York: George Braziller, 1987), 94.

3. Brown to author, 6 February 1994.

4. Brown, "Talking Profile," in Lawrence and Yau, *Brown*, 96.

Born, Hamilton, Alabama, 1941; attended David Lipscomb College, Nashville, Tennessee, 1960–1961; studied at the American Academy of Art, Chicago, 1962 and 1963–1964, and the School of the Art Institute of Chicago, 1962 and 1964–1968; lived in Chicago from 1962 with studio in New Buffalo, Michigan, from 1979; divides his time between Chicago and Carpenteria, California.

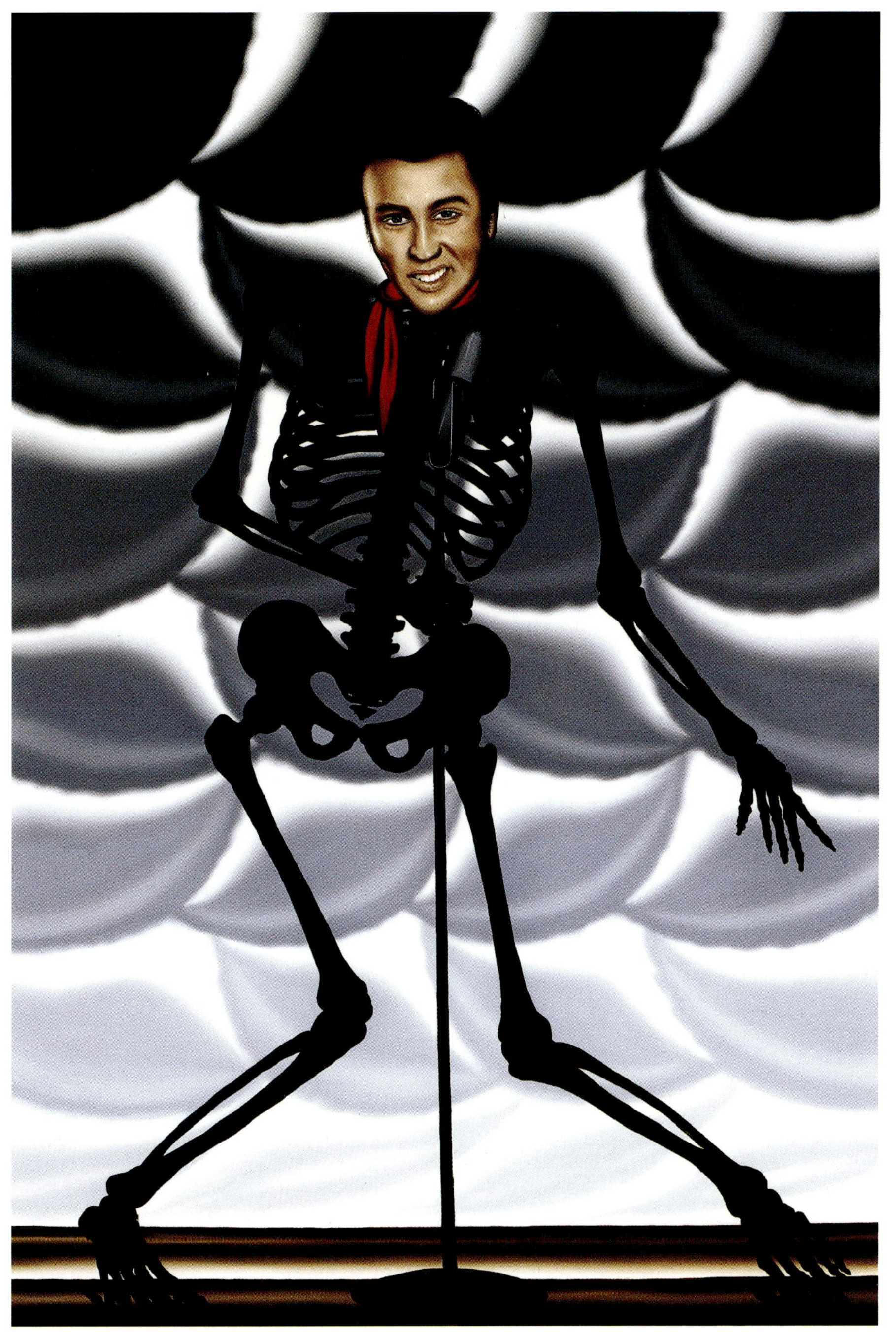

John Ahearn

born 1951

Marty Tinsley, 1984 [A]
acrylic on cast plaster, 26 × 20 × 8½ inches

Arthur Magill, 1984 [B]
acrylic on cast plaster, 21 × 12 × 4 inches

Robert Dawson, 1984 [C]
acrylic on cast plaster, 39 × 27 × 11 inches

Emma Lois McNeil, 1984 [D]
acrylic on cast plaster, 28 × 24 × 8 inches

Erick or Derick Locke, 1984 [E]
acrylic on cast plaster, 26½ × 22 × 8 inches

Claude Davis, 1984 [F]
acrylic on cast plaster, 21 × 23 × 6½ inches
Museum purchase with funds donated by the Arthur and Holly Magill Foundation

The realization that art can be more than a framed canvas or a sculpture on a pedestal led some artists to create environments, or physical surroundings that engulf the viewer in a synergistic aesthetic experience. The tableaux sculptors Edward Kienholz and George Segal exemplify this trend. Using unorthodox materials, they often combine such objects as tables and chairs, an automobile, a movie marquee, a tiled bathtub, and a diner counter to create compellingly staged scenarios. Within these settings their forlorn human figures appear frozen and incapacitated, evoking a sense of the loneliness and isolation of modern life.

Other artists, including Duane Hanson, John de Andrea, and John Ahearn, have concentrated more on painted cast figures and reduced the predominance of props. Using polyvinyl resins, both Hanson and de Andrea make realistic human replicas. Whereas de Andrea focuses on lifelike nudes, Hanson creates vignettes featuring ordinary individuals: housewives in curlers, janitors with brooms, and sunbathers with beach towels. Ahearn, in contrast, neither manipulates his viewers nor satirizes his sitters; instead he has become a community activist by involving his subjects in the art-making process. After graduating from Cornell University, Ahearn moved to New York to pursue a career in filmmaking. As part of this work he made masks and other special effects before he began to cast images of his friends. In 1979 he became affiliated with Fashion Moda, a storefront art center in the South Bronx, one of New York's most underprivileged neighborhoods. There he met young Rigoberto Torres, who had some casting experience in his uncle's religious statuary factory.

Together Ahearn and Torres create a form of community theater; Ahearn, with his background in painting and film, is complemented by Torres, with his casting abilities and contacts in the neighborhood. The actual process of making the mold happens under the watchful eyes of the community, often on the sidewalk in front of the artists' work space. The model breathes through straws while a gel is applied to the body; after an interval of about twenty minutes, this layer is peeled away and becomes the mold for plaster casts. Using a color snapshot of his subject as a reference, Ahearn paints facial details, skin, clothing, and props. Many of the finished casts are displayed on walls throughout the neighborhood, bringing recognition to the sitters. In addition, each sitter retains a copy of his likeness. Although initially called "The Headhunter" when he moved to the South Bronx, Ahearn has gained the confidence of his community. Yet he, the outsider, also recognizes the moral dilemma of his success and worries about exploiting his neighbors: "I think the number-one personal problem is, what right do I have as a white person to represent a black or Hispanic person?"[1]

In 1984 Ahearn visited Greenville, South Carolina, where he produced six bust-length figures. Two of the individuals, Claude Davis and Arthur Magill, were connected with the Museum: Davis, a sculptor, worked at the Museum as exhibitions preparator; and Magill is a long-standing benefactor. Ahearn went to Magill's home and remembers: "He greeted us at the door wearing a red plaid bathrobe and I asked to take a Polaroid of him. Later he agreed to let me 'work with him.' His wife was a little nervous about his prospects of surviving the ordeal but we did it anyways."[2] With Davis's assistance, Ahearn searched for other subjects, going to the Phillis Wheatley Community Center and to an elementary school, where he encountered identical twins. Ahearn, himself a twin, responded to them immediately: "I was shocked to see two absolutely identical twins both with bright gold complexions and very intense green eyes. They seemed eager to participate in our sculpture project. When the actual casting began, one told the other 'You go first.' But later the 'bossy one' wouldn't do it. So there is just one." Robert Dawson was discovered while Ahearn was out driving. "I picked up a drifter hitchhiking. I got him some wine and we made his portrait over the next two days." Ahearn met Marty Tinsley and Emma Lois McNeil at the Fine Arts Center and the Phillis Wheatley Center, respectively, where he engaged them in his project.

The Greenville group is, in its way, a cross section of the community, as are the likenesses Ahearn renders in the Bronx. All of the figures are animated, both by pose and by the intensity of their brightly painted surfaces. Each figure is shown in a characteristic manner, particularized with eyeglasses, jewelry, hats, and other articles of clothing. Davis, for instance, is depicted holding one of his own sculptures, a device reminiscent of the attributes saints hold in religious statues.

Ahearn's relationship to his Greenville subjects is different from the communal bond he typically forms with his South Bronx sitters. Like the painters who incorporated graffiti imagery and methodology in their paintings, Ahearn's work is of the street and its people, and he labors to return it to them. "I've said that I love every person I've casted, and that is fact. The people I've casted have given me more life experiences than any art education or college could hope to do. The key to my work is life—life casting."[3]

1. Ahearn, as quoted in Richard Goldstein, "The Headhunters of Walton Avenue," in Marilyn Zeitlin, Richard Goldstein, and Michael Ventura, *South Bronx Hall of Fame* (Houston: Contemporary Arts Museum, 1991), 86.

2. This and subsequent quotations from Ahearn to author, December 1993.

3. Ahearn, as quoted in Peter Frank and Michael McKenzie, *New, Used, and Improved: Art for the '80s* (New York: Abbeville Press, 1987), 35.

Born, Binghamton, New York, 1951; bachelor of fine arts degree, Cornell University, 1973; moved to New York, 1973; took up residence in the South Bronx, 1979; resides, South Bronx.

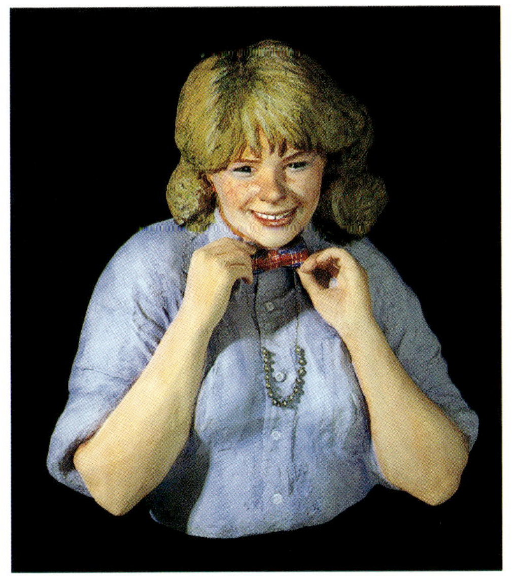
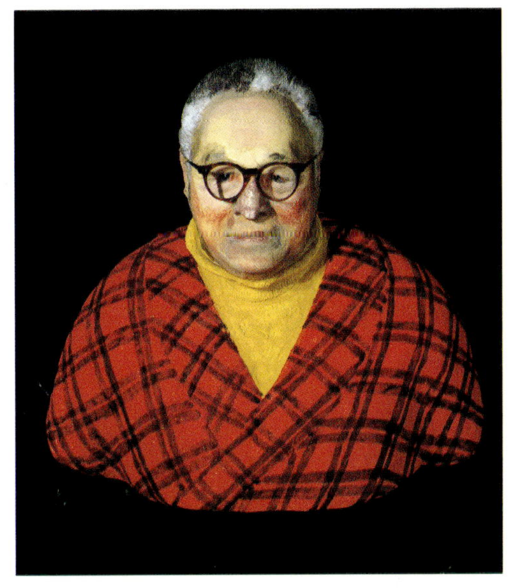
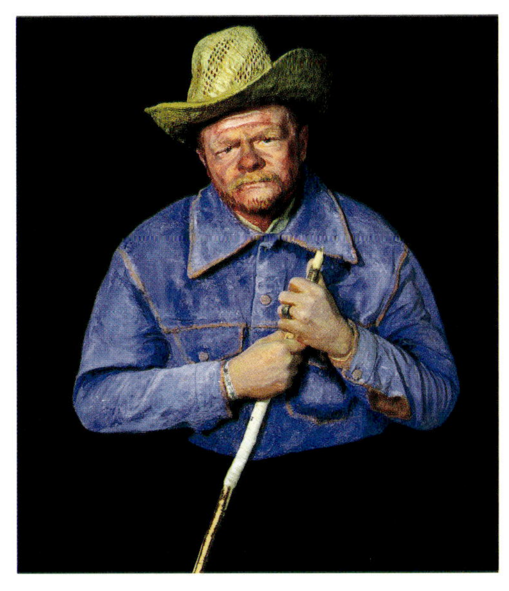
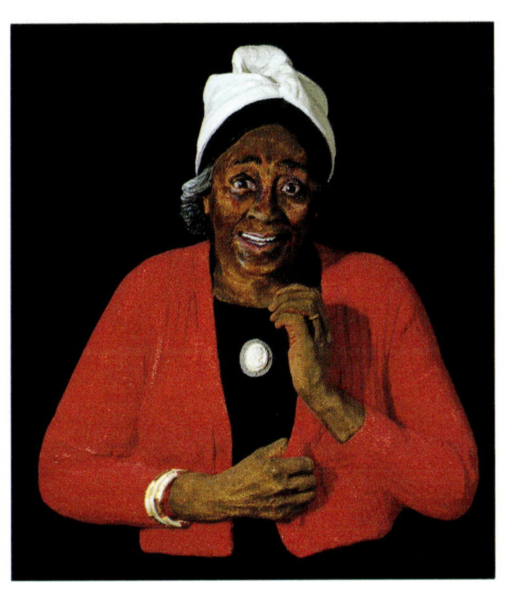
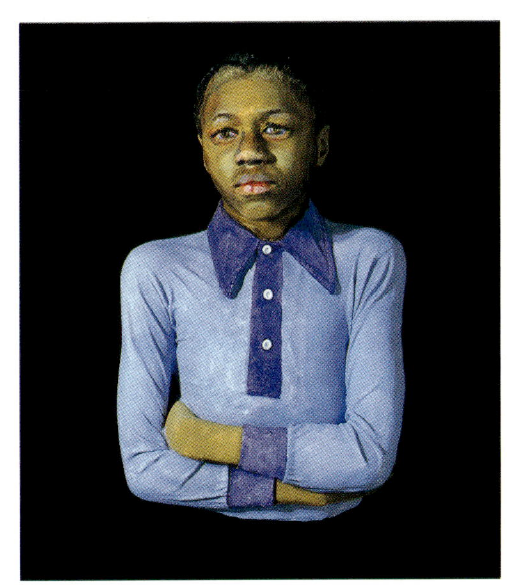
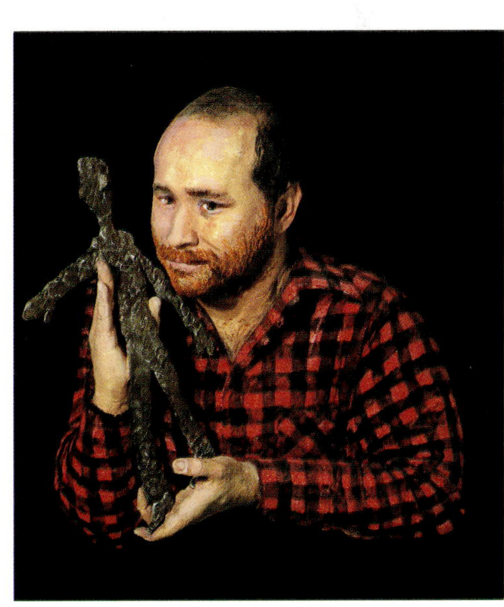

Daisy Youngblood

born 1945

Romana, 1987

bronze, edition of 3, 21 × 8¼ × 10 inches
signed, lower right: *D. Youngblood 3 / 3 / Empire Bronze Art Foundry*
Museum purchase with funds donated by the Arthur and Holly Magill Foundation

As many painters in the 1980s renewed their interest in figurative art, a small group of sculptors likewise embraced the human figure. Counter to the trend of monumental, abstract sculptures designed for public spaces, these individualistic sculptors pursued more modest, personal statements. Leonard Baskin, for example, skilled in printmaking and the book arts as well as in carved wood and bronze, often creates hybrids of man and bird. In these haunting images Baskin addresses such temporal human issues as suffering, death, and spirituality. Baskin admits that many of his torturous figures are autobiographical. Similarly, Mary Frank indulges in fragmented human imagery that is at times sensual, provocative, and playful, and at other times ominous. Her chosen material is clay, and she is credited with investing the medium with an artistic viability apart from its long-standing craft tradition.

Daisy Youngblood shares a number of qualities with both Baskin and Frank. Like Baskin, Youngblood is fascinated by the relation of man and animal and often transposes animal body parts to human figures to create an uneasy, restless synthesis. Similar to Frank, Youngblood prefers the immediacy of shaping clay, but in contrast to Frank's sophisticated and elegant works, Youngblood's possess a primeval quality. In their rounded contours and hollowness, they suggest that they have evolved from ancient vessels.

A native of Asheville, North Carolina, Youngblood has lived in Italy, France, and Costa Rica as well as in the American Southwest. The exposure to non-European traditions is reflected in both her imagery and her medium. Concerned with spirituality and the essence of life, she deals with the fundamental tensions between man and animal, male and female. She explains: "The imagery of my sculpture is not meant to be either allegory or metaphor, it is visual language that remains open. One should not get stuck in interpretation, but here are some clues as to how I use that language. Goat, snake, and horse are all masculine in that they bring with them masculine ways of relating: work, competition, aggression, separation."[1]

Youngblood relates personally to each of her sculptures, developing her content either from dreams and her own experiences or from friends. The source for *Romana* was a close friend whom she visited in Rome. Youngblood explains, "I had struggled with Romana's head for a long time when Ganesh [the Hindu elephant deity associated with wealth and earthly desire] appeared and fit perfectly. There was a strong downward pull about my sensual friend, both alluring and sad, the trunk brought the energy down and even fed it a circulatory motion. The pain of an ancient family history and heroin addiction saturated an otherwise creative feminine spirit."[2] The result is a potent combination of beast and human; the male, represented by the phalluslike trunk, is fused with the female's lithe body with its diminutive breasts. While living in New York in the late 1960s, Youngblood became involved in the Jungian Institute and immersed herself in Jungian psychology, which may explain the significance of gender interplay in her work.

Many of Youngblood's figures appear spiritually haunted, and several, in their limblessness and contorted forms, resemble the bodies discovered in the excavations at Pompeii. Like those ancient Romans who were the victims of a destructive volcano, Youngblood's baked clay figures reveal the artist's firing process. The artist's desire for permanence and solidity may be reflected in *Romana,* one of her few works to be converted into bronze. In the translation from clay to bronze, *Romana* retains the original's fragility and the same hollow quality, reinforced by the added weight of the metal. The castings were supervised by the artist, who also oversaw the finishing. Youngblood has carefully worked with the surface patina to emulate the color and texture of the original low-fired clay.

That Youngblood's form and content are individualistic is evident. What may be less clear is her own utter involvement in each piece, and how the organic evolution is both a labor and a passion. She has written: "The pieces took a long time, sometimes two years on a particular movement, because for them to develop I would have to develop. There was little separation between life and art or waking and sleeping (dreaming was a strong influence); the sculptures were a place of rest, vessels for my transformation. When they were finished, I no longer needed them; I could let go and relate to other people through them."[3]

---

1. Youngblood, "Notes," in Judith Stein and Paula Marincola, *Daisy Youngblood* (Glenside, Pa.: Beaver College Art Gallery, 1992), unpaginated.

2. Youngblood to author, 19 January 1994.

3. Youngblood, "Notes."

Born, Asheville, North Carolina, 1945; attended Virginia Commonwealth University, Richmond, 1962–1966; lived in New York, 1966–1984, and Costa Rica, 1984–1991, with periods in Italy and France; resides in Arizona and Costa Rica.

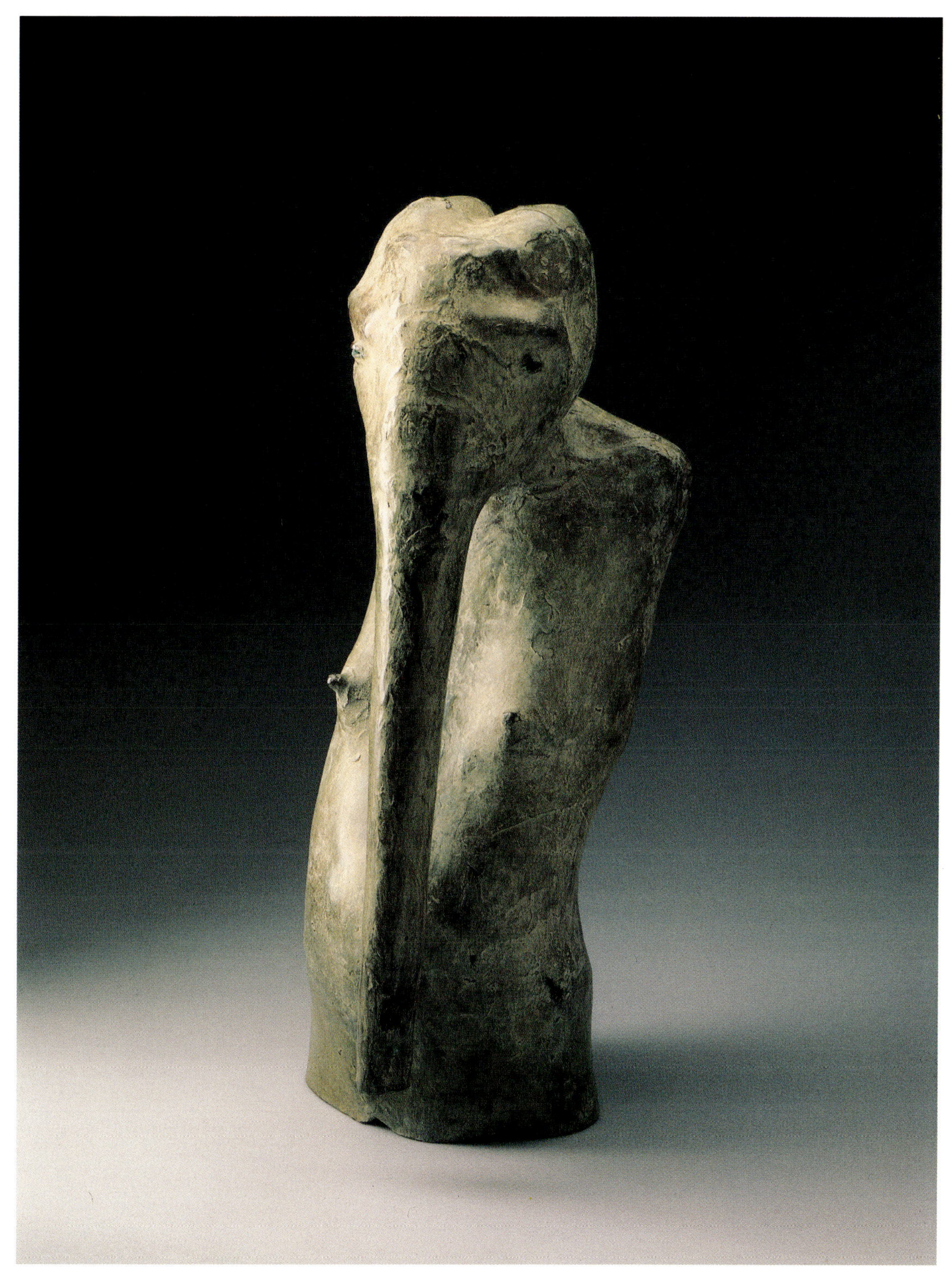

Leonard J. Koscianski

born 1952

The Kill, 1987

oil on canvas, 48 × 64 inches
signed, lower left: *Leonard Koscianski / '87*
Museum purchase

The 1980s witnessed an unprecedented expansion of the art scene and a chaotic proliferation of artistic trends. In all its various manifestations—museums, galleries, schools, studios, auctions, publications—the art world boomed. The settlement by artists and galleries of New York's Soho loft district along with the sale at auction of Vincent van Gogh's *Irises* for more than $54 million are only two hallmarks of the great surge of activity—and money—that characterized the decade. From this thriving culture emerged a new generation of young artists, many of whom managed to breathe new life into old styles. Thus, the press acclaimed and categorized artists as Neo-Expressionist, Neo-Geo, Neo-Surrealist, and Post-Modernist.

Whereas the Abstract Expressionists capitalized upon the automatism of Surrealism, they rejected its penchant for representational imagery. The subsequent reintroduction of recognizable subject matter under the auspices of both Pop Art and Photorealism was revived in the 1980s by a small group of artists who began again to explore the fertile ground of dreams and the subconscious. Eric Fischl plumbed the depths of Freudian sexual innuendo in the suburbs; Mark Tansey satirized art history by illustrating its egocentrism; and Leonard Koscianski created nightmare scenarios of bestial conflict in small town America.

Koscianski was born in Cleveland, Ohio, and received his bachelor of fine arts degree from the Cleveland Institute of Art in 1977. Part of his time there was spent at the nearby Cleveland Museum of Art, where he studied the techniques and content of old-master paintings. Two years later he earned his master of fine arts degree from the University of California at Davis, where he served as a studio assistant to Wayne Thiebaud, well known for his Pop Art images of cake and ice cream. Thiebaud reinforced Koscianski's appreciation for the old-fashioned preparation of oil paintings with an earth-colored preliminary ground, followed by cool-toned underpainting and a built-up layering of glazes. Koscianski labored with the process and in the 1980s achieved his first successes with academic depictions of vicious dogs fighting among brambles. During this time he taught at the University of Tennessee, Knoxville, and later at the University of Maryland.

Although Koscianski also paints birds, fish, and landscapes with solitary figures, he has made a specialty of portraying canines. In the tradition of Aesop, Koscianski employs his animals as surrogates for humanity. But his dogs, more wolflike than canine, have shed their traditional role and instead symbolize ferocity rather than faithfulness. Koscianski renders them as genuine beasts, often turning on one another in acts of rage or self-defense. They allude in clear, primal terms to the violence in modern society.

Koscianski most often stages his scenes in the woods, where trees are bare and the lighting is harsh. In the background loom the hard geometric forms of houses, usually identical, suggestive of suburban tract housing. This reference to suburbia, often touted as the refuge from urban ills, is disturbing: evil, in the form of snarling beasts, lurks just beyond its borders. The houses, in turn, have no doors, becoming simultaneouly inescapable prisons and unreachable safe havens.

In the Museum's painting, *The Kill,* the most compelling element is the animals' gnashing teeth. Heightened by dramatic lighting, deep, rich background colors, and strong diagonals, the tension is palpable. Motion is suspended, and both the cause of the fight and its final outcome are unknown. The animals are ensnared in their own mindless bestiality.

Such themes are not uncommon in the history of art, and Koscianski has expressed admiration for such artists as Peter Paul Rubens, Eugène Delacroix, and George Stubbs. Stubbs, who made his reputation by painting horse portraits for the English gentry, is best known today for his images of horses being savagely attacked by lions. In these paintings, Stubbs captured the reflex reaction of the victim toward his attacker, a response mirrored in *The Kill* by the dog on the right. But whereas Stubbs romanticized the ancient conflict of beasts, Koscianski creates a sinister fantasy that parallels the haunting specter of modern horror movies and the cold reality of violence in American society.

Born, Cleveland, Ohio, 1952; attended the University of Detroit and University of Cincinnati before earning bachelor of fine arts degree from Cleveland Institute of Art, 1977; master of fine arts degree, University of California, Davis, 1979; taught at University of Tennessee, Knoxville, 1980–1984, and the University of Maryland, College Park, 1984–1987; resides, Annapolis, Maryland.

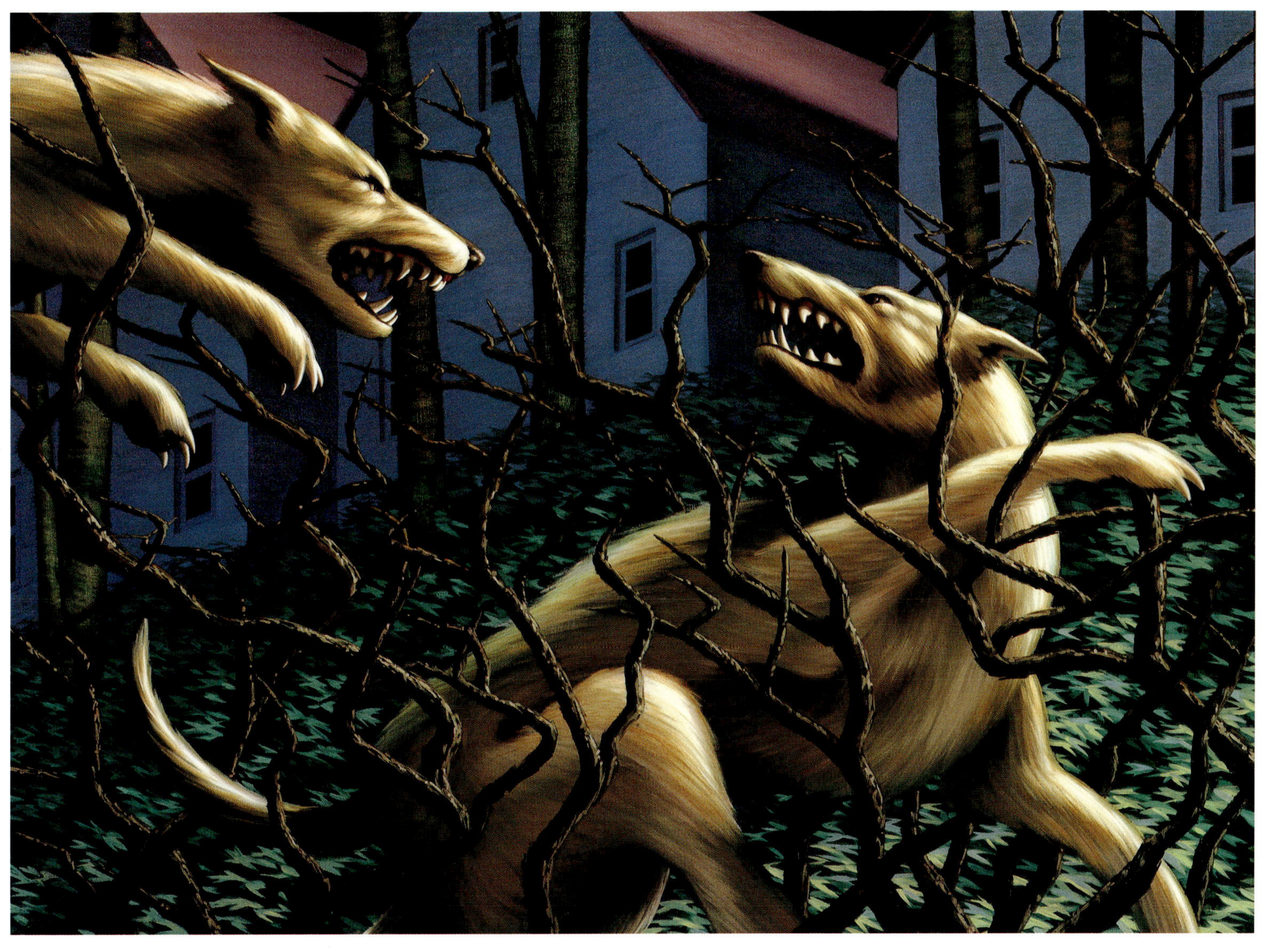

Scott Richter

born 1943

Surrogate, 1987

acrylic on carpet, 96¼ × 72 inches, and beeswax, plywood, and wire, 38 × 20 inches
Museum purchase

Collage, the arrangement of disparate fragments of paper, photographs, and other flat materials, is conceptually linked to its three-dimensional counterpart, assemblage. Whereas collages are two dimensional and are presented like drawings, in frames and usually under glass, assemblages are akin to sculpture. They can either be freestanding, like sculpture or environmental tableaux, or they can be hung on a wall like bas-reliefs. Closely connected to the Dada ideology, assemblages are generally composed from existing, prefabricated materials. They are exemplified by Joseph Cornell's boxes in which the artist carefully placed, among other things, photographs, scraps of wallpaper, small toys, marbles, and forms resembling architectural elements.

When Jasper Johns and Robert Rauschenberg affixed such three-dimensional objects as paintbrushes and pieces of furniture to their canvases, they invented a painterly hybrid of assemblage, often called "combines." Artists of the 1980s, including David Salle, Julian Schnabel, and Scott Richter, have continued this trend of blurring the conventional categories of art.

A native of Atlanta, Georgia, Richter earned his bachelor of fine arts degree in industrial design from the Parsons School of Design, New York. He considers himself virtually self-educated as an artist, and although he teaches drawing at the Cooper Union School of Art, New York, he does not believe art can be taught; he maintains: "you don't choose art; art chooses you. Some people call it a curse."[1] Exploiting his knowledge of photography, painting, and sculpture, he thrives on experimenting with various materials, often seeking the unpredictable. Using his sculptural skills, he fabricates objects from beeswax, plywood, and canvas, among other materials, creating works that defy easy categorization.

The inspiration for the Museum's work, *Surrogate,* derives from his school days and a photograph of a friend at Parsons. Richter painted this deadpan image in an imposing scale on the underside of carpeting, a substance with more body than canvas. It hangs loosely suspended, the bottom edge free from support. Almost serendipitously he joined the painting with the upturned vaselike object, a form that relates to several of his abstract torso sculptures. Richter constructed the form from wire, which he filled with foam insulation and coated with shiny beeswax. Like Johns and Rauschenberg before him, he is purposefully unorthodox in his use of materials. In *Surrogate* Richter integrates in a Neo-Dada manner the vessel he created with imagery derived from Photorealism, especially the enormous portraits by Chuck Close. This marriage of an ambiguous three-dimensional form with a highly realistic facial image forces a dynamic tension; the enigma is further enhanced by the figure whose gender remains unclear.

Richter has been recognized for both the theatricality of his works and their sense of humor, although it is, at times, ambivalently presented. Unlike most artists who name a piece after its completion, Richter actually starts with the title. While he admits that not all titles work and that he has changed a few, Richter uses them as a vehicle to get motivated. The title *Surrogate* refers to the illusory nature of metaphor. Richter is content if this baffles the viewer, explaining: "It's the same problem when we look at someone else, and wonder what they think."[2]

---

1. Interview with author, 14 February 1994.

2. Interview with author, 14 February 1994.

Born, Atlanta, Georgia, 1943; bachelor of fine arts degree, Parsons School of Design, New York, 1970; taught at State University of New York at Purchase, 1978–1984; teaches, Cooper Union School of Art, 1983 to the present; moved to Weston, Connecticut, 1990; resides in Weston.

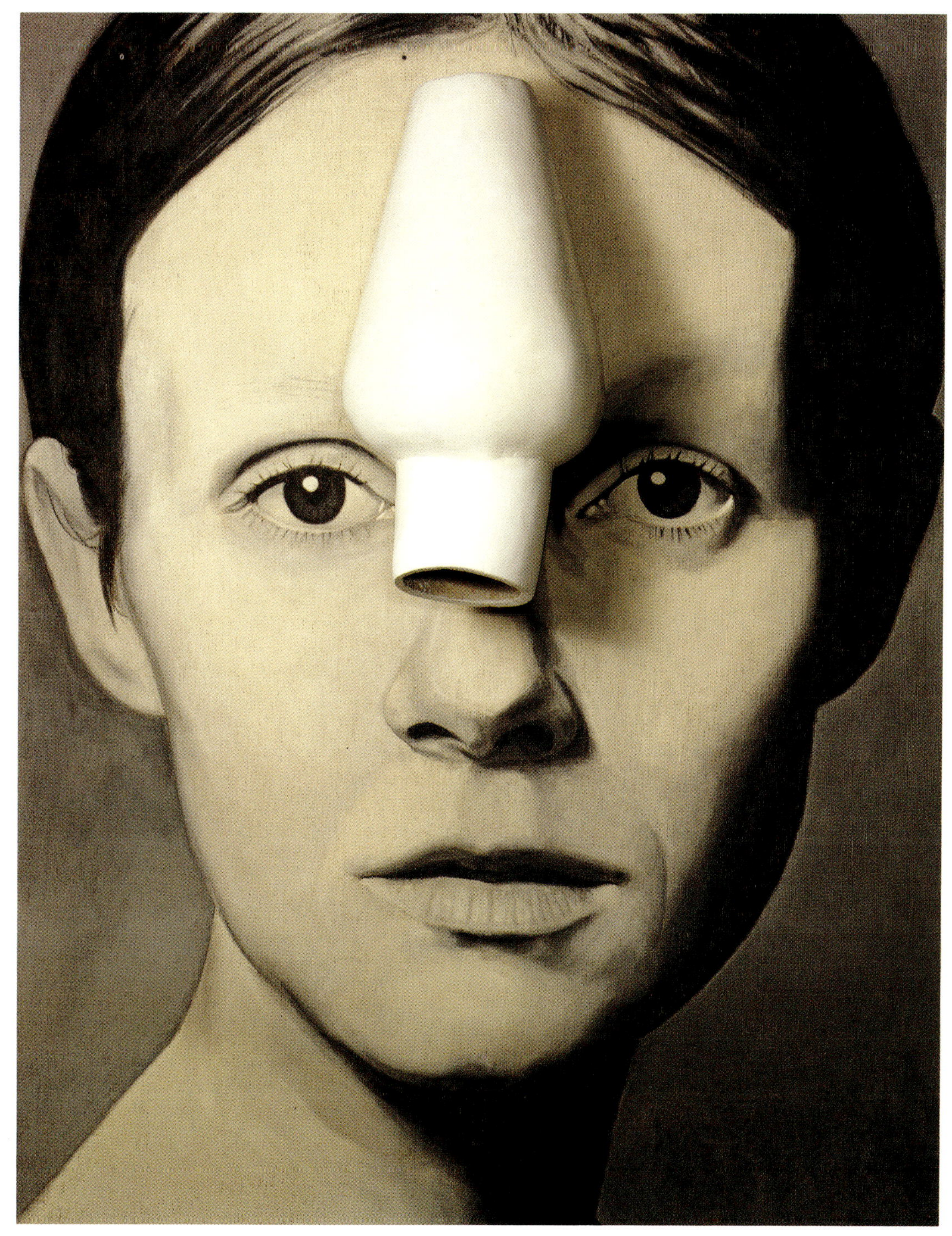

Philip Wofford

born 1935

Heart of the Woods, 1988

oil and acrylic on canvas, 78½ × 87½ inches
signed, on reverse: *1988 / Philip Wofford*
Museum purchase with funds donated by the Arthur and Holly Magill Foundation and gift of Albert Fried, Jr., and Philip Johnson (by exchange)

As avant-garde movements become mainstream, even newer avant-garde movements evolve from the negative reactions to or the positive extensions of their sources. Thus, Pop Art, in its assertion of everyday imagery, and Minimalism, in its serene geometry and reductiveness, can be viewed as divergent responses to Abstract Expressionism. At the same time, however, that Abstract Expressionism provoked rebellion, it remained a model of inspiration for many young painters.

Under the direct influence of the Abstract Expressionists, Philip Wofford has sustained a compellingly personal style of abstract imagery wrought in heavily textured surfaces. As a student in Arkansas, Wofford was introduced to Jackson Pollock's methodology by his high school art teacher, who brought to class a 1949 *Life* magazine article, "Jackson Pollock: Is He the Greatest Living Painter in the United States?" She also encouraged her students to experiment with pouring enamel paint. Later, Wofford studied at the University of Arkansas in Fayetteville, where Philip Guston visited and encouraged Wofford to be more expansive and adventuresome. Wofford encountered Abstract Expressionist painting firsthand in 1956 while spending a summer in New York. Enraptured with New York, he moved there in 1958, and thoroughly immersed himself in the art scene of galleries, artists' studios, and such hangouts as the Cedar Bar, which was frequented by many of the Abstract Expressionists over the years. Despite the great attraction of New York, Wofford has taught at Bennington College in southern Vermont since 1969.

Wofford acknowledges a number of turning points in his life; in the mid-1960s he reached an impasse in his painting, so he abandoned it and made sculpture. When he returned to painting two years later, he was "struck by the sheer physical struggle and the long-term patience that painting requires."[1] During a trip to New Mexico in 1968, Wofford was impressed by the magnitude and drama of the landscape and by Native American culture. In 1991 he traveled to the Yucatán and encountered the highly textured reliefs found on Mayan temples. Those influences led him to enhance the texture of his paintings even more, bringing the surface work forward by adding a wide variety of such materials as seeds, corks, charred wood, and rusty metal.

Living in upstate New York and traveling to Bennington, Wofford has been surrounded by some of this country's most beautiful natural scenery. This exposure seems to be reflected in a number of his works, including the Museum's *Heart of the Woods.* Like both Pollock and Willem de Kooning, who admitted the landscape qualities of their work, Wofford hints at such natural forms as trees, mountains, and streams. All these elements, however, are totally consumed by his heavily encrusted surface and the rhythmic patterns in the paint. Wofford's muscular application of paint, with brush and palette knife or squeezed directly from the tube, is captivating and results in textures sometimes as much as an inch thick. The critic and contemporary art historian Donald Kuspit has assessed Wofford's painterliness: "Wofford's gestures are also far from soothing; almost violent in their vigor. . . . There is painting to satiety here, but the plenitude of the paint does not make the work any less limber. What Wofford offers is Titanic assertiveness—an expressionistic dynamic suggestive of a time when giants strode the earth, shaking it with their primitive motion."[2]

Kuspit's invoking the primitive is apt; like the Navaho sand painters, whom Wofford is known to admire, the artist shapes his medium into rivers and valleys of texture. Certain strokes are repeated, creating patterns that are often hard edged and angular, like the gouged marks on African sculpture. In addition, Wofford's colors are glistening and rich; they exude a pulsating intensity of their own. In *Heart of the Woods,* the composition itself is energetic; a swath of yellow-orange pigment sweeps across the canvas and intersects with staccato diagonal strokes. The whole is restless and emotive, in keeping with the classic Abstract Expressionist aesthetic that Wofford embodies.

1. Wofford to author, 10 March 1994.

2. Donald Kuspit, *Philip Wofford: New Paintings* (New York: Frumkin/Adams Gallery, 1988), unpaginated.

Born, Van Buren, Arkansas, 1935; graduated from the University of Arkansas at Fayetteville, 1957; studied at the University of California, Berkeley, 1957–1958; moved to New York, 1958; teaches, Bennington College, Bennington, Vermont, 1969 to the present; resides, Hoosick Falls, New York.

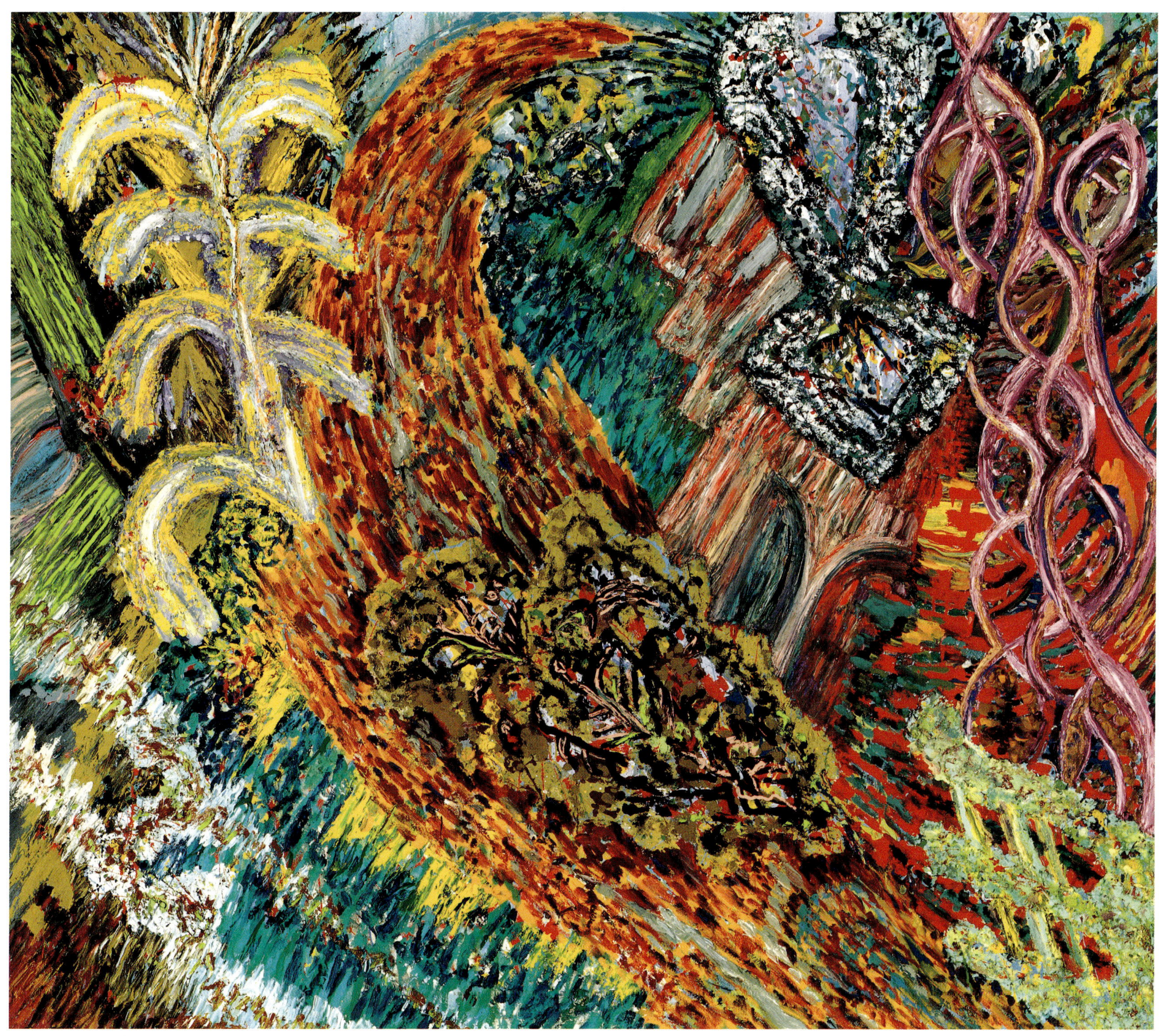

James William (Bo) Bartlett III

born 1955

Lamb, 1990

oil on linen, 88 × 70 inches
Museum purchase with funds provided by The Museum Association, Inc., and the National Endowment for the Arts

Notwithstanding the compelling drive of modern art toward extreme formalism, the influence of the academic tradition remains potent. The masters of the Italian Renaissance continue to be a rich source of inspiration despite the secularism of contemporary art. In particular, Piero della Francesca, who was not fully appreciated until the mid-twentieth century, served as a model for the synthesis of timeless, heroic values with everyday life. Several artists, including Alfred Leslie and Jack Beal, revived painting in a realistic vein, wedding contemporary iconography with a Renaissance-derived monumentality. Leslie's group figural compositions are theatrical and passionate, evoking the influence of Giotto. In an allegorical series about the virtues and vices, Beal shows the temptations of modern life in a manner reminiscent of the Baroque painter Caravaggio.

In his indebtedness to academic and Renaissance precedents Bo Bartlett resembles Leslie and Beal, but he creates works that are highly individualistic and often mysterious in their import. His large-scale canvases reveal both the pageantry and the tragedy of modern life. Initially, Bartlett depicted nudes and undertook portrait commissions; a turning point came after he heard a debate about a nuclear accident. Subsequently, his images have addressed disasters, disease, devastation, and even nuclear holocausts.

A native of Columbus, Georgia, Bartlett went to Florence in his late teens to study privately. Upon his return, he attended the Pennsylvania Academy of the Fine Arts, an institution steeped in tradition. There he encountered the legacy of the long-departed Thomas Eakins, whose emphasis on life drawing and anatomy are renewed in Bartlett's work. In the spirit of Eakins, Bartlett pursued anatomical studies at the Philadelphia College of Osteopathic Medicine.

In its inscrutable quietude, *Lamb* is typical of Bartlett's work. Whereas other paintings detail the drama of several figures who interact, *Lamb* focuses upon a solitary, iconic young man. Without employing standardized attributes, the image is simultaneously Christ-like and personal, timeless and contemporary. Directly confronting the viewer, the figure proffers a flayed and footless lamb, an overt reference to sacrifice, as well as to Christ as the Lamb of God. His gaze is penetrating and transfixing as well as imploring. Like the central subject of a Renaissance altarpiece, the figure dominates the scene with his erect verticality. The background provides only a glimpse of an ambiguous rocky landscape, with a vista extending toward water. Without specific references, the implication is that this is the Holy Land, or a wasteland following a nuclear explosion. In keeping with the latter interpretation, the sky radiates a warm, eerie glow, and the figure appears to stand at the end of a desolate highway.

The content of *Lamb* remains oblique and subject to a variety of interpretations, but the style of the painting is reassuringly familiar and conventional. Painted within the sphere of academic realism, *Lamb* is a testament to Bartlett's training in Florence and Philadelphia. His method is systematic, beginning with quick sketches in a sketchbook, followed by preliminary oil studies. Although his paintings are dominated by figures, he sometimes devotes himself to the setting first, adding people later.

In keeping with his traditional style and technique, Bartlett champions a conventional view regarding the role of art. He maintains: "There are a lot of different purposes for art. You can like one form for decorative purposes. You can like another because it makes you feel a certain way—to consider things, to make you question. That's when art starts to be a positive force in the world. It has to be life affirming."[1]

---

1. Bartlett, as quoted in William P. Scott, "Bo Bartlett: A Young Realist with Ambitions," *American Artist,* September 1986, 118.

Born, Columbus, Georgia, 1955; studied in Florence with Ben Long, 1974; attended the Pennsylvania Academy of the Fine Arts, 1975–1981; studied anatomy at the Philadelphia College of Osteopathic Medicine, 1977–1978; resides, Bala Cynwyd, Pennsylvania.

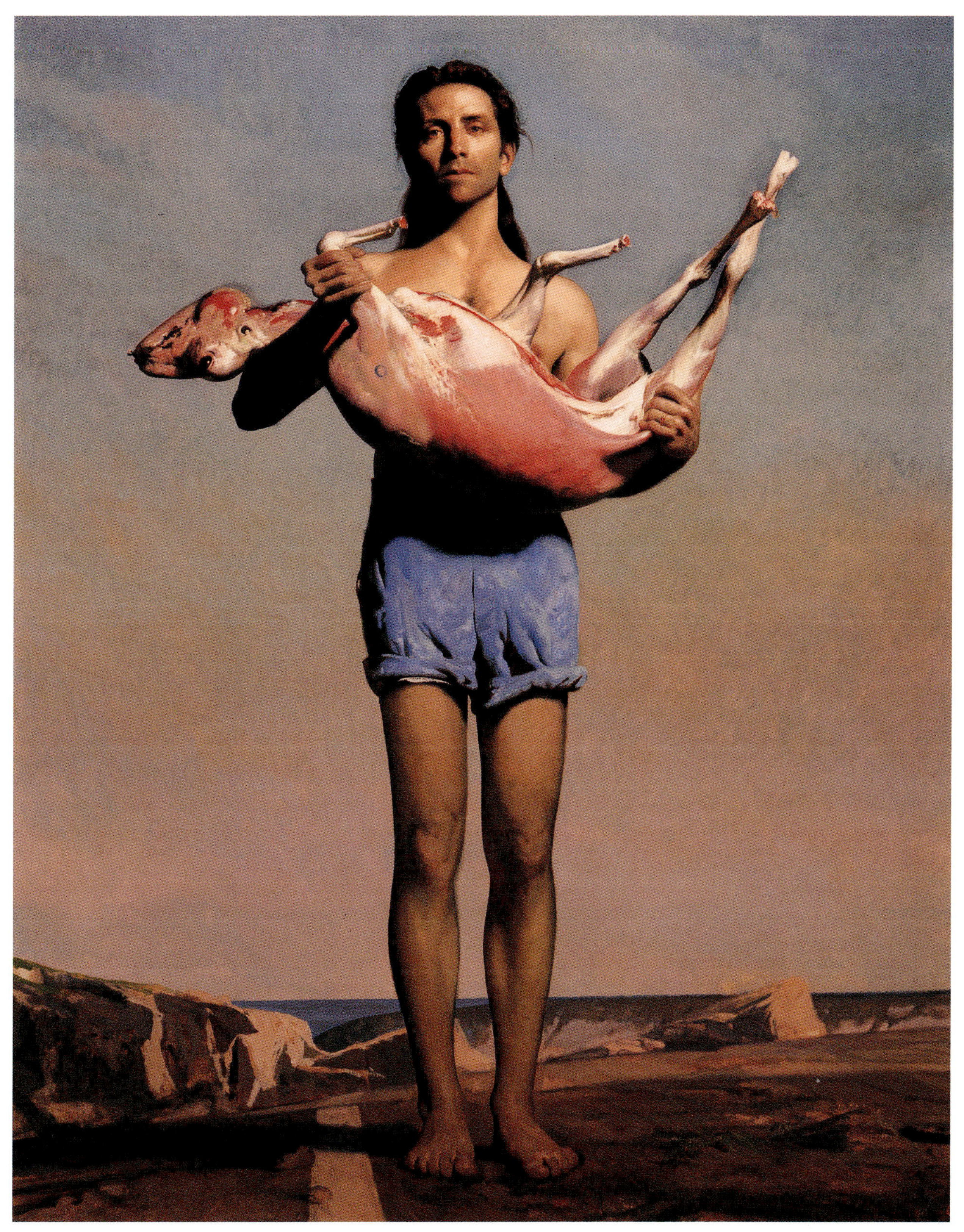

Emmett Williams

born 1925

***Portrait of Jasper Johns*, 1992**

mixed media, 59¾ × 47½ inches
signed, on reverse: *Emmett Williams, 1992*
Museum purchase with funds from the
Arthur and Holly Magill Purchase Fund

During its heyday in the 1960s, the Fluxus movement operated on an international stage, intermingling visual arts with music, performance, poetry, and objects from everyday life. Like its precursor, Dada, Fluxus was at times politically charged, anti-intellectual, and tongue-in-cheek. The term *Fluxus* implies fluidity, with an emphasis on association and improvisation; furthermore, its scatological definition was not lost on the Fluxus participants. Much of the movement's artistic output consisted of mass-produced handbills, posters, and announcements, which are by nature ephemeral. One of the American forerunners of the Fluxus movement was the program at Black Mountain College near Asheville, North Carolina, where John Cage, Merce Cunningham, and Buckminster Fuller formed a dynamic and creative collective.

In 1962 the first Festa Fluxorum was held in Wiesbaden, Germany, spearheaded by George Maciunas, the avowed leader and primary propagandist of the movement. He defined Fluxus as distinct from traditional art that "must appear to be complex, pretentious, profound, serious, intellectual, inspired, skillful, significant and theoretical. . . . [Fluxus must be] simple, amusing, unpretentious, concerned with insignificance, require no skill or countless rehearsals, have no commodity or institutional value."[1] Strict historians of Fluxus believe the movement ended with Maciunas's death in 1978; however, numerous artists, including Yoko Ono, Nam June Paik, and Emmett Williams, have continued to work in a Fluxus-inspired mode.

Williams, a native of Greenville, South Carolina, claims to have published the first story on Fluxus. In retrospect, Williams's vehicle, *The Stars and Stripes,* the daily newspaper of the United States Armed Forces, was an unlikely place for such publicity. Williams's article seems to have resulted, like much of Fluxus, from a fortuitous accident. At the time Williams was in Darmstadt, Germany, serving as a feature writer for the newspaper. Although not a visual artist, Williams was a committed Fluxus participant and performer; his forte was poetry and writing. He taught subjects ranging from Critical Studies at the California Institute of the Arts to Creative Aquatics at Mount Holyoke College.

The Museum's work is one of a dozen portraits of figures instrumental to the Fluxus movement, all of whom Williams knew personally: Maciunas, Cage, Paik, Joseph Beuys, Marcel Duchamp, Richard Hamilton, Claes Oldenburg, Robert Rauschenberg, Daniel Spoerri, Jean Tinguely, and Jasper Johns. Each portrait is an emblematic, and enigmatic, tribute to a major artist of the twentieth century. The underlying concept of the portraits reverts to a 1962 Fluxus performance piece by Williams, entitled the *Alphabet Symphony,* in which the letters of the alphabet were replaced by twenty-six objects or activities. In each portrait, an alphabet extends across the top, below which is placed a ready-made object gathered from a junk shop, flea market, or Williams's own collection of souvenirs. In some instances the association is obvious, as in the use of an old advertising sign for Japp's Hair Rejuvenator, an obvious allusion to Johns's nickname, Jap. At other times the artist is needed to decipher his code.

In his homage to Jasper Johns, Williams has created an image with multiple layers of significance. Like Williams, Johns has strong ties to the South, specifically to South Carolina. This is reflected in the use of a specimen box for the letter *S.* It purportedly contains caps and a bullet salvaged from a Civil War–era blockade runner grounded off Fort Moultrie in Charleston Harbor. Williams explains: "Everybody knows that Jasper [grew up] in South Carolina, and old Fort Moultrie was located not too far away from Edisto Island, where he had a beach house and studio for many years."[2]

Johns was of pivotal importance to the evolution of Pop and Conceptual Art to which Fluxus is closely tied. Williams's use of product labels and advertising is tied specifically to Pop Art, which relied heavily on both. He makes a specific reference to Johns's lifelong series devoted to the flag, that icon of American patriotism that Johns transformed into an art object. For the *S* in Johns, Williams alludes obliquely to the flag image by selecting a small encapsulated booklet about an art project. According to Williams: "The final *S* is a tribute to the Stars and Stripes, so central to Jasper's oeuvre. But here Old Glory is made out of cement, the work of an eccentric artist in Kansas who once upon a time built an entire Garden of Eden—all out of cement."

Several of the objects arranged by Williams are intimately involved with the making of art, a subject that Johns himself had undertaken on many occasions. For example, Williams explains, "*P* is for powder, and this fragile packet of Superior Quality Extra Brilliant Palegold Bronze Powder trademarked with a star and crescent is the very thing you'd expect in a sculptor's studio; . . . *N* is another reference to the craft of painting—Nine-Life Brush Cleaner. The trademark is a Cat and Brush."

The object that projects the most from the surface is the flat-top head of a mannequin, an overt reference to Johns's *Target with Plaster Casts* in which segments of facial casts are arranged above a target. Williams has added a bloody bandage over one eye to indicate that the head was hit instead of the target. In addition to alluding to Johns's work, Williams may be relating this image to his own Fluxus performances in which he threw darts, either at the back of an upright piano or at balloons attached to steaming teakettles. On one dart-throwing occasion Williams inadvertently started a fire, which he succeeded in stomping out "in a lively dance . . . [which] the attendant fireman in the wings, happily, thought was part of the act."[3]

Perhaps the emblems standing for two of the vowels come closest to the Fluxus spirit, ranging from obtuse to obvious: "*E* is for enigma, and this highly polished bronze winking face is nothing if not enigmatic. . . . The *O* object is a playful little red man moulded onto a piece of glass. *O* is for obvious." As portraiture the representation of Johns is mercurial and unconventional, just like the Fluxus movement. It exemplifies Williams's genius at concrete poetry, where words or names are given tangible qualities. Like much of late-twentieth-century art, its success relies heavily on the viewer's foreknowledge and understanding of indirect allusions, becoming a sublime example of "art for art's sake."

---

1. Maciunas, as quoted in Emmett Williams, *My Life in Flux—and Vice Versa* (London: Thames and Hudson, 1992), 41.
2. This and subsequent explanatory quotations derive from a statement written by Williams to the Museum, May 1994.
3. Williams, *My Life,* 22.

Born, Greenville, South Carolina, 1925; attended Kenyon College, Gambier, Ohio, 1943 and 1947–1949; served, United States Army, 1943–1946; lived and worked in France, Germany, and Switzerland, 1949–1966; editor, New York, 1966–1970; taught at the California Institute of the Arts, Valencia, 1970–1972, the Nova Scotia College of Art and Design, 1972–1974, and Harvard University, 1977–1980; moved to Berlin, 1980; resides, Berlin.

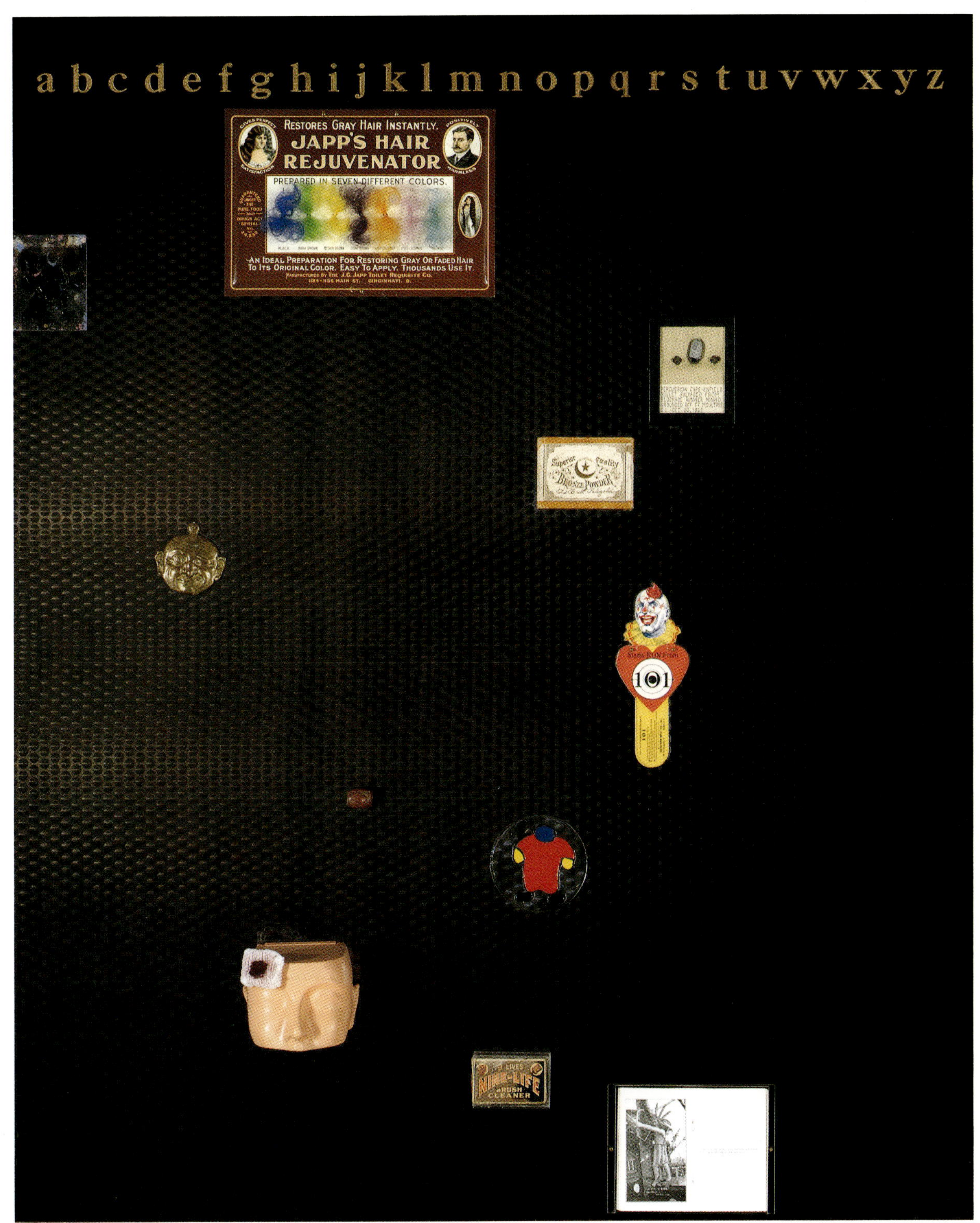
a b c d e f g h i j k l m n o p q r s t u v w x y z
RESTORES GRAY HAIR INSTANTLY.
JAPP'S HAIR REJUVENATOR
PREPARED IN SEVEN DIFFERENT COLORS.
AN IDEAL PREPARATION FOR RESTORING GRAY OR FADED HAIR TO ITS ORIGINAL COLOR. EASY TO APPLY. THOUSANDS USE IT.
Superior Quality
BRONZE POWDER
101
NINE-LIFE
BRUSH CLEANER

Carrie Mae Weems

born 1953

untitled from the *Sea Islands Series*, 1992

three tinted photographs, 1 in edition of 10: 20 inches diameter; 20 inches diameter; 20 × 16 inches
Museum purchase with funds donated by the Arthur and Holly Magill Foundation

untitled from the *Sea Islands Series*, 1992

two silver print photographs, two text panels, 1 in edition of 10: each 20 × 20 inches
Museum purchase with funds donated by the Arthur and Holly Magill Foundation

One natural extension of Conceptual Art, a form driven by ideas instead of by aesthetics, was the incorporation of text into works of art. Designed to complement or extend the imagery, rather than to elucidate its content, the texts often provide visual interest as well. Ultimately derived from Dada, this strategy became a standard practice for many post-modern artists, especially those who address contemporary sociopolitical issues in their work.

The device of employing texts with photographs was especially fruitful for a number of African-American women, who may have consciously created work that stands in strong contrast to paintings by white males. The most outspoken artists in this regard are Adrian Piper, Lorna Simpson, and Carrie Mae Weems. Weems's work, for example, broaches universal and profound concerns relating to identity, feminism, family relations, and the heritage of African-Americans. In her installations each work of art forms part of a thematic network with others, developing a broader narrative.

Weems's ancestors were Mississippi sharecroppers who migrated to the Northwest. The artist was born in Portland, Oregon, and was educated on the West Coast, earning a bachelor of fine arts degree at the California Institute of the Arts, Valencia, followed by a master's degree in photography at the University of California at San Diego. Reaching beyond the concerns of studio art, Weems obtained her master's degree in African-American folklore from the University of California, Berkeley; this experience dramatically altered the content of her work.

One notable result of her studies at Berkeley has been the *Sea Island Series,* a project in which she pursues her origins and reflects upon folk traditions. Isolated from the mainland, these small islands off the coast of South Carolina and Georgia have fostered and preserved a culture and a language with strong ties to the west coast of Africa. Weems visited the area with the express purpose of finding her roots; "went looking for Africa" is a phrase repeated throughout the installation. Capturing her reaction to the Sea Islands, one inscription reads: "Went looking for Africa / and found Africa here. . . . In the songs of St. Simons / Along the highways of Jekyll / In the gardens of Johns / In the graveyards of Hilton Head."

Weems's installation begins with the outright appropriation, or borrowing, of mid-nineteenth-century daguerreotypes of slaves belonging to B. F. Taylor, a major planter and slaveholder in Columbia, South Carolina. Initially taken to serve the ethnographic studies of Louis Agassiz, the likenesses show the figures half-length and nude, in a manner that purports to be scientific—they were merely specimens to Agassiz—but that in reality resembles modern criminal mug shots. The original daguerreotypes by J. T. Zealy are in the collection of the Peabody Museum at Harvard University. Weems has cropped the images slightly and enlarged them to life size, a transposition that makes them even more compelling. She has also tinted some of them blue, a process that relates to her earlier series *Colored People,* in which the artist pointedly satirizes the designation of people by the color of their skin. In the well-researched pursuit of her own roots, Weems curiously makes use of the work of Agassiz, who sought to establish distinct and hierarchical origins for eight different racial groups. Whereas Agassiz's research was used to justify slavery and to champion white supremacy, Weems co-opts his material to reconstruct African-American integrity, values, and cultural contributions. Ironically, her appropriation of Agassiz's photographs seeks to redress the dehumanization of slavery and to expose the propaganda that supported it.

The largest component of the *Sea Islands Series* consists of Weems's groups of straightforward black-and-white photographs and related texts. In their directness and apparent detachment the photographs resemble the work of Walker Evans, who captured the South during the Depression in a series memorialized by the publication *Let Us Now Praise Famous Men.* Although the majority of Evans's photographs depict single figures or family groups, he also recorded the humble shacks of the poor white sharecroppers and their sign-laden store-fronts. Weems similarly documents various business establishments on the Sea Islands.

The photographs are accompanied by texts, many presenting folk adages, local legends, or word-plays. In the Museum's work the etymological source for Gullah, a term used to describe the language and the culture of the Sea Islands, is shown to derive from Angola, thus clearly connecting coastal Carolina with Africa. This linkage is likewise asserted in the text relating to peanuts, which were initially brought to the United States by Africans. Weems's project, one of restoration and celebration, is summarized in her text: "Went looking for Africa and found it lurking quietly along the shore of the Carolinas, the inland of Georgia, the delta of Mississippi, the hills of Oakland, the malls of Newark, the plateaus of Arizona."

Born, Portland, Oregon, 1953; bachelor of arts degree, California Institute of the Arts, Valencia, 1981; master of fine arts degree, University of California, San Diego, 1984; master's degree in African-American folklore, University of California, Berkeley, 1991; taught at Hampshire College, Amherst, Massachusetts, 1987–1991, Hunter College, New York, 1988–1989, and the California College of Arts and Crafts, Oakland, 1991; resides, Oakland.

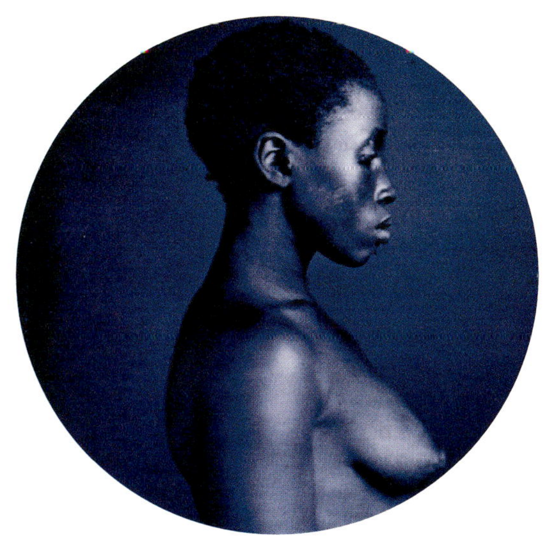

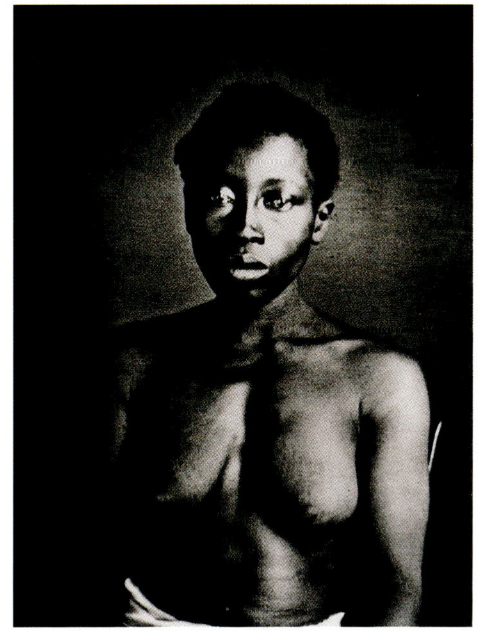

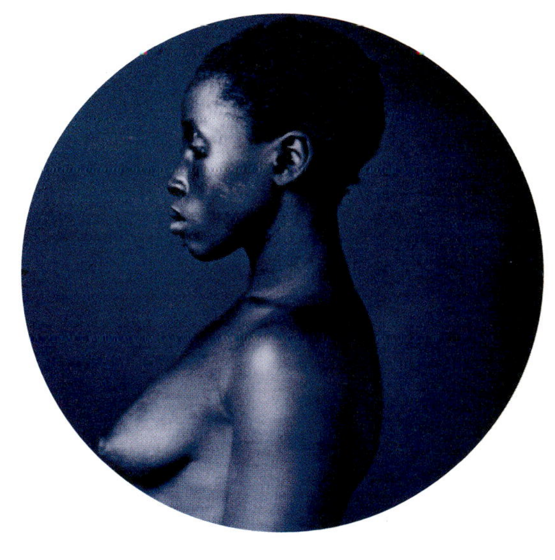

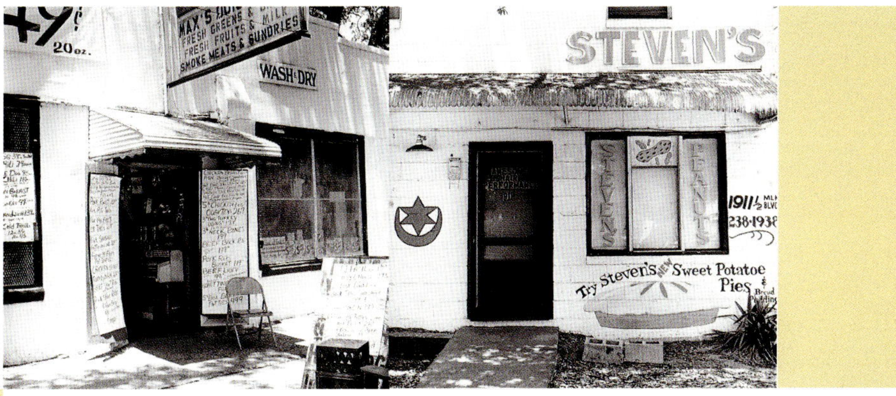

MPINDA
NGUBA
GOOBERS
PEANUTS

GOLA
ANGOLA
GULLA
GULLAH
GEECHEE

Stephen Scott Young

born 1957

The Veterans, 1993

watercolor on paper, 22¼ × 30 inches
signed, upper right: *S. S. Young / '93*
Gift of The Museum Association, Inc., with funds donated by Corporate Partners and Director's Circle Members: Carolina First Bank; the Daniel-Mickel Foundation; Laura E. duPont; Greenville News–Piedmont Company; Mr. and Mrs. M. Dexter Hagy; Hughes Development Corporation; Mr. and Mrs. Hurdle Lea; Mr. and Mrs. Stanton D. Loring; Mr. and Mrs. E. Erwin Maddrey II; Mr. and Mrs. John Martin; Mary Burnet M. Pearce; W. Thomas Smith; Director's Associates: Mr. and Mrs. Russell E. Dyer; Mr. and Mrs. R. Glenn Hilliard; Insignia Financial Group, Inc.; Mr. and Mrs. Bernard Kaplan; Mr. and Mrs. William W. Kehl; Dr. and Mrs. Jeffrey G. Lawson; Dr. and Mrs. Edward K. Lominack; Alice and Hal Lonnecker; Mary Louise Mims; Mr. and Mrs. Philip S. Patrick; Dorothy P. Peace; Mr. and Mrs. John D. Pellett, Jr.; Portman Marina, Inc.; Mr. and Mrs. C. Niles Ray; Mr. and Mrs. James M. Shoemaker, Jr.; Glenn and Jan Spears; Mr. and Mrs. Harry B. Ussery; Charles and Andrea Volpe; Mr. and Mrs. Richard Furman Watson, Jr.; Millie and Wilson Wearn

Many American painters have been closely identified with specific locales. This sense of place emerged as early as the Hudson River School and was sustained by Albert Bierstadt in California and by Winslow Homer in Maine. In the twentieth century, American Scene painters like Grant Wood and John Steuart Curry were intimately connected with their localities, often celebrating the distinctiveness of individual regions. Similarly, Andrew Wyeth, who in his painting restricts himself to two places, has made Chadds Ford, Pennsylvania, and Cushing, Maine, familiar and internationally famous.

In this same tradition, Scott Young portrays the tropics. A Hawaiian by birth, Young has made Florida his home since his midteens. After attending Flagler College in St. Augustine, Young studied printmaking at the Ringling School of Art in Sarasota. He has also adopted the Bahamas, where his wife's family lives, as a second home and makes regular visits there to paint. In the manner of Homer and Wyeth, he familiarizes himself with the landscape and the people, the light and the color, so that he can paint them with empathy and conviction.

Again like Homer and Wyeth, Young prefers the watercolor medium, which allows quick, on-the-spot sketches. Young's painting process begins with exploring a neighborhood, discovering its interesting aspects, perhaps engaging some residents in conversation, and then setting about capturing on paper the essential qualities of his subjects, first in swift graphite drawings. He enhances a few of these with watercolor, adding color and detail. With these studies in hand, he returns to his studio to create larger, more finished sketches and ultimately the final work. Despite his commitment to realism, Young does not use photographs as an aid, preferring instead to edit and alter according to his artistic needs. Often he combines elements from different scenes, synthesizing them into a harmonious whole. Few viewers are aware of this artistic license; most are convinced by his realism that each scene is a straightforward documentation.

Although Young paints landscape, still life, and genre scenes, his forte is the portrayal of figures, either singly or in small groups. His greatest success has been with the young and the old, perhaps because they have more time to spend with the artist and are less self-conscious. He uses his settings—porches, old barn doors, picket fences—to frame his subjects. In *The Veterans* the rectilinearity of the posts, door, and balusters gives the composition a certain solidity. On this stage is enacted a quiet and poignant drama, the relaxed interaction of two friends—one gestures while the other listens intently. Between them, at the center, is a dark rectangle marking the house's interior, which also serves to separate one figure from the other. This motif of distance and emptiness betrays Young's debt to Wyeth.

Young has rendered *The Veterans* with a broad range of detail and a variety of techniques. Such elements as the clothespin on the mailbox are painted with an apparent desire for completeness. These details, along with the sitters' faces, are painted with precision using the drybrush technique. A method favored by both Young and Wyeth because it resembles tempera painting, drybrush results from the artist squeezing most of the water from the brush. Other areas in the painting are more loosely rendered. These freely painted passages take advantage of the medium's transparent properties and correspond to areas that reflect light.

Invited to Greenville, South Carolina, in connection with his solo exhibition, *In the American Tradition,* Young was encouraged to seek out subject matter that appealed to him. Like Homer who painted in the Adirondacks, the Caribbean, and along the coast of Maine, Young is eager to demonstrate his versatility. *The Veterans* is the first in a series of works commissioned by the Greenville County Museum of Art to create a *Portrait of Greenville.* This was not, however, Young's first painting to employ the flag and explore the topic of patriotism; as the son of a wounded Vietnam veteran, Young is sensitive to the ideal of military duty.

On a side street of a Greenville neighborhood, Young encountered Willie Norris and Dewitt Jackson, two local residents and World War II veterans. Because it was Memorial Day weekend, it was only natural that the two reminisced about their war experiences, and the artist was their captive audience. As Young recounts, "It was a delightful day, actually the kind of day that makes me glad to do what I do. It [was] the kind of rare moment that I wait for, but comes occasionally at best."[1]

---

1. Young to author, March 1994.

Born, Hawaii, 1957; attended Flagler College, St. Augustine, 1975–1977, and the Ringling School of Art, Sarasota, Florida, 1978–1981; resides, Jupiter, Florida.

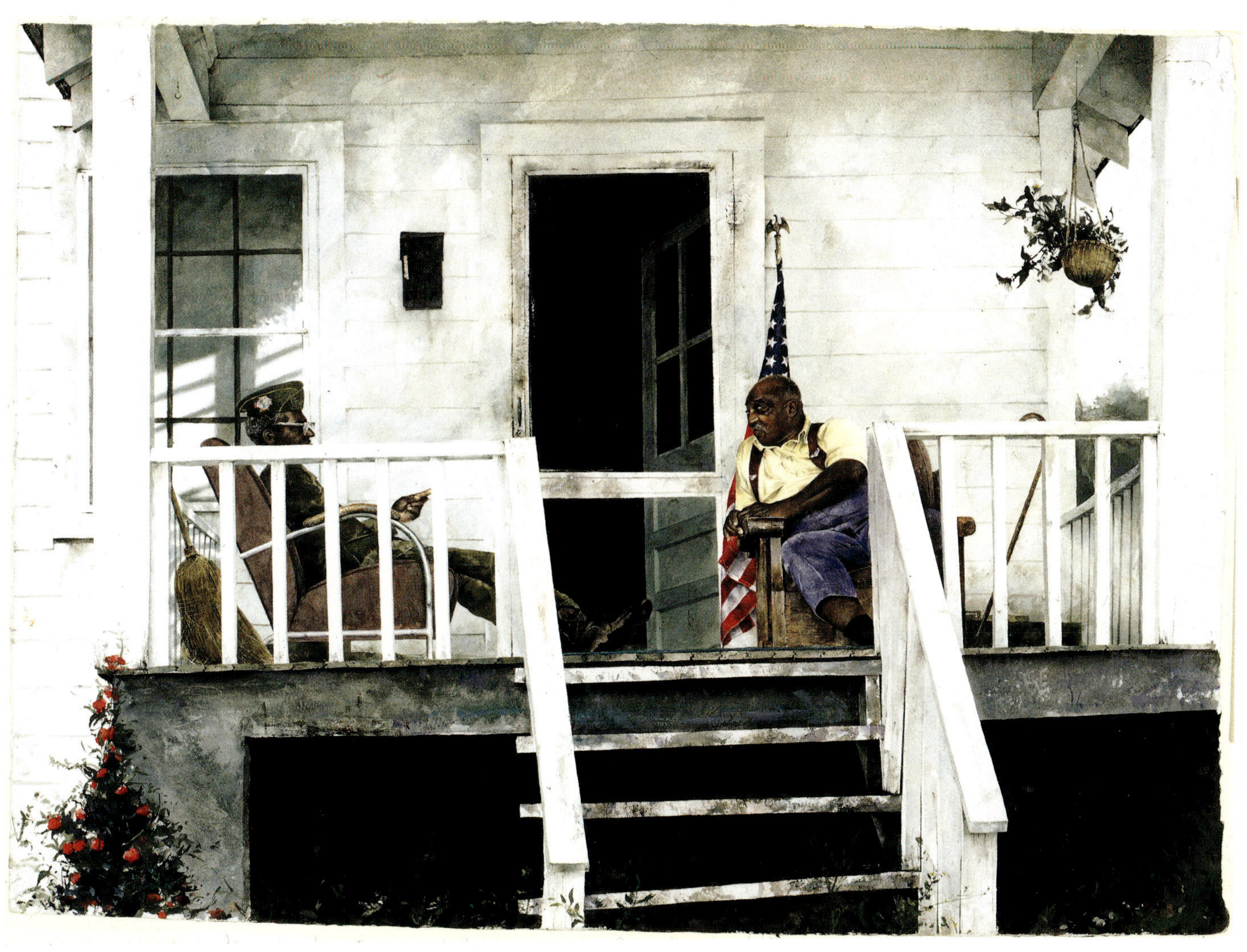

Evan Carter Wilson

born 1953

Holly and Arthur Magill, 1992

oil on canvas, 70 × 60 inches
signed, lower right: *Evan Wilson, 92*
Gift of the Friends of Holly and Arthur: Dr. and Mrs. Jerry Acosta; Mr. and Mrs. Dannitte Beattie; Dan and Brenda Bruce; Mrs. Alfred Burgess; Mr. and Mrs. Julian S. Bush; Mr. and Mrs. R. E. Coleman; Fannie Iselin Cromwell; Dr. Arthur and Jeanet Dreskin; Rhea and Nancy Eskew; Grace and Frank Espey; Keller and David Freeman; Mr. and Mrs. Alester G. Furman III; Dorothy and George M. Grimball; Mr. and Mrs. Caldwell Harper; Mr. and Mrs. R. Glenn Hilliard; Shirley and Francis Hipp; Elizabeth W. Houston; Richard Ingram; Mr. and Mrs. William W. Kehl; Mr. and Mrs. E. H. Kittredge, Jr.; Mary and Jeff Lawson; Mr. and Mrs. Guy Lipscomb; Ed and Sister Lominack; Hal and Alice Lee Lonnecker; Karen and Mike Mathers; John A. McCarroll; Mrs. George E. McDougall; Mr. and Mrs. G. Bruce McPherson, Jr.; Buck Alston Mickel; Mr. and Mrs. Charles C. Mickel; Minor and Buck Mickel; Carl and Allison Muller; Mr. and Mrs. Edgar M. Norris; Edward and Beaufort Cheves Olechovsky; Hunter and Peggy Park; Lillian and Henry Parr; Mary Burnet M. Pearce; Mr. and Mrs. John D. Pellett, Jr.; David Sz. Pollitt; Mr. and Mrs. F. Dean Rainey, Jr.; Dr. and Mrs. Harold E. Shaw, Jr.; Ann Cheves and Gordon B. Sherard, Jr., Cheves, Gordon III, and Reid; Mr. and Mrs. James M. Shoemaker, Jr.; J. Alden Simpson; Brooks Sloan; Charlotte and Ned Sloan; W. Thomas Smith; Jeannie and Tom Styron; Mr. and Mrs. T. H. Suitt; K. Tsuzuki Family; Virginia S. Uldrick; Fred and Jo Ann Walker; Richard and Lee Watson; Millie and Wilson Wearn; Harriet and Tommy Wyche

The earliest widely accepted form of fine art in this country was portraiture, and despite serious competition from the photograph, painters have not abandoned the portrait as a viable subject. Two post–World War II artists, widely different in their stylistic approach, have made portraiture their specialty: Chuck Close and Alice Neel. Close, linked with the Photorealists, makes larger-than-life frontal images of himself and friends. Projecting slides onto a gridded canvas, he enlarges the face to such an extent that it virtually becomes a monumental and depersonalized abstraction. Neel, by contrast, rendered psychologically penetrating and unidealized likenesses of her sitters in a freely painted style. She often posed her subjects nude, eliminating the distractions of clothes and creating unorthodox and slightly awkward likenesses. The portraiture of Close and Neel, however, does not fulfill the conventions of formal portraiture in the manner of Thomas Sully, George Healy, or John Singer Sargent.

Evan Wilson, although not solely a portraitist, sees himself as continuing that tradition: "I like more classic things. Basically I am a painter who learned a traditional technique, by copying the masters. I try to continue the tradition of representational painting—not photorealistic—but a painterly technique, done from life."[1] Of all painters Wilson admires Sargent the most, and he seeks to emulate Sargent's method in his portraits as well as in his other work.

A native of Tuscaloosa, Alabama, Wilson attended the North Carolina School of the Arts, the Maryland Institute, and the Schuler School of Fine Art. While close to Washington, D.C., he scrutinized the paintings at the National Gallery of Art, especially those by Sargent and Anthony van Dyck. His instructors placed a great deal of emphasis on preparation, to the extent that Wilson still regularly grinds his own pigment. Proud to be conservative, he aligns himself with classical musicians and ballet dancers who stress traditional craft and technique. In addition to commissioned portraits, Wilson paints landscapes, interiors, and nudes.

In his double portrait of Holly and Arthur Magill, Wilson has limited the amount of visual information to a few carefully selected items. The portrait was commissioned by friends of the Magills as a tribute to their generosity to Greenville and their support of the Greenville County Museum of Art. Thus the portrait takes on a ceremonial role, and in realizing this, Wilson has simplified and generalized the setting, allowing his composition to focus upon the Magills. Wilson also had to confront the challenges of a double portrait: to give both sitters equal importance and to capture their relationship. To this end Wilson immersed himself in the Magills' lives, painting daily in their living room and enjoying their hospitality at mealtime for almost six weeks.

In addition to his concern for traditional techniques, Wilson's other preoccupation is light. Wilson explains: "Quite often, the handling of light in a painting really makes the painting work successfully. The glow of morning light can establish the feeling of warmth in a painting of a mother and child, and the raking light of dusk can dramatize the forms of a landscape."[2] Emulating Sargent's method, Wilson places his canvas alongside his subject, so that both reflect the same angle and quality of light. In the portrait of the Magills, light serves to unify the composition as well as to highlight important areas. The entire scene is bathed in the cool northern light that enters the Magills' home, while certain critical elements, their faces and hands, the urn, and the right side of the frame in the background, are accented.

With the Magills' input Wilson chose the objects that would accompany them in their portrait: a large brass vessel, a favorite example of Holly Magill's needlework, and *Maternité,* by Mary Cassatt, a prized possession that hangs in their foyer. Other elements are kept to a minimum, including the setting itself, which is a neutral olive green. The selection of this color purposefully serves as a foil to Holly Magill's bright red suit and Arthur Magill's red sweater. Whereas the urn and needlework in the lower left foreground are important vehicles for entering the composition, the Cassatt pastel unites the painting. Hanging above and between the Magills, it connects them visually as well as emotionally. The maternal intimacy of Cassatt's painting is mirrored directly below in the Magills' handclasp and aptly symbolizes the couple's nurturing of the cultural life of Greenville.

1. Wilson, interview with author, February 1994.

2. Wilson, with M. Stephen Doherty, "Create a World inside a Painting," *American Artist,* November 1990, 79.

Born, Tuscaloosa, Alabama, 1953; studied at the North Carolina School of the Arts, Winston-Salem, 1970–1973, College of Art at the Maryland Institute, Baltimore, 1972–1975, and Schuler School of Fine Art, Baltimore, 1975–1976; resided in Florence, 1978–1981; lived in New York, 1981–1988; moved to Cambridge, New York, 1988–1994; resides, Hoosick Falls, New York.

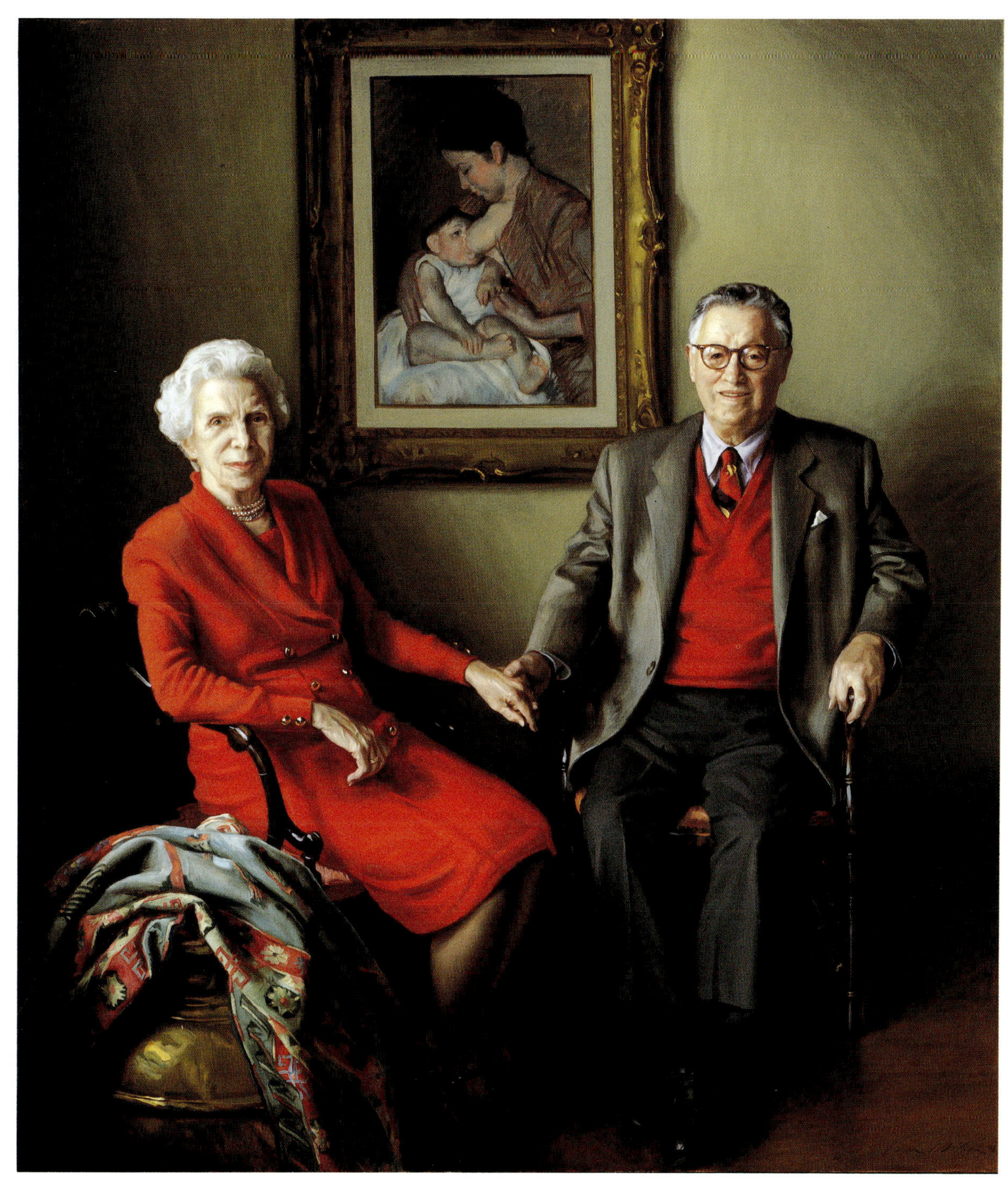

Bibliography

General

Acton, David, Karen F. Beall, and Clinton Adams. *A Spectrum of Innovation: Color in American Printmaking, 1890–1960*. Worcester, Mass.: Worcester Art Museum, 1990.

Adamson, Jeremy Elwell, et al. *Niagara: Two Centuries of Changing Attitudes, 1697–1901*. Washington, D.C.: The Corcoran Gallery of Art, 1985.

Arnason, H. H. *History of Modern Art: Painting, Sculpture, and Architecture*. Englewood Cliffs, N.J.: Prentice-Hall; New York: Harry N. Abrams, 1968.

Ausfeld, Margaret Lynne, et al. *Eight Southern Women*. Greenville, S.C.: Greenville County Museum of Art, 1986.

Avery, Kevin J. *Church's Great Picture: The Heart of the Andes*. New York: The Metropolitan Museum of Art, 1993.

Ayres, William S. *Picturing History: American Painting, 1779–1930*. New York: Rizzoli and Fraunces Tavern Museum, 1993.

Bearden, Romare, and Harry Henderson. *A History of African-American Artists: From 1792 to the Present*. New York: Pantheon Books, 1993.

Beckham, Sue Bridwell. *Depression Post Office Murals and Southern Culture: A Gentle Reconstruction*. Baton Rouge: Louisiana State University Press, 1989.

Blaugrund, Annette, et al. *Paris 1889: American Artists at the Universal Exposition*. Philadelphia: Pennsylvania Academy of the Fine Arts, 1989.

Boime, Albert. *Thomas Couture and the Eclectic Vision*. New Haven: Yale University Press, 1980.

Brown, Milton W. *The Story of the Armory Show*. Greenwich, Conn.: New York Graphic Society, 1963.

Burke, Doreen Bolger. *American Paintings in the Metropolitan Museum of Art. Vol. 3. A Catalogue of Works by Artists Born between 1846 and 1864*. New York: The Metropolitan Museum of Art, 1980.

Burke, Doreen Bolger, et al. *In Pursuit of Beauty: Americans and the Aesthetic Movement*. New York: The Metropolitan Museum of Art, 1986.

Campbell, Mary Schmidt, et al. *Harlem Renaissance: Art of Black America*. New York: Studio Museum in Harlem, 1986.

Canaday, John. *Mainstreams of Modern Art*. New York: Holt, Rinehart, and Winston, 1964.

Chambers, Bruce W. *Art and Artists of the South: The Robert P. Coggins Collection*. Columbia: University of South Carolina Press, 1984.

Conner, Janis, and Joel Rosenkranz. *Rediscoveries in American Sculpture: Studio Works, 1893–1939*. Austin: University of Texas Press, 1989.

Craven, Wayne. *Colonial American Portraiture: The Economic, Religious, Social, Cultural, Philosophical, Scientific, and Aesthetic Foundations*. Cambridge: Cambridge University Press, 1986.

Craven, Wayne. *Sculpture in America*. Newark: University of Delaware Press, 1968.

Danly, Susan. *Telling Tales: Nineteenth-Century Narrative Painting from the Collection of the Pennsylvania Academy of the Fine Arts*. Philadelphia: Pennsylvania Academy of the Fine Arts, 1991.

Davidson, Abraham A. *Early American Modernist Painting, 1910–1935*. New York: Harper & Row, 1981.

Dunlap, William. *A History of the Rise and Progress of the Arts of Design in the United States*. 1834. Reprint. 3 vols. New York: Benjamin Blom, 1965.

Edwards, Lee M. *Domestic Bliss: Family Life in American Painting, 1840–1910*. Yonkers, N.Y.: Hudson River Museum, 1986.

Eldredge, Charles C. *American Imagination and Symbolist Painting*. New York: Grey Art Gallery and Study Center, New York University, 1979.

Fairbrother, Trevor J., et al. *The Bostonians: Painters of an Elegant Age, 1870–1930*. Boston: Museum of Fine Arts, 1986.

Fink, Lois Marie. *American Art at the Nineteenth-Century Paris Salons*. Washington, D.C.: Smithsonian Institution Press, 1990.

Flint, Janet Atlic. *Provincetown Printers: A Woodcut Tradition*. Washington, D.C.: Smithsonian Institution Press, 1983.

Fort, Ilene Susan, and Michael Quick. *American Art: A Catalogue of the Los Angeles County Museum of Art Collection*. Los Angeles: Los Angeles County Museum of Art, 1991.

Gerdts, William H. *American Impressionism*. New York: Abbeville Press, 1984.

Gerdts, William H. *Art Across America: Two Centuries of Regional Painting, 1710–1920*. 3 vols. New York: Abbeville Press, 1990.

Gerdts, William H. *Painters of the Humble Truth: Masterpieces of American Still Life, 1801–1939*. Tulsa, Okla.: The Philbrook Museum of Art; Columbia: University of Missouri Press, 1981.

Harris, Mary Emma. *The Arts at Black Mountain College*. Cambridge, Mass.: MIT Press, 1987.

Homer, William Innes. *Alfred Stieglitz and the American Avant-Garde*. Boston: New York Graphic Society, 1977.

Hoopes, Donelson F., and Nancy Wall Moure. *American Narrative Painting*. Los Angeles: Los Angeles County Museum of Art, 1974.

Howat, John K., et al. *American Paradise: The World of the Hudson River School*. New York: The Metropolitan Museum of Art, 1987.

Hunter, Sam, ed. *An American Renaissance: Painting and Sculpture since 1940*. Fort Lauderdale, Fla.: Museum of Art, 1986.

Jacobs, Michael. *The Good and Simple Life: Artist Colonies in Europe and America*. Oxford: Phaidon, 1985.

Johns, Elizabeth. *American Genre Painting: The Politics of Everyday Life*. New Haven: Yale University Press, 1991.

Kingsley, April. *The Turning Point: The Abstract Expressionists and the Transformation of American Art*. New York: Simon & Schuster, 1992.

Kuspit, Donald B., et al. *Painting in the South, 1564–1980*. Richmond: Virginia Museum of Fine Arts, 1983.

Levin, Gail, and Marianne Lorenz. *Theme and Improvisation: Kandinsky and the American Avant-Garde, 1912–1950*. Dayton, Ohio: Dayton Art Institute, 1992.

Manthorne, Katherine Emma. *Tropical Renaissance: North American Artists Exploring Latin America, 1839–1879*. Washington, D.C.: Smithsonian Institution Press, 1989.

Marling, Karal Ann. *Wall-to-Wall America: A Cultural History of Post Office Murals in the Great Depression*. Minneapolis: University of Minnesota Press, 1982.

Marter, Joan M., Roberta K. Tarbell, and Jeffrey Wechsler. *Vanguard American Sculpture, 1913–1939*. New Brunswick, N.J.: Rutgers University, 1979.

Meisel, Louis K. *Photo-Realism*. New York: Harry N. Abrams, 1985.

Melosh, Barbara. *Engendering Culture: Manhood and Womanhood in New Deal Public Art and Theater*. Washington, D.C.: Smithsonian Institution Press, 1991.

Nygren, Edward J. *Views and Visions: American Landscape before 1830*. Washington, D.C.: The Corcoran Gallery of Art, 1986.

Pennington, Estill Curtis. *A Southern Collection*. Augusta, Ga.: Morris Museum of Art, 1992.

Perlman, Bennard B. *The Immortal Eight: American Painting from Eakins to the Armory Show, 1870–1913*. Westport, Conn.: North Light Publishers, 1979.

Poesch, Jessie. *The Art of the Old South: Painting, Sculpture, Architecture, and the Products of Craftsmen, 1560–1860*. New York: Alfred A. Knopf, 1983.

Quick, Michael. *American Expatriate Painters of the Late Nineteenth Century*. Dayton, Ohio: Dayton Art Institute, 1976.

Reynolds, Gary A., and Beryl J. Wright. *Against the Odds: African-American Artists and the Harmon Foundation*. Newark, N.J.: The Newark Museum, 1989.

Rosen, Randy, and Catherine C. Brawer. *Making Their Mark. Women Artists Moving into the Mainstream, 1970–1985*. New York: Abbeville Press, 1989.

Rubinstein, Charlotte Streifer. *American Women Artists from Early Indian Times to the Present*. Boston: G. K. Hall, 1982.

Rutledge, Anna Wells. *Artists in the Life of Charleston: Through Colony and State from Restoration to Reconstruction*. 1949. Reprint. Columbia: University of South Carolina Press, 1980.

Saunders, Richard H., and Ellen G. Miles. *American Colonial Portraits, 1700–1776*. Washington, D.C.: Smithsonian Institution Press, 1987.

Schimmel, Paul, et al. *The Figurative Fifties: New York Figurative Expressionism*. Newport Beach, Calif.: Newport Harbor Art Museum, 1988.

Schweizer, Paul D., ed. *Masterworks of American Art from the Munson-Williams-Proctor Institute*. New York: Harry N. Abrams, 1989.

Seckler, Dorothy Gees. *Provincetown Painters, 1890's–1970's*. Syracuse, N.Y.: Everson Museum of Art, 1977.

Seitz, William C. *Art in the Age of Aquarius, 1955–1970*. Compiled and edited by Marla Price. Washington, D.C.: Smithsonian Institution Press, 1992.

Shapiro, David, ed. *Social Realism: Art as a Weapon*. New York: Frederick Ungar, 1973.

Spassky, Natalie, et al. *American Paintings in the Metropolitan Museum of Art. Vol. 2. A Catalogue of Works by Artists Born between 1816 and 1845*. New York: The Metropolitan Museum of Art, 1985.

Stich, Sidra. *Made in USA.: An Americanization in Modern Art, the '50s & '60s*. Berkeley: University of California Press, 1987.

Truettner, William H., ed. *The West as America: Reinterpreting Images of the Frontier, 1820–1920*. Washington, D.C.: Smithsonian Institution Press, 1991.

Weinberg, H. Barbara. *The Lure of Paris: Nineteenth-Century American Painters and Their French Teachers*. New York: Abbeville Press, 1991.

Weisberg, Gabriel P. *Beyond Impressionism: The Naturalist Impulse*. New York: Harry N. Abrams, 1992.

Wilmerding, John, et al. *American Light: The Luminist Movement, 1850–1875*. Washington, D.C.: National Gallery of Art, 1980.

Wilson, Richard Guy, Dianne H. Pilgrim, and Richard N. Murray. *The American Renaissance, 1876–1917*. Brooklyn: The Brooklyn Museum, 1979.

Specific Artists

AHEARN

Zeitlin, Marilyn, Richard Goldstein, and Michael Ventura. *South Bronx Hall of Fame: Sculpture by John Ahearn and Rigoberto Torres*. Houston: Contemporary Arts Museum, 1991.

ALBERS

Weber, Nicholas Fox, et al. *Josef Albers: A Retrospective*. New York: The Solomon R. Guggenheim Foundation, 1988.

ALLSTON

Bjelajac, David. *Millennial Desire and the Apocalyptic Vision of Washington Allston*. Washington, D.C.: Smithsonian Institution Press, 1987.

Craven, Wayne. "The Grand Manner in Early Nineteenth-Century Painting: Borrowings from Antiquity, the Renaissance and the Baroque," *The American Art Journal* 11, no. 2 (April 1979): 4–43.

Flagg, Jared B., ed. *The Life and Letters of Washington Allston*. 1892. Reprint. New York: Benjamin Blom, 1969.

Gerdts, William H., and Theodore E. Stebbins, Jr. *"A Man of Genius": The Art of Washington Allston (1779–1843)*. Boston: Museum of Fine Arts, 1979.

Richardson, Edgar Preston. *Washington Allston: A Study of the Romantic Artist in America*. Chicago: University of Chicago Press, 1948.

AMINO

Gilbert, Gregory. *Leo Amino Sculpture, 1945–1974, in the Collection of the Jane Voorhees Zimmerli Art Museum*. Rutgers, N.J.: Zimmerli Art Museum, 1985.

ANDERSON

Driscoll, John Paul. *Walter Anderson: Realizations of the Islander*. Ocean Springs, Miss.: Estate of Walter Anderson, 1985.

Sugg, Redding S., Jr., ed. *The Horn Island Logs of Walter Inglis Anderson*. Jackson: University Press of Mississippi, 1985.

ANSHUTZ

Webster, Sally. "Thomas Anshutz: The Philadelphia Connection." *Arts Magazine*, November 1979, 139.

BARTLETT

Sweet, Christopher. *Bo Bartlett*. New York: P. P. O.W. Gallery, 1990.

BEAL

Shanes, Eric. *Jack Beal*. New York: Hudson Hills Press, 1993.

BEAUCHAMP

Kuchta, Ronald A., April Kingsley, and Robert Beauchamp. *Robert Beauchamp: An American Expressionist*. Syracuse, N.Y.: Everson Museum of Art, 1984.

BEARDEN

Murray, Albert, and Dore Ashton. *Romare Bearden, 1970–1980*. Charlotte, N.C.: Mint Museum of Art, 1980.

Schwartzman, Myron. *Romare Bearden: His Life and Art*. New York: Harry N. Abrams, 1990.

BELLOWS

Peck, Glenn C., and Gordon K. Allison. *George Bellows and the War Series of 1918*. New York: Hirschl & Adler Galleries, 1983.

Quick, Michael, et al. *The Paintings of George Bellows*. Fort Worth: Amon Carter Museum, 1992.

Wasserman, Krystyna. "George Bellows' War Lithographs and Paintings of 1918." Master's thesis, University of Maryland, 1981.

BENGLIS

Krane, Susan. *Lynda Benglis: Dual Natures*. Atlanta, Ga.: High Museum of Art, 1991.

BIDDLE

Biddle, George. *An American Artist's Story*. Boston: Little, Brown and Company, 1939.

Pennigar, Martha. *The Graphic Work of George Biddle with Catalogue Raisonné*. Washington, D.C.: The Corcoran Gallery of Art, 1979.

BOLOTOWSKY

Breeskin, Adelyn D. *Ilya Bolotowsky*. New York: The Solomon R. Guggenheim Foundation, 1974.

BRECKENRIDGE

Vogel, Margaret. *The Paintings of Hugh H. Breckenridge (1870–1937)*. Dallas: Valley House Gallery, 1967.

BROWN, FREDERICK

Bass, Ruth. *Frederick Brown*. New York: Marlborough Gallery, 1987.

BROWN, ROGER

Kahan, Mitchell Douglas, Dennis Adrian, and Russell Bowman. *Roger Brown*. Montgomery, Ala.: Montgomery Museum of Fine Arts, 1980.

Lawrence, Sidney, and John Yau. *Roger Brown*. New York: George Braziller, 1987.

BRUCE

Agee, William C., and Barbara Rose. *Patrick Henry Bruce: American Modernist*. New York: The Museum of Modern Art; Houston: The Museum of Fine Arts, 1979.

BRUSH

Morgan, Joan B. *George DeForest Brush, 1855–1941: Master of the American Renaissance*. New York: Berry-Hill Galleries, 1985.

BULTMAN

Kingsley, April. *Fritz Bultman: A Retrospective*. New Orleans: New Orleans Museum of Art, 1993.

BURCHFIELD

Baur, John I. H. *Life and Work of Charles Burchfield, 1893–1967: The Inlander*. Newark: University of Delaware Press, 1982.

CATESBY

Catesby, Mark. *Natural History of Carolina, Florida, and the Bahama Islands Containing Two Hundred and Twenty Figures of Birds, Beasts, Fishes, Serpents, Insects and Plants by the late Mark Catesby, F.R.S.* 1771. Reprint. Savannah, Ga.: Beehive Press, 1974.

Comstock, Helen. "An Eighteenth-Century Audubon." *The Magazine Antiques*, June 1940, 282–284.

CHAPMAN

Chamberlain, Georgia Stamm. *Studies on John Gadsby Chapman: An American Artist, 1808–1889*. Annandale, Va.: Turnpike Press, 1963.

CHRISTO

Vaizey, Marina. *Christo*. New York: Rizzoli, 1990.

DAINGERFIELD

Hobbs, Robert. *Elliott Daingerfield: Retrospective Exhibition*. Charlotte, N.C.: Mint Museum of Art, 1971.

Pennington, Estill Curtis, and J. Richard Gruber. *Victorian Visionary: The Art of Elliott Daingerfield*. Augusta, Ga.: Morris Museum of Art, 1994.

DE KOONING

Bledsoe, Jane K., et al. *Elaine de Kooning*. Athens: Georgia Museum of Art, University of Georgia, 1992.

DE RIVERA

Ashton, Dore, and Joan M. Marter. *José de Rivera: Constructions*. New York: Grace Borgenicht Gallery, 1979.

DONOHO

Gerdts, William H., Jeffrey W. Andersen, and Helen A. Harrison. *En Plein Air: The Art Colonies at East Hampton and Old Lyme, 1880–1930*. East Hampton, N.Y.: Guild Hall; Old Lyme, Conn.: Lyme Historical Society, 1989.

Pisano, Ronald G. *G. Ruger Donoho (1857–1916): A Retrospective Exhibition*. New York: Hirschl & Adler Galleries; Southampton, N.Y.: Parrish Art Museum, 1977.

DUVENECK

Neuhaus, Robert. *Unsuspected Genius: The Art and Life of Frank Duveneck*. San Francisco: Bedford Press, 1987.

Quick, Michael. *An American Painter Abroad: Frank Duveneck's European Years*. Cincinnati: Cincinnati Art Museum, 1987.

FRASER

Severens, Martha R., and Charles L. Wyrick, eds. *Charles Fraser of Charleston: Essays on the Man, His Art, and His Times*. Charleston, S.C.: Carolina Art Association/Gibbes Art Gallery, 1983.

FRERICHS

Williams, Benjamin F., and Hildegard J. Safford. *William C. A. Frerichs, 1829–1905: A Retrospective Exhibition*. Raleigh: North Carolina Museum of Art, 1974.

GAUL

Hoobler, James A. *Gilbert Gaul: American Realist*. Nashville: Tennessee State Museum, 1992.

Reeves, James F. *Gilbert Gaul*. Huntsville, Ala.: Huntsville Museum of Art, 1975.

GODWIN

Hobbs, Robert, and Gerald Nordland. *Judith Godwin Paintings: 1953–1992*. New York: Marisa del Rey Gallery, 1992.

GOLDTHWAITE

Breeskin, Adelyn Dohme. *Anne Goldthwaite, 1869–1944*. Montgomery, Ala.: Montgomery Museum of Fine Arts, 1977.

Breeskin, Adelyn Dohme. *Anne Goldthwaite: A Catalogue Raisonné of the Graphic Work*. Montgomery, Ala.: Montgomery Museum of Fine Arts, 1982.

GORKY

Lader, Melvin P. *Arshile Gorky*. New York: Abbeville Press, 1985.

Rand, Harry. *Arshile Gorky: The Implications of Symbols*. 1981. Reprint. Berkeley: University of California Press, 1991.

GRAVES

Kass, Ray, Duncan Phillips, and Theodore F. Wolff. *Morris Graves: Vision of the Inner Eye*. Washington, D.C.: The Phillips Collection, 1983.

GROOMS

Ratcliff, Carter. *Red Grooms*. New York: Abbeville Press, 1984.

GUGLIELMI

Baker, John. *O. Louis Guglielmi: A Retrospective Exhibition*. New Brunswick, N.J.: Rutgers University Art Gallery, 1980.

GUSTON

Feld, Ross. *Philip Guston*. New York: George Braziller, 1980.

Storr, Robert. *Philip Guston*. New York: Abbeville Press, 1986.

GWATHMEY

Piehl, Charles K. "Robert Gwathmey: The Social and Historical Context of a Southerner's Art in the Mid-Twentieth Century." *Arts in Virginia* 29, no. 1 (1989): 2–15.

HEADE

Stebbins, Theodore E., Jr. *The Life and Works of Martin Johnson Heade*. New Haven: Yale University Press, 1975.

HEALY

De Mare, Marie. *G. P. A. Healy: American Artist*. New York: David McKay Company, 1954.

HENRY

McCausland, Elizabeth. *The Life and Work of Edward Lamson Henry, N.A., 1841–1919*. 1945. Reprint. New York: Da Capo Press for Kennedy Graphics, 1970.

JOHNS

Bernstein, Roberta. *Jasper Johns' Paintings and Sculptures, 1954–1974*. Ann Arbor, Mich.: UMI Research Press, 1975.

Castleman, Riva. *Jasper Johns: A Print Retrospective*. New York: The Museum of Modern Art, 1986.

Crichton, Michael. *Jasper Johns*. New York: Harry N. Abrams, 1977.

Francis, Richard. *Jasper Johns*. New York: Abbeville Press, 1984.

JOHNSON

Powell, Richard J. *Homecoming: The Art and Life of William H. Johnson*. Washington, D.C.: Smithsonian Institution Press, 1991.

JOHNSTON

Alexander, Forsyth, ed. *Henrietta Johnston: Who Greatly Helped by Drawing Pictures*. Winston-Salem, N.C.: Museum of Early Southern Decorative Arts, 1991.

Middleton, Margaret Simons. *Henrietta Johnston of Charles Town, South Carolina: America's First Pastellist*. Columbia: University of South Carolina Press, 1966.

KEY

Harrison, Alfred C., Jr. "Bierstadt's *Bombardment of Fort Sumter* Reattributed." *The Magazine Antiques*, February 1986, 416–422.

KOHLMEYER

Kessler, Jane, and Whitney J. Engeran. *Ida Kohlmeyer: Thirty Years*. Charlotte, N.C.: Mint Museum of Art, 1983.

KOSCIANSKI

Heller, Tom. *Leonard Koscianski*. Newport Beach, Calif.: Newport Harbor Art Museum, 1984.

LAWRENCE

Brown, Milton W., and Louise A. Parks. *Jacob Lawrence*. New York: Whitney Museum of American Art, 1974.

Wheat, Ellen Harkins. *Jacob Lawrence: American Painter*. Seattle: University of Washington Press, 1986.

LEE

Henkes, Robert. *American Women Painters of the 1930s and 1940s: The Lives and Works of Ten Artists*. Jefferson, N.C.: McFarland & Company, 1991.

LEWANDOWSKI

Riehlman, Franklin, and Glenn C. Peck. *Edmund Lewandowski: Fifty Years of Painting*. New York: H. V. Allison Galleries; Greenville, S.C.: Greenville County Museum of Art, 1990.

LOUIS

Fried, Michael. *Morris Louis*. New York: Harry N. Abrams, 1979.

Elderfield, John. *Morris Louis*. New York: The Museum of Modern Art, 1987.

McCRADY

Marshall, Keith. *John McCrady, 1911–1968*. New Orleans: New Orleans Museum of Art, 1975.

McFEE

Baker, John. *Henry McFee and Formalist Realism in American Still Life, 1923–1936*. Cranbury, N.J.: Associated University Presses, 1987.

MELCHERS

Dreiss, Joseph G. *Gari Melchers: His Work in the Belmont Collection*. Charlottesville: University of Virginia Press, 1984.

Lesko, Diane, et al. *Gari Melchers: A Retrospective Exhibition*. St. Petersburg, Fla.: Museum of Fine Arts, 1990.

MILLS

Rutledge, Anna Wells. "Cogdell and Clark Mills, Charleston Sculptors." *The Magazine Antiques*, March 1942, 192–193, 205–207.

MYERS

Myers, Jerome. *Artist in Manhattan*. New York: American Artists Group, 1940.

NEWMAN

Landgren, Michael. *Robert Loftin Newman, 1827–1912*. Washington, D.C.: Smithsonian Institution Press, 1974.

NOBLE

Birchfield, James D., Albert Boime, and William J. Hennessey. *Thomas S. Noble, 1835–1907*. Lexington: University of Kentucky Art Museum, 1988.

NOLAND

Moffett, Kenworth. *Kenneth Noland*. New York: Harry N. Abrams, 1976.

O'KEEFFE

Messinger, Lisa Mintz. "Georgia O'Keeffe." *The Metropolitan Museum of Art Bulletin* 42, no. 2 (Fall 1984).

Eldredge, Charles C. *Georgia O'Keeffe: American and Modern*. New Haven: Yale University Press, 1993.

Cowart, Jack, Juan Hamilton, and Sarah Greenough. *Georgia O'Keeffe: Art and Letters*. Washington, D.C.: National Gallery of Art, 1988.

PARRISH, DAVID

Kahan, Mitchell Douglas. *David Parrish*. Montgomery, Ala.: Montgomery Museum of Fine Arts, 1981.

PERRY

Gibbs, Linda Mary Jones. "Enoch Wood Perry, Jr.: A Biography and Analysis of His Thematic and Stylistic Development." Master's thesis, University of Utah, 1981.

POLK

Simmons, Linda Crocker. *Charles Peale Polk, 1767–1822: A Limner and His Likenesses*. Washington, D.C.: The Corcoran Gallery of Art, 1981.

RANNEY

Ayres, Linda. "William Ranney." In *American Frontier Life: Early Western Painting and Prints*. Fort Worth: Amon Carter Museum; Cody, Wyo.: Buffalo Bill Historical Center, 1987.

Pennington, Estill Curtis. *Passage and Progress in the Works of William Tylee Ranney*. Augusta, Ga.: Morris Museum of Art, 1993.

RAVENSCROFT

Wolf, Amy J. *New York Society of Women Artists 1925*. New York: ACA Galleries, 1987.

RICHARDS

Koch, Mary Levin. "The Romance of American Landscape and the Art of Thomas Addison Richards." *Georgia Museum of Art Bulletin* 8, no. 2 (1983): 3–36.

ROSENQUIST

Goldman, Judith. *James Rosenquist*. New York: Viking Penguin, 1985.

Tucker, Marcia. *James Rosenquist*. New York: Whitney Museum of American Art, 1972.

SCARBOROUGH

Hennig, Helen Kohn. *William Harrison Scarborough: Portraitist and Miniaturist: "A Parade of the Living Past."* Columbia, S.C.: R. L. Bryan, 1937.

SIMKHOVITCH

Marquesee, Janet. *Simka Simkhovitch, 1893–1949: Paintings*. New York: Janet Marquesee Fine Arts, 1987.

SMITH

Vevers, Tony. *Houghton Cranford Smith: The Provincetown Paintings*. Provincetown, Mass.: Provincetown Art Association and Museum, 1991.

Wilkin, Karen. *Houghton Cranford Smith, 1887–1983: Early Landscape Studies*. New York: Grace Borgenicht Gallery, 1990.

SPEIGHT

Sellin, David. *Francis Speight: A Retrospective*. Washington, D.C.: Taggart, Jorgensen and Putnam, 1986.

STEVENS

Poesch, Jessie, and Thomas W. Styron. *Will Henry Stevens*. Greenville, S.C.: Greenville County Museum of Art, 1987.

SULLY

Biddle, Edward, and Mantle Fielding. *The Life and Works of Thomas Sully (1783–1872)*. Lancaster, Pa.: Wickersham Press, 1921.

Fabian, Monroe H. *Mr. Sully, Portrait Painter: The Works of Thomas Sully (1783–1872)*. Washington, D.C.: Smithsonian Institution Press, 1983.

TAYLOR

Severens, Martha R. *Anna Heyward Taylor: Printmaker*. Greenville, S.C.: Greenville County Museum of Art, 1987.

THEUS

Middleton, Margaret Simons. *Jeremiah Theus: Colonial Artist of Charles Town*. Columbia: University of South Carolina Press, 1953.

Severens, Martha R. "Jeremiah Theus of Charleston: Plagiarist or Pundit?" *The Southern Quarterly: A Journal of the Arts of the South* 24, nos. 1–2 (Fall–Winter 1985): 56–70.

TURNER

Rabbage, Lewis Hoyer. *Helen M. Turner (1858–1958): A Retrospective Exhibition*. Cragsmoor, N.Y.: Cragsmoor Free Library, 1983.

WALKER

Trovaioli, August P., and Roulhac B. Toledano. *William Aiken Walker: Southern Genre Painter*. Baton Rouge: Louisiana State University Press, 1972.

WEBER

North, Percy, and Susan Krane. *Max Weber: The Cubist Decade, 1910–1920*. Atlanta, Ga.: High Museum of Art, 1991.

WEEKS

Ganley, Kathleen Duff, and Leslie Paddock. *The Art of Edwin Lord Weeks (1849–1903)*. Durham: University Art Galleries, University of New Hampshire, 1976.

Thompson, D. Dodge. "Edwin Lord Weeks, American Painter of India." *The Magazine Antiques*, August 1985, 246–258.

WEEMS

Kirsh, Andrea, and Susan Fisher Sterling. *Carrie Mae Weems*. Washington, D.C.: National Museum of Women in the Arts, 1993.

WEST

Pennington, Estill Curtis. *William Edward West, 1788–1857: Kentucky Painter*. Washington, D.C.: National Portrait Gallery, 1985.

WIGHT

Shepherd, Elizabeth, and Stephen Prokopoff. *Sudden Nature: The Art of Frederick S. Wight, 1902–1986*. Los Angeles: Wight Art Gallery, University of California, 1991.

Wight, Frederick S. *South*. New York: Farrar & Rinehart, 1935.

WILEY

Pennington, Estill Curtis. *Southern Impressionist: The Art of Catherine Wiley*. Nashville: Tennessee State Museum, 1990.

WILLIAMS

Hendricks, Jon. *Fluxus Codex*. New York: Harry N. Abrams, Inc., 1988.

Williams, Emmett. *My Life in Flux—and Vice Versa*. New York: Thames and Hudson, 1992.

WOFFORD

Martin, Jean. "Philip Wofford Joins Gallery." *Allan Frumkin Gallery Newsletter*, Fall 1987.

WOODRUFF

Stoelting, Winifred. "Hale Woodruff, Artist and Teacher: Through the Atlanta Years." Ph.D. diss., Emory University, 1978.

YOUNG

Leeds, Valerie Ann. *Stephen Scott Young: In the American Tradition*. Palm Beach, Fla.: John Surovek Gallery, 1993.

YOUNGBLOOD

Stein, Judith, and Paula Marincola. *Daisy Youngblood*. Glenside, Pa.: Beaver College Art Gallery, 1992.

Index

Page numbers in *italics* refer to illustrations.